A Handbook for Wellbeing Policy-Making

A Handbook for Wellbeing Policy-Making

History, Theory, Measurement, Implementation, and Examples

PAUL FRIJTERS AND CHRISTIAN KREKEL

OXFORD
UNIVERSITY PRESS

OXFORD
UNIVERSITY PRESS

Great Clarendon Street, Oxford, OX2 6DP,
United Kingdom

Oxford University Press is a department of the University of Oxford.
It furthers the University's objective of excellence in research, scholarship,
and education by publishing worldwide. Oxford is a registered trade mark of
Oxford University Press in the UK and in certain other countries

First Edition published in 2021

Impression: 1

Published in the United States of America by Oxford University Press
198 Madison Avenue, New York, NY 10016, United States of America

British Library Cataloguing in Publication Data
Data available

Library of Congress Control Number: 2020949071

ISBN 978–0–19–289680–3

DOI: 10.1093/oso/9780192896803.001.0001

Printed and bound by
CPI Group (UK) Ltd, Croydon, CR0 4YY

Foreword

'The life and happiness of the people is the sole legitimate object of government.' So said Thomas Jefferson. It was perhaps the greatest idea of the modern age—that we judge our societies by how much our citizens are enjoying their lives. And the role of public policy is therefore to create the conditions which maximize their wellbeing.

The idea is over two hundred years old. But until recently there was no scientific way of implementing the idea, using actual numbers. However, thanks to the new science of wellbeing, all that is changing, and so is the attitude of politicians. Thanks to the leadership of the OECD, all member countries now measure the wellbeing of their citizens on an annual basis.[1] And recently the European Council called on its member states to 'put people and their wellbeing at the centre of policy design'.[2] Some countries are already doing this, including New Zealand, Scotland, and Iceland.

But the main constraint in applying this great Enlightenment principle is the lack of easily accessible numbers and a clear methodology. This book is an outstanding effort to remedy that shortcoming. It lays out the way forward for all policy-making. Where the policy involves money, the money should be allocated to policies which generate the most wellbeing per unit of expenditure. And similar principles apply to tax and regulation.

This book supplies not only a methodology but also a good array of numerical estimates which policy analysts can use in applying the methodology. And the book is also deeply thoughtful—it is not a cookbook but an intellectual guide to the many problems which arise in any policy analysis.

Paul Frijters has been one of the leading thinkers on wellbeing for many years, and Christian Krekel is a promising scholar from the younger generation. The What Works Centre for Wellbeing made a good choice in supporting this work, which supplies a critical need. The authors have provided us with the tools. Now lets us put them to use.

Professor Lord Richard Layard
London School of Economics

October 2020

[1] Durand (2018). Countries' Experiences with Well-being and Happiness Metrics. In J. Helliwell, R. Layard and J. Sachs (eds), *Global Happiness Policy Report*. New York: Sustainable Development Solutions Network.

[2] Council of the European Union (October 2019). The Economy of Wellbeing: Creating Opportunities for People's Wellbeing and Economic Growth. P. R. Committee. Brussels: Council of the European Union. Draft Council Conclusions on the Economy of Wellbeing.

Preface

This book follows the tradition of the Enlightenment thinkers to see the wellbeing of the population as the ultimate goal of government. What is new is that we openly look at how to implement this goal by using direct measures of the subjective wellbeing of the population, rather than inferred measures which have dominated hitherto. Over fifty years of analysis with millions of respondents in nearly all countries of the world has uncovered general patterns that are useful and robust to the critique that subjective wellbeing has limited accuracy and is easily manipulated.

We invite the reader on a journey with a clear historical purpose, which is to grapple with the difficulties of truly enacting the ideal that has underlined our system of government for centuries. This book should be understood as part of that journey: just a step along the way.[3]

The first out of five chapters covers the basic idea of how wellbeing policy-making would work, including a discussion of how it would fit in with democracy and the reality of bureaucracies. It sets out a suggested roadmap for how wellbeing can become more integrated in a national public service, both that of the United Kingdom and of other countries. This part is for anyone with a general interest in policy and wellbeing, but will already be familiar to most practitioners.

Chapter 2 synthesizes the knowledge the literature has yielded on wellbeing. It discusses measurement, basic findings, some of the main theories, and some of the open questions. It ends with a mental framework for how to see wellbeing within the wider socio-economic context, which is then applied to mental health programmes and the question of how we could think about the expenditures of different government departments. This part is useful for anyone professionally interested in how to improve the wellbeing of the general population, their employees, or others in their care.

Chapter 3 presents the methodology for wellbeing policy evaluations and appraisals,[4] developing technical standards and covering many implementation issues like double-counting, the optimal use of literature, and some of the practicalities of how to count what. This part is useful for those professionally interested in quantifying the wellbeing effects of some policy or intervention,

[3] While the writing of this book was co-sponsored by seven UK government departments and agencies, this book reflects the authors' own opinions and is not officially endorsed by any government.

[4] An evaluation is an *ex post* assessment of how an actual policy or intervention worked out. An appraisal is an *ex ante* assessment of a policy or intervention contemplated.

which includes regulations. It is the most technical part and could serve as a guidance for experts if wellbeing policy is to be implemented, with many examples to show how it would work in practice, and with lists of available datasets and advice on how to integrate findings using different wellbeing measures.

Chapter 4 discusses existing approaches to policy evaluation and appraisals, particularly cost-benefit analyses as they are practiced in the United Kingdom and elsewhere, but also wellbeing frameworks and approaches from around the world. This again is a largely technical discussion that is useful for those currently doing policy evaluations and appraisals, including business cases, impact cases, or multi-criterion approaches. We derive and discuss the most appropriate ways of monetizing wellbeing impacts in current standard cost-benefit analyses, and we compare the QALY (quality-adjusted life-years) approach with the WELLBY (wellbeing-years) approach. The discussion on wellbeing frameworks and approaches from around the world is useful for those thinking of pushing their own country or organization towards a particular wellbeing measurement system, as it lays out what type of bureaucratic culture fits with different wellbeing approaches.

Chapter 5 discusses seven examples, six of which are examples from UK government departments, the Welsh government, and other groups that funded this book. These examples show how a wellbeing orientation changes what one looks at and how one calculates things. They include the question of optimal survey design, the issue of how to evaluate the Hull City of Culture 2017 project from a wellbeing perspective, a Welsh vocational traineeship programme, a Stone Henge oriented programme to help people who suffer from chronic mental ill health, a study into the impact of commuting on people's lives, and the Heathrow airport expansion evaluation. A seventh example is an evaluation of the policy responses to the Covid-19 pandemic by governments around the world, comparing the costs and benefits of different policies by translating all effects into one unit of account: wellbeing.

Acknowledgements

This book is largely the result of a project that started in November 2018 as an ESRC grant with co-funding by UK government departments and agencies[5] via the What Works Centre for Wellbeing. There were three rounds of writing and feedback, culminating in final workshops to disseminate the methodological recommendations. On top of that were several further rounds of feedback and additions due to the reviewer and editor comments at Oxford University Press. The main additional work added in those last rounds was to make the book more international rather than solely UK-focused.

This book thus stands on the shoulders of many who gave their time and energy to make it a good guide for wellbeing policy-making.

We would like to thank Nancy Hey, Deborah Hardoon, and Sarah McLennan from the What Works Centre for Wellbeing. They opened doors, pulled off the immense logistical puzzle of juggling many stakeholders and institutions to pave the way for this endeavour, put up with our initial ignorance of the world of policy, and guided us to what's possible and what's useful in that world. We beg their forgiveness for the remaining imperfections and hope that they and their successors at the What Works Centre for Wellbeing will feel they co-own the result and will re-shape the material when the need calls for it: this was always meant as a living document, so we hope book 1.0 will be followed by many extensions and updates.

Next, we would like to thank all the academics who put in such an effort to wade through the many early versions and provided useful comments, corrections, and suggestions to make sure we are as academically honest as possible. We adopted most of the comments and quietly ignored the few we couldn't. So thanks to Richard Cookson and his team of health economists at York; Mark Bryan, Sara Connolly, and Kevin Daniels from the What Works Centre for Wellbeing: Work and Learning Evidence Programme (ESRC grant number: ES/N003586/1); Andrew Oswald from Warwick; Gigi Foster from the University of New South Wales; Richard Layard from the London School of Economics and Michael Plant from Oxford; and Carol Graham from the Brookings Institution. Because of useful What Works Centre for Wellbeing discussions at management meetings, and

[5] Including Arts Council England; Department for Business, Energy and Industrial Strategy; Department for Digital, Culture, Media and Sport; Department for Transport; Department for Work and Pensions; Historic England; Sport England; the Ministry of Housing, Communities and Local Government; and the Welsh government.

other Centre events, we would also like to acknowledge the other evidence programmes of the What Works Centre for Wellbeing: Communities (ESRC: ES/N003756/1) and Culture and Sport (ES/N003721/1).

We would also like to thank the many government economists, policy-makers, and analysts who provided comments, critiques, and suggestions to earlier versions. In particular, we want to thank those who gave advice on the general structure and whole chapters. So thanks to Phillip Ball and his team at the UK Department of Digital, Culture, Media and Sports; Iven Stead and his team at the UK Department for Transport; Adala Leeson and her team from Historic England; and Cara Maguire and her team at the UK Department for Business, Energy and Industrial Strategy. This version differs markedly from the previous versions mainly due to their feedback on how things work in practice.

Naturally, we thank Ekaterina (Katya) Oparina and Pierce Gately for excellent research assistance. We thank the team at the Centre for Economic Performance (CEP) at the London School of Economics, including Harriet Ogborn and Jo Cantlay, who helped smooth the way. Clément Béllet and Andrew Clark, co-authors who wrote pieces from which we extensively quote, also deserve a special thanks.

Of course, we also thank the sponsors who paid the bills. These include the Economic and Social Research Council (ESRC grant number: ES/N003683/1) which was supplemented by equal-matched public-sector funding via the What Works Centre for Wellbeing. The Australian Research Council Future Fellowship (ARC: FT130100738) also deserves mentioning as a lot of the groundwork for the frameworks and analysis in this book was developed in the period of this grant (2013–16).

The team at Oxford University Press also provided invaluable help; special thanks to Adam Swallow and Eleanor Capel-Smith.

These kinds of endeavours inevitably involve the support of loved ones, so Paul thanks Erika Turkstra and Christian thanks Herta Wagner-Krekel, Klaus Krekel, and Claryn Kung.

Contents

List of Figures

List of Tables

Quick Preview of the Main Ideas

The fundamental idea of this book is that we should measure societal progress in terms of additional wellbeing to the population. The unit of measure is the WELLBY: one unit of life satisfaction on a 0-to-10 scale for one person for one year.

We advocate the adoption of an institutional trajectory to absorb the key lessons that millions of observations in over a hundred thousand studies in nearly all countries of the world have given us as to how to increase wellbeing. The road ahead would involve embedding experimentation and measurement as a normal activity in the public sector, as well as structures to learn do's and don'ts of experimentation. It would involve the adoption of whole lists of estimated effects of policy-sensitive circumstances (like health, employment, or air pollution) on wellbeing, as well as a process via which better measures and better estimates can replace items on any endorsed list. It would involve generating frameworks for thinking about how this or that issue should be seen in wellbeing terms (such as how mental health or parenting skills relate to wellbeing), as well as a process for updating those frameworks.

This book makes many specific suggestions for these elements and advocates particular numbers, such as the threshold for the marginal social production costs of a WELLBY against which new policies could be judged. It also suggests how wellbeing analysis could simply be added to existing cost-benefit analyses by adopting a willingness-to-pay number for the value of a WELLBY, illustrating this with examples from different UK departments and agencies as well as organizations from around the world.

As a preview of the analyses this book is ultimately trying to normalize and lead to, consider Figure 0.1 below. This figure shows estimates for how cost-effective fifteen different interventions in different countries are in terms of WELLBY per £. It includes examples of very different types of interventions, ranging from workplace interventions (the STAR intervention in the United States), to health interventions (a mental-health intervention targeting depression in Pakistan), to environmental interventions (reduction of air pollution by retrofitting fossil-fuelled power plants in Germany), to subsidies for medicine (the NICE item), to cultural interventions. It thus shows how policies in very different domains can be compared on a single metric—the WELLBY—using the unifying concept of wellbeing.

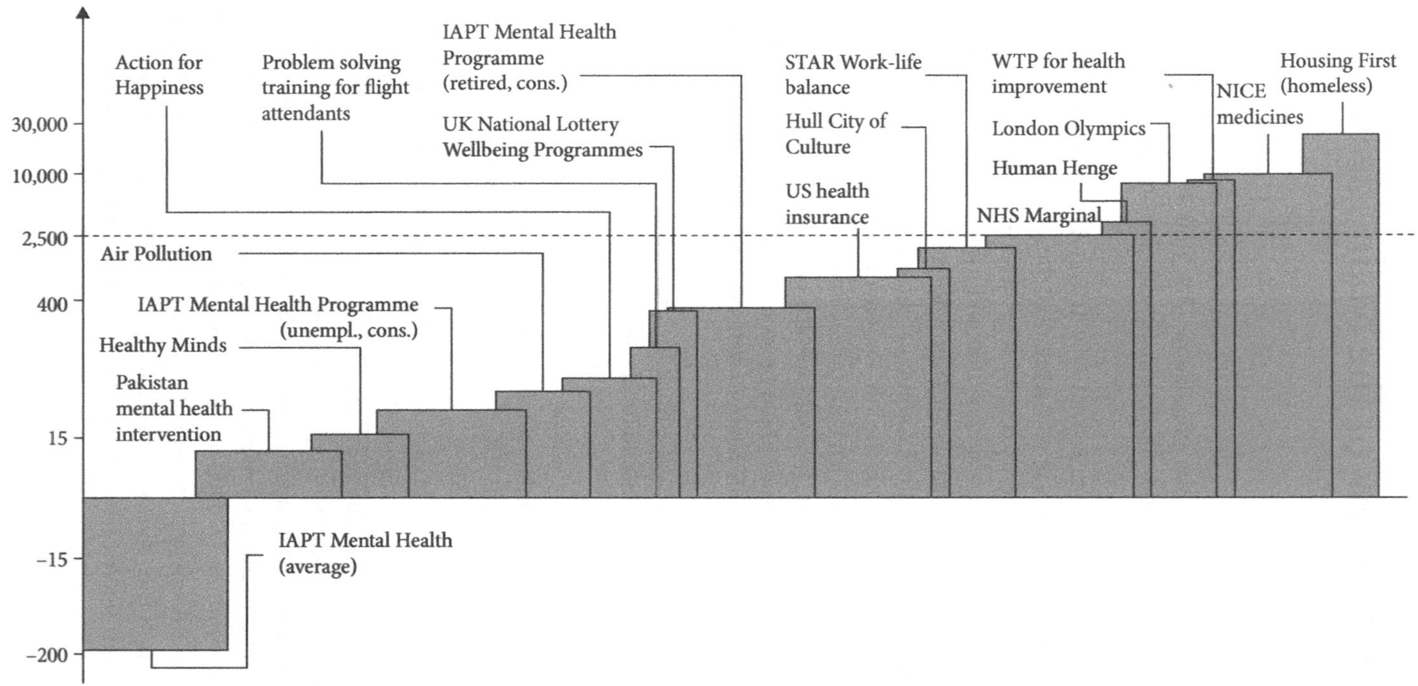

Figure 0.1 Cost per WELLBY of interventions at work, in the environment, and government services

Source: Own illustration based on own calculations.

This is not the place to discuss these fifteen interventions in depth as they are only for illustrative purposes and the actual value-for-money estimates are highly uncertain.

Yet, some crucial ideas that are used in this figure and some basic information to understand the figure are:

- A WELLBY is one unit of life satisfaction on a 0-to-10 scale for one person for one year. See chapter 2.
- Costs are in terms of net £ to the public purse as they would apply to the United Kingdom (so UK prices on things like housing). The net costs include up-front costs and flows into or out of the public purse, including changes in taxes and benefits. See chapter 3.
- All monetary effects that are not on the public purse are included in the WELLBY effect, which hence involves a translation from consumption levels to wellbeing. See chapter 4.
- The calculation requires assumptions on how the WELLBY relates to other major non-material factors, such as employment (chapter 2), mental and socio-emotional skills (chapter 2), health (chapter 4), culture (chapter 5), and so on.
- The breadth of the interventions shown in this figure entails a very basic guess as to how much up-front public costs would be involved if one would scale up the intervention to the level of the whole population. So a 'thin' intervention, like an employee work-planning intervention, is one which we do not believe would cost more than £1 billion in total when scaling it up. The 'thick' interventions are those that could include more than £10 billion of public money up front.
- The scale is logarithmic, meaning that vertical space translates to £ proportionally.
- The dotted vertical line shows the suggested threshold for adoption by the public sector. This threshold is derived from additional physical health spending in the United Kingdom on things like cancer treatments. See chapters 3 and 4.

The appendix in chapter 3 talks through the main assumptions and descriptions of the fifteen interventions in Figure 0.1, with references to the key studies from which estimates were taken.

1
The Case for Wellbeing as the Goal of Government and Constraints on Policy-making

Preview

This chapter is for readers interested in the general push to include wellbeing in governments' policy-making institutions. We discuss the origin of the idea that governments should care about wellbeing; how wellbeing is already incorporated in many policy evaluations and appraisals; how a wellbeing-oriented state bureaucracy fits in with the democratic process; and how the realities of policy-making often limit the use of formal wellbeing analyses and give rise to the importance of general knowledge about wellbeing amongst all decision-makers.

To start off, we give a quick synopsis of the basic vision at the heart of this book: what 'more wellbeing' would mean for policy-making and what steps would need to be taken to realize it. It is this basic vision which will unfold in the different chapters that follow and which forms our basic motivation. The chapter ends with a quick overview of the institutional trajectory yet to be undertaken to have wellbeing policy embedded in the government machinery.

Quo Vadis? The Basic Idea

The basic idea of 'more wellbeing' means that governments and policy-making institutions should openly adopt an actual measure of wellbeing and make the wellbeing of the population the primary objective of policy-making.

In many ways, GDP plays the role today of what we envision to be played by wellbeing in the future. True, a higher GDP is known to be somewhat good for wellbeing and all kinds of outcomes one expects to increase wellbeing in the long run, such as health and education (Weimann et al., 2015). Yet, there are more things to life than just market goods. A pure focus on GDP misses the harm economic activity can do to, for example, social relationships or the environment. In this sense, a broader perspective is needed—particularly since the main material bottlenecks that were so important in previous centuries dominated by poverty

A Handbook for Wellbeing Policy-Making: History, Theory, Measurement, Implementation, and Examples. Paul Frijters and Christian Krekel, Oxford University Press (2021).
DOI: 10.1093/oso/9780192896803.003.0001

and deprivation have now been largely overcome, at least in many middle to high-income countries and for large shares of the population.

One of the most often used measures of individual wellbeing that the scientific literature has come up with is life satisfaction.[1] The Office for National Statistics (ONS) in the United Kingdom, for example, has included the following Likert-scale question in more than forty datasets since 2011, with hundreds more around the world including a similar version:

> 'Overall, how satisfied are you with your life nowadays?'
> 0 means 'not at all', 10 'completely'.

This question, or close variants of it, has been posed to millions of UK residents and tens of millions of people around the world ever since the Likert scale was introduced in the 1930s, roughly at the same time that GDP measurement was introduced.

The question is subjective, and that is precisely the point of going towards wellbeing measurement: our lives are subjective and what we value as individuals is subjective.

One way to interpret this question is that answers consist of a vote by individuals as to how well they are doing in their life. This may be seen as augmenting voting for political parties, which happens only infrequently and is only a broad signal of what the population wants. Having information on how individuals evaluate their lives gives much more information on what they actually value and how their lives can be improved.

Using subjective information alongside electoral information is normal already in the public service. A hospital does not ask patients which health policy they favour, but rather how their health is in order to ascertain their needs. This is also the central idea of measuring wellbeing—that we take seriously how people judge their own lives to ascertain how we might help improve those lives.

There are many alternative measures and indices one could use to measure the wellbeing of individuals or whole countries. Besides GDP, examples include: literacy and numeracy rates, health outcomes, suicide rates, crime, or indices that aggregate hundreds of individual items.

Although there is information in each wellbeing measure and index, these alternatives are often not particularly useful for either central trade-offs or actual policy scenarios. Indices with hundreds of questions behind them, such as the

[1] On language: because the history of wellbeing in Western thought has such a long tradition, different words have been used over time and the meaning of words differ from period to period and from scholar to scholar. We will use the words *subjective wellbeing, wellbeing, life satisfaction*, and *happiness* interchangeably but will be more precise in how they subtly differ when we talk about measurement in chapter 2.

Sustainable Development Goals (SDGs), are simply too cumbersome to measure for many individuals in many scenarios, making them too unwieldly for any small or medium-level policy scenario. For central trade-offs, any multi-item index faces the issue of how to choose the weights between its components: how to determine how much, say, infant mortality is worth vis-à-vis literacy and numeracy rates? In current practice, the weights are made up ad hoc (Gruen, 2017), but a more proper weighting would need a clear choice for what is regarded as the best indicator of what people truly want. We argue that life satisfaction is the best candidate at present, though one should over time think of a process of challenge and updates should better measures emerge.

What makes life satisfaction appealing is that individuals have no trouble or hesitation in answering it.[2] Moreover, it is cheap to collect and a realistic option for nearly all datasets. Answers to the life-satisfaction question correlate positively with almost everything one intuitively thinks would be good for wellbeing, such as social relationships (Powdthavee, 2008), health (Helliwell et al., 2020), or wealth (Headey and Wooden, 2004). Happier individuals are more productive (De Neve and Oswald, 2012; Oswald et al., 2015), more pro-social (Drouvelis and Grosskopf, 2016), less often sick (Cohen et al., 2006), and live longer (Diener and Chan, 2011; Steptoe and Wardle, 2011). Most individuals agree in surveys asking them what they find important that life satisfaction fits their overall goal in life (Benjamin et al., 2012). Finally, individuals who are more satisfied with their lives are more likely to view the current government favourably (Ward, 2019), making life satisfaction a natural objective for elected politicians.

Although we argue that life satisfaction is the best single measure we have at present, it has many flaws and its use requires careful knowledge of survey design and statistical analysis. Measures of life satisfaction can be easily manipulated by priming individuals to think of something positive before asking them about their satisfaction with life (see, for example, Diener et al. (2013) for a summary of this effect in past studies). Answers are coarse in the sense that individuals give whole numbers and not something in between. Individual variation is high such that even at the individual level one needs many measurement points to say anything with confidence. There are strong seasonal, survey-specific (Smith, 1979), and age-specific effects (Pawlowski et al., 2011).

Importantly, individuals with higher life satisfaction are more likely to have all kinds of other good outcomes, which makes it difficult for researchers to separate

[2] For example, the missing rate for responses to questions on life satisfaction in the British Household Panel Survey (BHPS) across waves is about 2 per cent (Powdthavee, 2008). Similarly, for the Canadian General Social Survey (GSS) and the Canadian Community Health Survey (CCHS), between 96 per cent and 99 per cent of survey participants offered a valid response to the question on life satisfaction during the period from 2003 to 2011. See: https://www150.statcan.gc.ca/n1/pub/11f0019m/2013351/part-partie1-eng.htm#h2_4.

the effects of circumstances on life satisfaction from the effects of selection of more satisfied individuals into these circumstances. For example, while partners and jobs increase life satisfaction, it is also true that the more satisfied individuals find it easier to have partners and jobs, making it difficult to infer causality from wellbeing data.

Nevertheless, we now have over eighty years of experience with analysing life satisfaction, an experience that has led to more than 170,000 studies into its determinants. There is a growing body of robust studies looking at natural and quasi-natural experiments, randomized controlled trials, and large-scale analyses of what improves the wellbeing of individuals, households, communities, and whole countries (Diener et al., 2018).

In essence, this is what the wellbeing literature holds as a promise to the public sector: a huge existing and expanding database of relevant knowledge of what truly matters to individuals, a measurement-based understanding as to what degree specific factors and domains matter, and an empirical toolkit to ascertain both what is going on at present and to track the effects of policies over time in both small and large populations.

Throughout this book, we propose a vision of a self-aware and continuously measuring public sector that uses life satisfaction as the key link between its policies and the overall wellbeing of the population.

This vision offers different outlooks to different government institutions:

1. For some of the major public-service departments, such as social protection and health, life satisfaction can be the *direct goal of policy*. Departments, councils, and various other institutions can monitor the wellbeing of the population under their care and experiment continuously with new programmes or change old ones, finding out in an evolutionary manner what works best in what situation. Central information hubs like *What Works Centres* could help keep track of what has been tried and what has been found to work or not.
2. For other departments, including some major spending departments, life satisfaction can be the *indirect goal of policy*, while focusing directly on something more specific. Transport and the environment, for example, could aim primarily at the particular goals they have (like a reduction in commuting time or an improvement of air quality), basing themselves on established connections between those particular goals and wellbeing. This is probably the practical way forward for many departments which lack the individual capacity to figure out how their enterprise enhances the wellbeing of the whole population. They would need to be supplied with centrally vetted numbers as to how much their individual aims increase population

wellbeing, and what the rules of thumb are as to the external effects they would need to look out for.

3. For 'enabling departments' whose activities are by nature broad and lack a clearly defined group of clients, like defence or national audit institutions, wellbeing offers a narrative and a set of somewhat imprecise linkages between their activities and the wellbeing of the population. It is not realistic to expect the defence budget or the budget for national art to be based on exact estimates of the wellbeing value of a piece of military equipment or art. Yet, both can be grounded somewhat in a wellbeing narrative that makes their overall place in the scheme of things clear and that, perhaps in a process of decades, can become more precise. We know, for example, that a sense of cultural distinctiveness and pride, which is one of the goals of national art, helps to engender more social cohesion as it promotes a sense of shared culture and goals. Pro-social behaviour, tax morale, adherence to laws, and even the willingness to fight for one's country are higher in populations which share a strong common identity (Frijters and Foster, 2013), which in turn gives a rationale to jointly celebrated national events. Just how much wellbeing this ultimately generates will remain extremely speculative, but that does not mean it is trivial or should be ignored. Wellbeing thus offers a general route towards the longer-term accountability of enabling departments.
4. In all departments, knowledge of how wellbeing is increased in the workplace and in organizations more generally is of practical and direct self-interest in terms of how they organize their own workplaces and those they oversee. Here again, knowledge could be assembled and vetted by central information hubs like What Works Centres.
5. In all departments, wellbeing can be used to inform the general public and civil servants as to how pleasant it is in different areas as well as in different parts of the state bureaucracy. This already happens to a large degree, but can be integrated in management, local accountability, and job-search procedures even more than is already done at present. Budgets can, for example, be presented in terms of wellbeing effects and their distribution, as a form of wellbeing accountability to the population.
6. For analysts inside departments, the existing and rapidly expanding wellbeing literature offers an alternative source of estimates of value that can either augment standard cost-benefit analyses (CBAs) with wellbeing insights or completely replace them with explicit wellbeing cost-effectiveness analyses. Central allocation of funds can thus rank different policies in terms of their overall wellbeing value for money, leading to a funding cut-off point given by the last project still funded.

7. A central pool of knowledge used to train the next generation of analysts and policy-makers inside departments and state-affiliated organizations can be maintained in an open and constant conversation with academics and civil society. How to organize an open knowledge base that can be updated via challenge and new insights, and yet maintain a running set of guidelines based on the best knowledge at any moment, is as of yet uncertain. The model could follow the Intergovernmental Panel on Climate Change (IPCC) process within which climate scientists are included in a political process to come up with authoritative consensus numbers on the trajectory of the earth's climate. This would be too cumbersome and expensive to do for more than a few key wellbeing numbers, so one might down the line envisage a more disaggregated operation. The Linux and Wikipedia experiments, with open-source coding that are initially open to all experts in the world but that over time started to seal off compartments owned by specialized groups in academia and the civil service, would perhaps be a good model to follow for most of the wellbeing knowledge. Also, many of the techniques and habits for wellbeing improvement are generic statistical and scientific tools that could be maintained by groups that have no affinity with wellbeing themselves. New institutions that help local groups in setting up how to gather and analyse data over time need to know little about wellbeing but rather should know about experimental techniques and the do's and don'ts of things like database management.

Above is merely a sketch of what a wellbeing orientation could look like for the public sector. The basic idea is one of a state bureaucracy that is more aware of data and of the effects of policies and practices on wellbeing, and that is open to experiment constantly in order to find improvements. The challenge is just how an organization can learn from thousands of experiments that are too far apart for any single individual or group to fully understand. In that challenge, wellbeing is the natural linking-pin to maintain overall policy integrity: by generating and adopting overall frameworks based on a current best-practice measure of wellbeing, the system as a whole can slowly become more rational and improve wellbeing outcomes from its investments.

A Brief History

Preamble

The general study of happiness has deep philosophical roots and is part of the classical Western discussions surrounding the 'good life' and the Greek concept of 'eudemonia'. It has resonances in non-Western streams of thought too, such as

Buddhism. Let us suffice with a brief look at what has happened the last few centuries in Anglo-Saxon thought and in economics, which dominates the world of policy.[3]

The key take-away is that it has been completely normal in the last three hundred years in Western philosophical thought to assume that the nation state should orient itself towards improving the happiness of the population, loosely understood as a mental state of individuals. The only question has been whether it is feasible and sensible to truly set up a system to do this, or whether instead to rely more on proxies like economic growth and physical health as objectives for government policy.

A Brief History of Anglo-Saxon Thought and Early Happiness Theories

Since the Enlightenment, it has become widely accepted that governments should serve the interests of their populations. The idea of the social contract between the governors and the governed now dominates Western political thought, originating in the seventeenth and eighteenth century with Thomas Hobbes, John Locke, and Jean-Jacques Rousseau.[4]

These Enlightenment traditions have earlier counterparts in the city states of Italy and, of course, the thinking of the ancient Greeks, including Aristotle, who declared happiness to be the meaning and purpose of life.

In the United Kingdom and the United States, the social contract came to mean that the goal of government was the happiness of the people. Prominent early contributors in the United Kingdom were eighteenth- and nineteenth-century philosophers like Jeremy Bentham, John Stuart Mill, and Francis Edgeworth.

John Locke argued in *An Essay Concerning Human Understanding* (1689) that 'the highest perfection of intellectual nature lies in a careful and constant pursuit of true and solid happiness'. Jeremy Bentham advocated that societies should orient themselves towards the 'greatest happiness of the greatest number' (in *A Fragment on Government*, 1776). David Hume extended this notion to all human activity when he wrote 'The great end of all human industry is the attainment of happiness' (Hume, 1742). In the same year that Bentham enthused the importance of happiness, the US Declaration of Independence (1776) declared 'Life, liberty and the pursuit of happiness' as inalienable rights. Thomas Jefferson elevated 'the care of human life and happiness' to be the only legitimate object

[3] This historical exposition draws on Frijters et al. (2020) where the basic arguments and practicalities around wellbeing as the goal of government are presented and discussed by thirteen experts from various disciplines.

[4] There are many reviews of the philosophy and history of the use of wellbeing indicators as the objective of government. Recent contributions include Stiglitz et al. (2011) and O'Donnell et al. (2014).

of good government, and George Washington thought governments should concern themselves with the 'aggregate happiness of the society'.

Some nineteenth-century utilitarians already made attempts to measure the relation between direct pleasurable or displeasurable inputs on happiness. Long discussions were had in the nineteenth century about 'ideal utilitarianism', 'hedonistic value theory', and other forms of utilitarianism that took the internal experiences of humans as central to the goal of society. Concurrently, early psychophysicists started experimenting with stimulus-response models of well-being and formulated the Weber-Fechner law of response-stimulus, essentially postulating a logarithmic relationship between stimuli (say, stress) and psychological response (say, pleasure or pain). Interestingly, the logarithmic function is still the dominant functional form today to describe the relationship between income and happiness.

Adam Smith, the founder of modern economics, added an important constraint to the pursuit of happiness. He wanted people to concern themselves with the happiness of only those in their own group, not the whole of humankind. In Chapter III of the *Theory of Moral Sentiments* (1759),[5] he summarized this position as follows:

> The administration of the great system of the universe, however, the care of the universal happiness of all rational and sensible beings, is the business of God and not of man. To man is allotted a much humbler department, but one much more suitable to the weakness of his powers, and to the narrowness of his comprehension; the care of his own happiness, of that of his family, his friends, his country: that he is occupied in contemplating the more sublime, can never be an excuse for his neglecting the more humble department; and he must not expose himself to the charge which Avidius Cassius is said to have brought, perhaps unjustly, against Marcus Antoninus; that while he employed himself in philosophical speculations, and contemplated the prosperity of the universe, he neglected that of the Roman empire.

This constraint delineates the objective of a national government to be the happiness of its citizens, and raises the crucial questions of the pursuit of *national* happiness and the necessity of government to create a national identity. It also comes with the practical problem of having to be somewhat clear about who is in the relevant population, both now and in the future.

Many Western democracies followed this tradition and have long mandated that new policies should serve the interests of the population, although not using

[5] Of course, Adam Smith said a lot more about the responsibilities of individuals and government, so the quote is not the whole of his position, but it neatly summarizes the general thrust of utilitarian thought as practiced in the United Kingdom.

the word 'happiness' but 'wellbeing' or 'social welfare'. In the United Kingdom, this can be most clearly seen in the Her Majesty's Treasury (HMT) *Green Book*, which is the guide for all departments as to how to argue for resources for new policies. It states that 'economic appraisal is based on the principles of welfare economics', referred to in the *Green Book* as 'social value' (p. 5).

A Brief History of Happiness Measurement

In the nineteenth century, utilitarians did not yet have at their disposal large-scale instruments to measure the happiness of the population and were hence largely confined to small-scale experiments on stimulus-response, or deductions from observations and introspection.

In the early twentieth century, new measurement tools were developed, in particular the Likert scale (1932, 1934) where people were asked to rate a psychological outcome on an ordered scale with some minimum and some maximum that were given emotive labels (like 'completely satisfied', 'very happy', or 'very unhappy'). Likert scales remain the dominant measurement devices in use today, though the number of variations in terms of scaling, terminology, and applications has become large.

From the point of view of the preceding forms of measurement, using Likert scales to measure happiness has several distinguishing characteristics: (i) individuals themselves are taken as the sole and ultimate judges of the quality of their life; (ii) individuals are taken to be able and in the frequent habit of judging their life as a whole; (iii) the scales adopt an explicit lower- and an explicit upper-bound on what people can answer; and (iv) the number of possible answers is finite, meaning that happiness is measured in discrete intervals.

Each of these features has come under severe criticism, but the Likert scale remains the dominant form of measurement today for the same reason why it was developed in the 1930s: it is both politically and morally imperative to take individuals' own opinions as core considerations for how they are doing in life, and in order to be useful they must have bounded scales which give numbers that one can then add up and compare.[6]

We will revisit the question of how reasonable these elements are later in this book, but we can mention that the core arguments are a combination of political expediency and evolutionary plausibility. Politically, one has to treat individuals as equal, independent of their own personal belief systems or different ways they

[6] Adding up the answers to subjective questions which different people give at different points in time is generally referred to as taking the underlying numbers as *cardinal*, i.e. comparable between people and over time, and as being linearly additive.

might experience life. On the other hand, evolution has equipped humans with the habit of self-evaluation as a means of improving their choices (Felson, 1993) and these evaluations are somewhat observable to others via both verbal and non-verbal communication, like smiles and frowns.

Apart from individual scales, the other main measurement tool developed in the twentieth century that is still widely used is an aggregate of individual items, such as a question module leading to an index. There is no dominant index of wellbeing, however, merely a large wilderness of different ones. An example is the twelve-item General Health Questionnaire (GHQ12) developed by Goldberg et al. (1997), which poses twelve questions, including whether respondents feel happy, and which researchers then aggregate and sometimes interpret as an alternative measure of happiness (see Clark and Oswald (1994), for example). The Satisfaction with Life Scale (SWLS) developed by Diener et al. (1985) is popular within the discipline of psychology, though not in economics. The Comprehensive Quality of Life Scale (ComQol) developed by Cummins et al. (1994) is another example of an index derived from multiple single items.

At the national level, there exist even more indices aimed at monitoring wellbeing. Amongst hundreds, we can mention the Human Development Index (HDI), the Bhutan Happiness Index (Ura et al., 2012), the Macau Quality of Life Reports (Rato and Davey, 2012; Davey and Rato, 2012), or the Gallup Well-Being Index (Skopec et al., 2014). These are based on aggregations of a set of characteristics deemed desirable for individuals or whole countries, such as life expectancy or literacy and numeracy rates, and are often labelled 'wellbeing'. Stiglitz et al. (2011) document many such indices relating to quality of life, recommending that users pick the index that best fits their purpose but singling out the simple life-satisfaction question as the most useful measure if one is looking for a summary measure.

It is in hindsight interesting that the measurement tools for happiness in use today were developed at almost exactly the same time that measures of GDP were developed by economists like Simon Kuznets (in the mid-1930s, to better steer the war effort), with actual measures of GDP appearing at almost the same time (in the late 1940s). The fundamental contributions on happiness measurement thus came from previous generations of psychologists.

What has mainly happened during the last fifty years or so is a wide proliferation of new measures that are variations of the previous ones. This includes the notion of domain satisfactions, such as satisfaction with 'work', 'the environment', or 'yesterday's conference dinner'. It also includes the new field of internet-mediated measures of 'likes' and 'dislikes', 'numbers of stars', or degrees of 'agreement' with various statements. These all follow the notion of Likert scales in the sense that they provide bounded answers which are, in practical terms, just added up over people to generate aggregate scores that are subsequently advertised and used as indicators of overall sentiments.

One of the most important thinkers in the field of happiness measurement amongst the current generation is Daniel Kahneman, who has been pivotal in the development of the Day Reconstruction Method (DRM). The DRM elicits happiness at the end of the day as an aggregate of period-specific happiness experienced throughout that day (Kahneman et al., 2004). This method has not yet seen great uptake as it suffers from two important limitations. First, it is time-intensive in that respondents need to complete detailed diaries at the end of the day, making it an expensive measure. Second, it may suffer from recall bias in that people may be better or worse at remembering specific periods, which makes the results difficult to interpret. And, from a policy perspective, it sometimes yields seemingly counterintuitive results, for example, that people who are in unemployment do not experience less happiness than people who are in stable jobs.

A more modern version of the DRM that overcomes some of its limitations is the Experience Sampling Method (ESM). The ESM is typically based on a downloadable mobile phone app that asks users—at random times during the day—to report their feelings of happiness while recording their locations, activities, and companions. While this solves issues around recall bias, the method is more prone to selection: not only are individuals who download the app typically younger, more educated, and tech savvy than the general population, selection also occurs at the time of reporting when respondents choose to reply (or not) to random pings (which may be correlated to happiness). Nevertheless, the DRM and the ESM are some of the few real innovations of recent decades in happiness measurement.

Daniel Kahneman has also been highly influential when it comes to the interpretation of happiness measures as 'decision utility' (i.e. the happiness we think we will experience when making a decision) as opposed to 'experience utility' (i.e. the happiness we will actually experience as a consequence of making a decision), with the difference between both typically interpreted as a failure in hedonic forecasting. The dichotomy between decision and experience utility remains influential to this day (Kahneman et al., 1997).

A useful dichotomy between wellbeing measures at the individual level is that there are measures intended to ascertain a flow of instantaneous experiences (experiential measures like happiness or anxiety) and reflective measures of wellbeing (evaluative measures like life satisfaction). It now seems increasingly likely that more instantaneous measures differ strongly from reflective measures in terms of their drivers because they have a different purpose: immediate emotions, like anger and jealousy, aid decision-making in the very short run, whilst reflective deliberations on how life is going are more useful for planning purposes. These more reflective measures are the more natural objects of policy-making, but there is also useful information in measures of immediate experiences.

A Brief History of Practical Assumptions and their Implications for the Economics of Happiness

Economists have long had a somewhat schizophrenic relationship with happiness which persists up to this day. On the one hand, most economists, and certainly the profession as a whole, feel uneasy about any specific candidate measure of happiness because they quickly spot the main problems involved in these measures and the strong assumptions required to use them in practice. Yet, on the other hand, economists have the role of coming up with actual numbers about the advantages and disadvantages of different policies. This forces them into an implicit stance on what matters to people, which means they either must assume they know the answer without measurement or adopt some implicit measurement.

This ambiguous relationship was not always there. In the nineteenth century, Adam Smith's quote on how individuals should help their groups maximize overall happiness was the mainstream position in economics. Classic utilitarians such as Jeremy Bentham and Francis Edgeworth advocated the same goal: that economists should measure what it is that people enjoy and base their theories and policy prescripts on the principle of maximizing the happiness of individuals or some relevant group as a whole. There were no population-wide actual measures in the nineteenth century, but this was certainly the ideal.

This position changed with the marginalist revolution of the late nineteenth century and the subsequent move away from the attempt to measure individual mental states towards the formulation of general equilibrium theory, followed by the axiomatization of preferences and choice under uncertainty. This counter-movement had a strong proponent in Lionel Robbins, who declared that economists should not be involved in questions of ethics and should leave the measurement of the inner lives of people to others, doubting that it could ever be done in a scientific way. Robbins (1932), in his treatise on the significance of economics, accepted the implication that economics "is incapable of deciding between the desirability of different ends. It is fundamentally distinct from Ethics" (p. 152). People were acknowledged to have feelings and desires, but it was deemed outside the realm of economics to take measures of their actual feelings and desires as valuable outcomes.

Despite prominent dissenters throughout the twentieth century (including Ragnar Frisch and Jan Tinbergen, the first Nobel Prize winners in economics), Robbins' position was more or less the dominant position until relatively recently.

Economists in diverse fields simply assumed the shape of the utility function and declared utility immeasurable by any means other than observable consumer choices, and even these merely identified preference orderings and not any absolute measure of utility that could meaningfully be used by policy-makers as the basis of trade-offs *between* people. As Wansbeek and Kapteyn (1983) succinctly said during this period:

> Utility seems to be to economists what the Lord is to theologians. Economists talk about utility all the time, but seem not to have hope of ever observing it this side of heaven. In micro-economic theory, almost any model is built on utility functions of some kind. In empirical work little attempt is made to measure this all-pervasive concept. The concept is considered to be so esoteric as to defy direct measurement by mortals. Still, in a different role, viz. of non-economists, the same mortals are the sole possessors of utility functions and they are able to do incredible things with it [. . .]. As a result, there is a giant gap between theory and empirical work.

Throughout the 1970s and 1980s, there were some contributions by economists to use direct measures of utility, including Easterlin (1974), Scitovsky (1975), and Layard (1980), but they had relatively little influence on the profession until recently. Only in the 1990s did the study of happiness as a potential measure of utility amongst economists start to take off, with the main early interest being the question of whether economic growth increases happiness. Amongst psychologists and sociologists, it had long been argued that money and happiness were but weakly related (see Cantril (1965), for example), but such insights did not permeate economics.

The stance of Lionel Robbins created a huge problem for economists in government, as it is impossible to devise policies that do not involve trade-offs between people, requiring some implicit notion of 'cardinal utility' with which one might say that gains outweigh losses. As Ragnar Frisch said in 1964: 'To me the idea that cardinal utility should be avoided in economics is completely sterile . . . there are many domains of economic theory where it is absolutely *necessary* to consider the concept of cardinal utility if we want to develop a sensible sort of analysis.'

The profession tried to side-step this conundrum by focusing on the supposed possibility of 'Pareto improvements', which denote the situation in which policies improve the outcomes of some people without damaging the outcomes of others. However, the Pareto principle provides only a partial ordering of policies and, most importantly, policies that affect millions of people are never unanimously approved of. As a result, the Pareto principle is seldom practically used for policy evaluation and appraisal in mainstream government applications.

A related alternative is known as the 'Kaldor-Hicks' principle, which, roughly speaking, argues that economists should worry about the overall size of the economic pie, and that it is left to politicians to determine its appropriate redistribution so that no one is left behind. In this line of thinking, a good economic policy increases the economic pie, which then allows for a Pareto improvement where someone is made better off while no one is made worse off. Whether the increased pie is then actually redistributed in a way that is Pareto-improving is deemed a matter for policy-makers. One problem with this approach is that the 'pre-redistribution' pie would need to include everything that affects wellbeing, including externalities. So one cannot presume that the economic pie is the only thing that matters for wellbeing unless it has shown to be so in an accepted measure of wellbeing! Hence, the Kaldor-Hicks principle does not alleviate the issue of finding a proper measure of wellbeing that goes beyond material goods: all the principle does is to separate the potential wellbeing improvements from the decision of who gets the improvements, not the basic problem of measuring whether something is an improvement at all. One cannot know what the pre-redistribution 'wellbeing pie' is unless one measures it.

In some ways, the Kaldor-Hicks principle is still an important train of thought within government today, where the practice in many policy evaluations and appraisals is to look at changes in the 'total economic surplus', which, roughly speaking, relates to the economic pie. Economic surplus, in turn, is deduced largely via the revealed willingness-to-pay in markets, or via the stated willingness-to-pay elicited through survey methods such as contingent valuation or choice experiments.

Where this has become stuck most visibly is when it comes to redistribution and externalities between people that are not measurable as economic surplus. To assess the wellbeing effects of redistribution, it is necessary to adopt some explicit notion of how much additional resources affect the wellbeing of the poor relative to the wellbeing of the rich. It is difficult to make this assessment without taking a direct stance on cardinal utility. When it comes to externalities, and particularly externalities in the emotional realm (for example, hurt or discomfort), actual measurement needs to be at the individual level (where the experience takes place) and one needs to assume comparability between individuals to arrive at an overall measure of what has happened to the whole population.

Moreover, for externalities that individuals are not necessarily aware of (for example, certain forms of pollution) or would admit to (for example, jealousy or shame), one cannot rely on market prices or the stated willingness-to-pay to get a measure of how strong these are: one needs to measure their presence and strength by measuring the wellbeing of individuals, seeing how these change due to the actions of others.

Interestingly, the current position on distributional matters in government (at least in the United Kingdom) already appeals to life satisfaction as the best-candidate measure of individual wellbeing: the official weighing scales via which changes in the incomes of the poor are to be multiplied relative to changes in the incomes of the rich are (roughly) logarithmic, which is explicitly motivated by the basis that life satisfaction relates to incomes in a (roughly) logarithmic manner.[7] Moreover, when it comes to the monetary valuation of externalities or 'intangibles' for which there exists no given market price, current practice within government often includes the implicit willingness-to-pay via the estimated effects of externalities on life satisfaction. By trading off their effects with that of income and calculating the marginal rate of substitution, one can derive a monetary equivalent. We will discuss this more extensively in chapter 4, but note here that there exists a wide range of such studies in the wellbeing literature, including on air (Levinson, 2012; Ferreira et al., 2013; Ambrey et al., 2013) and noise pollution (Van Praag and Baarsma, 2005; Rehdanz and Maddison, 2008; Fujiwara et al., 2017), landscape amenities or disamenities (Ambrey and Fleming, 2011; Kopmann and Rehdanz, 2013), land use (Bertram and Rehdanz, 2015; Krekel et al., 2016), and even terrorism (Frey et al., 2009). The current practice on both distributional analyses and the monetary valuation of intangibles, therefore, already makes the implicit assumption that life satisfaction is a valid and cardinal measure of individual wellbeing, and that it is desirable to optimize it.

In sum, economists have long accepted the direct measurement of wellbeing, except for a brief period of about sixty years or so (starting from the mid-1930s) when the headline approach was to prefer an indirect measurement of utility via observed consumer choices and GDP to a direct measurement via mental states. In actual policy evaluations and appraisals, economists in practice often accepted self-reported wellbeing measures as cardinal utility, but this is often only implicitly done and certainly not the mainstream economic teaching of today. Slowly, economists are re-joining psychologists and others who have never let go of the idea of direct measurement and who have pushed for the inclusion of direct measures in many surveys.

The Tide of History: The Shift That Favours Wellbeing?

It is useful to think of underlying historical shifts that favour a wellbeing orientation in policy. One old but major and slow shift is the move towards consumerism and the one-man-one-vote rule of democracy: voters and populations have over the last two hundred years increasingly started to view democratic politics and the economy as providers of things they want as individuals. That means they have come to expect democratic institutions to be interested in what they want.

[7] The 2018 HMT *Green Book* (p. 78) proposes a value of 1.3 for the elasticity of the 'marginal utility of income', based on the life-satisfaction regressions in Layard et al. (2008).

The effect of democratic principles is equally true for the law, which supposedly applies equally to everyone, and in terms of access to public services, like education and health. While reality is less egalitarian than the ideal behind democracy or the law, the continued importance of these institutions increases the sense amongst people that these institutions are there to serve them and their interests. They are equals amongst many, at least in principle.

The increase in social programmes since the Second World War exemplifies the greater degree to which populations are 'serviced' by their governments and the state machinery, slowly replacing many other group structures that provided these services previously. This consumerist 'social contract' between citizens and those with representative roles naturally fits a philosophy of the greatest happiness. We now have Western governments spending about 40 per cent of GDP (OECD, 2020), a large slice of which goes to education, health, and welfare, replacing churches that previously supplied care for the poor or charities that ran schools. A government philosophy of the greatest happiness for all fits this focus on the population's needs and desires.

Another major and more recent shift has been the emergence of the internet and the provision of freely available information more generally. The choice set has increased tremendously in recent decades, both in terms of what people can consume and how they can invest their time. There are far more music songs available for free than one can listen to, more types of cars than one can test-drive, more magazines than one can read, more types of coffee than one can drink, more fields of study than one can learn about, and more holiday destinations than one has weekends in a year.

This widened choice set has generated a fundamental problem of cognitive overload. Humans simply cannot truly review all possible choices and pick the one best for them. We all must rely on easier heuristics that need less effort to pick something we are likely to enjoy.

One solution that the internet has come up with has been to aggregate subjective feedback to rank alternatives: many of us follow the stated likes and dislikes of those who have made choices before us. Many of us judge the trustworthiness of a seller on Amazon by the average ratings they received on previous sales. Many of us follow the music others have judged positively as witnessed by their aggregate downloads, perhaps weighted by how much these others are like us in various dimensions (for example, previous choices or tastes). Many of us follow the recommendations of others when it comes to bars, restaurants, and hotels, as measured in average 'likes' and 'stars' and other forms of subjective feedback. A common strategy is to look at aggregate information on subjective ratings of different options and then pick something near the top. That is also how internet search engines now work.[8] In essence, the aggregated subjective consumer experience of others has become an organizational force in itself for our choice behaviour.

[8] See Béllet and Frijters (2019) for an analysis of how such social media measures of wellbeing relate to more traditional, survey-based measures.

Younger generations are completely used to thinking of choice as something one does on the basis of the simple average of the evaluations of others, and to add one's own ratings to things one has tried oneself and liked or not. The younger generation votes many times a day, such as on how satisfied they have been with their teacher, their coffee, or their shoes. This makes it a small step for the younger generation to think of government programmes in the same way: one judges based on one's own experiences and one trusts the aggregate stated experience of others as a valid signal of how one would experience something oneself.

'Satisfaction' is a key phrase used for the subjective experience of goods and services, events, and even people. How satisfied one is with their drink, their dinner, or their conference is now a standard question many people encounter daily. The average scores are used to judge the quality of bars, restaurants, or conference organizers. What was once seen as heretical in mainstream economics—the idea that one should simply take the average of stated satisfaction levels as informative of how good one thing was over another—is now a lived reality experienced by many people (including economists themselves). It was not imposed but has grown from the bottom up. For the younger generations, the idea that changes in society as a whole should be judged similarly is natural. They have grown up with the benefits and pitfalls of subjective feedback, cognizant of its uses and limits.

A related shift, which is ultimately more a consequence of other shifts rather than an independent one, has been the need within service-oriented government bureaucracies to find a means of prioritizing different types of expenditure. More projects are suggested for finance than can be financed, leading to the need to have an overall objective to evaluate the relative merit of different options. For example, within the National Health Service (NHS) in the United Kingdom there has been a need for an overarching objective. Measures as simple as 'health' or 'mental health' but also more complex ones such as 'quality-adjusted life-years' (QALYs) have been proposed and implemented, but there is a clear argument to go towards a more whole-of-life view and look at what patients themselves find most important for their lives: their evaluation with life as a whole.

Although the need for an overarching objective need not arrive at wellbeing because one might well use a religious doctrine or the interests of a particular group to define that overarching objective, it is again the case that within the ideal of one-man-one-vote, the logical focus is the interests of the population. Some notion of the wellbeing of the population, therefore, lends itself as the focus of service-oriented government bureaucracies.

In sum, a truly fundamental new shift towards the acceptance of averaged subjective evaluations has been due to the explosion of choice and the resulting need for simplified measures to help people choose. That need is being filled with aggregated measures of satisfaction. The underlying information increase is still ongoing and makes the continued and increased use of aggregate wellbeing measures likely. The explosion of choice itself arises from many things, ranging from new inventions in computing, to reduced transportation costs between countries that makes increased specialization possible, and thus proliferation of goods and services to choose from. They can be seen as 'fundamental economic forces' over which no individual country or ideological group has much control.

Where these trends bite first for government are highly visible service-oriented programmes that need to allocate scarce resources over potential sub-programmes. This is both true for central and for local governments. Accordingly, such programmes should serve as the focus for quick wins and new methodologies that might eventually be rolled out elsewhere.

How Wellbeing Could Fit into Policy Evaluations and Appraisals

How does policy-making work, roughly speaking? And where would wellbeing fit in? What would it add? To answer these questions, we look at the example of the United Kingdom.

As in many other countries, the United Kingdom has, broadly speaking, two types of decision-makers, complete with two systems of selecting them.

At the top of the democratic political system are the elected national politicians who represent smaller areas, their constituencies. Information about what their constituents find important is generated in the democratic system, via direct communication between politicians and their electorates but also via democratic competition between politicians who offer voters different policy platforms. The democratic process tells us what the population, which constitutes the ultimate judge, values.[9]

On the other side is the civil service, organized mainly in individual departments. Civil servants have their own processes for hiring and promotion, and arguably have—to a certain extent—an independent mandate towards the wellbeing of the population. Their role is to help elected politicians enact the policies on which they were elected *and* select the best policies for the population.[10]

Both sides have sources of information to help them in this policy development process, including a national statistical agency, a large number of somewhat independent research institutes, the international scientific literature on various matters, and, of course, the training they have when they enter their jobs. Because there are many more civil servants than politicians and because they are more specialized, the role of the civil service is more contemplative.

[9] Of course, the democratic process serves many other functions, including the selection and scrutiny of those with representative power.

[10] Put more formally: the civil service role is to provide independent and impartial advice to the government of the day as set out in the Civil Service Code. The interest of officials and analysts in wellbeing is to provide the best possible policy advice.

Policies at the national level are set in the intersection of elected politicians and the civil service, using a variety of mechanisms and processes. Over decades, the system of policy formation has become complex and specialized.

The practice of policy-making involves numerous small and large decisions made every day in numerous government-related institutions, most of which do not involve the conscious knowledge of elected politicians, who by and large deal more with the bigger issues and the broad direction of policy. As a result, senior civil servants and others who are connected to the public sector all have some 'decision-making power'.

University managers are a good example of decision-makers with some independent power (over buildings, courses, recruitment, etc.) who are not truly civil servants but still connected to the overall policy process, for example because their funds mainly derive from national policies around students and research grants. Universities are thus a good example of a long-term oriented set of institutions that are, arguably, meant to serve the interests of the country by looking after teaching and research. They are somewhat independent and somewhat regulated, part clients and part lobbyists, led by traditions that sometimes go back hundreds of years and by the latest guidelines on how to apply for government funding.

There are similarly numerous authorities with some decision-making power, many of which will be largely unknown to some readers, such as the thirty-odd navigation authorities in the United Kingdom that are responsible for rivers and canals, or Her Majesty's representatives in Commonwealth countries around the world.[11] They continuously make decisions and rules without significant input from elected politicians, who only get informed and involved in particularly contentious or important matters. Many of these authorities are officially charities, such as the National Trust.

Some institutions, such as the Bank of England or Scotland Yard, are deliberately put at arm's length of politicians to increase their independence from short-term political goals. Similarly, there are independent authorities that are more or less operating without daily political oversight, such as the National Lottery or the British Broadcasting Corporation (BBC). Some of them have their own sources of income and their own decision procedures on how to spend it.

Cabinet is the main decision-making body for UK Government. However, there exists no central place where everything is known and discussed for the simple reason that society is just too complex.

Not only is there no central place that decides on everything, but the data that exist on aggregate circumstances are often not understood. For instance, only

[11] For an example of the complex relationships these somewhat independent authorities have with central and local government, see: https://www.waterways.org.uk/news_campaigns/campaigns/ea_navigations/navigation_authorities.

specialists know how GDP is truly estimated because the technical appendices on how it is put together count hundreds of pages. Few journalists reporting on GDP figures would know, for instance, that corrections are made on the basis of how many public holidays fall on a weekend in a particular year, or that there are vintages of GDP figures, such that there are in fact several consecutive GDP figures for any period. We have never seen a politician discuss the smoothing parameters used to derive an estimated flow of imports to put into the national accounts. How life expectancy and population figures are truly derived will similarly be a mystery to all but a few specialists who spent years studying such matters.

As a result, many decisions are made locally and much of the information used to make decisions is imperfect and difficult to understand. Nevertheless, decisions *are* made, they are (somewhat) informed, and there is a general push to increase and improve the information base.

Knowledge of what improves wellbeing, in principle, can be used by all decision-makers, ranging from elected politicians who decide on major new welfare programmes to university office clerks who decide on the purchase of office supplies. There are lots of sources of wellbeing information for all the various decision-makers, ranging from books to dedicated institutions like the What Works Centre for Wellbeing in the United Kingdom.

The national set-up is mirrored by local decision-making, with elected councillors on the one hand and a local public sector on the other. There, both sides also come with their own preferred means of obtaining information and some degree of an independent mandate to look after the wellbeing of the local population, with only the bigger and more visible decisions truly taken by elected politicians, and even then, often on the advice of their civil servants.

It is in this cauldron of professional civil servants negotiating, leading, and following elected politicians that major policies get decided. Lots of policies then become embedded in separate institutions and whole systems in society (e.g. the legal system) who further develop and enact them.

During implementation, many further decisions are taken as intention meets reality: few policies work out 'on the ground' as they were originally intended. Laws get reinterpreted and refined. Much of the policy process is then about steering institutions and policies towards a fairly vague 'better direction', motivated often more by visible problems than a utopian envisaged 'effect of a policy'.

This stylized sketch of policy-making will be fleshed out more when we come to actual methods for policy evaluation and appraisal, where the negotiations between spending departments and resource-deciding units in the Treasury are paramount. Yet, it serves to remind us that the practice of policy-making is far too complex for most people to completely understand, and hence to guide in any but a crude sense. This does not mean that 'anything goes' or that one should not aim for greater precision and evidence—far from it!—but we should not confuse targets and ideals with an imperfect reality that only changes slowly.

The purpose of policy-oriented wellbeing inquiry is then to help the various decision-makers at different levels of government, which boils down to approximately right strategic advice for those in charge of broad strategies, and more practical advice for those making choices on the ground.

There are many decision-makers for whom a knowledge of wellbeing is of less use because their mandate and role are already clearly defined. Someone whose main task it is to clean the street has little need to know environmental policy, and is more usefully served by a good broom. So too is knowledge of wellbeing virtually irrelevant to a homicide detective or the engineers designing the steel cables of a new bridge. Their role is not sensitive to the kind of additional information offered by direct wellbeing measurement, although, arguably, measuring their wellbeing at work can help design work environments that are more conducive to their job satisfaction and productivity.

Direct wellbeing measurement then mainly has the potential to inform policy-making at the highest level in terms of where the broad gains in terms of wellbeing might be; to help spending-departments decide on competing projects; and to help those in charge of any area with large amounts of discretion surrounding public services for people with some notion as to what is likely to improve wellbeing.

Why not rely solely on the information and judgement of voters as evidenced in elections? What are the differences between what is learned from the democratic process and the scientific process?

Elections and Information

Elections and representative democracy channel information about what the population believes is in its interest towards the decision-makers at various levels of society. Political activism and involved citizenry are related mechanisms to move the hand of decision-makers in the 'right' direction.

Yet, just like common sense might not be enough to know what is in our best interests, so too are there limitations as to how much decision-makers can learn from what the population votes for. The population as a whole might not know how to improve their wellbeing, just as the population as a whole might not know how a jet engine works or what the best foreign policy might look like. Political debate and decision-making can furthermore be dominated in the short run by special-interest groups who want something that benefits them at the expense of the overall wellbeing of society, leaving a role for decision-makers outside of the political process.

The complexity of life, the possibility that special-interest groups try to manipulate information streams, and the limited understanding of all of us lead to specialization in the gathering of evidence and synthesis of that evidence.

There is thus a role for scientific inquiry into the drivers of wellbeing, and a role for translation of that evidence into various levels of decision-making.

This should not be seen as an alternative to the democratic process, but rather a logical aspect of it: just as all major political parties support scientific councils and the existence of specialized ministries for all sorts of public activities (education, health, transport, defence, etc.), so too can a population decide that its state bureaucracy be mandated to aim for its long-run wellbeing. This is indeed precisely what the civil service has adopted as its mandate for many decades and what has been a standard theme in Western political philosophy for centuries.

Elections and scientific inquiry are then two complementary means of upholding the social contract between the governors and the governed, with elections a quicker and more responsive way of learning about the interests of a population, and scientific inquiry and long-run policy-making belonging to the more sober and reflective institutions of the state.

The Realities of Policy-making and the Use of Wellbeing Information

A Quick Sketch of How Wellbeing Cost-effectiveness Might Work

In wellbeing cost-effectiveness analysis, one works out for any proposed policy how large the wellbeing benefits are likely to be and compares them with the net public costs involved, implementing those policies with the best value for money first. To rank and then choose projects on the basis of how much benefit one obtains relative to costs is a normal task of treasuries, but it is also a staple activity in many departments, agencies, and organizations that have to allocate a given budget over many competing claims. Not all large expenses are decided in this way, but many are.

Apart from policies that cost money, there are also rules and regulations that do not immediately cost 'scarce funds' but which also need to be based on a wellbeing calculus.

This stylized picture of decision-making is of a rational centre that calmly decides on spending plans, thereby locking down a lot of actions further down the line. It fits in with top-down decision-making based on all the relevant information, guided by a joint goal of the wellbeing of the population.

Just how to do this is not that easy because there is the question of what policies would improve wellbeing, how to design them, how to implement them, and also how to organize the work itself.

We discuss the question of how one might do wellbeing cost-effectiveness analysis in chapter 3. Here, we sketch some of the characteristics of the realities of policy-making and how incorporating wellbeing information and a more pro-wellbeing culture might improve them.

One-off Decisions versus 'Holding Processes': The Role of Budget Wars

The basic policy rule of funding projects with high value for money simplifies decision-making to a single moment in time when some major yes-no decision must be taken. The presumption is that one uses an informed opinion on the most important costs and benefits associated with a reasonably well-defined policy.

Sometimes though, a policy is not decided upon in one go, but rather is 'put on ice' for a while, waiting for the right time to be championed. Departments and councils often have lists of what they would want to do if more funding was available. Transport departments often have plans for roads, railways, harbours, and other infrastructure investments 'on ice' waiting for particularly persuasive ministers or favourable economic conditions to materialize. Social spending departments often too have lists of things they want to do, such as particular new programmes or trials.

These 'wish lists', to some degree, reflect a deep learning of departments and a form of knowledge that is independent of the political process: units within departments, councils, or large organizations have become convinced that something is worthwhile to pursue and push for those programmes when the right political circumstances favour it.

The reality of budget processes also creates another reason why items on wish lists are spent: sometimes, departments and other institutions find themselves with budgets that need to be spent in a hurry lest they no longer have the power to spend them. Items on the wish list that can be spent in a hurry are then more likely to be pushed through (particularly if they can be dressed up as something else, for example a minor extension to an existing programme).

This may sound odd and inappropriate, but it is a fairly standard happenstance in any large institution, including large commercial companies: budgets largely get allocated by central processes on the basis of what was spent in previous years, and not necessarily on what is truly needed for some outcome in a year. This gives rise to budget 'accidents', for instance because some planned expense did not materialize, or some asset was sold off for more than anticipated. The well-known 'postcode lottery' in the NHS in the United Kingdom is a good example of this, reflecting the reality that in some areas a surplus of resources to spend on health emerged such that many more treatments are available, whilst in others there is an acute shortage such that there are fewer services and larger waiting times. That divergence happened because in some areas more elderly people with needs came to settle than in others, something that is somewhat accidental from the point of view of individuals. Hence, those 'lucky enough' to live in a postcode area with accidentally high resources get better care than others who did not 'win' the right postcode lottery.

One might think that some kind of 'central unit' inside ministries, councils, or large organizations would try to spot budget accidents in lower-down units in order to claim the additional funding and redistribute it. These central units indeed in many cases do just that, but they do not have the control and information to truly spot all budget accidents. There is almost invariably some discretion at lower levels to 'hide' budget accidents and spend them on things deemed worthwhile to pursue at the local level.

The reality of large organizations, both public and private, is therefore often a kind of race between the budget-spending and revenue-raising units inside organizations. The central units try to claim as much of the revenue and of the accidental lower spending as possible, whilst the revenue units try to keep some of the money supposedly to ensure the revenue stream, and the spending units claim that over-spending is due to unforeseen additional problems whilst hiding under-spending.

This is a subtle game and one should not believe that strict bureaucratic rules are going to perfectly solve them, even in cases that look open and shut. For instance, consider something as seemingly clear-cut as selling an asset, such as selling an old property. Surely, one could think, the central unit would know exactly what the market price was and would demand from the local unit to do the sale? If there was any ambiguity, surely the central unit would just organize the sale itself, insisting on some transparent procedure?

In a complex environment, there is invariably some discretion due to superior local knowledge. So, for instance, the local unit selling the property might know the buyers and would know how to negotiate important elements of the sale, such as whether the buyer is going to organize the clean-up of the grounds and the transport of stationery to other buildings in exchange for a lower sales price. The 'value' of that kind of arrangement will truly be known only to the local unit, creating a potential windfall in terms of the costs the local unit no longer has to make and can thus spend on other things, as long as they look like 'transport'.

This reality of bureaucratic life—the game of hide and seek with budgets—involves a kind of arms' race between central units and lower-down units that is highly dependent on the culture of the institution and the trustworthiness at all levels of the institution. It is precisely in this game that investments into trust and some notion of 'shared identity and shared values' can pay off.

In an institution full of workers who are truly committed to the same overall goal, accidental budget under-spending or over-spending will have hardly any real effect. All workers, in essence, monitor that the funds are spent on what is considered worthwhile to pursue, so the lower-down budget manager who discovers an accidental financial gain has little alternative but to either spend it on a clearly worthwhile lower-down project or else pass the windfall along to other units. Her judgement would be trusted, and expensive and disruptive monitoring could be avoided.

In an institution based on distrust, where senior management is somewhat at loggerheads with units and workers, windfall gains are more likely to be hidden and spent on things deemed worthwhile locally but not as a whole. This need not involve any malice, but can, for instance, involve local spending units 'hiding' funds in order to have 'spare funds' for worthwhile causes in the future. Monitoring by the centre is likely to be higher then, creating an 'us versus them' mentality.

Those who have never been in budget wars usually underestimate how prevalent and important they are. They really do determine much of daily life in many bureaucracies. This is implicitly acknowledged by the 2018 HMT *Green Book* in the advocated practice of having an 'optimism discount' whereby claimed anticipated benefits are reduced to reflect the likely pro-spending bias of the proposers.

There are various forms in which money can be hidden from sight. To give some actual examples of what is quite normal in large organizations, here are some personal examples from the academic departments Paul worked in:

- In some departments, carpets get changed and walls re-painted years in a row, not because there is anything wrong with the previous carpets or walls, but simply because this is a quick way to spend a significant amount of money in a hurry, ensuring that the budget for future years is not cut.
- In other departments, money is hidden via additional appointments of individuals to share the core activity (teaching), effectively reducing the amount that everyone needs to teach. Again, this ensures that the budget for ensuing years is kept at the same level and that there is a lot of 'slack' in the budget in the form of additional personnel who are not necessarily needed.
- Yet in other departments, staff are asked in the last few weeks of a budget cycle whether they would not like an additional screen, or whether there would be any forms of spending on data or casual workers that could be 'brought forward'. The object again is to avoid a budget cut by a central unit looking for possible cuts.
- In several places, local budget managers deliberately try to run a small deficit whilst central units try to reduce the budget anyway. This reflects the fact that some departments are often the 'cash-cows' of others, leading to the necessity to not merely hide money, but also to overspend so as to actually make a loss, all in order to protect the budget.
- In several places, discretionary funds (research funds, consulting fees, etc.) are 'hit' by a surprise increase in taxation from the central units, leading to long-term distrust and creative hiding behaviour.

- Often, some departments play the game better than others, with the worst departments having overworked lecturers and no money for copying machines, whereas the better-organized ones are throwing lavish conferences with fully paid high-profile guests to hide their surpluses.

What is important from a wellbeing point of view about this game of 'budget hide and seek' is the importance of the values shared throughout the organization as to what is 'worthwhile'. In selfish and distrustful places, accidental surpluses are often spent on 'bad' projects (like carpets and paint), whilst in organizations with a strong social conscience that is shared throughout, accidental surpluses are spent on things that are much more sensible (like bringing forward expenses that one is going to make anyway). In the most collegial places, lower-down units fear future budget problems much less and are hence happier to give up accidental surpluses to other units, whilst in the least collegial places the central units resort to highly distortionary tactics (like imposing surprise new taxes or taking away previous entitlements).

Wish lists and budget accidents thus exemplify an important nuance to the basic policy rule of funding projects with high value for money: the quality of actual spending is tied up with the general ethos and culture of institutions. Good institutions have good wish lists and spend accidental surpluses well. There is thus real value in having a pro-wellbeing culture throughout organizations, including the civil service. The more the overall aim is openly adopted, talked about, and shared, the harder it is for central units and local units to make bad decisions without push-back.

The continuous nature of policy work raises another question: is it really as simple as pushing a 'yes' button on a policy at the right time and then just sit back to see it unfold?

One-off versus Continuous Decisions

The basic policy rule of funding projects with high value for money depicts projects as large, one-off spending decisions that, once made, set a whole train of decisions in motion with no surprises and no additional decisions to be made down the line.

For relatively small decisions, such as to fund a small community project, this depiction is reasonable, although, of course, if projects are small, there is the question whether a formal process that lines up all the supposed costs and benefits of a decision is really worth the time put into it. Along these lines, policy evaluation and appraisal guidelines often require better and more comprehensive evidence for larger spending proposals than smaller ones.

For large decisions though, such as to fund a whole mental health programme for millions of people, or to revise the curriculum for secondary schools, the basic depiction is inadequate. The reality of large programmes and of decisions involving many 'moving parts' is that a plethora of decisions are made after the 'green light' is given at some higher level.

To illustrate how one decision depends on many others, let us think of a hypothetical decision to change the curriculum in the United Kingdom for local-authority-maintained schools, which is monitored by the Department for Education. Suppose for the sake of illustration that the department wants to, or is told to by politicians, to change the content of the science curriculum.

One does not just decide on a supposed improvement, even if one does start out with a reasonable idea as to who is going to do the improvements and how much this is going to cost. The amount of people involved in rewriting the books alone number in the hundreds, and each of the rewriters have some discretion as to what they will write. After all, the whole basis of the notion of 'expertise' is that the person applying the expertise has discretion.

The schools supposed to implement the curriculum have their own decisions to make, such as how to prepare for the change, how to inform pupils and parents, and how to train the teachers who are going to implement the new curriculum. Will existing teachers be paid over-time to learn the new material? Will the old books be used alongside the new ones with a list of changes? What prices for the new books can be negotiated with the publishers? Are they going to be held responsible for including those 'verified changes'? Who is going to write the new exams and ensure that the level of the exams is appropriate? Just where exactly is the boundary going to be put that defines the additional material?

When one thinks about something as complicated as school curricula, it should be clear that there are many institutions involved that must make their own decisions as to how to implement the change. Thousands of principals, school boards, committees, education experts, and parent stakeholder groups are involved and the changes can take years, with delays and adjustments along the way quite likely.

The initial 'decision' to go ahead with the changed curriculum is thus not the final decision, but more like the starting point of a complicated process in which lots of institutions and individuals are involved. The implementation involves budget wars (who is getting the money?), price negotiations (how much money does an expert want to rewrite the book?), and lots of coordination between many institutions (who is going to do what?). One can imagine the logistical nightmare involved.

The only reason that in the United Kingdom this kind of decision does not lead to complete chaos is because many of the institutions and decision-makers involved 'mean well', i.e. they do work towards the common goal of improving the curriculum. As a result, budget wars are kept in line, price negotiations go via reasonably well-established guidelines, and the process is coordinated somewhat amicably. Social trust and shared ideals reduce coordination difficulties.

However, the true nature of implementing complicated policies brings many aspects to the fore that are important:

- In reality, many decisions are not made democratically at all, but by lots of individuals and institutions, not merely civil service institutions (think of school boards and outside experts). This means that any orientation towards wellbeing as the ultimate goal would have to be 'carried' by many of the individual decision-makers to truly happen. It is simply not the case that 'the top' gets to decide on wellbeing without the rest being important. On the contrary, wellbeing matters to the degree that the combined opinions of all the decision-makers value it. The top matters more, but others feed into the process.
- There are many points at which the system can change its mind or change tack, implying that the originally envisioned timelines and goals are often not followed exactly as planned. Trust and competency at all levels then matter for the outcome, not just the competency of the original decision-makers.
- The degree to which the whole 'community' of institutions and individuals required to 'make something work' are on board is crucial. As a result, buy-in and communication matters.
- Large areas almost inevitably have 'vested interests' involved where (groups of) individuals enjoy special privileges that they will want to defend. In our example, these are the education experts or book publishers with whom book prices need to be negotiated.

One might think that such problems automatically get resolved if there is enough attention given to 'communication', 'stakeholder engagement', 'integrated planning', and more of these cooperative principles. Yet, that is often naïve because the reality in many cases is that incentives are misaligned and opinions can be irreconcilable. The opportunity to grab resources in budget wars may lead to an inevitable adversarial dynamic and may require some degree of initial top-down steam-rolling of budget allocations.

The reality of budget wars and of 'vested interests inside the system' who have privileges to defend can derail many projects. It is not the focus of this book to discuss that reality in great detail because the landscape of insiders and special interests differs by area and over time, but it is important to note that they complicate matters a lot.

Again, the complexity and dynamism of the realities of the policy development process highlight the value in having a pro-wellbeing culture: the more different actors at different points in the process share the same ultimate goal—to increase the wellbeing of those they are responsible for—the less do frictions along the process as well as insiders and special interests ultimately matter.

Societal Changes and the Policy Discovery Process

The world is forever changing and things that are a good idea at one point in time are not invariably a good idea at another. The type of schooling appropriate in the nineteenth century would not work in the twenty-first, for instance because parents now already teach children many learning habits (like enjoying reading) that had to be newly taught in the nineteenth century.

Not merely is there continuous change in lots of unexpected directions, but the possible things to do are near infinite. This influences how one thinks of evidence. For instance, one might think that a large (experimental) trial can show whether, say, a large mental health programme is cost-effective or not. Certainly, there are expensive trials with exactly that purpose. However, if one thinks more carefully about it, what is evaluated in any trial is far less clear than any headline suggests.

Take the Improving Access to Psychological Therapies (IAPT) trials in Doncaster and Newham in the United Kingdom in 2008, for example, after which a whole new, nationwide public service was set up. These trials did not only involve particular treatments for particular patients after specific mental health conditions were attested. Instead, there was a whole system of public service delivery, which included methods of hiring personnel and a system of measurement as well as adjustment to small and large problems as they emerged. This involved rules on part-time work and what to do with staff who had sick children. They needed policies on violent patients and the outlay of the rooms in which the therapy took place. The list goes on.

These trials, therefore, operated in a particular environment which involved everything relevant to patients and healthcare professionals, from particular treatments to simple things such as how patients would be greeted. The information flow, such as where patients could find information about treatments and their eligilibity, was particular. The training of the healthcare professionals involved numerous small and large choices, ranging from how to arrange the seats in the training sessions to how to ensure the trainees learnt what was most useful. In reality, therefore, the evaluation of the IAPT trials was really an evaluation of a set of thousands of particular choices in an environment that was unique in many ways.

Since the exact circumstances of the IAPT trials will never repeat themselves again, one can wonder what has really been shown. To a purist, one cannot say much with any certainty about anything based on a trial, or any other type of experiment that is not perfectly replicable. This is simply because nothing of the past *is* perfectly replicable: the circumstances, the people, and a whole lot of idiosyncratic choices will be different even for supposedly identical experiments. Hence, to the true purist, there is no such thing as 'evidence-based policy', for the simple reason that all evidence is outdated and not perfectly applicable to any future situation. It should be clear, though, that no bureaucratic system can function if it refused to learn anything from past experiments. So what do people do?

One invariably relies on some notion of what is important for the outcomes when judging the information content in a trial or experiment. That judgement is what identifies the believed 'active ingredients' that make something a success or not. In practice, one also relies on presumed knowledge in many different dimensions about numerous choices as to what is 'the best thing to do'. That current practice will include methods of hiring, working together, communicating, or measuring. In the background will be presumptions on what optimal training schedules, paid sick leave, or education looks like. Trials and experiments in that sense merely 'check' whether a particular choice in one multi-dimensional direction improves matters or not. From the presumed knowledge of the world it is then deduced what the active new ingredients were that lead to the success (or lack thereof), whilst relying on 'business as usual' in the vast majority of choices involved.

This delimits the role and use of outside information and experimental learning: most of the knowledge of 'what works' is embedded in the 'business as usual' and in principles of good practice. A proposed intervention is thereby really a bundle of particular new elements that form the core of the proposal, combined with the 'business-as-usual' in all other elements. It is simply presumed by the decision-maker, and usually also the proposer, that the whole myriad of additional decisions will conform to some notion of current practice.

Yet, new information emerges all the time about how many aspects of what is normal can be improved: wellbeing-at-work plans aim to improve what is normal practice in terms of how people work together; office engineers aim to improve the layout of offices, ventilation systems, and other elements of normal office life; education experts are collecting information from around the world as to how training might be improved in particular areas; fads in management and bureaucratic control come with great speed, some proving useful and some not. Normality itself is subject to experimentation and challenge on a continuous basis.

What this means is that it is not very fruitful to think of public services or any other form of production as being essentially decided in one great moment of discovery. Rather, one uses the knowledge presumed in current practice and expertise to map out what one thinks is the best way ahead in any area, largely implements that best-guess plan as best as one can, and then evaluates and experiments from where one has gotten to in order to find the best way ahead. A simple way to depict this kind of discovery process is illlustrated in Figures 1.1, 1.2, and 1.3, whereby the decision-maker is trying to get to the top of a

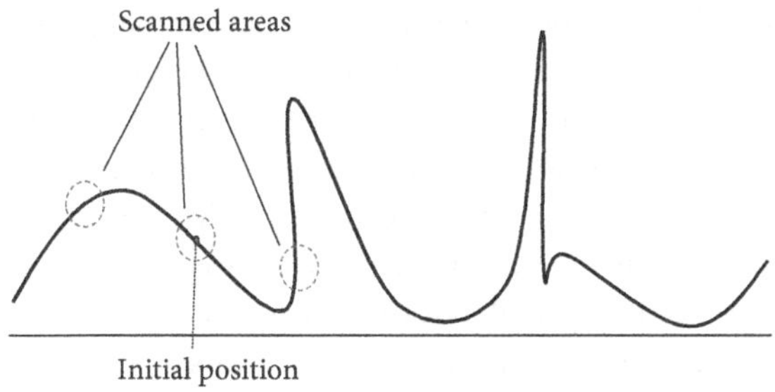

Figure 1.1 Illustrative policy discovery processes when knowledge of possibilities is imperfect: Policy discovery process 1
Source: Own illustration.

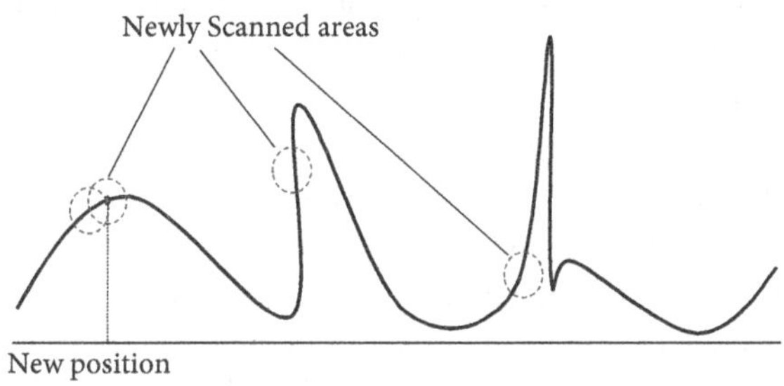

Figure 1.2 Illustrative policy discovery processes when knowledge of possibilities is imperfect: Policy discovery process 2
Source: Own illustration.

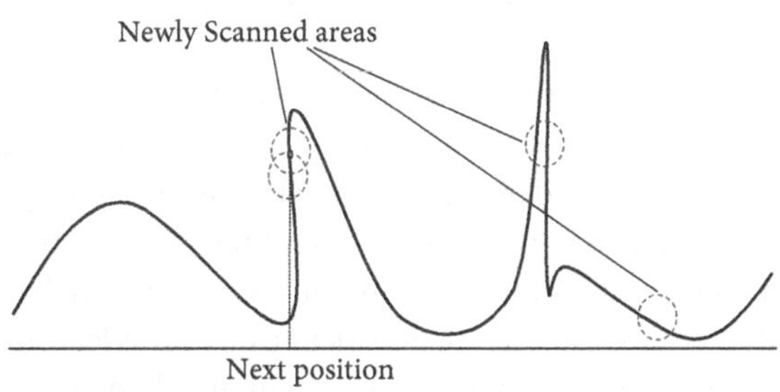

Figure 1.3 Illustrative policy discovery processes when knowledge of possibilities is imperfect: Policy discovery process 3
Source: Own illustration.

mountain by vaguely scanning the landscape that is in particular directions and moving towards the highest point found in this scanning process. Going to the highest point found and then rescanning, a different direction emerges as optimal, leading to a whole iteration of moves.

In Figure 1.1, the decision-maker is at a certain initial position, able to scan local areas and two more areas a bit further away, whereby scans are denoted by the dotted circles. These 'scans' can include formal experiments, particular experience, or other forms of learning. Maximizing, the decision-maker moves to the highest point scanned, which happens to be at the left. From that position, new local scans and scans of further away areas are conducted, depicted in Figure 1.2, revealing a new possible optimal position to go to. That then leads to a new position which forms the basis of further scans, and so on.

The point of this simple illustration is that there is an inevitability of sub-optimality about our knowledge: only slowly does the system learn about local possible improvements and potential large changes, updating knowledge all the time and requiring new experiments (which are the scans in the example) to see where next improvements might be possible. In reality, of course, the actual landscape is changing continuously so the situation is even less certain and more difficult than depicted.

What does a wellbeing orientation mean for this policy discovery processs? Pragmatically, it means that knowledge of where improvements in wellbeing are likely to be found would be useful for decision-makers at any level, because it helps with searching in the right direction. It also means that some shared notion of how wellbeing is affected by circumstances would help in spotting the wellbeing strengths and weaknesses in 'business as usual' and thus in gradually optimizing general systems.

Special Interests and the Wellbeing Policy Rule

One of the major problems with special interests is that they actively try to distort policies for their own good, potentially against the interests of the wider population. The more organized and resourced special-interest groups are, the more difficult it is to enact what is in the best interest of the public rather than give in to these groups. One encounters this when it comes to centrally buying medicines, where special interests are often clear outsiders (for example, international pharmaceuticals, an issue we discuss in more detail in chapter 3), but one finds organized special interests in almost every major policy area. Special interests are particularly difficult because they are part of 'us'.

Machiavelli already noted this in his famous treatise on how to run the Italian city states of the sixteenth century. His money quote on the difficulties of reform is rightly famous:

> It ought to be remembered that there is nothing more difficult to take in hand, more perilous to conduct, or more uncertain in its success, than to take the lead in the introduction of a new order of things. Because the innovator has for

> enemies all those who have done well under the old conditions, and lukewarm defenders in those who may do well under the new. This coolness arises partly from fear of the opponents, who have the laws on their side, and partly from the incredulity of men, who do not readily believe in new things until they have had a long experience of them. (In *The Prince*, 1532)

One can read 'special interests' to mean those Machiavelli describes as 'all those who have done well under the old conditions'.

Machiavelli's advice on how to implement reforms is then almost the exact opposite of how many public policy bodies currently organize the formation of policy, which involves a lot of 'stakeholder management', 'community involvement', 'integrated planning', and so on. This encourages opposition to reforms according to Machiavelli, who recommends taking everyone as much by surprise as possible, and to inflict all the painful things in one go:[12]

> Injuries, therefore, should be inflicted all at once, that their ill savour being less lasting may the less offend; whereas, benefits should be conferred little by little, that so they may be more fully relished. (ibid)

This lesson is not only insightful as to how to deal with special interests, but also speaks to the general design and timing of many policies and bundles of policies. In effect, Machiavelli is predicting that the political effect of negative things is less in total if they are bundled, whilst the wellbeing benefits of positive things are higher when unbundled and spread out over time. There is indeed the saying in the general nudge movement to 'unbundle gains and bundle losses'.

These lessons of Machiavelli are rightly famous, for they warn us that easy wins do not, usually, exist. Things of real importance face opposition and lots of consultation is likely to mobilize that opposition. A final quote:

> He who looks carefully into the matter will find, that in all human affairs, we cannot rid ourselves of one inconvenience without running into another.

In the context of the previous quotes, this one can be interpreted as saying that there is nothing unusual about special interests who defend their privileged positions. How special-interest groups will react to policies, either helping or frustrating them, is then an important consideration in policy design, though usually a hidden element because the problem is hidden as well: special interests invariably argue that their objections to something are not due to selfishness but

[12] Of course, always taking everyone by surprise may create a culture of uncertainty, which may have negative impacts on its own, for example when it comes to long-term investments. The right balance must be found.

from their regard to the interest of all.[13] Navigating this requires intimate local political knowledge and skill. The issue underscores the general importance of having many individuals in many areas interested in the same outcome: wellbeing.

Conclusion and the Way Ahead

The idea that governments should care for the wellbeing of the population is rooted in history and has arisen in many cultures. What is relatively new is the presence of a large mass of information on what affects wellbeing, measured as the evaluation by individuals themselves as to how their life is going. This information is increasingly accurate at the average level because of large datasets and a plethora of studies using quasi-experimental and experimental designs, though it should always be kept in mind that wellbeing remains volatile and relatively easy to manipulate at the individual level. Just like voting, it is inherently subjective. As for voting, that is precisely its strength and purpose.

To base more decision-making in government on wellbeing can and perhaps should happen at different levels. At the top, where large budgets are decided, it makes sense to rank possible policies on the basis of how much wellbeing is bought at what net costs to the public purse. In many departments that have to decide on the budgets of other entities, like schools or hospitals, the idea of basing a decision on expenditure on some explicit notion of how much wellbeing can be bought for that level of expenditure is equally sensible. At the lower level and in each organization itself, knowledge of what changes wellbeing can improve how organizations work and thereby the design and implementation process of policies.

What this needs is both a measurement apparatus and the capacity to learn from and adapt to the findings of policy evaluations. In each domain, there needs to be information on the wellbeing of those supposedly affected, or at least an in-depth understanding of the literature on how wellbeing is affected by different policies in that domain. To truly become self-learning, the state bureaucracy needs to have systems of experimentation that are quick and cheap to run when it comes to small policies, and that are sophisticated and standardized when it comes to large ones. This needs knowledge throughout the state bureaucracy of measurement and of quasi-experimental and experimental methods. It needs registries of experiments, complete with reasonable assessments of the findings of policy evaluations, by analysts who are trained and familiar with wellbeing.

None of this is trivial. Indeed, there is no state bureaucracy in the world that has truly come to grips with how to become self-learning based on experimentation

[13] Frijters and Foster (2013) speak at length about this and give many examples in Europe and elsewhere of how selfish motivations get dressed up as being in the interest of everyone.

and data. A key issue is that if one were to completely standardize experiments and require them to be registered according to the latest scientific insights, even trivially small experiments will become overly expensive, which would reduce rather than stimulate experimentation. A challenge in setting up a self-learning state bureaucracy based on experimentation and data is, therefore, to keep experiments cheap and easy to run, but nevertheless allow others to learn from them, which requires some notion of collecting and analysing them.

One idea to do this is to have an 'Evaluator General', a term coined by the Australian economist Nicholas Gruen (2018). In essence, the Evaluator General would be some kind of helpdesk within the state bureaucracy for how to collect data, design experiments, and learn from them. The idea is not to create an avalanche of paperwork but that staff of the Evaluator General would be embedded in various departments to help them collect their data and run their experiments, much like IT used to be run with local branches helping people with their computers until the time came that groups were functional enough in these skills themselves.

The various 'What Works Centres' in the United Kingdom are a good example of this kind of thinking: central hubs where the lessons learnt in various areas are gathered, translated, and then disseminated to those who have use for them.

The general picture of how to organize self-learning is akin to the idea of botanical gardens, particularly how they functioned in the nineteenth century: new species of plants were sent to a central hub, Kew Gardens in London, from which saplings and seeds were sent out to the smaller botanical gardens in the whole Empire, available to the farmers and large estates in the colonies and trading posts. Together with the seeds and the saplings, these places would also be the depository of knowledge of how to grow them and how to improve on them further. Particularly successful breeds would then again get sent to the centre.

Botanical gardens have lost their central role in agriculture, though seed banks and genetic labs have taken over much the same function. The basic idea is to copy this example for wellbeing and other social outcomes in the United Kingdom: local usage and local experimentation, combined with central stores of information and learning.

Particular to wellbeing, there needs to be more training in a central body of wellbeing knowledge, including knowledge of the main datasets, the main lessons learned hitherto, the main bottlenecks, and some shared technical standards on how to apply wellbeing knowledge in policy evaluations and appraisals.

What is also needed is agreement on standardization, as well an institutional mechanism to accredit numbers and lessons learned from previous work on wellbeing. This includes questions like the appropriate discount rate, the appropriate monetization of wellbeing effects, and the basic unit of wellbeing. We will touch upon these points in more detail in the chapters to follow. Whatever one starts out with, though, is likely to be challenged and improved over time, and some regard must be taken to allow improvements to overtake what is already being done without disrupting all the processes that became dependent on the previous standards.

There can be movement at various levels: some of the lessons of wellbeing can be taken on board in the form of particular policies reasonably quickly, whilst others might take longer to come to fruition, including how to integrate more of a wellbeing orientation into the entire policy development process throughout government. Also, adapting the internal machinery of policy-making to a wellbeing orientation, requires some notion of how wellbeing information can augment the analysis and evaluations done presently, as well as some transition path towards a fuller implementation of wellbeing information into new processes.

Hence, there is much to do in the coming decades when it comes to wellbeing and policy-making.

Literature

Ambrey, C. L., and Fleming, C. M. (2011). Valuing Scenic Amenity Using Life Satisfaction Data. *Ecological Economics* 72: 106–15.

Ambrey, C. L., Fleming, C. M., and Chan, A. Y.-C. (2013). Estimating the Cost of Air Pollution in South East Queensland: An Application of the Life Satisfaction Non-market Valuation Approach. *Ecological Economics* 97: 172–81.

Béllet, C., and Frijters, P. (2019). Big Data and Wellbeing. *World Happiness Report 2019*. New York: Sustainable Development Solutions Network.

Benjamin, D. J., Heffetz, O., Kimball, M. S., and Rees-Jones, A. (2012). What Do You Think Would Make You Happier? What Do You Think You Would Choose? *American Economic Review* 102(5): 2083–110.

Bentham, J. (1776). *A Fragment on Government*. Oxford: Clarendon Press.

Bertram, C., and Rehdanz, K. (2015). The Role of Urban Green Space for Human Well-being. *Ecological Economics* 120: 139–52.

Cantril, H. (1965). *The Pattern of Human Concerns*. New Brunswick: Rutgers University Press.

Clark, A. E., and Oswald, A. J. (1994). Unhappiness and Unemployment. *Economic Journal* 104(424): 648–59.

Cohen, S., Alper, C. M., Doyle, W. J., Treanor, J. J., and Turner, R. B. (2006). Positive Emotional Style Predicts Resistance to Illness after Experimental Exposure to Rhinovirus or Influenza A Virus. *Psychosomatic Medicine* 68(6): 809–15.

Cummins, R. P., Mccabe, M., Romeo, Y., and Gullone, E. (1994). The Comprehensive Quality of Life Scale (Com-QOL): Instrument Development and Psychometric Evaluation on College Staff and Students. *Educational and Psychological Measurement* 54: 372–82.

Davey, G., and Rato, R. (2012). Subjective Wellbeing in China: A Review. *Journal of Happiness Studies* 13(2): 333–46.

De Neve, J.-E., and Oswald, A. J. (2012). Estimating the Influence of Life Satisfaction and Positive Affect on Later Income Using Sibling Fixed Effects. *Proceedings of the National Academy of Sciences* 109(49): 19953–8.

Diener, E., and Chan, M. Y. (2011). Happy People Live Longer: Subjective Well-Being Contributes to Health and Longevity. *Applied Psychology: Health and Well-Being* 3: 1–43.

Diener, E., Emmons, R. A., Larsen, R. J., and Griffin, S. (1985). The Satisfaction with Life Scale. *Journal of Personality Assessment* 49: 71–5.

Diener, E., Inglehart, R., and Tay, L. (2013). Theory and Validity of Life Satisfaction Scales. *Social Indicators Research* 112(3): 497–527.

Diener, E., Lucas, R. E., and Oishi, S. (2018). Advances and Open Questions in the Science of Subjective Wellbeing. *Collabra: Psychology* 4(1): 15.

Drouvelis, M., and Grosskopf, B. (2016). The Effects of Induced Emotions on Pro-social Behaviour. *Journal of Public Economics* 134: 1–8.

Easterlin, R. (1974). Does Economic Growth Improve the Human Lot? Some Empirical Evidence. In David, R., and Reder, R. (eds), *Nations and Households in Economic Growth: Essays in Honor of Moses Abramovitz*. New York: Academic Press, pp. 89–125.

Felson, R. B. (1993). The (Somewhat) Social Self: How Others Affect Self-appraisals. *Psychological Perspectives on the Self* 4: 1–26.

Ferreira, S., Akay, A., Brereton, F., Cuñado, J., Martinsson, P., Moro, M., and Ningal, T. F. (2013). Life Satisfaction and Air Quality in Europe. *Ecological Economics* 88: 1–10.

Frey, B. S., Luechinger, S., and Stutzer, A. (2009). The Life Satisfaction Approach to Valuing Public Goods: The Case of Terrorism. *Public Choice* 138(3–4): 317–45.

Frey, B. S., and Stutzer, A. (2018). *Economics of Happiness*. Dordrecht: Springer International Publishing.

Frijters, P., Clark, A. E., Krekel, C., and R. Layard (2020), A happy choice: wellbeing as the goal of government. *Behavioural Public Policy* 4(2): 126–65.

Frijters, P., and Foster, G. (2013). *An Economic Theory of Love, Groups, Power and Networks*. Cambridge: Cambridge University Press.

Fujiwara, D., Lawton, R. N., and MacKerron, G. (2017). Experience Sampling in and around Airports. Momentary Subjective Wellbeing, Airports, and Aviation Noise in England. *Transportation Research Part D: Transport and Environment* 56: 43–54.

Goldberg, D., Gater, R., Sartorius, N., Ustun, T., Piccinelli, M., Gureje, O., and Rutter, C. (1997). The Validity of Two Versions of the GHQ in the WHO Study of Mental Illness in General Health Care. *Psychological Medicine* 27: 191–7.

Gruen, N. (2017). What Have Wellbeing Frameworks Ever Done for Us? *The Mandarin*. Available at: https://www.themandarin.com.au/84848-nicholas-gruen-what-have-wellbeing-frameworks-ever-done-for-us/#fn5.

Gruen, N. (2018). The Case for an Evaluator General? *The Mandarin*. Available at: https://www.themandarin.com.au/content/uploads/2018/11/Nicholas-Gruen-Evaluator-General-Submission-2018.pdf.

Headey, B., and Wooden, M. (2004). The Effects of Wealth and Income on Subjective Well-being and Ill-being. *Economic Record* 80: S24–S33.

Helliwell, J. F., Huang, H., Wang, S., and Norton, M. (2020). Social Environments for World Happiness. *World Happiness Report 2020*. New York: Sustainable Development Solutions Network.

Hume, D. (1742). *Essays, Moral and Political*.

Kahneman, D., Krueger, A., Schkade, D., Schwarz, N., and Stone, A. (2004). A Survey Method for Characterizing Daily Life Experience: The Day Reconstruction Method. *Science* 306: 1776–80.

Kahneman, D., Wakker, P., and Sarin, R. (1997). Back to Bentham Explorations of Experienced Utility. *Quarterly Journal of Economics* 112: 375–406.

Kopmann, A., and Rehdanz, K. (2013). A Human Well-being Approach for Assessing the Value of Natural Land Areas. *Ecological Economics* 93: 20–33.

Krekel, C., Kolbe, J., and Wüstemann, H. (2016). The Greener, the Happier? The Effect of Urban Land Use on Residential Well-being. *Ecological Economics* 121: 117–27.

Kuznets, S. (1937). Report to the U.S. Congress: National Income, 1929–35.

Layard, R. (1980). Human Satisfactions and Public Policy. *Economic Journal* 90(363): 737–50.

Layard, R., Mayraz, G., and Nickell, S. (2008). The Marginal Utility of Income. *Journal of Public Economics* 92(8–9): 1846–57.

Levinson, A. (2012). Valuing Public Goods Using Happiness Data: The Case of Air Quality. *Journal of Public Economics* 96(9–10): 869–80.

Likert, R. (1932). A Technique for the Measurement of Attitudes. *Archives of Psychology* 140: 1–55.

Likert, R., Roslow, S., and Murphy, G. (1934). A Simple and Reliable Method of Scoring the Thurstone Attitude Scales. *The Journal of Social Psychology* 5: 228–38.

Locke, J. (1689). *An Essay Concerning Human Understanding*.

Machiavelli, N. (1513). *The Prince*.

Murdoch, P. J. (1908–67). Papers of Sir Keith Murdoch, Manuscript reference no.: MS 2823/34.

OECD (2020). OECD Data—General Government—General Government Spending. Available at: https://data.oecd.org/gga/general-government-spending.htm.

O'Donnell, G., Deaton, A., Durand, M., Halpern, D., and Layard, R. (2014). Well-being and Policy. London: Legatum Institute.

Oswald, A. J., Proto, E., and Sgroi, D. (2015). Happiness and Productivity. *Journal of Labor Economics* 33(4): 789–822.

Pawlowski, T., Downward, P., and Rasciute, S. (2011). Subjective Well-being in European Countries—on the Age-specific Impact of Physical Activity. *European Review of Aging and Physical Activity* 8(2): 93–102.

Powdthavee, N. (2008). Putting a Price Tag on Friends, Relatives, and Neighbours: Using Surveys of Life Satisfaction to Value Social Relationships. *The Journal of Socio-Economics* 37(4): 1459–80.

Rato, R., and Davey, G. (2012). Quality of Life in Macau, China. *Social Indicators Research* 105(1): 93–108.

Rehdanz, K., and Maddison, D. (2008). Local Environmental Quality and Life-satisfaction in Germany. *Ecological Economics* 64(4): 787–97.

Robbins, L. (1932). *An Essay on the Nature and Significance of Economic Science.*

Scitovsky, T. (1975). Income and Happiness. *Acta Oeconomica* 15(1): 45–53.

Skopec, L., Musco, T., and Sommers, B. D. (2014). A Potential New Data Source for Assessing the Impacts of Health Reform: Evaluating the Gallup-Healthways Well-Being Index. *Healthcare* 2(2): 113–20.

Smith, A. (1759). *Theory of Moral Sentiments.*

Smith, T. (1979). Happiness: Time Trends, Seasonal Variations, Intersurvey Differences, and Other Mysteries. *Social Psychology Quarterly* 42(1): 18–30.

Steptoe, A., and Wardle, J. (2011). Positive Affect Measured Using Ecological Momentary Assessment and Survival in Older Men and Women. *Proceedings of the National Academy of Sciences* 108(45): 18244–8.

Stiglitz, J. E., Sen, A., and Fitoussi, J. (2011). Report by the Commission on the Measurement of Economic Performance and Social Progress. European Commission.

HM Treasury (2018). Guidance on How to Appraise and Evaluate Policies, Projects and Programmes. Available at: https://assets.publishing.service.gov.uk/government/uploads/system/uploads/attachment_data/file/685903/The_Green_Book.pdf.

Ura, K., Alkire, S., Zangmo, T., and Wangdi, K. (2012). An Extensive Analysis of GNH Index. Available at: http://www.grossnationalhappiness.com/

Van Praag, B., and Baarsma, B. (2005). Using Happiness Surveys to Value Intangibles: The Case of Airport Noise. *Economic Journal* 115(500): 224–46.

Wansbeek, T., and Kapteyn, A. (1983). Tackling Hard Questions by Means of Soft Methods: The Use of Individual Welfare Functions in Socio-Economic Policy. *Kyklos* 36(2): 249–69.

Ward, G. (2019). Happiness and Voting Behavior. *World Happiness Report 2019.* New York: Sustainable Development Solutions Network.

Weimann, J., Knabe, A., and Schöb, R. (2015). *Measuring Happiness: The Economics of Well-Being.* Cambridge, MA: MIT Press.

World Happiness Reports (2012 to 2019). Available at: http://worldhappiness.report/.

2

Wellbeing Measurement and Policy Design—Measures, Key Findings, and Wellbeing Frameworks

Preview

This chapter is for readers who wish to know what matters for wellbeing, and in particular for those who wish to design policies in order to improve it.

We start with an extensive discussion on the measurement of wellbeing, covering both prevalent current measures and promising future ones, after which we present some key findings and rules of thumb on what influences wellbeing. We then organize the wellbeing lessons for governments by discussing the relation between wellbeing and four areas where government is very active: the provision of basic comforts, the regulation and production of experience goods and skills, the importance of status concerns, and social identities. This come with rules of thumb on how to recognize possible improvements and some indication as to what would be good value for money in terms of interventions.

This chapter also discusses frameworks of wellbeing to aid appraisals, evaluations, and overall policy thinking in different areas. We present a mental framework that embeds wellbeing into the whole economy (a capital framework) and then apply the theories and general framework to mental health and relationship-type interventions. We end with a taxonomy of thinking about wellbeing in government departments, including departments directly oriented towards some aspect of wellbeing (like health) and others that are oriented towards enabling the government to function (like tax authorities) or towards identity (like culture).

Direct Measurement of Wellbeing

We start with the Enlightenment idea that individuals are the sole judges of their lives. This ideal puts individuals at the top of the judgement pyramid, making wellbeing an inherently subjective matter. The wellbeing of a society is then some function of the subjective wellbeing of all its members, i.e. the wellbeing as judged

A Handbook for Wellbeing Policy-Making: History, Theory, Measurement, Implementation, and Examples. Paul Frijters and Christian Krekel, Oxford University Press (2021). © Paul Frijters and Christian Krekel.
DOI: 10.1093/oso/9780192896803.003.0002

by the individuals themselves, where in a classic democracy every person counts exactly equally: one person, one vote. Subjective wellbeing is sometimes called *directly measured wellbeing*, and it is what we refer to when we use the term 'wellbeing'.

The purpose of measuring wellbeing in society is to learn how to improve 'our' circumstances. It thus presupposes that life and society are complex and that we cannot automatically know what would improve our lot: we have to measure and analyse. We might intuitively know of some basic requirements for high levels of wellbeing, such as the absence of violence and disease, but beyond that, the presumption is that we need better evidence than common sense to guide us.

The direct measurement of wellbeing is, therefore, an additional tool for those who make choices that affect others: the logical basis of benevolent longer-term decision-making. Direct measurement is not the only tool, and several strategies with the same goal can exist alongside each other.

Principles of Direct Measurement

Direct measurement of wellbeing grapples with the inherently subjective nature of how people evaluate and experience their lives, as opposed to trying to infer it indirectly from observing how people behave. Yet, the concept of wellbeing is not very precise in the minds of people, begging the question of what any measurement then really means.

At the outset, one should not expect to have perfect measures of wellbeing, because the very concept is an abstraction, i.e. a tool that we need as decision-makers but that might not exist in the way we imagine it inside every individual.[1] The issue then hinges on whether there are reasonable measures of wellbeing that tell us something robust about how people are doing in life which we were not already aware of.

We face somewhat of a chicken-and-egg problem: direct measurement is only useful if it tells us something we did not yet know, yet how can we judge whether a candidate measure indeed tells us something of interest if we were not already convinced of the unexpected outcome? How can we distinguish a good measure of wellbeing from a bad one?

[1] Krueger and Schkade (2008) review around a dozen studies that looked at the degree to which a measure of wellbeing at one point in time relates to another measure for the same individual some time later, i.e. the test–retest relationship. Even when measured the same day or the same week, the correlation between two measures (including life satisfaction and experiential measures such as happiness) is no higher than 0.6. Test–retest correlations are higher for multiple-item summed scales (e.g. 0.8 for Ed Diener's seven-item Satisfaction with Life Scale, measured two months apart), but that may come at the expense of being less clearly interpretable.

Simply put, we look for whether a measure corresponds 'on the whole' to what our prior knowledge of individuals and the world expects us to see. If there are measures for which we can tentatively say 'yes' to that requirement, we can add practical criteria (i.e. cheap to collect and easy to explain) and engage in a trajectory whereby we 'try out' the unexpected implications of our preferred wellbeing measure. We gradually learn whether or not we indeed get something useful that we can trust.[2]

One criterion is that a candidate measure of wellbeing should be intuitive: because wellbeing is the subjective assessment of a person's life, we expect any candidate measure to be, roughly, agreed upon by individuals. In other words, individuals should recognize a good measure as a reasonable summary of how they are doing. A candidate measure should capture what individuals would want for someone they really care about, like their own grandchildren.

Because we expect individuals to be responsible citizens with some agency over their lives, we also expect that individuals, broadly, are already trying to maximize their wellbeing. Their measured wellbeing should be affected by the fortunes of those they love and identify with, and whom they take into account in their decisions.

The behaviour of individuals should also tally with a candidate measure of wellbeing so that individuals who know how something will affect their lives will behave in such a way as to optimize it. If individuals know, for example, that eating poisonous berries is bad for them, they should not do so and the measured wellbeing should be lower for those who accidentally do eat them. Similarly, a good measure should be somewhat predictive of behaviour, for example, people should be seen to use their political influence towards increasing their wellbeing.

Because individuals communicate their likes and dislikes about the world in a myriad of observable ways, including smiles, language, and adaptive social behaviour, we also expect a candidate measure of wellbeing to be, roughly, in line with these forms of wellbeing-related communication.

As resources are limited, it is important that data on any candidate measure of wellbeing is relatively cheap to collect, that the measure is relatively easy to understand, transparent in terms of analysis, and robust to manipulation. Importantly, because we would like to say something definite and make a practical step ahead, after discussing wellbeing in one way or another for ages, we would like a measure to have been available and analysed enough to say something concrete about how to improve individual and societal wellbeing.

Having said what is desired, it is also handy to consider what a candidate measure of wellbeing does not necessarily need. Importantly, it is not necessary to be accurate at the individual level. This makes it different from diagnostic measures of mental health, for example. What is important, however, is that it

[2] These issues have been debated by many authors. See Alexandrova (2016), for example.

points in the right direction if measured amongst enough people over time. We particularly do not want it to be grossly and systematically 'wrong'.

Likewise, it is not important whether a measure would be immediately obvious to our ancestors who never saw a survey question. Just because a concept is new does not mean that people from an earlier age would not have understood its significance. Our ancestors would also not have known how to drive a car, but they would have seen the point in transportation.

We thus arrive at an extensive wish list for a candidate measure of wellbeing.

The Main Candidate Measure of Wellbeing

None of the many hundreds of candidate measures of wellbeing we currently have fits all the requirements on our wish list. Whether we ask people if they are happy several times a day, use the impression individuals give when they see their doctor, use a checklist of twenty-odd things that sound good, or simply observe how often individuals smile or communicate with their bodies, we do not fully capture everything we want.

There is a front-runner, though, advocated by a report by the Legatum Institute (O'Donnell et al., 2014), the Stiglitz-Sen-Fitoussi Commission/Sarkozy Report (Stiglitz et al., 2011), and the (OECD, 2013): life satisfaction. The canonical measure is a simple question that has asks: 'Overall, how satisfied are you with your life nowadays?' Answers range from 0 ('not at all') to 10 ('completely satisfied').

Variants of this question ask how 'happy' respondents are with their life as a whole rather than 'satisfied', or prompt them to answer on a different scale or in terms of verbal labels. The Cantril ladder-of-life question, which asks respondents to rate themselves on a ladder whereby 0 denotes the 'worst possible' and 10 the 'best possible life', also has a high correlation with life satisfaction in Western countries, as do some question modules that aggregate a set of questions, such as asking both about regular life satisfaction and whether someone finds their life worthwhile or meaningful.[3]

The crucial ingredients in a life-satisfaction question are (i) to ask about life as a whole, (ii) to be unspecific with regards to timing, (iii) to have a clearly ordered set of answering options with more than a handful of options, and (iv) to use a recognizable phrase that makes it clear an evaluation is sought in terms of what an individual finds important.[4]

[3] Clark (2016) finds that, in the United Kingdom, the measure of life satisfaction has a raw 0.7 correlation with the measure of eudemonia (i.e. whether someone thinks his or her life is worthwhile). He also shows that there is a 0.9 correlation between the determinants of life satisfaction and those of eudemonia. Clark (2016) suggests they are similar constructs, particularly from a policy point of view (where it is more about what changes and thus explains the construct rather than its absolute level).

[4] Bond and Lang (2019) find that, under certain circumstances, ordered probit findings from wellbeing measures can be reversed by lognormal transformations. However, the authors use a measure with a small scale. Arguably, this issue becomes less important in practice when scales are larger (for

The life-satisfaction question scores well on most of these aspects: it is predictive of many things we would intuitively think are associated with wellbeing, such as marital stability (Carr et al., 2014; Margelisch et al., 2017), longevity (Koivumaa-Honkanen et al., 2000; Chida and Steptoe, 2008; Diener and Chan, 2011; Steptoe and Wardle, 2011), support for the current political constellation (Ward, 2019), or labour productivity (De Neve and Oswald, 2012; Oswald et al., 2015). Individuals pick life satisfaction more often than different possible other things they could want, like 'knowledge', 'career or goal attainment', or 'income', cf. Adler et al., 2017). It is positively associated with desirable outcomes, such as being in a partnership (Jakobsson et al., 2004; Kesebir and Diener, 2009; Gustavson et al., 2016), social relationships (Powdthavee, 2008), physical and mental health (Layard et al., 2013; Layard, 2018), employment (Clark and Oswald, 1994; Blanchflower and Oswald, 2004), or social status (Alpizar et al., 2005; Anderson et al., 2012).

The life-satisfaction question is easy to collect, easy to answer, easy to interpret, and has been collected for millions of respondents in nearly all countries of the world, starting more than fifty years ago. Crucially, life satisfaction seems to be a better predictor of important life choices than other candidates, such as more 'experiential measures' like answers to how happy someone is right now (Benjamin et al., 2012).

Is life satisfaction picking up something that exists outside of surveys, though? Do individuals evaluate their own life in the absence of surveys? Do they communicate that evaluation to others, consciously or unconsciously?

Here too the answer is 'yes'. Individuals communicate how they feel about the world via expressed emotions, verbal communication, and behaviour. Humans have always done this, just as all other primates: social life inherently involves reading other people and signalling how we feel, what we want, and how we see the world. We evolved to observe and communicate our feelings and wishes as a species, for example by using the forty-three muscles in our face to create smiles and frowns.

Social skills require us to judge how happy someone else is without asking them, and we know from many surveys that people are remarkably good at guessing how satisfied their partner is, or a person they only briefly see. This is true for good reasons: those who can read others better make fewer mistakes in social interactions. Our evolution as a social animal has honed our ability to read the feelings and mental states of those we interact with.[5] So we humans indeed are

example, from zero to ten). Moreover, there is evidence showing that simple data manipulations (that is, looking at the median rather than the mean) are sufficient to eliminate this issue and restore most stylized facts observed in wellbeing data (Chen et al., 2019).

[5] Evolution has also honed a keen ability to mislead others in a race between deception and decipherment. Some scholars believe that the importance of being able to tell lies convincingly to others was so important that it lead to self-deception mechanisms whereby individuals first convince themselves of lies so as to be more believable to others (Von Hippel and Trivers, 2011). This highlights the importance to measure wellbeing without incentives for concealment.

in the habit of evaluating life and communicating this evaluation. Using life satisfaction as a direct measure of wellbeing, researchers are simply trying to pick up this habit of socially active and aware humans in order to evaluate how they are doing, which is probably why the self-reported life satisfaction of individuals correlates highly with judgements made by third persons observing these individuals.

Yet, individuals can lie about their life satisfaction in surveys, which they might well do if it is advantageous to do so. It is also fairly easy to nudge survey respondents into a higher or lower answer, for instance by reminding them of something positive or negative in their life just before asking them about their life satisfaction. Deaton (2012) showed large changes in US wellbeing in the Gallup US Daily Poll which ran from 2008, with some of these large changes caused by changes to the questions asked just before life satisfaction. As a consequence, it is preferable to either start or end a survey with the question on life satisfaction and to employ a consistent methodology for asking the question over time and across surveys.

The manipulability of life satisfaction means that researchers down the line may look for some combination of a question on life satisfaction augmented with physiological measures that are harder to manipulate. Yet, at the moment, the available physiological measures (like numbers of smiles or cortisol, which is a steroid hormone responsive to stress) are far less accurate than life satisfaction and come with problems of their own: they are more expensive to collect and analyse, more volatile, bring with them a host of ethical issues and issues of data protection, and are often uncorrelated with large areas of life that people care about in their decision-making.

Arguably, the main alternatives to life satisfaction do worse in terms of our wish list. For instance, asking individuals how they feel right now, and then aggregating responses to that question over a period of days, weeks, or months, often yields seemingly counterintuitive results. Such 'experience-sampling' may show that the unemployed are happier than the employed despite being more likely to have much lower life satisfaction. This finding essentially comes from the result that individuals report not enjoying time spent at work, with those being out of work spending more time on activities they find more enjoyable (Knabe et al., 2010; Flèche and Smith, 2017). What this misses, however, is that the unemployed are actually looking for jobs and strongly signal low wellbeing (for example, they are more likely to have been diagnosed with depression, cf. Clark et al., 2018). Moreover, 'experience-sampling' can be expensive, only available for selective groups who answer at selective times, and only in a few countries.

Daniel Kahneman, who won the Nobel Prize in economics and who spent many years working on measures of instantaneous happiness (leading to the Day-

Reconstruction and ultimately, down the line, the Experience-Sampling Method) argued in a recent 2018 interview with Haaretz:[6]

> People do not want to be happy the way I've defined the term—what I experience here and now. In my view, it's much more important for them to be satisfied, to experience life satisfaction, from the perspective of 'What I remember', of the story they tell about their lives.

Importantly, the inability of experience-sampling to fully measure what people themselves find important indicates that wellbeing is not about a particular feeling or emotion, or even about a particular stream of feelings, such as surface-level feelings ('mood').

The differences between measures has alerted researchers to the fact that individuals can, in fact, have many feelings simultaneously and that it is possible for individuals to have fleeting feelings of happiness without being content, fulfilled, or happy about their life as a whole. Researchers have learned that there really are respondents who smilingly engage in their supposedly favourite leisure activities all day and yet are miserable about their life as a whole, desperate to change their circumstances, as reflected in clinical measures of mental ill health. The requirement of a useful measure of wellbeing that it is recognized and accepted as important by individuals themselves, hence moves us away from measures of momentary experiences and towards a cognitive evaluation of how a person thinks about his or her life.

Other alternative measures of wellbeing, like national indices based on large sets of life conditions, likewise struggle with some of the basic requirements. They are either not about how individuals think about their lives (such as GDP) or else artificially impose a weighting between what is important (such as adding years of education and life expectancy with equal weighting to an index), or use ambiguous variables (like housing prices which are good for some but bad for others). They fail the intuitive test that wellbeing should be what individuals want for their own grandchildren: it is normal to want our grandchildren to live a long and happy life, but less so to want them to score high on an index with thirty items.

We will discuss some of these alternative measures of wellbeing in more detail later this chapter, and discuss some aggregate indices in greater depth in chapter 4, where we focus more on the context in which measurement takes place, and hence the question of what makes a good measure for a particular purpose.

Life satisfaction can thus be argued to be the best measure of wellbeing we have at this moment, but it is not perfect: it is quite variable at the individual level over time and there is no obvious verification we can use to prevent manipulation if

[6] Available at: https://www.haaretz.com/israel-news/.premium.MAGAZINE-why-nobel-prize-winner-daniel-kahneman-gave-up-on-happiness-1.6528513.

individuals have an incentive to lie, such as if they would get more money when identified as 'wellbeing poor' via their self-reports.[7]

The variability of life satisfaction means that one needs hundreds, if not thousands, of individuals in different circumstances to say something reasonably certain about the wellbeing effects of those different circumstances. This rules out life satisfaction as a means of figuring out within a few weeks what might matter for a few individuals. Theories of wellbeing would be much more useful in those cases than small-scale data, but robust theories by design are limited to areas that are familiar and fed by observations on thousands.

Yet, life satisfaction can still be the linking pin between small-scale experiments and wellbeing, but then only in situations where one can draw upon a more reliable measure of outcomes that has a known relation with life satisfaction in circumstances where nothing else changes. An example would be experiments on Alzheimer patients who are no longer able to communicate themselves, but for whom one relies on the judgements of their carers. The known relation between those third-person judgements and life satisfaction (known from other large-scale studies) can then be relied upon to evaluate the effectiveness of experiments without direct measurement of wellbeing.

Life satisfaction can also be the linking pin between the particular objectives of some government department or agency and the role of that organization for government as a whole. If one, for instance, knows the effect of physical health or heritage on wellbeing (via all channels), then the institutions just oriented on physical health or heritage can calculate any effect they know can impact on the wellbeing of the nation.[8]

Alternative Measures of Wellbeing in Greater Depth

Experiential Measures

Experiential measures are an alternative to life satisfaction as a cognitive, evaluative measure of wellbeing. Experiential measures differ from evaluative ones in that they try to look at how individuals experience their lives in each moment, and then add up those experiences to come to a composite measure of someone's wellbeing.

There are many such experiential measures, ranging from momentary or periodic experiences sampled through diaries or mobile phone apps to sentiments

[7] This is less important than it would seem at first glance: usually, policy would be based on the expected change in wellbeing as evidenced by previous experiments and literature findings, gathered before wellbeing became important for policy and usually involving individuals with no clear reason to lie about their wellbeing. It is thus only for adaptive policies based on wellbeing feedback that the problem of manipulability arises. An example of an adaptive policy would be to lay off lecturers with particularly dissatisfied students. These kinds of policies invite manipulation.

[8] A first attempt at reasonable conversion numbers between life satisfaction and popular health measures is taken by Layard (2016). We will generate some new conversion numbers in chapters 3 and 4.

derived from Twitter or Facebook to biometric measures to automatic surveillance via cameras or voice recognition. These measures were recently surveyed by Béllet and Frijters (2019) in the context of the explosion of big data and the many uses that commercial companies now make of subjective information.

We discuss the two most promising ones: (i) momentary or periodic experiences sampled through diaries (the so-called Day-Reconstruction Method or DRM, which was championed by Daniel Kahneman) or through mobile phone apps (the so-called Experience-Sampling Method or ESM, which is basically the digital cousin of the DRM), and (ii) facial emotion recognition.

Momentary or Periodic Experiences Let us first discuss the Day-Reconstruction Method (DRM). This method has been around for about two decades now and there are a lot of data available on the related wellbeing measures. There is knowledge on its measurement, comparability between different measures, and 'validation' in terms of whether conclusions based on the DRM are actually palatable to individuals.

A typical DRM diary includes at least the following two elements as shown in Figure 2.1. These excerpts from surveys describe the two steps involved in arriving at an experiential wellbeing measure for a single day. In a first step, individuals are asked to describe their day in terms of episodes that are loosely labelled. A 24-hour day could, for instance, involve the episodes sleep, breakfast, commute, work, commute, dinner, leisure, and sleep again. Some respondents give far more episodes while most report fairly large chunks during the day as an episode, partially in order to get the questionnaire over with quickly. In a second step, individuals are asked more details about each episode, such as who else was involved and whether they combined various activities. Crucially, a respondent is asked to evaluate each episode on some kind of satisfaction scale. A prevalent way in which this leads to a summary measure is to take the evaluations of each episode and weigh them with the length of time spent in each episode.

There are several problems with this approach, both practical and in terms of legitimacy. Practical problems include that it takes a long time for individuals to complete these diaries and many respondents take shortcuts, do not fill in the whole diary, or simply refuse to participate at all in a survey of such length. Besides such issues of sample selection, there are also issues of selective reporting of certain episodes—think of culturally sensitive episodes such as being intimate. Equally problematic, there are major differences between what someone feels in the moment or when asked to remember an episode later: an episode is evaluated very differently in hindsight than it was evaluated in the moment (Lucas et al., 2012). Unfortunately, that change is not as simple as an episode being remembered as less fondly than it was experienced: in hindsight individuals value things differently than they value those same things in the moment, particularly elements to do with social approval and goals in life. For example, social

On the next pages, we ask you to please break down your day yesterday in single episodes. Give each episode a brief name (e.g. 'working', 'havng breakfast' or 'shopping') and write down the approximate times at which each episode began and ended.

Number	Episode Name	Time it began	Time it ended
☐	☐	☐	☐
☐	☐	☐	☐
☐	☐	☐	☐
☐	☐	☐	☐

This is episode number ...., which began at .... and ended at ....

8. Were you interacting with anyone during the episode, and if yes, how? Please also check the intensity of the interaction!

		in person	on the phone	Email/Chat	intense	quick
0) No one	☐					
1) spouse/partner	☐	☐	☐	☐	☐	☐
2) your children (under age 10)	☐	☐	☐	☐	☐	☐
3) parents/ relatives	☐	☐	☐	☐	☐	☐
4) friends	☐	☐	☐	☐	☐	☐
5) co-workers	☐	☐	☐	☐	☐	☐
6) clients/customers	☐	☐	☐	☐	☐	☐
7) boss	☐	☐	☐	☐	☐	☐
8) Other people (________) *please specify!*	☐	☐	☐	☐	☐	☐

9. How satisfied were you during this episode?

Not at all — Very much

☐ 0 ☐ 1 ☐ 2 ☐ 3 ☐ 4 ☐ 5 ☐ 6 ☐ 7 ☐ 8 ☐ 9 ☐ 10

Figure 2.1 Excerpt from DRM surveys
Source: Kahneman et al. (2004).

disapproval may be worse in hindsight than in the moment. Yet, social disapproval may strongly guide future behaviour. It is therefore not clear whether the experience in the moment is 'more valid' than the remembered experience later.

Some of these problems come out when looking at high-level associations. An early study by Knabe et al. (2010) using DRM data for Germany found that the unemployed were no less satisfied with their average days than the employed, though those unemployed were in worse mental health and did not intend to remain unemployed. Yet, those who became unemployed did not see a reduction in their valuation of the average day, despite all the usual observed problems with unemployment, including higher divorce rates and depression.

The same problems apply to other types of experience sampling, including using apps from mobile phones or sentiments from Twitter or Facebook. They all ask for an immediate evaluation of the day, the last ten minutes, or something equivalent, and they all have similar problems of not corresponding all that strongly with what people remember, nor do they correspond all that strongly with what people on reflection want in important life domains (especially work and social status). It is increasingly clear that short-run emotions and experiences have short-run purposes, i.e. to help the individual make quick decisions relating to immediate threats and opportunities. They differ from how individuals make longer-term plans which require more of an overall assessment of complex situations and what the better decisions are.

Facial Emotion Recognition Facial recognition technology is based on the face having forty-three muscles, many of which are involved in the expression of emotions and evaluative judgements. If faces portray what we feel and what we value, why not use observations on faces to arrive at a measure of wellbeing?

This picture (https://www.youtube.com/watch?v=TrgNKGjSyxA), taken from a scientific project that is active in this area, illustrates computer-aided facial recognition:[9] a computer programme analyses the orientation of the lips, the width of the eyes, pupil dilation, the flattening of the nose, and so on, and then ascribes emotional states to the sum of these facial elements. The idea is that if one could observe someone on a permanent basis, the average emotion inferred from these facial expressions could be used as a wellbeing measure.

The key things to note about facial recognition are:

1. No such measure actually yet exists or has been used. So there simply is no actual continuous measure of someone's experiential wellbeing based on

[9] Using the Facial Action Coding System (FACS) developed by Paul Elkman. For more information, see: https://www.scribd.com/document/18649644/Facial-Action-Coding-System-Khappucino-s-Tutorial; and https://www.paulekman.com/facial-action-coding-system/.

facial recognition as of today. Rather, at best, one can talk about the prevalence of various emotions in a day.

2. The methodology is not yet advanced enough to analyse the emotions of moving individuals: they basically have to be still in front of a camera to be somewhat accurate, which is why border controls now use facial recognition techniques. Yet, following a face moving in a crowd and deducing its emotions while that face is at an angle, partly concealed, and often has other things in front of it, is something no computer software is yet capable of.
3. Even if one were to work out the average emotions of a crowd or an individual during a period, emotions have limited democratic legitimacy and correspondence to what individuals on reflection want: meaning and worthwhileness are very poorly correlated with emotional facial expressions (for examples of how facial expressions can be misleading, see Barrett et al., 2019).
4. There is no literature that tells us how various circumstances affect a facial-recognition derived measure of wellbeing, let alone a large literature on the causal elements. It will probably take years for facial-recognition literature to reach maturity.
5. Hence, at present, facial recognition is largely something that might be useful in the future of wellbeing research and policy, perhaps as an augmentation tool useful in very confined spaces, where one can imagine some use for a crowd-emotion measure.

Informed Preferences Finally, we should mention the long-standing interest of economists and others in the notion of 'informed preferences', together with the desire to measure them as the basis of public policy.

It is important to realize that neuroscientists have not found a single place in the brain that houses preferences: when making choices, people do not 'look up their preferences' in some internal full map. Rather, they apply all kinds of complicated heuristics that involve situational cues (what the immediate choice situation alerts them to) and longer-running interests (their 'plans', expectations, and reflections). Choices hence do not really reveal preferences: rather, they establish the individual's preferences at that moment in time. Since people can change their minds, such as about the political party they support or the breakfast they like, their 'preferences' are in constant flux.

Hence, at best, the notion of informed preferences is one that describes what individuals would really want if they thought about it a long time. To some extent, that is what conversations about someone's life and whether they are satisfied with it are exactly about: to find out whether they are satisfied with their life and thus 'prefer it' in the sense of not having much desire for a different life at that moment.

Yet, many philosophers and economists actively look for measures that are closer to some notion of what people really on reflection want than a single question on life satisfaction. There are many different attempts to create measures of wellbeing that capture what life individuals prefer and how much weight there is attached to various circumstances in that implied wellbeing.

The basic idea behind these measures is best illustrated by looking at an example: the suggestion by Benjamin et al. (2014). Their suggestion is to have a weighted average of many life goals, where the weights are determined by an aggregation of how individuals trade them off in hypothetical scenarios posed in surveys.

To get an idea of how this goes, note that they select 136 different aspects of life, including such life goals as 'how full of beautiful memories your life is', 'you not feeling depressed', 'your ability to have and raise children', and 'your ability to dream and pursue your dreams'. In order to find out how to weigh each of these 136 different aspects into a composite index, they ask four thousand Americans to fill in a survey with many hypotheticals hypotheticals on trade-offs between these different aspects. An example is shown in Figure 2.2.

This means that they let individuals make actual choices that vary outcomes in two dimensions at a time, which then reveals how much respondents are willing to trade off one dimension for another. By making some additional assumptions on functional form, they estimate for each of the 136 dimensions how much weight the average respondent gives to that dimension relative to others, which then allows them to calculate a final score.

Imaging you are **making a personal decision**, and that you face a choice between two options: Option 1 and Option 2. The two options are predicted to have different effects over the next four years but to have the same effects after tjat. The table below lists these predicted differences in the next four years. Please assume that anything not listed in the table would be marked "about equal" if it were listed.

Click here to see the instructions again

	OPTION 1				OPTION 2		
	much higher	somewhat higher	slightly higher	about equal	slightly higher	somewhat higher	much higher
how happy you feel						X	
you not feeling anxious			X				

Between these two options, which do you think you would choose?

OPTION 1			OPTION 2		
Much prefer Option 1	Somewhat prefer Option 1	Slightly prefer Option 1	Slightly prefer Option 2	Somewhat prefer Option 2	Much prefer Option 2
o	o	o	o	o	o

Figure 2.2 Example of Hypothetical Scenario Survey
Source: Benjamin et al. (2014).

This procedure is typical for many attempts at measuring informed preferences, which is that weights on outcomes are inferred from choices in hypothetical scenarios. Note that the choices are very abstract and likely to be poorly understood by many: what does a respondent think of when asked to consider for a period of the 'next four years' to 'not feel anxious'? Would they think this meant never feeling anxious at all for the entire four years? Would it mean they think feeling less anxious than usual? Would it mean they think they have a low level of anxiety relative to the rest of the population? Basically, one does not know how respondents interpret such a question, and it is likely that each respondent interprets such a question quite differently.

What this means is that these are not concrete choice situations, as if someone is buying this car or that car. Individuals are asked to choose between life trajectories for ensuing years labelled in ways that are difficult to interpret, in 136 dimensions no less. The logic of a conversation, and thus a survey, is that individuals will try their best to answer based on their understanding of what might be meant, but it should be doubted all the respondents share a common understanding of all 136 dimensions. Moreover, the fact that they are asked to trade off one dimension with another immediately will be understood by the respondents as implying they should think of them as opposing dimensions between which there is a trade-off. They might not have thought about these dimensions as separate from each other at all before being asked, and thus are basically guided by the survey to presume they are different.

There are thus several difficulties with this method and the use of the ensuing measure as a guide for policy-making and budget trade-offs:

1. Answering questions on 136 dimensions takes a lot of time and resources, whether one gets some respondents to answer thousands of questions, or gets hundreds of thousands to answer only a few: it takes an awful lot of measurement to get an individual value of wellbeing from this approach.
2. To be useful, one would then need a whole literature on how circumstances affect the resulting measure. Since many of the 136 dimensions do not have a large backing literature, this effectively means one is back at point zero in terms of wellbeing for policy, setting back the agenda by decades.
3. It is unlikely that weights between 136 dimensions remain stable over time, or that they are invariant to policies and cultural shifts, so one would not only need to know the effects of circumstances on each of the 136 dimensions, but also on the effects of their weight in a composite index of those dimensions. To see the importance of culture, we can suffice by pointing out that the life goal 'your ability to dream and pursue your dreams' will not mean much to (non-American) cultures not used to thinking of lives as dream pursuits.

4. Individuals are known to have great difficulties in answering hypotheticals because it requires a lot of imagination. It is subject to what is known as affective forecasting biases and the sheer mental effort of imagining a whole different life. This general problem has been often discussed in the context of health hypotheticals that underlie the QALY method, but the general point is that many individuals are just not good at imagining themselves in very different circumstances and make huge mistakes forecasting how they would feel in those circumstances.

In short, the method seems impractical for current decision systems. It is theoretically appealing in economics and philosophy, but too cumbersome, speculative, culturally specific, and high-dimensional for practical use. These objections convey one of the great advantages of asking individuals to evaluate their lives, which is that they do not have to imagine a different life but can simply report how they think about the one they are living.

This does not mean one needs to completely abandon the idea of informed preferences, but one should probably abandon the idea that it is a practical idea to measure preferences on a continuous basis. Rather, one can pursue the idea in a more detached high-level manner by trying to see what people on reflection think about their whole life (Clark et al. (2008) pursue this idea much further; Frijters et al. (2020) also link life satisfaction to a contractarian philosophy).

Key Implementation Questions: What Do We Assume When We Aggregate Life Satisfaction?

With a particular measure of wellbeing in mind, the question arises as to how one can derive the aggregate wellbeing of the population from all individual observations at different times.

The classical utilitarian approach is to take the answers to the question on life satisfaction at face value and to treat them as cardinally comparable numbers, i.e. to sum up all the values of all the citizens. One would do the same when considering lifetime values, by summing up the discounted values in each year of life for any individual into a 'lifetime life-satisfaction' number. The basic unit is then a WELLBY (wellbeing-adjusted life-year): one unit of life satisfaction on a 0-to-10 scale for one person for one year. The wellbeing value of a policy change is the expected change in WELLBYs for the population. It can then be compared with the costs.

This approach is already implicitly adopted when researchers and analysts talk about changes to average life satisfaction over time in a country, or when they try to explain differences in averages across countries. Any discussion using average life satisfaction treats the individual observations on life satisfaction as comparable over people and over time.

What assumptions are we making when we just add up the individual observations and how reasonable are those assumptions?

The first assumption is that individuals themselves treat life satisfaction as cardinal (we call this 'internal comparability'), i.e. that a one unit change means the same increase to them anywhere on the scale, such that there is the same change in wellbeing when they go from a 4 to a 5 as they do from an 8 to a 9.

There are two basic reasons to think this assumption is reasonable. The first stems purely from the logic of language: asking individuals to give responses in terms of numbers automatically makes them think of these answers as if the characteristics of numbers apply to them. So just as individuals treat different prices and weights on a single cardinal scale, asking them for a number leads individuals to treat life-satisfaction responses on a single cardinal scale. Kapteyn (1977) and Parducci (1995) discuss this argument at length.

Researchers have looked to corroborate this intuition. One approach is to ask individuals whether they would be willing to trade off years spent in different life satisfaction states in a cardinal manner. In particular, they have asked respondents whether they would, for instance, prefer a life with two years spent in a state worth an 8 out of 10 on the life-satisfaction scale to one year worth a 9 and one year worth a 6. If the answers are cardinally comparable, the two years spent in a state worth 8 should be worth an 8 on average, whilst the alternative should be worth a 7.5 and thus less valued. Peasgood et al. (2018) indeed find that, in hypothetical trade-offs, the stated life-satisfaction numbers are, roughly speaking, treated as cardinally comparable, i.e. the trade-offs are close to linear.

A related idea is to look at the test-retest relationship: Krueger and Schkade (2008) find that there is, on average, a 0.6 correlation between two measures of life satisfaction for the same individual when they are two weeks apart (illustrating the high degree of variability in life satisfaction).[10] Importantly, though, they look at whether the change in the wellbeing measure relates to the initial level of that measure. The idea is that if individuals interpret the measure as cardinal, then changes in a short period of time should be equal in all directions, because whatever happens to change their answer should be somewhat equal in both the positive and the negative realm. In particular, it should be equally likely than an individual goes from an 8 to a 9 as going from a 3 to a 2 or from a 6 to a 7. Whilst it is clear that an individual who is at the very extremes (0 or 10) can only change in one direction, Krueger and Schkade (2008) do find for their sample of 230 respondents that the

[10] Lucas and Donnellan (2012) look at the test–retest reliability of life satisfaction for around seventy thousand individuals in four countries. When they treat the 'occasion-specific' variation as real (in the sense that it is not a mistake but a reflection of the specificity of how the day and the occasion make them evaluate their life), the reliability is around 0.7. When the occasion-specific variation is treated as an error, the reliability is again around 0.6.

changes were equally likely for the middle 80 per cent of their sample, which lead them to cautiously say that they could not reject the hypothesis of 'homoscedasticity in errors', which can be seen as weak evidence for cardinality.[11]

Another argument to support internal comparability is the evolutionary argument for why we have evaluative capacities in the first place and why humans communicate these evaluations with others: in order to effectively communicate and read others well, it is necessary that they share the same understanding and use numbers to convey information in the same way (Kapteyn, 1977). This accentuates the argument on the logic of language: when numbers are used to compare outcomes between individuals, they should be expected to convey cardinal information.

The main evidence in this line of reasoning comes from studies that have used third parties to corroborate life-satisfaction answers of individuals (Sandvik et al., 1993). It turns out that, for example, individuals do reasonably well at guessing the life-satisfaction answers of their family members. The judgement of interviewers also aligns well with what individuals themselves say. Similarly, the judgements of third-party individuals who get to see videos or written statements of individuals aligns similarly well (see Frijters et al. (2020) for references). From this high degree of 'cross-rater validity', there thus appears to be a degree of observability of the wellbeing of individuals which also relies on a joint interpretation of language (i.e. a 9 has to be a high number for both the individual and their family members as well as for random strangers). Clark (2016) discusses this point in greater detail.

The second assumption when adding up individual observations of wellbeing is that answers are comparable between individuals (we call this 'external comparability'), i.e. that we can treat a 6 from one person the same as a 6 from another one. There are two different arguments in favour of this:

1. The first is along the lines of the arguments above, which is that the joint use of language forces the same interpretation on answers in a language community. Just like people's internal conception of 'a chair' or 'a table' gradually start to mean the same thing amongst people in the same language community, so too do individual feelings and mental processes become labelled in a comparable way. One piece of evidence for this is that virtually everyone answers these questions, and does so quite quickly (about five seconds, on average): they must know what is meant.[12] Additional evidence for this thinking comes from the experience of regular (economic) migrants.

[11] In their study, they applied their heteroscedasticity tests to net affect (which has more than eleven possible responses) based on evaluations of activities in particular time periods (the previous day).

[12] Another interpretation for this finding could be that individuals answer the question on life satisfaction so quickly because they do not understand it. However, this would lead to a much higher number of non-responses. Typically, the number of non-responses is very low.

In the World Happiness Report 2018, John Helliwell and colleagues found evidence from around the world that 'regular' migrants (i.e. not refugees) within twelve months of moving from one country to another had assimilated to about 75 per cent of the life evaluation (measured by the Cantril ladder, a close relative to life satisfaction) in the destination country. Their finding held for migrants from any large region of the world to any other, despite different uses of language and the possibility that life satisfaction meant something different in different cultures. The uniformity of assimilation strongly suggests three things: life-satisfaction answers are not merely comparable across individuals, but even across cultures; life satisfaction varies strongly due to national circumstances that migrants are also subject to; and individual life satisfaction is highly variable and not set in stone during childhood or due to some individual setpoint.

2. A different argument for interpersonal comparability comes from the rationale for looking at wellbeing in the first place: interpersonal cardinality is a cornerstone of the democratic ideal to take each individual equally seriously. The only way to respect the equal-value ideal of democracy is to count every person's life satisfaction as equally valuable, irrespective of possible differences in the inner lives of individuals. Within that argument, it does not matter whether some individuals experience far more pleasure than others because their brains are wired differently. Taking different individuals as equals requires us to ignore potential between-individual variability in their internal wiring when it comes to how much they matter for collective action. Thus, we should treat life satisfaction as interpersonally comparable for the same reason that each vote in an election counts equally: not because each vote is given for the same reason and reflective of the same feelings, but simply because each person should count equally in terms of collective decision-making.

There are important objections to life satisfaction and alternative wellbeing measures we quickly want to mention. One common objection is that the answers are bounded rather than open-ended, which might force lots of individuals to give a score on the boundary rather than their true open-ended feeling (which lies outside of the scale). Another is that the answers are in terms of whole numbers between 0 and 10 rather than decimals (such as 6.5).

The boundedness of the scale, cemented in the 1930s, is crucial in order to receive meaningful averages. Just think of the converse: if you give individuals open-ended questions to life satisfaction, how does one aggregate someone who says a 0.0003 and someone else who says −2,013,032? One can't. Boundedness thus respects the need to obtain comparable answers. Moreover, typically no more than 10 per cent of respondents in any region of the world are at the top end of the scale (see, for example, Figure 2.1 in the World Happiness Report 2017). Thus, practically, it is not a large impediment that the scale is bounded. Additionally, it may be that individuals in fact experience their world through perceptive abilities that are bounded, meaning that a bounded scale is warranted even if one would be interested in some notion of 'actual level of feelings'.

To expand on this last point, our sensory system has a minimal and a maximal perceptibility for senses: individuals can only hear sounds if they are sufficiently loud, and there is a maximum sound level they can perceive above which their ear sustains damage. Individuals can similarly perceive a minimum level of light, weight, temperature, or speed. Above their maximums, nerves burn out or are firing at a maximum rate, i.e. our brain can only handle a certain maximum stimulus. Whilst it is the case that our senses adjust to the background level and variability, it remains the case that there are minimal and maximal levels to our perception (Gazzaniga and Ivry, 2013). It is intuitive to assume that the same goes for whatever feeds into evaluations of our life.

Historically, whole-number answers of Likert scales exist for practical reasons: to limit the number of options when some interviewer had to record the answers of an interviewee on paper. This practical reason is no longer relevant in the days of computer-based interviews, though respondents find it much easier to give whole-number answers than something in-between, so non-response rates are much lower for questions that allow only whole numbers than asking individuals to give any value between 0 and 10: when given a choice, almost no one gives fractional responses like 7.319. The penchant of respondents to prefer whole answers was already discovered very early on in the development of the Likert scale in the 1930s (Chyung et al., 2018). Indeed, many respondents are prone to answer round numbers for many questions anyway (including their age) and there is a lot of variation in life-satisfaction answers between individuals and over time. Thus, it hardly matters for applications whether individuals are constrained to whole numbers or not.

It is important to mention that the list of objections to life satisfaction is almost as large as the list of objections to GDP. The more seriously life satisfaction is taken, the faster and more numerous the objections arise. The objections stimulate the search for different measures of wellbeing, just as there are now many alternatives to GDP. This search for improvements should go on, yet should not stop current measures from being used. The search for perfection should not impede actual improvements.

Influences of Survey Design on Wellbeing Measures

As mentioned earlier, survey design can have important influences on how respondents answer the life-satisfaction question. When it comes to survey mode, for example, we know that respondents tend to give higher scores when an interviewer is present (either face-to-face or on the phone), as opposed to filling out a survey and mailing it back to an anonymous survey firm. We also know that item ordering matters: items preceding the life-satisfaction question may prime respondents to answer (consciously or unconsciously) in a certain way, whereby the influence can go in either direction depending on the type of framing or the strength of emotional content.

Framing of the life-satisfaction question in general matters, especially whether the question text and scale reminds respondents of social comparisons, as is the case with the Cantril ladder-of-life question (i.e. life evaluation), which tends to yield lower scores than the standard life-satisfaction question as the question text may induce social comparisons with idealized, higher-up social groups. Finally, there are important situational factors (including place and time-of-day, which seem to matter more for experiential as opposed to evaluative measures like life satisfaction) and cultural factors that matter for how respondents answer to wellbeing questions in surveys.

Table 2.1 gives an overview of the effects of survey design characteristics on the measured level of life satisfaction, including directionality of influence, key studies, and short descriptions. The general lesson to be kept in mind is that consistent, standardized, and best-practice survey design (in the sense of having consistent priming and framing) matters. But there are also influences outside the scope of the analyst such as situational and cultural factors. These influences underline once more the importance of having a large sample to 'net out' such influences, to the extent possible, in average scores of wellbeing.

Stylized Facts on Wellbeing

We start with some key facts we know about wellbeing, from here on understood as life satisfaction, using the example of the United Kingdom. Figure 2.3 shows the current distribution of life satisfaction, recorded on a scale from 0 to 10, in the United Kingdom and two other European countries, taken from the Gallup World Poll.[13]

We see that the biggest difference between Denmark and the United Kingdom or France is not at the very bottom (in the 0-to-2 range) but for the low-to-middle and top group: Denmark has fewer people in the 3-to-6 range than France or the United Kingdom. This suggests that improvements in the 'somewhat unsatisfied' region can be made in the United Kingdom, possibly by adopting the key ingredients in the policies of the Danes.

[13] The Gallup World Poll uses the Cantril ladder of life, which is also termed 'life evaluation' and which is a close relative to life satisfaction. We refer to life satisfaction for simplicity.

Table 2.1 Effects of survey design characteristics on the measured levels of life satisfaction

Characteristic	Directionality of effect	Key studies	Description
Survey mode	Upward effect for survey modes that lend themselves to more engagement between interviewer and interviewee.	Schwarz, N., Strack, F., Hippler, H. J., and Bishop, G. (1991) The Impact of Administration Mode on Response Effects in Survey Measurement. *Applied Cognitive Psychology* 5(3): 193–212.	Certain survey modes (e.g. face-to-face) may induce higher responses from participants who may be susceptible to a social desirability bias.
		Dolan, P., and Kavetsos, G. (2016). Happy Talk: Mode of Administration Effects on Subjective Well-Being. *Journal of Happiness Studies* 17(3): 1273–91.	Looking at the difference between face-to-face and phone interviews, Dolan and Kavetsos (2016) find that, relative to face-to-face interviews, phone interviews induce higher responses.
Item order (priming due to preceding items)	Depends on content of the preceding item. Effects are often small and can be somewhat eliminated by the inclusion of a buffer or transition question.	Deaton, A. (2012). The Financial Crisis and the Well-being of Americans. 2011 OEP Hicks Lecture. *Oxford Economic Papers* 64(1): 1–26.	Deaton (2012) reports an item-order effect using data from the Gallup Healthways Well-being index. People's responses to life-satisfaction questions were lower when political questions were preceding the life-satisfaction questions, although a 'buffer' or transition question between the two largely eliminated the effect. Certain questions may thus frame the way individuals think about the successive life-satisfaction question (e.g. political questions may lead one to judge their responses relative to political or societal affairs).
		Strack, F., Martin, L. L., and Schwarz, N. (1988). Priming and Communication: Social Determinants of Information Use in Judgments of Life Satisfaction. *European Journal of Social Psychology* 18(5): 429–42.	Impacts of item order are stronger when preceding items frame successive life-satisfaction questions in a particular way. For instance, the question 'are you worried about crime in your neighbourhood?' will have more effect

			than a non-emotional question like 'do you have a friendly relationship with your neighbours?'
Framing of questions (anchoring, choice of scale)	Downward effect for anchors that induce one to judge their situation relative to an ideal benchmark.	Bjørnskov, C. (2010). How Comparable Are the Gallup World Poll Life Satisfaction Data? *Journal of Happiness Studies* 11(1): 41–60. Lim, H. E. (2008). The Use of Different Happiness Rating Scales: Bias and Comparison Problem? *Social Indicators Research* 87(2): 259–67. Cummins, R. A. (2003). Normative Life Satisfaction: Measurement Issues and a Homeostatic Model. *Social Indicators Research* 64(2): 225–56.	The question text and scale can have an impact on respondents' answers to life-satisfaction questions. Responses to life-satisfaction scales are normally restricted to a closed interval, with a maximum. Anchoring that pushes one to evaluate their life relative to an ideal standard, such as 'the best possible life' (used in the Cantril ladder-of-life question to describe the maximum) may yield lower life-satisfaction responses compared to simpler questions with a weaker 'cognitive' state anchor (i.e. the standard 'how satisfied are you' question).
Polarity of responses (unipolar versus bipolar)	Upward effect for bipolar measures.	Mazaheri, M., and Theuns, P. (2009). Effects of Varying Response Formats on Self-ratings of Life-Satisfaction. *Social Indicators Research* 90(3): 381.	Mazaheri and Theuns (2009) suggest that respondents have some difficulty rating life dissatisfaction using bipolar scales.
Day-of-week (weekend versus weekdays)	Measures of positive affect are higher on weekends and holidays than on weekdays though there is no day of the week effect for life satisfaction.	Helliwell, J. F., and Wang, S. (2014). Weekends and Subjective Well-being. *Social Indicators Research* 116(2): 389–407.	Leisure and time use are key explanatory factors for the phenomenon that positive affect is higher at weekends. This is derived from the fact that individuals can

Continued

Table 2.1 *Continued*

Characteristic	Directionality of effect	Key studies	Description
			engage in more social activities and spend more time with family and friends on weekends.
Situational factors	Will be positive or negative depending on the nature of the 'priming' activity.	Suh, E. M., Diener, E. D., and Updegraff, J. A. (2008). From Culture to Priming Conditions: Self-construal Influences on Life Satisfaction Judgments. *Journal of Cross-Cultural Psychology* 39(1): 3–15. Oishi, S., Schimmack, U., and Colcombe, S. J. (2003). The Contextual and Systematic Nature of Life Satisfaction Judgments. *Journal of Experimental Social Psychology* 39(3): 232–47. Strack, F., Schwarz, N., Chassein, B., Kern, D., and Wagner, D. (1990). Salience of Comparison Standards and the Activation of Social Norms: Consequences for Judgements of Happiness and their Communication. *British Journal of Social Psychology* 29(4): 303–14.	Situational factors, such as whether the person holding the interview is friendly or whether someone just had a cup of coffee, can be altered or primed to make them more salient at the moment the life-satisfaction question is asked. This may prime certain information within the respondent which will alter how they evaluate their response to the life-satisfaction question.

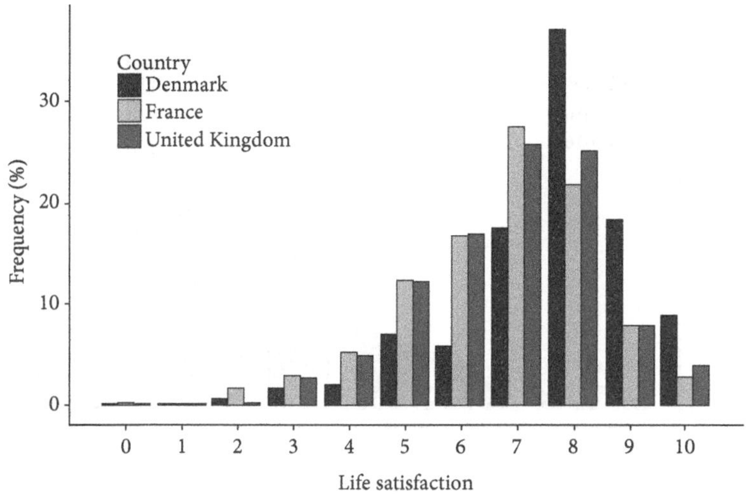

Figure 2.3 Frequency distribution of life satisfaction in the United Kingdom, France, and Denmark
Source: Gallup World Poll, 2016.

The figure also shows that the mean taken over the three countries is about 7.5, that few individuals are at the very top, and that the United Kingdom has a higher share of individuals who are less satisfied with their lives. Compared to Denmark, UK citizens are, on average, less happy, but compared to France, they are happier.

If we combine the nationally representative, longitudinal household data for the United Kingdom from the British Household Panel Survey in 1996 with Understanding Society from 2010 to 2016 (both of which measure life satisfaction on a 1-to-7 scale) in Figure 2.4, we see clear changes in wellbeing over time.

The figure shows that life satisfaction has improved quite strongly in the United Kingdom during the last twenty years, illustrating that average life satisfaction across the population does change over time. The improvement has been particularly due to a reduction in the middle group (4s and 5s) towards the higher group (6s), which is also what we see in the official statistics by the ONS in the United Kingdom. In the last six years, there has been a marked reduction in the share of the population living in misery (1s and 2s).[14]

We do not really know what has driven the improvement in average life satisfaction in the United Kingdom during the last twenty years, though it might be low unemployment and more and better treatment of mental health

[14] Note that one would probably not come to the same conclusion if one looked only at the change in life satisfaction for those who remain in the British Household Panel Survey, as this group gets older and there may be insufficient new intake into the panel. Thus, being cautious about just how one concludes that life satisfaction has increased matters. In this case, we take arguably the most representative dataset and simply aggregate the responses in each survey year.

Figure 2.4 Frequency distribution of life satisfaction in the United Kingdom
Source: British Household Panel Survey, 1996; Understanding Society, 2010 to 2016.

problems. Both have direct and indirect benefits: lower unemployment and improved mental health benefit the whole family and social circle.

Of course, the Covid-19 crisis had a strong negative effect on life satisfaction in the United Kingdom and elsewhere and so the data above are not quite up to date. We will discuss the use of wellbeing methods to illuminate aspects of this crisis in chapter 5 when we apply the techniques of this book to different policy questions, including Covid-19 lockdowns. The advantage of these techniques, and WELLBY methodology in particular, is that it allows one to combine the diverse effects of the Covid-19 crisis (premature deaths, loneliness, unemployment, fear, etc.) into a single number: the overall wellbeing of the population. Getting a single number that summarizes a policy allows one to judge what should be done at what point and to compare the outcomes of different policies, something impossible to do without a methodology to combine outcomes in different domains. In fact, as we shall argue in chapter 5, the Covid-19 crisis shows the great importance of using the WELLBY methodology to base policy and decision-making on.

Key Lessons on Wellbeing

Some Key Findings from around the World

A first hint at what policies might raise wellbeing can be gleaned by looking at what explains the differences in life satisfaction between individuals: the variation

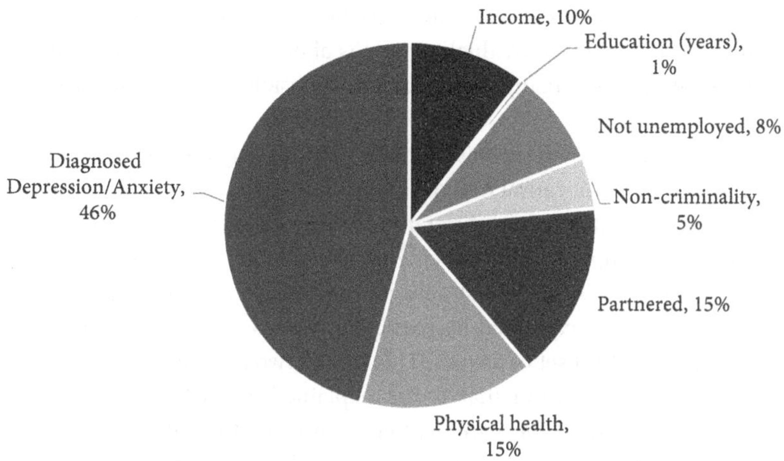

Figure 2.5 The contribution of different socio-economic factors to explained adult life satisfaction in the United Kingdom

Source: British Household Panel Survey, cross-section, beta-coefficients; taken from Table 16.1 Clark et al. (2018).

within the population tells us what can be changed by moving individuals from the worst to the best possible circumstances.

Figure 2.5 is again based on the British Household Panel Survey: it shows what explains adult life satisfaction amongst all adults aged twenty-five and above:[15]

The figure shows the importance of different areas of life in explaining adult life satisfaction. Note that only about 19 per cent of adult life satisfaction can be explained by these different factors in the first place: other factors are either not captured (due to missing variables in the data), largely fixed (like genes), or highly transient (like the weather). So whilst mental health captures about 46 per cent of the explained variance in adult life satisfaction, it in fact 'only' explains about 9 per cent of the variation in 'raw' life satisfaction ($= 0.46 \times 0.19$), which corresponds to the basic rule of thumb that the correlation between mental health and life satisfaction is about 0.3.

The figure is based on the partial correlation coefficients in an equation in which life satisfaction (standardized) is regressed on log household income per capita, years of education, whether or not the respondent is unemployed, number of criminal convictions (times −1), whether the respondent is partnered, the number of physical health conditions, and whether the respondent has been diagnosed as suffering from depression or anxiety (all likewise standardized). The square of each coefficient measures the fraction of the variance of life

[15] What is shown are the relative contribution of squared beta-coefficients into the explained variation.

satisfaction explained by the respective variable. As the figure shows, the fraction of variance explained by individual income is about 11 per cent. More important are social relationships (being partnered and in a job) and, by far, health (especially mental health).

One should view these results as no more than vaguely indicative, though. They are not based on careful causal designs but only correlations, i.e. regressions of life satisfaction on indicators of the different life areas. Hence, it is not at all clear that one would get the supposed improvements in wellbeing if the factors shown here were truly improved. Also, one should be mindful of what the pie chart shows, which is the variation explained by particular factors within the total amount of variation explained by a set of factors. This misses two crucial aspects: it misses the 81 per cent of the variation that is not explained at all by *any* of the factors included, be it because of measurement error or lack of variables themselves, and all the factors that hardly vary at the country level, which will include basic needs and things like national security.

Similar analyses are possible going back to schooling and pre-school experience, and they can help guide the search for policy options using a more holistic, life-course perspective on wellbeing.[16]

We next look at what explains the variation in national average life satisfaction across countries, as opposed to average individual life satisfaction within a particular country. We know from cross-country regressions that a high percentage of variation in national average life satisfaction across countries can be explained (about 80 per cent, see Table 8.1 in Clark et al. (2018), for example). However, a major problem is that many of the factors which have a positive impact on life satisfaction are highly correlated with each other, such that one can easily explain that 80 per cent with almost anything that picks up some notion of national wealth, the quality of governance, and the quality of the environment. This has led to long-running controversies on which factors matter for national average life satisfaction.

The latest and arguably most comprehensive study into the various country-level factors important for life satisfaction comes from a paper by Arie Kapteyn and colleagues from RAND in the United States (Kapteyn et al., 2019): the authors run several regressions using the Gallup World Poll including 150 countries since 2008, focusing on the contribution of country-level factors to national average life satisfaction (measured as the Cantril ladder-of-life, as is typical in the Gallup World Poll). Table 2.2 shows the individual life satisfaction that can be explained by macro-level factors, supressing, for simplicity, the remainder of the authors' regression table that includes individual-level factors similar to the ones shown in Figure 2.5 for the United Kingdom.

[16] See, for example, Lordan and McGuire (2019), Adler (2016), and Fergusson and Horwood (2001) for school interventions with a wellbeing rationale.

Table 2.2 Effects of GDP per capita, household income, and public goods

	(1)	(2)	(3)	(4)	(5)	(6)
Log GDP	0.380***	0.084				0.104
	0.031	0.086				0.097
Log household income			0.442***	0.228***	0.059	0.037
			0.035	0.013	0.077	0.082
Log of relative income			−0.211***		0.174**	0.196**
			0.037		0.078	0.082
Life expectancy		0.027***		0.023***	0.026***	0.025***
		0.006		0.007	0.007	0.007
Log of health expenditures		−0.002		−0.022	0.041	−0.013
		0.101		0.095	0.097	0.108
Log of education expenditures		0.05		0.044	0.067	0.047
		0.07		0.075	0.073	0.074
Average years of schooling		0.001		−0.008	0.001	0
		0.018		0.019	0.019	0.018
Corruption perception index		−0.005**		−0.006***	−0.005**	−0.005**
		0.002		0.002	0.002	0.002
Environmental health index		0.008**		0.008**	0.008**	0.009**
		0.004		0.004	0.003	0.004
Observations	**86,819**	**86,819**	**86,819**	**86,819**	**86,819**	**86,819**
Pseudo R-squared	0.066	0.067	0.073	0.074	0.074	0.074

Notes: Ordered probit. Standard errors below each estimated coefficient. The year of the observed variable is the survey year (e.g. log GDP in 2012 for a respondent surveyed in 2012). Linear extrapolation is used for education expenditures for Saudi Arabia and Yemen in 2014.

Source: Kapteyn et al. (2019).

Before we discuss these macro-level factors, let us discuss an apparent puzzle in how much variation is explained. The very bottom of this table shows the proportion of variance explained, which is only 6.6 per cent to 7.4 per cent in different columns. This is much lower than the 80 per cent that we argued could be explained by between-country variation, and even lower than the 19 per cent that could be explained by within-country variation in the United Kingdom (even though the full regression includes many of the same variables). How can all of this be consistent at the same time?

The main thing to bear in mind is that the underlying variation is now the variation of life satisfaction at the individual level in the whole world, rather than the average variation at the country level or the variation at the individual level within a single country. That world variation is far higher. Hence, 6.6 per cent of world variation may in fact be between 40 per cent and 70 per cent of average variation at the country level (Kapteyn et al., 2019). Similarly, individual characteristics are neither as well measured across the world as they are within the United Kingdom, nor necessarily equally important as they are within the United Kingdom, so that the same headline individual drivers explain much less at the world level than at the level of a single (developed) country.

Let us then look at the importance of macro-level factors. The first column shows how GDP is strongly related to national life satisfaction if you use it as the only explanatory variable. Importantly, columns 2 and 6 show that the contribution of GDP reduces to 25 per cent of its raw effect if one includes measures of welfare, good governance, and the quality of the environment. The environment, in turn, relates to mental health (see Bowler et al. (2010) for a review of evidence). Similarly, by comparing column 5 to column 4, one can see that the contribution of individual income reduces by around 75 per cent if one also takes relative income (which in this study is the income of the individual relative to the median household income) into account: an estimated 75 per cent of the effect of individual income is due to comparisons with others. This may, of course, be different at lower levels of average income (as in less developed countries) or at lower levels of the income distribution within developed countries: at lower levels, increases in income may buy more wellbeing as these may be used to satisfy basic comforts rather than being geared towards status races.

Kapteyn et al. (2019) dovetails with some of the stylized understanding in the academic literature, evidenced by a survey of twenty-nine leading wellbeing researchers around the world who were asked in the April 2018 World Wellbeing Panel poll whether they agreed with the statement: 'Is the main effect of economic growth on national wellbeing via employment and public welfare programs?' Twenty-four out of twenty-nine panellists agreed, with the four dissenters adding small caveats, such as that it depended on whether economic growth was inequality-neutral.

As an important example that even in poor countries GDP increases may not on their own lead to wellbeing increases, consider the case of China and India in the last thirty years. Easterlin et al. (2017) showed that life satisfaction in fact dropped in China during the 1990 to 2005 period, when incomes grew by at least 300 per cent. The life-satisfaction drop was largely attributable to the collapse of the social safety net in the early 1990s, only for a new social safety net to emerge in the late 2000s. So the increase in uncertainty among the vulnerable due to the collapse of safety nets more than outweighed the effects of rising incomes among those able to take advantage of growth opportunities.

Exactly the same drop in life satisfaction is currently being observed in India, where the informal social safety nets in families and communities have come undone in the growth spurt that India is currently experiencing: the expectation for India too is now that the wellbeing increases of higher national incomes will materialize only when these higher incomes start being used for a new and more effective social safety net (see chapter 3 in the World Happiness Report 2017). We will return to China's and India's growth periods and its implications for wellbeing when discussion basic comforts later in this chapter. For now, we want to note that, in short, higher national incomes over the longer run may eventually translate into higher wellbeing, but in the medium run, which in the case of China and India has meant several decades, incomes may go up whilst wellbeing goes down.

We should reiterate the central caveat to this list of macro-level factors: one can get a similar amount of variation explained between countries by using many different sets of factors (see chapter 6 in the World Happiness Report 2019, in which the authors use a different set of factors to have about 80 per cent variation explained between US states). The generic issue is that many positive macro-level factors are strongly correlated with each other: things like the rule of law and the absence of conflict, good governance, high public service provision or high productivity, all move together. When putting a few of these factors in a regression, one likely picks up the contribution of many more.

A key problem with Kapteyn et al. (2019), as with many others that have tried to look at correlates of national wellbeing, is a lack of random variation in macro-level factors, making it difficult to pick them apart as causal factors. To get closer to causality has been one of the central concerns in the academic literature related to wellbeing, just as it has emerged as a central concern in the whole of the social sciences. Unpicking causal mechanisms requires more than merely looking at variation at either the individual or the aggregate level. To get consensus on a believed effect, the mechanisms have to 'work' at the individual level, the aggregate level, and need to be born out in experimental or quasi-experimental designs. If we find that the typical effect of a variable on life satisfaction in one study goes in another direction than the effect in another which differs in at least one of these aspects (between individuals; between countries; in experimental or quasi-experimental designs), it is difficult to have confidence in our knowledge of how a specific factors affects life satisfaction. The worry is that the variable simply picks up something closely related to it.

One source of information is thereby seldom seen as enough. Looking at one particular source is then mainly useful in terms of an initial orientation for where improvements can be made, and for what might be a causal effect.

However, if we do find that a specific factor has the same kind of effect in various datasets, types of data, and methods used, we can more readily assign causality to that. There are quite a few factors for which we now do this such as, for instance, health or unemployment: whether you look at between-individuals, within-individuals over time, between-countries over time, or somewhat random shocks, we consistently find that life satisfaction goes up with good health and down with unemployment.

Quality of Life or Length of Life?

So far, we have focused on what affects the level of life satisfaction, but we should at least pay some attention to length of life. Naturally, the question arises whether the biggest gains in wellbeing are in improving the quality of life or the length of life.

Put simply, the lifetime life satisfaction of a person can be written as:

Lifetime wellbeing = Average life satisfaction * Length of life

which means that life-satisfaction improvements can come from increases in average life satisfaction or from increases in length of life.[17]

Life expectancy in the last fifty years has increased dramatically in the United Kingdom, as it has in nearly all countries around the world. Figures 2.6 and 2.7 shows male and female life expectancy taken from the ONS. They show that life expectancy has increased in the last thirty years by about six years for females and 8.5 years for males. That is almost a 10 per cent improvement. Figure 2.8 presents an even longer time-series, which shows that life expectancy increased from about forty years in 1841 to over eighty years at present, a remarkable increase.

Thus, from this change in life expectancy alone, per-person lifetime life satisfaction has roughly doubled during the past 170 years. The changes that have been credited for this increase are varied, but include several policy-sensitive trends:

[17] There is evidence that higher life satisfaction is associated with longer length of life, a strong effect that remains no matter what objective health variables are controlled for (Frijters et al., 2011). See Steptoe and Wardle (2011) for similar findings.

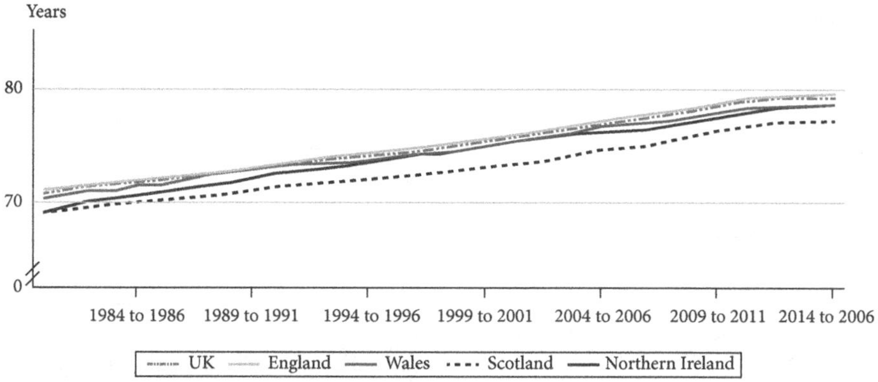

Figure 2.6 Life expectancy at birth in years for males in the United Kingdom
Source: ONS, National Life Tables, UK: 2014 to 2016.

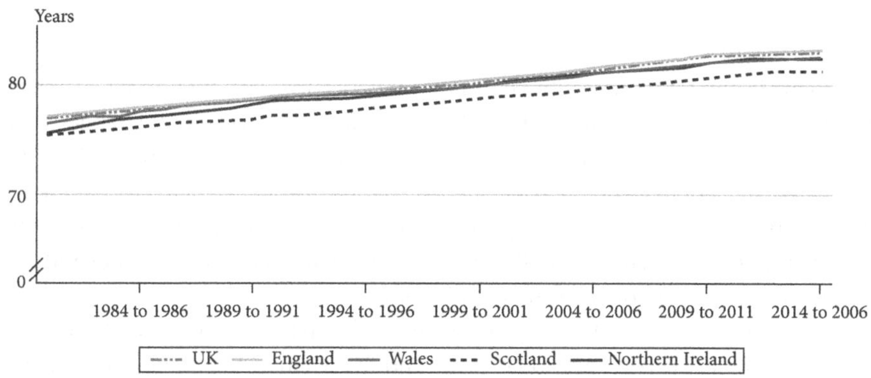

Figure 2.7 Life expectancy at birth in years for females in the United Kingdom
Source: ONS, National Life Tables, UK: 2014 to 2016.

1. Reductions in infant and child mortality due to improved hygiene, inoculations, reduced reliance on open-fire cooking at home, improved pregnancy behaviour (i.e. no alcohol or smoking during pregnancy), and improved pre-natal and natal care.
2. Less exposure to infectious diseases via greater availability of clean water, sewage works in cities, and applied knowledge of infections.
3. Increased resistance due to greater availability of better food, less physically strenuous work, and fewer children.
4. Blood-thinners (statins) that have reduced the deaths from heart disease in the 50–70 age range dramatically during the past thirty years.

Some of these changes were found out to be important only later, such as the extremely detrimental role of open-fire cooking at home, which was highly

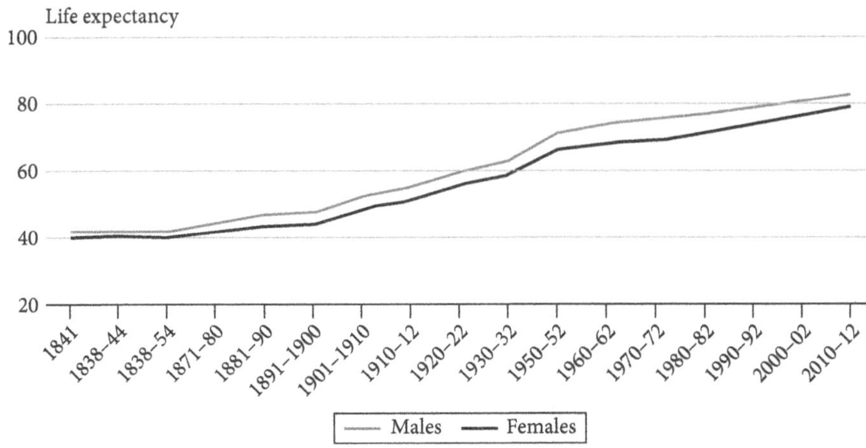

Figure 2.8 Period expectation of life at birth in years in England and Wales
Source: ONS, English Life Tables No. 17: 2010 to 2012.

prevalent in the late nineteenth century and associated with high levels of infant mortality (McKeown and Record, 1962; Matossian, 1985). Yet, other changes were the direct result of conscious investments by individuals and governments into the health of the population, such as the greater use of statins and anti-smoking campaigns. Clean water and sewage works were also directly provided by governments, requiring enormous public capital investments that would be beyond the means of the vast majority of the population.

Are there obvious further improvements to be made? Looking at the United Kingdom, the life expectancy today is around 81, whereas the highest life expectancies in the OECD are around 83 in countries like Japan, Italy, or Spain. Demographers and health professionals are not sure what causes these differences, but possible contributing factors are diet, pollution, leaded water pipes, high levels of stress, as well as more fixed factors such as climate (for example, the flu is worse in colder climates). None of these are easy to address but many can be affected by policies, so there is probably some scope for policy-induced improvements.

An interesting and policy-relevant question is whether there is a strong reason to fear the ageing of our societies: fertility rates have decreased and individuals live longer, so the population pyramid has turned upside down, with older people now outnumbering younger ones. The main fear, which was quite strong in some policy circles until recently, is that ageing would lead to a huge increase in the dependency ratio. This fear of an unmanageable increase in the number of old people who need constant care has subsided somewhat in the last two decades: whilst individuals have indeed become older, the proportion of years spent in ill health has remained almost constant, as Figure 2.9 shows.

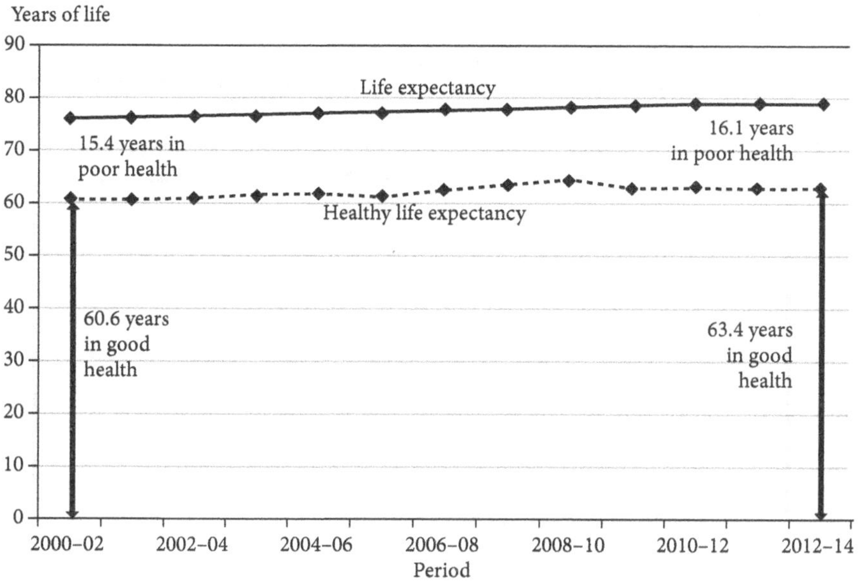

Figure 2.9 Life expectancy, healthy life expectancy, and years spent in poor health from birth for males

Source: ONS, available at: https://www.gov.uk/government/publications/health-profile-for-england/chapter-1-life-expectancy-and-healthy-life-expectancy.

This figure calculates the number of years that men are expected to live in good health and in poor health over time, where good health is assessed by individuals themselves, i.e. whether they state that they are in 'good or excellent health'. Hence, this graph uses a subjective notion of health, just as life satisfaction is a subjective notion of wellbeing.

The share of years spent in poor health remained fairly stable: 20 per cent in 2000–02 versus 20 per cent in 2012–14. Women too have seen increases in years spent in good health, although they spend, on average, 26 per cent of their years in self-assessed poor health (see Figure 2.10 for women).

It is not merely self-assessed good health years that are rising. Individuals are also working longer and remain active for longer. For example, the average 'age of withdrawal' from the labour market increased by about two years for both men and women between 1995 and 2012, about half of the increase of life expectancy. Simply put, old people are mainly looking after themselves.

The fears of demographers and economists have not proven correct so far, but this is not to dismiss the role of policy in addressing their fears: part of the reason for the increase in the length of working lives have been policy changes, such as, for example, an increase in the age at which individuals retire, which was at 62.5 a generation ago (60 for women, 65 for men) and will be over 68 for both sexes in the United Kingdom after 2025.

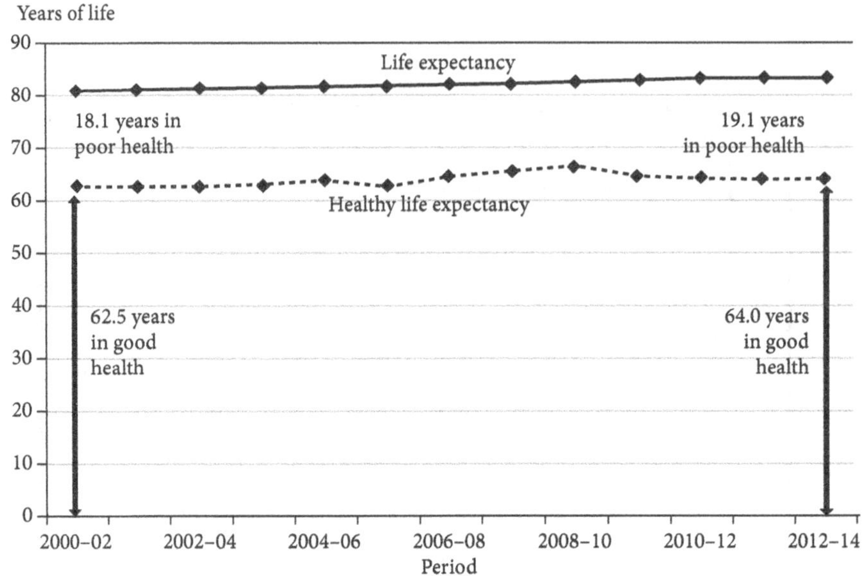

Figure 2.10 Life expectancy, healthy life expectancy, and years spent in poor health from birth for females

Source: ONS, available at: https://www.gov.uk/government/publications/health-profile-for-england/chapter-1-life-expectancy-and-healthy-life-expectancy.

Another policy reaction throughout many developed countries has been to increase total healthcare spending from about 5 per cent of GDP in 1970 to 8.9 per cent in 2016 (Huber, 1999; OECD, 2017). This growth might well continue, which makes it important to use a broader criterion to allocate spending than physical health, which makes up no more than one third of WELLBYs (see Huang et al. (2018) and Figure 2.5 above).

Estimates of Key Wellbeing Effects

The literature on wellbeing has become vast and the 'Bibliography of Happiness' by Ruut Veenhoven lists thousands of correlates of happiness. Yet, for policy purposes, we ideally want to have causal estimates based on research designs that are robust.[18]

We argue that a useful approach would be to have an interactive process in terms of 'agreed-upon metrics and causal effects'. The idea is that, first, the state bureaucracy should adopt a current metric for wellbeing, which we argue to be life

[18] This section draws on Frijters et al. (2020).

satisfaction until this measure can be improved upon. Then, it should maintain and regularly update a list of believed effects of various policies and circumstances on its chosen metric of wellbeing. Such a list is crucial in terms of setting policy priorities within and between different government departments and in terms of having a consistent process for generating internal estimates of how much a complex policy increases wellbeing and via which channels. There are many ways the updating process could happen, but the idea is similar to the current practice of government departments in having appraisal guidelines. A regular shared list of evidence-based effects would form part of a government-wide appraisal guideline.

Because this list would be so influential in setting priorities, its elements must be arrived at via a transparent process and improvements should be argued based on scientific rigour. The example of the Intergovernmental Panel on Climate Change (IPCC) process for generating a consensus number in terms of climate change is a good example of how governments can channel science into a competitive process for arriving at overall figures. The list would always be provisional and subject to caveats and disagreements, but that is to be expected in any explicit or implicit priority-setting. Having open lists and debates can only improve upon the gut feeling that would otherwise pervade.

To kick-off this process, Table 2.3 offers a list of effects taken from Frijters et al. (2020). Many of the figures on the list come from studies that employ natural or quasi-natural experiments to establish causality of the identified effects. In what follows, we take the example of the long-run impact of income on life satisfaction to explain how figures are typically arrived at.

Example: The Long-run Wellbeing Benefits of More Money—What We Now Know from a Swedish Lottery

A fundamental question for the economics of wellbeing is just how much wellbeing one unit of money can buy when individuals have become used to higher levels of financial resources. This is the number that matters when we think of higher levels of consumption over the longer run. It does not account for the elation or disappointment associated with unexpected fluctuations in financial resources, an effect that fades within a year or so (Frijters et al., 2011). Related to the question of how much wellbeing additional financial resources can buy for an individual is the question how much wellbeing additional financial resources at the individual level can buy at the collective level.

The standard story in the literature has so far been that more income to an individual does buy more life satisfaction, but not much and largely at the expense of the life satisfaction of others (jealousy). Not surprisingly then, a 2018 snap-survey of fifty wellbeing experts in the World Wellbeing Panel found a large

Table 2.3 A selection of key findings from the literature on life satisfaction

	Change	Effect on 0–10 life satisfaction	Dynamics	Key literature references[e]	Confidence in effect and causality
Work	From employment to unemployment	–0.46 (UK) –0.71 (Ger)	Immediate effect higher, then reducing, but no adaptation	UK: [1] Tbl 4.2 Ger: [1] Tbl 4.2.	High. Large effects found in longitudinal studies, cross-sections, recession-related, and employment shock-related (plant closures)
	From unemployment to out-of-labour force	+0.32 (UK) +0.57 (Ger)	Unknown	UK: [1] Tbl 4.2	Effect very robust in cross-section and panels, but causality unclear
	From no commute to one-hour car commute	–0.01 (UK) –0.15 (Ger)	Unknown	UK: [2] Ger: [3]	Low. Findings disputed and causality unclear. No RCTs
	From car commute to walking commute (time)	Insig. (UK) Insig. (Ger)	Unknown	UK: [2] Ger: [3]	Medium: results from fixed-effects estimation. No RCTs
	From full-time employed to part-time employed and wanting more hours	–0.17 (W. Europe)	Largely permanent, particularly strong effect for men	[16]	Effect very robust in cross-section and panels, but causality unclear
	From full-time employed to part-time employed and *not* wanting more hours	+0.07 (W. Europe)	Largely permanent, particularly strong effect for women	[16]	Effect very robust in cross-section and panels, but causality unclear
	Being in a white-collar job (e.g. managers, officials, clerical, or office workers) versus a blue-collar job (e.g. construction, transport, or farming)	Approx. +0.80 (worldwide)	Unknown	[16]	Effect very robust in cross-section and panels, but causality unclear
Finances	Doubling of household income	+0.16 (UK) +0.5 (E-Ger) +0.3 (Sweden)	Persistent effect with elation peak	UK: [1] Tbl 2.1 Ger: [4a] Sweden: [4b]	High. Effect found in panels, cross-sections, and shock-related (lotteries) research designs. Height disputed and income measurement problematic
Education	Extra year of compulsory education	–0.03 (UK)	Persistent effects	UK: [5]	High for UK, since effect found from 1972 UK compulsory

					school changes. Marginal result also found in other Western countries
Relationships	From single to partnered/married	+0.28 (UK) +0.1 (Ger)	Permanent effect, with initial peak	UK: [1] Tbl 5.2 Ger: [6]	High. Ubiquitous finding around the world
	From never married to married at 50	+0.2 (UK)	Permanent effect, high initial peak	UK: [1] Tbl 9.1	Medium: cohort study findings, causality unclear
	From partnered to separated	−0.40 (UK)	High initial effect, then some adaptation	UK: [1] Tbl 5.2	High as found everywhere, but most find new partners so do not stay separated. Separated men suffer more
Health	From healthy to poor physical health (self-rated)	−1.08 (UK) −0.96 (Ger)	Permanent effect, but initial peak as well	UK: [7], Tbl 4, column 2 Ger: [6][a]	High as found everywhere, including due to health shocks
	From depression to full mental health (4 points on a 0–12 scale)	+0.71	Permanent, little evidence of a peak	UK: [1] Tbl 16.2	High as found everywhere, including in large clinical trials
Crime	A doubling of fear of crime	−0.30 (Europe)[b]	Unknown	[8]	Medium: panel-data based, often replicated, but drivers of fear not exogenous
	Victim of violent crime	−0.40 (Australia)	Effect largely in year 1	[9]	High, but specific: effects are for unanticipated events that were recorded
Environment	Increase of 10 in SO_2 (μ g/m^3)	−0.08 (Ger)	Unknown	[10]	High: effects driven by unanticipated changes in power plant emissions due to policy
	Increase of 10 in PM_{10} (μ g/m^3)	−0.05 (US)	Unknown	[11]	Medium to high: effects of air pollution sufficiently exogenous for single individual
	Increase of 1 hectare of green space within 1 kilometre around household	+0.007 (Ger) +0.003 (UK)[c]	Seems permanent	Ger [12], UK [13, 14]	Medium to high: panel-data based but no clear-cut exogenous variation, similar results by studies in UK
		−0.04 (Ger)	Unknown	[12]	

Continued

Table 2.3 *Continued*

	Change	Effect on 0–10 life satisfaction	Dynamics	Key literature references[e]	Confidence in effect and causality
	Increase of 1 hectare of vacant land within 1 kilometre around household				Medium: panel-data based, but no clear-cut exogenous variation
	Construction of wind turbine within 4 kilometres around household	−0.14 (Ger)	Seems temporary: effect disappears after 5 years	[15]	High: wind turbine construction exogenous for household in surroundings, difference-in-differences design with treatment at multiple points in time
Various	From 0 to 8 portions of fruit and vegetables per day	+0.20 (Aus)	Effect lasts while treatment lasts	[17]	Medium: fixed-effect estimation consistent with small RCTs and public health campaign results, but magnitude very unclear
	Hosting the Olympic Games for residents in the host city	+0.07 (UK)	Effect temporary around event	[18]	Strong: Olympic Games exogenous for single resident in host city, difference-in-differences design with treatment and control group

Notes: [a] Based on a 3-point change on a 1–5 self-report measure of health. [b] Derived from relative effect of fear of crime versus the effect from unemployment in a log-odds setting. [c] Converted from 1–7 to 0–10 scale of life satisfaction. [d] Converted from 1–3 to 0–10 scale of life satisfaction. [e] References are provided at the end of the chapter.

majority agreeing with the statement that increases in productivity were better spent on improved public services than on more private consumption.[19]

Yet, we all still want to know just how much wellbeing we as individuals gain if we become richer and have become used to more money. The 'best' previous data on that question came from studies of UK lottery winners, such as Gardner and Oswald (2007) who found modest effects at best. The key problem with that study and the many subsequent ones in different countries that followed was that they had few lottery winners who won substantial amounts, and that individuals who won small amounts were often gamblers, and hence different from the general population. Gamblers were bound to pick up small prizes now and then, but the effects of those small wins are hard to separate from the losses they incur on all the bets that did not pay off, or from the fact that they were gamblers for unrelated reasons. The average 'lottery win' in Gardner and Oswald (2007) was thus under £40 and only sixty-five people in their data won more than £1,000.

A 2020 Swedish study from the University of Stockholm by Erik Lindqvist and colleagues managed to find 3,362 lottery winners with average prizes close to $100,000 (Lindqvist et al., 2020). The unusual thing about that study is not merely that they were able to find so many lottery winners, but also the nature of the lottery itself: they look at a lottery amongst all members of the Swedish Labour Party, which included nearly half of the population in the period of the lottery wins (1990 and onwards). Hence, these lottery winners were not gamblers but rather accidental lottery participants who were 'typical Swedes' and who received large wins that were worth over half their lifetime incomes in hundreds of cases. It is an almost ideal type of 'experiment' to study the effect of more income on, arguably, average people (in Sweden).

The drawback of their study is that they were not able to follow individuals before and after the lottery, but started to observe them only at least four years after they won the lottery. Hence, the study misses all the short-run gains from winning the lottery, such as the elation that comes with such a gain. Nevertheless, the researchers were able to ascertain their physical health, mental health, life satisfaction, and how they spent the money in the years following their lottery wins. They were able to match these winners with people from the same pool of potential winners, i.e. the lottery participants who did not win, allowing them to look at long-run effects.

Their results illuminate many aspects of wellbeing economics: first, the additional money had no effect on health, neither physical nor mental, which goes against the quite universal finding that individuals with higher incomes also have better health in many developed countries. The main reason for such a 'null result' of a random income increase is that Sweden has a decent national health system that is available to all citizens ('universal health coverage'). There are thus not

[19] See the World Wellbeing Panel at https://www.barcelonagse.eu/research/world-wellbeing-panel/ for this survey and others.

many physical health services that additional money can buy, at least not for adults.[20] The same explanation probably holds for the lack of additional mental health benefits: when the social safety net works well, mental health problems are not due to lack of income. These are policy-relevant insights.

Yet, there is a marked effect on life satisfaction, even after twenty years: a 10 per cent increase in lifetime income buys about 0.04 points in life satisfaction measured on a 0-to-10 scale every remaining year of life. That may not sound much, but it is easily twice as much as one usually finds income to matter in many Western European countries. The probable reason for this high effect indicates that more 'regular' studies of income and life satisfaction suffer from statistical problems, such as that individuals who are particularly happy in a year under-report their actual incomes because they may feel less need to mention the money they made (see Clark et al. (2008) for a discussion).

Equally interesting is that the study finds that Swedish lottery winners spend their additional financial resources quite sensibly: they did not spend it in one go, but effectively saved up the vast majority and only slowly spent the resources, partially via working fewer hours and partially via higher consumption (for example, more holidays or buying a house). The idea that people are careless with money and spend a winning in a big splurge seems not true, at least not for Swedes. In the same vein, data on *un*conditional cash transfers to poor individuals in Kenya show that these households are also 'quite' sensible (Haushofer and Shapiro, 2016).

The fact that lottery winners significantly reduced their working hours tells us that, before their wins, they were indeed working longer hours than they would have wished, probably to keep up their consumption levels. Maybe they have been trying to keep up with their neighbours beforehand. If that is true, then their non-winning neighbours are likely to have been jealous, as was, for instance, found in a recent study of lottery winners in the Netherlands (Kuhn et al., 2011), where the neighbours of those who won a luxury car were found to be more likely to buy a new luxury car themselves.

The findings of this simple study are thus quite profound for wellbeing economics: the authors find that a 10 per cent increase in income increases life satisfaction by 0.04 points on a 0-to-10 scale, which is thereby the new benchmark for what the long-run effect of income on individuals' wellbeing is. The lack of any effect on physical and mental health suggests further that, in many developed countries, we should not expect all that much health benefits from increasing

[20] We may note that the same is unlikely to apply to the United States where universal healthcare does not exist in the same way as in Sweden or the United Kingdom. Concomitantly, Currie et al. (2007) find a much stronger income-health gradient for the United States than for the United Kingdom, consistent with the idea that health correlates positively in the United Kingdom mainly because of reverse causality (healthier people are more likely to earn more), while in the United States additional money seems to buy crucial health services that the poor lack. Johnston et al. (2009) confirm this by looking at objective health measures (hypertension) alongside self-reported health.

average income more: an efficient and equitable health system manages to largely overcome the advantage of money.[21]

The study and its interpretation also illustrate that the wellbeing literature must be read in the context of a wider social science literature and a country's institutional context.

Whilst individual pieces of research and knowledge of specific wellbeing-relationships are important in policy-making (as evidence will always point to specific pieces), for many purposes we need more than just single numbers. We need general lessons that are likely to hold outside of the context in which they were originally found. It is general lessons that are relied upon when designing policies, that populate checklists, and that form frameworks.

General Wellbeing Lessons for Policy: Theory, Evidence, and Implications

The wellbeing literature is vast. We here organize what we have learned from the literature by putting findings into the context of four theories: cause-and-effect frameworks that can be the basis of design and extrapolation. We present these theories together with some of the best available evidence on them, the policy implications that result from them, and the checklists associated with them.

The first two theories relate to basic comforts and experience goods (goods of which one only knows what benefits they hold after consuming them), which both offer fairly straightforward advice. Loosely speaking, many governments in developed countries already implement most of the insights relating to basic comforts, though many developing countries and a few developed countries do not. Hence, insights relating to basic comforts are the least controversial and offer the least general new insight for many readers, but working through their logic and the evidence base is still important as it will show that the wellbeing literature supports and strengthens the case for public service provision in many areas. Insights on experience goods are beginning to take pace in policy-making right at this moment because this is where the low-hanging fruit which is least controversial and disruptive is in terms of wellbeing. Yet, as we shall see, the full implications of the wellbeing evidence on experience goods are not yet implemented and there are many insights that will take years to be fully absorbed into policy-making.

[21] Wilkinson and Pickett (2010) also argue that beyond a certain income level health benefits cease to accrue. Of course, this is not to say that there are not huge inequalities in income within many countries, which may, for those at the bottom of the income distribution, lead to inequalities in health outcomes.

The last two theories relate to status-seeking and belonging, which offer policy implications and checklists that strongly challenge the status quo of policy-making and even the self-image of our society. Because of the controversial nature of these theories, we pay particular attention to the evidence base we have on them so that readers can more properly decide on their merits.

Finally, we suggest possible intermediary steps between how policy is evaluated now and how it would be evaluated if the wellbeing lessons were fully taken on board.

Basic Comforts

The first theory argues that there are such things as basic comforts that are necessary requirements for wellbeing at the individual level. These include food, water, shelter, access to basic healthcare, security, lack of noise or air pollution, and other items that are recognized as universally positive across human cultures and societies. Their importance is not controversial, though the question of who exactly should provide them under which circumstances is.

In terms of evidence that basic comforts truly matter, we can first point to evidence on differences across countries: all the world's happiest countries have a sizeable state-provided social safety net (see the country rankings in the World Happiness Reports from 2015 to 2020, for example). As we have already seen in the previous section, individuals with higher levels of basic comforts tend to be more satisfied with their lives. We can also point to evidence on changes over time: individuals who suffer shocks to any basic comfort are markedly less satisfied with their lives (see Frijters et al. (2011) for various negative life events). For example, we know that health shocks, criminal events, or financial distress are all bad for wellbeing. This also applies to countries as a whole: hunger and lack of safety in Venezuela in recent years has led to a relatively sudden and large drop in life satisfaction in the country (see World Happiness Report 2018, chapter 2).

An interesting and instructive case study is that by Coupe and Obrizan (2016). The authors looked at different provinces in Ukraine and compared them before and during the civil war, finding large decreases in life satisfaction in the provinces with heavy fighting whilst seeing no decline in other provinces. They claim that living in a war zone is associated with a drop in happiness of about 0.6 on a 0-to-10 scale, which is roughly equivalent to the drop a rich person in Ukraine would experience when becoming poor.[22]

[22] Their effects are expressed in terms of whether a person has ticked the boxes 'rather happy' or 'happy' in response to the question 'Do you consider yourself a happy person?', whereby these boxes are the top two out of six. The probability of high answers drops fifteen percentage points in war zones. If we make the rough assumptions on how that scale would translate to a 0-to-10 scale (applying the

Another study of how improvements in basic comforts increase wellbeing is that by Cesur et al. (2017). The authors looked at the introduction of basic healthcare in Turkey. They took advantage of the fact that in 2005 basic and universal access to GPs was rolled out throughout the country in a staggered manner (in some provinces earlier than in others). In their own words, their calculations show that 'each family physician saves about 0.15, 0.46, and 0.005 lives among infants, the elderly, and children aged 1–4 per province every year.' For each physician to essentially save 0.6 lives every year is, of course, an extremely cost-effective policy.

Similarly, Kim and Koh (2018) showed how the introduction of additional health insurance coverage (similar to Obamacare) in Massachusetts in 2007 increased wellbeing significantly and permanently, by more than one point of life satisfaction per year per additional person covered.[23] Importantly, they found that, when a similar health insurance cover was taken away in Tennessee, there was a roughly equal decline. Their findings are important because they showed that the wellbeing effect was not subject to adaptation, nor to jealousy: the whole state showed a clear increase in life satisfaction when health coverage increased, and this increase remained stable over time.

A study by Finkelstein et al. (2012) followed an experiment in health insurance by the state of Oregon in wich a random group of around 35,000 low-income individuals were drawn by lottery to get Medicaid. The randomized design allowed the authors to show that health insurance did not merely work well because it reduced anxiety and increased basic health services, but also because it cut out many 'mistakes' made by uninsured individuals who often failed to get cheap and effective treatments. Providing basic comforts has, therefore, several effects on both behaviour, consumption, and feelings of stress, none of which appear to reduce over time or be subject to the jealousy of others.

From other experimental studies we now know that providing basic housing to families within the communities in which they live improves wellbeing similarly (Galiani et al., 2017), and that crime is detrimental to the wellbeing of both the individual and the neighbourhood (Johnston et al., 2018).

Strong suggestive evidence for how important basic comforts are comes from the growth-experience in China and India. In China, the huge growth after 1978 is now believed to have been accompanied by a decrease in life satisfaction from 1985 to 2002, only recovering after that (Easterlin et al., 2017). This may sound wondrous if one realizes that from 1985 to 2002 the economy grew well over 300

Parducci (1995) equal-interval assumptions and a roughly normal distribution around the third option), this becomes roughly 0.6.

[23] They find a point estimate of 0.7 per person covered on a scale from 1 to 4. Translated to a 0-to-10 scale using the Parducci (1995) method, this is about 1.5. Note that this effect was found by looking at changes in the average levels, not by looking at the same individuals over time, implying that external benefits to others are included.

per cent and that nearly any objective indicator (education, health, and longevity) increased substantially. Yet, we know of this period that the early growth transition included the break-up of the previous social safety net inside communities and state-run companies. As a result, families were left to fend for themselves as previous pensions, work, and health systems broke down. So whilst, on average, material living standards improved tremendously, the anxiety and uncertainty associated with the lack of a social safety net actually lead to a large reduction in wellbeing that was only reversed once the state started to set up new social safety net structures in the 2000s, guaranteeing basic comforts.

Exactly the same thing now appears to be underway in India: despite huge improvements in the economy and all its associated benefits, wellbeing in India is declining so much that the world average has actually decreased during the past five years (World Happiness Report, 2018). This too is now argued to happen because of the loss of the previous community-based social safety nets. As with China, the expectation is that things will eventually improve at a higher level than before, but this might take a generation, showing a large trade-off in terms of the dynamism of transitions and levels of wellbeing.

The essential take-away is thus that the wellbeing literature lends strong support for what is completely accepted in many developed countries: the provision of basic comforts by the state increases overall wellbeing permanently and strongly.

Implications and Checklists

Whenever a supposed basic comfort is lacking, one should go over a simple checklist:

- Is this a basic comfort that would be recognized as positive in any culture and society?
- Is the provision lacking relative to what well-functioning communities provide?
- Who would be best placed to provide it? Is it cost-effective for the state to provide it?

The last question, of course, goes to the fundamental question of what the state is good at and whether there is value for money to provide the basic comfort or whether it is better just to leave the need unmet. As a rule of thumb, the state is good in providing standardized services, which is why it is so heavily involved in education, health, and personal social services throughout the world.

To give a brief snapshot of wellbeing cost-effectiveness, the UK Department of Health and Social Care assumes as an internal estimate that it can produce a QALY via the NHS for about £15,000 (Claxton et al., 2015; Lomas et al., 2019; see also Department of Health and Department of Education, 2017). We know that an additional year of life in excellent health is worth around six WELLBYs, which, in turn, implies that the NHS currently buys a WELLBY at a rate of £2,500 in 2019 values.[24] At present, that would be the logical cost-effectiveness threshold to ask of policies targeting basic comforts. We discuss wellbeing cost-effectiveness analysis in great detail in chapters 3 and 4.

There are a few caveats to this checklist and its implications. For one, the division between a basic comfort and other things people want is not always clear. For instance, irregular noise is welcome if it is a concert, but unwelcome if it is an airplane engine. Violence is unwanted when it is criminal but wanted in a boxing match. Another important caveat is that experimental evidence is invariably not about one single thing. As always in social science, an experiment bundles a large number of goods that are provided at the same time. Health-care provision by the state is, for instance, not merely about health, but also about relieving the anxiety that one could be financially ruined by having to pay private health providers in case of an unexpected health shock. It is also a form of acknowledgement that a community is part of a larger whole. Hence, the interpretation of experiments is always provisional because it requires the active ingredients to be borne out similarly in different contexts. When it comes to basic comforts, this seems to be the case: a vast amount of evidence that varies in lots of different aspects documents the importance of basic comforts for wellbeing. Yet, with anything new to the list of basic comforts, this caveat should be kept in mind.

Experience Goods and Skills

The textbook definition of an experience good is a product or service whose product characteristics, such as price or quality, are difficult to observe in advance, but ascertained upon consumption. A good example is a new drink that one has not tried before: one does not know if one likes it before one tries it. By consuming that drink, its characteristics get revealed. After trying, the good becomes a regular consumption good that one might buy again, but before trying it is an experience good. Similarly, there are experience skills, which denote skills whose value people do not know beforehand. This includes, for example, the value of learning a new instrument or a new language: one only knows the full value of such skills after learning them, not before.

For many experience goods and skills, individuals can make a reasonable guess as to whether they will enjoy them by seeing how others react to them and what others claim to get out of them.

[24] This uses the current best estimate that the zero point of life satisfaction at which an individual is indifferent between living or not is a 2 on a 0-to-10 scale and that the average year spent in good health is worth an 8. See chapter 4 for a more detailed description of these numbers including background studies.

For the purpose of this book, we are only interested in a particular subset of experience goods and skills: not only must their characteristics be difficult to observe, but individuals must also be somewhat sceptical about their value because they entail some characteristics that go against social norms or that even suggest a negative value to individuals or society at large. One could call them experience goods and skills with 'misleading characteristics', but we will simply call them experience goods and skills. Hence, an experience good or skill will be understood here as something that would potentially benefit many individuals, but these individuals can neither anticipate this nor believe it beforehand. The key role of the state is then to determine that something truly is as beneficial as is claimed, ascertain that people are sceptical about it, and then either try to convince people that it is truly beneficial, or else take up its provision and teaching itself.

A good example of such an experience skill are certain forms of selflessness. Individuals can see the loss to their own consumption in being more selfless, which means there is a visible cost, whereas the claimed benefit is less visible. Yet, there are by now many experiments on how certain forms of selflessness can be enforced in a manner that surprises those forced into them, whilst at the same time benefiting those forced and their wider communities.

An early experiment is Dunn et al. (2008). As the abstract to their study states, 'we found that spending more of one's income on others predicted greater happiness both cross-sectionally (in a nationally representative survey) and longitudinally (in a field study of windfall spending). Finally, participants who were randomly assigned to spend money on others experienced greater happiness than those assigned to spend money on themselves.'

What the authors did was to randomly assign individuals in a firm to spend their bonus (around £4,000, on average) on a list of charitable spending items, and others to spend it on themselves. When they followed them up two months later, they found that the group forced into pro-social spending was still significantly happier compared to the other group. This runs counter to standard economic theory, which predicts that happiness should decrease as individuals in this group are on a lower utility level due to less income.

The study was, of course, on a small group spending a peculiar type of windfall income. However, somewhat to the surprise of the literature, the same results have now been found in a large variety of circumstances of pro-social behaviour, including modes of giving time (Whillans et al., 2017) or money (Whillans et al., 2016), together with evidence that individuals expect the opposite in terms of effects:

- The effects were found in a sample of delinquent youths, as well as ex-offenders and toddlers (Hanniball et al., 2019).
- The effects were found whether it concerned money that was presented as a bonus or whether individuals had to work for it themselves (Geenen et al., 2014).

- The effects were found across a variety of cultures, including for higher-stakes amounts in developing countries (Aknin et al., 2013).
- When bystanders are asked whom they expect to become happier after giving, the typical finding is that they expect the group that receives money to spend on themselves to be happier (Dunn et al., 2008).

As a result of these findings, scholars are now experimenting in companies with variations on this theme, such as having co-workers do each other favours in an open system of favours that is encouraged and adopted by management. An illustrative example of this comes from a Spanish firm (Chancellor et al., 2018), where the authors found the whole firm became happier and more productive as a result of this community-enhancing intervention.

One should certainly see this as an example of an experience good, but one that is a package: in each of the experiments, it was not merely the case that groups of individuals were strongly encouraged to be selfless, but authority was also on board in that it played an active part. The visible approval of authority to help their organizations become more of a community via open internal charity is probably at least as important as the selflessness itself.[25]

A good example of institutions that have long recognized and implemented these lessons are International Baccalaureate (IB) schools. There, all pupils have to spend a certain number of hours on volunteering and doing good in the local community, which comes with the obligation to document this. It is a clear example of selflessness validated by a hierarchy, seen as a good thing by parents and communities.

It is fairly obvious how this lesson could be extended across communities, firms, and institutions countrywide. For example, government could implement such practices internally almost immediately, just as any other private and public institution could.

Some caveats to this example are important: selflessness is easy to abuse and to orient towards selfish goals by authorities. Moreover, a strengthened sense of community can itself become a vehicle for other desires of a group, such as a more equal say in the running of a place, which may not be wanted by authorities. Also, more community life comes with having to deal with the shocks and pressures that come with stronger social ties. Within certain legal systems, those things are basically a liability for management. Having more selflessness, therefore, depends on an authority that can be trusted and that does not oppose community life.

[25] The package aspect may be an important factor why pure laboratory experiments on this, like Falk and Graeber (2020), obtain conflicting results on the relationship between happiness and giving: when forcing random people into acts of pro-social behaviour without authority that backs that up, and a social environment where the experiences are shared and where one can see others being pro-social, the effects may be different. We will revisit this point again when we discuss the importance of belonging later in this chapter.

Finally, there is the question as to whether extrinsically motivating selflessness may crowd out a given level of intrinsic motivation, so that, when the extrinsic incentive is taken away, selflessness vanishes (even below levels that were present *before* the extrinsic incentive has been set up). This is an important area of research with currently mixed results.

In general, it is particularly easy to make false claims about experience goods. Basically anything that does not work is liable to cloak itself in the mantra of being an experience good ('trust me, try me, you will be amazed'). Evidence is particularly important when it comes to public recognition of something as an experience good.

The most surprising experience goods are those for which there are good reasons for humans to be innately sceptical about and yet which are in fact genuine. When it comes to selflessness, it is easy for others to demand it from us for their own benefit, and hence a degree of scepticism is healthy, particularly in adversarial situations.

What Other Experience Goods and Skills Can We Point to?

An important previous example of an experience skill was the knowledge that passive smoking exists and is harmful. In the 1950s, that information was not believed by many people who heard about it, and hence the market for locations where smoking was permitted had not included this information in its price. The benefits of smoking (the pleasant sensations associated) were easier to observe and experience, with the claimed cost to health being far less easy to observe, making many smokers naturally sceptical of the supposed health costs. The reluctance to believe that a widespread practice would harm others was also natural, leading to passive smoking not priced into decisions as much as it merited: customers to pubs would not include the detrimental effect of passive smoking; parents would not include the passive smoking effects on their children; and individual smokers would not include the health costs to others in their calculus.

The main job of the government for decades was to verify, certify, and then disseminate the information that smoking was truly bad and that, likewise, passive smoking was highly detrimental to health. Alongside information campaigns also emerged new regulations to limit passive smoking and to reduce the number of smokers, which included regulations on advertising, price increases for tobacco products, as well as outright bans on smoking in public places.

Sixty years on, the culture around smoking has changed entirely. Not only are individuals and families completely convinced of the negative effects of smoking and passive smoking, but new social norms have arisen in which the actual effects of smoking have been incorporated. For instance, smoking in the presence of children has become taboo for many people; non-smoking rules have appeared in many companies; and special zones have been created to confine smokers when they pursue their smoking habits. Individual and collective behaviour have adjusted to what was once information only believed by a few: that (passive) smoking really is bad for health.

Other important examples of experience skills are particular mental health and socio-emotional skills. For example, cognitive-behavioural therapeutic approaches to depression and anxiety had been studied for generations before the UK policy community was finally convinced of their general value and set up the Improving Access to Psychological Therapies (IAPT) programme in 2010 (Clark, 2018). What is perhaps even more remarkable than that it took the UK decades to act on the evidence that was coming out of dozens of trials was that it took other countries even longer. Now that the UK has rolled out the IAPT programme, several other countries have followed suit since and they look likely to be followed by many more.

Why did it take so long for governments to believe that mental health problems were amenable to cognitive-behavioural interventions? We think it is because individuals not only have a hard time admitting they have a mental health problem, but also that they have an even harder time imagining that they can re-orient their own thought processes and behaviours in such a way that their mental health would strongly improve. The latter requires admitting there is something they do not know and that they have never experienced as well as believing that they could learn it from someone else. Scepticism is understandable in such circumstances, both amongst mental health sufferers and policy-makers. Consequently, it took an extraordinary amount of evidence to overcome that scepticism.

Socio-emotional skills are also, to some extent, experience skills. The Incredible Years parenting programme for young children with conduct disorder is a good example of the genre: this programme trains parents who have children with conduct disorder how they can improve their interaction with their children and with each other (Leijten et al., 2013). As with selflessness and mental health skills, it now seems that socio-emotional skills have strong, life-long benefits, to the surprise of parents and educators alike. Again, the basic pattern for initial scepticism is the same: parents with disruptive children are not naturally prone to think of their relationship skills as part of the problem, nor that anyone else could offer ways of improving them which they could learn. Hence, in this realm too, the basic invisibility of these skills combined with scepticism make them an experience skill.

There is another category of experience goods on the horizon: knowledge of environmental circumstances, particularly air pollution which leads to worse mental health. Here too, there is increasing information on the detrimental effects of air pollution on mental health that are not entirely believed by the population but where governments can start to improve outcomes already. Because people may not yet believe this, air pollution may only partially be internalized in housing prices, implying that conventional market-based measures may not (yet) pick them up, just like they would not have picked up the effects of passive smoking in the 1960s.

One of the best causal studies on in this area is by Luechinger (2009) on life satisfaction and SO_2 levels in Germany during the period 1985 to 2000. The author was able to use nationally representative data from the German Socio-Economic Panel Study (SOEP), which has been following more than thirty thousand individuals in eleven thousand households every year from 1984 onwards. This was combined with detailed local information about the levels of atmospheric SO_2, which were quite high in the 1980s, on average (46.9 microgram per cubic metre in 1985, for example), dropping substantially afterwards (to 5.3 microgram per cubic meter in 2000, for example).

To identify causal effects, Luechinger (2009) was able to use unanticipated changes in legislation pertaining to power plants for the whole of Germany, enforced differentially over time in different areas (that is, first in West Germany and later in East Germany as it only became part of the unified Germany in 1991). Using information on wind directions, the author was able to map who was affected to what degree at what time, everywhere in Germany, as a result of these legislative changes. An instrumental variable approach was used to estimate the causal effect of SO_2 levels on life satisfaction. It turned out to be fairly linear and constant, with an increase in SO_2 concentration of 10 micrograms per cubic metre affecting life satisfaction by a minimum of –0.05 points on a 0-to-10 scale. The author then calculated the willingness-to-pay both from changes in life satisfaction and from changes in rental prices. The study showed that no more than 5 per cent of the effect of air pollution was priced in the value of rental prices, strongly suggesting individuals were simply not convinced or aware of the strong effect of air pollution on wellbeing.

Similar findings are now starting to pop up in other circumstances: Zhang et al. (2017) obtain similar results for air pollution on cognitive performance, whereas Dolan and Laffan (2016) obtain similar results on different measures of mental health. Importantly, these effects are over and above the better-known physical health effects of these air pollutants and in fact of greater importance for wellbeing.

Crucially, similar to air pollution, noise pollution from airports is not affecting house prices by the amount one would expect from its actual effect (Fujiwara et al., 2017). As with air pollution, the likely explanation is that individuals are just not convinced of the strong negative effects of irregular noise on their mental health, even if it actually occurs. For noise pollution, especially irregular noise from planes, awareness is probably less of an issue than for air pollution where some pollutants might be odourless and invisible. It is not so much that individuals consciously lie to themselves, but rather that they may not attribute the small negative changes in mental health to noise. At the individual level, the effect is small enough that individuals may either not notice it much or may simply ascribe it to dozens of other confounding factors (like time or day-of-week).

As with mental health skills, considerations around air pollution are now starting to show up more and more in urban planning and design around the world because authorities are becoming convinced of the evidence that the benefits of reduced air pollution are an experience good.

There are, at present, several identified experience goods and skills that are being considered by policy-makers in their design of new policies and programmes. Around the world, these are probably the lowest-hanging fruits in terms of identified wellbeing interventions. The fact that the population is still sceptical but that the scientific evidence is growing is exactly why they represent the lowest-hanging fruits: the population has not yet itself taken up these goods and skills because they do not really know about or believe in them. Hence, the obvious task is to either accredit their existence and effects, as with passive smoking, or to simply provide them, as with basic education, which some centuries ago was also an experience good.

Because it is an active area, one should not lose sight of the fact that there are many claims out there regarding mental health and socio-emotional skills with little backing. 'Resilience training', for instance, is widely implemented and the word 'resilience' widely used, but there are different definitions as to what resilience is; mixed evidence on whether the programmes set up to increase it actually work; or that resilience truly improves life outcomes (see Etilé et al. (2019) for a recent review and new evidence). Resilience is thus a candidate experience skill, but not yet in the same category as parental skills training or cognitive behavioural therapy for depression and anxiety because it requires more evidence on its effectiveness.

There is an active market in services that promise good skills, essentially claiming to be an experience skill. The market has both truly useful services and snake oil programmes pretending to be useful. The ease with which anyone can claim their programme works is precisely what makes the scientific process so important and what gives governments a clear role: to separate the wheat from the chaff, accredit that which truly works whilst discrediting that which does not, and to promote take-up of what works.

Experience goods and skills are usually win-win in terms of public investments, i.e. they are both wellbeing-increasing and money-saving. This was true in the case of passive smoking, where reductions in smoking rates both lead to large increases in wellbeing directly because smokers are found to be unhappier than smokers (cf. Odermatt and Stutzer, 2015) and indirectly because of increased length of life. At the same time, there were probable reductions to public health costs because dying from smoking is very expensive to the health system.

There are other benefits from selflessness and increases in wellbeing: we already mentioned that higher wellbeing translates into higher productivity, less sickness, and higher longevity. However, we also know that more selflessness and higher wellbeing is likely to translate into more volunteering, higher tax morale, less littering, and more pro-social behaviour in general (see Lane (2017) for a review).

There is a timing issue with many experience goods and skills. Once a government is successful in convincing a population of their effects, it stops being necessary to push the message. One sees this with passive smoking: when what was once believed to be untrue starts to be accepted as truth by the many, governments no longer have to drag people along because what was once an experience good or skill has become a normal good or skill. At that point, governments will be dragged along by the demands of their populations. Parents and communities will themselves tell the next generation of the value of these goods and skills, eliminating the need for governments to do so.

Today, the situation applies to forms of knowledge concerning selflessness, mental health and socio-emotional skills, and environmental pollution: many do not believe the claims made about what we know about these things and hence the population does not fully incorporate it in its behaviour. This also works in the opposite direction: sometimes large parts of the population believe something has an effect that actually does not, such as that inoculations cause autism, and it is partially the job of governments to disseminate information about what is truly the case.

The general role of the government is then to provide and disseminate credible information on experience goods and skills (partially via an oversight structure) and to organize their production in a standardized manner. The first step in this process is for governments to absorb the evidence that something which claims to be an experience good or skills truly is one.

Implications and Checklists

It is obvious what can be done about the experience goods and skills discussed above. More generally though, there is a particular checklist to be followed with any candidate experience good or skill:

- Is this truly an experience good or skill? The three tests are:
  1. Is a sizeable proportion of the population sceptical about the claimed effect?
  2. Is the candidate experience good or skill in essence poorly visible such that verification is an issue, or is its value difficult to verify *ex ante*?
  3. Is there good evidence that an intervention works and can be taught to a group even when that group is somewhat sceptical?
- How effectively can the candidate experience good or skill be provided relative to other goods and skills?

- Is there a need and a role for accreditation structures or is there a good case for actual direct provision?
- Can we think of win-wins? For example, can one organize selflessness to provide experience goods or skills to others?[26]

The important caveat to bear in mind here is that 'everyone and their dog' might claim their intervention is an experience good or skill—simply because it has the basic characteristic that it needs to be tried before its value can be ascertained. Hence, there will be long queue of candidates demanding to be tried. Part of the reason it took decades for governments to become convinced of certain mental health skills was that it was so easy to claim to be in this class of goods.

This practically forces some degree of scepticism on policy-makers: before considering the expense of trials, let alone possible roll-outs, candidates will need to have considerable evidence to even make it to the status of 'promising enough to run a large trial'.

Status-seeking

In the *Theory of Moral Sentiments* (1759), Adam Smith rhetorically asked: 'To what purpose is all the toil and bustle of this world?' He answered: 'It is the vanity, not the ease, or the pleasure, which interests us.'

Adam Smith's concept of vanity roughly corresponds to what we now call a 'status orientation', a 'positional good', a 'contest good', or even 'greed'. To Adam Smith, signalling status was a basic motivation of humans, something we could not as a society successfully repress but that had enormous consequences for all of us.

Crucially, Adam Smith realized that we could direct vanity towards things that are socially validated. Hence, Adam Smith's policy prescription regarding vanity was revolutionary at the time. He wrote: 'The great secret of education is to direct vanity to proper objects', meaning that the community as a whole can and therefore should consciously shape and direct vanity.

We now know that Adam Smith was right in terms of the ubiquitous and inevitability of 'status-seeking', as well as its malleability in terms of direction. Indeed, we now know that states, in many ways, direct status-seeking, for example, by giving out yearly honours to those who have done something they approve of, with the only real question being how to do this even better.

[26] This is more or less what the free 'Exploring What Matters' curriculum of the Action for Happiness charity is set up to do. See our discussions under 'Belonging' below.

The key thing to note is that we now think of status-seeking as a basic competitive motivation that is there for good evolutionary reasons: those who do not seek to out-do those around them lose out in the evolutionary battle for resources and partners with those who are competitively motivated. Competition, in turn, is in terms of relative, not absolute outcomes: to win mates, one has to do better than others. This insight is now part of basic teaching on evolution (Buss, 2016).

Animal studies provide interesting experiments on this basic insight. A famous video https://www.youtube.com/watch?v=-KSryJXDpZo shows how one monkey is initially perfectly happy to do a specific task (returning a rock to the experimenter) in exchange for a cucumber.[27] Yet, when that monkey sees another monkey getting rewarded for the same task with a grape, which is more desirable than a cucumber, then the first monkey in a subsequent round refuses the payment of a cucumber for the same task. What was initially deemed enough payment turns into something inferior, and the cucumber gets thrown at the experimenter whilst the offended monkey rattles his cage in frustration at not also receiving a grape. It is a beautiful example of what economists call a 'consumption externality', by which is meant that the value of a good is affected by what someone else consumes.

We now know that this behaviour is ubiquitous amongst social animals (Chodosh, 2017) and that we see it in almost every walk of life amongst humans.[28]

If you, for instance, ask students in visual descriptions (vignettes) whether they would rather be at the top of one society with a relatively low income, or in the middle of another with a much higher income, over 50 per cent opt for being at the top of the poorer society despite the fact that their purchasing power is much lower (Mujcic and Frijters, 2013). The authors show that this is also seen in other hypothetical scenarios. For example, when being asked, participants state that they would prefer to be 'at the top of a hill rather than on the slopes of a mountain'. It appears that our brains are specifically geared towards relative evaluations (Fliessbach et al., 2007). Mattan et al. (2017) review extensive evidence on how humans quickly sensitize to what they think others have and start evaluating their own outcomes accordingly.

The enormous implications for wellbeing and policy from the great importance of status motivations was recognized very early on in both economics and other social sciences. Veblen (1899) already realized that there is a strong zero-sum aspect to development if status concerns apply. He recounted many anecdotes from antiquity where the motivation of dictators and commoners was to out-do

[27] See Brosnan and De Waal (2003) for more information.

[28] See Clark et al. (2008) for a wide survey and Alpizar et al. (2005) for survey and experimental evidence on the ubiquity of relative comparisons across all types of consumption, including holidays.

others. After all, the Old Testament does not for nothing warn against coveting what others have. Karl Marx remarked: 'A house may be large or small; as long as the surrounding houses are equally small it satisfies all social demands for a dwelling. But if a palace rises beside the little house, the little house shrinks into a hut' (as quoted by Lipset (1960), page 3).

The implications of the status race for the (relative unimportance of the) size of the economic pie was exactly the argument of Richard Easterlin, who in 1974 boldly asked: 'Does economic growth improve the human lot?' He acknowledged that many earlier thinkers asked the same question (such as Moses Abramovitz in 1959), and postulated that economic growth only brought greater average happiness to a country up to a fairly low level of income, after which there was almost no further happiness coming from further economic growth as long as basic comforts were met.

Easterlin (1974) did not have much data as evidence, but he could show that average happiness levels in the United States after the 1940s had not increased whilst GDP kept growing steadily and strongly. He could draw on surveys in rich countries (initially discussed by Cantril in 1965), which suggested that several of the happiest countries around the world were no more than middle-income countries.

The idea that economic growth does not necessarily generate much noticeable additional happiness in developed countries has since been confirmed many times for many countries, including most OECD countries (Easterlin, 2015). There have, of course, been counter-claims, which include some of the works by the authors of this book (Frijters et al., 2004), but it remains the case that the United States have witnessed economic growth without much happiness growth during the last sixty years. There is also little indication that happiness growth in some other rich countries has had much to do with income. What is now known, as we saw with basic comforts, is that it matters whether a country provides a basic social safety net, usually paid for by taxes on reasonable levels of economic development. So economic growth can buy happiness, but it depends on how it is spent.

Notably, the United Kingdom has seen its life satisfaction increase almost continuously during the past fifteen years despite income levels dropping due to the Global Financial Crisis. Hence, Easterlin's main contention and his main explanation have stood the test of time, with the only controversy remaining to what degree Easterlin's hypothesis holds. We know, for instance, that populations care about how rich their country is relative to others, which means that there is still some national benefit to higher incomes even if there would be no effect anymore at the international level (Proto and Rustichini, 2013).

Importantly, this insight has been the mainstream position in the literature on poverty for a long time. Sen (1983) reflected on a large body of scholarly study when he advocated that we should interpret 'poverty', which really is a state of low material welfare and unhappiness, as an inherently relative phenomenon. This position is still dominant today in terms of the measurement of poverty by means of counting people as poor when their income is below half the mean or median in their country (the definition used by the OECD). The proportion of people below half-mean or half-median does not change if everyone's income increases by the same amount, thus decoupling economic growth from poverty reduction if one adopts a relative definition of poverty.

We have more recently learned that what is important to humans is not necessarily what they have relative to others, but what they have relative to what they *see* others having, much like the monkey becoming jealous only when he sees the other monkey having a grape rather than a cucumber. Visibility matters because it makes comparisons salient, so it is quite possible to have happy countries with high levels of underlying wealth inequality (for example, several countries in Latin America) where the daily experience of people is to not see this wealth inequality.

Two recent studies illustrate the importance of visibility. Kuhn et al. (2011) used an unusual aspect of the Dutch postcode lottery, in which every month a random person in a postcode was given a new car independent of whether they were actually taking part in the lottery or not. The authors sent research assistants to the neighbours of these accidental car-winners, finding out that six months later, each of the neighbours were 6 per cent more likely to have also bought a new car. They found no such effect for the neighbours of those who won the regular lottery and (usually) did not buy a new car.

Another example of the importance of visibility comes from Perez-Truglia (2018): the author used the happenstance that in 2001 Norwegian tax records became easily accessible online, allowing everyone in the country to observe the incomes of everyone else. This additional visibility was via an app. In the ensuing years, the app started to be widely used such that there was a huge spike in related search terms on the day that new tax data came out. Perez-Truglia (2018) showed that the importance of income for life satisfaction increased by about 30 per cent in this period relative to Germany (which had no such visibility of tax data). Importantly, the Norwegian government was so dismayed at the increased importance of materialism that it shut down the easy visibility of the tax data. Hence, the example shows both the importance of visibility in the status race, as well as an actual policy countermove that was undertaken as a result.[29]

[29] The importance of visibility has long been recognized by the term 'conspicuous consumption' coined by Veblen in 1899. Indeed, recent papers showing the great importance of how visible goods are for their income elasticity and for labour supply choices are Heffetz (2011) and Frijters and Leigh (2009). Heffetz (2011) essentially asks a group of individuals how visible particular forms of consumption are, and shows that these ratings are strongly related to income elasticities for those goods in the general population (the more visible, the more people spend extra income on it). Frijters and Leigh (2009) show that when mobility is higher in US states due to more migration, all groups respond by

A careful reading of the history of taxation shows many instances of both trying to tax status goods in order to raise revenue, as well as its sometimes unintended consequences.

London is a beautiful example of this genre. When William III of Orange took over, in 1696, he instigated a tax on the number of windows that properties had, which at the time was a simple tax to verify and collect. The number of windows was at the time pretty much in direct proportion to the size of the building, so he was in a sense directly taxing status-related consumption goods as large mansions had to pay a lot more than small sheds. Yet, the longer-term result of his tax was that dwellings started to have far fewer windows and that owners started to brick-up some of them, a salutary lesson for those who might think taxing status is a simple thing to do.

A recent paper by Butera et al. (2019) on 'social recognition', which is understood to be conferring social status to something, summarizes many experiments around the world that now exist with actively assigning status to people and activities:

> Recent field experiments confirm that public recognition of individuals' behavior does, indeed, have substantial effects on behavior in a number of economically important domains. Examples include increasing charitable and political donations (Perez-Truglia and Cruces, 2017) by recognizing the donors; increasing tax compliance by publicising it to neighbours (Perez-Truglia and Troiano, 2018); affecting education and career choices by manipulating the observability to one's peers (Bursztyn and Jensen, 2015; Bursztyn et al., 2017, 2019); increasing employee productivity by publicising ranks (Barankay, 2011; Ashraf et al., 2014; Bradler et al., 2016); increasing voter turnout by publicising voting records to neighbours (Gerber et al., 2008); increasing childhood immunisation by publicising progress through the bracelets given to children (Karing, 2019); increasing the sign up rates for energy conservation programmes (Yoeli et al., 2013); and increasing the take-up of credit cards by making them a status signal (Bursztyn et al., 2018).

Hence, the visibility of status goods not only matters, but is a quite intricate policy tool in many areas. Things are not quite as simple as being able to turn status on and off: to be credible, there have to be mechanisms for continued recognition. Yet, the principle that status has a major behavioural and satisfaction effect on individuals is now well-established, leading to a clear public interest in discounting some of the increase in individual status as zero-sum for society as a whole.

If we now think of consequences, one should realize how important taxing status already is in many countries, and how many activities countries are engaged

working longer hours as status is more easily signalled by visible consumption goods (such as houses or cars) than less visible leisure goods that take longer to observe (such as education or theatre visits).

in can be reinterpreted as trying to direct status-seeking, or 'vanity' as Adam Smith called it. For one, the state gives out status to people on the basis that they have contributed to society. This happens every year in the United Kingdom, for example, with the 'honours roll' where people who have contributed to society are honoured for their contribution. That is an open signal of status. Perhaps most importantly, and blatantly, the state honours those who fight for the country. Most villages and neighbourhoods in countries around the world have statues honouring those who died in wars, in a well-understood open attempt at giving status to those who were willing to run enormous personal risks for the community as a whole. In a very real way hence, the state and communities indeed can be said to 'direct vanity'.

Hence, status not only matters, but the state is dependent on taxing status-oriented activities and is often quite active in deciding what activities to confer status on and what activities to openly shame and punish. The question, therefore, is not how to reduce status-seeking activities, but simply whether we can improve on the current list of status menu prices, adjust visibilities, and orient status concerns to even better activities.

Private persons, and the private sector more generally, are also involved in consciously conferring and encouraging status. Families will naturally try to confer some status on pro-family activities whilst private companies will naturally try to increase the degree to which their products and services are seen as status goods because this is what increases their demand.

It is then mainly public goods and unbranded basic commodities that lack status as there exists no active agent that tries to confer status to them. Hence, status races mainly apply above the level of minimum welfare provided by the state. Anything that is recognizably above this minimum and from which a private provider attempts to gain by increasing its desirability is likely to have a strong status component. That status component can be invested in by marketing, awards, or pricing.

Implications and Checklists

The primary implication for policy is that further increases in private consumption levels in many developed countries are likely to be largely zero-sum in terms of relative consumption levels and not themselves of interest under a rational wellbeing orientation that looks at average population wellbeing. What this concretely means is that any increase or decrease in consumer or producer surplus that is somewhat visible to others should be subject to an 'Easterlin Discount' in terms of the change in overall societal surplus counted in cost-effectiveness and CBAs, impact studies, business cases, and so on. This is not to say that individuals and firms should not invest in private consumption and wealth anymore, but simply that private consumption and wealth would be valued less in policy evaluations and appraisals from a public policy perspective if policy has the average population wellbeing as objective.

If one starts from the status quo in which increases in economic surplus are not discounted for any consumption externality and are treated on a par with changes in taxation or the valuation of environmental goods, then the adoption of an Easterlin Discount would change matters a lot. If one, for instance, were to adopt a 50 per cent Easterlin Discount on any form of private consumption and wealth, then this would mean that all current valuations would have to be adjusted in the sense that all changes in visible consumer and producer surplus would have to be reduced by 50 per cent. This would not hold for valuations of intangibles or the environment as long as these are not private or visible consumption goods: it is precisely the visibility to others that matters, not the visibility of what belongs to everyone (like the environment), nor intangible goods that cannot be seen (like mental health or socio-emotional skills), nor forms of consumption open to almost everyone (like some basic comforts).[30]

Later in this book, we will spell out what this means in particular case studies, but can mention here that the calculated economic surplus changes in housing improvement projects or airport expansions, which are clear examples of visible surplus that would be subject to an Easterlin Discount. Ideally, the precise Easterlin Discount factor comes from scientific evidence on private consumption externalities that is transparent and open to debate. It is also possible to apply different Easterlin Discounts to different private consumption goods, although this, arguably, might lead to distortions in terms of strategic manipulation due to recategorizations of goods. Here too, the precise factor should stem from scientific evidence. In any case, one wants, ideally, a clear rule that is difficult to circumvent to avoid distortions in labelling. A practical approach would start with a discount factor that is roughly right (ideally a single number), allowing for exceptions where good evidence can be brought to light. Highly visible private consumption and wealth could be discounted 50 per cent in policy evaluations and appraisals, invisible ones not discounted at all.[31]

Naturally, the question then becomes what is highly visible? The 'selfie test' seems a good rule of thumb: if someone can believably brag about it on Instagram by taking a selfie with it, it is a visible consumption good subject to status considerations. This, of course, includes cars and houses, but also a holiday in the Alps or in

[30] It is possible to be both jealous of what someone else has and still wish that good for them for other reasons, such as when they are family or when one thinks it is good for people to have those things (such as employment). That said, there might be positive consumption externalities and negative consumption externalities on the same good.

[31] Alpizar et al. (2005) tried to uncover consumption bundle-specific degrees of relativities, but it is unlikely that their findings are accurate because they rely on their subjects (students in Costa Rica) being completely rational about relativity. Moreover, relativity is not fixed but can quickly change with visibility (as evidenced by the Norway tax experiment, cf. Perez-Truglia, 2018).

a fancy resort. What it would not include are improved socio-emotional skills, a more sustainable climate, or a quiet time with loved ones: as soon as one starts taking selfies of a quiet time with loved ones, it ceases to be quiet time.

Taking account of status considerations would thus lead to a clear and across-the-board change in how state bureaucracies calculate the value of increases in private consumption and wealth, subjecting such changes to a uniform Easterlin Discount with exceptions only when there is strong scientific evidence emerging for a number that differs from the default. Since the whole country can brag about anything that is seen to belong to the whole country, such as national museums and national accomplishments (like winning sports events), those kinds of public consumption and wealth should not be subject to a discount, at least not as counted by national agencies.

Another policy implication is a different approach to 'vanity-related' aspects of educational curricula or equivalent programmes inside organizations. One, for instance, wants to direct status-seeking more towards the good of the community and towards outcomes that individuals can achieve, rather than towards outcomes they usually cannot achieve or that come at great cost to the community. This needs to be argued on its merits in each case, but one can, for instance, reasonably argue that the advocacy of impossible body images in magazines and elsewhere—a form of directing status to a particular body shape—is detrimental to the health of young girls and should be curtailed.

The basic checklist then is:

- As an adjustment to current methodology, an Easterlin Discount may be applied to all changes in the relevant private economic surplus, unless there is a clear case that the good at hand is largely invisible to others and thus not a status good per se. The discount does not apply to tax revenue from which public goods are paid as these are not privately owned.
- What are the current ways in which an organization is promoting some forms of status-seeking and discouraging others? What are the full external effects of these orientations? If detrimental, status-seeking activities may be taxed or discouraged in some other way. If positive, they may be encouraged, particularly if the benefits are felt by the community as a whole.

An important caveat concerns government investments that are themselves similar to those of private investors. When a private investor receives a return that is a (visible) economic surplus, that return may be subject to an Easterlin Discount when it comes to how society would value it, just as an Easterlin Discount would hold for private investments. When the government invests in productive capacity, however, this should in contrast be seen as a straightforward investment in future tax revenue. The relevant question then simplifies to whether a tax investment now comes at the benefit of a higher rate of return in terms of future tax revenue compared to other government investments. Effectively, current public goods are traded off for future public goods, in which case one does not want to apply a discount to either.

Belonging

When it comes to belonging, we mean the importance of social relationships, community ties, feelings of connections to other people, and the quality of interpersonal relations.

Ed Diener, in chapter 6 of the 2019 Global Happiness and Well-Being Policy Report, summarized the current state of the wellbeing literature as follows:

> If there is a single 'secret' to happiness, it is to be found in high quality social relationships. This finding emerges time and again in the research literature.

Social relationships exist in social groups, some small (like nuclear families), some medium-sized (like local communities), some very large (like religions and countries). Individuals are part of many groups and have many social relationships with others in those groups, flitting in and out of groups as well as in and out of relationships. Both the quantity and quality of those relationships matter.

Importantly, statistical agencies are currently not well set up to record the flow and stock of social relationships, or their quality. A typical example of how they are often measured is given by the surveys organized by the University of Hull surrounding the Hull 2017 initiative, when Kingston upon Hull was the UK City of Culture hosting close to three thousand events in 2017. The researchers were interested in how the celebrations in Hull would affect measures of belonging in Hull and thus conducted fairly large (about 2,800 respondents) surveys before, during, and after 2017. In these surveys, they asked respondents about the extent to which they agreed with certain statements or asked them direct questions about belonging such as: 'I am proud to live in Hull', 'Members of the community listen to you', 'I feel connected to my local community', 'How often do you use Facebook', or 'How often you feel lonely'.

Questions in other surveys that may proxy for belonging include the classic general social trust question of the form: 'Do you generally trust individuals in your neighbourhood/city/country', or how many friends individuals have or whether they have at least one friend they could rely on in case of an emergency. The English Longitudinal Study of Ageing (ELSA), for example, has followed over time how many friends people report to have, how positive people feel around those friends, and how they communicate with them.[32] An interesting stylized fact for the United Kingdom is that community trust has increased over time, probably

[32] For a description and many studies, see https://www.elsa-project.ac.uk/.

a major factor in the general increase in wellbeing in the United Kingdom over the past years.[33]

Hence, statistical agencies do try to measure the stock of community relationships by asking individuals about their number of friends and means of communication with others. What is difficult to observe, though, is both sides of these relationships, how they came about, what allowed them to occur, and what might break them up. The lack of data on such things reflects the difficulty of observing an actual relationship as well as the difficulty of defining and finding such things as 'friendship groups' or 'communities'. Statistical agencies usually work off lists of individuals and households; they lack a list of current communities or relationships and hence do not have an obvious way to sample them or predict their emergence.

As a result, our understanding of how relationships arise, are maintained, and of their emotional content is largely based on a large amount of observational cases studies and on comparisons across large groups, leading to somewhat vague stylized facts like 'Latin American culture has warmer social ties', where both the notion of a Latin American culture and the notion of a warm social tie is imprecise because both are in the eyes of the beholder. Nevertheless, slow progress is being made and there is hope that in the future statistical agencies will get a better handle on actual interactions between people and thus relationship formation (for instance, by collecting information on whole neighbourhoods or communities).

A well-known example of an attempt to measure social relationships in a whole community is the Framingham Heart Study in the United States, which tracked about five thousand individuals in the town of Framingham via health clinics, keeping tabs on who was friends with whom. The researchers were still not observing the relationship formation directly but at least looked at dynamics. Fowler and Christakis (2008) found that happy individuals were often found in groups, partially because happy people befriended other happy people, which we also see, for instance, in partnership and marriage in general (the happier are more likely to get married; cf. Ferrer-i-Carbonell and Frijters, 2004). Fowler and Christakis (2008) found that having a happy friend living within a mile was highly predictive of own levels of happiness, and that the loss or gain of friends strongly co-moved with decreases or increase in happiness, respectively.

This concurs with the general lesson we know from migration flows around the world, where the 2018 World Happiness Report found that economic migrants within a year of arrival had caught up 75 per cent with the level of life satisfaction in the country they had migrated to. The underlying data for that claim were

[33] For a primer on some of the data available and options for measuring 'community wellbeing', see the United Kingdom's What Works Centre for Wellbeing scoping report in Bagnall et al. (2017). Moreover, Bagnall et al. (2019) discuss what can be done in terms of physical infrastructure (i.e. parks, design of buildings, etc.) to improve the formation of social relationships. Charles Montgomery's (2013) book 'Happy City' is another good, general interest read in this field.

cross-sectional, meaning that they did not observe individuals pre- and post-migration, but the finding nevertheless strongly suggests, especially since it was found in several datasets, that migrants quickly partake in whatever causes low or high levels of wellbeing in the destination country. This fits the general idea that a lot of wellbeing is tied up with the general quality of social relationships and the ease with which these relationships are made in a country, leading to the question of how relationship formation can be improved.

Other examples of the importance of social relationships for wellbeing, which were summarized and referred to in chapter 6 of the 2019 Global Happiness and Well-Being Policy Report, include:

- Latin America is unusually happy, particularly places like Costa Rica and Columbia. Despite high levels of violence and medium levels of income, these places provide basic social safety nets and have warm social communities where enjoyment of life is openly advocated (Rojas and García, 2017).
- The quality of interpersonal relationships (such as the relationship with management) is a strong predictor of job satisfaction (Matzler and Renzl, 2006). It is even more important than pay.
- Shocks that disrupt communities create huge medium-term loss to wellbeing, though not necessarily in the long run. As we saw already, this loss was observed in China in the 1990s and 2000s, and is now being observed in India. This is partially about anxiety due to insecurities surrounding basic comforts, but also about the loss of a social-group attachment. We can see in China, for instance, that the rural-urban migrants are more miserable than those who remain in the countryside, despite the fact that their income is more than double and even though these migrants do usually return home (Frijters and Meng, 2012). What they miss in the cities they work in is their community.
- At the personal level, relationships with spouses, children, parents, and friends show up as strong predictors of wellbeing, with negative shocks to loved ones (for example, the death of a child or the spouse) amongst the most negative life events that can happen to people (Oswald and Powdthavee, 2008; Frijters et al., 2011).
- A strong co-movement of levels of wellbeing within a large community, particularly a whole country: there are (temporary) spikes in happiness when a country 'wins something' (for example, a football match) and sustained slumps if the country and its ideology is seen to 'lose' (such as the collapse of communism, cf. Easterlin, 2015).

'Belonging' thus includes having good social relationships, including a joint sense of identity. Important indicators of high levels of belonging are community trust, cohesion, willingness to contribute to the community, and indicators of an active and warm social life. The basic theory is that individuals enjoy being an active contributor and a valued member of social groups. It is best if the appreciation is real because what is contributed is truly wanted by others, cementing social ties between people.[34]

Individuals are members of many groups at the same time, forming new groups (like families) and transitioning between groups (from school to employment), including virtual groups. The basic relation to wellbeing is the same in all of them though: when individuals cannot contribute or feel that they and their actions are not appreciated by their groups, their wellbeing suffers. Sometimes that is a good thing in the short run, such as when it gets them to join a different group where they fit better. However, long-term disconnection with others involves loneliness, alienation, resentment, and desperation.

The working ingredients in all three of the previous theories above have an element of belonging in them: having certainty about basic comforts provided makes people feel valued and part of something; selflessness and other socio-emotional skills in the area of experience goods or skills partially work so well because they create communities and the skills to be active in them in a sustainable way; and part of the pain of low status (or even poverty) is the feeling of no longer belonging and being valued by society. The importance of feelings of connection and harmony between the individual and his or her groups hence cannot be overstated, despite those concepts being somewhat vague and difficult to measure at present.

The essential object of collective action by much larger groups (such as the state) is then to organize the rules of the game and circumstances such that there is a healthy ecology of group formation and destruction, and hence social capital formation (bonding capital within groups and bridging capital between them), with virtually everyone slotting in somewhere they want and are wanted.[35] The many difficulties include the fact that groups are not necessarily set up with the benefit of the whole in mind (criminal gangs are groups too!); that there is a basic tendency for sub-groups to start to see others as outsiders when there is a benefit to the insiders in doing so; that groups need to be seen to punish deviations from social norms they maintain so as to remain functional; and that group membership is nearly always exclusive (someone is left outside, by definition).

The state and collective institutions are involved in all aspects of group formation, for example by providing education in the language used to communicate

[34] Although we use slightly different terms to keep consistency with the rest of the book, our line of argument basically follows Turner et al. (1994), Haslam (2004), Haslam et al. (2010), and Frijters and Foster (2013).

[35] Here, capital is used in terms of a stock of something that can be added to and reduced, and that is used in some function of production to produce outcomes. Relationships between people can be seen as such a thing: they require time investments to form and can also be destroyed by both sides of a relationship. Moreover, they give those in relationships flows of services (like joint enjoyment of friendship activities). Thus, relationships can be viewed as a type of social capital stock.

within groups, by providing the legislation of the rules governing the formation and dissolution of many groups (think of divorce and bankruptcy, or registered societies), by creating groups that have specific tasks for which they receive budgets, by creating separate institutions, by disseminating collective information via media, or by maintaining collective stories of the past (heritage).

We offer a checklist of five points that any policy-maker, analyst, or manager in the civil service can ask in connection with belonging that is relevant to wellbeing:

1. Permission: 'Do we give the people we serve permission to have a high wellbeing via warm social relationships?'
2. Engagement: 'Do we walk the walk on wellbeing ourselves in that we are seen as part of the group that values it?'
3. Information: 'Do we know the wellbeing of groups and do we communicate that knowledge, showing that we think it matters?'
4. Identity narratives: 'Is the story of who we are conducive to wellbeing?'
5. Creation and destruction: 'Have we got the right communities and (sub-) communities?'

We turn to each of these points below.

Permission

The importance of permission comes from the wish by individuals to be valued by others. This makes them look to authority and group power structures for an open signal that what they want and can contribute is openly valued.[36] This extends to the wish to be happy as well: if authority treats wellbeing as something that is not truly valued, group members will take their cue from that and value it less too. Indeed, they may erect cognitive barriers to even thinking constructively about their own happiness.

So giving permission matters: namely, to notice that it is truly 'okay' to work on one's own wellbeing and that of others and that this is liberating and validated. We see this in the selflessness experiments mentioned previously where people to their own surprise enjoyed the community aspect of helping others when they notice that they truly had permission.

A good example of this are the self-help activities of the Action for Happiness charity, and in particular, the eight-week 'Exploring What Matters' course, evaluated by Krekel et al. (2020). The intervention consists of volunteers leading group discussions for ninety minutes, eight weeks in a row, with around fifteen people

[36] Ellemers et al. (2004) talk extensively about the psychology of leadership and the crucial role managers play in constructing the group identity of a workplace or an organization. Haslam et al. (2010) give many examples of how leadership creates identity and that leadership needs to maintain one that works well.

per group. These groups openly talk about topics such as 'What makes a happy life?', 'Can we be happier at work?', or 'Can we create a happier society?' The group discussions are occasions in which participants give themselves and others permission to really treat the question of their own happiness and that of others seriously.

The impact evaluation employed a waitlist randomization protocol, looking at how the life satisfaction and mental health of about seventy people who went through this curriculum compared to that of about seventy other people who enrolled at the same time but went through the curriculum six months later. The study found that the curriculum increases life satisfaction of the treatment group by a whole point on a 0-to-10 scale compared to the control group, an effect that was even slightly higher eight weeks after the course had finished, suggesting that there is no adaptation and return to baseline. There was a strong reduction in depressive symptoms and anxiety as well.

There are many other studies with similar content (reviewed in Layard (2020), for example), but the key point to note here is that permission matters: what individuals believe is acceptable to truly mull over can be altered by the reaction of others, particularly the top.

Hence, a policy implication is to give permission to be happy, as simple as that, in terms of openly valuing wellbeing and social relationships while not undermining that permission by being dismissive about it in a noticeable way.

Engagement

Closely related to openly giving permission to be happy is being seen to 'walk the walk', i.e. to implement wellbeing-improving changes in one's own neck of the woods when there are clear opportunities to do so. This includes one's own workplace, but also, of course, the groups and communities one may have influence with.

Engagement can take many forms, ranging from setting up selflessness interventions like the ones described previously, to being supportive of initiatives of others in this direction if they work well. It essentially involves the application of the three main wellbeing theories described before, incorporating new insights as they emerge.

Engagement also involves the application of some of the main things we know about sustaining cooperation within groups: to be seen to punish those who harm wellbeing and to reward those who increase it.[37] Part and parcel of that can be things like—for example, by conferring status—openly valuing those who manage to improve the wellbeing of others, including their own staff and colleagues.

[37] See Haslam et al. (2010) for more details.

Information

The formation of social relationships can be seen in a similar way as the creation of jobs: like any relationship, jobs involve at least two parties (employer and employee), may not last long, and generate benefits for both sides. Just as with jobs, the various parties in social relationships have to be able to find each other. In the case of jobs, that includes information on characteristics of both job offers and job seekers.

A key aspect of improving the market for social relationships is thus to measure wellbeing and its key drivers related to belonging at the organizational level.

This already happens on a large scale in the United Kingdom, for example, both for the public and the private sector. Compared to other countries, it is probably fair to say that the United Kingdom leads the world in openly available information on the wellbeing of staff. At the Institute for Government, for example, one can find the wellbeing levels of workers in various public sector institutions across the United Kingdom.[38] At Glassdoor, one can find similar information about various private sector employers.[39] At 80,000 Hours, one can see the judgement of a charity as to how individuals can best spend their lives to increase the happiness of the world.[40]

The purpose of this information is both to have an idea as to the current state of wellbeing in any organization relative to that of others, so one knows which place is doing well and which is not, and to provide information for those trying to find a group to belong to, job-wise. This latter role is thus of optimal matching of individuals to groups, in this case employers. It is an example of how information is used to deliberately influence the formation of groups, not merely to inform existing groups of whether it is likely that they can improve matters.

The principle of wellbeing measurement and of the communication of that measurement in order to foster groups with higher wellbeing can, of course, be extended beyond its current level. It is already normal in Welsh schools, for example, to measure life satisfaction and various aspects of social relationships within schools, partly to help schools identify opportunities for improvement and partly to help parents and pupils choose schools. Yet, this does not happen in English schools.[41] Open measurement is also not yet, as far as we know, a tool to compare and measure what goes on in prisons or youth institutions. It is not yet open information anywhere as to how satisfied different types of patients fare in different hospitals.[42] It is not yet normal for every manager to track information as to how staff is doing

[38] https://www.instituteforgovernment.org.uk/explainers/location-of-civil-service.

[39] https://www.glassdoor.co.uk/Reviews/index.htm.

[40] https://80000hours.org/.

[41] See, for example: https://dera.ioe.ac.uk/24929/3/151211-children-young-people-wellbeing-monitor-2015-en_Redacted.pdf.

[42] There is, however, a lot of information available on health in the United Kingdom, such as via the Care Quality Commission.

under his or her care, let alone to make that information available. Hence, information and optimal matching in terms of wellbeing can likely be further improved.

Identity Narratives

As Haslam et al. (2010) noted, managers create stories as to what the group is and does. Any state institution also does this. The state as a whole is pivotal in the creation and maintenance of the story of 'all of us', i.e. the population of a country.

Taking again the example of the United Kingdom, let us first remind ourselves of the many ways in which the state actively propagates a story of the country and its various smaller communities. There are, for instance, listed national sports events that are mandatorily offered to free-to-air TV channels such as ITV or the BBC (for example, the Wimbledon finals, the Olympic Games, or the Grand National). There are National Parks, National Trails, and National Heritage sites. There are national symbols such as the flag and the anthem, national holidays, national commemorations, a national language, national defence, a national broadcaster, even a quasi-national religion (the Church of England and the Church of Scotland). And, of course, there is the monarchy.

By comparison to other European countries, the United Kingdom has relatively 'heavy' forms of national identity-bearing institutions, reflecting the many centuries in which power was centralized strongly under the monarchy and now parliament. The idea that a monarch is the head of the church is, for instance, quite unusual in Europe. The notion of the Queen's representatives in regions and whole countries is similarly a strongly unitary and centralized approach to identity that is unusual in Europe. Yet, on the other hand, the United Kingdom lacks a few identity-creating and maintaining institutions that are seen as pivotal in many other EU countries, such as a single national school curriculum, which is particularly important to identity when it comes to history.

Like most other countries, the idea of a united territory and population is integrated into UK democracy: only UK citizens can vote for the parliament and can stand for election. There is thus such a thing as the UK 'demos'. This is, of course, normal in many countries, but noting it should remind us that the United Kingdom in fact does in many areas have an active approach to the maintenance of a single unifying identity.

We give this reminder of the role of the state in creating and maintaining a national identity to show that questions of identity and tensions between different identities are at the very heart of the state in the United Kingdom. One might think that the creation and maintenance of a national identity are outside of the scope of state action, but this is not true: pretty much all smaller groups and identities are bound by the general legal system that sets the rules of the game for group interactions and expressions of identity. Moreover, the state creates new groups actively, such as by setting up new institutions or funding local groups to grow. Finally, the state is heavily involved in identity-creating activities, such as education and the use of a shared language.

If we think of the national identity aspect of belonging as an engineering problem, the general question is what the ideal mix of cultural diversity is between individuals, communities, and the country as a whole; and what the optimal configuration of state institutions and responsibilities is given a certain level of cultural diversity.

From international comparisons, we have a reasonable suspicion about the belonging-elements of the happiest countries (like the Scandinavian countries): they have a national story that is inclusive in the sense that there are no innate barriers to any citizen in those countries joining the notion of 'us'.[43] Around that national story, individual communities and regions have their own identities and stories, but more in the nature of 'variants of' rather than 'rivals to' the overall national identity, without any separatist movements. There appears to be a spectrum of possibilities within which high levels of wellbeing are possible.

The countries with an extremely uniform identity and thus quite low diversity include Japan and South Korea, both collectivist countries. They have high levels of GDP, strong pro-social behaviour in the population, and are well-governed. However, they have relatively low levels of wellbeing compared to Northern Europe and Latin America. One explanation for this is that the strong unitary identity implicit in collectivism is constrictive to its populations such that there is not enough room for personal development and enjoyment, constraining the warmth of many social relationships (Suh and Oishi, 2002). Maybe they are not selfish enough.

On the other extreme, there are the 'fractured countries' in Africa where colonial boundaries created countries with highly dissimilar regional identities, leaving no overarching identity that binds these regions, leading to disruptions ranging from tensions to full-blown civil war (this is a well-researched area, see Keller (2014), for example).

The happier countries in between these extremes have a reasonably strong shared identity, although there is a spectrum in which degrees of federation can keep the whole together whilst leaving individual regions and communities a larger sense of distinctiveness. Hence, the more diverse the smaller identities, the more federal the system should probably be to regulate these differences. If separate communities and regions do not have some identity of their own, local public good provision and community cohesion are low.

Within this spectrum, there are quite happy countries, like the federal Swiss or the somewhat less federal Finns, and somewhat unhappy countries and regions,

[43] This means, for instance, that citizenship is not exclusively defined by bloodlines ('ius sanguinis').

like Portugal or the Balkan countries, which are possibly unhappy due to major economic disruptions (Portugal) or cultural factors (Balkans).

Whether a country has the right balance is difficult to ascertain empirically. What matters is that there are wellbeing benefits of cohesion arising from a shared identity, as well the quite well-known ways in which that shared identity is actively shaped and could further be shaped.[44]

How could one create more cohesion? One could foster more uniformity in beliefs, attitudes, or behaviours via education and create more shared experiences and interests via mixing communities and a joint story of 'us' that people can identify with and look up to. The policy options to increase or decrease community cohesion are varied: one could have a mixing model of a national army (France) versus regional regiments (United Kingdom); mixing students around the country via regional specialization in universities (Netherlands) versus all-purpose universities everywhere (Australia); mixing government staff around departments; introducing a national history and culture curriculum; organizing school trips to national museums; having a national (social) service; having a more federal model if the regional differences are large; and maintaining a reputation that the law and political favours indeed fall equally to everybody everywhere (and are not, for instance, biased towards a capital city).

However, there are a few basic tensions, too: achieving more commonality requires conscious investments in the story of 'us', which is costly, also because it needs to be maintained (Haslam et al., 2010); existing identities and communities have a competing story that would have to be replaced, which comes with short-run losses that may be worse if the local communities feel they are being harmed. The gains to common identity are long-run and there is a short-run free-riding incentive; greater community life comes with the problems of community life which require additional structures to cope with—a necessary cost for some institutions (for example, the army, which has to cater for families) and probably not cost-effective in others (for example, private firms). The more there is a joint story of us, the more will the majority demand to share in the wealth of the whole, which threatens the wealth and the status of those at the top, implying that greater uniformity is not politically neutral.

Identity stories and changes in the sense of belonging are generated throughout the country, so it is not always clear that the state needs to push a joint story or whether enough cohesion emerges anyway. The United States, for instance, has a strong national narrative and there is also a natural pull towards images of success, so a country doing conspicuously well will have more cohesion-forming. Also, perceived dangers to the population, as we are now experiencing in the Covid-19

[44] Frijters and Foster (2013) describe this in great detail. Haslam (2004) and Haslam et al. (2010) also provide relevant insights.

crisis, can translate into a push towards more social cohesion. In sum, there are basic tensions between regions, time-periods, and social layers.

What would a rational approach to identity look like? There would need to be a measurement of tensions: how much people feel part of the same country? How proud are they to belong? What were the last things that made them feel good about the country? What made them feel bad? Do they feel everyone in their country is treated equally? Ideally, one wants to know the hierarchy of identification when it comes to neighbourhood, larger community, regions, or the state. There should also be a measurement of instruments: heritage sites, mixed communities, intermarriage, or shared events. Finally, there should be a rational appraisal of the total benefits of the application of various instruments.

Creation and Destruction

Have we got the right groups and how much does it matter if some current group identity is dissolved? This question comes up in many circumstances, including the drawing of regional boundaries, displacement when there are natural disasters or major infrastructure projects, as well as the creation and destruction of groups via budgets (as a rule of thumb, every budget maintains or creates at least one group around its expenses). It is also a natural aspect of a market economy that firms (which usually also create work communities) get created and destroyed over time by competitive pressures, involving the policy question as to whether they should be 'rescued' when they fail.

As we have argued by now, the main rule is the one already in operation: does the current set of groups perform a useful function or could a different group with a different orientation add more to national wellbeing? One should expect the dissolution of any group to cause pain in the short run (via the destruction of social ties in those groups) but since people want to feel truly valued, it will often be the case that it is better to follow the longer-term strategy of going with what is sustainable: people will often find places in new groups.

An important 'unknown' in this regard is just how fast group formation goes in the absence of state intervention. The 'natural rate of group formation' that arises out of a 'group matching function' matters especially for the question of how bad it is to actively dissolve groups. The higher the natural rate, the less one needs to worry about all but the largest negative shocks to the social system. One might think of this natural rate of group formation as corresponding to the notion of the resilience of the overall social system. This then contrasts with individual resilience, which is about weathering individual shocks, and national resilience, which is about weathering all types of shocks, not just shocks to particular sub-groups.

In Sum

Belonging is probably the most important ingredient of wellbeing and the one that we are least sure about as a research community, despite years of active deliberation and many books on the subject. This is because groups come in many shapes and sizes, and they form and dissolve quickly. To estimate how wellbeing may be changed via some belonging-oriented intervention is tremendously difficult.

For some of the five points offered in our checklist (permission, engagement, information, identity narratives, and creation and destruction), it should be fairly clear from the theories described previously what to look at and what can be done (as in the case of information and permission). But on this issue of identity and group creation, one essentially needs deep knowledge of individual and social processes, as well as wellbeing, economics, and politics.

A rational national approach to identity formation is at the moment still futuristic. The question of 'who we could be' remains wide open.

What We Do Not Yet Know or Are on the Fence about

The four theories above represent what we know with most certainty, at least in terms of what matters and what the policy levers and checklists are. However, there are also large areas of decision-making in which governments operate where we have little idea what the right way forward is from a wellbeing perspective. Hence, we want to briefly mention a few studies and areas where there are blind spots in our knowledge.

Caring for the Homeless

Even the richest countries have a small population at the bottom of the ladder, including the homeless. Can they be effectively helped?

One would think that spending lots of resources on the homeless is always a good thing. Surely, the wellbeing of a homeless person can only increase if one, for instance, gives them a home and organizes intensive psychological and regular health services?

It appears not to be this straightforward. A randomized controlled trial in Canada brought out the difficulties with this approach, summarized in Stergiopoulos et al. (2015).

The Canadian trial was large, similar in scope and intention to the UK Housing First programme, and involved a quite extensive group of agencies to measure and track outcomes. Some 2,148 homeless individuals across Canada, with new cases starting during the 2009 to 2011 period, were randomly assigned to intensive housing-and-social-support help (versus 'normal help') for twenty-four months in the period 2011 to 2013. Every six months, they were extensively interviewed, with additional measures taken from public records. The key wellbeing outcome was life satisfaction on a 0-to-6 scale, although the study also included standard measures of health (the EQ5D) and many highly specific measures, for instance of substance abuse and criminal activity.

The results were somewhat surprising: those with intensive treatments were not more likely to stop substance abuse, had an equal or higher number of arrests, and were no better integrated in the community. The severity of their mental illness—a key target outcome—actually worsened for the intensively treated group in the first six months. The life-satisfaction benefits on a scale from 0-to-6 were an estimated 0.22 in the first year and 0.18 in the second compared to the control group. This is quite small for such a large intervention. For example, health insurance, which is far cheaper, is found to increase life satisfaction by at least twice that amount (cf. Kim and Hoh, 2018).

This Canadian study can be summarized by saying that many of the homeless individuals treated had severe behavioural difficulties that did not diminish by simply giving them a home or basic counselling. Drug abuse and other negative behaviours might actually increase as access to resources is enlarged. The study should make us wary that there is a simple solution for the problems of those at the bottom of the societal and psychological health ladder. Rather, it appears that we do not yet know enough about the extreme ends of the wellbeing spectrum.

Empowerment

It is intuitively plausible to think that giving more power to an individual or a group makes their life better: to 'empower' a group is an appealing slogan even when it is often unclear what that actually entails.

If one thinks of empowerment as giving higher relative status to a person or a group of persons, then the section above on status applies: more status is a good thing for the entity receiving it but, most likely, bad for everyone else around it because status is in fixed supply. Hence, the issue then boils down to the balance between benefits or disbenefits of the status-entailing empowerment that is encouraged, for example whether it leads to more taxes and more pro-social behaviour (good), or whether it leads to more disruptive behaviour (bad).

If one thinks of empowerment merely as 'more discretionary resources', then the large literature on income and wellbeing tells us the basic answers: more income is again a good thing for the entity receiving, whether an individual or a group. Yet, entities not being a part of the resource increase lose out as their relative status associated with income decreases. From a policy perspective, the issue then boils down to what the entity receiving more resources is likely to do with it compared to the entity from which the extra resources are taken, and whether, as result, aggregate wellbeing is increased.

If one thinks of empowerment as a legal concept, that is, as more 'rights' or fewer 'obligations', we suddenly find ourselves without a clear answer. A good example of ambiguous findings is the quite large literature on female empowerment, seen as an increase in legal rights. If you look across countries, Meisenberg and Woodley (2015) show that there is no systematic relationship between the gender life-satisfaction gap and the level of legal rights of women versus men. In other words, the difference in the life satisfaction of women and men is not directly related—at least at the country level—to differential legal treatments.

If one looks at changes over time in gender labour laws (like equal pay acts) or other gender-specific legislation, Batz-Barbarich et al. (2018) find no associated change in female life satisfaction either. Looking at the United States over time, Stevenson and Wolfers (2009) even find evidence for reduced female life satisfaction as their rights and incomes increase, something they ascribe to a concomitant rise in the expectations of females. The relationship between female empowerment, by giving more rights and imposing fewer obligations, and wellbeing, therefore, seems not straightforward.

These studies are all correlational. How about experimental evidence? Dahl et al. (2020) use the fact that in 2000 the German citizenship law changed such that immigrant children born in Germany would automatically obtain citizenship. The authors found that those female teenagers born a few weeks after the change (who thus had access to German citizenship) were much less satisfied with life than male teenagers from the same migrant community, or than females from the same community born a few weeks earlier (who thus had no access). Females with automatic access experienced greater cultural strife with their parents, actually leading them to do worse at school rather than better.

One can read these results negatively and positively. Negatively, one could note that there seems to be no straightforward, unidirectional long-run wellbeing gain from greater empowerment and perhaps even a reduction in the medium-run. Positively, one could note that there is no clear loss to the wellbeing of males from female empowerment, neither in the short run nor long run. One could also speculate that particular forms of gender power balance are optimal for the long-run operation of the country as a whole, a feedback effect that is hard to prove or disprove. The jury is hence still out on wellbeing benefits of empowering large groups.

The Spillover Effects of Unemployment

We know that unemployment is highly detrimental to an individual, partially so by policy design since it is important to the state that individuals are keen to engage in taxed employment. Whatever the reason though, the unemployed feel less valued and their sense of belonging is threatened. As a result, the unemployed are either desperate to find another job (the intended effect) or prone to give up the world of paid employment altogether. During a period of unemployment, the unemployed are less socially active, partly due to the stigma of being unemployed (see Gallie et al. (2003), for example).

We know that there is little adaptation to unemployment, and that the effect of unemployment on wellbeing remains roughly constant over time for the unemployed (Clark et al., 2008). In fact, there might even be scarring: even when regaining employment, the formerly unemployed do not reach the previous wellbeing level they had before entering unemployment (Lucas et al. 2004; Mousteri et al., 2018).

What is unclear, however, is the effect of an individual's unemployment on the whole community. This is because there are three strong forces in operation, which go in different directions. The first is that the family and friends close to the unemployed share in that persons' misery, either because they empathize or because they are shunned (McKee and Bell, 1986). The second is the fear that those still employed and those hoping for jobs experience when unemployment in the country or the region is made salient, by members of their communities becoming unemployed, a potentially strong anxiety effect. The third is the fact that family and friends may move on, forming new social relationships and engaging in other social activities to fill their lives with.

Clark et al. (2018) claim that the total effect of unemployment on others is three times the amount on the unemployed individual herself, studying changes in life satisfaction in regions hit by different unemployment shocks. Looking at changes in countries over time, Di Tella et al. (2003), amongst others, find effects of unemployment that were also far greater than could be rationalized by the effect on individuals alone.

Yet, on the other hand, the bounce-back of average life satisfaction in the United States within twelve months of the advent of the Great Financial Crisis, which increased unemployment by over five percentage points (taking a decade to return to baseline), made it clear that multiplier effects of unemployment might well be quite short lived (Deaton, 2012). What this means is that we do not yet truly know just how high the social multiplier on unemployment really is or how long it really lasts.

Caring for the Elderly and Community Support Systems in General

One of the biggest surprises about wellbeing in many developed countries during the last two decades or so has been its strong increase, particularly amongst the elderly (Veenhoven, 2018). This has been associated with a real increase in measured community cohesion (in particular trust in the community and community satisfaction, cf. Tov and Diener, 2009; Helliwell and Wang, 2010; Bagnall et al., 2017; Atkinson et al., 2020). What makes this particularly surprising—at least in the United Kingdom—is that in this period there has been a reduction in state services for the elderly, including the withdrawal of many local and national services (Lupton and Burchardt, 2016).

However, the high levels of life satisfaction and community cohesion seem to indicate that the reduction in state services in one area of the welfare state has been, partly or completely, absorbed by something else. We do not truly know how it has been absorbed and do see some indicators of social stability decrease since 2016, such as, for example, knife crime and problems with juveniles in the United Kingdom.

The key unknown element here is just how quickly and to what degree non-state actors pick up the roles abandoned by the welfare state. We saw in China, and right now in India, that it takes the state decades to pick up the slack when previous structures stop providing insurance and basic public goods to the population. In the reverse scenario, we saw in Eastern Europe how it took civil society a decade to pick up the slack from the collapse of the central state (Foa and Ekiert, 2017). We know, therefore, that huge social shocks take a decade or more to be absorbed. But how quickly are much smaller shocks absorbed? As noted before for the case of elderly care, we do not yet know the answer.

One unknown is the speed with which communities form new social bonds if the previous bonds with the state (which includes local councils) are severed by an external shock. The second unknown is whether communities and families have truly taken up 'the slack' or whether it has been other services that thereby have come under more strain: the police, social workers, or the health care professionals. We have few answers to these questions because it is extremely difficult to measure the notions of strain and slack.[45] At the same time, it is possible that confounding factors have concurrently counterbalanced the cuts, such as wealth increases amongst the elderly.

What the example shows is that we do not know how resilient or stressed public services and communities actually are. Since their wellbeing is higher, which is universally found to be positively correlated with lack of stress and higher resilience, one would suspect that communities were in fact more resilient and less stressed at the start of 2020 than before. More deeply though, we do not know the capacity of the social system to absorb wellbeing-related shocks, or the speed with which this happens. Part of the problem is that we do not yet think of communities in such an integrated capital-stock-type way.

[45] Of course, this does not mean that there are no opinions on the subject. However, since within a state system calls for more resources easily take the form of claims of crisis and strain, the truth is difficult to ascertain.

Hence, in many cases, we do not really know what would happen with or without state intervention and aid for community programmes. That hampers sensible 'cost-effectiveness analysis', 'cost-benefit analysis', or 'impact analysis', which all require some notion of what would happen if the state did not do something—a counterfactual scenario that is unobservable.

An Economic Framework and Some Applications

Policy-makers and analysts often have to come up with a framework that places the problem at hand in the most relevant context: the various objects of interest are related to the elements that have most effect on them and that either need to be taken into account or could be changed via policies. Less important elements are left out. The framework then captures the causality between the most important elements. From frameworks, which we could also call 'models' or 'theories of change', one gets a better idea of what data to use, how to use them, and where to look for the sub-questions and estimates one needs for policy evaluation and appraisal.

There are plenty of economic and social science frameworks for all kinds of problems. We cannot possibly provide a wellbeing framework that replaces them all: frameworks have a 'horses for courses' element to them and the set of useful ones needs time to be built up. It is thus a matter of long usage that will ultimately lead to appropriate wellbeing frameworks for different problems and sub-problems. Here, we only want to give a general economic framework with two more detailed applications that illustrate the theories introduced above and that exemplify the kind of thinking that becomes normal when one adopts individual measures of wellbeing as the source of information on what matters.

First, we give a framework that embeds wellbeing in a national economic perspective. It is reasonably close to the way the OECD envisages the national economic system (Fitoussi and Durand, 2018a, 2018b; Llena-Nozal et al., 2019) and is also one of the directions that New Zealand has thought of with respect to wellbeing (Treasury, 2019). It is not a ready-to-go framework as its constituent elements would need a lot of work to truly operationalize, but it is useful as a means of thinking how wellbeing fits together at the macro-level. This general framework is then used to put wellbeing into a standard economic context, which allows us to give a general heuristic for designing policies related to wellbeing. The two applications apply the offered heuristic. The first application centres around the IAPT programme in the United Kingdom, a framework we actually applied, leading to estimates of IAPT cost-effectiveness. We do not give the full evaluation here but do comment on the framework as an example of the application of the four main theories. The second application centres around childhood conduct disorders and the Incredible Years parenting programme, a framework we have developed. Again, we do not fully describe the evaluation, but do use it to illustrate how that framework applies basic theories and rules of thumb.

An Integrated Economic Model of Wellbeing

So far, we have avoided stances on how the world works and have therefore not presented specific models of wellbeing. The reason for this is that social science is not united in the appropriate view of the world, with many competing disciplines and literatures disagreeing with each other. By avoiding an explicit stance, this book allows individuals from diverse backgrounds to adopt wellbeing into their thinking and decision processes.

Nevertheless, the reality is that the world of policy evaluation and appraisal and other techniques for decision-support systems inside government is dominated by economists. It is, therefore, important to at least sketch how wellbeing could fit into standard economic thinking about the economic system and the role of the state therein. Hence, we first augment the standard view of production to include the key investments and issues related to wellbeing, after which we sketch, using an imperfect-competition and imperfect-rationality lens, the role of the state in policies related to wellbeing. Our approach is, in essence, a generalization of the wellbeing approach taken by the OECD and the natural capital approaches (see Bright et al. (2019), for example) already adopted in some places. Such approaches are not really operational, nor is it likely they will be operational in the near future, but it is still important to sketch how wellbeing and the economic system roughly fit together.

The National Socio-economic System

Since at least the time of Frank Ramsey (1928), economics has viewed the level of output of a country, including all its goods and services, as related to stocks and flows of input factors into a production process. The original factors considered were physical capital and labour. Over time, economists have added other factors of production, gradually adopting the insights of other social sciences into a more nuanced set of 'capital'. These additions include, for example, human capital, social capital, and quite a few others (see Frijters and Foster (2013) for a discussion). The reason to view the economic system in this way is that it recognizes that the state is heavily involved in investments that can be suitably named 'production factors'. Education, in which the state is heavily involved in, is, for instance, universally recognized as an investment into human capital. The state is also directly involved in building infrastructure and other forms of physical capital.

To integrate wellbeing in this type of model requires only minor changes to this established way of economic thinking. The key additions involve the recognition that the state needs to self-replicate a group identity, and the main social linkages

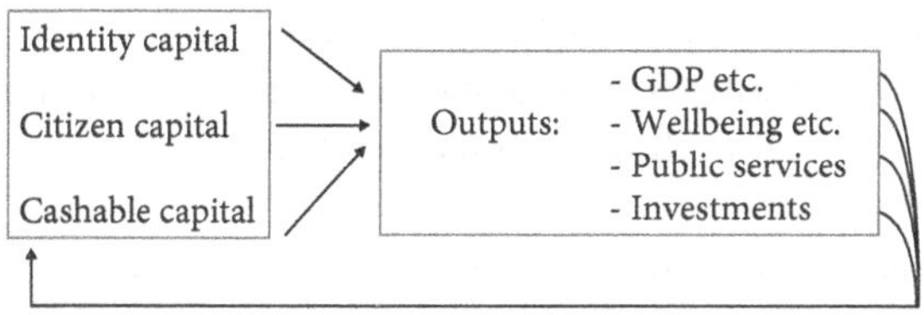

Figure 2.11 The national socio-economic capital-production-investment cycle
Source: own illustration.

and skills directly related to wellbeing. Diagrammatically, we could envisage a national socio-economic system as a self-replicating cycle of capital inputs that lead to outputs, including the investments that flow back into capital stocks as shown in Figure 2.11.

Outputs here are meant to be generic and may include anything produced by citizens and their organizations, which is why the diagram (rather colloquially) refers to 'GDP etc.' or 'Wellbeing etc.'. Health, education, housing, and many other things are thus included, in principle. By adopting particular production functions for the different outputs, this diagramme could become a standard 'growth model' in economics. By having a more complicated set-up with competing producting entities that individually produce outcomes, one obtains a standard competitive model.

Identity Capital: 'Who Are We?'

Identity capital refers to the stock of social relationships, shared identity, and protective institutions. In the case of national policy, the identification is with the country as a whole. The prime functions of identity capital are to define 'us', i.e. the strength of a common identity.[46] Its components are:

- Social capital: This is a broad term by which we mean the emotional bonds in communities, levels of trust, and informal institutions via which individuals recognize each other as belonging to the same larger group.
- Unity of purpose: This denotes the degree to which the members of the whole have a shared understanding about the purpose of their communal structures, particularly the role of the state.
- National pride: This denotes the degree to which individuals take pride from being part of their community.

[46] In standard economics textbooks, this factor is missing because standard economics takes preferences for granted, as if a person is born a UK citizen, not educated as one. A lot of institutions and policies concern identity, necessitating an explicit treatment of how national identity self-replicates. Although the terms used in this section will be unfamiliar to many economists, these arguments have been long-standing in the literatures on socialization (Banks, 1978; A. Hargreaves, 1978; D. H. Hargreaves, 1978) and social identity theory (Ellemers and Haslam, 2012).

- Defining institutions and beliefs: This denotes the stock of cultural, formal, and informal institutions that define the shared notion of a national community, as opposed to those of other countries.

The country as a whole and its constituent communities continuously make investments into identity capital. This includes investments in the national language, the national history, national events, or national symbols. These investments often go via the education system which perpetuates a joint story of a shared language, a shared history, and a shared set of attitudes, beliefs, and behaviours. One could even see the Royal Family, a national broadcaster, or the army as an identity-affirming and identity-defending set of institutions. Families and communities consciously make investments in identity capital, too, partly because they will do better when they 'fit in' by being sufficiently similar to others, partly because deviating from social norms of behaviour may result in wellbeing losses, either internally imposed when feeling out of place or externally when being punished for deviating behaviour.

The set of individuals identified as 'our citizens' have both rights and obligations via identity capital. A large country like the United Kingdom, for example, has multiple communities and some of those communities are in competition with a shared country-wide identity. Those communities will then make their own investments into their language and culture. As long as the culture and the story of the shared identity is not too distant from that of the UK-wide identity, these smaller community identities can augment the strength of the whole. If these smaller community identities become too distant from the whole, however, then there is a threat to the overall identity of the country.

We may note that a belief that one is part of a vibrant and successful entity is beneficial for wellbeing, as argued in the flourishing literature (Keyes and Haidt, 2003; Fischer, 2014). This makes it important for a country to have a positive self-image and narrative that allows citizens some degree of pride in who they are as a collective. Countries that felt they were in decline, such as the regions of the former Soviet Union in the early 1990s, witnessed great unhappiness and suffering, far beyond what would have been predicted from a decline in economic activity following the economic turmoil. Michael Ellman described the human suffering during this period, including high levels of mental anguish, alcohol abuse, suicide, and other visible signs of suffering related to the loss of a shared identity in his 1994 book *Katastroika*.

Identity investments are usually interwoven with other activities and functions, such as when education uses a common language to teach particular skills: via the use of a common language, the social identity connected to that language is strengthened even though the overt purpose might be to teach particular skills.

Identity capital ensures that what is eventually produced is shared as 'ours'. It is the main factor needed to motivate and engender national decision-making.

Citizen Capital: 'What Can We Do?'

Citizen capital is a broad term denoting what is internal to the national stock of citizens: their health, their knowledge, and their skills. Its components are:

- The labour force: Because nearly everyone is involved in some notion of work (including home production), this refers mainly to the stock of citizens.
- Human capital, which refers to the knowledge of how things work.
- Mental and socio-emotional capital, which refers to the knowledge and skills related to one's own mind and the minds of others.
- Executive capital, which refers to management knowledge, networks of power, or industrial relations. This can be loosely viewed as the knowledge of what combinations of people and factors can produce what outcomes. Economists have a large variety of concepts that capture similar things, like firm-specific capital, organizational capital, and relational capital (Frijters and Foster, 2013).
- Institutional capital, which refers to the current system of property rights and regulations and the knowledge of 'how things are done'.

In the early years, economists only considered labour and human capital, but have in recent decades recognized many other factors as relevant, such as non-cognitive skills and emotional intelligence (Cunha and Heckman, 2007; Cunha et al., 2010). Again, these capital stocks are subject to investments by individuals, families, communities, and the state. The stock of people is subject to births, deaths, and migration, all of which are intimately tied to government policy and public services. Education, including basic training and socialization within families, are prime vehicles for human capital investments and investments into the mental and socio-emotional capital of children. The latter includes notions of resilience, self-regulation, confidence, and other self-regarding and other-regarding skills.

Executive capital (or networks of power and knowledge) is invested in via networking and the command-and-control structures of organizations. Institutional capital is partly a matter of laws, and partly the outcome of economic contests.

Cashable Capital: 'What Do We Own?'

Cashable capital is a broad term denoting any kind of capital that can be touched or converted into money. Traditionally, economists only considered physical capital but it has now long been recognized that physical capital is only part of the production equation. The components of cashable capital are then:

- Physical capital, which includes buildings, machines, and other types of infrastructure.

- Natural capital and the ecology, which includes land, mineral wealth, the environment, the climate, and biodiversity.
- International political capital, which includes the international political power of a country to enforce policies at an international level as well as major alliances.

Investments into physical capital have been well studied and include investments by private entities (domestic and foreign) and the government. Natural capital levels are subject to degradation and investments, such as via land reclamation and erosion, greenhouse gas emissions, or sustainable management practices. Investments into international political capital are done by all individuals and groups in a country. National political alliances, including directly cashable ones like IMF drawing rights or the reputation for paying back loans, are a prime output of the political system and subject to both investments (for example, forging new alliances or maintaining property rights) and disruptions (for example, Brexit). One can view international political capital as capturing aspects of the identity of a whole country in a larger community of countries, in which a country has rights and obligations.

Capital Stocks, Flows, Outputs, and Wellbeing

The different factors of production combine to produce many things, including goods, services, capital, health, and ultimately, wellbeing. The study of how this production occurs and can be optimized will involve many academic disciplines.

Wellbeing is particularly related to identity capital as well as mental and socio-emotional capital. This is not to say that all the other capitals are irrelevant in the production of wellbeing, but our current state of knowledge points to these particular forms of capital as the areas where large gains are possible for relatively little costs. A potential reason could be rooted in particular market failures related to these types of capital when it comes to wellbeing.

The Status of This Framework

Variants of our framework are already reflected in existing frameworks around the world. The OECD integrated wellbeing model features similar types of capital and the report by the Commission on Wellbeing and Policy by the Legatum Institute (O'Donnell et al., 2014) groups drivers of growth in similar ways. The New Zealand natural capital approach features a similar setup.

However, these approaches are not yet truly implemented because there is no available measure for many of these capital stocks. There is no established measure for the mental and socio-emotional stock of skills. Moreover, there is no agreement for the amount of 'nature'. Finally, there is no clear measure of identity capital. This is not to deny the proliferation of indices for some of these capital stocks based on hundreds of constituent variables, but such indices do not clearly capture capital stocks nor is it clear how individuals, organizations, and governments can invest in them.

To make true progress would require a strong push in statistics to develop capital measures that are more clearly and directly related to the investments and actions of individuals, organizations, and governments. It is not too hard to envisage how this can be done for some of these forms of capital: there are, for instance, statistics on the number of people with particular skill levels for many countries, as well the mental health levels in the working-age population. Those can be marshalled to get at human and mental capital stocks of a population. Also, there are lots of measures of national parks, wildlife, and measures of stress of the natural environment for many countries. Yet, to consolidate and standardize that information into clear internationally comparable capital levels is an enormous task. Until this is fully accomplished, national socio-economic models such as the one sketched above are essentially thought models helpful to think about the system as a whole, and not yet practical models that yield estimated effects of different decisions.

We should openly say that it may be futile to truly try to make this general model operational, just as some have argued that economic growth models have had little use because the assumptions needed to group many disparate elements together into broad notions of capital make them irrelevant for any practical policy. The main usage of these kinds of general models is then to help us organize our thinking when it comes to actual problems.

An Economic Heuristic to Wellbeing-related Policy Design

The advantage of having a framework of how the national socio-economic system as a whole roughly works, even if that framework cannot be implemented yet, is that it suggests a checklist that one can apply when designing policies to address a particular problem that has arisen. A loose heuristic for wellbeing policy design based on the model ('theory of change') above is:

1. Is there really a problem, and if so, what is it? This is the classic issue of identifying whether there even is a problem to begin with. Comparing a situation with that in other communities and countries is often a good way of seeing whether there really is a problem and what entities usually solve that problem and in which way.
2. What are the main forms of capital involved? This step identifies the bigger picture, i.e. the different roles of the state and society that are involved.
3. What are the main market failures involved? This step identifies who is best placed to address the problem, and how. The generic strategy is to produce the key capital factor in short supply.

4. What is the most efficient means of producing more of the key capital factor involved and how is that believed to address the problem and wellbeing in general?
5. Experimentation and cost-effectiveness analysis to test the proposed solution and whether it represents good value for money.

Note that this heuristic is not restricted to the state, but works equally well for local communities and even households. Also note that the heuristic can be applied without it ever being the case that there is a national system of measurement of the various forms of capital, communities, or market failures: it is very much a heuristic that can be used at a quite local level that ties into national and international issues via habits of thought about capital levels, communities, etc. This makes it much more practical.

An Application: The IAPT Mental Health Programme

In 2016, we evaluated the IAPT Mental Health Programme in the UK, which required a framework for what was most important about the effects of the scheme.

The basic design of the IAPT programme is that those with particular mental health problems, primarily those with depression and anxiety, receive access to cognitive behavioural therapy (CBT) through their GP. CBT has been found to be remarkably effective in various large trials in reducing mental health problems, both in the short run and in the longer run, with some of the longest running trials of more than 40 months still finding large effects of around 60 per cent of the initial effect in terms of the primary mental health outcomes of the treated (Wiles et al., 2016).

The question arose as to what the costs and benefits of the IAPT programme were from a wellbeing perspective, which goes beyond the question of mental health outcomes of the treated: the question becomes how much wellbeing additional mental health is worth, and what the knock-on effects of improved mental health were on the whole population and the public purse including taxes and benefits. Figure 2.12 illustrates our way of thinking.

The figure shows the causal model we developed and applied to the nationally representative Understanding Society panel data in the United Kingdom, whereby the causal estimates came from the appropriate literature on wellbeing. Hence, each of the lines and elements in the figure above is populated with a particular causal estimate taken from a study in the scientific literature. For example, for the effect of mental health on employment, we assume that being relieved from depression increases the likelihood to be full-time employed by fifteen percentage points and actual hours worked by 6.6 per cent for those who worked at baseline (Rollman et al., 2005).

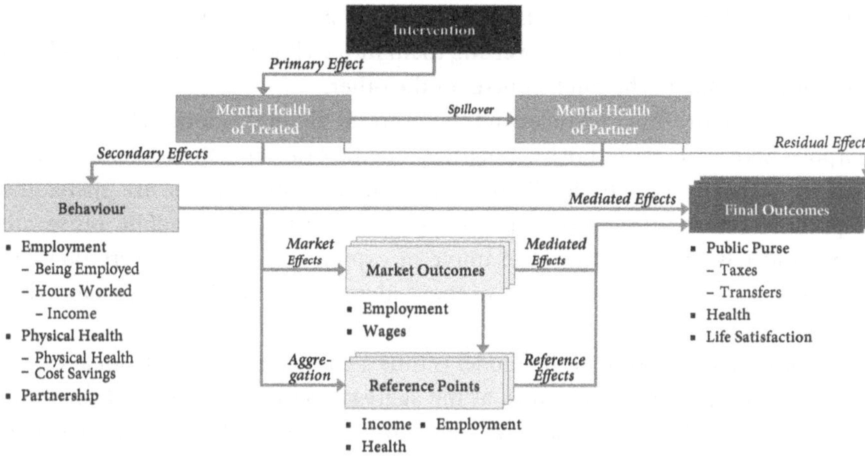

Figure 2.12 Overview of the IAPT programme analytical framework
Source: own illustration.

It is important to discuss what is included and what is not in this model. It is a fairly small model by comparison to some economic models, but it is meant to capture the key pathways. As one can see, the primary effect of the IAPT programme on the mental health of those treated is taken as the initial change to the whole system. The first additional element (which increases the total effects by about 10 per cent) is to also consider the effect on close social relationships, although in this case only the partner and not the children or friends. Those are probably also affected, but solid evidence on that is still lacking somewhat. We adopted a conservative approach and neglected these knock-on effects for the time being.

The main behavioural effects considered are on employment, partnerships, and physical health costs. This reflects the rule-of-thumb judgement that employment and close social relationships matter a great deal to wellbeing. Furthermore, employment matters greatly to the public purse. We should mention that these effects are not huge (10–20 per cent of the total effects on wellbeing). Of greatest importance are the reduced physical health costs, essentially arising because mental health sufferers incur greater costs for some physical health conditions than others: for example, they show up at the hospital more often, an aspect of anxiety. In fact, that channel dominates the public costs of the IAPT programme because it turns out that the estimates in the literature of how much additional physical health costs a mental health sufferer entails for the system are so large that the IAPT programme pays itself back within three years just on that account alone.

The model also includes macro-feedback effects around reference incomes (the income of one person versus the average in the neighbourhood) and even reference health, exemplifying the importance of status considerations. Finally, it brings together all effects by converting them into wellbeing on the one hand and costs and benefits to the public purse on the other.

There are many other nuances and things to say about this model, but the main purpose here is to show how it puts the four theories and their heuristics into practice: anxiety as a basic discomfort is there; status effects are there; the importance of social relationships is there; the costs to the public purse are there; and CBT itself is a great example of experience skills that were doubted for many decades until the weight of the evidence convinced policy-makers that they are truly good value for money.

The essential structure of the model is thus a combination of individual causal pathways and pathways that work at the aggregate level. We work out for those directly affected how a mental health improvement affects their most important life domains (health, social relationships, and employment), and then aggregate all these micro-level changes into a changed population average which, in turn, feeds into a macro-model that takes account of reference point effects and labour market shocks. The changed wages, employment levels, and reference point levels then feed back into the micro-model to determine wellbeing. This then becomes the new starting point of the subsequent period.[47]

Another Application: The Incredible Years Parenting Programme

As with the IAPT programme, we looked at schemes intended to improve mental and socio-emotional skills, sketching a model around the parenting module of the Incredible Years programme, effectively a programme offered to parents of disruptive children aged four to six.

The basic idea of the parenting module of the Incredible Years programme is to hone in on parents with children aged four to six with conduct disorders and to teach them parenting skills. The programme only selects parents who actively want to learn; instructors go through a manualized curriculum in around ten sessions with homework. Some of the main active ingredients are that these parents are shown that many other parents also have children with conduct disorders, teaching them to treat it almost like a puzzle: they learn how to become non-judgemental and more practical towards their children and themselves, treating conduct as something that can be invested in and consciously steered towards improvement. As with the IAPT programme, the results of various trials have been quite promising, though the literature is still based only on relatively

[47] See chapter 3 for results and a more detailed discussion of this IAPT programme evaluation.

small trials of a few hundred children (see Leijten et al. (2018) for a review of the literature).

The challenge was to come up with a wellbeing model that would extend the evaluation of this programme beyond the immediate effect on child conduct (the initial problem) to wellbeing and the public purse. Figure 2.13 illustrates our way of thinking.

This diagram is the blueprint of a quite complicated dynamic model with many elements and datasets in the background (not depicted), but the most important causal pathways are shown: the intervention is seen as a causal change in three different dimensions, i.e. the mental health of the parents; the relationship stability of the parents (because there are fewer problems and the parents themselves work better together); and the skills of the parents in managing their children and themselves.

The improved mental health effect then follows the framework of the IAPT programme as to its effects on the rest of their behaviour and society. The improved parental relationship and their skills then affect child emotional conduct, a causality that is the key focus of the few randomized controlled trials evaluated. In turn, the improved emotional conduct of the children has a direct effect on the same outcome (conduct) of siblings and classmates. That then feeds into improved education and improved mental health, which have long-term consequences because improved education means higher taxes and less costs to society for decades to come. Each of these causal pathways has been populated with estimates from the relevant literatures involved, which is not merely the health literature, but also the education literature and the literature on peer effects. Putting this model together thus requires expertise of several fields.

The key things to note are:

- The model embeds the model of the IAPT programme for the mental health effects, showing how a new framework can piggy-back on an existing one.
- The model homes in on close social relationships such as parents, siblings, and classmates. That turns out to matter immensely because the literature on disruptions in class and peer effects within families actually shows that spillovers are large, easily multiplying the initial effect by a factor of five if the counterfactual was no intervention of any kind. The peer-effect literature is a non-health and often non-experimental literature that may be easy to be missed by authors who design childhood interventions, partly because it would be expensive to track the entire peer group in any experiment. Hence, experiments often do not track close social relationships and one has to import the likely peer effects from the peer-effect literature. Strong peer effects basically arise because disruptive children can derail the learning and emotional health of an entire class if they are not addressed. To expel and neglect individual children with high conduct problems is even more

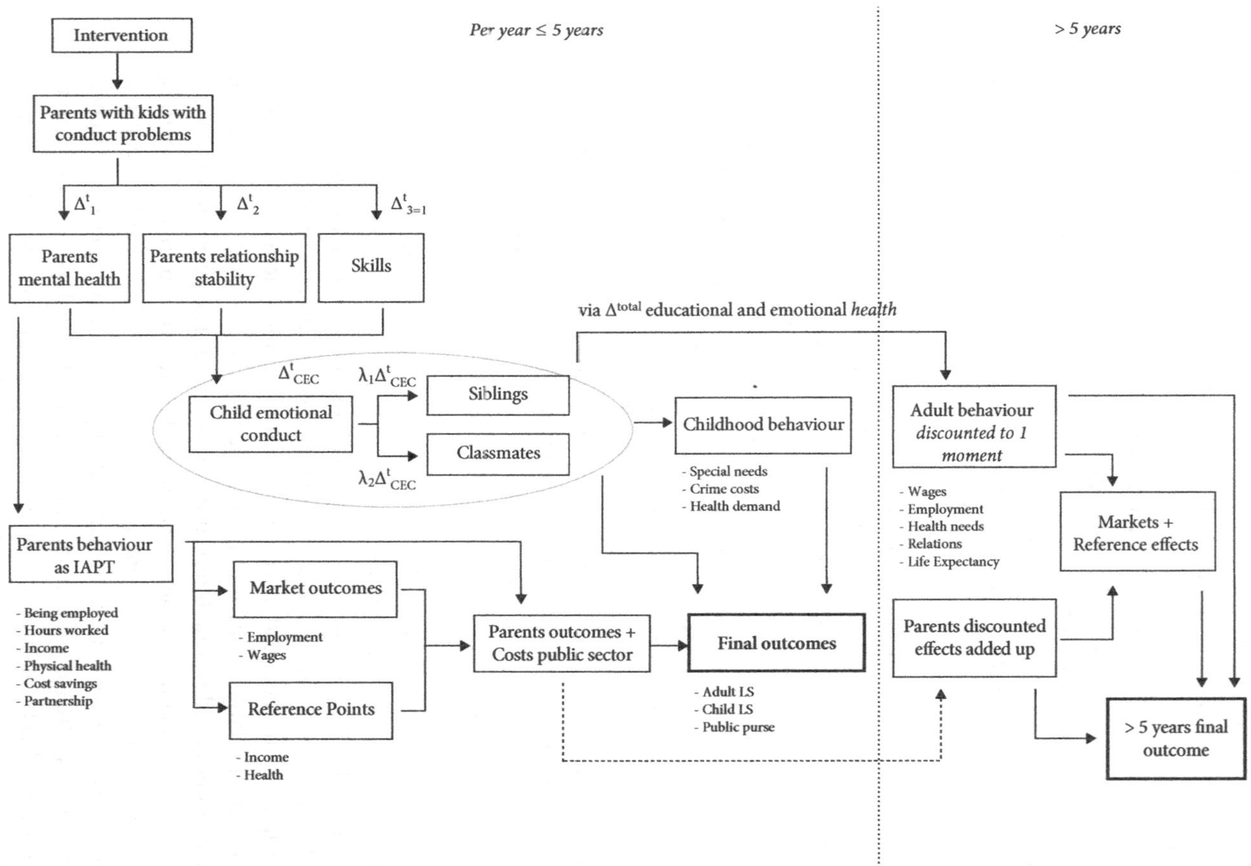

Figure 2.13 Overview of the Incredible Years analytical framework

Source: own illustration.

costly than giving them special care, as completely disregarding them is a prime causeway to even worse mental health problems and potentially even crime, with large associated societal cost.

- In terms of public costs, the key of the intervention is improved education which, in turn, pays itself back via higher taxes and lower social welfare payments later in life.

Hence, as with the IAPT programme, this model exemplifies how a wellbeing perspective always makes one think first of close social relationships as the key factor that drives wellbeing and where large additional effects are to be found that are often ignored in evaluations. The cost perspective forces one to recognize the importance of education and employment for the public purse, meaning that the main pathways one looks for are via public services that either generate or cost substantial amounts of funds (for example, health or crime and welfare versus tax receipts and pro-social behaviour).

We can mention here that the health-driven evaluations of such programmes (see Bonin et al. (2014) or Burns et al. (2007), for example) usually do not have a general equilibrium lens nor look at close social relationships. That is because the basic health model is patient-focused, reflecting the set-up of the national health service where it is the person in need who is looked at, not the wider environment that causes the problems or is strongly affected. In wellbeing, the close social relationships are, in contrast, the first thing one thinks of because it is usually them that multiply any initial effect to become larger or smaller.

A Taxonomy of Government Expenditures

With the theories and frameworks above in mind, we can make some headway into the question of what kind of expenditures governments typically engage in, which in turn suggests particular ways of showing what their overall wellbeing effect are.

Short-run Expenses on Wellbeing with Potentially Long-run Effects

Short-run expenses on wellbeing with potentially long-run effects include all types of short-run activities designed to make (part of) the population feel good. National festivities, one-off mega events (like the Olympic Games), and special handouts (like the 2020 Covid-19 furloughs) are included. Many types of health spending near the end of life can also be considered, as they are expenses towards the dignity of an individual and a community. Reducing pain and certain environmental externalities such as noise also has immediate pay-offs with potentially long-run effects.

Expenses That Are Long-run Investments into Private Wellbeing

Investments into physical and mental health, social relationships, housing, or the quality of the local environment are important examples of long-run investments into private wellbeing. The payoffs of these investments are not exclusively private, as investments in mental health and social relationships, for instance, often lead to reduced public health costs. Yet, the prime focus of these investments is individual wellbeing in the longer run. These expenses lend themselves to cost-effectiveness analyses informed by experiments.

Expenses That Increase the Economic Base of the Country

Expenses that increase economic growth or activity in general but that have no clear direct private wellbeing benefits should be seen as investments that increase the resources available for policies aimed at wellbeing. Their value thus lies in the general ability of public expenses to increase wellbeing.

Many forms of additional economic activity do, of course, increase private wellbeing, notably employment, which has a large effect and also increases the wellbeing of others (like family members or the wider community) by at least as much as it increases the private wellbeing of the individual.

Public education, which itself has been found to have a very small direct effect on wellbeing, is a prime example of an expense that increases the budget of the individual and the country, thereby indirectly increasing wellbeing.

Enabling Expenditures

Treasuries are an example of enabling departments, which are crucial for the operation of the government and the state. Without taxation, there is no government revenue and, ultimately, no government. Since government is a crucial part of the wellbeing of the country, it must have a treasury that is capable of taxing a large part of the economy and, in national emergencies such as Covid-19, raising vast sums.

There are other enabling departments, including parts of the home offices or ministries of the interior, national statistical agencies, school inspectorates, or even weather bureaus: without enabling departments capable of monitoring important aspects of life in a country and enabling the operation of the state itself, government cannot do its job. These departments create little wellbeing directly, but without them the rest of government could not exist.

If these functions are crucial, how should enabling departments be judged from a wellbeing perspective? When are they too big, too small, or lacking in some capacity? A judgement is unlikely to be fruitfully done on the basis of a simple wellbeing cost-effectiveness analysis because their effects on wellbeing are indirect.

There are, however, alternative ways of judging enabling departments, including benchmarking departments in one country against similar ones in other countries as well as using expert judgements about the potential benefit of a new capacity that could be acquired, such as new monitoring systems to enable internet taxation. Here too, one ideally would want to rely on well-documented experiments in this country or a comparable one to justify making large changes.

Expenses That Are Investments in the Strength of Collective Identities

Defence is an important example of an expense that is not directly related to wellbeing, nor with enabling in the same way as the revenue departments (at least during peace times), but is nevertheless a crucial component of a wellbeing-oriented strategy because it increases the ability of the population to pursue its wellbeing interests in this world. It can also be seen an investment in the strength of our joint identity as a country's citizens. If there were no external dangers to a country, defence spending could be much smaller, but in an international environment with competing national wills, a country must have a defence capability to thrive.

Other investments in identity are particular components of the education curriculum (language and history), national culture (museums and arts), national festivities and commemorations, national parks, and cultural representations in the rest of the world. There is some degree to which these investments might also 'pay themselves back' in terms of tourist activities, but this is largely not the point: even without foreign demand for domestic culture and identity, a country needs to invest in its national identity to retain a sense of common purpose.

A key question for empirical research is whether this is really an additional cost at all, or whether investments in identity are largely fixed at the national level: all humans have some identity and some form of continuous reminders and investments in it. Max Weber reminds us that countries are the winners of an evolutionary struggle between identities and that the winning identity must assert itself continuously to remain dominant (Weber, 1895/1994). Investments into the culture and in regional identities that support local governments then define the identities we now want to retain, keeping the growth of alternative identities at bay.

These investments relate to national pride, but also to community cohesion, social trust, and the degree to which citizens feel part of a joint enterprise. As such, there are long-run benefits to these investments for tax morale and a public good spirit, key aspects of any good system of governance. The more there is a general goal shared in all parts of the system, the less there is need to have an expensive system of accountability in which everyone is treated as a potential offender and that hence tracks everyone's behaviour. A shared goal allows the system to be based more on social trust and local decision-making, where punishment for bad behaviour is done locally by those who believe in the shared goal.

A shared goal of wellbeing is likely to increase community acceptance of the rule of law (if the laws are seen to be fair), and the degree to which people help each other and thus alleviate loneliness and poverty, amongst others. The extent of these long-run implications, and whether some investments are more cost-effective than others, is an important area of research. Moreover, the trade-offs between the strengths of different identities is a key area of research, including the question of what level of group is best placed to produce particular public goods (for example, local schools that may be run by local groups) and at what point local identities become competitors to a national identity.

Conclusion and the Way Ahead

This chapter presented and synthesized the current knowledge of how to improve wellbeing: what the main drivers of wellbeing are; the main theories of what matters and how that can be changed; and the rules of thumb in terms of designing policies and setting up frameworks to think about particular issues and interventions.

Thinking ahead of institutions needed to disseminate and improve these theories and frameworks, it is clear that wellbeing would need both academic groups and specialized groups inside a country's bureaucratic machinery that develop and maintain models and knowledge. That is what is normal in macro, health, education, or regulation economics, as well as in many other fields: whilst some academics work on the frontier and educate new cohorts of students to learn the basic knowledge gathered hitherto, the bureaucracy has its own units that maintain the knowledge of what matters most to them, including frameworks around particular policy issues and recurrent work. Importantly, training and the development of standards occurs within the state bureaucracy.

Developing standards is not innate to academia since there is no strong reason for academics to come to consensus opinions or numbers, but bureaucracies need standardized knowledge to have consistent and transparent policy-making that withstands criticism. Hence, developing standards is innately led by the state bureaucracy, possibly with input from academics.

None of these institutions yet exists for wellbeing. There are some embryonic institutions oriented somewhat towards this, however, such as the OECD Better Life Initiative that aims at standardization of what is measured, some working groups inside particular departments, and various intergovernmental relations between countries trying to institutionalize wellbeing, such as in New Zealand, the

United Arab Emirates, the United Kingdom, and others. However, there is at present no academic group delivering large numbers of well-trained students fully versed in all theories and techniques related to wellbeing, nor are there the jobs and the roles within state bureaucracies and large institutions to justify mass training in wellbeing. Institutions that maintain and further develop standards and frameworks are still similarly small.

There is thus still much to do, but the road map points towards gradual professionalization and institutionalization of wellbeing, following the examples of macro, health, education, or regulation economics that have become core state activities over time.

Literature

Abramovitz, M. (1959). The Welfare Interpretation of Secular Trends in National Income and Product. In M. Abramovitz, A. Alchian, K. J. Arrow, and P. A. Baran (eds), *The Allocation of Economic Resources. Essays in Honor of Bernard Francis Haley*. Stanford, CA: Stanford University Press, pp. 1–22.

Adler, A., (2016). Teaching Well-being Increases Academic Performance: Evidence from Bhutan, Mexico, and Peru. Available at: https://repository.upenn.edu/edissertations/1572/.

Aknin, L. B., Barrington-Leigh, C. P., Dunn, E. W., Helliwell, J. F., Burns, J., Biswas-Diener, R., . . . and Norton, M. I. (2013). Prosocial Spending and Well-being: Cross-cultural Evidence for a Psychological Universal. *Journal of Personality and Social Psychology* 104(4): 635.

Alexandrova, A. (2016). Is Well-being Measurable After All? *Public Health Ethics* 10(June): 1–15.

Alpizar, F., Carlsson, F., and Johansson-Stenman, O. (2005). How Much Do We Care about Absolute versus Relative Income and Consumption? *Journal of Economic Behavior and Organization* 56(3): 405–21.

Anderson, C., Kraus, M. W., Galinsky, A. D., and Keltner, D. (2012). The Local-ladder Effect: Social Status and Subjective Well-being. *Psychological Science* 23(7): 764–71.

Ashraf, N., Bandiera, O., and Jack, K. (2014). No margin, no mission? A field experiment on incentives for public service delivery. *Journal of Public Economics* 120: 1-17.

Atkinson, S., Bagnall, A. M., Corcoran, R., South, J., and Curtis, S. (2020). Being Well Together: Individual Subjective and Community Wellbeing. *Journal of Happiness Studies* 21(5): 1903–21.

Bagnall, A., South, J., Mitchell, B., Pilkington, G., Newton, R., and Salvatore, D. M. (2017). Systematic Scoping Review of Indicators of Community Wellbeing in the UK. What Works Centre for Wellbeing, London.

Bagnall, A. M., South, J., Southby, K., Di Martino, S., Pilkington, G., Mitchell, B., . . . and Corcoran, R. (2019). A Systematic Review of Interventions in Community

Infrastructure (Places and Spaces) to Boost Social Relations and Community Wellbeing. What Works Centre for Wellbeing, London.

Banks, O. (1978). School and Society. In L. Barton and R. Meighan (eds), *Sociological Interpretations of Schooling and Classrooms: A Reappraisal*. Driffield: Studies in Education Ltd., pp. 37–46.

Barankay, I. (2011). Rankings and Social Tournaments: Evidence froma Crowd-Sourcing Experiment. *Wharton Faculty Research Management Papers* 9-12-2011.

Barrett, L. F., Adolphs, R., Marsella, S., Martinez, A. M., and Pollack, S. D. (2019). Emotional Expressions Reconsidered: Challenges to Inferring Emotion From Human Facial Movements. *Psychological Science in the Public Interest* 20(11), 1–68.

Batz-Barbarich, C., Tay, L., Kuykendall, L., and Cheung, H. K. (2018). A Meta-analysis of Gender Differences in Subjective Well-being: Estimating Effect Sizes and Associations with Gender Inequality. *Psychological Science* 29(9), 1491–1503.

Béllet, C., and Frijters, P. (2019). Big Data and Wellbeing. *World Happiness Report 2019*. New York: Sustainable Development Solutions Network.

Benjamin, D. J., Heffetz, O., Kimball, M. S., and Rees-Jones, A. (2012). What Do You Think Would Make You Happier? What Do You Think You Would Choose? *American Economic Review* 102(5): 2083–110.

Benjamin, D. J., Heffetz, O., Kimball, M. S., and Szembrot, N. (2014). Beyond Happiness and Satisfaction: Toward Well-being Indices Based on Stated Preference. *American Economic Review* 104(9): 2698–735.

Bjørnskov, C. (2010). How Comparable Are the Gallup World Poll Life Satisfaction Data? *Journal of Happiness Studies* 11(1): 41–60.

Blanchflower, D. G., and Oswald, A. J. (2004). Well-being over Time in Britain and the USA. *Journal of Public Economics* 88(7–8): 1359–86.

Bond, T. N., and Lang, K. (2019). The Sad Truth about Happiness Scales. *Journal of Political Economy* 127(4): 1629–40.

Bonin, E. M., Beecham, J., Swift, N., Raikundalia, S., and Brown, J. (2014). Psycho-educational CBT-Insomnia Workshops in the Community: A Cost-effectiveness Analysis alongside a Randomised Controlled Trial. *Behaviour Research and Therapy* 55C(1): 40–7.

Bowler, D. E., Buyung-Ali, L. M., Knight, T. M., and Pullin, A. S. (2010). A Systematic Review of Evidence for the Added Benefits to Health of Exposure to Natural Environments. *BMC Public Health* 10(1): 456.

Bradler, C., Dur, R., Neckermann, S., and Non, A. (2016). Employee Recognition and Performance: A Field Experiment. *ZEW - Centre for European Economic Research Discussion Paper* 13–017.

Brosnan, S. F., and De Waal, F. B. (2003). Monkeys Reject Unequal Pay. *Nature* 425 (6955): 297–9.

Burns, T., Catty, J., Becker, T., Drake, R. E., Fioritti, A., Knapp, M., Lauber, C., Rössler, W., Tomov, T., van Busschbach, J., White, S., and Wiersma, D. (2007). The

Effectiveness of Supported Employment for People with Severe Mental Illness: A Randomised Controlled Trial. *The Lancet* 370(9593): 1146–52.

Bursztyn, L., and Jensen, R. (2015). How Does Peer Pressure Affect Educational Investments? *Quarterly Journal of Economics* 130(3): 1329–1367.

Bursztyn, L., Ferman, B., Fiorin, S., Kanz, M., and Rao, G. (2018). Status Goods: Experimental Evidence from Platinum Credit Cards. *Quarterly Journal of Economics* 133(3): 1561–1595.

Bursztyn, L., Fiorin, S., Gottlied, D., and Kanz, M. (2019). Moral Incentives in Credit Card Debt Repayment: Evidence from a Field Experiment. *Journal of Political Economy* 127(4): 1641–1683.

Bursztyn, L., Fujiwara, T., and Pallais, A. (2017). 'Acting Wife': Marriage Market Incentives and Labor Market Investments. *American Economic Review* 107(11): 3288–3319.

Buss, D. M. (2016). *The Evolution of Desire: Strategies of Human Mating.* London: Hachette.

Butera, L., Metcalfe, R., Morrison, W., and Taubinsky, D. (2019). The Deadweight Loss of Social Recognition. *NBER Working Paper* 25637.

Bright, G. A., Connors, E., and Grice, J. (2019). Measuring natural capital: Towards accounts for the UK and a basis for improved decision-making. *Oxford Review of Economic Policy* 35(1): 88–108.

Cantril, H. (1965). *The Pattern of Human Concerns.* New Brunswick: Rutgers University Press.

Carr, D., Freedman, V. A., Cornman, J. C., and Schwarz, N. (2014). Happy Marriage, Happy Life? Marital Quality and Subjective Well-being in Later Life. *Journal of Marriage and Family* 76(5): 930–48.

Cesur, R., Güneş, P. M., Tekin, E., and Ulker, A. (2017). The Value of Socialized Medicine: The Impact of Universal Primary Healthcare Provision on Mortality Rates in Turkey. *Journal of Public Economics* 150: 75–93.

Chancellor, J., Margolis, S., Jacobs Bao, K., and Lyubomirsky, S. (2018). Everyday Prosociality in the Workplace: The Reinforcing Benefits of Giving, Getting, and Glimpsing. *Emotion* 18(4): 507–17.

Chen, L.-Y., Oparina, E., Powdthavee, N., and Srisuma, S. (2019). Have Econometric Analyses of Happiness Data Been Futile? A Simple Truth about Happiness Scales. *IZA Discussion Paper* 12,151.

Chida, Y., and Steptoe, A. (2008). Positive Psychological Well-being and Mortality: A Quantitative Review of Prospective Observational Studies. *Psychosomatic Medicine* 70(7): 741–56.

Chyung, S. Y., Swanson, I., Roberts, K., & Hankinson, A. (2018). Evidence-based survey design: The use of continuous rating scales in surveys. *Performance Improvement* 57(5), 38–48.

Clark, A. E., and Oswald, A. J. (1994). Unhappiness and Unemployment. *Economic Journal* 104(424): 648–59.

Chodosh, S. (2017). Dogs and Wolves Both Get Sad When You Do Not Treat Them Fairly. *Popular Science*. Available at: https://www.popsci.com/dogs-wolves-inequity.

Clark, A. E. (2016). SWB as a Measure of Individual Well-being. In M. Adler and M. Fleurbaey (eds), *Oxford Handbook of Wellbeing and Public Policy*. Oxford: Oxford University Press, pp. 518–52.

Clark, A. E. (2018). Four Decades of the Economics of Happiness: Where Next? *Review of Income and Wealth* 64(2): 245–69.

Clark, A. E., Diener. E., Georgellis, Y., and Lucas, R. E. (2008). Lags and Leads in Life Satisfaction: A Test of the Baseline Hypothesis. *Economic Journal* 118(529): F222–F243.

Clark, A. E., Flèche, S., Layard, R., Powdthavee, N., and Ward, G. (2018). *The Origins of Happiness: The Science of Wellbeing over the Life Course*. Princeton, NJ: Princeton University Press.

Clark, A. E., Frijters, P., and Shields, M. A. (2008). A Survey of the Income Happiness Gradient. *Journal of Economic Literature* 46(1): 95–144.

Clark, D. M. (2018). Realizing the Mass Public Benefit of Evidence-based Psychological Therapies: The IAPT Program. *Annual Review of Clinical Psychology* 14: 159–83.

Claxton, K., Martin, S., Soares, M., Rice, N., Spackman, E., Hinde, S., . . . and Sculpher, M. (2015). Methods for the Estimation of the National Institute for Health and Care Excellence Cost-effectiveness Threshold. *Health Technology Assessment* 19(14): 1.

Coupe, T., and Obrizan, M. (2016). The Impact of War on Happiness: The Case of Ukraine. *Journal of Economic Behavior and Organization* 132: 228–42.

Cummins, R. A. (2003). Normative Life Satisfaction: Measurement Issues and a Homeostatic Model. *Social Indicators Research* 64(2): 225–56.

Cunha, F., and Heckman, J. J. (2007). The Technology of Skill Formation. *American Economic Review* 97(2): 31–47.

Cunha, F., Heckman, J. J., and Schennach, S. M. (2010). Estimating the Technology of Cognitive and Noncognitive Skill Formation. *Econometrica* 78: 883–931.

Currie, A., Shields, M. A., and Price, S. W. (2007). The Child Health/Family Income Gradient: Evidence from England. *Journal of Health Economics* 26(2): 213–32.

Dahl, G. B., Felfe, C., Frijters, P, and Rainer, H. (2020). Caught between Cultures: Unintended Consequences of Improving Opportunity for Immigrant Girls. *NBER Working Paper* 26674.

Deaton, A. (2012). The Financial Crisis and the Wellbeing of Americans 2011. OEP Hicks Lecture. *Oxford Economic Papers* 64(1): 1–26.

De Neve, J. E., and Oswald, A. J. (2012). Estimating the Influence of Life Satisfaction and Positive Affect on Later Income Using Sibling Fixed Effects. *Proceedings of the National Academy of Sciences* 109(49): 19953–8.

Department of Health and Department of Education (2017). Transforming Children and Young People's Mental Health Provision: A Green Paper Impact Assessment (IA). Available at: https://assets.publishing.service.gov.uk/government/uploads/system/uploads/attachment_data/file/664442/MHGP_IA.pdf.

Diener, E., and Chan, M. Y. (2011). Happy People Live Longer: Subjective Well-being Contributes to Health and Longevity. *Applied Psychology: Health and Well-Being* 3 (1): 1–43.

Di Tella, R., MacCulloch, R., and Oswald, A. (2003). The Macroeconomics of Happiness. *Review of Economics and Statistics* 85(4): 809–27.

Dolan, P., and Kavetsos, G. (2016). Happy Talk: Mode of Administration Effects on Subjective Well-Being. *Journal of Happiness Studies* 17(3): 1273–91.

Dolan, P., and Laffan, K. (2016). Bad Air Days: The Effects of Air Quality on Different Measures of Subjective Well-being. *Journal of Benefit-Cost Analysis* 7 (1): 147–95.

Dulleck, U., and Kerschbamer, R. (2006). On Doctors, Mechanics, and Computer Specialists: The Economics of Credence Goods. *Journal of Economic Literature* 44 (1): 5–42.

Dunn, E. W., Aknin, L. B., and Norton, M. I. (2008). Spending Money on Others Promotes Happiness. *Science* 319(5870): 1687–8.

Easterlin, R. A., Wang, F., and Wang, S. (2017). Growth and Happiness in China, 1990–2015. *World Happiness Report 2017*. New York: Sustainable Development Solutions Network.

Easterlin, R. (1974). Does Economic Growth Improve the Human Lot? Some Empirical Evidence. In R. David and R. Reder (eds), *Nations and Households in Economic Growth: Essays in Honor of Moses Abramovitz*. New York: Academic Press, pp. 89–125.

Easterlin, R. A. (2015). Happiness and Economic Growth—The Evidence. In W. Glatzer, L. Camfield, V. Møller, and M. Rojas (eds), *Global Handbook of Quality of Life*. International Handbooks of Quality-of-Life. Dordrecht: Springer, pp. 283–99.

Ellemers, N., and Haslam, S. A. (2012). Social Identity Theory. In P. A. M. Van Lange, A. W. Kruglanski, and E. T. Higgins (eds), *Handbook of Theories of Social Psychology*. Thousand Oaks, CA: Sage Publications, pp. 379–98.

Ellemers, N., De Gilder, D., and Haslam, S. A. (2004). Motivating Individuals and Groups at Work: A Social Identity Perspective on Leadership and Group Performance. *Academy of Management Review* 29(3): 459–78.

Ellman, M. (1994). The Increase in Death and Disease under 'Katastroika'. *Cambridge Journal of Economics* 18(4): 329–55.

Etile, F., Frijters, P., Johnston, D., and Shields, M. (2017). Modelling Heterogeneity in the Resilience to Major Socioeconomic Life Events. *PSE Working Papers* halshs-01485989.

Falk, A., and Graeber, T. (2020). Delayed Negative Effects of Prosocial Spending on Happiness. *Proceedings of the National Academy of Sciences* 117(12): 6463–8.

Fergusson, D., and Horwood, L. (2001). The Christchurch Health and Development Study: Review of Findings on Child and Adolescent Mental Health. *Australian and New Zealand Journal of Psychiatry* 35(3): 287–96.

Ferrer-i-Carbonell, A., and Frijters, P. (2004). The Effect of Methodology on the Determinants of Happiness. *Economic Journal* 114: 641–59.

Finkelstein, A., Taubman, S., Wright, B., Bernstein, M., Gruber, J., Newhouse, J., Allen, H., and Baicker, K. (2012). The Oregon Health Insurance Experiment: Evidence from the First Year. *Quarterly Journal of Economics* 127(3): 1057–106.

Fischer, E. F. (2014). The Good Life: Aspiration, Dignity, and the Anthropology of Wellbeing. Stanford, CA: Stanford University Press.

Fitoussi, J.-P., and Durand, M. (2018a). Beyond GDP: Measuring What Counts for Economic and Social Performance. Paris: OECD Publishing. Available at: https://www.oecd.org/corruption/beyond-gdp-9789264307292-en.htm.

Fitoussi, J.-P., and Durand, M. (2018b). Beyond GDP: Advancing Research on Well-being Metrics beyond GDP. Paris: OECD Publishing. Available at: http://www.oecd.org/publications/for-good-measure-9,789,264,307,278-en.htm.

Flèche, S., and Smith, C. (2017). Time Use Surveys and Experienced Wellbeing in France and the United States. *OECD Statistics Working Paper* 2017/7.

Fleurbaey, M., and Blanchet, D. (2013). *Beyond GDP: Measuring Welfare and Assessing Sustainability*. Oxford: Oxford University Press.

Fliessbach, K., Weber, B., Trautner, P., Dohmen, T., Sunde, U., Elger, C. E., and Falk, A. (2007). Social Comparison Affects Reward-related Brain Activity in the Human Ventral Striatum. *Science* 318: 1305–8.

Foa, R. S., and Ekiert, G. (2017). The Weakness of Postcommunist Civil Society Reassessed. *European Journal of Political Research* 56: 419–39.

Fowler, J. H., and Christakis, N. A. (2008). Dynamic Spread of Happiness in a Large Social Network: Longitudinal Analysis over 20 Years in the Framingham Heart Study. *BMJ* 337: a2338.

Frijters, P., Clark, A. E., Krekel, C., and Layard, R. (2020). A Happy Choice: Wellbeing as the Goal of Government. *Behavioural Public Policy* 4(2): 126–65.

Frijters, P., and Foster, G. (2013). *Economic Theory of Greed, Love, Groups, and Networks*. Cambridge: Cambridge University Press.

Frijters, P., Haisken-DeNew, J. P., and Shields, M. A. (2004). Money Does Matter! Evidence from Increasing Real Income and Life Satisfaction in East Germany Following Reunification. *American Economic Review* 94(3): 730–40.

Frijters, P., Johnston, D., and Shields, M. A. (2011). Happiness Dynamics with Quarterly Life Event Data. *Scandinavian Journal of Economics* 113(1): 190–211.

Frijters, P., and Leigh, A. (2009). Materialism on the March: From Conspicuous Leisure to Conspicuous Consumption. *Journal of Socio-Economics* 37(5): 1937–45.

Frijters, P., and Meng, X. (2012). Are Optimistic Expectations Keeping the Chinese Happy? *Journal of Economic Behaviour & Organisation* 81(1): 159–71.

Fujiwara, D., Lawton, R. N., and MacKerron, G. (2017). Experience-sampling in and around Airports: Momentary Subjective Wellbeing, Airports, and Aviation Noise in England. *Transportation Research Part D: Transport and Environment* 56: 43–54.

Galiani, S., Gertler, P. J., Undurraga, R., Cooper, R., Martínez, S., and Ross, A. (2017). Shelter from the Storm: Upgrading Housing Infrastructure in Latin American Slums. *Journal of Urban Economics* 98(C): 187–213.

Gallie, D., Paugam, S., and Jacobs, S. (2003). Unemployment, Poverty and Social Isolation: Is There a Vicious Circle of Social Exclusion? *European Societies* 5(1): 1–32.

Gardner, J., and Oswald, A. J. (2007). Money and mental wellbeing: a longitudinal study of medium-sized lottery wins. *Journal of Health Economics*: 26(1), 49–60.

Gazzaniga, M., and Ivry, R. B. (2013). *Cognitive Neuroscience: The Biology of the Mind.* Fourth International Student Edition. New York: W. W. Norton.

Geenen, N. Y., Hohelüchter, M., Langholf, V., and Walther, E. (2014). The Beneficial Effects of Prosocial Spending on Happiness: Work Hard, Make Money, and Spend It on Others? *Journal of Positive Psychology* 9(3): 204–8.

Gerber, A. S., Green, D. P., and Larimer, C. W. (2008). Social pressure and voter turnout: Evidence from a large-scale field experiment. *American Political Science Review* 102(1): 33–48.

Glassdoor (n.d.). Available at: https://www.glassdoor.co.uk/Reviews/index.htm.

Gustavson, K., Røysamb, E., Borren, I., Torvik, F. A., and Karevold, E. (2016). Life Satisfaction in Close Relationships: Findings from a Longitudinal Study. *Journal of Happiness Studies* 17(3): 1293–311.

Hanniball, K. B., Aknin, L. B., Douglas, K. S., and Viljoen, J. L. (2019). Does Helping Promote Well-being in At-risk Youth and Ex-offender Samples? *Journal of Experimental Social Psychology* 82: 307–17.

Hargreaves, A. (1978). The Significance of Classroom Coping Strategies. In L. Barton and R. Meighan (eds), *Sociological Interpretations of Schooling and Classrooms: A Reappraisal.* Driffield: Studies in Education Ltd., pp. 17–46.

Hargreaves, D. H. (1978). Whatever Happened to Symbolic Interactionism. In L. Barton and R. Meighan (eds), *Sociological Interpretations of Schooling and Classrooms: A Reappraisal.* Driffield: Studies in Education Ltd., pp. 7–22.

Haslam, S. A. (2004). *Psychology in Organizations: The Social Identity Approach.* Thousand Oaks, CA: SAGE Publications Inc.

Haslam, S. A., Reicher, S. D., and Platow, M. J. (2010). *The New Psychology of Leadership: Identity, Influence and Power.* London: Psychology Press.

Haushofer, J., and Shapiro, J. (2016). The Short-term Impact of Unconditional Cash Transfers to the Poor: Experimental Evidence from Kenya. *Quarterly Journal of Economics* 131(4): 1973–2042.

Heffetz, O. (2011). A Test of Conspicuous Consumption: Visibility and Income Elasticities. *Review of Economics and Statistics* 93(4): 1101–17.

Helliwell, J. F., and Wang, S. (2010). Trust and Well-being. *NBER Working Paper* 15911.

Helliwell, J. F., and Wang, S. (2014). Weekends and Subjective Well-being. *Social Indicators Research* 116(2): 389–407.

Huang, L., Frijters, P., Dalziel, K., and Clarke, P. (2018). Life satisfaction, QALYs, and the monetary value of health. *Social Science & Medicine* 211, 131–136.

Huber M. (1999). Health Expenditure Trends in OECD Countries, 1970–1997. *Health Care Financing Review* 21(2): 99–117.

Institute for Government (n.d.). Available at: https://www.instituteforgovernment.org.uk/explainers/location-of-civil-service.

Jakobsson, U., Hallberg, I. R., and Westergren, A. (2004). Overall and Health-related Quality of Life among the Oldest Old in Pain. *Quality of Life Research* 13(1): 125–36.

Johnston, D. W., Propper, C., and Shields, M. A. (2009). Comparing Subjective and Objective Measures of Health: Evidence from Hypertension for the Income/Health Gradient. *Journal of Health Economics* 28(3): 540–52.

Johnston, D. W., Shields, M. A., and Suziedelyte, A. (2018). Victimisation, Well-being and Compensation: Using Panel Data to Estimate the Costs of Violent Crime. *Economic Journal* 128: 1545–69.

Kahneman, D., Krueger, A., Schkade, D., Schwarz, N., and Stone, A. (2004). A Survey Method for Characterizing Daily Life Experience: The Day Reconstruction Method. *Science* 306: 1776–80.

Kapteyn, A. (1977). *A Theory of Preference Formation*. PhD Thesis.

Kapteyn, A., Montgomery, M., Smith, J. P., and A. van Soest (2019). Life Satisfaction within and across Countries: The Role of Societal Capital and Relative Income. Keynote address at the SABE conference in Dublin, 2 September.

Karing, A. (2019). Social Signaling and Childhood Immunization: A Field Experiment in Sierra Leone. *mimeo*.

Keller, E. J. (2014). *Identity, Citizenship, and Political Conflict in Africa*. Bloomington, IN: Indiana University Press.

Kesebir, P., and Diener, E. (2009). In Pursuit of Happiness: Empirical Answers to Philosophical Questions. In *The Science of Well-being: The Collected Works of Ed Diener*. Dordrecht: Springer, pp. 59–74.

Keyes, C. L. M., and Haidt, J. (2003). *Flourishing: Positive Psychology and the Life Well-lived*. Washington, DC: American Psychological Association.

Kim, S., and Koh, K. (2018). Does Health Insurance Make People Happier? Evidence from Massachusetts' Healthcare Reform. *IZA Discussion Paper* 11879.

Knabe, A., Rätzel, S., Schöb, R., and Weimann, J. (2010). Dissatisfied with Life But Having a Good Day: Time-use and Well-being of the Unemployed. *Economic Journal* 120(547): 867–89.

Koivumaa-Honkanen, H., Honkanen, R., Viinamäki, H., Heikkilä, K., Kaprio, J., and Koskenvuo, M. (2000). Self-reported Life Satisfaction and 20-year Mortality in Healthy Finnish Adults. *American Journal of Epidemiology* 152(10): 983–91.

Krekel, C., Ward, G., and De Neve, J.-E. (2019). What Makes for a Good Job? Evidence Using Subjective Wellbeing Data. In M. Rojas (ed). *The Economics of Happiness*. Berlin: Springer, pp. 241–68.

Krekel, C., De Neve, J. E., Fancourt, D., and Layard, R (2020). A Local Community Course That Raises Mental Well-being and Pro-Sociality. *CEP Discussion Paper* 1671.

Krueger, A., and Schkade, D. (2008). The Reliability of Subjective Well-being Measures. *Journal of Public Economics* 92: 1833–45.

Kuhn, P., Kooreman, P., Soetevent, A., and Kapteyn, A. (2011). The Effects of Lottery Prizes on Winners and their Neighbors: Evidence from the Dutch Postcode Lottery. *American Economic Review* 101(5): 2226–47.

Lane, T. (2017). How does happiness relate to economic behaviour? A review of the literature. *Journal of Economic Behavior & Organization* 68: 62–78.

Layard, R. (2016). Measuring Wellbeing and Cost-effectiveness Analysis Using Subjective Wellbeing. What Works Centre for Wellbeing. Available at: https://whatworkswellbeing.files.wordpress.com/2016/08/common-currency-measuring-wellbeing-series-1-dec-2016.pdf.

Layard, R. (2018). Mental Illness Destroys Happiness and Is Costless to Treat. *Global Happiness Policy Report*. Global Happiness Council, pp. 26–51.

Layard, R. (2020). *Happier*. London: Penguin Random House.

Layard, R., Chisholm, D., Patel, V., and Saxena, S. (2013). Mental Illness and Unhappiness. In J. F. Helliwell, R. Layard, and J. D. Sachs (eds), *World Happiness Report* 2013. New York: Sustainable Development Solutions Network, pp. 38–53.

Leijten, P., Gardner, F., Landau, S., Harris, V., Mann, J., Hutchings, J., . . . and Scott, S. (2018). Research Review: Harnessing the Power of Individual Participant Data in a Meta-analysis of the Benefits and Harms of the Incredible Years Parenting Program. *Journal of Child Psychology and Psychiatry* 59(2): 99–109.

Leijten, P., Raaijmakers, M. A., de Castro, B. O., and Matthys, W. (2013). Does Socioeconomic Status Matter? A Meta-analysis on Parent Training Effectiveness for Disruptive Child Behavior. *Journal of Clinical Child and Adolescent Psychology* 42(3): 384–92.

Lindqvist, E., Östling, R., and Cesarini, D. (2020). Long-Run Effects of Lottery Wealth on Psychological Well-Being. Review of Economic Studies: 87(6), 2703–26.

Lim, H. E. (2008). The Use of Different Happiness Rating Scales: Bias and Comparison Problem? *Social Indicators Research* 87(2): 259–67.

Lipset, S. M. (1960). *Political Man: The Social Bases of Politics*. Garden City, NY: Doubleday.

Llena-Nozal, A., Martin, N., and Murtin, F. (2019). The Economy of Well-being: Creating Opportunities for People's Well-being and Economic Growth. *OECD Statistics Working Paper* 2019(2). Available at: http://www.oecd.org/officialdocuments/publicdisplaydocumentpdf/?cote=SDD/DOC(2019)2&docLanguage=En.

Lomas, J., Martin, S., and Claxton, K. (2019). Estimating the Marginal Productivity of the English National Health Service from 2003 to 2012. *Value in Health* 22(9): 995–1002.

Lordan, G., and McGuire, A. (2019). Widening the High School Curriculum to Include Soft Skill Training: Impacts on Health, Behaviour, Emotional Wellbeing and Occupational Aspirations. *IZA Discussion Paper* 12439.

Lucas, R. E., Clark, A. E., Georgellis Y., and Diener, E. (2004). Unemployment Alters the Set Point for Life Satisfaction. *Psychological Science* 15(1): 8–13.

Lucas, R. E., and Donnellan, M. B. (2012). Estimating the Reliability of Single-item Life Satisfaction Measures: Results from Four National Panel Studies. *Social Indicators Research* 105: 323–31.

Luechinger, S., (2009). Valuing Air Quality Using the Life Satisfaction Approach. *Economic Journal* 119(536): 482–515.

Lupton, R., and Burchardt, T. (eds) (2016). *Social Policy in a Cold Climate: Policies and their Consequences since the Crisis.* Bristol: Policy Press.

Mandel, A. (2018). Why Nobel Prize Winner Daniel Kahneman Gave Up on Happiness. *Haaretz.* Available at: https://www.haaretz.com/israel-news/.premium.MAGAZINE-why-nobel-prize-winner-daniel-kahneman-gave-up-on-happiness-1.6528513.

Margelisch, K., Schneewind, K. A., Violette, J., and Perrig-Chiello, P. (2017). Marital Stability, Satisfaction and Well-being in Old Age: Variability and Continuity in Long-term Continuously Married Older Persons. *Aging and Mental Health* 21(4): 389–98.

Matossian, M. K. (1985). Death in London, 1750–1909. *The Journal of Interdisciplinary History* 16(2): 183–97.

Mattan, B. D., Kubota, J. T., and Cloutier, J. (2017). How Social Status Shapes Person Perception and Evaluation: A Social Neuroscience Perspective. *Perspectives on Psychological Science* 12(3): 468–507.

Matzler, K., and Renzl, B. (2006). The Relationship between Interpersonal Trust, Employee Satisfaction, and Employee Loyalty. *Total Quality Management and Business Excellence* 17: 1261–71.

Mazaheri, M., and Theuns, P. (2009). Effects of Varying Response Formats on Self-ratings of Life-Satisfaction. *Social Indicators Research* 90(3): 381.

McKee, L., and Bell, C. (1986). His Unemployment, her Problem: The Domestic and Marital Consequences of Male Unemployment. In S. Allen, S. Waton, K. Purcell, and S. Wood (eds), *The Experience of Unemployment.* Basingstoke: Macmillan.

McKeown, T., and Record, R. G. (1962). Reasons for the Decline of Mortality in England and Wales during the Nineteenth Century. *Population Studies* 16(2): 94–122.

Meisenberg, G., and Woodley, M. A. (2015). Gender Differences in Subjective Wellbeing and their Relationships with Gender Equality. *Journal of Happiness Studies* 16(6): 1539–55.

Montgomery, C. (2013). *Happy City: Transforming Our Lives Through Urban Design.* London: Penguin.

Mousteri, V., Daly, M., and Delaney, L. (2018). The Scarring Effect of Unemployment on Psychological Well-being across Europe. *Social Science Research* 72: 146–69.

Mujcic, R., and Frijters, P. (2013). Economic Choices and Status: Measuring Preferences for Income Rank. *Oxford Economic Papers* 65(1): 47–73.

Odermatt, R., and Stutzer, A. (2015). Smoking Bans, Cigarette Prices and Life Satisfaction. *Journal of Health Economics* 44: 176–94.

O'Donnell, G., Deaton, A., Durand, M., Halpern, D., and Layard, R. (2014). Wellbeing and Policy. Legatum Institute, London.

OECD (2013), How's Life? 2013: Measuring Well-being. Paris: OECD Publishing. Available at: http://dx.doi.org/10.1787/9789264201392-en.

OECD (n.d.). Health at a Glance 2017: OECD Indicators. Paris: OECD Publishing. Available at: https://www.oecd.org/els/health-systems/Health-at-a-Glance-2017-Chartset.pdf.

Office for National Statistics (2015). English Life Tables No.17: 2010 to 2012. Available at: https://www.ons.gov.uk/peoplepopulationandcommunity/birthsdeathsandmarriages/lifeexpectancies/bulletins/englishlifetablesno17/latest.

Office for National Statistics. (2017). National Life Tables, UK: 2014 to 2016. Available at: https://www.ons.gov.uk/peoplepopulationandcommunity/birthsdeathsandmarriages/lifeexpectancies/bulletins/nationallifetablesunitedkingdom/2014to2016#life-expectancy-at-birth.

Oishi, S., Schimmack, U., and Colcombe, S. J. (2003). The Contextual and Systematic Nature of Life Satisfaction Judgments. *Journal of Experimental Social Psychology* 39 (3): 232–47.

Oswald, A. J., and Powdthavee, N. (2008). Death, Happiness, and the Calculation of Compensatory Damages. *Journal of Legal Studies* 37(S2): S217–S251.

Oswald, A. J., Proto, E., and Sgroi, D. (2015). Happiness and Productivity. *Journal of Labor Economics* 33(4): 789–822.

Parducci, A. (1995). *Happiness, Pleasure, and Judgment: The Contextual Theory and its Applications*. Hillsdale, NJ: Lawrence Erlbaum Associates.

Peasgood, T., Mukuria, C., Karimi, M., and Brazier, J. (2018). Eliciting Preference Weights for Life Satisfaction: A Feasibility Study. Mimeo.

Perez-Truglia, R. (2018). The Effects of Income Transparency on Wellbeing: Evidence from a Natural Experiment. *NBER Working Paper* 25622.

Perez-Truglia, R., and Guillermo, C. (2017). Partisan Interactions: Evidence from a Field Experiment in the United States. *Journal of Political Economy* 125(4), 1208–43.

Perez-Truglia, R., and Troiano, U. (2018). Shaming tax delinquents. *Journal of Public Economics* 167, 120–37.

Powdthavee, N. (2008). Putting a Price Tag on Friends, Relatives, and Neighbours: Using Surveys of Life Satisfaction to Value Social Relationships. *Journal of Socio-Economics* 37(4): 1459–80.

Proto, E., and Rustichini, A. (2013). A Reassessment of the Relationship between GDP and Life Satisfaction. *PLOS ONE* 8(11): e79358.

Public Health England (2017). Life Expectancy and Healthy Life Expectancy. In *Health Profile for England: 2017*. Available at: https://www.gov.uk/government/publications/health-profile-for-england/chapter-1-life-expectancy-and-healthy-life-expectancy.

Ramsey, F. P. (1928). A Mathematical Theory of Saving. *Economic Journal* 38(152): 543–59.

Rojas M., and García Vega J. J. (2017). Wellbeing in Latin America. In R. Estes and M. Sirgy (eds), *The Pursuit of Human Wellbeing*. International Handbooks of Quality-of-Life. Dordrecht: Springer, pp. 217–55.

Rollman, B., Belnap, B., Mazumdar, S., Houck, P., Zhu, F., Gardner, W., Reynolds III, C., Schulberg, H., and Shear, M. (2005). A Randomized Trial to Improve the Quality of Treatment for Panic and Generalized Anxiety Disorders in Primary Care. *Archives of General Psychiatry* 62: 1332–42.

Sandvik, E., Diener, E., and Seidlitz, L. (1993). Subjective Well-being: The Convergence and Stability of Self-report and Non-self-report Measures. *Journal of Personality* 61: 317–42.

Schwarz, N., Strack, F., Hippler, H. J., and Bishop, G. (1991). The Impact of Administration Mode on Response Effects in Survey Measurement. *Applied Cognitive Psychology* 5(3): 193–212.

Sen, A. (1983). Poor, Relatively Speaking. *Oxford Economic Papers* 35(2): 153–69.

Smith, A. (1759). *Theory of Moral Sentiments*.

Steptoe, A., and Wardle, J. (2011). Positive Affect Measured Using Ecological Momentary Assessment and Survival in Older Men and Women. *Proceedings of the National Academy of Sciences* 108(45): 18244–8.

Stergiopoulos, V., Gozdzik, A., Misir, V., Skosireva, A., Connelly, J., Sarang, A., Whisler, A., Hwang, S. W., O'Campo, P., and McKenzie, K. (2015). Effectiveness of Housing First with Intensive Case Management in an Ethnically Diverse Sample of Homeless Adults with Mental Illness: A Randomized Controlled Trial. *PLOS ONE* 10(7): e0130281.

Stevenson, B., and Wolfers, J. (2009). The Paradox of Declining Female Happiness. *American Economic Journal: Economic Policy* 1(2): 190–225.

Stiglitz, J. E., Sen, A., and Fitoussi, J. (2011). Report by the Commission on the Measurement of Economic Performance and Social Progress. Brussels: European Commission.

Strack, F., Martin, L. L., and Schwarz, N. (1988). Priming and Communication: Social Determinants of Information Use in Judgments of Life Satisfaction. *European Journal of Social Psychology* 18(5): 429–42.

Strack, F., Schwarz, N., Chassein, B., Kern, D., and Wagner, D. (1990). Salience of Comparison Standards and the Activation of Social Norms: Consequences for

Judgements of Happiness and their Communication. *British Journal of Social Psychology* 29(4): 303–14.

Suh, E. M., Diener, E. D., and Updegraff, J. A. (2008). From Culture to Priming Conditions: Self-construal Influences on Life Satisfaction Judgments. *Journal of Cross-Cultural Psychology* 39(1): 3–15.

Suh, E. M., and Oishi, S. (2002). Subjective Wellbeing across Cultures. *Online Readings in Psychology and Culture* 10(1).

Tov, W., and Diener, E. (2009). The Well-being of Nations: Linking Together Trust, Cooperation, and Democracy. In E. Diener (ed), *The Science of Well-Being*. Dordrecht: Springer, pp. 155–73.

Treasury, N. Z. (2019). The Wellbeing Budget. Available at: https://treasury.govt.nz/sites/default/files/2019-05/b19-wellbeing-budget.pdf.

Turner, J. C., Oakes, P. J., Haslam, S., and McGarty, C. (1994). Self and Collective: Cognition and Social Context. *Personality and Social Psychology Bulletin* 20: 454–63.

Van Praag, B., and Baarsma, B. (2005). Using Happiness Surveys to Value Intangibles: The Case of Airport Noise. *Economic Journal* 115(500): 224–46.

Veblen, T. (1899). *The Theory of the Leisure Class*. New York: Macmillan.

Veenhoven, R. (2018). Subjective Well-being in Nations. In E. Diener, S. Oishi, and L. Tay (eds), *Handbook of Well-being*. Salt Lake City, UT: DEF Publishers, pp. 1–15.

Von Hippel, W., and Trivers, R. (2011). Reflections on Self-deception. *Behavioral and Brain Sciences* 34(1): 41–56.

Ward, G. (2019). Happiness and Voting Behavior. In J. F. Helliwell, R. Layard, and J. D. Sachs (eds), *World Happiness Report 2019*. New York: Sustainable Development Solutions Network, pp. 46–65.

Weber, Max (1895/1994). The Nations State and Economic Policy (Freiburg Address). In P. Lassman and R. Speirs (ed. and trans.), *Weber: Political Writings*. Cambridge: Cambridge University Press.

Welsh Government Social Research (2015). Children and Young People Wellbeing Monitor for Wales 2015. Available at: https://dera.ioe.ac.uk/24929/3/151211-children-young-people-wellbeing-monitor-2015-en_Redacted.pdf.

Whillans, A. V., Dunn, E. W., Sandstrom, G. M., Dickerson, S. S., and Madden, K. M. (2016). Is Spending Money on Others Good for your Heart? *Health Psychology* 35 (6): 574–83.

Whillans, A. V., Dunn, E. W., Smeets, P., Bekkers, R., and Norton, M. I. (2017). Buying Time Promotes Happiness. *Proceedings of the National Academy of Sciences* 114 (32): 8523–27.

Wiles, N., Thomas, L., Turner, N., Garfield, K., Kounali, D., Campbell, J., Kessler, D., Kuyken, W., Lewis, G., Morrison, J., Williams, C., Peters, T., and Hollinghurst, S. (2016). Long-term Effectiveness and Cost-effectiveness of Cognitive Behavioural Therapy as an Adjunct to Pharmacology for Treatment-resistant Depression in

Primary Care: Follow-up of the CoBalT Randomised Controlled Trial. *Lancet Psychiatry* 3:137–44.

Wilkinson, R., and Pickett, K. (2010). *The Spirit Level: Why Equality Is Better for Everyone*. London: Penguin.

World Database of Happiness. Available at: https://worlddatabaseofhappiness.eur.nl/hap_bib/bib_fp.php.

World Happiness Reports (2013 to 2019). Available at: http://worldhappiness.report/.

World Wellbeing Panel (n.d.). Available at: https://www.barcelonagse.eu/research/world-wellbeing-panel.

Yoeli, E., Hoffman, M., Rand, D. G., and Nowak, M. A. (2013). Powering up with indirect reciprocity in a large-scale field experiment. *Proceedings of the National Academy of Sciences* 110 (Supplement 2): 10424-29.

Zhang, X., Zhang, X., and Chen, X. (2017). Happiness in the Air: How Does a Dirty Sky Affect Mental Health and Subjective Well-being? *Journal of Environmental Economics and Management* 85: 81–94.

Zhang, X., Chen, X., and Zhang, X. (2018). The Impact of Exposure to Air Pollution on Cognitive Performance. *Proceedings of the National Academy of Sciences* 115(37): 9193–7.

80,000 Hours (n.d.). Available at: https://80000hours.org/.

References to Table 2.2

1. Clark, A. E., Flèche, S., Layard, R., Powdthavee, N., and Ward, G. (2018). *The Origins of Happiness*. Princeton: Princeton University Press.
2. Dickerson, A., Hole, R. A., and Munford, L. A. (2014). The Relationship between Wellbeing and Commuting Revisited: Does the Choice of Methodology Matter? *Regional Science and Urban Economics* 49: 321–9.
3. Stutzer, A., and Frey, B. S. (2008). Stress That Doesn't Pay: The Commuting Paradox. *Scandinavian Journal of Economics* 110: 339–66.
4. Frijters, P., Haisken-DeNew, J. P., and Shields, M. A. (2004). Money Does Matter! Evidence from Increasing Real Incomes and Life Satisfaction in East Germany Following Reunification. *American Economic Review* 94: 730–40.
5. Clark, A. E., and Jung, S. (2017). 'Does Compulsory Education Really Increase Life Satisfaction? *Inha University Institute of Business and Economic Research Discussion Paper* 2017–6.
6. Ferrer-i-Carbonell, A., and Frijters, P. (2004). How Important Is Methodology for the Estimates of the Determinants of Happiness? *Economic Journal* 114: 641–59.
7. Frijters, P., Johnston, D. W., and Shields, M. A. (2014). Does Childhood Predict Adult Life Satisfaction? Evidence from British Cohort Surveys. *Economic Journal* 124: F688–F719.

8. Hanslmaier, M. (2013). Crime, Fear and Subjective Wellbeing: How Victimization and Street Crime Affect Fear and Life Satisfaction. *European Journal of Criminology* 10: 515–33.
9. Johnston, D. W., Shields, M. A. and Suziedelyte, A. (2017). Victimisation, Wellbeing and Compensation: Using Panel Data to Estimate the Costs of Violent Crime. *Economic Journal* 128: 1545–69.
10. Luechinger, S. (2009). Valuing Air Quality Using the Life Satisfaction Approach. *Economic Journal* 119: 482–515.
11. Levinson, A. (2012). Valuing Public Goods Using Happiness Data: The Case of Air Quality. *Journal of Public Economics* 96: 869–80.
12. Krekel, C., Kolbe, J., and Wuestemann, H. (2016). The Greener, the Happier? The Effect of Urban Land Use on Residential Wellbeing. *Ecological Economics* 121: 117–27.
13. White, M. P., Alcock, I., Wheeler, B. W., and Depledge, M. H. (2013). Would You Be Happier Living in a Greener Urban Area? A Fixed-effects Analysis of Panel Data. *Psychological Science* 24: 920–8.
14. Alcock, I., White, M. P., Wheeler, B. W., Fleming, L. E., and Depledge, M. H. (2014). Longitudinal Effects on Mental Health of Moving to Greener and Less Green Urban Areas. *Environmental Science and Technology* 48: 1247–55.
15. Krekel, C., and Zerrahn, A. (2017). Does the Presence of Wind Turbines Have Negative Externalities for People in their Surroundings? Evidence from Wellbeing Data. *Journal of Environmental Economics and Management* 82: 221–38.
16. De Neve, J.-E., and Ward, G. (2017). Happiness at Work. In J. F. Helliwell, R. Layard, and J. Sachs (eds), *World Happiness Report*. New York: Sustainable Development Solutions Network, pp. 144–77.
17. Mujcic, R., and Oswald, A. J. (2016). Evolution of Wellbeing and Happiness after Increases in Consumption of Fruit and Vegetables. *American Journal of Public Health* 106: 1504–10.
18. Dolan, P. H., Kavetsos, G., Krekel, C., Mavridis, D., Metcalfe, R., Senik, C., Szymanski, S., and Ziebarth, N. R. (2019). Quantifying the Intangible Impact of the Olympics Using Subjective Well-Being Data. *Journal of Public Economics* 177: 104043.

References to Table 2.3

Cummins, R. A. (2003). Normative Life Satisfaction: Measurement Issues and a Homeostatic Model. *Social Indicators Research* 64(2): 225–56.

Diener, E., Inglehart, R., and Tay, L. (2013). Theory and Validity of Life Satisfaction Scales. *Social Indicators Research* 112(3): 497–527.

Krueger, A. B., and Schkade, D. A. (2008). The Reliability of Subjective Well-being Measures. *Journal of Public Economics* 92(8–9): 1833–45.

Lim, H. E. (2008). The Use of Different Happiness Rating Scales: Bias and Comparison Problem? *Social Indicators Research* 87(2): 259–67.

Mazaheri, M., and Theuns, P. (2009). Effects of Varying Response Formats on Self-ratings of Life-satisfaction. *Social Indicators Research* 90(3): 381.

Nikolova, E., and Sanfey, P. (2016). How Much Should We Trust Life Satisfaction Data? Evidence from the Life in Transition Survey. *Journal of Comparative Economics* 44(3): 720–31.

3

Wellbeing Policy Evaluation and Appraisal

Data, Methods, Literature, Rules of Thumb, and Technical Standards

Preview

This chapter offers a methodology for those readers who are tasked with actually conducting wellbeing policy evaluations and appraisals, including wellbeing cost-effectiveness and cost-benefit analyses (CBAs), impact assessments, or business plans. We first give a simple and fairly non-formal exposition of how wellbeing cost-effectiveness works. We then set up the methodology formally and discuss the various technical standards and issues that might arise when implementing them, for example double-counting of impacts. We illustrate the methodology using various examples, ranging from simple to more technical. We also introduce and discuss data sources related to wellbeing, with a particular focus on the United Kingdom at present but also beyond, as well as rules of thumb and matters associated with the use of evidence and literature on wellbeing more generally.

We do not discuss here in depth how wellbeing cost-effectiveness analysis (CEA) relates to current CBA, or the various methodologies advocated by different government departments and agencies. That is left for later chapters. The essential purpose of the methodology described here is to be able to formulate figures such as Figure 3.1, which summarizes findings discussed in various subsections of this chapter.

The figure shows estimates for how cost-effective fifteen different interventions are in terms of WELLBYs per £. Its scale is logarithmic so vertical space translates to £ proportionally. The dotted vertical line ('NHS Marginal') shows the currently used suggested threshold for adoption by the public sector. This threshold comes from additional physical health spending by the National Health Service (NHS) in the United Kingdom.

The figure includes examples of very different types of intervention, ranging from workplace interventions (the STAR intervention), to environmental interventions (air pollution), to subsidies for medicine (the NICE item), to cultural interventions. It thus shows how policies in different areas can be compared on a single metric using wellbeing as the unit of account. It also deliberately includes estimates of interventions in other countries, which may be relevant for

A Handbook for Wellbeing Policy-Making: History, Theory, Measurement, Implementation, and Examples. Paul Frijters and Christian Krekel, Oxford University Press (2021).
DOI: 10.1093/oso/9780192896803.003.0003

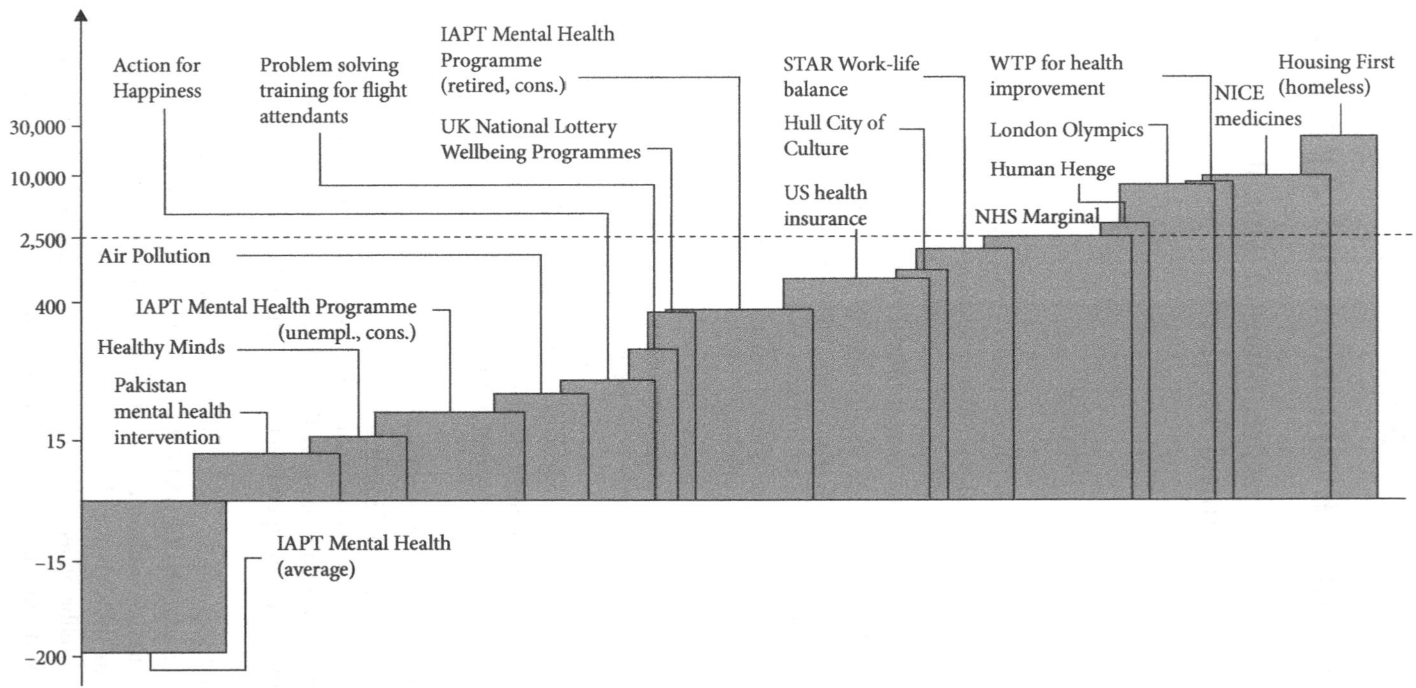

Figure 3.1 Cost per WELLBY of interventions at work, in the environment, and government services

Source: Own illustration based on own calculations.

development aid decisions (an intervention in Pakistan), but also because some public goods and services may be so basic in developed countries such as the United Kingdom (for example, basic health provision) that we can really only see their full value by looking at what their recent introduction in other countries actually leads to in terms of wellbeing impacts.

This is not the place to talk about the fifteen interventions in depth because many of these numbers will come out of calculations later in this chapter and the underlying methodology is one of its main purposes. Yet, we should already mention a caveat here that the actual value-for-money estimates are highly uncertain so that this graph is largely for illustrative purposes.

In any case, some crucial ideas that are used in Figure 3.1, and some basic information to understand the figure, are:

- A WELLBY is one unit of life satisfaction on a 0-to-10 scale for one person for one year. See chapter 2 for details.
- Costs are in terms of net £ to the public purse as they would apply to the United Kingdom (that is, UK prices for things like housing). The net costs include up-front costs and flows into or out of the public purse, including changes in taxes and benefits. The methodology can be generalized to any other currency in the world.
- All monetary effects that are not on the public purse are included in the WELLBY effect, which hence involves a translation from consumption levels to wellbeing levels. See chapter 4 for details.
- The wellbeing cost-effectiveness calculations typically also look at knock-on effects beyond the primary outcome, which requires assumptions on how a WELLBY relates to other major non-material factors, such as employment (chapter 2), socio-emotional skills (chapter 2), health (chapter 4), or culture (chapter 5).
- The width of the intervention shown in Figure 3.1 entails a very basic guess as to how much up-front public costs would be involved if one scaled up the intervention to the level of the whole population. Often, this remains a guesstimate because publications on interventions are silent about implementation costs, which makes cost-effectiveness calculations difficult. A 'thin' intervention (for example, the workplace problem-solving intervention) is one where it is rather unlikely that large amounts of money need to be invested up front when scaling the intervention up, whereas the opposite is probably the case for 'thick' interventions such as the London Olympics.

Appendix E talks through the main assumptions and descriptions of the fifteen interventions in this figure, providing references to the key studies from which the estimates are derived.

A Non-formal Introduction to Wellbeing CEA

The rationale behind wellbeing CEA is to compare the net public costs of a policy with its net benefits in terms of WELLBYs (one unit of life satisfaction on a 0-to-10 scale for one person for one year). The optimal policy rule is to implement a policy if:

$$\text{Net Additional Wellbeing Benefits} - \lambda * \text{Net Additional Public Costs} > 0 \quad (1)$$

The net benefits are in terms of changes in WELLBYs and include all the effects of a policy, both direct and indirect, and thus require a judgement as to how long the effects of a policy will lead to changes in wellbeing and what effects on wellbeing are going to be important. The public costs include all the changes to the public purse, both positive and negative. Additional tax receipts due to a policy count as negative costs, while increased costs in any part of the system are positive costs. The additional costs of a policy could involve increased usage of health and education, or increased take-up of welfare benefits or tax avoidance.

If there are many policies to consider that satisfy the optimal policy rule, but one does not have the budget to fund all of them, the basic idea is to fund those with the highest ratio of benefits to costs until the budget runs out. A system of ranking alternatives in terms of their cost-effectiveness and then funding those ranked highest until the budget runs out leads to an implicit λ determined by the last funded project: it gives the opportunity value of public money, or the amount of WELLBYs a unit of money can buy. A higher value of λ means that the policies which get enacted need to have, on average, higher value for money. A democratic political system that decides on a ceiling on public spending (for example, via a fiscal rule) thereby indirectly decides on λ.

Note that, in an ideal scenario, one would not trade off budgets with wellbeing but only maximize wellbeing: there would then be no term with public costs necessary, merely net wellbeing, where all changes in incomes and budgets would be calculated in terms of their ultimate effects on wellbeing as well. In this ideal scenario, one would simply implement all policies with positive WELLBY effects. One would automatically know what the opportunity costs (or benefits) are of greater government revenues, such that any revenue-related wellbeing is included in the calculation of the net effect of a policy. The reason that this ideal scenario would not lead to 100 per cent taxation is that the WELLBY effects of increased taxation would be part of the net benefits calculation: excessive taxation would at some point lead to lower economic growth, less actual taxes, less private consumption, and thereby, reduced wellbeing, as implied by the Laffer curve.[1]

[1] The Laffer curve is a hump-shaped curve describing the relation between tax rates and tax receipts. The key aspect is that tax receipts start decreasing at some level of tax rates well below 100 per cent because economic activity moves away to other countries or ceases entirely because individuals and companies start preferring leisure over work.

Yet, in practice, many of the negative effects of tax increases are difficult to ascertain and are the subject of intense political debates. Also, policies are typically evaluated or appraised one by one, simply because it is difficult to take account of all potential policies at once, making it more practical to take a budget as given and to have the importance of other policies reflected in the marginal value of the public purse. A feature of a dual system of governance, whereby policies are shaped by a combination of elected politicians and more permanent civil servants, is that the debate about the budget largely takes place in the political arena. Large changes in budgets will involve bureaucratic implementation but are invariably politicized.

This does not mean at all that wellbeing arguments are unimportant for setting the budget. Rather, the opposite. But wellbeing arguments then have to openly appear in the political debate where the budget is decided, not the bureaucratic arena. For the civil service as a whole, the budget is then more or less given and the main discretion is at the margins of how to spend wisely, leading to a single λ for all spending units (such as government departments or agencies).

Note that the optimal policy rule generalizes to the case in which net benefits can be negative but may be counter-balanced by a negative change in public costs. The prime example is cuts in public services. It also generalizes to different types of policies, including policies that have no significant public costs such as regulations. Similarly, there are policies with no noticeable effect on WELLBYs that nevertheless are beneficial to have because they come with negative public costs (public cost savings), which may free up funds for wellbeing-generating policies.

Let us consider some of the most important nuances to the optimal policy rule, starting with the problem that one policy may change the environment for another policy.

Choosing from Multiple Possible Policies in Multiple Spending Units

The optimal policy rule is useful if there are many policy to choose from because the basic idea is to implement the policies which have the highest value for money first, until the available budget runs out and the last policy implemented satisfies the constraint of having a zero total effect.

Yet, one policy often affects the value of another policy. A school bus, for instance, cannot be seen as independent of there being a school: they complement each other. Transportation, schooling, and housing policies also naturally complement each other, as do many others. This means that two policies viewed in isolation may not represent value for money while taken together they may.

One needs a process to recognize the complementarities between policies so that one can consider larger policies that combine smaller ones. In the examples above, it would mean that transport and some other decision (for example, on education or housing) have to be seen together in terms of policy packages. This may sound easy, but 'inter-departmental cooperation' is not a trivial thing for the civil service in most countries, particularly when policies combine more than two spending units simultaneously, let alone if they involve different administration levels as well (for example, national, regional, or local).

Policies that transcend different departments and levels of decision-making may lead to competency and budget battles: who gets to decide on what and who gets to spend what? The reality of inter-departmental policy design and budget-setting may be just as strong as budget fights in parliament. There is nothing new about this: leaderships of institutions often look to expand the scope of their activities, which may lead to coordination and competency problems when the design of new policies falls within the responsibilities of several institutions. Yet, these are known problems and countries such as the United Kingdom have several mechanisms for trying to deal with them (for example, interdepartmental commissions).

One mechanism is for departments that champion particular policies to work out how it would affect other departments, both in terms of costs and benefits.[2] This is a piecemeal approach, because each department is taking the activities of the other departments as given rather than subject to a joint exploration, but it is at least a start. Another mechanism is for politicians or civil servants to recognize that some policies might involve many institutions of the state and to set up particular groups to come up with an optimal overarching policy. This happens regularly when it comes to complex social spending, such as care for the elderly, or at local levels when it comes to such things as crime prevention.

There are also dedicated institutions where knowledge about policies that involve many institutions is brought together. The Central Planbureaus in Northern Europe were explicitly set up to be a place where diverse interests and institutions could get together with scientists to 'plan' optimal policies for the country as a whole. Different countries have different institutions: the Germans have a council of five economists directly advising the Chancellor (the Council of Economic Experts) on economic policy, the French have Planbureaus, and the Dutch have scientific advisory councils and Planbureaus. The United Kingdom has a system of inquiries initiated by top politicians and bureaucrats. There are also mechanisms inside large state institutions to recognize complementarities

[2] This is supposedly mandatory, but there is, of course, no easy way to enforce it because the knowledge of how things work is partly specific to an area. If it were clear how activities of one institution are complementary to those of others, one would not need separate institutions to begin with.

between spending units, such as working groups involving senior management. The aim of such consultation and integration is to come up with policies that take advantage of possible complementarities while reducing coordination and competency problems.

From the point of view of wellbeing optimization, the ideal is to consider all reasonable policies when conducting wellbeing CEA, including combinations of smaller ones, and then to apply the optimal policy rule to fund the most cost-effective ones first. Yet, institutions should be in place to recognize unanticipated realities afterwards and smooth out problems. Knowledge of wellbeing helps recognize probable complementarities between different policies of different institutions, such as the link between air quality (affected by policies of many different departments and decision units) and mental health.

When Costs and Benefits Are Risky or Uncertain

In principle, a policy simply has a net benefit and a net public cost. In reality, however, neither the costs nor the benefits of a policy are certain. This problem is inherent in all choices, which invariably requires two acts of imagination: one needs an idea as to what is going to happen if one path is chosen, and another idea as to what would otherwise happen if something else, or even nothing, is chosen. There is risk in all the benefits and costs no matter what and it is often not known which choice is riskier either.[3]

The first way to deal with risk is to read the optimal policy rule 'in expectation' and to judge a possible new policy by the expected benefits and the expected costs, i.e. the average effect they will have across future 'states of the world'. In such cases, it is equally important to consider whether a policy can be undone if things go wrong. Some policies cannot be undone once in motion without huge costs, such as large infrastructure projects that involve contracts and land clearing with *ex ante* contractual financial obligations. In other cases, policies can be undone relatively easily, such as benefits or tax changes. Moreover, one sometimes knows early on in the implementation what the effects are going to be, and sometimes one never fully knows the effects a policy has had.

When a policy is easily reversible and its effects are easily observed during implementation, the optimal policy rule is obvious: as soon as it becomes clear that, in reality, the costs are going to be much higher than expected, and the benefits much lower, one simply cancels the policy if it is contractually possible.

[3] In most cases, we can attach some probability to costs and benefits, which formally describe these decisions as decisions under risk. There are, however, cases in which we cannot even attach probabilities, such as how a pandemic such as Covid-19 might affect the national health system. In such cases, we speak of (Knightian) uncertainty, because we do not even know the underlying parameters of a model (or the model itself).

Yet, in that pristine world, where one could quickly cancel policies when the true costs and benefits start to become known, before large costs have been made, the risk in outcomes fundamentally changes the optimal policy rule.

You see, if one would truly find out quickly what effects a policy is going to have, one more or less wants to start implementing any policies that have some possibility of high value for money: one simply reverses those policies that did not work out. In effect, this is precisely the point of experimentation, which is a low-cost way of trying out a policy and seeing whether it is worth implementing it more widely. The real cost of such small-scale experimental implementation is that wider implementation is postponed until the results of the experiments become known. So if we can easily reverse something, we may want to try it even if the expected benefits are negative or not cost-effective: it depends on the cost of trying and the odds of getting a positive surprise.

In the less pristine case that policies cannot be easily undone without significant costs, for instance because one has made *ex ante* contractual financial obligations that ensure a future flow of costs, the costs of failure are far higher than for policies that can easily be reversed. This is also the case if one never truly learns what effect a policy has had and hence has no way to decide afterwards to stop the policy, in which case one is essentially stuck with the effects and costs as they are.

Many policies have effects that we do not truly know, simply because the world is too complex, and in many cases the policies involved are costly and high profile. For instance, does a nuclear deterrent truly work? Do increased prison sentences really deter crime? Does increased taxation deter economic activity? Do subsidies to national museums increase the level of identification within the country and thus tax morale? Different governments and different departments within governments have opposing beliefs about the answers to these very difficult questions. We often cannot be sure. Under this kind of persistent uncertainty, one relies, in practice, on some implicit view of how the world truly works (or applies some other, often non-quantitative decision rules for decisions under uncertainty).[4] That view, which can be debated and is subject to new knowledge about the world, is then the default belief as to what would happen if particular policies are implemented.

From the point of view of a rational planner who wishes to implement the best policies, risk gives rise to a cost of risk that depends on visibility and reversibility. When policies have effects that are neither visible nor reversible, the optimal policy rule remains as before. But when policies are visible in effects and are reversible in implementation, they in effect have a positive return to risk: the possibility of a very high cost-effectiveness merits them being tried out to see whether they work. Risk thus gives rise to asymmetric experimentation: one tries

[4] These methods are not the focus of this book. For an introduction to decision-making under (deep) uncertainty, see Kochenderfer (2015), for example.

out the reversible policies that have low expected return but some possibility of high returns, while one only implements the irreversible policies with non-verifiable outcomes if their expected returns are high enough.

What if we are not the only ones making strategic decisions though?

When Costs and Benefits Are Subject to Negotiation

The optimal policy rule on wellbeing takes the monetary costs of a policy as given. This is appropriate when it comes to building a bridge or a hospital, in which case we do roughly know what the costs are and we cannot change the costs of the material or the labour involved. It is appropriate in the many areas of policies where prices of inputs are given. But how do we think about cases when prices are the results of negotiations?

Governments are not like individual households, which have to take prices in the world as given: governments have clout and can negotiate with large companies and institutions about the prices of things. These companies have a mind of their own and will pre-empt and react to governments' choices. What then?

A particularly important example is where governments buy pharmaceutical medicines on behalf of the population. The United Kingdom, for example, spends around £20 billion per year on medication via the National Institute for Health and Care Excellence (NICE), which has to approve the use and the price of medicines in the United Kingdom.[5] It is hence a 'monopsonist': the sole effective purchaser. This means it has market power and could demand lower prices from suppliers. The way that NICE negotiates with suppliers of medicine, usually large pharmaceutical companies that negotiate with many governments around the world, is effectively to advertise the optimal policy rule above. The current stance is that if the cost-benefit ratio is better than around £25,000 to £30,000 per healthy year of life (quality-adjusted life-year, or QALY), then the medicines are approved for use in the United Kingdom.

Is this not exactly what we advocate, merely using a health criterion (QALY) rather than a wellbeing criterion (WELLBY)? In this case, unfortunately no, because openly advocating what one is willing to pay is the surest way to 'lose' negotiations. Many previous authors have commented upon this, most recently Wang et al. (2018) who also mention several previous studies that argued how an advertised specific threshold is a bad idea in negotiations.[6]

[5] We acknowledge that NICE has many responsibilities and activities. In this chapter, we exclusively talk about its role concerning approvals for pharmaceutical medicines.

[6] This is a heated debate, which also includes the argument that pharmaceutical companies need to make profits in order to invest in research and development. This is not the place to discuss all those nuances as they have been extensively discussed elsewhere.

To see the essential problem, suppose you really like beer and announce at your local brewery that you would be willing to pay that brewery £100 per pint. The first time you do this, the brewery owner might let you buy the pint for the advertised price of, say, £5. Yet, at some point in time, there is a good chance that the brewery owner starts to increase the price. If he really believes you, he is going to charge you £99.99 for a pint, even though his own costs are still below £5.

According to Wang et al. (2018), this is more or less what has happened with pharmaceutical prices in the United Kingdom and much of the rest of the world: pharmaceutical companies have started to charge what governments are maximally willing to pay. In Australia, this is around $50,000 per QALY. In the United Kingdom, it is around £25,000 per QALY. Pharmaceuticals have, as rational actors, started to believe the advertised willingness-to-pay by the medicine monopsonist and have started to ask for exactly that, regardless of what their true production costs are.

Hence, the result is that the United Kingdom may have had the same medicines for a fraction of the price, because many are cheap to produce, if it was not for its negotiation techniques. This means, in turn, that there could have been more additional, wellbeing-generating public goods in other spheres.

New Zealand looked very carefully at the Australian system, which preceded the UK system by some ten years, and decided to do it differently. They effectively capped the total amount spent on medicines and gave the regulator the power to negotiate with pharmaceutical companies, giving them the power to not buy particular medicines at all. And there is the rub.

In a price negotiation, one's ability to negotiate a low price depends strongly on the ability to walk away from the negotiation. Pharmaceutical companies are under no obligation to sell to a country and can thus credibly threaten to walk away from the table. In order to avoid paying the maximum one would be willing to pay, countries would have to be able to credibly threaten to walk away from the table as well. Is this not foregoing a clear possible advantage? Does this not mean that a policy is turned down which is above the threshold?

The essential insight here is that there is a better policy possible than merely 'paying the price demanded'. The superior policy is where one includes the bargaining itself into the policy process: a policy that says 'we will offer half our actual maximum willingness-to-pay and stick to that maximum' has a higher expected return than the policy of offering the maximum willingness-to-pay, especially if there are multiple rounds of negotiation. Including bargaining thus changes the (expected) costs of all policies that have negotiated costs in them, thereby changing the mix of policies one considers funding, and ultimately changing the cut-off point λ.

The reason why one reduces the expected costs in almost every case where one bargains over a price is that the expected surplus of the strategy 'offer half the surplus on the table' is always positive as soon as there is some chance the other side will take the offer. The expected surplus of offering the maximum is zero no matter whether the offer is accepted or not. That zero-surplus could also be achieved by simply reducing the budget and giving the money back to the population to spend as they wish.[7]

The rule to 'offer half' is, of course, arbitrary. One could alternatively offer a third, or perhaps some amount that depends on the costs of making the product, or some other, more complicated formula. The key point is not whether to offer exactly half, but to have some mechanism to offer less than the maximum willingness-to-pay and to stick to that stance, i.e. to run the conscious risk of 'no sale'.

There is a reason why New Zealand is one of the few countries capable of consciously running a risk of 'no sale': in many other countries, the politics of openly running a 'no sale' risk are very difficult in the case of medicines. Patient groups and pharmaceutical companies directly lobby the government and the general public to have their favourite medicines allowed. As a result, for medicines with particular visibility, prices are often far higher than the maximum willingness-to-pay. For instance, for Pompe disease, the cost of medicines in Australia are equivalent to around £300,000 per QALY. For that amount of money, one may help many others by preventative means. The difference is, however, that reducing the suffering of others may be less visible beforehand or even known with certainty afterwards.

The visibility of the benefits or costs of decisions is hence important politically, even though to the rational wellbeing maximizer, visibility should not matter: the suffering of many should matter more than the suffering of one. However, human sympathies and sensibilities do not quite work that way, as we focus on the needs that are visibly in front of us, rather than the somewhat vaguer suffering of unnamed others. The Covid-19 crisis was a clear case of the emotive power of an immediate threat to a defined population, with visible suffering in terms of physical health, whilst the suffering of those hit by the policies to contain Covid-19 were much less visible since it was mostly in the domains of mental health and social isolation or loneliness.[8]

This is a general conundrum that shows up in many areas of policy: the needs of the visible weigh greater on our minds than the needs of others who are anonymous, who are in the future, or who we find it difficult to identify with. This is precisely why in many areas we have developed institutions that are blind to this distinction. The legal system is symbolized by a woman with a blindfold precisely to symbolize the unemotional application of a principle designed to benefit

[7] In the case that the budget is optimal.

[8] One of the authors estimated in March 2020 that this high visibility meant at least fifty unseen victims were tolerated in order to save one highly visible one. Miles et al. (2020) came to similar conclusions.

everyone equally, taking out the role of emotions and privilege, thereby avoiding miscarriages of justice. The founding principle of the NHS in the United Kingdom is similarly of equal access by rich and poor, young and old. Reality is, of course, never quite the same as the ideal, but many countries do set up institutions to be 'fair' and removed from daily political considerations.

Both the policy rule and the institutional environment in which rules are made depend, therefore, on whether we face 'a strategic opponent'. The example of medicines illustrates several nuances to the optimal policy rule above:

- When prices are subject to negotiations, the threshold that is openly advertised should be higher than the true λ in order to drive down the price.
- Visible suffering that can be mobilized towards a political outcome weighs higher politically than anonymous suffering, which makes the case for institutions that make impartial decisions without immediate political oversight.
- Different countries have set up different institutions for the same basic problem, which means that one could potentially learn from successful examples elsewhere.

What goes for medicines also goes for other policies in which negotiations can have real impacts on prices, such as trade negotiations, large infrastructure projects, large purchases of equipment, or large land purchases. The design of the institutions that negotiate about prices have to, therefore, carefully consider the issue of independence of daily politics and the willingness to run the risk of 'no deal'.

What holds for costs can also hold for benefits: negotiations with large companies, other countries, or large local institutions involve many potential benefits to the population, including, for example, decisions on cultural and social projects. There too, the application of the optimal policy rule requires careful thought about the negotiation strategy.

With this non-formal exposition in mind, we can now turn to the same material in greater technical depth. In what follows, we first go over the basic wellbeing CEA methodology. Then, we expand it to include a range of issues that may come up in practice, including risk or uncertainty, continuous process versus one-off decisions, multiple outcomes, or pathways choices. This methodology section is best read in conjunction with the example section later in this chapter which clarifies, giving real-world examples, how wellbeing CEA can be done in practice and what difference a wellbeing perspective would make compared to CEA based on traditional outcomes.

Wellbeing CEA Methodology

The relevant outcomes can be divided into *intermediate outcomes* X_{it} for individuals i at times $t \geq 0$ and *final outcomes* Y_{it}. Intermediate outcomes can include, for example, relationships with others, health conditions, employment characteristics, or simply consumed goods and services. X_{it} is a large vector of such intermediate outcomes (1 to K). Likewise, final outcomes Y_{it} are thought of as a set of outcomes: wellbeing, taxes paid, and costs to the public purse, including costs of the intervention. We denote the wellbeing outcome as W_{it} and the net public costs (public costs incurred minus taxes paid) as C_{it}. These are one-dimensional, with wellbeing measured in units of life satisfaction per person per year (WELLBYs) and costs in the current value of a unit of money in the respective country (we assume, for simplicity, £ sterling throughout our examples). Life satisfaction is typically obtained from surveys, and in particular, from a single-item 11-point Likert scale question asking respondents: "Overall, how satisfied are you with your life nowadays?". Answer categories range from 0 ("not at all") to 10 ("completely").[9]

Time t is typically measured in years, although only out of convention, as datasets often have yearly observations and budget cycles are yearly (or in bulks of years). The basic methodology, however, is not constrained to measure intermediate and final outcomes in years; any other time frame would also be valid as long as appropriate changes are made so as to keep outcomes comparable in terms of time frame.

In the simple, generic case, the question we ask is: how cost-effective in terms of wellbeing is an intervention that is set in motion at a single point in time ($t = 0$) and that is then associated with a set of outcomes for a given group of individuals? The key comparison is between outcomes that would occur from $t = 0$ onwards to some final date T if the intervention happens, i.e. the *intervention scenario*, versus if it did not, i.e. the *status quo scenario*. We use the word *intervention* here in a broad sense to denote any major plan of activities that require significant resources (for example, a policy) or some form of permission (for example, a regulation).

Typically, policy analysts do not know the exact outcomes with or without the intervention as the anticipated outcome of any course of action is always unobservable. One thus has to either infer both outcomes or their difference from the literature, policy trials, or from an assumed view of the world. Here, we initially assume, for simplicity, that analysts do know X_{it}, W_{it}, and C_{it} for the

[9] The basic methodology generalizes to cases in which a different measure of wellbeing is used, for example if a policy-maker decides to adopt a different measure or if an improved measure becomes available.

whole population under both the intervention scenario and the status quo scenario.[10]

Outcomes under the status quo scenario are denoted as X^0_{it}, W^0_{it}, and C^0_{it}, whereas outcomes under the intervention scenario are denoted as X^1_{it}, W^1_{it}, and C^1_{it}. The effects of the intervention are then captured in each period by $(X^1_{it} - X^0_{it})$, $(W^1_{it} - W^0_{it})$, and $(C^1_{it} - C^0_{it})$. The wellbeing cost-effectiveness, *CE*, of the intervention is equal to:

$$\mathrm{CE} = \frac{\text{Net Additional Wellbeing Benefits}}{\text{Net Additional Public Costs}} = \frac{\sum_t (1-\rho^w)^t \sum_i sw_i * (W^1_{it} - W^0_{it})}{\sum_t (1-\rho^c)^t \sum_i (C^1_{it} - C^0_{it})} \tag{2}$$

where:

$$sw_i = \text{social weight of individual i}$$
$$\rho^W = \text{wellbeing discount rate}$$
$$\rho^c = \text{cost discount rate}$$

The first important element of this equation is $\sum_t$, which denotes a summation over the overall time period. This requires policy analysts to have a duration in mind in which the intervention is supposed to have an effect. The choice for the overall time period is essentially determined by the periods in which the main effects are believed to accrue. For long-term investments such as infrastructure or education, the overall time period will typically be at least fifty years. For very short-lived interventions such as a major sports event, we would usually be thinking of a year or even shorter.

The second element is $(1-\rho^W)^t$, which is the weight given to wellbeing benefits in periods after $t = 0$. The wellbeing discount rate $\rho^W > 0$ is the pure social discount rate pertaining to individuals in the future plus a catastrophic risk premium.

The social discount rate is a judgement on how much the present matters more than the future. In the United Kingdom, for example, it is customary to choose a pure social discount rate of 0.5 per cent. Moreover, in a CBA framework, it is customary to add a 1 per cent catastrophic risk premium to the social discount rate. The basic idea is that there is a possibility of systemic failure in which case all investments into the future become worthless. When thinking of wellbeing benefits in a CEA framework, the same issue applies: there is a certain probability that major events overtake the system in which investments are made and that, as a

[10] This presents the problem as a deterministic one, whereby it is certain which individuals will be affected. One can easily generalize the problem to probabilistic interventions in which individuals have a probability of being affected by an intervention such as, for example, a probability of receiving treatment. In this case, the basic formulas look more cumbersome but are not fundamentally very different. We present the deterministic case first and the generalization later on.

result, the projected wellbeing benefits no longer apply. Summing social discount rate and catastrophic risk premium, we obtain $\rho^W = 0.015$. Note that double-counting should be avoided: because the formula includes the probability of catastrophic risk, one should not, at the same time, include a monetized catastrophic risk term when calculating the wellbeing benefits pre-discounting. We discuss this issue in greater detail later on.

Next, $\sum_i$ denotes a summation over (the relevant sub-group of) the population. This requires analysts to make a choice which (sub-group of) the population is relevant and, by omission, which is not. Many moral choices become explicit or implicit in the choice of whom to include in $\sum_i$. The natural default is the population of the country, that is, the *demos* that makes up the country's democracy and whose political will is represented in parliament either currently or in the foreseeable future as in the case of children. Note that the formula is generalizable to account for both positive wellbeing changes to some parts of the population and negative wellbeing changes to others.

It is often impractical to include the whole population in any calculation based on data pertaining to individuals. One reason is that there is often no easily available dataset that covers the entire population, except perhaps a microcensus, which is often only conducted every couple of years. Another reason is that an inclusion of the whole population would require analysts to take an explicit stance on how everybody in the country will be affected over the whole duration of the intervention. This is a tall order, particularly if the intervention envisioned is small.

Practically, therefore, the relevant population will either be a representative group of individuals who 'stands in' for the population as a whole, a hypothetical population that 'stands in', or else some fraction of the sub-group of the population that is believed to be affected by the intervention. Large-scale surveys with appropriate survey weights to make the sample nationally representative can form the basis of a representative population. Depending on the intervention, sub-groups of the population can be as small as the members of a local sports club or as large as the population of a city.

Whatever analysts choose as the relevant population, they need to make quite strong implicit assumptions on who matters and who is affected.[11] For instance, if one does not include the future population that is yet to be born or to migrate to the country in $\sum_i$, then it is implicitly deemed irrelevant for the intervention at hand. Leaving aside practical limitations as to what one can and cannot know or foresee, strong moral assumptions are unavoidable in any actual calculation because the alternative, which is to do full justice in every calculation to all possible groups one cares about, would require enormous additional resources

[11] The basic methodology also generalizes to including both humans and animals.

(which, in the worst case, would not be available to spend on these groups then, an ineffective use of public resources).[12] Therefore, the choice of $\sum_i$ will often only be 'vaguely right'.

sw_i is the social weight pertaining to each individual i. Again, this is a moral choice. Under classic utilitarianism, it is normal to count everybody as equal and thus to have $sw_i = 1$ for every individual in the 'demos'. However, one could argue that some individuals should matter more than others, either because of some higher status accrued to certain individuals or because one cares more about their wellbeing increase than others. For instance, one could care more about alleviating misery than raising the wellbeing of those already at high levels of wellbeing, in which case sw_i would be higher for those with low initial levels of wellbeing.

The final element in the numerator is $(W_{it}^1 - W_{it}^0)$, which is the wellbeing change of individuals i at times t, derived as the difference between the wellbeing under the intervention scenario (W_{it}^1) and the wellbeing under the status quo scenario (W_{it}^0). As one is only interested in changes, one in principle does not need to truly take a stance on what the level of either W_{it}^1 or W_{it}^0 is for an individual: only the change is relevant.

The denominator is the net additional public costs, denoted as $\sum_t (1 - \rho^c) \sum_i (C_{it}^1 - C_{it}^0)$. Again, there is a choice to be made for $\sum_t$. This need not be the same as in the numerator as it is perfectly plausible that changes to the public purse occur earlier or later than changes to wellbeing. In many cases, for instance, there would be an immediate up-front cost with no significant future effects on public costs while wellbeing benefits might take years to materialize. An example would be new equipment to improve palliative care for individuals in nursing homes, which makes life more pleasant for many terminally ill patients: the costs are up front while the patients who benefit include people in the far future, with little expected change on the public purse relative to the status quo scenario later on.

The cost discount rate ρ^c need not be the same as the wellbeing discount rate ρ^W even though it is normal practice to assume that the discount rates on costs and benefits are the same. We here discuss what seems the optimal approach to

[12] Indeed, it is practically impossible to even include the whole population of a country for the simple reason that it is not known precisely at any moment who is in the population for a variety of reasons. Some individuals with passports or a claim to a passport might be living abroad without exercising that claim. Some living in the country believed to be citizens and behaving like citizens might not actually have a valid claim. At any moment in time, large numbers of citizens are abroad while large numbers in the country are citizens of other countries. At any moment in time, migration status is deliberated for many individuals, and there will be many individuals who themselves do not quite know which citizenry applies to them because they are, for instance, of mixed ancestry and have not yet looked up their rights. It is entirely normal in most policy analyses to ignore all this, involving in practice many moral choices that are almost never made explicit.

wellbeing CEA and later what the differences are with normal practice in government.

The reason to have a different discount rate for public costs than for wellbeing is simple: the discount rate on the cost side is less of a moral issue and more an issue of the costs of financing: a £ spent today rather than tomorrow is more costly because of interest rates.[13] Within our economic system, in most cases, the cost of financing is to a large degree driven by the interest rate operating on global financial markets and hence is only to a limited degree a matter of national policy.

The best way to see this is to imagine the intervention as being decided on by a country as a single entity. The money then comes from raising public debt or, in the case that available money is spent on something, not reducing the public debt. Explicitly or implicitly, therefore, the interest on public debt is the relevant interest rate. The question then is what real interest rate will need to be paid on money spent in one year. Real interest rates on ten-year UK treasury bonds in 2018, for example, were at a historic low of around 0.5 per cent. However, from a long-term point of view (for example, looking back at the last one hundred years or so), 2 per cent is a typical estimate for the real interest rate.

The issue of catastrophic risk is also important for the cost discount rate, though in this case the notion of what is 'catastrophic' is subtly different than for wellbeing. In case of the numerator, the risk was one of some large disruption under which the envisioned wellbeing changes would not occur at all. In case of the denominator, the 'risk' is that the financial costs assumed to occur in the future do not occur at all. Those are not necessarily the same risks: in the case of building a road, for instance, the costs will be subject to the catastrophic risk of earthquakes or some other collapse of the transport system such that a half-finished road will not be completed and hence the supposed future costs are not made. The risks on the benefit side could include the death of the population so that there is no one to use the road. Arguably, the latter 'catastrophic risk' is far less likely.

Given the current interest rates, there is an argument to be made that the current relevant cost discount rate ρ^c to be 1.5 per cent (0.5 per cent long-run interest rate plus 1 per cent financial catastrophic risk premium), though—given historical interests rate over the long-run—one could also argue for 3.0 per cent (2 per cent long-run interest rate plus 1 per cent financial catastrophic risk premium), or anything in between. Finally, the default choice, simply to be consistent with current practice, is to set the two discount rates equal to each other, i.e. $\rho^W = \rho^c$.

Note that, because net public costs include both potential cost reductions (such as via higher taxes or reduced welfare benefits) as well as increased public expenses

[13] Of course, there is also inflation. When referring to costs throughout this chapter, we mean to refer to them in real terms, that is in terms of the purchasing value of £ today.

in the future, one has to be careful about how catastrophic risks are applied to different forms of costs made at different points in time. While the collapse of the financial system one year from now might, for instance, render all loans null and void, thus leading to a write-off in terms of any current expenses, such a 'catastrophe' is unlikely to nullify the increased tax receipts in twenty years' time due to higher human capital (future tax receipts). Yet, in practice, it is not realistic to assign different probabilities to different types of catastrophic risks that pertain to different costs and wellbeing changes. The default is to apply the same discount rates to all aspects of the calculation.

The next element in the denominator is $\sum_i$ (pertaining to cost changes), which will almost never be the same $\sum_i$ in the numerator (pertaining to wellbeing changes). This is because one will typically be thinking of the total effects on the public purse pertaining to the whole of the UK population. Think of the up-front cost of a large public programme, for example: such up-front costs are typically borne by the whole population as an entity. Apart from clear costs and cost reductions that accrue to the system as a whole, there still is a choice to be made by analysts as to where to look for public costs and public costs savings that are likely to occur as a result of the intervention. The $\sum_i$ term in the denominator (pertaining to costs) thus needs to include the individuals whose changed behaviour is likely to lead to significant changes in taxation or take-up of welfare benefits.

Note the absence of a social weighting term sw_i in the evaluation of the public costs. That is because, to the public sector as a whole, spending a £ costs a £ no matter from which departmental budget, council budget, or budget of a public organization it comes from. The lack of weighting thus adopts a 'whole-of-government' approach. Note that we are here not talking about monetary costs to private individuals or private entities, which in a wellbeing CEA methodology all show up in the wellbeing effects of an intervention and thus automatically involve distributional issues: only monetary costs borne by the public sector are seen as 'costs' in wellbeing CEA. All else goes via the wellbeing effects.

The final item in the denominator is $(C_{it}^1 - C_{it}^0)$, which is the change at the individual level in the draw on the public purse: it can be denoted in terms of actual costs made up front and over time, or in terms of the monetary equivalent of utilization of public services such as the healthcare or education system. Increased tax receipts due to the intervention are a negative cost, as are reductions in the utilization of public services.[14]

[14] Although we do not want to dwell too much on the comparison with analyses currently done by UK government departments and devolved administrations, a UK policy analyst commented on how current CBA does differ: 'The current webTAG position is that changes in government revenues are perceived in factor prices and are then uprated by the market price adjustment factor (MPA) before inclusion in the cost benefit analysis. This applies to changes in indirect taxation revenue, which feature in the numerator to the Benefit Cost Ratio (BCR), and changes in DfT related expenditure both capital

The result of the calculation, *CE*, is then the ratio between the change in net additional wellbeing benefits and the change in net additional public costs. The higher this number, the greater the value for money. A rational, wellbeing-maximizing policy-maker then ranks candidate interventions from highest to lowest value for money, and implements them from top to bottom until the fixed budget runs out, yielding a value of *CE* that is equal to λ: it is the opportunity value of public money, or the amount of WELLBYs a unit of public money can buy. More formally, we can refer to this value as the minimum social production costs of a WELLBY.

How to Choose What to Fund

When there are many possible interventions, the first thing to do is to gauge which ones are truly distinct, could be fruitfully combined, or axed. If there are multiple possible interventions designed to achieve the same thing (say prisoner recidivism programmes) but one has more benefits and less costs, clearly dominating the others, one can normally disregard the dominated interventions. It is also possible that some interventions should be combined because they would achieve better outcomes jointly than separately, a situation that, for instance, is often true when thinking of tackling social disadvantages which manifest themselves in many domains that interact and that thus require different tasks. This will often become clear in the design and pre-evaluation stage of a policy, but may be learned only afterwards as well.

For simplicity, we assume that the remaining interventions are the most effective ones in their respective domains and that there are no obvious improvements to be made by either combining them or getting rid of those that are dominated by an alternative in the same domain. The situation we then have is illustrated in Figure 3.2 below, where each dot represents a distinct and feasible intervention, associated with net discounted costs in £ on the horizontal axis and a discounted wellbeing change in WELLBYs on the vertical axis. The graph has four quadrants.

and revenue, which feature in the denominator of the BCR' (Laird and Mackie, 2017, page 1). This exemplifies how in current government analyses the notion of benefits often includes some actual effects on the public purse that would normally be considered as positive or negative costs (not doing so effectively presumes the wellbeing benefit of a £ spent by a private individual and the government to have equal wellbeing value, which is a bold empirical claim that almost begs the question what the supposed benefit of government is if it does not have higher returns to spending than individuals). One may argue that, at the margin, the returns should become the same under rational policy-making, but one cannot presume they are the same. Indeed, we argue in chapter 4 that the marginal social production costs of a WELLBY are only about 25 per cent of the marginal private production costs, which coincides with what is at present already presumed for the NHS (the private willingness-to-pay for a QALY is currently taken to be about four times the marginal social production costs).

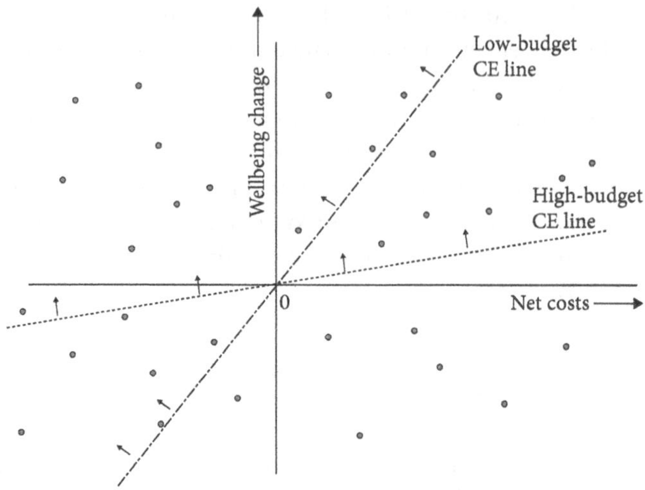

Figure 3.2 Wellbeing cost-effectiveness decisions when budgets are high or low
Source: Own illustration.

The right-bottom quadrant is made up of interventions that accrue net costs and have negative wellbeing changes. These are interventions one should never consider, no matter what the budget is. Interventions in the left-top quadrant are interventions that save money and have positive wellbeing changes. Since these are, by prior assumption, the most effective interventions in their respective domains, they should, normally speaking, all go ahead. The real choices pertain to projects that have (a) positive net costs and positive wellbeing changes (top-right quadrant) and (b) save money and have negative wellbeing changes (bottom-left). The reason to agree to go ahead with interventions that have negative net costs and negative wellbeing changes is to free up funds for programmes that have higher wellbeing benefits.[15]

The optimal policy rule depends on the implicit value put on the use of public funds. Recall equation (1): an intervention should go ahead if the social surplus of the intervention is positive. That is,

$$\text{Net Additional Wellbeing Benefits} - \lambda * \text{Net Additional Public Costs} > 0$$

where the left-hand side is the social surplus and λ denotes the wellbeing value of a unit of net public costs. λ ideally captures—taking the example of the United

[15] We here abstract from the possibility of an exact budget constraint and lumpy projects such that one, for instance, cannot, at the margin, finance the most cost-effective programme because a less effective one has a lower overall cost that does not exceed the exact budget constraint. The optimal knapsack problems associated with choosing how to allocate an exact budget to buy particular items are computationally difficult but not all that relevant for government as a whole, which funds thousands of distinct programmes, in which case it is reasonable to presume that funding the most cost-effective programmes first identifies the marginal cost-effectiveness threshold by the last project funded.

Kingdom—the agreed-upon, minimal UK-wide benefit of every £ spent for any public programme anywhere in the country. It is the conversion value between money and wellbeing. In the case that all interventions have positive costs, the optimal policy rule is simply to fund the interventions for which the cost-effectiveness ratio (CE) is higher than λ. Within the logic of rational spending of government funds, λ should be the number of WELLBYs per £ produced by the marginal intervention that is funded, i.e. the inverse of the marginal social production costs of a WELLBY.

Equivalently to having the rule to fund everything with positive social surplus, one can define the public's maximum willingness-to-pay for an intervention that leads to a particular amount of WELLBYs as:

$$WTP_{public} = \frac{\text{Net Additional Wellbeing Benefits}}{\lambda} \qquad (3)$$

which yields the monetized value of wellbeing benefits of an intervention. This would be the willingness-to-pay by the government, which might differ quite strongly from the willingness-to-pay of an individual, which will typically be higher because it is more costly for individuals to increase their wellbeing than it is for the government. We will discuss in more detail which λ to use for different types of analyses in chapter 4, where we discuss the overlap and differences between wellbeing CEA and other approaches to public funding decisions.

When λ is high, the opportunity value of funds is high, which means that new interventions displace something else with a high level of wellbeing cost-effectiveness. For a new intervention to be funded, that intervention would thus have to have a higher wellbeing cost-effectiveness than what it displaces. In Figure 3.2, this situation is captured by the steep dotted line going through the origin (point '0', i.e. the intersection between the cost and the wellbeing axes). It can be denoted as the *low-budget line*. Only interventions to the left of that line should go ahead, which include all interventions with negative net costs and positive wellbeing changes, as well as some interventions that have negative net costs and negative wellbeing changes and some interventions that have positive net costs and positive wellbeing changes.

When λ is low, the opportunity value of funds is low, which means that new interventions displace something else with a low level of wellbeing cost-effectiveness. For a new intervention to be funded, that intervention would thus have to only go above that lower wellbeing cost-effectiveness. In Figure 3.2, this situation is captured by the dotted line going through the origin, which is less steep. It can be denoted as the *high-budget line*. Interventions to the left of that line should go ahead, which again includes all interventions that have negative net costs and positive wellbeing-changes, as well as just one intervention that has negative net costs and negative wellbeing changes and many interventions that have positive net costs and positive wellbeing changes.

Where Does λ Come from?

The parameter λ denotes the wellbeing opportunity value of public funds. It is implicitly given by the least favourable intervention to be funded that exhausts the available budget. In terms of Figure 3.2 above, λ can be found by looking for the least steep line at which the available budget is entirely spent.

Yet, in the longer run, the budget itself is not a given but subject to public choice. Ideally, the only real optimal policy rule should be that any change is acceptable if it raises national wellbeing. The effects of changes of budgets on wellbeing then simply become part of the calculation.

Thus, ideally, both the budget and λ themselves derive from the long-run optimization of wellbeing in the country. Taking the example of the United Kingdom, their level is then given by the point at which an additional £ of public resources raised has zero wellbeing benefits, however that extra resource is raised. Public resources can increase via additional economic activity that is taxed, via increases in tax rates, or via decreases in spending. Yet, it should remain the case that, at the margin of the additional £ gained by any public action (that is, more taxes or less spending), the net long-term wellbeing change should be zero.

This does not mean that the value of λ should ideally be zero, because funds are never infinite and it can be the case that raising more funds might have negative wellbeing effects itself. Likewise, it is possible that wellbeing is maximized when the budget is maximized, where any change would only reduce public resources. This will be the optimal case if all public spending at the margin has wellbeing benefits while taxation has no wellbeing costs. The optimal budget is then the point at which additional taxes lead to lower economic activity such that the net additional taxes are zero. This is known in economics as the maximum of the *Laffer curve* which denotes the relation between tax rates and tax revenue, and has the important feature that, at some point, higher tax rates reduce tax revenues as taxable economic activity is discouraged. When taxation or other methods of raising public revenue have negative effects on wellbeing, the optimal budget is likely to be lower than maximum possible budget. λ is then the marginal wellbeing benefit of spending at the level of the optimal budget.

In practice, from a wellbeing perspective, we do not yet understand the economic and political system well enough to determine the long-run wellbeing or long-run economic effects of changes to the budget. One might say the system as a whole uses trial-and-error to find optimal public budgets, guided more by political pressures than rational policy. The pragmatic approach is then to take the available budget as the outcome of the political process, and to focus the wellbeing efforts on the question of how best to allocate the given budget, which in turn implies a particular λ.

A Few Key Reflections

The basic wellbeing CEA methodology made several implicit choices and embedded circumstances that need to be pointed out for a full understanding.

Why a Sum of Wellbeing over Time?

The basic wellbeing CEA methodology involves a sum of individual wellbeing over time, for which a short-hand notation (that neglects discounting and social weights) is $\sum_t W_{it}$. The motivation is that a sum over time comes closest to the notion of the lifetime wellbeing of an individual.

Yet, if one thinks of the different reasons for why life satisfaction is the most suitable candidate measure of W_{it} we have at the moment, it is not immediately clear at all that one should care about a sum of life satisfaction over time, that is $\sum_t W_{it}$.

If one considers the argument that life satisfaction is a strong predictor of political behaviour (voting for or against the incumbent; cf. Liberini et al., 2017; Ward, 2019; Ward et al., 2020) and thus an expression of the political will of an individual, then a self-interested politician would logically care about the life satisfaction of the voting population at the next election. What the life satisfaction is between elections or of non-voters is not obviously of concern to such a politician, since the system is set up for the politician to care about being (re-)elected at a particular point in time. (In this argument, we focus on politicians rather than bureaucrats in the civil service, which are less determined by the political business cycle and may have more complex motivations.) The counterargument to this is that election incentives are a means to an end in themselves, where the end is more the wellbeing of the entire population throughout their lives. Yet, there is an obvious tension between the incentives given to politicians via the political business cycle and any longer-term aim.

If one then considers the argument that life satisfaction is a reasonable measure of how someone thinks he or she is doing, including (somewhat of) an assessment of what happened in the past and expectations for the future, then the question arises why one would need future wellbeing at all and not just look at W_{i0} for the relevant population. If life satisfaction was some kind of aggregation of experiences over life, one should not aggregate again over these aggregations, one can argue, but merely aim to increase W_{i0}. Much like in classic utility theory one would care about the current measure of lifetime utility.

The main counterarguments to this are that (i) different individuals are likely to have different time frames in mind when they answer the life satisfaction, which makes W_{i0} much less comparable across individuals than $\sum_t W_{it}$, (ii) individuals cannot be realistically expected to know at this moment what all the chosen policies in the future are going to be and hence considerations of policy must involve the notion of future life satisfactions as expected to evolve with or without policies, and (iii) we do not merely care about how individuals think about their lives now but also have some regard for what they will think in the future, which is likely to differ due to the cognitive burden when taking into account how changes will affect them.[16]

What about Adaptation?

A strong feature in the literature on psychological measures of wellbeing (be it life satisfaction, happiness, anxiety, or mental wellbeing) is that individuals adapt to circumstances such that a permanent change in intermediate outcomes has only a temporary effect on wellbeing. At the very least, the immediate effect of a permanent change is often much higher than the long-run effect, something we see, for instance, with physical impairments but also with changes in income levels.

The basic wellbeing CEA methodology generalizes to this feature, by looking at discounted sums of wellbeing whereby everything is measured in terms of discounted lifetime effects. Whether changes in circumstances then have a permanent or temporary effect on wellbeing is a purely empirical question, which makes it important to hold that distinction in mind when looking at the claimed effects of a policy. Note that this does not necessarily mean that if something does not show up in individual life satisfaction it is without value to the public because it may show up as affecting life expectancy (hence affecting the sum of wellbeing) or net public costs including taxes and welfare spending.

Why Not a Cost-benefit Calculation?

The central inequality in equation (1) compares net additional wellbeing in WELLBYs with net additional public costs in £ and thus combines two different units of accounts. Why not convert one into the other such that one either only compares wellbeing with wellbeing, or £ with £? This would then be either a 'wellbeing-augmented CBA' (when wellbeing and all other factors are converted into £) or a 'wellbeing CBA' (when £ and all other factors are converted into wellbeing). We will look at these differences in more detail in chapter 4, but note

[16] To see this point at its most basic level, suppose that there are two types of individuals, one that rationally scans all possible futures and answers the life-satisfaction question as if it is expected lifetime utility, and another individual who sees no further ahead than a day (a highly myopic individual). If one were to use W_{i0} for both individuals, this would be an accurate approximation for the first person but hugely misleading for the second. Yet, in both cases $\sum_t W_{it}$ would be an accurate approximation of their lifetime utility: in expectation $\sum_t W_{it}$ is the same as W_{i0} for the rational individual while $\sum_t W_{it}$ approaches expected lifetime utility the more time periods one includes in $\sum_t$.

here that the optimal policy rule is set up to fit the generic problem of a budget-constrained decision-maker who simply has to choose how to allocate funds over different demands.

The key problem with converting £ into wellbeing is that the shadow value of funds (which one might think of as the Lagrangean multiplier in an optimization problem) is unlikely to remain fixed over time, and its value is extraordinarily difficult to pin down because it involves, in principle, all the effects of increasing or decreasing budgets at any point in the future. A practical approach to this is to take the budget as roughly fixed and driven by the political process, which then leads to a particular λ in every period.

The key problem with converting wellbeing into £ is basically the same, but in reverse: because the wellbeing value of funds changes, the £ value of wellbeing also changes over time. More practically, the methods to calculate them from individual choice behaviour yield a rather wide range of possible values, essentially depending on whether one takes an individual or societal perspective (which requires one to include consumption externalities), whether one looks at invisible or visible spending (spending to which attention is drawn has far more wellbeing effects than other costs), and whether one looks at short-run or long-run spending. We will revisit this issue in depth in chapter 4.

Wellbeing CEA methodology bypasses both these issues and takes the pragmatic approach of comparing spending over all different destinations, simply asking where the highest return is for the available budget in that period. It separates the problem of the value of public money from the problem of the value of wellbeing.

Generalizations and Recommended Technical Standards

The above is a very idealized illustration of how to spend a finite amount of public funds on a set of potentially worthy interventions. It depicted a very pristine case where things were known for certain, decisions were all or nothing, and there was actual information on all relevant changes to wellbeing and costs. Almost no actual wellbeing CEA will be as pristine as this, just as no existing policy evaluation and appraisal will be as pristine either. We next discuss some common short cuts and generalizations relevant to many, if not all, actual analyses.

Splitting up Groups and Time Periods

One difficulty is often that the different sources of evidence for the effects an intervention might have are not derived from the same groups of people. One might, for instance, have primary information from a randomized controlled trial about how a school intervention changes outcomes for pupils' behaviour, and yet have no information in that study on how the parents and siblings are affected.

Yet, behavioural issues with children could have large benefits to parents shown in a different study. How does one deal with this?

A key generalization is to split up the affected population into manageable groups of people. In the case of the school intervention, this could be:

$$\sum_i sw_i{}^*(W_{it}^1 - W_{it}^0) = \sum_{pupils}(W_{it}^1 - W_{it}^0) + \sum_{parents}\Delta W_{it} + \sum_{siblings}\Delta W_{it} \tag{4}$$

This splits up the group whose wellbeing is deemed relevant into three different sub-groups: pupils, parents, and siblings. In this example, one is likely to know both W_{it}^1 and W_{it}^0 for the pupils because this is what a proper randomized controlled trial does: a proper trial has a control group that allows one to say what W_{it}^0 would be for the individuals in the absence of an intervention, as well as a treatment group that actually measures W_{it}^1 such that one can calculate the average causal effect of the intervention on the wellbeing of the treated $(W_{it}^1 - W_{it}^0)$. In this example, one does not know, however, the actual parents or siblings because they were missing from the trial. Nevertheless, one might be able to obtain a good estimate for $\sum_{parents}\Delta W_{it}$ and $\sum_{siblings}\Delta W_{it}$ because one does know what has changed in the lives of the pupils. If one can find good evidence on what effect a behavioural improvement of students has on their parents and siblings (for example, from the related literature), then one can effectively deduce the likely change for the wellbeing of parents and siblings given the intervention at hand.

Mathematically, one might thus have a good idea as to what ΔX_{it} is for a set of pupils where the relevant X_{it} could, for instance, be conduct problems or exam results. We will loosely call this *behaviour*. If one then knows what $\frac{\partial W_{parent,t}}{\partial X_{child,t}}$ is, that is, the change in wellbeing of the parents when one of their children's behaviour improves due to an intervention at school (found in another study), then one can know $\sum_{parents}\Delta W_{it}$ as it equals $\sum_{pupils}\Delta X_{it}\sum_{\text{parents of i}}\frac{\partial W_{parent,t}}{\partial X_{child,t}}$. The same holds for siblings.

When doing this, one has to be careful to get the main elements right: one has to have some idea as to how many parents the students have (which can differ between school types), and it has to be reasonable that the effect on the wellbeing of the parents found in some outside study would also hold in this case, that is, the situation in which the result was found in the outside study should in its key characteristics resemble the situation at hand.[17]

In the same manner as one can split the population into distinct sub-groups, one can also split the overall time period into distinct periods. For instance, in the

[17] Another issue is that the measure of behaviour is often not the same across studies. This could mean that the behavioural improvement found in the main study would need to be 'translated' into the supposed behavioural improvement used in the outside study. A common and often reasonable approach is to check that the behavioural measures roughly measure the same underlying constructs, and then to presume that a standard deviation in one is equal to a standard deviation in the other.

same schooling intervention one might want to include the long-run wellbeing benefits of improved schooling outcomes, despite the fact that the randomized controlled trial itself does not follow individuals for twenty years and hence does not actually report on long-run wellbeing benefits. Then, one effectively would need to split the overall time period into the observed and an unobserved future time period:

$$\sum_t \sum_{pupils} (W_{it}^1 - W_{it}^0) = \sum_{\text{study period}} \sum_{pupils} (W_{it}^1 - W_{it}^0) + \sum_{\text{rest of life}} \sum_{pupils} \Delta Education_i * \frac{\partial W_{it}}{\partial Education_i} \quad (5)$$

This now treats the problem quite differently in different time periods, with full information on wellbeing in the period for which there is information (the study period) and a best-estimate approach for the rest of life, which takes a key indicator of what the intervention achieved from the randomized controlled trial (changed education) and then combines that indicator with outside information of how much education changes wellbeing in the long run. The latter can be denoted as $\frac{\partial W_{it}}{\partial Education_i}$. Taking the example of the United Kingdom, cohort datasets such as the National Child Development Study (NCDS) or the 1970 British Cohort Study (BCS) allow us to have some idea as to how much education (and behavioural improvements) affect later-life wellbeing.

Note that this is not the first-best, because one ideally would want all the relevant information from a single source of evidence (ideally a randomized controlled trial) in which everything is measured. Unfortunately, such cases are exceedingly rare, if only because it makes the original studies very expensive if they have to follow more groups over longer periods of time. Hence, one is almost always forced to combine information from different sources as a second-best in practice.

On the cost side, it is nearly always important to split up groups that incur costs: directly affected individuals, employers, or the taxpayer. The two main reasons to split up groups is that information on costs is usually group-specific rather than individual-specific and that analysts are usually interested in a breakdown between entities where financial costs and cost savings occur.

Time, Forecasting, and Backcasting

The overall time period chosen implies a judgement as to how long an intervention is thought to have an effect. Yet, so far, the example we have seen has been about how the overall time period might be split up into different periods. In many cases, it makes more sense (and imposes far less assumptions) to do exactly the opposite, that is, try and work out what effect an intervention would have had *in the past.*

Of course, suggested interventions are invariably aimed at the future. Yet, all the evidence on what an intervention might do is always from the past; the future has many uncertain elements in it that one might not want to speculate on. Explicitly or implicitly, any forecast makes a stand on what future is expected. An alternative to trying to calculate what an intervention might have as costs and wellbeing benefits in the future is, therefore, to calculate what it might have had in the past, effectively taking it as likely that a similar effect will happen if the intervention were to occur in the future. One could, for instance, try and work out what the wellbeing cost-effectiveness of an intervention would have been over the last five years. We call this *backcasting*, to differentiate it from forecasting.

A key advantage of backcasting is that the past is known, implying that one does not have to guess the status quo scenario, which one would have to do in the case of forecasting. In the case of backcasting, one can rely on past data and effectively compare the actual outcomes from the past with those one thinks would have happened under the intervention scenario. In many ways, this is the honest thing to do, as any trial and evidence does exactly that: it looks at what happened in the past.

Backcasting is particularly useful when one wants to take into account a large number of causal pathways that require a deeper knowledge about the circumstances individuals find themselves in. For instance, childhood interventions involve many different individuals (for example, parents, siblings, classmates, or teachers) and the effects of changes spilling over from a child onto others are dependent on circumstances (for example, socio-economic status or schools). Thus, if one is interested in the effects of changes on many different individuals, one needs to calculate wellbeing and cost changes for many different individuals under many different circumstances. An easy way to go about this is to look at the past using data that have lots of specific information in order to trace how an intervention would have changed variables in those circumstances.

In the discussion of the Improving Access to Psychological Therapies (IAPT) mental health programme later in this chapter, we will give a detailed example of backcasting, combined with split populations. Note that backcasting can also be combined with forecasting, by splitting the overall time period into a study period and a rest of life.

Risk or Uncertainty

All elements of wellbeing CEA contain elements of risk or uncertainty: which individuals to include, which overall time period to consider, which wellbeing benefits and costs to include. How does one deal with risk or uncertainty?

We should remind ourselves of equation (1) and what the optimal policy rule is: we adopt an intervention if the surplus of the intervention is positive:

$$\text{Net Additional Wellbeing Benefits} - \lambda * \text{Net Additional Public Costs} > 0$$

Here, the λ is such that the least beneficial project to be funded has a surplus of just above zero. If the budget is not exhausted at some initial level of λ, then one can decrease λ so as to fund more interventions that together exhaust the budget.

Risk changes very little about the optimal policy rule because all that risk does is to change the rule to that of expected surplus:

$$\text{Expected Net Additional Wellbeing Benefits} - \lambda * \text{Expected Net Additional Public Costs} > 0 \quad (6)$$

This denotes that one should use expected wellbeing benefits and costs changes, but otherwise adopt the same rule, because that is the rule that maximizes the expected surplus from the choice of interventions. In case the risk around the original case is symmetric, i.e. that there is as much possible unexpected upside as downside, risk has no effect at all and can be ignored.[18] Often, however, one cares about risk because of a fear of a large negative downside, particularly if the costs involved are large and the claimed surplus is small.

There are many ways to take account of and report risk. Analysts can, for instance, calculate and report the standard deviations around the expected wellbeing benefits as well as the expected costs. Moreover, they can nominate a 'worst case scenario' that depicts, say, the average of the bottom 5 per cent of all possible outcomes. Likewise, analysts can report the percentage of possible outcomes in which the intervention is not cost-effective.

The sources of risk are sometimes known, sometimes not. If one uses estimates of effects from randomized controlled trials or the literature, one usually has some information on the risk in those estimates. One could thus make 'draws' from the distribution that those estimates come from, calculate the relevant statistics using different draws, and then report the outcomes of particular draws (for example, the average, the best, or the worst draw). Such methods are well elaborated in the statistics literature and can be applied to wellbeing CEA just as effectively.

Sources of uncertainty pertain to how the world works and what the future looks like, which is particularly important when looking at the far future. Three examples of wellbeing-relevant questions with unknown answers (and largely unknown probabilities) are: how likely is it that the world of work is completely disrupted by digital technology, automation, and artificial intelligence so that old structures become obsolete? What are the most important pathways in which future international migration affects the wellbeing of the current population? What are the long-run consequences of the Covid-19 pandemic for social relationships? To all three, the answer is that we do not know and that we have no obvious way of knowing how negative the consequences are if we ignore them.

[18] Note that here we are talking of symmetry in the risk in terms of effects on wellbeing and costs. Risk-aversion and distributional issues are already included in the wellbeing outcome which means that symmetry in the risk of a particular input might not translate to symmetry in terms of risk in wellbeing.

Usually one proceeds from the running assumption that the future will look like the past few years, meaning that one tries to improve past outcomes.

Risk or uncertainty are, therefore, innate features of policy-making. The question is how much effort one wants to put into evaluating and discussing all possible sources of risk or uncertainty. A pragmatic approach is to evaluate and discuss the main sources that one believes are relevant to an intervention, to make an informed judgement as to how a bad outcome in that dimension would change the bottom line or would change how the intervention should be implemented, and to suggest where further analysis might be most informative.

Endogenous Costs

As we discussed in the non-formal introduction of the basic wellbeing CEA methodology, costs often come from a bargaining situation and are not set in stone. This includes situations in which private companies are involved that deliver specialized services. The prices charged by private companies can come from auctions, a procurement procedure, or some other form of negotiation. Automatically, costs are then not fixed (assuming that the government is a monopsonist) and dependent on the outcome of a strategic bargaining situation.

In our illustrative diagram of interventions with net costs and wellbeing changes, the surplus of the intervention denoted by an asterisk (*) can be calculated as the horizontal distance between that point and the decision curve given by the budget line, which we can also refer to as *zero-surplus line*. This distance is denoted in Figure 3.3 below as A:

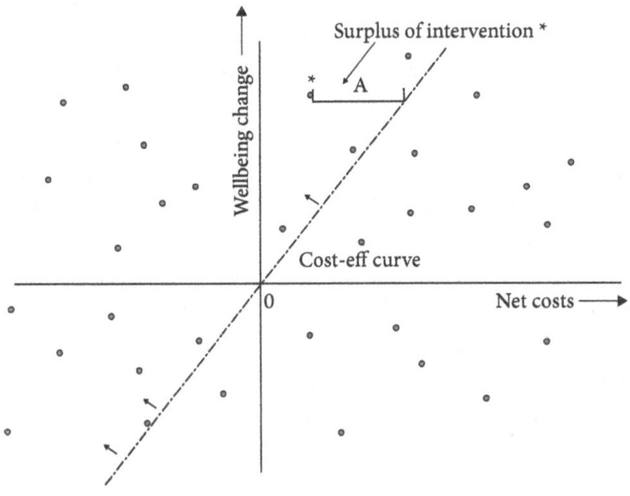

Figure 3.3 Wellbeing cost-effectiveness decisions: results of bargaining
Source: Own illustration.

The distance A between the zero-surplus line given by a particular λ is the additional cost that the agency delivering the intervention could 'charge' while remaining cost-effective. It is the surplus accruing to the public under the 'old' price. If the intervention's cost was driven by the price asked by a private company that maximizes profits, then the logical thing to do for that private company would be to increase the price until the zero-surplus line was reached. This would, of course, also be a danger for all other projects, meaning that there is the possibility that all private companies implementing interventions would want to 'charge' the maximum they can get away with, which would bring all costs up to the zero-surplus line, as denoted in Figure 3.4 above. The cost of each intervention would then reach the public's willingness-to-pay.

This is not merely a theoretical possibility, as our example on pharmaceutical purchases in the United Kingdom from before has shown: by implicitly advertising a cost-effectiveness threshold of around £25,000 to £30,000 per QALY, pharmaceutical companies have started asking for prices close to it, leading to prices for medicines that are above costs in many situations. Jena and Philipson (2009) argued that a 'reimbursement policy based on endogenous cost-effectiveness levels may therefore bear little relationship to efficient use of scarce medical resources.' A recent study of the medicine-reimbursement systems in United Kingdom and Australia found that the use of an explicit threshold by NICE led to significantly higher costs (Wang et al., 2018). Given the huge costs of medicines, the loss due to openly advertising and enforcing a high willingness-to-pay is likely to cost the United Kingdom billions.

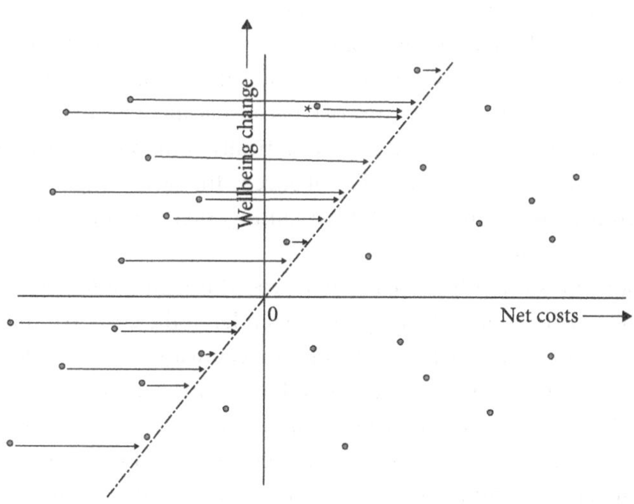

Figure 3.4 Wellbeing cost-effectiveness decisions: danger of escalating costs
Source: Own illustration.

The danger of openly advertising a country-wide λ to be used in procurement processes should not be underestimated because the problem experienced in pharmaceutical purchases might easily spill over to other sectors that rely on private providers for public services that have significant market power. The problem of bargaining with many different providers in many different interventions about possible prices does not have a straightforward answer, except in the highly improbable case that the decider has so much information about all the costs that he or she can simply offer a low price that is known to be sufficient to attract providers. That kind of scenario exists only in almost perfect markets. In all other situations, costs will not be well known, and the issue arises as to how best to design the bargaining situation to maximize total surplus and thereby the overall wellbeing of the population. Private providers will usually have an incentive to ask for more than their actual costs and to hide information on their actual costs.

How to minimize public costs in strategic bargaining situations is a vast area of active research that falls outside the scope of this book. Klemperer (2004) gives a general treatise on how to design procurement auctions in cases when information about costs is imperfect and a decider wants to maximize surplus via strategic bargaining. The key insight to keep in mind is that one is likely to pay too much if one is not prepared to walk away from the negotiation at a point below one's maximum willingness-to-pay.

At a conceptual level, bargaining over costs expands the notion of what an intervention is to include the bargaining process itself. An intervention is hence a combination of things one wants to do and a procedure to minimize the possible costs associated with them. Bargaining then is as much a core part of an intervention as all other parts, and is potentially subject to risk or uncertainty, experimentation, and incremental optimization. For instance, a road-building intervention can include the policy rule that one will offer no more than £X per kilometre of road of a certain quality, where £X should be well below the maximum willingness-to-pay.

Mathematically, bargaining creates risk because it includes the possibility of no agreement, which means that one is automatically thinking of an expected wellbeing CEA, where there is a probability of successful bargaining and a probability of no deal. In the case of unsuccessful bargaining, there are no wellbeing changes due to the intervention.

Large institutions often have particular procedures to guide negotiations with outside parties such as compulsory 'going to tender' if the costs are above a certain threshold. In many cases, such as with pharmaceuticals and tax negotiations, the bargaining situation is a prime area where large gains can be made. One should, therefore, take the process via which costs arise seriously as an area to be optimized in the design phase of the intervention. Pragmatically speaking, this means that it is rarely optimal to have a publicly advertised optimal policy rule to fund all interventions with a certain cost-effectiveness in the case that one is procuring major parts of an intervention from partners who can alter their prices strategically. One explicitly wants to think about how to maximize expected total surplus via bargaining systems.

Reversibility and Gambling with Disruption

Reversibility changes wellbeing CEA in a fundamental way because a reversible intervention is really a combination of two interventions: the intervention up until the reversible moment and the intervention after that moment. The second intervention is only possible if one has chosen the first, but not the other way around.

To see how reversibility changes the relevant cost-effectiveness calculation, let us first introduce some notation and, for simplicity, assume that the intervention has a fixed, but unknown, wellbeing benefit and cost in each time period and that the intervention could run until period T. One only learns the benefits and costs after some initial time which is after 0 but before T, at which point one can axe the programme at no further cost. The wellbeing benefits come from a cumulative distribution function denoted as $g(w)$, whereas the costs come from a cumulative distribution function denoted as $h(C)$. The reversible intervention is, by assumption, reversible at time $t = 1$.

The expected wellbeing changes until $t = 1$ are $W_{before} = E_g\{W\}$ and the expected net costs are $C_{before} = E_h\{C\}$. At $t = 1$, one learns what the true wellbeing benefits W and costs C per period are. The optimal action at $t = 1$ is to continue with the intervention if and only if $W > \lambda C$, and else stop. The expected surplus of adopting the intervention in period $t = 0$ is:

$$\begin{aligned} &W_{before} - \lambda C_{before} + [\text{option value}] \\ &= W_{before} - \lambda C_{before} + \\ &p(W > \lambda C) * \frac{(1-\rho) - (1-\rho)^{T+1}}{\rho} * E_{g,h}(W - \lambda C | W > \lambda C) \end{aligned} \tag{7}$$

where $W_{before} - \lambda C_{before}$ are the expected wellbeing benefits minus costs in the first period, $p(W > \lambda C)$ denotes the probability that the intervention turns out to be cost-effective, and $\frac{(1-\rho)-(1-\rho)^{T+1}}{\rho} * E_{g,h}(W - \lambda C | W > \lambda C)$ denotes the discounted surplus (wellbeing gains minus costs) conditional on the surplus being positive. This expected surplus formula has important characteristics. For one, the option value $p(W > \lambda C) * \frac{(1-\rho)-(1-\rho)^{T+1}}{\rho} * E_{g,h}(W - \lambda C | W > \lambda C)$ is always positive, simply because there is some probability that the intervention is unexpectedly cost-effective. Also, it is perfectly possible that $W_{before} - \lambda C_{before}$ is negative, meaning that the intervention is expected to be a bad decision in the first period. The expected surplus for the whole period can still be positive, however, due to the option value.

Reversibility has the nature of a gamble: if something is reversible, one has the benefit that the gamble could lead to a future pay-out even though that is unlikely. The gamble comes at the cost that it requires one to try it for some time before one finds out the true value. This is also the clue as to the relevance of this kind of possibility: where one only learns over time what the wellbeing benefits and net costs are by implementing an intervention. The gamble is then like a large experiment that one does not expect to be a success but that might be a success.

The logic also goes in reverse: one can axe a programme which one currently believes might be cost-effective if there is a good possibility that it is in fact not cost-effective, but one can only find out by axing it. If one intends to resurrect the programme if it is revealed it to be cost-effective after axing it, then terminating a current programme in an attempt to learn its true cost-effectiveness can be sensible under certain circumstances.

The crucial element here is then the possibility that the cost-effectiveness of some programmes can only be known when they are implemented or axed. One might think this is unusual, but our societies are so complex that it is actually not: those who benefit most from current programmes might only reveal themselves when something is axed because they then complain. There are programmes of which the cost-effectiveness is unknown and where only a large disruption is likely to unearth whether they work or not. Sometimes that is a risk worth taking, sometimes not.

Life and Death

So far, we have not been explicit about how to count additional years of life in a wellbeing context. Yet, nearly all large policies have an effect on the number of people alive in the population, either by preventing deaths, affecting the birth rate, affecting the mortality rate, or in some other way that affects life and death. This is obviously an emotional issue, but inevitable because every large project includes risks, particularly in the area of infrastructure and health, but also essential social services.

The basic methodology is the same as before: one makes initial choices as to who counts as part of the relevant population, which can include future generations. Then the question each period arises as to how the intervention affects $(W_{it}^1 - W_{it}^0)$, which denotes the wellbeing under the intervention (W_{it}^1) minus that under the status quo (W_{it}^0). If the status quo is where someone is dead or not born at all, then $W_{it}^0 = 0$.

This does raise the practical issue of what level of measured wellbeing is equal to zero. If one takes life satisfaction as the best available measure, the question is then what level of life satisfaction is equal to death (or non-existence)?

Importantly, the answer cannot be that the lowest possible number on the life-satisfaction scale is equal to not living, because that effectively rules out the possibility that people can live in circumstances that are worse than death. In the health economics literature, it has long been realized that there are health states worse than death and that some people may live in such terrible health states that death may seem preferable to them: their QALYS are negative.[19] In order to allow for terrible lives worse than death, the 'zero point' of life satisfaction has, therefore, to be higher than zero on a 0-to-10 scale.

Yet, just where on the 0-to-10 scale is life not worth living? There is no accepted answer to this question, but the literature has made attempts to answer it. Frijters (1999) already speculated about this issue and suggested that one should ask respondents whether they think their life would be worth living if they had to continue living in their present circumstances. The level of life satisfaction at which individuals would no longer think it would be worth carrying on would then be a suitable empirical measure of the 'zero-point' in life satisfaction.

Recently, Tessa Peasgood and colleagues of Sheffield University did something similar: they asked about 100 random persons near Sheffield if additional years of life spent in particular levels of life satisfaction would be worth living. Respondents had to indicate, for example, if they would prefer five more years of life living with a life-satisfaction level of 3 or simply not living further at all. They varied the hypothetical trade-offs, finding that at a life-satisfaction level of 2 about an equal number of respondents choose death over continued life (Peasgood et al., 2018), which denotes the point at which the marginal respondent is indifferent. While it would be important to do this study more thoroughly and with a much larger sample, the best estimate, at least at the moment, for the zero-point is thus a life-satisfaction level of 2.

This does not imply by all means that individuals below a life-satisfaction level of 2 are suicidal because individuals in a current life state worse than death may still hope for improvement, or may not have the disposition to take their own life even if they find it worse than death.

Note that it is important for the evaluation of continuation of life that one should not presume additional years of life are spent in full health or high life satisfaction, but rather one should presume them at the most likely level appropriate to their circumstances. When thinking of life-extending investments one should thus count the additional years at the level most likely to arise, not some imagined, overly high level.

Choosing Pathways in Evaluation and Design

When calculating the likely effect of an intervention on the population, one is effectively deciding on what the most important elements and pathways are. One is thus building a model of how the world works in that particular area, ideally

[19] The QALY as measured with the EQ5D can go below −0.5.

based on some theory of change. The model can be simple or complicated, but one probably does not get it perfectly right.

The following heuristic is useful, both when thinking of designing interventions and in trying to identify the most important pathways of a particular intervention:

1. Make a distinction in the relevant time period between three groups: the directly affected, those closest to the directly affected, and the population as a whole. One identifies the directly affected by the headline purpose of the intervention: what does the intervention aim for, whose lives are supposed to be affected, and how? Crucially, this requires an understanding of the status quo, because one needs to have an idea as to what would have happened without the intervention as only that identifies whose lives are affected the most. One identifies those closest to the directly affected by the simple question of who they interact with most (for example, loved ones, colleagues, or neighbours). Identifying the population as a whole is usually simpler, albeit not entirely trivial either, as our discussion on whom to include at the beginning has shown.
2. For each of the three groups, write down the five most important effects of the intervention on them that one intuitively expects. The pathways must be distinct enough so that one is not counting the same thing over and over, but truly counts additional effects. This is where the general thinking in the social science literature is the most valuable, because the literature gives clues as to the main wellbeing-relevant effects on individuals and the effects that people have on each other (externalities).[20]
3. Chase up one's own intuition with a casual look at the literature: what evidence or strong clues are there for the size of the effects? What does the literature related to the one consulted say about the strongest effects of these interventions and the envisioned linkages?
4. Work out the supposed timing of these effects: when do the effects emerge and how long do they last?
5. Do the same for costs as for the wellbeing benefits: who incurs what costs at what moments in time? What are the five most important sources of costs for the three groups? Again, the main pathways found in the literature might surprise one.

[20] For instance, we know for the population as a whole that additional consumption is almost irrelevant for wellbeing, though this is not true for the individual consuming more. Yet, since ultimately we are interested in the net effect on the wellbeing of the whole population, this knowledge helps eliminate a factor many would otherwise think of. On the other hand, we know that, in general, siblings and peers strongly affect each other's behaviour and that there are likely to be strong positive and negative externalities between them, meaning that one wants to have the literature on those effects at one's fingertips when deciding on pathways.

6. Redo steps 1 to 5 until one has a relatively coherent story as to main effects, externalities, costs, and population-wide effects. If effects quickly become less large as one goes from main effects to other effects, or from the directly affected to the indirectly affected, one can reduce the number of pathways and groups looked at. Conversely, if more than five pathways or three groups truly seem important, find evidence on more pathways and more groups. The eventual outcome of this is a model, which can be verbal or formal. This model can then be applied to data if applicable.
7. Get feedback from people who are knowledgeable but lukewarm and see whether they find the model plausible (this is a form of independent review). An approach that is more and more applied in the social sciences is adversarial feedback: try to get feedback specifically from people who are known to be non-supportive and sceptic about the intervention in question or about the methodology itself. Return to steps 1 to 6 if necessary.
8. Put in effort to get the best actual estimates on each of the pathways and costs, and work out what the effects are on the identified population in the identified time period.

The same steps can be done in design, though design is far more expansive and difficult because it requires one to think of many practicalities ('how would we implement this'). In the design stage, one is less constrained because one can still change the planned intervention, which in some sense adds to the problem of evaluation. As a result of the greater possibility space, one needs to run though the initial steps 1 to 6 more quickly and hence a bit more shallow, involving more relevant feedback earlier, only doing detailed benefits and costings for the best case.

Yet, at heart, design, evaluations, and appraisals are all acts of the imagination that require an interaction between how the world is imagined to go on without the intervention (the status quo) and images of how the world could be under the proposed change.

Avoiding the Double-counting of Effects When Doing Pathway Analyses

A classic problem with modern social science is that there are different sub-literatures focusing on parts of a larger problem, often in isolation of what other groups are looking at. Take as an example income and health. You have some research groups looking at the question of how income affects physical health, and others at how physical health affects income. The question of how mental health affects income is then another question, where physical health and mental health are neither the same nor totally different.[21]

[21] Take, for instance, problems with sleep, which are both a physical health problem and a mental health problem. It can also be caused by physical or mental issues.

Now, suppose that one has an intervention in mind that alleviates some physical health problem, like hip pain. How much wellbeing would that be worth? It is a relatively straightforward question in that it is clear who the primary beneficiary is (the patient with the hip problem) and one can additionally get a pretty good idea of how long the benefit would last, what the costs to the health system are, and who the additional beneficiaries are likely to be (for example, spouses).

If one were to trace the pathways, there is the great temptation to take pathways that are very similar to each other, such as the direct benefits of improved physical health on wellbeing, the effects of improved mental health on wellbeing, the effects of more income on wellbeing due to better health, and the effects of more income due to mental health. Each of these four pathways could easily be quantified via an existing literature that would give reasonable estimates as to how large the effects were, how long they lasted, and who in particular would benefit more.

Yet, it would be a clear case of double-counting: because physical health and mental health are not completely unrelated, one cannot simply add up the wellbeing benefits of greater physical health separately from the wellbeing benefits of greater mental health. The estimates for each separately contain an element of the other. Similarly, the estimates of the benefits to income of greater physical health are not completely independent from the estimates of the benefits to income of greater mental health. Finally, there is the issue of how to separate the 'direct effects' to wellbeing of health (via either mental or physical) from the indirect ones (via income).

How should this be done? Ideally, one would want a large randomized controlled trial in which one group received the intervention and another did not, where within both groups one measures their wellbeing over time, as well as their physical health, mental health, and incomes. One would then not bother about calculating wellbeing effects via health or income and simply take the observed improvement in wellbeing as the best number for the overall wellbeing improvement. One would still use the income improvement, but then not as a pathway to wellbeing but rather as relevant to the costs of the intervention because increased incomes mean increased taxation, which is a negative public cost (a saving). One would not look at the health-wellbeing pathways at all if one had the direct evidence on wellbeing.

In reality, however, such trials are rare. As a result, one will usually have to deduce the wellbeing effect from the known health effect of an intervention, coupled with outside literature knowledge on how health affects wellbeing and income. What to do then?

In this more limited data scenario, one has to make clear what the primary and secondary channels are through which the intervention affects wellbeing. It would be normal to think of the wellbeing benefit of improved physical health as the most important channel of a hip operation. The estimate on that effect found in the literature would be counted in full. One would also want to include an effect of improved mental health, but then one needs evidence on the mental health effects *conditional* on the physical health effect. This will often require one to trawl through the underlying studies to see how their results were derived, making sure to pick the identified effect that keeps physical health constant (that is, which controls for physical health in the respective multivariate regression analysis). With those two pathways accounted for, one should then *not* additionally add the two mentioned indirect pathways via income *unless* the previously identified health effects were explicitly *conditional* on income.

What this more deeply means is that one needs to immerse oneself in the question of what the evidence actually shows in terms of effects. This is not trivial because it requires a deep knowledge of research processes and how to read the research output, sometimes in different literatures using different methods. The generic questions are about the sources and limitations of findings: what is the variation that the underlying study is based on, and what factors are kept constant or not? Double-counting can only be avoided if the pathways are either completely independent, or if one uses as evidence information wherein the other pathways contemplated are 'shut down', by being conditional on the other key variables.

This issue only gets more complicated when one considers behavioural spillovers, different groups, and longer overall time periods. In principle, each pathway is like an envisioned mini-intervention where one thing is presumed to be changed independent of the rest of the system, and where one is interested in how that change subsequently affects some other part of the system. A proper accounting of the interrelations will invariably need a good understanding of how the original studies were conducted, sometimes adding pathways that were not mentioned in these studies.

The conservative approach to double-counting on the benefit side is the old saying 'when in doubt, kick it out', such that a pathway is not included if there is a likelihood that it is already included in the other pathways. In particular, this will go for any 'reflection' pathway, such as when the reduced hip pain in a patient improves relationship quality with their spouse, which then improves the health of the original patient again. While such a reflective pathway is quite possibly there, it is both likely to be relatively small and likely to be part of the effect found in the original study anyway because it will have been part of the effects that lead to the observed overall health improvements.

The same issue shows up on the cost side, such as when one does not want to include both the likely effect on taxes or benefits via observed improvements in income, as well as direct estimates of changes in benefits or taxes (it would have to be one or the other).

Unfortunately, it is not always the case that 'simpler is better' because a choice to look at very few pathways might, for instance, miss out negative feedback effects under which any original effect may be nullified. This is, for instance, salient when it comes to jealousy, which we know is important when it comes to consumption goods like housing or cars: one grossly overestimates the wellbeing benefits to society of consumption upgrades, i.e. bigger cars and bigger houses, if one only looks at the effects on those who upgraded and fails to look at those in their surroundings who did not. Hence, when it comes to negative feedback loops, the conservative approach is not 'when in doubt, leave it out' but rather the opposite: 'when in doubt, it counts'.

The issue of double-counting can only really be satisfactorily solved through a correct model of how the world works, including all the main interactions. Social science does not really yield that degree of certainty about complicated social processes, so limited heuristics like those outlined above are one pragmatic way of going forward.

Recommended Technical Standards

In order to have a consistent use of wellbeing CEA across different organizations and areas, the different users need to have an agreed list of technical standards. Table 3.1 summarizes the suggestions from the previous sections.

What this means is that the sum of WELLBYs, which is the maximand of the state, is now $\sum W = \sum (LS - ZeroPoint)$. Next, we discuss the issue of discounting in greater depth.

Table 3.1 Recommended technical standards

Description	Recommendation
Preferred measure of wellbeing	WELLBY: 1 unit of life satisfaction on a 0-to-10 scale for 1 person for 1 year
Child wellbeing (<10 years)	Carer's judgement of life satisfaction
Wellbeing of incapacitated	Carer's judgement of life satisfaction
Death	Life satisfaction of 2 on a 0-to-10 scale
Financial discount factor	Long-term treasury real bond rate
Wellbeing discount factor	1.5% (0.5% pure time preference + 1% catastrophic risk premium)
Easterlin Discount on economic surplus	75% (perhaps initially 50%)
Long-term income effect on individual	1% increase in annual net household income = 0.004 WELLBYs
Minimum social production cost of a WELLBY, λ	1/ £2,500 in 2019 £
Individual willingness-to-pay for a WELLBY	£9,000 in 2019 £

Source: Own illustration.

Further Notes on Discounting

In the literature on discounting for public sector projects (see Freeman et al. (2018) or Gollier (2012), for example), it is perfectly normal to start with a Ramsey rule which states that the social discount rate SDR is:

$$SDR = \delta + L + \eta g \tag{8}$$

where:

$$\delta = \text{pure time discount}$$
$$L = \text{catastrophic risk premium}$$
$$g = \text{real growth rate}$$
$$\eta = \text{elasticity of marginal utility of consumption}$$

which in the case of the UK HMT Green Book would boil down to 3.5 per cent as the assumptions are that the pure time discount is 0.5 per cent, the catastrophic risk premium is 1 per cent, the real growth rate is 2 per cent, and the elasticity of the marginal utility of consumption is 1. As Freeman et al. (2018) state, this is 'appropriate for discounting costs and benefits measured in consumption units'. Freeman et al. (2018) also make clear that other countries have quite different approaches and different discount rates, meaning that the UK methodology is not universally shared, particularly because the UK approach involves 'calibrating' the underlying social welfare function. We should mention that, while Freeman et al. (2018) consider various additions and alterations to the previous assumptions in the UK HMT Green Book, they recommend staying with the 3.5 per cent discount rate.

Now, it is important to realize the background to the Ramsey rule, which is that Ramsey assumed that money and consumption were interchangeable, and that the problem was to come up with a cut-off rule for projects that would merit funding versus those that would not. Ramsey was thus focused on using part of the economic pie today (in the form of investments in monetary terms, seen as the same as consumption terms) to generate a larger economic pie in the future (with everything in the future added up in terms of consumption, too). This required answers to two very different questions: (i) the question of how much the collective cares about consumption in the future versus consumption now, and (ii) the question of how high the return is on the last project still funded. Given that consumption is not utility and that the marginal utility of consumption reduces when the level of consumption increases, the cut-off rate Ramsey came to thus needed to include a consideration of how much one cares about utility tomorrow versus utility today, and how much marginal utility of consumption tomorrow will differ from that today.

The Ramsey rule provides a very particular answer to these questions: it is effectively presumed that the opportunity cost is such that economic growth is

2 per cent and that anything that promises more utility than would be given by that growth rate is a good project, and anything that promises less utility is a bad project. The possibility of a catastrophic risk then essentially entails a risk that there is no entity that enjoys utility tomorrow, or that something else unforeseen derails all the costs and benefits in terms of consumption.

Wellbeing CEA differs from this depiction in two ways: most importantly, the benefits are directly in terms of wellbeing, i.e. 'utility' in the language of the Ramsey-rule literature.[22] This means that there is no such term as ηg, simply because any change in the marginal utility of consumption is already embedded in the calculation of the wellbeing benefits. There is hence no 'correction factor' needed or appropriate when the benefits are directly in terms of wellbeing. Yet, pure time discounts and catastrophic risk remain relevant, which is why the appropriate rate for discounting wellbeing would be 1.5 per cent within the logic of the UK HMT Green Book.[23]

The second important difference is that in wellbeing CEA, the cost part is in monetary terms while we do not yet know how the wellbeing opportunity cost of money will change over time. Unlike for the Ramsey rule, it is not appropriate to assume that we know the cut-off point for projects to fund and projects not to fund because part of the objective is to actually find out what the relevant opportunity costs are. We cannot already presume to know the answer to the question of what the appropriate return on money would need to be.

Implicit in the Ramsey rule is that the utility benefit of a unit of real monetary costs reduces over time, which would mean that the marginal wellbeing benefits of government expenditure would decline. Within the Ramsey rule, the rate of that decline can be pinned down by long-run growth and particular parameters on risk aversion (depending on the utility function chosen). However, these assumptions are inappropriate for wellbeing CEA as we really do not know the long-run growth rate of wellbeing, or the changing marginal wellbeing benefits of government expenditure.[24] What then?

[22] There is an ongoing debate about whether wellbeing can be equated to utility or is just a component in an individual's utility function, amongst others. This debate is largely unsettled, and there is evidence supportive of both viewpoints. By and large, experimental evidence suggests that individuals consistently rank wellbeing (almost regardless of measure) higher than other outcomes (for example, income), except for health (Adler et al., 2017).

[23] Note that the UK Department of Health and Social Care uses the same 1.5 per cent when it aggregates health improvements over time, applying the same logic: as a final outcome, health does not have diminishing marginal utility in the future due to general increases in consumption, so that the 2 per cent additional discount does not apply. We advocate the same logic for wellbeing.

[24] For rich countries like the United Kingdom, the most likely answer is that the long-run growth rate of wellbeing per individual per year is zero. Moreover, the marginal wellbeing value of more individual consumption is likely to be zero as well (because the consumption externalities to others off-set individual gains). All the gains would be in terms of public goods, breaking the symmetry between

There are many possible ways forward. A pragmatic one is to choose a possible counterfactual for the costs of monetary funds, which includes both costs in the future (which are potentially negative) and up-front costs. Since part of the objective is to find out how much a stand-alone project is worth in terms of wellbeing benefits and financial costs today, one approach is to view the country as an entity that can borrow and lend to foreign investors at the real interest rate embedded in long-term treasury bonds. Within that viewpoint, the real value of a stream of monetary costs (some of which could be negative) spread out over time is the real value today applying the real interest rate in operation today, where, of course, the real interest rate itself may reflect things like changes in the marginal benefit of money. This essentially treats a project as if its funding is self-contained, either with actual money set aside for costs made in future years or borrowed against expectations of future returns. The appropriate discount rate is then the international real interest rate for the entity making the expenditure (for example, the UK government).

Now, a problem with this approach is that the break in the symmetry of discount rates for monetary costs and wellbeing benefits could lead to absurdities in terms of long-run trade-offs. For instance, if the market interest rate is lower than the wellbeing discount rate, then one would be willing to trade off an arbitrarily high loss of wellbeing for a finite monetary gain in the far future. Alternatively, if the market interest rate is higher than the wellbeing discount rate, one would be willing to have an arbitrarily high monetary cost for a finite wellbeing gain in the far future. These kinds of absurdities are standard when one compares two entities that are discounted at different rates.

Yet, while such absurdities then indeed hold, we should note that there are absurdities in any system of discounting combined with mechanical rules. For instance, in the current CBA logic, if it were the case that a new investment arose in which the rates of return were higher than the current discount rate but the benefits would only arise in an arbitrarily far future, say ten generations from now, then one 'should' invest the whole of the economic pie in it. It should be clear that no generation is truly going to forego all its own consumption for the benefits of ten generations ahead, independent of how high those benefits would be, so one then arrives at an absurdity in terms of the implications of a particular decision rule (i.e. maximize discounted costs less benefits).

Practically, if absurd choices truly arose, one would, of course, immediately consider the validity of the simplifying assumptions made to obtain actual discount rates and to obtain the decision rule.

individual private consumption and government expenditure (which are simply added together when calculating GDP). If we take wellbeing seriously, we need to break that presumed equivalence.

The Easterlin Discount

A decision has to be made as to how much of the individual benefit of additional material resources to include as a social benefit. The problems are negative consumption externalities, also termed as conspicuous consumption, status considerations, or simply jealousy. We discussed the huge evidence base for this phenomenon in chapter 2, but in accounting practice there needs to be a decision on how much the individual benefit is offset by relative status concerns in the whole population.

Richard Easterlin, who set this debate off in 1974, has ever since maintained that the discount should be 100 per cent, i.e. that the only benefit of more individual income is more taxes and that there is no residual benefit of greater private consumption in terms of wellbeing: it is all about status. Others in the literature are less absolute about this, but even the critics of Richard Easterlin, such as Angus Deaton or Betsey Stevenson and Justin Wolfers, agree that there is a large status effect. As discussed in chapter 2, a recent study by Kapteyn et al. (2019) suggests some 75 per cent of the effect of individual income on national wellbeing disappears if one additionally accounts for relative income (i.e. the income of others in a society or those like the individual). Yet, whilst it is widely accepted that status effects are large, there is no agreed-upon number as it is extremely difficult to pin down.

The proposed technical standard to start with in this book is to discount all increases in additional private consumption from additional economic activity by 75 per cent, i.e. to count only 25 per cent as an addition to the wellbeing of the country. From a political point of view, it is probably more expedient to start with a lower number, but we here simply advocate the default that seems the most reasonable one in rich countries like the United Kingdom where the state provides for most basic comforts. In a developing country, one should probably have a much lower default discount.

Importantly, as with all default standards, they cannot be taken as sacred. Rather, exceptions to the default should be argued on the basis of particular scientific evidence, such as evidence that some form of private consumption or wealth really involves much less or much higher levels of negative consumption externalities. We will show in the IAPT example later in this chapter how one could implement a subtle version of the Easterlin Discount, with different discounts applying to different forms of private consumption via explicitly modelled local reference points (although in that example the effective Easterlin Discount is still 75 per cent).

Note that this recommendation holds for additional private consumption and wealth, not for additional government spending that leads to public goods that are in principle available to everyone. This reflects the argument in chapter 2 that what is available to almost everyone is not subject to status considerations. An

Easterlin Discount also does not apply to expenses that are meant to increase the standing of the country amongst other countries because status considerations between populations are not equally relevant to national wellbeing (at least not to 75 per cent).

Anything that is actively marketed is likely to have a strong status element because private providers have strong incentives to try and attach status to the consumption of their products and services since that increases demand. As a rule of thumb, therefore, the Easterlin Discount should apply to anything with a market price on it.

A tricky class of private consumption goods are services and social positions that individuals are prepared to pay for, like marriage, education, or even employment. After all, it is perfectly possible for one person to be jealous of the partner someone else has, the college someone else goes to, or the job someone else has. Individuals can be willing to spend large amounts on obtaining such services. How to deal with this?

The proposed technical standard is to count all expenses towards such services and social positions as subject to the same Easterlin Discount, meaning that all private expenses into marriage, education, or even employment would be discounted in terms of their contribution to the national wellbeing by 75 per cent. It is possible and perhaps even probable that some services are more status-oriented than others, but that would then have to be shown by solid scientific evidence.

How to deal with investments? Private investments can be seen as less consumption today (which should be subject to the Easterlin Discount) leading to higher consumption in the future (which should also be subject to the Easterlin Discount). Public investments are like investments made for the whole population by the whole population, and hence with no obvious internal negative consumption externality (again, the jealousy of those in other populations does not count).

Note that things like the existing welfare state, which is partly about higher levels of consumption but partly also about providing a social safety net and hence taking away anxiety of destitution and social isolation, has its own wellbeing rationale. Changes to the welfare state should preferably be based on good randomized controlled trials or other strong evidence as to the likely effects. As chapter 2 discussed, the ability of key public services like health insurance or basic social safety nets to take away anxiety has not been found in the literature to go at the expense of those already well off. Hence, the Easterlin Discount should not apply to them. Also, the very fact that their rationale is to provide a social safety net to all takes away the status element because if everyone is covered, there are no status considerations.

The proposed technical standard, therefore, is to take all public expenses leading to things in principle offered to the whole population, like access to road or welfare, as exempt from the Easterlin Discount. Of course, if the state makes specific expenses that benefit only a small number of people and the rest is explicitly excluded, then that transfer to particular individuals should certainly be subject to the Easterlin Discount.

An Important Unknown: The Value of Enabling Collective Action

Some activities increase the wellbeing of a population, while others enable the state to exist and function. Enabling activities include the investments into the cohesion of the country and the functioning of the state itself. Key institutions that are primarily about enabling include, for example, the tax office or the ministry of defence, but also areas like heritage. Their primary role is less to generate direct wellbeing benefits to the population and more to create a sense of unity and joint purpose that is an input into the operation of the country itself, for instance, leading to higher tax morale and willingness to contribute to the good of the country.

In the case of tax morale, one could assign an indirect wellbeing value to activities that increase it, for instance by counting the wellbeing effect of more taxation as opposed to more private consumption (which is the opportunity cost of taxes). However, paying taxes is not the only means by which people give their time and talents to the good of the group as a whole. Nor is it immediate what the actual value is of several activities aimed at the strength and safety of the collective.

Defence is a case in point. In order to assign a wellbeing value to the marginal £ spent on defence one has to take a stand on what would happen without that marginal £, which, in turn, depends on the change in probability of some defensive breach and the likely wellbeing consequences of that breach. Such calculations have never been done as far we know, and it is difficult to envisage how they would be done because it requires taking a stance on complex developments that are difficult to predict, involving the likely reactions of other countries and agents. There may be risk analyses, but probably not in terms of actual probabilities. Nevertheless, the complexities of getting a good estimate of the wellbeing value of marginal defence spending has not stopped the United Kingdom or any other country in the past from investing in defence.

A similar difficulty arises with the enabling effects of heritage, shared values, and a stronger sense of community and joint national purpose. We know it is crucial for any sense of 'us' and hence for collective action, but just how crucial? Similarly, just how much wellbeing surplus is there due to the current ability to take collective action versus possible alternatives, such as from more independent regions or more integration into international structures? To make rational decisions on these matters that allow for trade-offs with other expenses, we need a reasonable framework to estimate the value of enabling activities, particularly the marginal enabling activities.

The default to a rational evidence-based approach in the case that the evidence is in terms of a general knowledge of how the world works, but not in terms of actual effects on measurable outcomes, is probably political and democratic judgement. A simple way of saying this is that if there is no clear expertise on something, one reverts to decision-making via the considered average view of everybody: if no one really knows, one goes with what everyone thinks they know.

Use of Literature in Wellbeing CEA When Developing Policy: Basic Issues and an Example

Literature study is a core part of the job of analysts and researchers, taught in universities and elsewhere. It is a key resource when one is developing policy. The context of wellbeing CEA for policy development purposes adds three additional elements to the simple question 'what does the literature say about this?':

(i) A policy focus means one needs to keep the limitations and practicalities of policy development in mind;
(ii) The question of what one is looking at is not set in stone but co-dependent on what one finds;
(iii) One is interested in the likely life-time effects on the whole population, not merely a particular sub-group.

We suggest ten steps one can go through to come to a considered answer to the question of how some intended increase in X changes the wellbeing of the population. Here, X is shorthand for some intermediate outcome initially envisaged to address a particular policy issue. To make this concrete, the example we are using is public secondary-school education, where the hypothetical intervention is to increase the maximum school-leaving age in the population (relative to the prevailing number of years as the status quo).

The provision of education, particularly for young children, is a core task of the state in most countries. The question whether it should provide for more education arises in many contexts, such as in debates about compulsory schooling, extensions of vocational education, subsidies and arrangements around university expansion, and new institutions around adult education. There has also been a recent push towards decreasing the school-entry age, and there is huge demand for pre-school and early childhood education services in many countries around the world.

Education involves both short-run and long-run effects. The short-run effect of education is the educational experience itself: schooling replaces other activities, such as formal work, which is an economic 'opportunity cost'. Schooling is also a daily activity with positive and negative characteristics, involving social interactions and compulsory elements (for example, exams). One main long-run effect is on labour market outcomes which accrue during the whole remaining lifetime.

Education also changes an individual: it socializes him or her to fit into particular groups, communities, and the country and international community.

This means that education is a good example of an investment made by society as a whole that has incredibly complicated effects on both individuals and society, many of which are hard to know with precision. Despite these uncertainties, however, every high-income country in the world invests heavily in education and has hit upon the basic belief that educating individuals for more than twelve years, on average, is a good thing for both those individuals and society.

Education is, therefore, a good case study of how wellbeing thinking can be applied to a general area of policy. We want to go over the basic case for more education, understood particularly as mandating individuals to stay in school until at least the age of sixteen, although the general reasoning applies to other types of educational investments as well.

The proposed literature checklist consists of the following steps:

1. What is the best and most convincing evidence on the effect of an increase in *X* on individual wellbeing over the life course?
2. Reflect on that evidence: what is the source of variation relied on? Do the key numbers make sense given how we think the world works? How well does that variation fit the potential policy changes we are interested in at the moment? Do the affected individuals in these studies look like the individuals that would be affected in the policy changes we are currently interested in?
3. If the answers to step 2 are 'no' or 'not really', then re-do step 1 until one has arrived at the best evidence for the kind of policy one is thinking of doing. Note that this is not an exact process because it relies on some notion of 'distance' between people studied in the literature and people affected by a future policy, who are unlikely to be exactly the same. Also, there is some notion of 'distance' between the source of evidence in the past and the type of policy we have in mind for the future, which are again unlikely to be exactly the same. Thus, some implicit theory of 'what really matters' is always present when thinking of evidence. The more explicit that theory, the better, as a more explicit theory can be updated with more evidence.
4. Decide on the most important pathways via which *X* might have an effect on the wellbeing of others. This minimally includes the effect of *X* on the public purse and the effect of *X* on close relations (for example, parents, partners, children, peers, or the community). This mapping out of the possible pathways again reflects implicit knowledge of how the world works and should thus include the thinking of the literature and the dominant theories therein.
5. Do steps 1 to 3 for each of the pathways via which *X* affects others.

6. Decide on the most important general equilibrium and long-term effects of an increase in X on the wellbeing of the current and future generations. Again, this relies on a judgement as to what the most important aspects of the macro environment are.
7. Do steps 1 to 3 for each of the chosen general equilibrium and long-term effects.
8. Add up the likely effects to an overall effect as well as its distribution: who gains, who loses? Compare the wellbeing effects with the costs, leading to an overall wellbeing cost-effectiveness and a wellbeing cost-effectiveness from different points of view (for example, society, a region, the first five years).
9. Reflect further on how the actual policy might be designed and implemented, with an eye on amplifying those pathways that lead to more wellbeing. This requires institutional knowledge of what is politically possible. Knowledge of the key wellbeing-sensitive areas helps in improving the policy and its delivery. Knowledge of pro-wellbeing ways of working also helps.
10. To get a full picture of the likely effects of the intervention and how it might be implemented, reflect on the system that would have to implement the changes and how they would react to the anticipated distribution and timing of effects: what are the incentives in place and how would that lead the implementing machinery to react? For instance, are there incentives for various parts of the implementing machinery to accentuate quick gains at the expense of longer-term gains and how would they achieve this? Are the outcomes of certain groups more important to those implementing the intervention and how would that affect outcomes?

Different elements on this checklist might be done by different people and, of course, the checklist can be part of an interactive system whereby a policy is deliberated by different stakeholders. That said, this checklist is not necessarily something an individual analyst works out on his or her own, but more thought steps recommended. Next, we apply these steps to education in a quick, organic manner: we construct a narrative on education that includes all these steps.

Example: Education and Wellbeing

Education, in a broad sense, has long been regarded as an excellent investment for individuals and society, particularly science, technology, engineering, and mathematics (STEM) subjects. The real rate of return on an extra year of secondary education or a year of university study has been estimated to be around 6 per cent per year (see the review by Psacharopoulos and Patinos (2018), for example), which is a far higher rate of return than what government bonds or the stock market have been offering during the past ten years, where 2 per cent to 3 per cent returns are now normal.

Yet, unless one assumes that individuals do not make rational investment decisions or are otherwise financially constrained, it is not so clear whether more education increases an individual's wellbeing, i.e. their life satisfaction. Rational people who are maximizing should not underinvest in education. One might think that there is an innate joy to knowing more and expanding one's mind, but from a quick look at international data across countries it appears perfectly possible to have a happy low-educated population: to know more does not obviously make you happier since more knowledge comes with problems too, such as additional expectations or more risks one is aware of.

While the consensus has long been that the higher educated are a bit happier than the less well educated (see Argyle (1999), for example), this has usually been explained by the fact that the higher educated score better in almost everything, including social relationships and health, so that causality runs more from the fact that better-resourced and healthier people are both happier and have more education. At a certain point, more education is likely to yield negatives: it means more years of low income during the investment period and brings about higher expectations because one now compares oneself to others in a higher-education group. Thus, if you look at the studies that track how the circumstances of people change as they are forced into more education than they wanted to invest in, you can get a basic idea of the impact of more education on the reluctant.

The cleanest study on this topic has been by Clark and Jung (2017) who track over four thousand individuals in the British Household Panel Survey (BHPS) subjected to a change in UK education laws in 1972 which made it compulsory for all children to stay in school until they were at least 16 years old. The authors compare around 1,850 individuals who turned sixteen just before September 1, 1973 (i.e. before the educational law was changed), with about 2,500 who turned sixteen after that date (i.e. after the law was changed), to estimate the causal effect of education on life satisfaction, assuming that individuals around the cut-off are otherwise comparable. They found that the group which was forced into additional years of education earned around 6 per cent more labour income per year, the same rate of return as the general literature on education finds. That is important because more income also means more taxes paid, which, in turn, may go to improved public services. In a lifetime income sense, the 6 per cent increase is worth roughly estimated around £50,000, and, in turn, leads to about £20,000 more taxes (assuming a 40 per cent tax rate). If spent on improved health services, for example, this increase in taxes could buy 1.3 QALYs[25] or eight WELLBYs.[26]

[25] Claxton et al. (2015) estimate that the NHS can generate one year of additional life in reasonable health at the price of around £12,936 (in 2008 £), which is around £15,000 in 2019 £ (Claxton et al., 2015; Lomas et al., 2019; see also Department of Health and Department of Education, 2017).

[26] One QALY is worth approximately six WELLBYs, using the rule of thumb that average life satisfaction for people in good health (i.e. a QALY of one) is about 8 while 2 is the life-satisfaction level

Importantly, however, life satisfaction reduced by about 0.1 points on a 0-to-10 scale for the group that was forced into additional education, which, in turn, was largely due to a decrease in mental health in that group. This fits the notion that (some of) those forced to be in school another year may now sort into different occupations and may learn to compare themselves with others who are in school for longer (and also in different occupations), which may increase their expectations and reduces their enjoyment of a particular economic outcome. At the same time, occupations at the higher end of the educational spectrum may yield other negatives, such as, for example, higher stress levels or less desirable working hours, which may contribute to the decrease in overall life satisfaction.

This decrease in life satisfaction is borderline significant, but taken at face value is quite large: a 0.1 decrease in life satisfaction on a 0-to-10 scale per year amounts to six points over a sixty-year post-school life, which, in turn, is a loss of six WELLBYs. The authors themselves note that other authors looking at the same data with slightly different methods actually find a slightly positive life-satisfaction effect, which they attribute to the fact that others look at just a small window in life as opposed to the overall life course (i.e. the effects are not constant throughout life).

If we then ask about the effect of more education on physical health, the best information comes from compulsory schooling changes in other European countries. Brunello et al. (2016) found for twelve European countries which had compulsory schooling changes that health behaviour indeed improved for those forced into more education: smoking rates and alcohol abuse rates were lower, and exercise habits were better. Still, the effect of education on the probability of low health were small (around 3 per cent to 6 per cent).

If we look at mortality, the same methodology of looking at compulsory school changes has been used by Gathmann et al. (2015). The authors looked at changes in eighteen European countries over 100 years and found that an extra year of schooling bought no more than 0.5 years of life for men and even less for women, concluding that the effect of education on mortality was not significantly different from zero. Half a year of additional life would be worth around four additional WELLBYs, which, if it only held for men, would mean two additional WELLBYs per average affected individual.

Now, if we add this up, then an extra year of compulsory schooling increases lifetime income by roughly £50,000. It also improves health and health behaviour by a small amount (3 per cent to 6 per cent), which, normally, also means a small reduction in public health-care costs. These individuals live at least as long. The gains of an additional year of compulsory schooling would, therefore, be worth in the order of seven to ten WELLBYs over the life course.

deemed equivalent to death and thus a QALY of zero. We will discuss this conversion in more detail in chapter 4.

On the other hand, compulsory schooling changes forced individuals into something they may not otherwise have done, which seems costly to them in terms of life satisfaction, probably via increased unfavourable comparisons, changes in occupational sorting, or differences in later-life working conditions. That effect is a negative of about six WELLBYs for the person forced into another year of education. This is counterbalanced by an increase of about three WELLBYs via reduced mortality and improved health for those individuals, who thus lose three WELLBYs in terms of their own lifetime wellbeing.

If we then reflect on the likely societal effects surrounding these changes at the individual level, we can say that the effects on lifetime income are likely to carry over to the country as a whole: the increased income is probably from increased productivity that comes with more education and does not come at the expense of others. The same is likely to hold for improved health behaviours. If anything, the advantage of improved individual behaviour is likely to have add-on benefits to children, dependents, and peers (Behrman and Stacey, 1997).

On the other hand, the negative effect on life satisfaction via changes in comparisons or occupational sorting is likely to be counterbalanced by a positive effect on others with higher education as their comparisons improve: adding individuals at the bottom of the income scale is bad for the status of those added to the bottom but good for the status of the higher-up. This negative effect is, therefore, likely to wash out, probably entirely: since status is a zero-sum game, any gain or loss for some group washes out at the population level (Moldovanu et al., 2007). This adds another six WELLBYs to the gains of more education. The net loss per individual forced into another year of education is then two (for men) to six (for women) WELLBYs, counterbalanced by a benefit of around eleven WELLBYs for the rest of society (five plus six WELLBYs), yielding a total net benefit of seven WELLBYs.

In terms of the political economy of more education, the trade-offs are clear: the chief beneficiary of more education is the tax system, which is not the same as the education department which would organize the additional education. That said, the chief group of beneficiaries are essentially living in the future while it is the current generation of taxpayers who would do the investing.

On balance, therefore, the current literature strongly suggests that additional education is a net benefit to society as a whole on any metric: income, health, or wellbeing. While the individual forced into more education is likely to experience a small wellbeing loss, the rest of society gains substantially, particularly the next generations.

The most important question for policy, on which the general case rests, is whether the increased taxation is indeed spent on wellbeing-improving public goods and services. The case for particular types of additional education mainly rests on whether there is still a productivity case for more education than the education that is already enjoyed: there is no obvious other loss in sight than the direct costs of education and the opportunity costs of the time involved, so this question is all about whether it makes economic sense.

Reflection on the Checklist in the Education Example

The reader hopefully noticed the crucial importance of knowledge of the wellbeing literature and a wider knowledge of how the world works in this example: when selecting the important pathways, there was an explicit reaching out to knowledge of what was important. This was particularly salient at the boundaries of our knowledge. The uncertainties in the process were hopefully also clear: the limitations of the key studies on which the narrative was based, such as the uncertain translation of lessons from one type of data (returns to education, social comparisons, and occupational sorting) to another type of question (macroeconomic effects of higher average education). The reliance on broad literature judgements, such as in the case of the rate of return to education or the zero-sum nature of status games, also meant a reliance on whole fields of study.

The discussion tried to be as reasonable as possible, but we hope the reader can see that it would be child's play to come up with fifty objections on each part of the reasoning: is it really reasonable to use information on education reforms a generation ago to say something about more education now? Are all the claimed effects the same for men and women? Does state-provided education have the same effect as private-provided education? Should we not actually be concerned with even longer-term effects of education and its associated production effects such as fertility rates and the depletion of the natural resources of the planet? These questions are all valid, but are either only important if we know more about the precise policy under consideration, or else make the question too broad to tackle analytically. The final paragraphs made it clear how the discussion on the general case for education informed us about where to look at in particular cases. The discussion also included departmental and generational incentives.

There was not much open discussion in the example on economic rationality, i.e. the question of why individuals make choices and where the role of the government was in guiding those choices. Yet, implicitly, the case was made that around the world it has been governments that have led their populations into more education and that this was a good thing for the populations as a whole, even though households might lose out in the short run (because their children were at school rather than helping in production) and the individuals might lose out in the short run (because they could not spend time in a job or on some other activity that appealed more to them). The case for education was strongly based on the benefits to others via more public services paid for by additional taxes and the general positive effects of more education on behaviour, such as better health-related behaviour and less crime.

General Issues in Assessing the Quality of Evidence in a Study

There are several general statistical principles which are important for assessing claims about the causal impact on any outcome. The generic problem is that claims about effects are based on statistical analyses of data in the past that include variation in the supposed driver of wellbeing and some measure of wellbeing. When the variation in the driver of wellbeing is not completely random or of the type that an intended policy would create, causal claims may or may not be valid (a problem of internal validity) or carry over to other areas (a problem of external validity).

The following challenges arise whenever one looks at the impact of something on wellbeing (or any other outcome) in a study:

- The policy variable is often correlated with unobserved factors about the individual leading to selection bias. Likewise, reverse causality (leading to bias) will occur if happier people select into the policy or programme rather than the other way around.
- Appropriate controls: this will depend on the factor of interest, but most likely include controls to account for selection into the policy, including permanent factors not caused by the factor of interest or temporary factors which, in theory, could be caused by the factor of interest as long as they are measured before. Include individual fixed effects wherever possible.
- How to interpret the wellbeing impact—who is affected, by how much, and for how long?
- There is often measurement error, so wellbeing and policy variables need to be measured accurately, at least when summed up over many observations, or else there is a likely bias.
- Marginal changes (for example, one-off visits and events) are less likely to produce realistic figures for evaluative measures of wellbeing.

The challenges can be addressed in several ways. In general, the confidence in estimates tends to be highest:

- Where estimates come from well-designed randomized controlled trials in which wellbeing has been measured.
- Where there are naturally occurring conditions that replicate randomization such as natural experiments, randomized encouragements, availability of instrumental variables, or threshold randomizations (regression discontinuity or kink approaches). This often requires longitudinal data, although this is not always the case. Examples from the wellbeing literature include educational expansions, lottery wins, regulations on disclosures of tax records, or other regulatory changes.

In most policy settings, the change in question is endogenous and happens for a reason, often related to wellbeing. In such cases, there is a hierarchy of quality of evidence where one can put more confidence in:

- Techniques using credible sources of random variation like the policy intervention in mind (prevalent techniques are usually centred around an argued random source of variation and include difference-in-differences, regression discontinuities or kinks, or instrumental variable approaches).
- The better studies allow one to control for the impact of exogenous individual unobserved factors that have caused the treatment of interest (including hereditary factors), or exogenous area-specific factors when using geographical information.
- In all cases, judgements about the causal structure will be involved: it would need to be backed up with a clear logic, consistent with theories from social science in general, and ideally, triangulated with other estimates, including, for example, market prices, and across sources of variation (within-person, between-person, across regions, across time, or across similar changes in slightly differently worded variables).

One can have less confidence in:

- A one-off cross-sectional analysis of choices which are deliberated, including, for example, diet, choices of one-off goods purchases, or choices of one-off services purchases.
- Estimates of a change in a global measure such as life satisfaction where the change is marginal (for example, an additional visit to a museum) rather than a change in state (for example, the frequency of visits).

One should have almost no confidence in small trials on relatively trivial interventions using measures which are prone to measurement error.

A good example of what one can and cannot trust was given by the question of what the initial wellbeing changes were following lockdowns and other policies meant to contain the Covid-19 virus. The studies that were more trustworthy according to the rules above were those with consistent designs pre-Covid and post-Covid, which furthermore were able to identify groups afflicted with unexpected restrictions (like groups of 'essential workers' allowed to keep on working versus 'non-essential workers' forced to stop working). Such more reliable studies were, for instance, the ONS wellbeing surveys in the United Kingdom or the Gallup wellbeing surveys in the United States, both showing a sudden drop in life satisfaction of at least 0.6 on an 0-to-10 scale in the three months of the initial policy response.

What was far less reliable were the many studies that were set up after the advent of Covid-19 and that hence were unable to compare the situation during the policy intervention period with a time before, at least not for the same survey population using the same survey methodology.

Preliminary Rules of Thumb on Wellbeing Effect Sizes

In every scientific discipline, researchers learn to recognize results that are out of the ordinary and thereby suspect, leading them to look more closely at the claimed effects. A recent example was the 2011 claim by a group of Italian researchers (Adam et al., 2012) that they found neutrinos that moved faster than light, an erroneous claim that was eventually found to be due to a faulty time-measurement system.[27] During the period when this 'opera result' was being verified with new experiments, there were dozens of theories proposed for why the claim might be right, but Jim Al-Khalili, a professor of physics at the University of Surrey, was sceptical enough to pledge to eat his boxer shorts on live television should the claim indeed hold to be true.[28] He was relying on years of theoretical and empirical knowledge that practically ruled out the possibility that faster-than--light-neutrinos could exist, leading him to be confident that the claim would be proven false eventually. He was following the old scientific dictum that extraordinary claims need extraordinary evidence.

While data eventually must be decisive, wellbeing researchers too have developed several rules of thumb as to what is in the realm of the believable when it comes to claims about wellbeing, allowing them to judge whether a particular claim is believable or not. A non-exhaustive list of some of the current rules of thumb pertaining to life satisfaction, measured on a 0-to-10 scale, meant to be used as a checklist for analysts as to whether a study or a dataset is believable, is as follows:

1. Any survey that asks for a specific *X* in the fifteen minutes leading up to the life-satisfaction question is bound to find an unusually high effect of that *X* on life satisfaction which is probably wrong (as it made *X* atypically salient). That is, one either asks about life satisfaction before revealing the specific *X* that the survey is really interested in (the first-best), or else asks about all the major areas of life before asking about life satisfaction, ideally with some emotionally neutral questions just before the life-satisfaction question (the second-best).

[27] See https://phys.org/news/2012-03-italian-physicist-faster-than-light-resigns.html.

[28] See https://www.theguardian.com/commentisfree/2011/nov/23/faster-speed-of-light-boxers and https://www.theguardian.com/science/2011/sep/23/physicists-speed-light-violated.

2. The difference between a relatively satisfied and a relatively unsatisfied Western country is easily two points on the 0-to-10 life-satisfaction scale, with the Northern European countries (for example, Denmark or Finland) at the high end and Southern or Eastern European countries (for example, Romania or Bulgaria) at the low end. Any dataset that shows much lower differences is suspect.
3. The differences in average life satisfaction can differ substantially depending on how the sample was collected, easily by one point. For example, the United Kingdom scores 6.5, on average, in the 2015 Gallup World Poll while, at the same time, 7.6 in the ONS data based on a much larger and more representative sample of the population (it is mainly due to where the life-satisfaction question was posed and how the interview was conducted, and partly due to the fact that the Gallup World Poll asks the Cantril ladder-of-life question as opposed to the common life-satisfaction question).[29]
4. Most large life events have only temporary effects on life satisfaction lasting less than two years, even for highly emotional losses like the deaths of loved ones. The events that have longer-lasting effects are those that people would naturally be reminded of or where they regularly pay attention to, such as continuing unemployment or mental ill-health like depression or anxiety. Most people bounce back from negative shocks though, to some extent even from unemployment (although there is evidence for scarring: those who regain employment after a period of unemployment remain on a permanently lower level of life satisfaction, cf. Lucas et al., 2004; Mousteri et al., 2018).
5. Unemployment has a strongly negative effect (around half to one point on the 0-to-10 life-satisfaction scale), as does bad health (ditto) (see Clark et al. (2018) and the references therein). Any dataset that finds something different is suspect in terms of its definitions of either work, health, or wellbeing. Because the difference between retirement and unemployment (conditional on income) lies in the expectations of the individual and society, we generally expect strong negative life-satisfaction effects for individuals who cannot match the norms of proper behaviour expected of them by their comparison group. With any other finding, the first suspicion is measurement error and the second is that the surveyed individuals do not see themselves as part of the same comparison group that disapproves of their situation.

[29] See http://ourworldindata.org/happiness-and-life-satisfaction for the Gallup World Poll results put in a world cultural context, where life satisfaction is measured using the Cantril ladder-of-life question. The 2015 ONS results are available in several publications, including https://www.ons.gov.uk/people populationandcommunity/wellbeing/bulletins/measuringnationalwellbeing/july2017tojune2018.

6. The largest shocks on life satisfaction have to do with personal relationships (for example, deaths of loved ones or loss of social status), meaning that any claim of huge effects of small purchases or temporary experiences (like going to a theatre or visiting a national park having a 0.1 annual life-satisfaction effect) are highly unlikely.
7. One-off highs and lows, such as terrorist events or national sporting success, have very short-lived effects (days, perhaps weeks).
8. 'Hawthorne effects', i.e. the warm glow of being part of a programme designed to help something while in reality being just a placebo, can be up to 0.5 for six months (Seligman et al., 2005). Hence, up until that level it is not clear that a programme has a sustained effect any higher than the social science equivalent of a placebo.[30]
9. One-off social inclusion programmes, like those of the National Lottery (for example, a series of cooking classes) can raise life satisfaction by up to 0.5 points for six months (CLES and NEF, 2013), but should be expected to then tail off again.
10. Additional mental or socio-emotional skills can have decades-long effects on wellbeing (see the seven-year Pakistani-village follow-up trial on cognitive behavioural therapy for post-partum depression by Gajaria and Ravindran (2018), for example). Still, sustained effects above one point are unusual and improbable.
11. No more than 30 per cent of life-satisfaction variation within the UK population is fixed, which thus limits the role of genes and personality (Frijters et al., 2014; Okbay et al., 2016). This also means that any claim that a childhood intervention will radically change life satisfaction of a whole population is unlikely to hold.
12. The within-population standard deviation of life satisfaction is usually just below two, and is around that for almost any sub-population, like employees of a firm or people living in a neighbourhood. In other words, there is no such thing as an easily identifiable large group where everyone has a very similar level of life satisfaction (so any claim based on that possibility is likely false).
13. Estimated effects of income based on variation in reported income in standard panels or cross-sections are usually around 0.1 to 0.2 for a unit of log income (at least in developed countries like the United Kingdom). In the United States, this is closer to 0.3. Any wellbeing measure that shows much lower effects is unlikely to be too similar to life satisfaction. Any higher effect is probably either due to better income measurement or a

[30] There is, of course, nothing wrong with positive placebo effects, but they should be as cheap as possible and perhaps not offered by the state at all. People are probably the best judges themselves of what placebo works best for them. There is a huge private market for placebo effects.

more status-sensitive measure of wellbeing. This low effect in most data also means that controlling for income hardly changes the coefficients of most other effects (except things that are very closely related to long-run income such as education).

14. The determinants of very low levels of life satisfaction look very similar to the determinants of the average (Ferrer-i-Carbonell and Frijters, 2004; Clark et al., 2018). Even papers critical of simple averaging find that it makes little difference for the 0-to-10 life-satisfaction scale (Bond and Lang, 2019). Thus, for practical purposes, treating life satisfaction as a cardinal variable yields similar results to ordinal techniques (like ordered probit) but is far easier to implement and interpret.
15. In the raw data, there is usually a dip in life satisfaction around mid-life, preceded by happier childhoods (which end sooner for females) and followed by a life-satisfaction boost in retirement (tailing off before death) (Blanchflower, 2020). The ONS data in the United Kingdom show this pattern very clearly. It is also generally the case that this pattern closely mimics the reverse of suicide rates. In other words, suicide rates are higher for age groups with lower average life satisfaction. This strongly underscores the likelihood that life satisfaction is comparable over ages and that it measures something humans care strongly about.
16. Year-on-year changes in national life satisfaction are usually small (less than 0.2) except around highly visible negative protracted events (examples include the Covid-19 crisis which led to a drop of about 0.6 in the United Kingdom, on average; or the start of the Great Financial Crisis in the United States in 2008; or the collapse of the Soviet Union in 1990). Any claim of huge up-swings in normal times are unlikely.
17. We typically cannot explain more than 15 per cent of the variation between individuals in a region by individual-specific objective and health-related variables, including physical health, mental health, income, and demographics (see Argyle (1999), for example). We typically cannot explain more than 5 per cent of the changes in individual life satisfaction in any large sample (that is, samples with a few thousand individuals). Any claim of more explained variation then usually has included some variables very similar to life satisfaction such as, for example, satisfaction with certain life domains (job satisfaction, financial satisfaction, etc.) or satisfaction-dependent judgements ('I am unhappy with . . . '). Yet, we can typically explain close to 90 per cent of the variation in average life satisfaction between regions or countries over time. Causality in all cases is highly unclear, yet the combination suggests that a lot of variation in life satisfaction at the individual level is due to factors evenly divided over time and over populations (like classic measurement error, random mood swings, or genetic variations).

Wellbeing CEA Examples

In what follows, we show some stylized examples of wellbeing CEA. In doing so, we use rather simple spreadsheets into which the relevant figures are put. There is nothing particularly sophisticated about these and they are merely meant to illustrate how wellbeing CEA would look like in practice.

The generic template in Table 3.2 illustrates how things would look like in a basic wellbeing CEA: per time period, one works out how much several outcomes would change per person, where persons could be an intervention group or the whole population. One then gauges the importance of that change in outcome by using the wellbeing value of that outcome, usually relying on a good estimate of the causal effect of that outcome on wellbeing. One does this for several outcomes, including, usually, some notion of private consumption and wealth.

For private consumption and wealth, one also works out how much wellbeing that would create per individual (see chapter 4 for values, because this would not be the social costs of producing wellbeing but rather the actual effect of additional private consumption and wealth on life satisfaction, which means that the wellbeing value of one £ is actually much smaller than when using the social costs of production of wellbeing). One then implements an Easterlin Discount by taking 75 per cent of that wellbeing value, which one deducts from the wellbeing value of additional private consumption and wealth in the summation of the total wellbeing effect per person. Note again that one, in principle, could have a particular Easterlin Discount for any outcome, implying that outcomes 1 and 2 in Table 3.2 (which are not subject to an Easterlin Discount) are implicitly those not subject to a large status effect, such as depression or anxiety. Finally, one works out what the total public costs are, which will include items such as changes in taxation and welfare benefits as well as up-front costs. The key number is then the cost-effectiveness ratio in terms of WELLBYs per £ of public money.

If a private organization was calculating its cost-effectiveness, the relevant costs would not necessarily be the total public costs (although they could be if the private organization decides that this is what it also values) but will usually be the actual costs incurred by that organization. In this case, the resulting cost-effectiveness ratio is not the one relevant to the public, of course.

In what follows, we go over some examples of how this might work in practice and what the relevant cost-effectiveness ratios would look like for several recent policy examples. The examples below all show up in the headline cost-effectiveness curve in Figure 3.1, for which each individual value is explained in appendix E to this chapter.

Table 3.2 A template for wellbeing CEAs

Period		Period 1	Period 2	Period 3	Period 4	Period 5	Period 6	Combined-discounted total
Outcome 1								
LS value of outcome 1								A
Outcome 2								
LS value of outcome 2								B
LS value of additional private consumption/wealth								D
Easterlin Discount on LS value of consumption/wealth								0.75*D
..								
Overall LS effect per person								A+B+(1−0.75)*D
Total public cost per person								C
Cost-effectiveness per person	£ per unit of LS							(A+B+(1−0.75)*D)/C

Source: Own illustration.

Housing First

Housing First is a form of high-intensity support for the homeless, with authorities renting accommodation on the private market to help the homeless into permanent housing, with intensive ongoing mental health support. Targeting in the United Kingdom has been for high-problem cases.

No randomized controlled trial of this intervention exists for the United Kingdom, but Liam Wright and Tessa Peasgood of the community team at the What Works Centre for Wellbeing in the United Kingdom tried to generate a cost-effectiveness estimate by combining estimates from the effectiveness of a similar programme in Canada, with estimates of the costs for the United Kingdom.[31] Both those elements are highly uncertain, but it is an important policy area where the pressure is high to help the homeless and some idea of the cost-effectiveness of what is being tried is thus urgent. The Canadian experiment that resembles Housing First (and its comparison level of support) is summarized by Stergiopoulos et al. (2015).

The Canadian trial was large and involved an extensive group of agencies for measuring outcomes. Some 2,148 homeless individuals across Canada, with new cases starting from 2009 to 2011, were randomly assigned to intensive housing-and-social-support help (versus 'normal') for twenty-four months. The trial ran from 2011 to 2013. Every six months, the treated homeless were extensively interviewed, with additional measures taken from public records. The key well-being outcome was life satisfaction measured on a 0-to-6 scale, although the study also included standard measures of health (EQ5D) and many highly specific measures, for example, of substance abuse and criminal activities.

The results were somewhat surprising, in that the effects of the intensive treatment were far less positive than hoped for: those with intensive treatment were not more likely to stop substance abuse, had an equal or higher number of arrests, and were no better integrated in the community. The severity of their mental illness (a key target outcome) actually worsened for the intensively treated group in the first six months. The life-satisfaction benefits were estimated to be 0.22 in the first year and 0.18 in the second compared to the control group, which equated to an overall accumulated increase of 0.67 WELLBYs per participant for the whole period.

The UK costs of the quite similar Housing First programme have been strongly debated and multiple estimates exist. Bretherton and Pleace (2015) analysed nine pilots in the United Kingdom, collecting estimates of several cost items that predominantly look at the costs of supporting the homeless person and the accommodation they receive. Their numbers equate to an average cost for the

[31] This cost-effectiveness study was conducted by Wright and Peasgood (2018) as part of the What Works Centre for Wellbeing: Communities Evidence Programme (ESRC: ES/N003756/1).

two-year intensive programme of £ 2,994. In contrast, Blood et al. (2018) calculate what Housing First would cost in Liverpool based on the requirements of the Housing First programme in terms of direct support and auxiliary services: based on their estimates, the costs of the two-year programme would be £ 18, 681. Hence, the lower estimate of the cost per WELLBY is £ 4,491 and the higher estimate is £28,022. These are both several orders of magnitude higher than the marginal cost per WELLBY of the NHS of around £ 2,500.

Given the findings of the Canadian study, it is unlikely that this effectiveness will improve if criminal justice costs and substance abuse costs are included because those were not found to improve. Yet, there might be some health cost savings not estimated in the UK studies: in the Canadian experiment, there were fewer emergency hospitalizations amongst those in the more intensive group, although the change is probably not high enough to change the overall picture.

In terms of methodology, this simple example illustrates how effects and costs from different places and multiple time periods can be combined (see Table 3.3).

One should note some differences between this spreadsheet and the proposed generic template. For one, it merely lists several outcomes (days housed, EQ5D, and mental illness) without giving the life-satisfaction value of those outcomes. This is because life satisfaction was directly measured as an outcome, which is better than inferring the likely life-satisfaction value from the effect of several other intermediary outcomes. Hence, outcomes are merely shown for information. Another difference is that the table shows the life-satisfaction effect on a scale measured from 0 to 6, which is then translated into a scale from 0 to 10 by linearly scaling up the effect by a factor of 11/6. There are other (slightly better) conversion methodologies, but that is the most intuitive one as it treats the top and bottom possibilities as equal (see Frijters (1999) for other possibilities on converting scales).

Table 3.3 Wellbeing CEA: Housing First

Period	Year	2017	2018	Combined-undiscounted
Intended outcome	Days housed			298
Other outcome 1	EQ5D	1.51	0.08	1.59
Other outcome 2	Mental illness severity	−0.74	0.37	0.37
Overal LS effect per person	0-to-6 scale	0.22	0.18	0.40
	0-to-10 scale	0.37	0.30	0.67
Baseline cost total				£2,993.82
High cost estimate total				£18,681
Cost-effectiveness baseline	£ per unit of LS			£4,490.73
Cost-effectiveness high cost	£ per unit of LS			£28,021.50

Source: Own illustration based on own calculations.

Finally, note that it will, of course, often be important to also know the total value and cost of an intervention, not just the value and cost per person. Since we are here talking about a hypothetical UK intervention, though, there is no need to specify an exact scale of the programme. Moreover, for international and cross-programme comparisons, the cost-effectiveness ratio per person will typically be the key indicator one is interested in.

Socio-emotional Skills Training in the Workplace

Next, we look at the wellbeing cost-effectiveness of a socio-emotional skills training programme in the workplace, implemented by a private company.[32] We treat that programme as if it was implemented by the UK government, which means our cost estimates are estimates of what this programme would have cost in the United Kingdom.

The actual company had, of course, its own consideration of costs and benefits: a £ spent by a private entity is not a £ spent by the public. It has different opportunity values, and often simply entails a transfer from one private entity to another which are gains and losses to those entities but not to society. Thus, to 'translate' this private programme implemented by an Australian airline company (Qantas) into a cost-effectiveness figure, we assume that the UK government could mandate and implement the same programme with the same costs and benefits for private companies in the United Kingdom, at UK prices.

Like many organizations, the airline company runs various experiments for its employees. One such experiment—a socio-emotional skills training programme—was evaluated in a randomized controlled trial by Ayres and Malouff (2007). The programme consisted of 111 individuals who volunteered for a problem-solving training, fifty-six of whom randomly received the training and fifty-five did not, allowing the researchers to compare the outcomes of those who received it with those who did not but were otherwise comparable over time.

The content of the programme was some four weeks of training in managing time, diaries, and general goal-setting and planning techniques. There was an initial thirty-minute intake interview to discuss the problems experienced by employees, followed by homework and regular check-ups on the basis of that homework and ensuing follow-up questions and issues. There were surveys before and after, including the key outcomes of life satisfaction and job satisfaction.

The evaluation showed marked improvement in an index of problem-solving abilities. The intervention group improved 2.65 points on a 5-to-35 score termed

[32] This randomized controlled trial was identified in the systematic review undertaken by Watson et al. (2018) as part of the What Works Centre for Wellbeing: Work and Learning Evidence Programme (ESRC: ES/N003586/1).

'life satisfaction', relative to 0.82 for the control group. The intervention group also improved 1.57 points on a 5-to-25 score termed 'job satisfaction', relative to –0.11 for the control group.

If we equalize scales, this means an increase in life satisfaction of 0.72 points on a 0-to-10 scale. That is a very high effect that is likely to be dominated by observer effects of having been given special attention, besides some improvements in socio-emotional skills.

The costs of the training programme to the private company were basically the production foregone, the costs of the instructor, and some overhead to the organization. Note that these are not all costs to society but definitely costs to the company that commissioned the programme. In total, these costs were around £148 per participant.

The cost-effectiveness figures then depend to a very large extent on what one assumes about longer-term effects and spillovers from those affected. Since they are not studied in the research we are drawing from, one has to put in what seem like reasonable guesses based on what happened in other longer-term studies.

On the one hand, we know that improved socio-emotional skills can have long-term benefits, but on the other hand it is not likely that a four-week treatment with only thirty minutes of face time will have imparted life-changing skills that permanently increase life satisfaction by 0.72 points over the entire life course. In fact, we find that for many programmes, such as those funded by the UK National Lottery, that observer effects fade after the first few months. A conservative guess is that the effects dissipate after a year such that the total lifetime effect is 0.72 WELLBYs.

On externalities, if we presume that 80 per cent of the treated employees have a partner and that the spillover of their life satisfaction on their partners plus children is roughly 20 per cent (which is probably reasonable if you think of mental health spillovers, cf. Mervin and Frijters, 2014), there would be an additional 0.1152 WELLBYs from improved social relationships. Under these assumptions, we obtain Table 3.4.

Note that the outcomes for job satisfaction and problem-solving skills are shown but do not have any particular role in the cost-effectiveness calculation as they are already included in the outcome for life satisfaction.

Finally, note that are many uncertainties here and one could add more effects by putting in estimates from other studies, such as the effect of improved job satisfaction on productivity and job retention, which would probably improve the cost-effectiveness figure further. Still, given that it is a small study that has only a short time horizon, our purpose is not to show a strongly realistic bottom-line number but more to illustrate that one can generate cost-effectiveness figures even for small interventions. The example also illustrates how problem-solving skills training seems good value for money even amongst particular employee groups (here: flight attendants), who are not known as a particularly problematic group.

Table 3.4 Wellbeing cost-effectiveness analysis: Socio-emotional skills training

Period	Months	Period 1	Combined-undiscounted
Intended outcome	Problem-solving	3.6	3.6
Direct cost per person		148	148
Other cost per person			
External cost per person		0	0
Other outcome 1	0-to-10 JS direct	0.55	0.56
Other outcome 2	0-to-10 LS on externals	0.1152	0.1152
Direct LS effect on the treated	0-to-10 LS	0.72	0.72
Other LS effects per person		0.1152	0.1152
Overall LS effect per person	0-to-10 LS	0.8352	0.8352
Total internal cost per person			
Total cost per person to society		148	148
Cost-effectiveness	£ per unit of LS		177.20

Source: Own illustration based on own calculations.

Air Pollution in Germany

One of the best causal studies on wellbeing and pollution is the paper by Simon Luechinger on life satisfaction and SO_2 levels in Germany. Simon was able to use nationally representative data from the German Socio-Economic Panel Study (SOEP), which has been following more than thirty thousand individuals in eleven thousand households every year from 1984 onwards. He combined household data from the 1985 to 2003 period with detailed geographical information about the levels of atmospheric SO_2, which were quite high in 1985, on average (46.9 microgram per cubic metre), dropping substantially afterwards (to 5.3 microgram per cubic metre in 2000).[33]

To identify the causal effect of air pollution on life satisfaction, Simon exploited unanticipated changes in legislation pertaining to power plants over the whole of Germany, enforced differentially over time in different areas (first across West Germany and later across East Germany after Germany reunified in 1990). Using information on wind directions, he mapped who should be affected to what degree at what time, everywhere in Germany, as a result of these legislative changes. He could then use an instrumental variable approach to estimate the causal effect of

[33] The figures in this section originate from Luechinger (2009), coupled with additional data averages the author supplied at our request.

SO_2 on life satisfaction. That effect turned out to be fairly linear and constant, with an increase in SO_2 concentrations of ten micrograms per cubic metre affecting life satisfaction by a minimum of –0.05. He found that this was robust to various intricacies of his estimation strategy (for example, excluding specific regions or looking only at specific time periods). Simon then calculated the willingness-to-pay for a reduction in air pollution based on his estimates. His study is a landmark in terms of showing a convincing effect of a public policy on life satisfaction.

The costs of such an intervention require careful examination and we want to illustrate the general methodology with a simple back-of-the-envelope calculation, followed by a sketch of what a full wellbeing CEA would require.

Back-of-the-envelope Calculation

What the German government did was to require scrubbers to be added to power plants so that most of the SO_2 generated (about 69 per cent) was taken out. The US example of an actual market in SO_2 emissions in the 1990s and early 2000s reveals that cheaper interventions exist, for instance, by moving from one type of fuel to another that generates less SO_2 per unit of energy. From the point of view of air pollution, the effect is essentially the same. The experience with the American market has been that the costs of reducing emissions by a tonne of SO_2 is around $100 (with a huge range from $70 to over $200 per tonne during the years in which the SO_2 market was functional). When thinking of adopting the same intervention elsewhere, the actual costs the German government enforced are less relevant than the costs one would incur if they had adopted the most cost-effective measures, so we will use the $100 per tonne figure as the appropriate public costs for reducing emissions.

In 1990, the level of annual emissions was 5,485 kilotons and the level of SO_2 in the atmosphere was 19.0 milligrams per cubic metre. To reduce the level of SO_2 in the atmosphere by 10 milligrams per cubic metre would require a uniform proportionate cut in emissions of 2,887 kilotons per year. As stated above, this would produce a gain per person of 0.05 WELLBYs, or given a population in 1990 of 79.43 million, a total gain of 3.972 million WELLBYs. This gives us an estimated cost per WELLBY of around $72.7, or around £60 per WELLBY.

Even though we have taken conservative estimates, the uncertainty around this number is large and can go in both directions: the methodology does not count the improved numbers of years lived, nor the knock-on effects of the improved physical and mental health on both productivity and reduced costs to the health system. As we know from the United Kingdom, those effects are likely to be substantial.[34] Yet, on the other hand, the costs of reducing SO_2 might easily be more than double than $100 per tonne, particularly once the easier adjustments to

[34] See the following IAPT example in this chapter.

different fuels and scrubbers have been made. Still, even if the costs were ten times as high, the intervention would still be cost-effective at $730 (around £600) per WELLBY. Since there is still quite a way to go on reducing air pollution in the United Kingdom and elsewhere (the UK Clean Air Strategy 2019 aims to cut the harm of air pollution to human health by half), this type of intervention thereby is part of the low-hanging fruit in terms of wellbeing improvements yet to be enacted.

Exemplary Wellbeing CEA

We here conducted a simple wellbeing CEA. A full analysis would differ from this simple one in many ways:

1. It would include dynamics on the direct costs side. A policy to clean up power plants cannot be implemented just for one year and hence one would look at a whole plan of cleaning up, with costs incurred in different years.
2. It would include dynamics on the indirect (negative) costs side. The main benefits of the SO_2 reduction were through both physical and mental health improvements, not separated into those elements. These health improvements come with reduced costs to the health system and increased taxation via higher employment and productivity.
3. It would include dynamics on the total benefits side, including improved life expectancy and the improved life satisfaction of employment.

In Tables 3.5, 3.6, and 3.7 below, we illustrate the main effects one would want a reasonable estimate of in order to obtain a reasonable cost-effectiveness figure for this policy. We should mention that all these additional effects are expected to go in the same direction: they strengthen the policy case for addressing air pollution

Table 3.5 Assumptions

Assumptions	
1.50%	Discount rate for wellbeing benefits
3.50%	Discount rate for monetary costs
0.05	Change in LS on 0-to-10 scale from decrease of 10 micrograms per m3
55,000,000	Population affected by change in SO_2
0.008	Change in life years per person due to change in SO_2 – Example (Luechinger, 2009)
3.2	Measure of wellbeing for additional years of life (above 'misery')*
−0.7	Change in LS on 0-to-10 scale moving from employment to unemployment
50	Population moving from employment to unemployment

Notes: *A conservative approach is 7.6 (mean) – 4 (i.e. assuming that a life is 'worth living' only if it is greater than 4 on a 0-to-10 scale).

Source: Own illustration based on own calculations.

Table 3.6 Life satisfaction benefits

Life satisfaction benefits	**Year**	**1**	**2**	**10**
Reduction in SO_2 of existing life years	[change in life satisfaction on 0-to-10 scale x people affected]	275,000	275,000	275,000
Additional years of life due to health benefits	[additional years of life x people x measure of LS + 0.05]	143,000	143,000	143,000
Change in employment*	[number of people moving from employment to unemployment x −0.7]	−35	−35	−35
Change in prices*	[change in disposable income of consumers and owners who get the profits * marginal LS of income = change in disposable income* 0.3/ current disposable income level. Note there is no impact via house price changes because the study found those changes to be minimal]	42	42	42
Changes in relative consumption	[change in relative consumption due to changes in disposable incomes of consumers and owners who get the profits * marginal LS of relative consumption = −0.3/current average disposable income level]	−42	−42	−42
Total undiscounted life satisfaction benefits		417,965	417,965	417,965
Discounted life satisfaction benefits		411,788	405,703	360,147
Total				**3,854,550**

Note: *This split between employment and disposable income of consumers/owners depends on the elasticity of demand for the products as well as the economy-wide reaction to the change in employment in the sector affected.

Source: Own illustration based on own calculations.

because one can expect gains (rather than losses) in life expectancy and expect gains (rather than losses) in employment.

In terms of actual numbers, we have taken conservative figures, meant to keep the cost-effectiveness ratio relatively low (i.e. low benefits at higher costs). As a conservative calculation, our calculation actually uses an Easterlin Discount of 100 per cent rather than 75 per cent, although the income effects are extremely small so that it would not matter too much in this case and is merely stated for illustrative purposes. Also, purely for illustrative purposes, the example calculation deviates from the preferred assumptions on the value of life (with a 2 for death and

Table 3.7 Wellbeing CEA: Air pollution in Germany

Costs	Year	1	2		10
Costs of reduction in SO_2	[example number]	£60,000,000	£60,000,000	...	£60,000,000
Impact on company taxes	[the costs without a fully compensating subsidy would be based on elasticity of demand for the products with increased costs x rate of profit taxation]	£3,500	£3,500	...	£3,500
Reduced costs to the NHS	[reduced costs due to £-reduced admissions for physical and mental health related conditions—note that this is a complex calculation—example figure included here]		£38,000	...	£38,000
Total undiscounted costs		£60,003,500	£60,041,500	...	£60,041,500
Discounted costs		£57,974,396	£56,049,383	...	£42,564,549
Total					**£499,304,743**
Cost-effectiveness ratio					£129.54

Source: Own illustration based on own calculations.

an 8 for a healthy life) by using more conservative values (with a 4 for death and a 7.5 for a healthy life). Again, this is merely for illustrative purposes, to show how one can generate a lower-bound by picking lower values.

The methodology above can be, and has been, used for other forms of pollution because wellbeing CEA is one of the few ways of evaluating pollution that incorporates the large, but often not consciously realized (due to non-salience), mental health effects of pollution. This particular study is an example of how a wellbeing methodology can be combined with a national intervention to evaluate the impact of its effectiveness.

UK National Lottery Programmes

The UK Big Lottery funded a whole suite of wellbeing programmes from 2008 to 2013 to the tune of £160 million and followed this up from 2013 to 2015 with an additional funding of £40 million to fund fourteen portfolios, each consisting of three to thirty-four actual programmes. These programmes included a wide range of community-based activities, including cooking lessons for adults, sports events, and yoga sessions for parents-to-be. Similar activities are often subsidized by the state in some way or another, for example, via anti-loneliness or community engagement programmes. Hence, as a group of activities, it is interesting to know whether these UK Big Lottery-sponsored programmes were cost-effective or not.[35] They provide a benchmark for how much wellbeing can be 'purchased' at fairly short notice via community activities.

The most successful individual programmes identified were all targeting very particular groups: 'Branching out--Eco Minds',[36] 'Food and Fitness for Family',[37] and the 'Inspire Project',[38] with the evaluation based on rather small numbers of individuals followed (twenty to thirty individuals), which means that one should not put too much confidence in the findings pertaining to any particular programme. What is more useful is the evaluation of all the projects combined: as a whole, they represent what a large programme of broad wellbeing-oriented UK Big Lottery funding can achieve.

The evaluation was based on before-after changes in outcomes, meaning that there was no control group and that the effectiveness estimates were based on a 'business-as-usual' scenario in which there was no change in average wellbeing assumed. The evaluation of the first set of programmes consisted of 3,269 entry, 1,964 exit, and 572 follow-up questionnaires. This means a high rate of drop-out, with only one in six of those originally sampled filling in the final questionnaire. The second set of programmes started with 1,000 adults who did an entry questionnaire and ended up with 166 adults, a similar retention rate of only one in six.

The main wellbeing question was life satisfaction measured on a 1-to-10 scale. In the first set of wellbeing programmes, the average life satisfaction rose from 6.5 to 7.1 at follow-up three to six months after completion of the individual

[35] These programmes were evaluated by CLES Consulting and the Centre for Wellbeing at the New Economics Foundation (nef). The reports on the first and second wave of funded programmes can be found on the UK Big Lottery website (although they are now archived and must be requested): https://www.biglotteryfund.org.uk/-/media/Files/Research%20Documents/Wellbeing%20in%20England/National_Well-being_Evaluation_Final_Report%20August%202013.pdf and https://www.biglotteryfund.org.uk/-/media/Files/Research%20Documents/Wellbeing%20in%20England/er_eval_wellbeing_2_prog_evaluation.pdf.

[36] Described by the report as: Food-growing project for people with mental health needs, including training and providing community spaces. Participants were engaged for over half a year. The project also involved active travel. The evaluation was based on twenty individuals interviewed at the start, at the end, and three to six months later.

[37] Described as 'Food and Fitness for Families'—North West Networks for Healthy Living Weight management and cookery for families, with healthy food vouchers and awareness-raising. The programme targeted overweight adults and families with children. The evaluation was based on thirty-three individuals.

[38] Described as helping substance abusers improve life skills, increase self-esteem, and re-engage within the community. Participants were referred and engaged over twelve weeks, involving a full range of activities. The evaluation was based on thirty-one individuals.

programmes, while it rose from 6.2 to 7.0 in the second set of programmes. As a conservative estimate, these programmes, therefore, increased life satisfaction by 0.5 for six months, on average.

The report on the second set of programmes explicitly reports the number of beneficiaries and the costs: the second set of programmes reached 500,000 to a million participants (depending on who is counted as a participant; the survey covers the population most affected, dominated by the 500,000 participants of the programmes of the Children's Food Trust, which has since 2018 ceased operations and handed part of its work programme over to the British Dietetic Association). This means that the cost of the average programme per participant was a little under £100. As a very conservative estimate, this means that the UK Big Lottery-sponsored programmes bought one WELLBY at a cost of £400, on average, i.e. £100 per (0.5 * 0.5 WELLBYs). These costs-per-WELLBY were somewhat lower for females and mid-life individuals than for the rest of the population.

The evaluation reports include the simplest form of wellbeing CEA: they give a crude estimate of the life-satisfaction change of those directly targeted, make an assumption about how long the effects last, and compare that with the average costs. The uncertainties are great with this average number because of many issues with the methodology: the evaluation is not based on a comparison between a treatment group and a control group over time; those answering the follow-up surveys are unlikely to be random; and the targeting of survey respondents was done by programme managers who will have had particular incentives. Likewise, participants might have felt obliged to respond to surveys in a positive way. Nevertheless, this methodology is relatively simple to implement and represents a crude common impact-evaluation strategy.

There are reasons to suspect that the true wellbeing cost-effectiveness ratio is more beneficial than £400 per WELLBY. The back-of-the-envelope calculation above assumes a total lack of longer-term benefits from the programmes, many of which will have forged longer-term relationships and socio-emotional skills amongst participants. The methodology is also not set up to consider beneficiaries other than direct programme participants, which means improvements to families and communities are not measured. Cost savings in the public system from improved employment and health outcomes are also not considered but likely to exist, at least to some extent. A fuller analysis would have to consider these additional benefits, and also include all the same elements as in the air pollution example above.

The main reason to be cautious about the headline number is the lack of a control group and the likely selectivity of the group that was followed up after twelve months. Nevertheless, the programme was a large expense affecting many individuals and so the headline figure forms a baseline for how much wellbeing can be bought via large-scale, community-oriented group activities, even if that effect lasts no longer than twelve months. It can be compared to other festive activities paid for by the (quasi-) public sector, such as cities of culture or community festivals.

The IAPT Mental Health Programme

Our most comprehensive example comes from the United Kingdom. It is a fully fledged dynamic model with macro elements, public-cost feedbacks, multiple actors, multiple periods, and multiple outcomes, and particular attention paid to behavioural effects (while avoiding double-counting, of course).

In a preliminary report, Frijters et al. (2017) looked at what a hypothetical treatment of 25 per cent of depressed UK residents in 2010 would have meant for life satisfaction, mental health, and net public costs in the ensuing 2010 to 2015 period.[39]

The evaluation is based on two large randomized controlled trials in the United Kingdom. One is a forty-two-month follow-up for a large cognitive behavioural therapy (CBT) trial in seventy-three medical centres in three major UK cities, targeting patients with treatment-resistant depression (Wiles et al., 2016). In this study, the authors found that the effect of CBT forty-two months post-treatment was around 70 per cent of the initial effect, very similar to the improvement that remained after six months in a comparable trial in Chicago (Mohr et al., 2012). The implied effect in the UK trial was around three points on the General Health Questionnaire (GHQ12) score.

The second is a large pilot trial of the future IAPT programme in two test sites in Doncaster and Newham, United Kingdom, which found the same basic effect, though these trials used a slightly different measure of mental health than the GHQ12, i.e. the PHQ9. Both in terms of size and content, the evaluation is then of the likely effects of the IAPT treatment now being expanded to 1.5 million UK citizens. It is not exactly the same though, because we here evaluate what the effect would have been if applied equally in the whole of the United Kingdom (including Wales, where IAPT was not implemented), and in one year rather than spread out.

Figure 6 in Frijters et al. (2017) gives a diagrammatic summary of the causal structure of the model, while Figures 7 to 10 summarize the found effects of the intervention over the 2010 to 2015 period as opposed to the status quo scenario. We first discuss the model and then the results.

Figure 3.5 shows the causal model we used, which we applied to population representative Understanding Society panel data and where the causal estimates all came from the appropriate literature. For example, for employment, we assume that being relieved from depression increases the likelihood of being in full-time

[39] Available at the University of York: https://equipol.org/research/projects/lifesim/.

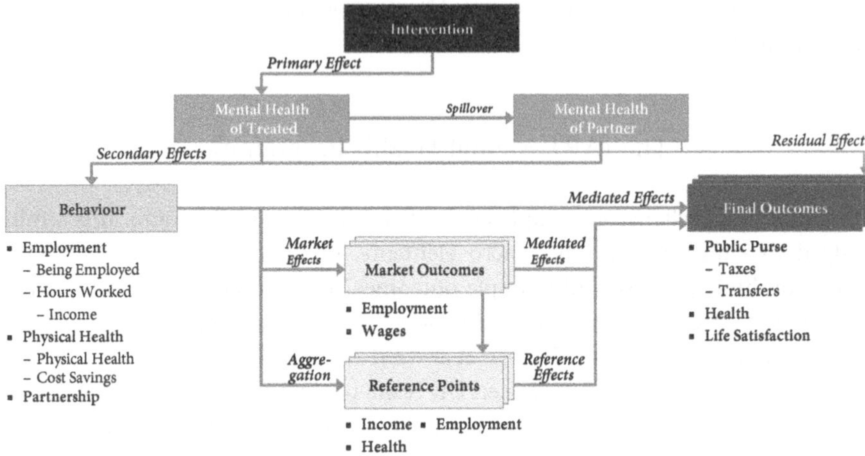

Figure 3.5 Causal structure of the model
Source: Own illustration.

employment by 15 percentage points and actual hours worked by 6.6 per cent for those who worked at baseline (Rollman et al., 2005).[40, 41] Physical health improvements are assumed to be low: +1.7 points on the SF12 physical health summary scale if patients remain out of depression, and +0.4 otherwise (Cho et al., 2010). Physical health-care cost savings, however, are typically large: we assume, following the literature for the United Kingdom, £720 per treated per year (Layard and Clark, 2014). How changes in these behavioural domains translate into changes in our final outcome, the wellbeing and health of the population, likewise stems from causal estimates from the relevant literatures.

For example, from the mental health literature, we know that the multiplier on changes to patient's mental health is positive such that improvements due to a hypothetical mental health intervention are amplified: Mervin and Frijters (2014) find a multiplier of around 0.15 on changes in mental health of partners.[42] From standard economic theory, we know that the multiplier on labour market behavioural changes is typically negative (in the short run), such that an

[40] We interpret these conservatively and only apply them to the unemployed, not non-participants. If one were to also apply them to non-participants, the labour market benefits would be far larger, but one may wonder if that is realistic given that labour force participation was already historically high during this period in the United Kingdom.

[41] Averaging across all participants (those who worked at baseline and those who did not), Rollman et al. (2005) find that actual hours worked increased by only 5.7 per cent. There was no significant change when looking at those who did not work at baseline in isolation. The increase by 15 percentage points pertains to participants who worked at baseline only. That said, the intervention keeps people in employment who would have otherwise dropped out due to mental ill health.

[42] Compared to the Qantas example earlier, this means we are not including likely effects on children here, partially because we think the average age of the IAPT group is likely somewhat higher than the flight attendants' group so the latter group is more likely to have young children.

increase in the labour supply of the treated due to a hypothetical mental health intervention would lead to reduced labour supply of complementary others as wages adjust. Indeed, Nickell and Saleheen (2017) find that a 10 per cent increase in labour supply amongst the low-skilled and medium-skilled (from an influx of migrants) leads to a 2 per cent drop in wages for those occupations, while Blundell et al. (2011) find that a 1 per cent drop in hourly wages decreases labour supply in the United Kingdom by around 0.4, on average. These two estimates of the labour demand and labour supply function can be combined to generate changes in overall wages and employment for the population due to the mental health interventions that would increase the number of potential workers in the United Kingdom (at both the extensive and intensive margin).

The essential structure of the model is thus a combination of individual causal pathways and pathways that work at the national level. We thus work out for those directly affected how a mental health improvement affects their main areas of life (employment, health, relationships), and then aggregate all these micro-level changes into a changed population average which, in turn, is fed into a macro-model that takes account of reference point effects and labour market shocks.

The reference effects are the same as the Easterlin Discount: changes in individual income are assumed to negatively affect the wellbeing of others such that only 25 per cent of the direct effect of individual income on individual wellbeing remains. In this analysis the same is taken to be true for health, where the individual benefits of health also lead to greater status concerns amongst others (using the estimates of Frijters and Mujcic, 2015), thus reducing the effective benefit of the health improvement on overall wellbeing by around 50 per cent, a conservative approach to benefits of the IAPT programme.[43] The changes in wages, employment levels, and reference point levels are then fed back into the micro-model to determine wellbeing, which becomes the starting point of the subsequent period.

This model is expressed entirely in differences: we do not model the baseline levels of any outcome but use the actual data averages over the 2010 to 2015 period for the counterfactual. We thus sidestep the difficulty of modelling many processes that lead to the status quo and focus exclusively on changes.

Figure 3.6 shows the hypothesized effects of the proposed intervention for those with a GHQ12 of four or above in 2010. The 3.5 reduction roughly halves the number of mental health problems experienced by the selected patients in 2010, and mental health problems reduce to very low levels for the remaining years as the improvement of 3.5 is added to the actual trajectory, which also shows a strong

[43] The actual implementation is more sophisticated in this model than a blanket 75 per cent Easterlin Discount on incomes and a 50 per cent discount on health benefits: the reference effects are presumed to operate on individuals who are similar to those affected in terms of age, gender, education, and location, leading to distributional patterns of these discounts (although in total still equal to a 75 per cent Easterlin Discount).

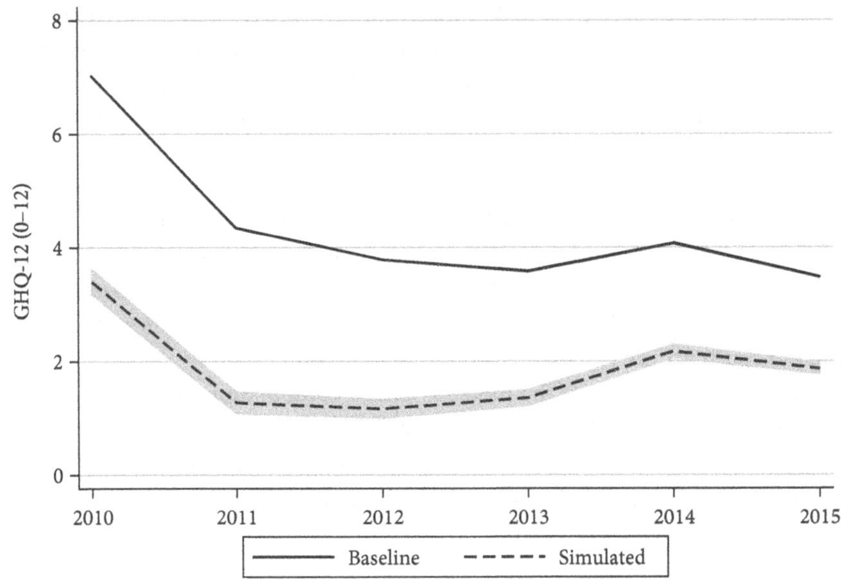

Figure 3.6 Reduction in GHQ12 scores of treated patients
Source: Own illustration based on own calculations.

recovery even without treatment. Note that Figure 3.6 depicts an optimistic scenario: in a more pessimistic scenario, treated individuals would relapse into depression at a particular relapse rate. For ease of exposition, we focus on the optimistic scenario here and note that CBT has been shown to have rather sustained, long-term impacts on mental wellbeing.

Figure 3.7 shows how introducing this intervention impacts the prevalence of depression in the whole population, whereby the reduction in prevalence of depression is much higher in the first year (around a 2.5 per cent point reduction in the population depression prevalence) than in later years (around a 1 per cent point reduction). This tapering reflects the fact that the hypothesized intervention is targeted to people who are depressed in 2010: many of them went out of depression without intervention while others became depressed who were not treated in our hypothetical scenario, reducing the effect of the modelled mental health improvement on actual rates of depression.

Figure 3.8 shows the estimated monetary returns of the intervention per treated individual and the pathways via which these returns materialize. By far the largest monetary return comes from a sharp reduction in the number of people with mental health problems going to hospitals and doctors with physical health problems, which is not because they are physically healthier (that effect is modest) but potentially because they are less anxious and more confident in their ability to deal with such problems themselves. This effect is modelled at the individual level, but the causality itself comes from the estimates in Layard and Clark (2014), who,

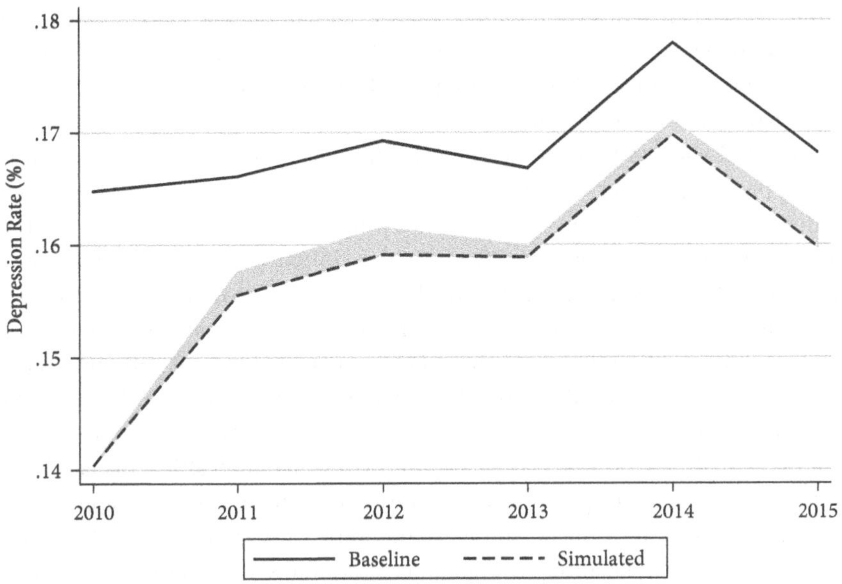

Figure 3.7 Reduction in depression rate of whole population
Source: Own illustration based on own calculations.

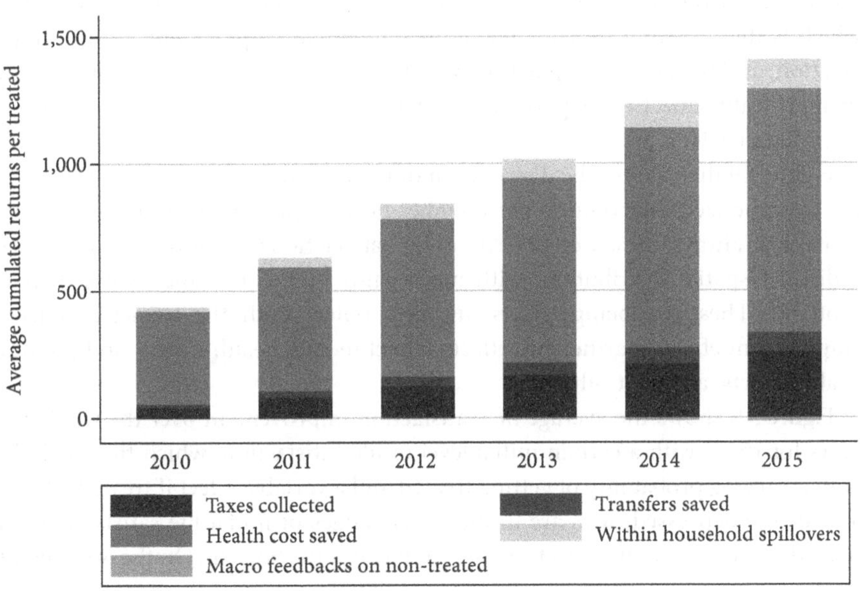

Figure 3.8 Monetary returns per treated patient
Source: Own illustration based on own calculations.

in turn, base themselves on the meta-analysis of Chiles et al. (1999): the authors reviewed ninety-one studies on the impact of psychological interventions (of various types) on medical service use published between 1967 and 1997, finding that treatment reduced the annual costs of medical service use by 20 per cent for physically ill with co-morbid mental ill health, yielding a net saving of £600 per treated patient per year. Due to a paucity of studies on medical service use cost savings, we take this figure at face value. Importantly, Carol Propper and co-authors (2019) report the same effect for the United Kingdom, finding reduced physical health costs in areas that introduced IAPT more quickly than others.[44]

The impact evaluation of the two Doncaster and Newham test sites for the IAPT programme found costs of about £650 per treated patient with, on average, twenty-two sessions of CBT (Layard and Clark, 2014). Given that the estimated monetary benefits are already over £1,000 after three years, the proposed intervention actually saves money as well as improves mental health. This is reflected in the headline graph (Figure 3.1) at the start of this chapter (see also appendix E).

Figure 3.8 also introduces some of the other causal pathways the model includes: increased taxation through increased rates of employment; reduced levels of welfare benefit take-up due to higher employment; taxation and benefit effects from the rest of the population as they are affected by the labour supply increase of the formerly depressed; and the monetary effects of the same channels as they emanate from a mental health benefit accrued by the partners of the treated (estimated to be 15 per cent of the original benefit to the treated). Figure 3.8 introduces some of the main themes of this proposed line of research, which is that we want to allow for improvements in employment, relationships, taxation, and the general population, which come from an initial improvement in mental health due to a hypothesized intervention based on actual randomized controlled trials.

Figure 3.9 then shows the distribution of the accumulated wellbeing benefits of the hypothesized intervention per member of the whole population, where wellbeing is, as always, measured in terms of life satisfaction on a 0-to-10 scale. We see a distinct spatial distribution, with more gains in London and Wales than in Scotland. These wellbeing effects, in turn, reflect both the monetary effects, employment effects, partnership effects, direct mental health effects, and physical health effects, amongst others.

Figure 3.9 shows the average life-satisfaction improvement over the whole five years for those with a certain initial level of life satisfaction, which thus includes both a varying probability of getting treated and a variable effect if treated. One in four of the depressed, who are in the lower ranges of initial life satisfaction, are treated, which makes the effects higher for those at the bottom. On the other hand,

[44] This analysis is not yet available publicly, but was presented in Rome in 2018 and is, according to personal correspondence with Carol Propper, forthcoming as a working paper.

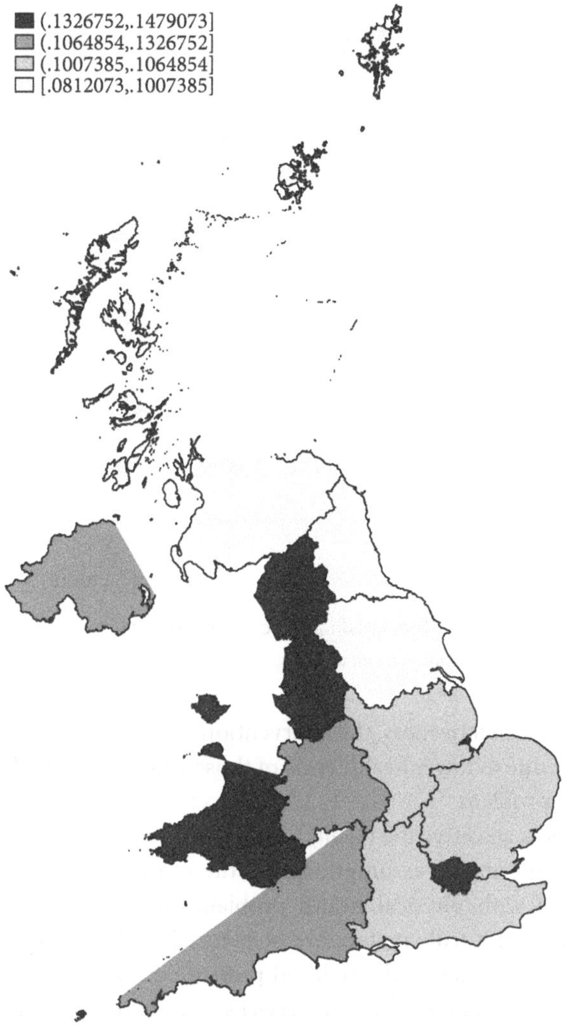

Figure 3.9 Distribution of regional life satisfaction changes per capita
Source: Own illustration based on own calculations.

the treatments have only a limited effect on mental health such that the most depressed individuals are less likely to be moved out of the depressed state.

Figure 3.10 shows how the average life-satisfaction improvement is higher for the lower range, and then in particular from the range that is close to the cut-off for depression (values between three and four for the GHQ12): those are the individuals who are likely to receive treatment and are likely to move out of depression if they are treated. Those with high levels of initial life satisfaction are less likely to be depressed and hence treated, while those with very low levels of life satisfaction are less likely to be lifted out of depression when treated.

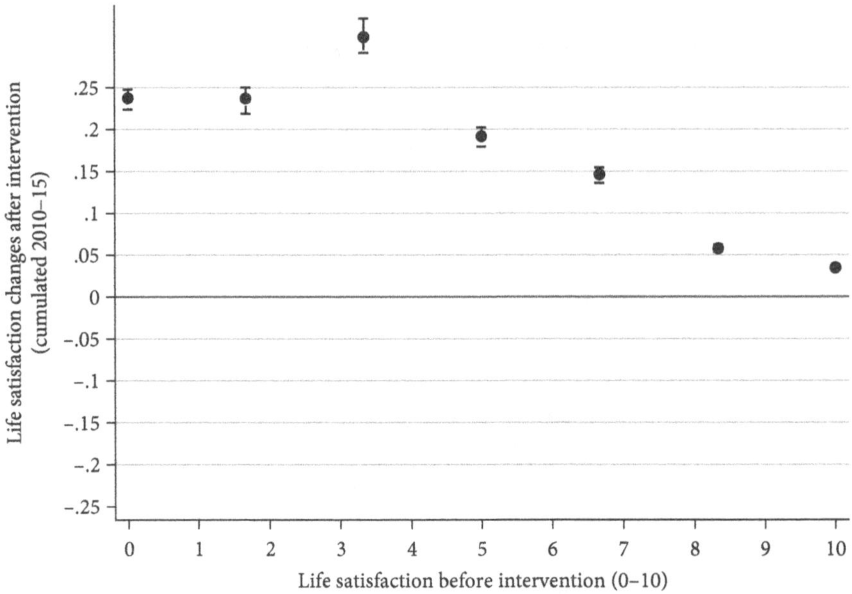

Figure 3.10 Distribution of life satisfaction changes per capita
Source: Own illustration based on own calculations.

In terms of cost-effectiveness, the intervention pays for itself within two to three years, primarily due to lower health costs of those who have both depression and a physical health problem.

We can see how sensitive the results are to the assumptions on the savings side, by making the alternative assumption that the reduced visits to health professionals by those with physical health problems that went through the IAPT programme would not truly materialize in reduced health costs or other valuable benefits. This recognizes that the reduced pressure on health professionals might be taken up by other demand for their services with unproven benefits (that is, the reduced visits will not result in fewer GPs or hospitals). This is an extremely negative view but is useful in giving a sense of robustness.

If we were to leave out the public health cost reduction channel (which in terms of cost-effectiveness dominates all other effects) for sensitivity, the cost per WELLBY would range from £40 per WELLBY (for those unemployed) to £410 per WELLBY (for those retired). These large differences come from the importance of mental health for the ability to hold a job, which matters much more for the unemployed than for those who are retired.

This example shows the current frontier of wellbeing CEA, requiring a combination of longitudinal information from (randomized controlled) trials, relevant literatures, and nationally representative datasets.

In terms of our template which summarizes the found effects for each intermediary and final outcome over time, the basic setup would look like Table 3.8.

Table 3.8 Wellbeing CEA template

		2010	2011	2012	2013	2014	2015
Direct cost per patient							
Health cast savings per patient							
Welfare/tax savings per patient							
Combined public purse effect per patient							
Costs external to NHS per person							
Treatment effect MH per patient							
Treatment LS change (direct, per patient)							
Partner effect MH per patient							
	LS change						
External effect MH per patient							
	LS change						
Employment increase patients							
	LS change						
Single decrease patients							
	LS change						
Health increase patients							
	LS change						
Income increase patients							
	LS change						
Employment increase partner							
	LS change						
Single decrease partner							
	LS change						
Health increase partner							
	LS change						
Income increase partner							
	LS change						
Employment changes external							
	LS change						
Single change external							
	LS change						
Health increase external							
	LS change						
Income increase external							
	LS change						
Reference income change							
	LS change						
Reference health change							
	LS change						
Reference employment change							
	LS change						
All non-direct effects LS per patient							
Overall LS effect per person							
Cost-effectiveness	£ per unit of LS						

Source: Own illustration.

We can now populate this spreadsheet with numbers, neglecting the physical health cost savings and for a moment not allowing for reference income or reference health effects (thus taking a more 'traditional' view of what to count). This hardly matters when it comes to Easterlin Discounts (reference effects) but does matter for the physical health costs savings, which are here implicitly treated as unlikely to truly materialize because the reduced physical health care demand by mental health sufferers will be filled by others in the queue. We obtain Table 3.9.

This, in turn, leads to the following bottom-line figures, which we view as upper-bound estimates of the costs per WELLBY (see Table 3.10).

Of course, we only offer these numbers and this methodology as illustrative of what a micro-macro wellbeing CEA of mental health interventions could look like. Nevertheless, the example combines the use of literature, multiple datasets, a dynamic framework, a causal structure, some regards for general equilibrium effects and consumption externalities, and merging techniques for results and variables that are not 100 per cent overlapping with the basic data. It thus represents the frontier at the moment.

Datasets on Wellbeing

Finally, it is important to say a little bit about the existing datasets in which wellbeing has been measured over the years, as well as about how to combine results from different datasets using slightly different actual questions.

The ONS in the United Kingdom has been mandated to integrate a standard set of evaluative, experiential, and eudemonic wellbeing indicators—the so-called *ONS-4* comprising life satisfaction, happiness and anxiety, and worthwhileness—in all of its surveys starting from 2011. Since then, a plethora of data on wellbeing in the United Kingdom has been accumulated through these surveys. Besides standard ONS instruments, there exist various datasets that have been initiated and maintained by different universities and research institutes in the United Kingdom. Wellbeing indicators have also been included in various datasets around the world, often from early on in national household panels such as the German Socio-Economic Panel Study (SOEP) or the Household, Income and Labour Dynamics in Australia (HILDA) panel.

Existing datasets can be broadly classified into longitudinal (panel and cohort data) and cross-section data. Besides differences in type of data, datasets also differ in terms of number of observations, frequency of sampling, and population coverage. Appendix A provides a general overview of existing datasets that include at least life satisfaction, appendix B provides a corresponding technical overview that gives particularly important details for each dataset, like the number of respondents, the type of information as to where respondents live, and the

Table 3.9 Wellbeing CEA calculations

		2010	2011	2012	2013	2014	2015
Direct cost per patient		650.00	0.00	0.00	0.00	0.00	0.00
Health cost savings per patient		473.92	150	192	146.67	168.51	150.70
Welfare/tax savings per patient		8.22	14.44	6.52	13.62	8.99	8.44
Combined public purse effect per patient		−167.86	164.44	198.52	160.28	177.50	159.14
Costs external to NHS per person							
Treatment effect MH per patient		−3.63	−3.09	−3.09	−3.09	−3.09	−3.09
Treatment LS change (direct, per patient)		0.62	0.50	0.45	0.48	0.50	0.48
Partner effect MH per patient		−0.54	−0.46	−0.46	−0.46	−0.46	−0.46
	LS change	0.08	0.06	0.08	0.06	0.08	0.07
External effect MH per patient		−0.27	−0.23	−0.23	−0.23	−0.23	−0.23
	LS change	0.04	0.03	0.04	0.03	0.04	0.03
Employment increase patients		2.33	2.09	1.68	1.94	2.50	2.23
	LS change	0.05	0.04	0.04	0.04	0.04	0.04
Single decrease patients		−0.02	−0.02	−0.01	−0.01	−0.01	−0.01
	LS change	0.01	0.01	0.00	0.00	0.01	0.00
Health increase patients		0.96	0.59	0.56	0.50	0.48	0.51
	LS change	0.12	0.07	0.06	0.06	0.06	0.06
Income increase patients		88.91	103.44	64.09	116.06	130.45	89.64
	LS change	0.08	0.08	0.05	0.07	0.08	0.07
Employment increase partner		0.20	0.38	0.14	0.20	0.63	0.06
	LS change	0.00	0.00	0.00	0.00	0.00	0.00
Single decrease partner		0.00	0.00	0.00	0.00	0.00	0.00
	LS change	0.00	0.00	000	0.00	0.00	0.00
Health increase partner		0.09	0.07	0.09	0.07	0.11	0.08
	LS change	0.01	0.01	0.01	0.01	0.01	0.01
Income increase partner		15.16	10.30	14.18	6.81	22.49	−1.26
	LS change	0.02	0.01	0.02	0.01	0.02	0.01

Continued

Table 3.9 *Continued*

		2010	2011	2012	2013	2014	2015
Employment changes external		0.10	0.19	0.07	0.10	0.31	0.03
	LS change	0.00	0.00	0.00	0.00	0.00	0.00
Single change external		0.00	0.00	0.00	0.00	0.00	0.00
	LS change	0.00	0.00	0.00	0.00	0.00	0.00
Health increase external		0.05	0.04	0.05	0.04	0.05	0.04
	LS change	0.00	0.00	000	0.00	0.00	000
Income increase external		7.58	5.09	7.04	3.37	11.18	−0.70
	LS change	0.00	0.00	0.00	0.00	0.00	0.00
Reference income change							
	LS change						
Reference health change							
	LS change						
Reference employment change							
	LS change						
All non-direct effects LS per patient		0.26	0.19	0.16	0.17	0.19	0.17
Overall LS effect per person		0.62	0.50	0.45	0.48	0.50	0.48
Cost-effectiveness	£ per unit of LS						329.94

Source: Own illustration based on own calculations.

Table 3.10 Wellbeing cost-effectiveness ratio

All non-direct effects LS per patient		0.26	0.19	0.16	0.17	0.19	0.17
Overall LS effect per person		0.62	0.50	0.45	0.48	0.50	0.48
Cost-effectiveness	£ per unit of LS						329.94

Source: Own illustration based on own calculations.

actual wellbeing questions included. Appendix C provides information on where to obtain the respective datasets and cites examples of studies that have been conducted with the different datasets. The list of datasets for the United Kingdom is exhaustive (taken from the UK Data Archive), while the mentioned international datasets are a selection of some of the most important ones.

Conversion between Different Scales and Indicators of Wellbeing

The life-satisfaction question sampled in all datasets run by the ONS in the United Kingdom asks respondents: 'Overall, how satisfied are you with your life nowadays?' Answer possibilities range from 0 ('not at all') to 10 ('completely'). Often, however, different datasets use different wording or scales. In other cases, there is no direct life-satisfaction question available at all, but only a sibling or a relative such as, for example, mental health.

The question then arises of how to translate one scale into another (for example, a 1-to-7 scaled life-satisfaction question into a 0-to-10 scaled one) or what is reasonable to assume about life-satisfaction changes when all that is available is a related construct. Various methods are available for translating scales, from simple linear transformations to more complex, non-linear approaches. Appendix D provides an overview of the most important approaches for rescaling as well as conversion factors advocated by reputable studies between a selection of related constructs and life satisfaction.

Conclusion and the Way Ahead

This chapter developed the basic methodology for wellbeing CEA, covering the main issues practitioners need to be aware of, including recommended technical standards, rules of thumb to avoid double-counting, design heuristics, and the use of relevant literature.

Looking ahead, one should see this basic methodology as a work in progress that will become more refined as wellbeing analyses become more commonplace.

One would, in particular, expect the public-cost side to require further improvement as there is, at the moment, surprisingly little information on how costly many outcomes are to the public purse. How much does the average divorce, layoff, low-skilled migrant, unemployed youth, discharged prisoner, or 70 year old with particular health problems cost the public purse, and via which pathways? You would think that we know the answers, yet we do not because it is incredibly complicated to trace the full costs of people and circumstances via public services, tax authorities, and welfare programmes. The connections between people, which are crucial when it comes to the full public costs of things like unemployment and crime, are often not part of a country-wide social model that would be needed to ascertain their full public cost. Lacking information on the cost side thus hampers all analyses, both those in the present and in the future. Such an endeavour is not wellbeing-specific but certainly important to it.

Further developments in methodology in wellbeing CEA itself can be expected to be rapid once it becomes more normal: new measurement tools will lead to different types of models and will open up new applications. There are also many technical challenges awaiting a fuller treatment, such as how to deal with different types of catastrophic risk, how to integrate the social models of wellbeing with existing models, such as standard economic models of the macroeconomy, or the environment. One can also envisage Bayesian methods becoming a normal way of incorporating soft wellbeing knowledge in the form of priors, and in terms of generating *ex post* uncertainty intervals.

There is hence much to be done.

Literature

Adam, T., Agafonova, N., Aleksandrov, A., Altinok, O., Sanchez, P. A., Anokhina, A., ... and Badertscher, A. (2012). Measurement of the Neutrino Velocity with the OPERA Detector in the CNGS Beam. *Journal of High Energy Physics* 10: 93.

Adler, M. D., Dolan, P., and Kavetsos, G. (2017). Would You Choose to Be Happy? Tradeoffs between Happiness and the Other Dimensions of Life in a Large Population Survey. *Journal of Economic Behavior & Organization* 139: 60–73.

Ayres, J, and Malouff, J. M. (2007). Problem-solving Training to Help Workers Increase Positive Affect, Job Satisfaction, and Life Satisfaction. *European Journal of Work and Organizational Psychology* 16(3): 279–94.

Argyle, M. (1999). Causes and Correlates of Happiness. In D. Kahneman, E. Diener, and N. Schwarz (eds), *Well-Being: The Foundations of Hedonic Psychology*. New York: Russell Sage Foundation, pp. 353–73.

Behrman, J. R., and Stacey, N. (1997). *The Social Benefits of Education.* Ann Arbor: University of Michigan Press.

Blanchflower, D. G. (2020). Is Happiness U-shaped Everywhere? Age and Subjective Well-being in 132 Countries. *NBER Working Paper* 26641.

Blood, I., Connery, P. Parmar, and Dulson, S. (2018). Conwy and Denbighshire Housing First Feasibility Study: Full Report. Ruthin, Conwy CBC and Denbighshire CC.

Blundell, R., Antoine, B., and Laroque, G. (2011). Labor Supply and the Extensive Margin. *American Economic Review* 101(3): 482–6.

Bond, T. N., and Lang, K. (2019). The Sad Truth about Happiness Scales. *Journal of Political Economy* 127(4): 1629–40.

Bretherton, J., and Pleace, N. (2015). Housing First in England: An Evaluation of Nine Services. York: University of York.

Brunello, G., Fort, M., Schneeweis N., and Winter-Ebmer R. (2016). The Causal Effect of Education on Health: What Is the Role of Health Behaviors? *Health Economics* 25, 314–36.

Chiles, C., Lambert, M., and Hatch, A. (1999). The Impact of Psychological Interventions on Medical Cost Offset: A Meta-analytic Review. *Clinical Psychology: Science and Practice* 6(2): 204–20.

Cho, H., Lavretsky, H., Olmstead R., Levin, M., Oxman, M., and Irwin, M. (2010). Prior Depression History and Deterioration of Physical Health in Community-dwelling Older Adults: A Prospective Cohort Study. *American Journal of Geriatric Psychiatry* 18(5): 442–51.

Clark, A. E., Flèche, S., Layard, R., Powdthavee, N., and Ward, G. (2018). *The Origins of Happiness: The Science of Well-Being over the Life Course.* Princeton, NJ: Princeton University Press.

Clark, A. E., and Jung, S. (2017). 'Does Compulsory Education Really Increase Life Satisfaction? *Inha University Institute of Business and Economic Research Discussion Paper* 2017–6.

Claxton, K., Martin S., Soares M., Rice N., Spackman, E., Hinde, S., . . . and Sculpher, M. (2015). Methods for the Estimation of the National Institute for Health and Care Excellence Cost-effectiveness Threshold. *Health Technology Assessment* 19(14): 1–503.

CLES Consulting and new economics foundation (2013). Big Lottery Fund National Well-being Evaluation. Available at: https://www.nurturedevelopment.org/wp-content/uploads/2016/01/National-Well-being-Evaluation-Final-Report-August-2013.pdf.

Department for Environment, Food and Rural Affairs (2019). Clean Air Strategy 2019. Available at: https://assets.publishing.service.gov.uk/government/uploads/system/uploads/attachment_data/file/770715/clean-air-strategy-2019.pdf.

Department of Health and Department of Education, (2017). Transforming Children and Young People's Mental Health Provision: A Green Paper Impact Assessment (IA). Available at: https://assets.publishing.service.gov.uk/government/uploads/system/uploads/attachment_data/file/664442/MHGP_IA.pdf.

Ferrer-i-Carbonell, A., and Frijters, P. (2004). How Important Is Methodology for the Estimates of the Determinants of Happiness? *Economic Journal* 114: 641–59.

Freeman, M., Groom, B., and Spackman, M. (2018). Social Discount Rates for Cost–Benefit Analysis: A Report for HM Treasury. Available on HM Treasury's Green Book website: https://www.gov.uk/government/publications/the-green-book-appraisal-and-evaluation-in-central-governent.

Frijters, P. (1999). Explorations of Welfare and Well-being. Tinbergen Institute Thesis, Thela Thesis, Amsterdam.

Frijters, P. (2020). The Corona Dilemma. *Club Troppo*. Available at: https://clubtroppo.com.au/2020/03/21/the-corona-dilemma/.

Frijters, P., Béllet, C., and Krekel, C. (2019). Micro-Macro Simulations for Wellbeing. Mimeo. Available at: https://equipol.org/research/projects/lifesim/.

Frijters, P., Johnston, D., and Shields, M. (2014). Does Childhood Predict Adult Life Satisfaction? Evidence from British Cohort Surveys. *Economic Journal* 124(580): F688–F719.

Frijters, P., and Mujcic R. (2015). Conspicuous Consumption, Conspicuous Health, and Optimal Taxation. *Journal of Economic Behavior & Organization* 111(C): 59–70.

Frijters, P., and van Praag, B. (1999). The Measurement of Welfare and Well-being: The Leyden Approach. In E. Diener, D. Kahneman, and N. Schwarz (eds), *Well-being: The Foundations of Hedonic Psychology*. New York: Russell Sage Foundation, pp. 413–33.

Gajaria, A., and Ravindran A. V. (2018). Interventions for Perinatal Depression in Low and Middle-income Countries: A Systematic Review. *Asian Journal of Psychiatry* 37: 112–20.

Gathmann, C., Jürges, H., and Reinhold, S. (2015). Compulsory Schooling Reforms, Education and Mortality in Twentieth-century Europe. *Social Science & Medicine* 127: 74–82.

Gollier, C. (2012). *Pricing the Planet's Future: The Economics of Discounting in an Uncertain World*. Princeton: Princeton University Press.

Jena, A. B., and Philipson, T. (2009). Endogenous CEA in Health Care Technology Adoption. *NBER Working Paper* 15032.

Jena, A. B., and Philipson, T. J. (2013). Endogenous CEA and Health Care Technology Adoption. *Journal of Health Economics* 32(1): 172–80.

Kapteyn, A., Montgomery, M., Smith, J. P., and van Soest, A. (2019). Life Satisfaction within and across Countries: The Role of Societal Capital and Relative Income. Keynote address at the SABE conference in Dublin, 2 September.

Klemperer, P. (2004). *Auctions: Theory and Practice*. Princeton, NJ: Princeton University Press.

Kochenderfer, M. J. (2015). *Decision Making under Uncertainty*. Cambridge, MA: MIT Press.

Laffer, A. B. (2004). The Laffer Curve: Past, Present, and Future. Available at: https://www.heritage.org/taxes/report/the-laffer-curve-past-present-and-future.

Laird, J., and Mackie, P. (2017). *The Treatment of Non-Recoverable VAT in Appraisal*. Final Report to the Department for Transport, London.

Layard, R., and Clark, D. (2014). *Thrive: The Power of Psychological Therapy*. London: Penguin Books.

Liberini, F., Redoano, M., and Proto, E. (2017). Happy Voters. *Journal of Public Economics* 146: 41–57.

Lomas, J., Martin, S., and Claxton, K. (2019). Estimating the Marginal Productivity of the English National Health Service from 2003 to 2012. *Value in Health* 22(9): 995–1002.

Lucas, R. E., Clark, A. E., Georgellis Y., and Diener, E. (2004). Unemployment Alters the Set Point for Life Satisfaction. *Psychological Science* 15(1): 8–13.

Luechinger, S. (2009). Valuing Air Quality Using the Life Satisfaction Approach. *Economic Journal* 119(536): 482–515.

Mervin, M. C., and Frijters, P. (2014). Is Shared Misery Double Misery? *Social Science & Medicine* 107: 68–77.

Miles, D., Stedman, M., and Heald, A. (2020). Living with COVID 19: Balancing Costs against Benefits in the Face of the Virus. *National Institute Economic Review* 253: R60-R76.

Mohr, M., Nybo, L., Grantham, J., and Racinais, S. (2012). Physiological Responses and Physical Performance during Football in the Heat. *PLOS ONE* 7(6): e39202.

Moldovanu, B., Sela, A., and Shi, X. (2007). Contests for Status. *Journal of Political Economy* 115(2): 338–63.

Mousteri, V., Daly, M., and Delaney, L. (2018). The Scarring Effect of Unemployment on Psychological Well-being across Europe. *Social Science Research* 72: 146–69.

Nickell, S., and Saleheen, J. (2015). The Impact of Immigration on Occupational Wages: Evidence from Britain. *Bank of England Working Paper* 574.

Office for National Statistics (2018). Personal Well-being in the UK: July 2017 to June 2018. Available at: https://www.ons.gov.uk/peoplepopulationandcommunity/wellbeing/bulletins/measuringnationalwellbeing/july2017tojune2018.

Okbay, A., Baselmans, B. M. L., De Neve, J.-E., Turley, P., Nivard, M. G., Fontana, M. A., . . . Cesarini, D. (2016). Genetic Variants Associated with Subjective Well-being, Depressive Symptoms, and Neuroticism Identified through Genome-wide Analyses. *Nature Genetics* 48(6): 624–33.

Ortiz-Ospina, E., and Roser, M. (2013). Happiness and Life Satisfaction. Our World in Data. Available at: https://ourworldindata.org/happiness-and-life-satisfaction.

Peasgood, T., Mukuria, C., Karimi, M., and J. Brazier (2018). Eliciting Preference Weights for Life Satisfaction: A Feasibility Study. Mimeo.

Psacharopoulos, G., and Patrinos, H. A. (2018). *Returns to Investment in Education: A Decennial Review of the Global Literature*. Washington, DC: The World Bank.

Rollman, B., Belnap, B., Mazumdar, S., Houck, P., Zhu, F., Gardner, W., Reynolds III, C., Schulberg, H., and Shear, M. (2005). A Randomized Trial to Improve the Quality of Treatment for Panic and Generalized Anxiety Disorders in Primary Care. *Archives of General Psychiatry* 62: 1332–42.

Seligman, M. E., Steen, T. A., Park, N., and Peterson, C. (2005). Positive Psychology Progress: Empirical Validation of Interventions. *American Psychologist* 60(5): 410–21.

Stergiopoulos, V., Gozdzik, A., Misir, V., Skosireva, A., Connelly, J., Sarang, A., Whisler, A., Hwang, S. W., O'Campo, P., and McKenzie, K. (2015). Effectiveness of Housing First with Intensive Case Management in an Ethnically Diverse Sample of Homeless Adults with Mental Illness: A Randomized Controlled Trial. *PLOS ONE* 10(7): e0130281.

Wang, S., Gum, D., and Merlin, T. (2018). Comparing the ICERs in Medicine Reimbursement Submissions to NICE and PBAC—Does the Presence of an Explicit Threshold Affect the ICER Proposed? *Value in Health* 21(8): 938–43.

Ward, G. (2019). Happiness and Voting: Evidence from Four Decades of Elections in Europe. *American Journal of Political Science* 64(3): 504–18.

Ward, G., De Neve, J.-E., Ungar, L. H., and Eichstaedt, J. C. (2020). (Un)Happiness and Voting in U.S. Presidential Elections. *Journal of Personality and Social Psychology*, forthcoming.

Watson, D., Tregaskis, O., Gedikli, C., Vaughn, O., and Semkina, A. (2018). Well-being through Learning: A Systematic Review of Learning Interventions in the Workplace and their Impact on Well-being. *European Journal of Work and Organizational Psychology* 27(2): 247–68.

Wiles, N., Thomas, L., Turner, N., Garfield, K., Kounali, D., Campbell, J., Kessler, D., Kuyken, W., Lewis, G., Morrison, J., Williams, C., Peters, T., and Hollinghurst, S. (2016). Long-term Effectiveness and Cost-effectiveness of Cognitive Behavioural Therapy as an Adjunct to Pharmacology for Treatment-resistant Depression in Primary Care: Follow-up of the CoBalT Randomised Controlled Trial. *Lancet Psychiatry* 3: 137–44.

Wright, L., and Peasgood, T. (2018). Cost-effectiveness of Housing First. What Works Centre for Wellbeing, London. Available at: https://whatworkswellbeing.org/wp-content/uploads/2020/01/housing-first-Cost-effectiveness-model-may2018_0158328900.pdf.

Literature for Appendix D

Abelson, R. P., and Tukey, J. W. (1963). Efficient Utilization of Non-numerical Information in Quantitative Analysis General Theory and the Case of Simple Order. *Annals of Mathematical Statistics* 34(4): 1347–69.

Baltatescu, S. (2002). Problems of Transforming Scales of Life Satisfaction. Euromodule Workshop, WZB Berlin, October 18–19, 2002.

Cohen, J. (1992). Statistical Power Analysis. *Current Directions in Psychological Science* 1(3): 98–101.

Cummins, R. A. (1995). On the Trail of the Gold Standard for Subjective Well-Being. *Social Indicators Research* 35(2): 179–200.

Cummins, R. A. (2005). On the Trail of the Gold Standard for Subjective Well-being. In A. C. Michalos (ed.), *Citation Classics from Social Indicators Research*. Dordrecht: Springer, pp. 537–58.

Hensler, C., and Stipak, B. (1979). Estimating Interval Scale Values for Survey Item Response Categories. *American Journal of Political Science* 23(3): 627–49.

Kalmijn, W. (2013). From Discrete 1 to 10 towards Continuous 0 to 10: The Continuum Approach to Estimating the Distribution of Happiness in a Nation. *Social Indicators Research* 110(2): 549–57.

Kalmijn, W. M., Arends, L. R., and Veenhoven, R. (2011). Happiness Scale Interval Study: Methodological Considerations. *Social Indicators Research* 102(3): 497–515.

Layard, R. (2016). Measuring Wellbeing and Cost-effectiveness Analysis Using Subjective Wellbeing. What Works Centre for Wellbeing, London.

Lim, H. E. (2008). The Use of Different Happiness Rating Scales: Bias and Comparison Problem? *Social Indicators Research* 87(2): 259–67.

Mazaheri, M., and Theuns, P. (2009). Effects of Varying Response Formats on Self-ratings of Life-satisfaction. *Social Indicators Research* 90(3): 381–95.

Mukuria, C., Rowen, D., Peasgood, T. and Brazier, J. (2016). An Empirical Comparison of Well-being Measures Used in UK. Research Interim Report RR0027, University of Sheffield and the University of York. Available at: http://www.eepru.org.uk/wp-content/uploads/2017/11/eepru-report-empirical-comparison-of-well-being-measures-nov-2016-048.pdf.

Powdthavee, N. (2012). 'Jobless, Friendless and Broke: What Happens to Different Areas of Life before and after Unemployment?' *Economica* 79(315): 557–75.

Shen, S. M., and Lai, Y. L. (1998). Optimally Scaled Quality-of-life Indicators. *Social Indicators Research* 44(2): 225–54.

Veenhoven, R. (2009). The International Scale Interval Study: Improving the Comparability of Responses to Survey Questions about Happiness. In V. Moller and Denis Huschka (eds), *Quality of Life and the Millennium Challenge*. Dordrecht: Springer, pp 45–58.

Veenhoven, R., Ehrhardt, J., Ho, M. S. D., and de Vries, A. (1993). *Happiness in Nations: Subjective Appreciation of Life in 56 Nations, 1946–1992*. Rotterdam: Erasmus University.

Appendix A: Data—General Overview

Table 3A.1 Data—General overview.

United Kingdom Data *(Descriptions by UK Data Archive, Adapted)*		
Dataset	**Description**	**Commissioned By**
English Longitudinal Study of Ageing	The English Longitudinal Study of Ageing (ELSA) study, which began in 2002 (though the sample was constructed from earlier data) is a longitudinal survey of ageing and quality of life among older people. It explores the dynamic relationships between health and functioning, social networks and participation, and economic position as people plan for, move into and progress beyond retirement. The study is funded jointly by UK government departments and the National Institute on Aging, in the United States.	Department for Work and Pensions (DWP)
Understanding Society	The Understanding Society study, or the United Kingdom Household Longitudinal Study (UKHLS), which began in 2009, is conducted by the Institute for Social and Economic Research (ISER), at the University of Essex. As a multi-topic household survey, the purpose of Understanding Society is to understand social and economic change in Britain at the household and individual levels. It is anticipated that over time the study will permit examination of short- and long-term effects of social and economic change, including policy interventions, on the general wellbeing of the UK population. The Understanding Society study is a successor to the British Household Panel Survey (BHPS). The BHPS sample forms part of Understanding Society from Wave 2 onwards.	Economic and Social Research Council (ESRC), Institute for Social and Economic Research (ISER), University of Essex
Wealth and Assets Survey	The Wealth and Assets Survey (WAS) is a longitudinal survey, which aims to address gaps identified in data about the economic wellbeing of households by gathering information on level of assets, savings, and debt; saving for retirement; how wealth is distributed among households or individuals; and factors that affect financial planning.	ONS
Active Lives Survey	The Active Lives Survey (ALS), commenced in November 2015. It replaces the Active People Survey, which ran from 2005 to 2015. The survey provides the largest	Sport England

	sample size ever established for a sport and recreation survey and allows levels of detailed analysis previously unavailable. It identifies how participation varies from place to place, across different sports, and between different groups in the population. The survey also measures: the proportion of the adult population that volunteer in sport on a weekly basis, club membership; involvement in organized sport/competition; receipt of tuition or coaching; and overall satisfaction with levels of sporting provision in the local community. The questionnaire was designed to enable analysis of the findings by a broad range of demographic information, such as gender, social class, ethnicity, household structure, age, and disability.	
Annual Population Survey	The Annual Population Survey (APS), which began in 2004, aims to provide data that can produce reliable estimates at local authority level. Key topics covered in the survey include education, employment, health, and ethnicity. The APS comprises key variables from the Labour Force Survey (LFS), all its associated LFS boosts and the APS boost sample.	ONS
Armed Forces Continuous Attitude Survey (AFCAS)	Information on the views and experiences of MoD personnel which helps shape policies for training, support, and the terms and conditions of service.	Ministry of Defence (MoD)
British Social Attitudes	The British Social Attitudes (BSA) survey series, which began in 1983, is designed to produce annual measures of attitudinal movements to complement information gathered from (a) large-scale government surveys that deal largely with facts and behaviour patterns, and (b) party political attitudes data produced by the polls. One of the main purposes of the BSA is to monitor patterns of continuity and change, and examine the relative rates at which social attitudes change over time.	National Centre for Social Research (NatCen)
Community Life Survey	The Community Life Survey was first commissioned by the Cabinet Office in 2012–13. It is an annual household survey conducted with adults resident in England, covering a range of topics including measures that are key to understanding society and local communities. These include volunteering, charitable giving, neighbourhood, civic engagement, social action, and subjective wellbeing. The survey incorporates a small number of priority measures from the Citizenship Survey, which ran from 2001 to 11. These measures were incorporated in the Community Life Survey so that trends in these issues could continue to be tracked over time.	Department for Digital, Culture, Media and Sport (DCMS)
		ONS

Continued

Table 3A.1 *Continued*

United Kingdom Data ***(Descriptions by UK Data Archive, Adapted)***

Dataset	Description	Commissioned By
Crime Survey for England and Wales	The Crime Survey for England and Wales (CSEW) (formerly the British Crime Survey) provides an important source of information about levels of crime, public attitudes to crime and other related issues. The results play an important role in informing government policy. The CSEW measures the amount of crime in England and Wales by asking people about crimes they have experienced in the last year. This includes crimes not reported to the police, so it is an important alternative to police records.	
English Housing Survey (formerly English House Condition Survey and Survey of English Housing)	The English Housing Survey (EHS) began in 2008–09, bringing together two previous housing surveys into a single fieldwork operation: the English House Condition Survey (EHCS) which ran every five years between 1967 and 2001 and became continuous from 2002 to 2007, and the Survey of English Housing (SEH) which ran from 1993/94 to 2007/08. Commissioned by the Ministry of Housing, Communities and Local Government (MHCLG), the EHS collects information from households on housing circumstances. It includes a household questionnaire, a physical assessment of the property and in some years, a desk-based market value assessment. A periodic follow-up survey of private landlords and agents (the Private Landlords Survey (PLS)) is conducted using information from the EHS interview survey.	Department for Communities and Local Government (DCLG)
Families Continuous Attitude Survey (FAMCAS)	Personal information on the MoD spouses in a number of areas including accommodation, healthcare, education and childcare, and deployment.	Ministry of Defence (MoD)
Family Resources Survey	The Family Resources Survey (FRS) is a continuous survey that was launched in 1992 to meet the information requirements of Department for Work and Pensions (DWP) analysts. The survey aims to: support the monitoring of the social security programme; support the costing and modelling of changes to national insurance contributions and social security benefits; and provide better information for the forecasting of benefit expenditure.	ONS, National Centre for Social Research (NatCen)

Food and You Survey	The Food and You Survey was commissioned by the Food Standards Agency (FSA) to collect robust information on the UK public's reported behaviour, attitudes, and knowledge towards food issues (such as food safety and healthy eating). A consortium comprising TNS BMRB, the Policy Studies Institute (PSI) and the University of Westminster carried out waves 1 and 2 of the survey in 2010 and 2012 respectively; wave 3 was conducted in 2014 by TNS BMRB. Wave 4 of the survey was conducted in 2016 by NatCen Social Research.	Foods Standards Agency
Graduate Outcomes Survey	Graduate Outcomes is the biggest UK annual social survey and captures the perspectives and current status of recent graduates. All graduates who completed a course will be asked to take part in the survey 15 months after they finish their studies. The survey aims to help current and future students gain an insight into career destinations and development.	Higher Education Statistics Agency (HESA)
Health Survey for England	The Health Survey for England (HSE), sponsored by the Information Centre for Health and Social Care and the Department of Health, began in 1991 and has been carried out annually since then. A number of core questions are included in every wave but each year's survey also has a particular focus on a disease or condition or population group, which are subsequently revisited at appropriate intervals in order to monitor change. The survey combines questionnaire-based answers with physical measurements and the analysis of blood samples. Blood pressure, height and weight, smoking, drinking and general health are covered every year. An interview with each eligible person in the household is followed by a nurse visit.	Department of Health and Social Care (DHSC), Health and Social Care Information Centre
Health Survey Northern Ireland	The Health Survey Northern Ireland was commissioned by the Department of Health in Northern Ireland and the Central Survey Unit (CSU) of the Northern Ireland Statistics and Research Agency (NISRA) carried out the survey on their behalf. This survey series has been running on a continuous basis since April 2010 with separate modules for different policy areas included in different financial years. It covers a range of health topics that are important to the lives of people in Northern Ireland today, and replaces the Northern Ireland Health and Social Wellbeing Survey (available from the UK Data Service under SNs 4589, 4590, 5710).	Northern Ireland Department of Health (DoH)
Labour Force Survey	The Labour Force Survey (LFS) is a unique source of articulated information using international definitions of employment and unemployment and economic	ONS

Continued

Table 3A.1 *Continued*

United Kingdom Data *(Descriptions by UK Data Archive, Adapted)*		
Dataset	**Description**	**Commissioned By**
	inactivity, together with a wide range of related topics such as occupation, training, hours of work, and personal characteristics of household members aged 16 years and over. As well as the main survey, several sub-sample and derived datasets are also produced, including longitudinal series and a Eurostat version of the dataset. Key variables from the LFS and its boost samples are also used to create the Annual Population Survey (APS).	
Living Costs and Food Survey	The Living Costs and Food Survey (LCF) began in 2008, replacing the Expenditure and Food Survey (EFS). The LCF, conducted by the Office for National Statistics, collects information on spending patterns and the cost of living that reflects household budgets across the country. A household expenditure survey has been conducted each year in the United Kingdom since 1957; from 1957 to 2001, the Family Expenditure Survey (FES) and National Food Survey (NFS) provided information on household expenditure patterns and food consumption. In April 2001 these surveys were combined to form the Expenditure and Food Survey (EFS), which completely replaced both series. From January 2008, the EFS became known as the Living Costs and Food (LCF) module of the Integrated Household Survey (IHS).	ONS
Living Well Index	What does it mean to live well? How well are we really living as a nation, and why? This study aims to provide the answers—by defining, measuring, and tracking, over a number of years, what it means to live well in Britain.	Sainsbury's, Oxford Economics, National Centre for Social Research (NatCen)
National Survey for Wales	The National Survey for Wales is carried out by the Office for National Statistics on behalf of the Welsh government. The survey is a key source of information for the Welsh government, other public sector organizations, and academics on the views and circumstances of people in Wales. It is carried out annually, face-to-face with a random sample of over 10,000 adults. Starting with the National Survey for Wales 2016–17, the survey design covers the topics of five predecessor surveys and has	Welsh Government

	therefore a longer interview than previous years. The predecessor surveys were: the first set of National Survey for Wales, which ran from 2012 to 15; the Welsh Health Survey; the Active Adults Survey; the Arts in Wales Survey; and the Welsh Outdoor Recreation Survey.	
Natural Survey on People and the Natural Environment	This survey provides information on how people use the natural environment, including the type of destination, duration, mode of transport, distance travelled, expenditure, main activities, motivations, and barriers to visiting.	Natural England
Opinions and Lifestyle Survey (formerly ONS Opinions Survey and ONS Omnibus Survey)	The Opinions and Lifestyle Survey, formerly ONS Opinions Survey or ONS Omnibus Survey, is a regular, multi-purpose survey which started operating commercially in 1990. It was carried out in eight months of the year until April 2005, when it began to run monthly. It was originally set up to meet the needs of government departments for a survey that used short and simple sets of questions, had greater statistical reliability than private sector omnibus surveys and a properly designed random sample. Each month's questionnaire consists of two elements: core demographic questions, and non-core questions that vary from month to month. From April 2012 the ONS Opinions Survey changed its name to the Opinions and Lifestyle Survey following the merger of some elements from the General Lifestyle Survey (GLF), which closed in January 2012.	ONS
Scottish Health Survey	The Scottish Health Survey (SHeS) began in 1995, with subsequent surveys conducted in 1998 and 2003. From 2008 to 11, commissioned by the Scottish Government, the survey has run continuously with a two-stage process—a personal interview for the full sample, followed by a nurse visit to one sixth of the sample, whereas previously a nurse visit had been offered to the whole sample. The aim of the SHeS is to gain knowledge about the health of the population of Scotland.	Scottish Government
Scottish Household Survey	The Scottish Household Survey (SHS), which began in 1999, is a continuous survey based on a sample of the general population in private residences in Scotland. It is financed by the Scottish Government. The aim of the survey is to provide representative information about the composition, characteristics, and behaviours of Scottish households, both nationally and at a more local level. The survey covers a wide range of topics to allow links to be made between different policy areas, with a particular focus on information to aid policy decisions on transport and social inclusion.From 1999 up to 2011 the survey followed a fairly consistent survey design.	Scottish Government

Continued

Table 3A.1 *Continued*

United Kingdom Data *(Descriptions by UK Data Archive, Adapted)*		
Dataset	**Description**	**Commissioned By**
	From 2012 onwards, the survey was substantially redesigned to include elements of the Scottish House Condition Survey (SHCS) including the follow-up Physical Survey component. More details can be found in the survey documentation.	
Scottish Social Attitudes Survey	The Scottish Social Attitudes (SSA) survey was launched in 1999, following the advent of devolution. Its aims are to facilitate the study of public opinion and inform the development of public policy in Scotland. In this it has similar objectives to the British Social Attitudes (BSA) survey.	Scottish Government
Taking Part Survey	The Taking Part survey was first commissioned by the Department for Culture, Media and Sport in 2005 and has run continuously since then. The survey originated in response to a need for consistent, high-quality national data on people's engagement with leisure, culture, and sport in England. The survey collects information on arts, heritage, museums and galleries, libraries, archives, and sports participation, as well as extensive socio-demographic information.	Department for Culture, Media and Sport (DCMS)
Time Use Survey	The United Kingdom Time Use Surveys were conducted in 2000–01 and 2014–15. The 2014–15 survey was conducted by NatCen and designed to be, as far as possible, compatible both with the 2000–01 survey (conducted by the Office for National Statistics) and with other European time use studies carried out since 2008 (not currently held at the UK Data Service). The 2014–15 study was deposited by the Centre for Time Use Research at the University of Oxford.The main aim of the surveys was to measure the amount of time spent by the population on various activities. The surveys provide an opportunity to inform a cross-section of policy areas as well as having interest for academia, social research centres, and the advertising and retail sector.	ONS, University of Oxford
Youth Social Action Survey	The Youth Social Action Survey aims to determine the proportion of young people involved in social action in the United Kingdom. It is planned to repeat the survey for six years from 2014 to 2020. The term 'youth social action', in this context, is defined as 'practical action in the service of others to create positive change' and covers a range of activities such as fundraising, supporting charities, tutoring and mentoring, supporting other people, and campaigning (excluding party political campaigning), tutoring/mentoring, and giving time to charity. The surveys will	Cabinet Office

	inform, and help to measure the progress of, the #iwill campaign run by Step Up To Serve, which aims to raise the number of 10–20 year olds in the United Kingdom involved in meaningful social action by 50 per cent by 2020. Further information is available from the #iwill website.The Youth Social Action Survey, 2015 is the second survey in the series and provides an update on how participation in social action is changing over time since 2014.	
1970 British Cohort Study	The 1970 British Cohort Study (BCS70) follows the lives of more than 17,000 people born in England, Scotland and Wales in a single week of 1970. Over the course of cohort members' lives, the BCS70 has broadened from a strictly medical focus at birth to collect information on health, physical, educational, and social development, and economic circumstances among other factors. The BCS70 is conducted by the Centre for Longitudinal Studies (CLS).	Economic and Social Research Council (ESRC), Medical Research Council (MRC), British Heart Foundation
Millennium Cohort Study	The Millennium Cohort Study (MCS), which began in 2000, is conducted by the Centre for Longitudinal Studies (CLS). It aims to chart the conditions of social, economic, and health advantages and disadvantages facing children born at the start of the twenty-first century. The study has been tracking the 'Millennium children' through their early childhood years and plans to follow them into adulthood. It also provides a basis for comparing patterns of development with the preceding cohort studies (the National Child Development Study (NCDS) and the 1970 Birth Cohort Study (BCS70)).	Economic and Social Research Council (ESRC), various government departments
National Child Development Study	The National Child Development Study (NCDS) is a continuing longitudinal study that seeks to follow the lives of all those living in Great Britain who were born in one particular week in 1958. Conducted by the Centre for Longitudinal Studies (CLS), the aim of the study is to improve understanding of the factors affecting human development over the whole lifespan. It collects information on physical and educational development, economic circumstances, employment, family life, health behaviour, wellbeing, social participation, and attitudes.	Economic and Social Research Council (ESRC), Medical Research Council (MRC), National Institutes of Health, Department for Work and Pensions (DWP)
Next Steps	Next Steps (also known as the Longitudinal Study of Young People in England (LSYPE1)) is a major longitudinal study that follows the lives of around 16,000 people born in 1989–90 in England. The first seven sweeps of the study (2004–10) were funded and managed by the Department for Education (DfE) and mainly focused on the educational and early labour market experiences of young people.The study began in 2004 and included young people in Year 9 who attended state and independent schools in England. Following the initial survey at age 13–14, the cohort members were interviewed every year until 2010. The survey data have also been	Economic and Social Research Council (ESRC), Department for Education (DfE)

Continued

Table 3A.1 *Continued*

United Kingdom Data *(Descriptions by UK Data Archive, Adapted)*		
Dataset	**Description**	**Commissioned By**
	linked to the National Pupil Database (NPD) records, including cohort members' individual scores at Key Stage 2, 3, and 4. In 2013 the management of Next Steps was transferred to the Centre for Longitudinal Studies (CLS) at the UCL Institute of Education and in 2015 Next Steps was restarted, under the management of CLS, to find out how the lives of the cohort members had turned out at age 25. It maintained the strong focus on education, but the content was broadened to become a more multi-disciplinary research resource. There are now two separate studies that began under the LSYPE programme. The second study, Our Future (also known as LSYPE2), began in 2013 and will track a sample of over 13,000 young people from the age of 13–14 annually through to the age of 20 (seven waves).	
Our Future	The Department for Education (DfE) commissioned the Our Future study (also known as the Second Longitudinal Study of Young People in England (LSYPE2)) at the beginning of 2013. It is one of the largest studies of young people ever commissioned.Our Future aims to follow a sample of young people through the final years of compulsory education and their transition from compulsory education to other forms of education, training, and employment. The survey will collect information about their career paths and about the factors affecting them; and provide a strategic evidence base about the lives and experiences of young people. There are now two separate studies that began under the LSYPE programme. The first study, Next Steps (also known as LSYPE1), began in 2004, and is managed by the Department for Education (DfE). In 2013 the management of Next Steps was transferred to the Centre for Longitudinal Studies (CLS) at the UCL Institute of Education, when the DfE launched Our Future.	Economic and Social Research Council (ESRC), Department for Education (DfE)

International Data

Dataset	Description	Commissioned By
Survey of Health Ageing and Retirement in Europe (SHARE)	The Survey of Health, Ageing and Retirement in Europe (SHARE) (whose first wave was administered in 2004) is a multidisciplinary and cross-national panel database. The survey collects a rich variety of micro-level data pertaining to respondents' health and socio-economic status and relating to participants' family and social ties.	Receives funding from the European Commission and the National Institute on Aging.
The Irish Longitudinal Study on Ageing (TILDA)	The Irish Longitudinal Study on Ageing (TILDA) is a large-scale nationally representative longitudinal study on ageing in Ireland and collects a wide range of information on the health, economic, and social circumstances of participants aged 50+.	Department for Health.
German Socio-Economic Panel Study (SOEP)	The German Socio-Economic Panel Study (SOEP) started in 1984, making it one of the longest-running panel studies globally. The study aims to support basic, applied, and policy-driven research by incorporating interdisciplinary insights in its design.	Deutsches Institut für Wirtschaftsforschung (DIW) receives funding from the Federal Ministry of Education and Research (BMBF) and from Germany's state (Länder) governments.
Household, Income and Labour Dynamics in Australia (HILDA)	The Household, Income and Labour Dynamics in Australia (HILDA) survey commenced in 2001 and collates information to help answer research questions related to three broad areas—income, labour markets, and family dynamics.	Department of Social Services
Panel Study of Income Dynamics (PSID)	The Panel Study of Income Dynamics (PSID) began in 1968, making it the longest-running longitudinal housing survey in the world. While originally the study was conceived as a vessel to study the dynamics of poverty and wealth, over the years the scope of the survey has expanded to cover areas related to health, wellbeing, wealth, philanthropy, and much more.	Office of Economic Opportunity (OEO) directed by the US Bureau of the Census
Health and Retirement Study (HRS)	The University of Michigan Health and Retirement Study (HRS) is a longitudinal study in the United States covering a representative sample of *circa* 20,000 older individuals. The survey generates data which can help to address research questions centred on aging and its associated challenges and opportunities.	Supported by the National Institute on Aging (NIA) and the Social Security Administration
General Social Survey (GSS)	The General Social Survey began in 1972 and collates information from a range of questions which cover among other things, demographic, behavioural, and attitudinal characteristics of respondents. The survey also covers psychological wellbeing.	National Data Program for the Social Sciences, National Science Foundation

Continued

Table 3A.1 *Continued*

International Data		
Dataset	**Description**	**Commissioned By**
European Social Survey (ESS)	The European Social Survey (ESS) is a cross-national survey which began in 2001. It is conducted every two years, in an attempt to quantify and collect data on the diverse range of attitudes, beliefs, and patterns of behaviour across European countries.	European Commission, European Science Foundation (ESF), national funding councils
Behavioral Risk Factor Surveillance System (BRFSS)	The Behavioral Risk Factor Surveillance System (BRFSS) is administered via telephone surveys, to collect information on health-related risks and behaviors. The survey represents the largest of its kind, completing over 400,000 adult interviews annually.	Centers for Disease Control and Prevention, supported by CDC National Center for Chronic Disease Prevention and Health Promotion, Health Resources and Services Administration, Administration on Aging, Department of Veterans Affairs, and Substance Abuse and Mental Health Services Administration
Gallup World Poll	Since 2005, the Gallup World Poll has surveyed residents across over 160 countries, collecting information on attitudes and behaviours, covering important issues such as employment, access to nourishment, wellbeing, and happiness.	Gallup partner with Fortune 500 companies, foundations and think tanks (e.g. World Bank, Sustainable Development Solutions Network, MetLife Foundation, Walk Free Foundation)
Russia Longitudinal Monitoring Survey—HSE	The Russia Longitudinal Monitoring Survey began in 1992. Data is collected on household expenditures and service utilization, health status, and pertinent community-level indicators. The second phase of the survey, which corresponds to the ongoing longitudinal survey, commenced in 1994.	The World Bank was the lead agency to fund the survey during phase 1, solely funding round 1, and jointly funding rounds 2–4 with the United States Agency for International Development (USAID). For phase 2, rounds 5–8, funding was from the USAID, and supported by the National Science Foundation, and National Institutes of Health (NIH).
China Health and Nutrition Survey	The China Health and Nutrition Survey began in 1989 and collected information on the health and nutritional status of Chinese residents. An interdisciplinary team of international researchers conducted the surveys.	National Institute for Nutrition and Health (NINH) at the Chinese Center for Disease Control and Prevention (CCDC), Chinese Ministry of Public Health

Appendix B: Data—Technical Details

Table 3A.2 Data—Technical details.

United Kingdom Data								
Dataset	Type	Observations	Frequency	Start	Population	Life-satisfaction Question	Regional Identifiers	Notes
English Longitudinal Study of Ageing	Panel	12,000	Annually	2002	England	'I feel satisfied with the way my life has turned out.' (2002–03)	GOR, OA, LLSOA, MLSOA, LAD	Includes ONS-4 standardized items (life satisfaction, happiness, anxiety, and worthwhileness) since 2012
Understanding Society	Panel	40,000	Annually	2009	United Kingdom	Satisfaction with Life Overall (2009–17)	National Grid Reference, GOR, OA, LLSOA, MLSOA, LAD, Statistics Wards, Others	
Wealth and Assets Survey	Panel	30,000	Bienially	2006	England, Scotland, and Wales	Satisfaction with Life (2006–12)	GOR, OA, LLSOA, MLSOA, LAD, Statistics Wards, Counties, Others	Includes ONS-4 standardized items (life satisfaction, happiness, anxiety, and worthwhileness) since 2011
Active Lives Survey	Cross-section	200,000	Annually	2015	England	'Overall, how satisfied are you with your life nowadays?' (2015–)	LAD, Others	Includes ONS-4 standardized items (life satisfaction, happiness, anxiety, and worthwhileness) since 2015
Annual Population Survey	Cross-section	320,000	Annually	2004	United Kingdom	'Overall, how satisfied are you with your life nowadays?' (2011–17)	GOR, OA, Unit Postcodes, Others	Includes ONS-4 standardized items (life satisfaction, happiness, anxiety, and worthwhileness) since 2011
Armed Forces Continuous	Cross-section	28,000	Annually	2007	United Kingdom		Unknown	Includes ONS-4 standardized items (life satisfaction,

Continued

Table 3A.2 *Continued*

United Kingdom Data								
Dataset	Type	Observations	Frequency	Start	Population	Life-satisfaction Question	Regional Identifiers	Notes
Attitude Survey (AFCAS)						'Overall, how satisfied are you with your life nowadays?' (2012–)		happiness, anxiety, and worthwhileness) since 2012
British Social Attitudes	Cross-section	3,000	Annually	1983	England, Scotland, and Wales	'All things considered, how satisfied are you with your life as a whole nowadays?' (2008, 2013)	GOR, Counties	
Community Life Survey	Cross-section	6,600	Annually	2012	England	'On a scale from 0 to 10, how satisfied are you with your life as a whole nowadays?' (2012–17)	GOR, OA, Statistics Wards, Counties, Others	Includes ONS-4 standardized items (life satisfaction, happiness, anxiety, and worthwhileness) since 2013
Crime Survey for England and Wales	Cross-section	50,000	Annually, Quarterly	1982	England, Wales	'Overall, how satisfied are you with your life nowadays?' (2012–)	LLSOA, MLSOA, Others	Includes ONS-4 standardized items (life satisfaction, happiness, anxiety, and worthwhileness) since 2012
English Housing Survey (formerly English House Condition Survey and Survey of English Housing)	Cross-section	13,300	Annually	2008	England	Satisfaction with Life Nowadays (2013–14)	GOR, LLSOA, Unit Postcodes	Includes ONS-4 standardized items (life satisfaction, happiness, anxiety, and worthwhileness) since 2013
Families Continuous Attitude Survey (FAMCAS)	Cross-section	Unknown	Annually	2009	United Kingdom	'Overall, how satisfied are you with your life nowadays?' (2012–)	Unknown	Includes ONS-4 standardized items (life satisfaction, happiness, anxiety, and worthwhileness) since 2012
Family Resources Survey	Cross-section	24,000	Annually	1992	United Kingdom	'How satisfied are you with your life now?' (2013–16)	GOR	
Food and You Survey	Cross-Section	3,100	Bienially	2010	United Kingdom	'Overall, how satisfied are you with your life nowadays?' (2014–)	GOR	Includes ONS-4 standardized items (life satisfaction,

								happiness, anxiety, and worthwhileness) since 2014
Graduate Outcomes Survey	Cross-section	700,000	Annually	2018	United Kingdom	'Overall, how satisfied are you with your life nowadays?' (2018-)	Unknown	Includes ONS-4 standardized items (life satisfaction, happiness, anxiety, and worthwhileness) since 2018
Health Survey for England	Cross-section	10,000	Annually	1991	England	'Overall, how satisfied are you with your life nowadays, where 0 is "not at all satisfied" and 10 is "completely satisfied"?' (2015–16)	GOR, Others	
Health Survey Northern Ireland	Cross-section	3,900	Annually	2010	Northern Ireland	'How satisfied are you with your life in general?' (2010–14)	Unknown	
Labour Force Survey	Cross-section	3,600	Quarterly	1973	United Kingdom	'Overall, how satisfied are you with your life nowadays?' (2011–17)	GOR, LAD, Others	Includes ONS-4 standardized items (life satisfaction, happiness, anxiety, and worthwhileness) since 2011
Living Costs and Food Survey	Cross-section	4,700	Annually	2008	United Kingdom	'Overall, how satisfied are you with your life nowadays?' (2014–16)	GOR, OA, LAD, Unit Post Codes, Others	Includes ONS-4 standardized items (life satisfaction, happiness, anxiety, and worthwhileness) since 2011
Living Well Index	Cross-section	8,250	Annually	2012	England, Scotland, Wales	'Overall, how satisfied are you with your life nowadays?' (2012–)	Unknown	Includes ONS-4 standardized items (life satisfaction, happiness, anxiety, and worthwhileness) since 2012
National Survey for Wales	Cross-section	10,000	Annually	2012	Wales	'Overall, how satisfied are you with your life nowadays?' (2009–10, 2012–17)	LAD, Others	Includes ONS-4 standardized items (life satisfaction, happiness, anxiety, and worthwhileness) since 2012
Natural Survey on People and the	Cross-section	45,000	Annually	2009	England		GOR	Includes ONS-4 standardized items (life satisfaction,

Continued

Table 3A.2 *Continued*

United Kingdom Data								
Dataset	Type	Observations	Frequency	Start	Population	Life-satisfaction Question	Regional Identifiers	Notes
Natural Environment						'Overall, how satisfied are you with your life nowadays?' (2012–)		happiness, anxiety, and worthwhileness) since 2012
Opinions and Lifestyle Survey (formerly ONS Opinions Survey and ONS Omnibus Survey)	Cross-section	1,100	Monthly	1990	England, Scotland, and Wales	'Overall, how satisfied are you with your life nowadays?' (2012–17)	GOR, Others	Includes ONS-4 standardized items (life satisfaction, happiness, anxiety, and worthwhileness) since 2011
Scottish Health Survey	Cross-section	5,300	Annually	1995	Scotland	'All things considered, how satisfied are you with your life as a whole nowadays?' (2008, 2009, 2010, 2011, 2013, 2014, 2015, 2016)	Others	
Scottish Household Survey	Cross-section	15,500	Annually	1999	Scotland	Satisfaction with Life as a Whole Nowadays (2009–10, 2011)	LAD, Others	
Scottish Social Attitudes Survey	Cross-section	1,500	Annually	1999	Scotland	Life Satisfaction (2007)	Others	
Taking Part Survey	Cross-section	8,400	Annually	2005	England	'Overall, how satisfied are you with your life nowadays?' (2013–)	GOR	Includes ONS-4 standardized items (life satisfaction, happiness, anxiety, and worthwhileness) since 2013
Time Use Survey	Cross-section	6,400	2000, 2015	2000	United Kingdom	Satisfaction with Life Overall (2014–15)	GOR, Counties	Includes ONS-4 standardized items (life satisfaction, happiness, anxiety, and worthwhileness) since 2014
		2,000	Annually	2014			GOR	

Youth Social Action Survey	Cross-section					United Kingdom	'Overall, how satisfied are you with your life nowadays?' (2014–)		Includes ONS-4 standardized items (life satisfaction, happiness, anxiety, and worthwhileness) since 2014
1970 British Cohort Study	Cohort	17,000		1970, 1975, 1980, 1986, 1996, 2000, 2004, 2008, 2012, 2016	1970	England, Scotland, and Wales	Satisfaction With Life So Far (1992, 1996, 2000, 2004, 2012)	GOR, OA, LLSOA, MLSOA, LAD, Statistics Wards, Others	
Millennium Cohort Study	Cohort	18,800		2001, 2004, 2006, 2008, 2012, 2015, 2018	2000	United Kingdom	Life Satisfaction (2001–03, 2015)	GOR, OA, LLSOA, MLSOA, Statistics Wards, Others	
National Child Development Study	Cohort	17,400		1958, 1965, 1969, 1974, 1981, 1991, 2000, 2002, 2004, 2008, 2013, 2020	1958	England, Scotland, and Wales	Life Satisfaction So Far (1995)	LAD, Counties, Others	
Next Steps	Cohort	16,000		2004, 2005, 2006, 2007, 2008, 2009, 2010, 2015	2004	England	'And how dissatisfied or satisfied you are about the way your life has turned out so far?' (2004–10)	GOR	
Our Future	Cohort	13,000		2013, 2014, 2015	2013	England	Overall Satisfaction with Life (2013–15)	GOR, LLSOA, LAD, Statistics Wards	

Continued

Table 3A.2 *Continued*

International Data

Dataset	Type	Observations	Frequency	Start	Population	Life-satisfaction Question	Regional Identifiers	Notes
Survey of Health Ageing and Retirement in Europe	Panel	140,000 (Wave 1-7)	Biennial	2004	27 European Countries and Israel[a]	'On a scale from 0 to 10 where 0 means completely dissatisfied and 10 means completely satisfied, how satisfied are you with your life?' (2011–)	Country of birth	While waves 1–2 deals with Mental Health and emotional health/wellbeing a question explicitly on life satisfaction was not introduced until wave 4
The Irish Longitudinal Study on Ageing	Panel	8,504	Biennial	2009	Ireland	'In a scale from 1 to 7, where "1" means strongly agree and "7" means strongly disagree; please say how much you agree or disagree with the following statement: I am satisfied with my life' (2009–)		In later waves of TILDA the question has been modified such that, '1' means strongly disagree and '7' means strongly agree
German Socio-Economic Panel Study (SOEP)	Panel	15,000 (households)	Annually	1984	Germany	'How satisfied are you today with the following areas of your life? (health, sleep, job, income, standard of living, dwelling, etc.)' (2003–)		Answer on a scale from 0 (completely dissatisfied) to 10 (completely satisfied)
Household, Income and Labour Dynamics in Australia (HILDA)	Panel	8,000 (households)	Annually	2001	Australia	'All things considered, how satisfied are you with your life? Again, pick a number between 0 and 10 to indicate how satisfied you are.' (2001–)		
Panel Study of Income Dynamics (PSID)	Panel	5,000 (households)	Annually from 1968 to 97 and biennially since.	1968	United States	'Please think about your life-as-a-whole. How satisfied are you with it? Are you completely satisfied, very satisfied, somewhat satisfied, not very satisfied, or not at all satisfied?' (2009–		

Health and Retirement Study (HRS)	Panel	20,000 (individuals)	Annually from 1992 to 1996, and then biennially after 1996.	1992	United States	'Please say how much you agree or disagree with the following statements: I am satisfied with my life.' (2004–)	The options are: Strongly agree, Agree, Slightly agree, Neither agree nor disagree, Slightly disagree, Disagree, Strongly disagree
General Social Survey (GSS)	Originally cross-sectional and has now switched to a combined repeating cross-section and panel-component design.	5,000	Annually from 1972–78, and 1982–91, and then biennially from 1994.	1972	United States	'All things considered, how satisfied are you with your life as a whole nowadays?' (2018–)	Options include: Completely satisfied, Very satisfied, Fairly satisfied, Neither satisfied nor dissatisfied, Fairly dissatisfied, Very dissatisfied, Completely dissatisfied From 1982 to 1989 respondents were asked 'For each area of life I am going to name, tell me the number that shows how much satisfaction you get from that area' ranging from 1 (A very great deal) to 7 (none).
European Social Survey (ESS)	Cross-section	All countries must aim for a minimum 'effective achieved sample size' of 1,500 or 800 in countries with ESS populations	Biennially	2001	36 countries across 9 rounds of the survey.	'All things considered, how satisfied are you with your life as a whole nowadays? Please answer using this card, where 0 means extremely dissatisfied and 10 means extremely satisfied.' (2002–)	Respondents are also asked, 'On a scale from 0 (Extremely unhappy) to 10 (Extremely happy): Taking all things together, how happy would you say you are?'

Continued

Table 3A.2 *Continued*

International Data								
Dataset	Type	Observations	Frequency	Start	Population	Life-satisfaction Question	Regional Identifiers	Notes
		of less than 2 million after discounting for design effects						
Behavioral Risk Factor Surveillance System (BRFSS)	Cross-section	BRFSS completes more than 400,000 adult interviews each year	Annually	1984	United States	'In general, how satisfied are you with your life?' (2005–17)		Answers on a 4-point scale from, 'Very satisfied' to 'Very dissatisfied'.
Gallup World Poll	Cross-section	The typical survey includes at least 1,000 individuals per country.	Depending on the country, Gallup conducts interviews on a semi-annual, annual, or biennial frequency.	2005	Over 160 countries	'All things considered, how satisfied are you with your life as a whole these days? Use a 0 to 10 scale, where 0 is dissatisfied and 10 is satisfied.'(2005–)		Some larger countries, such as China, sample sizes are at least 2,000. In some rare cases the sample size is between 500 and 1,000. Respondents are also asked to imagine a ladder with 11 rungs from 0 to 10, and higher rungs representing a better life, and then judge, where they are on the ladder today, where they were five years ago, and where they will be in five years time.
Russia Longitudinal Monitoring Survey—HSE	Panel	4,000 (households)	Annually since 1994 (with two exceptions—not asked in 1997 or 1999).	1994	Russia	'To what extent are you satisfied with your life in general at the present time?' (1994–)		Options are: 1 (Fully satisfied), 2 (Rather satisfied), 3 (Both yes and no), 4 (Less than satisfied), 5 (Not at all satisfied)

China Health and Nutrition Survey	Panel	4,400 (households) 19,000 (individuals)	Biennially from 1989–93, and then conducted in 1997, 2000, 2004, 2006, 2009, 2011, 2015.	1989	9 Provinces in China[b]	'How do you rate the quality of your life at present?' (2006–15)	Options: Very good, Good, Fair, Bad, Very bad

Notes: [a] Not every country has participated in every wave of SHARE. For details of which waves particular countries have participated in, seehttp://www.share-project.org/data-documentation/waves-overview.html. [b] See https://www.cpc.unc.edu/projects/china/about/proj_desc/chinamap.

Appendix C: Data—Download Links and Sample Studies

Table 3A.3 Data—Download links and sample studies.

United Kingdom Data		
Dataset	**Link**	**Example Study**
English Longitudinal Study of Ageing	http://beta.ukdataservice.ac.uk/datacatalogue/series/series?id=200011	Steptoe, A., Shankar, A., Demakakos, P. and Wardle, J. (2013). Social Isolation, Loneliness, and All-cause Mortality in Older Men and Women. *Proceedings of the National Academy of Sciences* 110(15): 5797–801.
Understanding Society	http://beta.ukdataservice.ac.uk/datacatalogue/series/series?id=2000053	Chanfreau, J., Lloyd, C., Byron, C., Roberts, C., R. Craig, R., De Feo, D., and McManus, S. (2013). Predicting Wellbeing. NatCen Social Research.
Wealth and Assets Survey	http://beta.ukdataservice.ac.uk/datacatalogue/series/series?id=2000056	Paya, I., and Wang, P. (2013). Wealth Fluctuations and Investment in Risky Assets: The UK Micro Evidence on Households Asset Allocation. *Journal of Empirical Finance* 38(Part A): 221–35.
Active Lives Survey	http://beta.ukdataservice.ac.uk/datacatalogue/studies/study?id=8223&type=Data%20catalogue	Brainard, J., Cooke, R., Lane, K., and Salter, C. (2019). Age, Sex and Other Correlates with Active Travel Walking and Cycling in England: Analysis of Responses to the Active Lives Survey 2016/17. *Preventive Medicine* 123: 225–31.
Annual Population Survey	http://beta.ukdataservice.ac.uk/datacatalogue/series/series?id=200002#!/abstract	Lawton, R. N., and Fujiwara, D. (2016). Living with Aircraft Noise: Airport Proximity, Aviation Noise and Subjective Wellbeing in England. *Transportation Research Part D: Transport and Environment* 42: 104–18.
Armed Forces Continuous Attitude Survey (AFCAS)	http://www.gov.uk/government/collections/armed-forces-continuous-attitude-survey-index	Elliott-Mabey, N., and Davison, H. (2019). UK Armed Forces Continuous Attitude Survey: A Short History and Description of a Key Strategic Information Tool. *Journal of the Royal Army Medical Corps* 165(2): 133–5.
British Social Attitudes	http://beta.ukdataservice.ac.uk/datacatalogue/series/series?id=200002	MacInnes, J. (2005). Work–Life Balance and the Demand for Reduction in Working Hours: Evidence from the British Social Attitudes Survey 2002. *British Journal of Industrial Relations* 43(2): 273–95.

Community Life Survey	http://beta.ukdataservice.ac.uk/datacatalogue/series/series?id=2000100	Appau, S., and Churchill, S. A. (2019). Social Integration and Subjective Well-being. *Applied Economics* 51(16): 1748–61.
Crime Survey for England and Wales	http://beta.ukdataservice.ac.uk/datacatalogue/series/series?id=200009	Maccagnan, A., Taylor, T., and White, M. P. (2019). Valuing the Relationship between Drug and Alcohol Use and Life Satisfaction: Findings from the Crime Survey for England and Wales. *Journal of Happiness Studies* 21(3): 877–98.
English Housing Survey (formerly English House Condition Survey and Survey of English Housing)	http://beta.ukdataservice.ac.uk/datacatalogue/series/series?id=200010	Lupton, R. (2016). The Influence(s) of Housing Policies on the Residential Moves of Families with Young Children. *Longitudinal and Life Course Studies* 7(3): 288–301.
Families Continuous Attitude Survey (FAMCAS)	http://data.gov.uk/dataset/4a2258fe-e618-4fed-94d5-765760638b0f/army-families-continuous-attitude-survey-famcas	Jervis, S. (2011). *Relocation, Gender and Emotion: A Psycho-Social Perspective on the Experiences of Military Wives*. London: Routledge.
Family Resources Survey	http://beta.ukdataservice.ac.uk/datacatalogue/series/series?id=200017	Brewer, M., Etheridge, B., and O'Dea, C. (2017). Why Are Households that Report the Lowest Incomes So Well-off? *Economic Journal* 127 (605): F24–F49.
Food and You Survey	http://beta.ukdataservice.ac.uk/datacatalogue/studies/study?id=8193&type=Data%20catalogue	Prior, G., Hall, L., Morris, S., and Draper, A. (2011). Exploring Food Attitudes and Behaviours in the UK: Findings from the Food and You Survey 2010. Food Standards Agency, London.
Graduate Outcomes Survey	http://www.graduateoutcomes.ac.uk/	Callender, C., and Dougherty, K. J. (2018). Student Choice in Higher Education—Reducing or Reproducing Social Inequalities? *Social Sciences* 7(189): 1–28.
Health Survey for England	http://beta.ukdataservice.ac.uk/datacatalogue/series/series?id=2000021	Stewart-Brown, S., Chandimali Samaraweera, P., Taggart, F., and Ngianga-Bakwin, K. (2015). Socioeconomic Gradients and Mental Health: Implications for Public Health. *British Journal of Psychiatry* 206(6): 461–5.
Health Survey Northern Ireland	http://beta.ukdataservice.ac.uk/datacatalogue/studies/study?id=7258	French, D., and McKillop, D. (2017). The Impact of Debt and Financial Stress on Health in Northern Irish Households. *Journal of European Social Policy* 27(5): 458–73.
Labour Force Survey	http://beta.ukdataservice.ac.uk/datacatalogue/series/series?id=2000026	Bell, D. N. F., and Blanchflower, D. G. (2019). The Well-being of the Overemployed and the Underemployed and the Rise in Depression in the UK. *Journal of Economic Behavior and Organization* 161: 180–96.

Continued

Table 3A.3 *Continued*

United Kingdom Data		
Dataset	**Link**	**Example Study**
Living Costs and Food Survey	http://beta.ukdataservice.ac.uk/datacatalogue/series/series?id=2000028	Monteiro, C. A., Moubarac, J.-C., Levy, R. B., and Canella, D. S. (2018). Household Availability of Ultra-processed Foods and Obesity in Nineteen European Countries. *Public Health Nutrition* 21(1): 18–26.
Living Well Index	http://www.basw.co.uk/system/files/resources/basw_90113-8.pdf	Sainsbury's (2017). The Sainsbury's Living Well Index: A Landmark Study Carried out by Oxford Economics and the National Centre for Social Research. Report.
National Survey for Wales	http://beta.ukdataservice.ac.uk/datacatalogue/series/series?id=2000029	Song, J., Fry, R., Mizen, A., Akbari, A., Wheeler, B., White, J., White, M., Lovell, R., Parker, C., Berridge, D., Stratton, G., Nieuwenhuijsen, M., Lyons, R., and Rodgers, S. (2018). Association between Blue and Green Space Availability with Mental Health and Wellbeing. *International Journal of Population Data Science* 3(4): 330.
Natural Survey on People and the Natural Environment	http://www.gov.uk/government/collections/monitor-of-engagement-with-the-natural-environment-survey-purpose-and-results	White, M. P., Pahl, S., Wheeler, B. W., Depledge, M. H., and Fleming, L. E. (2017). Natural Environments and Subjective Wellbeing: Different Types of Exposure Are Associated with Different Aspects of Wellbeing. *Health and Place* 45: 77–84.
Opinions and Lifestyle Survey (formerly ONS Opinions Survey and ONS Omnibus Survey)	http://beta.ukdataservice.ac.uk/datacatalogue/series/series?id=2000043	de Bell, S., Graham, H., Jarvis, S., and White, P. (2017). The Importance of Nature in Mediating Social and Psychological Benefits Associated with Visits to Freshwater Blue Space. *Landscape and Urban Planning* 167: 118–27.
Scottish Health Survey	http://beta.ukdataservice.ac.uk/datacatalogue/series/series?id=2000047	Robertson, T., and Watts, E. (2016). The Importance of Age, Sex and Place in Understanding Socioeconomic Inequalities in Allostatic Load: Evidence from the Scottish Health Survey (2008–2011). *BMJ Public Health* 16(126): 1–13.
Scottish Household Survey	http://beta.ukdataservice.ac.uk/datacatalogue/series/series?id=2000048	Parkes, A., and Kearns, A. (2006). The Multi-dimensional Neighbourhood and Health: A Cross-sectional Analysis of the Scottish Household Survey, 2001. *Health and Place* 12(1): 1–18.
Scottish Social Attitudes Survey	http://beta.ukdataservice.ac.uk/datacatalogue/series/series?id=2000049	Glendinning, T., and Bruce, S. (2006). New Ways of Believing or Belonging: Is Religion Giving Way to Spirituality? *British Journal of Sociology* 57(3): 399–414.

Taking Part Survey	http://beta.ukdataservice.ac.uk/datacatalogue/series/series?id=2000052	Rasciute, S., and Downward, P. (2010). Health or Happiness? What Is the Impact of Physical Activity on the Individual? *Kyklos* 63(2): 256–70.
Time Use Survey	http://beta.ukdataservice.ac.uk/datacatalogue/series/series?id=2000054	Chatzitheochari, S., and Arber, S. (2009). Lack of Sleep, Work and the Long Hours Culture: Evidence from the UK Time Use Survey. *Work, Employment and Society*. 23(1): 30–48.
Youth Social Action Survey	http://beta.ukdataservice.ac.uk/datacatalogue/studies/study?id=8037&type=Data%20catalogue#!/details	Taylor-Collins, E., Harrison, T., Thoma, S. J., and Moller, F. (2019). A Habit of Social Action: Understanding the Factors Associated with Adolescents Who Have Made a Habit of Helping Others. *International Journal of Voluntary and Nonprofit Organizations* 30(1): 98–114.
1970 British Cohort Study	http://beta.ukdataservice.ac.uk/datacatalogue/series/series?id=200001	Flèche, S., Lekfuangfu, W. N., and Clark, A. E. (2019). The Long-lasting Effects of Family and Childhood on Adult Wellbeing: Evidence from British Cohort Data. *Journal of Economic Behavior and Organization*. Doi: 10.1016/j.jebo.2018.09.018.
Millennium Cohort Study	http://beta.ukdataservice.ac.uk/datacatalogue/series/series?id=2000031	Gambaro, L., and Joshi, H. (2016). Moving Home in the Early Years: What Happens to Children in the UK? Longitudinal and Life Course Studies 7(3): 265–87.
National Child Development Study	http://beta.ukdataservice.ac.uk/datacatalogue/series/series?id=2000032	Cutler, D. M., and Lleras-Muney, A. (2010). Understanding Differences in health Behaviors by Education. *Journal of Health Economics* 29(1): 1–28.
Next Steps	http://beta.ukdataservice.ac.uk/datacatalogue/series/series?id=2000030	Green, R., and Ross, A. (2010). Young People's Alcohol Consumption and its Relationship to Other Outcomes and Behaviour. Department for Education. Report, DFE-RR005.
Our Future	http://beta.ukdataservice.ac.uk/datacatalogue/series/series?id=2000110	Not yet available

Continued

Table 3A.3 *Continued*

International Data		
Dataset	**Link**	**Example Study**
Survey of Health Ageing and Retirement in Europe	http://www.share-project.org/data-access.html	Mousteri, V., Daly, M., and Delaney, L. (2018). The Scarring Effect of Unemployment on Psychological Well-being across Europe. *Social Science Research* 72: 146–69.
		Arpino, B., Bordone, V., and Balbo, N. (2018). Grandparenting, Education and Subjective Well-being of Older Europeans. *European Journal of Ageing* 15(3): 251–63.
		Hansen, T., Aartsen, M., Slagsvold, B., and Deindl, C. (2018). Dynamics of Volunteering and Life Satisfaction in Midlife and Old Age: Findings from 12 European Countries. *Social Sciences* 7(5): 78.
The Irish Longitudinal Study on Ageing	https://tilda.tcd.ie/data/accessing-data/	Donoghue, O. A., McGarrigle, C. A., and Kenny, R. A. (2019). Who's in the Driver's Seat? Impact on Social Participation and Psychosocial Wellbeing in Adults Aged 50 and over. *Transportation Research Part F: Traffic Psychology and Behaviour* 64: 522–31.
		Turner, N., Donoghue, O., and Kenny, R. A. (2018). Wellbeing and Health in Ireland's over 50s, 2009–2016. TILDA Report.
German Socio-Economic Panel Study (SOEP)	https://www.diw.de/en/diw_02.c.222829.en/access_and_ordering.html	Headey, B. (2009). Yes We Can . . . : Happiness Levels Can Change, But Most Recent Changes Are in the Wrong Direction. *Weekly Report* 5(4): 26–30.
		Priem, M., and Schupp, J. (2014). Everyone Happy: Living Standards in Germany 25 Years after Reunification. *DIW Economic Bulletin* 4(11): 65–71.
		Kroh, M., Kühne, S., Kipp, C., and Richter, D. (2017). Income, Social Support Networks, Life Satisfaction: Lesbians, Gays, and Bisexuals in Germany. *DIW Economic Bulletin* 7(33/35): 335–45.
Household, Income and Labour Dynamics in Australia (HILDA)	https://dataverse.ada.edu.au/dataverse/hilda	Brown, S., and Gray, D. (2016). Household Finances and Wellbeing in Australia: An Empirical Analysis of Comparison Effects. *Journal of Economic Psychology* 53: 17–36.
Panel Study of Income Dynamics (PSID)	https://simba.isr.umich.edu/data/data.aspx	Senik, C. (2005). Income Distribution and Well-being: What Can We Learn from Subjective Data? *Journal of Economic Surveys* 19(1): 43–63.
		Sass, V., Kravitz-Wirtz, N., Karceski, S. M., Hajat, A., Crowder, K., and Takeuchi, D. (2017). The Effects of Air Pollution on Individual Psychological Distress. *Health and Place* 48: 72–9.

		Brown, G. D., and Gathergood, J. (2020). Consumption Changes, Not Income Changes, Predict Changes in Subjective Well-being. *Social Psychological and Personality Science* 11(1): 64–73.
Health and Retirement Study (HRS)	https://hrs.isr.umich.edu/data-products	Gilberto, J. M., Davenport, M. K., and Beier, M. E. (2020). Personality, Health, Wealth, and Subjective Well-being: Testing a Integrative Model with Retired and Working Older Adults. *Journal of Research in Personality* 87: 103959.
General Social Survey (GSS)	https://gss.norc.org/Get-The-Data	Davis, J. A. (2004). Did Growing up in the 1960s Leave a Permanent Mark on Attitudes and Values? Evidence from the General Social Survey. *Public Opinion Quarterly* 68(2): 161–83.
European Social Survey (ESS)	https://www.europeansocialsurvey.org/data/	European Social Survey. (2015). Measuring and Reporting on Europeans' Wellbeing: Findings from the European Social Survey.
Behavioral Risk Factor Surveillance System (BRFSS)	https://www.cdc.gov/brfss/annual_data/annual_data.htm	Cheung, F., and Lucas, R. E. (2014). Assessing the Validity of Single-item Life Satisfaction Measures: Results from Three Large Samples. *Quality of Life Research* 23(10): 2809–18.
Gallup World Poll	https://www.gallup.com/analytics/213617/gallup-analytics.aspx	De Neve, J. E., and Krekel, C. (2020). Cities and Happiness: A Global Ranking and Analysis. *World Happiness Report 2020*, 14. Harter, J. K., Schmidt, F. L., and Keyes, C. L. (2003). Well-being in the Workplace and its Relationship to Business Outcomes: A Review of the Gallup Studies.
Russia Longitudinal Monitoring Survey—HSE	https://www.hse.ru/en/rlms/availability	Decancq, K., and Lugo, M. A. (2012). Inequality of Wellbeing: A Multidimensional Approach. *Economica* 79(316): 721–46. Eggers, A., Gaddy, C., and Graham, C. (2006). Well-being and Unemployment in Russia in the 1990s: Can Society's Suffering Be Individuals' Solace? *The Journal of Socio-Economics* 35(2): 209–42. Grogan, L., and Koka, K. (2013). Economic Crises and Wellbeing: Social Norms and Home Production. *Journal of Economic Behavior and Organization* 92: 241–58.
China Health and Nutrition Survey	https://www.cpc.unc.edu/projects/china/data/datasets/data-downloads-registration	Bakkeli, N. Z. (2019). Older Adults' Mental Health in China: Examining the Relationship between Income Inequality and Subjective Wellbeing Using Panel Data Analysis. *Journal of Happiness Studies*, 21 (4): 1–35. Lee, Y. H., Shelley, M., Liu, C. T., and Chang, Y. C. (2018). Assessing the Association of Food Preferences and Self-reported Psychological Well-being among Middle-aged and Older Adults in Contemporary China: Results from the China Health and Nutrition Survey. *International Journal of Environmental Research and Public Health* 15(3): 463.

Appendix D: Conversion between Different Scales and Indicators of Wellbeing

There are many different methods in use to convert one scale into another. All of them share the characteristic of preserving any rank order so that higher on one scale means higher on the other. Since we are interested in how a scale that does not use a 0-to-10 scale can be translated into a 0-to-10 scale, the generic question is how to transform an answer A_i on some other scale into an appropriate level B_i on the 0-to-10 scale. If answer categories are not numerical but in terms of verbal labels or some other ordered manner (and it is clear what is higher and what is lower), a preceding step would be to simply replace the verbal or other labels into numerical numbers, usually starting with 0 (lowest) increasing by 1 with each higher step.

We lay out our preferred methodology but also mention several others.

Convert One Cardinal Life-satisfaction Scale into Another—Linear Transformation Using the Equidistance Assumption and Maximum Information Principle

- Simple way to convert scales using a unique formula
- Advocated by Parducci (1995) and Kapteyn (1977) on the basis that it respects an equal interval assumption within any scale and individuals maximize the information about themselves. The effective implication is that there is an equal amount of wellbeing below the lowest reported scale and above the highest reported scale as there is between adjoining points with the scale. So the 0-to-10 scale is assumed to have intervals between any two points equal to 1/11th of the total possible, with 1/22 spacing below the lowest possible answer category (0) and another 1/22 spacing above the highest possible (10).

The formula used for converting various-point scales into an 11-point scale is then:

$$B_i = \frac{0.5 + A_i - A_0}{A_n - A_0 + 1} \times (11) - 0.5 \tag{1}$$

where:

- B_i = transformed variable to 11-point scale
- A_i = value on the original scale
- A_0 = lowest possible score on the original scale
- A_n = highest possible score on the original scale

For a 7-point Likert scale[45] the corresponding transformed values are thus:

Original Scale (1–7)	1	2	3	4	5	6	7
Target Scale (0–10)	0.286	1.857	3.429	5	6.571	8.143	9.714

[45] Assuming equal intervals, with values from 1 to 7.

Properties of this transformation include:

- The formula is designed in such a way that the 'middle' points of the original and target scale coincide after transformation (i.e. '4' in the middle of the 1-to-7 scale corresponds to 5 in the middle of the 0-to-10 scale).
- There is an equal distance between any two categories in both the original and the resulting transformation (in the example, the stretching is a factor of 7/11 corresponding to the difference in the number of answer categories).
- The transformation preserves rank and relative distance of the original scale.
- Can be used to transform values assigned to rank-order categories.

An alternative approach involves transforming ratings and average values into corresponding percentages of the maximum possible score of the measurement scale (Cummins, 2005; Mazaheri and Theuns, 2009). This is done via rescaling by *Percentage of Scale Maximum Scores* (%SM), which standardizes data onto a 0-to-100 scale and which originated in Cummins (1995). Mazaheri and Theuns (2009) use the following formula:

$$\%SM = \frac{s - m}{M - m} \times 100 \tag{2}$$

where:

- s = score selected from the scale interval [m, M]
- m = minimum value of the scale
- M= maximum value of the scale

Another often-used transformation is to simply equate the maxima of the scales (so a 1 on a 1-to-7 scale is equated to a 0 on a 0-to-10 scale and a 7 is equated to a 10), but this has as the undesirable feature that for scales with very low numbers of answer categories (and hence with high proportions of the population answering them) one is over-estimating the percentage of people who are as satisfied as possible. Nevertheless, because of its simplicity it is also frequently used (e.g. by Veenhoven in his world database of happiness to convert different survey scales into each other).

Yet another often-used approach is to multiply A_i with the relative standard deviation ($=\frac{SD_B}{SD_A}$) where SD_A is the standard deviation observed in the population for the question to which A_i was an answer, and SD_B the standard deviation observed in the 0-to-10 measure transformed into. Whilst this is a very prevalent method for translating coefficients found in different studies using different scales, it has some important disadvantages. One is that the empirical standard deviation is specific to the population within the study, meaning that one cannot always presume the standard deviations in some small study to coincide with what it would be in the wider population (which is usually the population of interest).

Convert an Ordinal Life-satisfaction Scale into Another—Non-linear Transformations

There are many ways in which scales can be translated into each other using non-linear transformations. One prevalent possibility is to presume there is some distribution (like the normal distribution or a log-normal distribution) which fits the distribution of answers, and then basically translate A_i into some statistic of that distribution (see van Praag and Ferrer (2004), for examples).

We here mention an alternative approach developed by Veenhoven (2009):

- Within this framework, a response option is assumed 'to cover a subset of contiguous happiness values, one subset for each response option' (Kalmijn, 2013).
- Considering the case where happiness is measured on an X-point scale. Under this method, the continuum [0, 10] is divided into X connecting subintervals, each corresponding to a particular response option of the recorded level of happiness.
- A first step in this transformation is to ascertain where the boundaries are. This method is used when researchers assume the latent variable has a particular distribution and consider that observed categories correspond to separate segments under the density function of the latent variables.

Kalmijn (2013) describes the intricacies of this method as follows:

> The leading question with the set of alternative response options is presented to a group of native speakers, who were asked to identify the boundary between successive response options, e.g. between 'pretty happy' and 'not too happy' on a [0, 10] continuum, in which '0' ('10') represents the least (most) happy situation they could imagine and ignoring their own happiness situation. Each of these 'judges' estimates the three boundaries on the [0, 10] interval; they do so in the context of a particular series of response options in a particular language. The opinions of all judges on the same boundary are averaged, resulting in e.g. the happiness value 6.3 as the dividing point between 'not too happy' and 'pretty happy'. The mid-interval value of each subinterval is adopted as the secondary rating of this particular response option within the context of this particular leading question and this particular set of response alternatives, all formulated in this particular language and in this particular period of time.

Additionally, Kalmijn and Veenhoven (2011) discuss another method in which the 'existence of a latent happiness variable is postulated'. Under this method, any information on the population at large is always information related to the distribution of the latent variable. The authors suggest that the method is capable of converting 'sample observations of happiness, as it is measured by using a discrete ordinal scale of measurement, into estimates of the parameters of the happiness distribution in the population represented by the sample'.

There is also the potential to combine features of the two strategies from above, as well as using alternative strategies such as, maximin (Abelson and Tukey, 1963) or estimation from criterion variables (Hensler and Stipak, 1979).

Convert an Ordinal Life-satisfaction Scale into Closely Related Constructs

In what follows, we list conversion factors between life satisfaction and different questions that are (closely) related to life satisfaction. We interpret these alternative questions as weighing parts of life differently than life satisfaction does and hence capturing part of life satisfaction. As a result, it makes it appropriate to simply use a regression analysis of how each measure co-moves with life satisfaction in the general population because that identifies how, in the period of the estimation, factors of life relevant to both measures have changed and are reflected in different degrees in the two measures, revealing the strength of the overlap in that period.[46] The conversion factors should therefore be read as the average default associations.

Table 3.A4, which is taken from Mukuria et al. (2014) and reported in Layard (2016), shows conversion factors between life satisfaction and other (closely) related questions in different datasets, and one can see that they turn out—in most cases—quite comparable across data. The conversion factors are obtained by regressing life satisfaction (measured on or transformed to a 0-to-10 scale) on the respective related question alongside controls (having health conditions, being unemployed, age and age squared, gender, and whether a respondent was married or not). The first column shows the impact of the respective question on life satisfaction using standardized variables, the second column the impact of a one-unit change in the respective question on life satisfaction.

Apart from partial correlation coefficients (which control for observables), Tables 3.A5 and 3.A6, which are also taken from Mukuria et al. (2014), show simple Spearman correlation coefficients. Finally, Table 3.A7, which is taken from Powdthavee (2012), shows the coefficients of an individual fixed-effects regression of life satisfaction on different life domain satisfactions, using data from the British Household Panel Survey for the period 1996 to 2009. It thus gives the relative importance of different life domains for overall satisfaction with life.

[46] As a result of this perspective, one ideally wants to have measured relations from a long period that is representative of what one might expect in the future. Note that an alternative approach would be more tailored to whatever intervention one has in mind (i.e. the overlap in the particular domain of the intervention), but that would lead to different conversion factors by domain and is sensitive to definition of that domain.

Table 3A.4 Impact of different measures on life-satisfaction (0-to-10)

	Range of Variable	Health Improvement and Patient Outcomes		Multi-instrument Comparison		South Yorkshire Comparison Cohort over 65		Understanding Society	
		r	dLS/dX	r	dLS/dX	r	dLS/dX	r	dLS/dX
Wellbeing									
Worthwhile (ONS)	0–10	0.80	0.80	0.77	0.84	0.75	0.75		
WB-VAS[a]	0–10	0.82	0.490						
GHQ									
GHQ	0–36							−0.49	−0.21
GHQ positive	0–18							−0.40	−0.42
GHQ negative	0–18							−0.48	−0.30
Health									
EQ5D5L	(−0.6)–1	0.63	5.65	0.39	4.56	0.44	3.79		
WEMWBS[b]	16–70					0.68	0.13		
SWEMWBS[c]						0.66	0.26	0.50	0.25
ICECAP-0[d]	0–1					0.63	8.77		
ICECAP-A[e]	0–1			0.65	9.71				
EQ-VAS15[f]	0–10	0.70	0.80			0.59	0.60		

Notes: [a] Visual analogue scale (four statistics are over-rounded). [b] Warwick Edinburgh Mental Well-Being Scale. [c] Shortened Warwick Edinburgh Mental Well-Being Scale. [d] Investigating Choice Experiments Capability Measure for Older People. [e] Investigating Choice Experiments Capability Measure for Adults. [f] Short Form 12 or 36 Health Survey.

Source: Layard (2016), Adapted.

Table 3A.5 Spearman correlations between wellbeing, health, and social care measures (datasets: HIPO, MIC, and SYC65)

HIPO n=5,344	satisfaction	worthwhile	happy	anxious	ONS total	ONS positive total	Positive HIPO SWB total	Negative HIPO SWB total	
Life satisfaction	1.00								
Worthwhile	0.80	1.00							
Happy	0.84	0.80	1.00						
Anxious (recoded)	0.60	0.56	0.67	1.00					
ONS-4 total	0.91	0.88	0.93	0.80	1.00				
ONS-4	0.94	0.92	0.94	0.65	0.97	1.00			
Positive total	0.84	0.80	0.85	0.64	0.88	0.89	1.00		
Negative total	0.67	0.64	0.70	0.70	0.77	0.72	0.72	1.00	
EQ5D-5L	0.63	0.52	0.56	0.47	0.62	0.61	0.63	0.55	
SF-6D (SF-12)	0.72	0.62	0.68	0.58	0.74	0.72	0.73	0.67	
EQ-VAS	0.70	0.58	0.63	0.48	0.67	0.68	0.67	0.57	
SWB-VAS	0.82	0.73	0.79	0.61	0.83	0.83	0.84	0.68	
MIC n=6,808	**satisfaction**	**worthwhile**	**happy**	**anxious**	**ONS total**	**ONS positive total**	**Positive AQoL SWB total**	**Negative AQoL SWB total**	**ICECAP**
Life satisfaction	1.00								
Worthwhile	0.77	1.00							
Happy	0.76	0.72	1.00						
Anxious (recoded)	0.32	0.28	0.40	1.00					
ONS-4 total	0.87	0.82	0.88	0.64	1.00				
ONS-4	0.93	0.89	0.91	0.37	0.94	1.00			
Positive total	0.69	0.64	0.66	0.35	0.72	0.73	1.00		
Negative total	0.62	0.55	0.62	0.43	0.69	0.66	0.82	1.00	

Continued

Table 3A.5 *Continued*

HIPO n=5,344	satisfaction	worthwhile	happy	anxious	ONS total	ONS positive total	Positive HIPO SWB total	Negative HIPO SWB total	
ICECAP-A	0.65	0.58	0.60	0.31	0.65	0.67	0.81	0.74	1.00
EQ5D-5L	0.39	0.31	0.35	0.24	0.40	0.39	0.53	0.55	0.56
SF-6D (SF-12)	0.50	0.43	0.48	0.36	0.56	0.52	0.65	0.69	0.65
SF-6D (SF-36)	0.48	0.41	0.46	0.36	0.54	0.50	0.63	0.67	0.64

SYC65 n=1593	satisfaction	worthwhile	happy	anxious	ONS total	ONS Positive total	SWB Positive	total SWEMWB	SWEMWBS	ICECAP
Life satisfaction	1.00									
Worthwhile	0.75	1.00								
Happy	0.80	0.71	1.00							
Anxious (recoded)	0.50	0.43	0.57	1.00						
ONS-4 total	0.85	0.80	0.88	0.81	1.00					
ONS-4	0.92	0.89	0.92	0.55	0.92	1.00				
Positive total	0.79	0.76	0.77	0.50	0.79	0.84	1.00			
SWEMWBs	0.66	0.68	0.69	0.52	0.73	0.73	0.78	1.00		
WEMWBS	0.68	0.69	0.71	0.51	0.74	0.75	0.80	0.96	1.00	
ICECAP-O	0.63	0.59	0.60	0.47	0.65	0.65	0.71	0.68	0.70	1.00
EQ5D-5L	0.44	0.36	0.40	0.37	0.47	0.43	0.49	0.43	0.46	0.47
ASCOT	0.48	0.44	0.45	0.34	0.49	0.50	0.54	0.49	0.51	0.56
EQ-VAS	0.59	0.50	0.54	0.41	0.59	0.59	0.64	0.55	0.59	0.57
WB-VAS	0.74	0.65	0.70	0.50	0.74	0.76	0.76	0.68	0.71	0.69

Notes: strong: >=|0.5|, moderate: <|0.5 to >= 0.3|, weak: <|0.3 to >= 0.1 | (Cohen, 1992).

Source: Mukuria et al. (2014).

Table 3A.6 Spearman correlations between wellbeing scores and health (datasets, USoc wave 1 and HSE)

USoc n =37,602	**GHQ score**	**GHQ positive**	**GHQ negative**	**SWEMWBS score**	**Life satisfaction**	
GHQ score $^{\phi}$	1					
GHQ positive $^{\phi}$	0.86	1				
GHQ negative $^{\phi}$	0.95	0.65	1			
SWEMWBS score	−0.61	−0.50	−0.59	1		
Life satisfaction	−0.49	−0.40	−0.48	0.50	1	
SF-6D (SF-12)	−0.56	−0.47	−0.54	0.42	0.36	
HSE n = 5,709	**GHQ score**	**GHQ positive**	**GHQ negative**	**SWEMWBS score**	**WEMWBS score**	**Happy**
GHQ score $^{\phi}$	1					
GHQ positive $^{\phi}$	0.82	1				
GHQ negative $^{\phi}$	0.95	0.60	1			
SWEMWBS score	−0.64	−0.50	−0.62	1		
WEMWBS score	−0.66	−0.51	−0.63	0.96	1	
Happy	−0.59	−0.46	−0.58	0.56	0.56	1
EQ5D-3L	−0.46	−0.45	−0.40	0.36	0.39	0.34

Notes: strong: >=|0.5|, moderate: <|0.5 to >= 0.3|, weak: <|0.3 to >= 0.1| (Cohen, 1992). ϕ GHQ scores—high scores indicate poor wellbeing.

Source: Mukuria et al. (2014).

Table 3A.7 Domain satisfactions as predictors of life satisfaction, BHPS 1996–2009

Dependent variable: Life satisfaction	r	$\partial LS/\partial X$
Satisfaction with income of household	0.089	0.110
Satisfaction with flat/house	0.063	0.070
Satisfaction with job	0.041	0.086
Satisfaction with amount of leisure	0.055	0.070
Satisfaction with use of leisure	0.146	0.174
Satisfaction with spouse/partner	0.077	0.171
Satisfaction with social life	0.167	0.194
Satisfaction with health	0.138	0.172
Observations	107,501	107,501
R-squared	0.571	0.740

Notes: Robust standard errors in parentheses. Fixed effects included. $p<0.01$, ** $p<0.05$, * $p<0.1$.

Source: Layard (2016).

Appendix E: Headline Cost-effectiveness Graph and Justification of the Elements

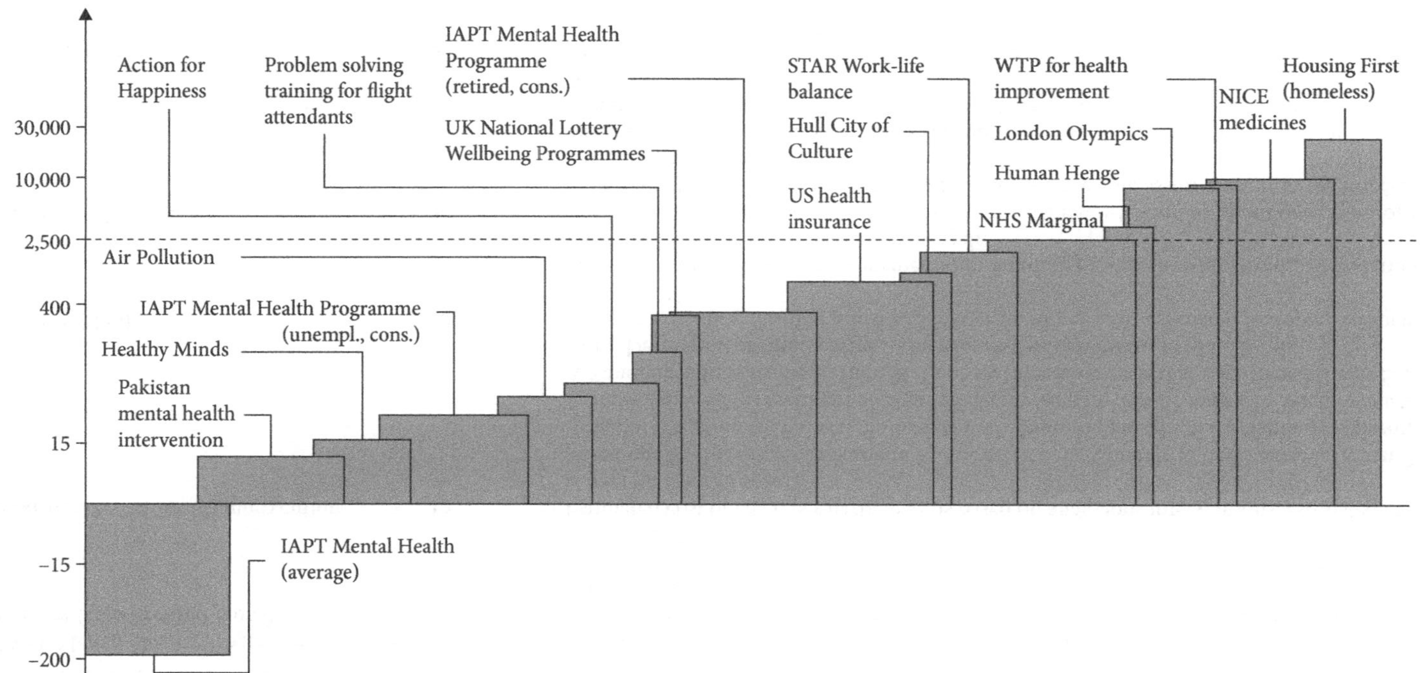

Figure 3.A1 Cost per WELLBY

Source: Own illustration based on own calculations.

Table 3A.8 Justification of each element of the headline cost-effectiveness graph

Element	£ per WELLBY	Description, Reference
IAPT Mental Health Programme: average/ unempl (cons)/retired (cons)	−198/40/410	Includes average estimates for all the participants, discussed in Section 'The IAPT Mental Health Programme' of chapter 3, as well as the estimates for the subgroups based on conservative assumptions. Based on: Frijters, P., Béllet, C., and Krekel, C. (2019). Micro-Macro Simulations for Wellbeing. Mimeo.
Pakistan mental health intervention	15	Estimated cost of £8.20 per participant is based on analogous interventions, estimated effect is 0.56 on 0-to-10 scale. Based on: N. Husain, F. Zulqernain, L. A. Carter, I. B., Chaudhry, B., Fatima, T., Kiran, N., Chaudhry, S., Naeem, F., Jafri, F., Lunat, S. U., Haq, M., Husain, C., Roberts, F., Naeem, A. Rahman (2017). Treatment of Maternal Depression in Urban Slums of Karachi, Pakistan: A Randomized Controlled Trial (RCT) of an Integrated Maternal Psychological and Early Child Development Intervention. *Asian Journal of Psychiatry* 29: 63–70.
Healthy Minds	22	Costs of providing training are at £23.50 per pupil per year, estimated four-year wellbeing effect is 0.27. Based on: https://educationendowmentfoundation.org.uk/public/files/Projects/Evaluation_Reports/Healthy_Minds_interim_paper.pdf.
Action for Happiness	80	The course costs £80 per participant, and it raises life satisfaction by about one point for up to two months post-treatment. The calculation is under the assumption that the impact remains constant for a year. Based on: Krekel, C., De Neve, J.-E., Fancourt, D., and R. Layard (2019). A Local Community Course. That Raises Mental Wellbeing and Pro-sociality. *CEP Discussion Paper 1671*.
Air pollution	60	Discussed in section 'Air Pollution in Germany' of chapter 3. Based on: Luechinger, S. (2009). Valuing Air Quality Using the Life Satisfaction Approach. *Economic Journal* 119(536): 482–515.
Problem-solving training for flight attendants	177	Discussed in section of 'Socio-emotional Skills Training in the Workplace' of chapter 3.

		Based on: Ayres, J., and Malouff, J. M. (2007). Problem-solving Training to Help Workers Increase Positive Affect, Job Satisfaction, and Life Satisfaction. *European Journal of Work and Organizational Psychology* 16(3): 279–94.
UK National Lottery Wellbeing Programmes	400	Discussed in section 'UK National Lottery Programmes' of chapter 3. Based on: New Economics Foundation (now archived and must be requested): https://www.biglotteryfund.org.uk/-/media/Files/Research%%20Documents/Wellbeing%%20in%%20England/National_Wellbeing_Evaluation_Final_Report%20August%%202013.pdf and https://www.biglotteryfund.org.uk/-/media/Files/Research%%20Documents/Wellbeing%%20in%%20England/er_eval_wellbeing_2_prog_evaluation.pdf
US health insurance	895	The programme allowed uninsured Massachusetts residents to purchase health insurance for $175 (£144) per month. The program lead to an improvement of SWB by 0.7 on a 4-point scale. Based on: Kim, S., and Koh, K. (2018). Does Health Insurance Make People Happier? Evidence from Massachusetts' Healthcare Reform. *IZA Discussion Paper* 11879.
Hull City of Culture	1,171	Discussed in section 'Case Study 3: The UK City of Culture' of chapter 5.
STAR Work-life Balance	1,893	The direct costs of the intervention are estimated in the order of $1,200 per worker. The effect on life satisfaction on a 0-to-10 scale is 0.075. The estimation is done under the assumption that the intervention would have a three-year effect and have an equivalent benefit for the rest of the family as the worker primarily affected.
NHS Marginal	2,500	Discussed in section 'Basic Comforts', 'Implications' of chapter 2. Based on: Claxton, K., Martin, S., Soares, M., Rice, N., Spackman, E., Hinde, S., . . . and Sculpher, M. (2015). Methods for the Estimation of the for Health and Care Excellence Cost-effectiveness Threshold. *Health Technology Assessment* 19(14): 1.
Human Henge	3,417	Discussed in section 'Case Study 2: The Human Henge Project' of chapter 5.
London Olympics	8,333	Estimates are based on a model, that employs the entire summer period of 2012 as the relevant treatment period and only account for wellbeing of Londoners. The total estimated cost is £9.3bn and the estimated life satisfaction effect is 0.14 on a scale from 0 to 10. Based on: Dolan, P. H., Kavetsos, G., Krekel, C., Mavridis, D., Metcalfe, R., Senik, C., Szymanski, S., and Ziebarth, N. R. (2019). Quantifying the Intangible Impact of the Olympics Using Subjective Well-Being Data. *Journal of Public Economics* 177: 104043.
WTP for health improvement	9,000	Discussed in section 'The Value of Wellbeing' of chapter 5. Based on: Huang, L., Frijters, P., Dalziel, K., and Clarke, P. (2018). Life Satisfaction, QALYs, and the Monetary Value of Health. *Social Science & Medicine* 211: 131–6.

Continued

Table 3A.8 *Continued*

Element	£ per WELLBY	Description, Reference
NICE medicines	10,000	Discussed in section 'On QALYs and WELLBYs' of chapter 4. Based on: https://www.nice.org.uk/process/pmg9/resources/guide-to-the-methods-of-technology-appraisal-2013-pdf-2007975843781
Housing First (homeless)	28,022	Discussed in section 'Housing First' of chapter 3. Based on: Blood, I., Connery, P., Parmar, and Dulson, S. (2018). Conwy and Denbighshire Housing First Feasibility Study: Full Report. Ruthin, Conwy CBC, and Denbighshire CC.

Source: Own illustration based on own calculations.

4

Wellbeing Cost-effectiveness Analysis and Existing Approaches

Preview

In this chapter, we compare our basic methodology for wellbeing cost-effectiveness analysis (CEA) with existing approaches to decide on public resource allocations in the United Kingdom and wellbeing frameworks from around the world.

The main comparison is with cost-benefit analysis (CBA) as it is practiced around the world inside state bureaucracies, taking the United Kingdom as our main focus. We discuss how CBA could be augmented with wellbeing insights and what the key differences are. This, in turn, suggests a list of changes that could be made to current CBA or, equivalently, a transition path between current CBA and wellbeing CEA.

We also compare wellbeing CEA with multi-criterion approaches as mandated by, for example, the Welsh Future Generations Act, as well as social rates of return analyses and business case scenarios or impact assessments. All the well-recognized caveats and nuances mentioned for wellbeing CEA, such as intricacies of bargaining negotiations over prices and the limited use of one-off decisions, also hold for these other approaches.

We start with a quick reminder of our basic methodology for wellbeing CEA, after which we sketch the current practice of CBA, highlighting the differences in a stylized, non-technical manner. We also sketch the relationship between WELLBYs (wellbeing-years) and QALYs (quality-adjusted life-years), deriving a proper translation between the two measures, which will culminate in the important distinction between the individual willingness-to-pay for a WELLBY and the social costs of producing a WELLBY.

We then answer some crucial questions as to how more wellbeing knowledge can be incorporated into existing approaches, including the question of the monetization of wellbeing effects for current-practice CBA. Here, we also discuss the old approach advocated in the UK HMT Green Book versus new insights on how individuals evaluate changes in incomes.

This chapter, just like the previous one, is targeted mainly at analysts who have to quantify how much benefits and costs are generated by future or existing

A Handbook for Wellbeing Policy-Making: History, Theory, Measurement, Implementation, and Examples. Paul Frijters and Christian Krekel, Oxford University Press (2021). © Paul Frijters and Christian Krekel.
DOI: 10.1093/oso/9780192896803.003.0004

policies and programmes. Yet, the chapter is also of interest to academics in the fields of health and wellbeing as it discusses in depth the differences between WELLBYs and QALYs, and how different findings in the wellbeing literature on the importance of money translate into different numbers used for various types of analyses in government practice. The discussion on wellbeing approaches from around the world is of importance to all those tasked with embedding wellbeing into their own country's public-sector systems.

A Reminder of Wellbeing Cost-effectiveness Analysis

The basic idea behind wellbeing CEA is to compare the net additional wellbeing benefits, measured in terms of WELLBYs (that is, one unit of life satisfaction on a zero-to-ten scale for one person for one year) with the net additional public costs of a policy. The optimal policy rule is to implement a policy if:

$$\text{Net Additional Wellbeing Benefits} - \lambda * \text{Net Additional Public Costs} > 0 \tag{1}$$

The net additional wellbeing benefits are expressed in terms of changes in WELLBYs and include all effects of a policy, both direct and indirect, and thus require a judgement as to how long the effects of a policy will last and what effects are going to be relevant. The net additional public costs include all changes to the public purse, both positive and negative. Additional tax receipts due to a policy count as negative costs, while increased costs in any part of the system are positive costs. The additional costs of a policy could involve increased utilization of health and education, or increased take-up of welfare benefits or a rise in tax avoidance.

As a stringent threshold to impose on other programmes, a conservative threshold for $(1/\lambda)$ is £2,500, which is essentially the marginal social production cost of a WELLBY (as we will discuss later). The equivalent amount of public funds that a change in wellbeing (denoted by ΔW) is then worth equals $\Delta W \times$ £2,500.

Existing CBA

CBA has a long tradition. It is said to have started with Jules Dupuit (1848) in the nineteenth century when he proposed a specific methodology to make the social spending case for building a bridge in France. Different countries have subtly different habits and rules, but there are many shared elements. General texts on CBA as it is applied throughout the world are Boardman et al. (2017) and Campbell and Brown 2016).

Even within a country, different departments and institutions practice different versions of CBA, including, for example, variations in what counts as a direct and an indirect cost. In the United Kingdom, there is a whole set of guidelines from HM Treasury (mainly via the UK HMT Green Book) as well as additional guidelines and estimates within departments and organizations.[1]

Yet, the principle of CBA is to maximize total value, so the differences all boil down as to what to count as value and how to calculate it. CBA then corresponds to a rule that proposes to implement a policy:

$$\text{Net Additional Benefits} > \text{Net Additional Public Costs} \quad (2)$$

Often, this is thought of as:

$$\text{Increase in Value of Consumption} > \text{Cost of Reduced Consumption} \quad (3)$$

There are particular nuances here, such as discount rates for things that happen in the future, and adjustments for risks, but the basic methodology requires the analyst to translate every effect into a consumption value, which used to be termed 'welfare', or 'utility', or 'social value'. The link to 'wellbeing' is that, in economics, consumption value was always meant to be based on what the value was to the consumer, i.e. 'wellbeing'.

In principle, if one uses WELLBYs as a measure of ultimate value in CBA and simply monetizes wellbeing appropriately, cost-benefit and wellbeing CEA are equivalent. CBA typically expresses all benefits and costs in monetary terms rather than wellbeing, but that does not mean that the approach is fundamentally different. It is only through the default setting of CBA, which involves an implicit view of the world and a monetization of wellbeing that actual differences with wellbeing CEA arise.

The wellbeing effects of any policy in CBA could show up either in the net additional public costs, which can include the monetary value of wellbeing losses, or in the net additional wellbeing benefits, which can include the monetary value of wellbeing gains. In principle, therefore, there need not be a difference in the optimal policy rules governing wellbeing CEA and CBA. Yet, in current practice, CBA employs habits one would not persist with in wellbeing CBA and which may lead to quite different conclusions.

[1] To name just a few, those developed by HM Treasury include CBA guidance for local partnerships: https://www.gov.uk/government/publications/supporting-public-service-transformation-cost-benefit--analysis-guidance-for-local-partnerships cost_benefit_analysis_guidance_for_local_partnerships.pdf, or for transport infrastructure: https://www.gov.uk/government/publications/webtag-tag-unit-a1-1-cost-benefit-analysis-may-2018; by the Bank of England for monetary and fiscal statistics: https://www.bankofengland.co.uk/-/media/boe/files/statistics/cost-benefit-analysis-of-monetary-and-financial-statistics; or by (various) local authorities, for example: https://www.greatermanchester-ca.gov.uk/what-we-do/research/research-cost-benefit-analysis/.

The main differences in assumptions between wellbeing CEA and current-practice CBA are that, in the latter, well-informed individuals are assumed to know what they want in all cases, public expenditure has the same marginal benefit as private expenditure, and there are no significant consumption externalities between individuals.

Within these assumptions, the price of goods and services is the prime measure of value as it reflects what the marginal consumer is willing to pay. When observable prices do not exist for some good or service, such as social relationships or the environment, the basic methododology for finding the value of that good or service is to measure consumers' willingness-to-pay in some other way, such as *indirectly* via observed prices of complementary goods or services (so-called *revealed-preference approaches*) or directly via hypothetical scenarios, including contingent valuation or discrete choice experiments (so-called *stated-preference approaches*).

By contrast, in wellbeing cost-effectiveness one attempts to measure the wellbeing effects of the goods and services one is interested in directly, without assuming that this coincides with how much individuals say they are willing to pay for those goods and services. One source of difference is that individuals are not always aware of the importance of things like the environment or social relations on their own wellbeing. Another is that there may be social conventions that one should not pay for certain things, like friendships or children, but that this is not a sign that they don't matter—rather the opposite.

One way to go back and forth between wellbeing analyses and CBA is via a crucial statistic for both approaches—the monetary value of wellbeing. Wellbeing CEA yields an implicit monetary value of wellbeing given by the minimum social production cost of wellbeing, i.e. $1/\lambda$: the last policy option funded that gives the implicit social cost. This is, in principle, unlikely to yield exactly the same monetary value of a WELLBY than the individual willingness-to-pay and it becomes an empirical question how much they differ.

We will next discuss where our initial recommended minimum social production cost of wellbeing ($1/\lambda$) comes from: the relationship between health (production costs) and wellbeing.

On QALYs and WELLBYs

The Minimum Social Production Costs of Wellbeing

An intuitive place to start looking for a seed value for the minimum social production cost of wellbeing ($1/\lambda$) is to ask how much wellbeing the public health system buys at the margin. In the United Kingdom, the public health system is run by the National Health Service (NHS), which has a huge spending programme with well-researched benefits and costs. Its minimum social production costs of a WELLBY would be a reasonable benchmark for other public expenses.

Health benefits in the UK are currently measured in terms of QALYs, where 'quality' is captured by survey questions on subjective health, primarily the EQ5D. Its five health dimensions, each measured using a set of items, are mobility, ability to care for self, ability to engage in usual activities, pain and discomfort, and anxiety and depression.[2]

A QALY of 1 relates to top answers across all five dimensions. A QALY of 0 is trickier and has basically been derived by asking individuals hypothetical trade-offs between more years of life in a particular health state versus less years of life in a better health state. Leaving aside issues pertaining to the hypothetical nature of this task, the logic is that rational individuals will reveal which health level is equivalent to death.

When assessing the relation between the QALY and the WELLBY, it is important to bear in mind that both have two dimensions: years of life and the quality of that life. The two are similar when it comes to an additional year of life, but different when it comes to how to measure the quality of life and thus what the trade-off is between elements going into that quality versus additional years of life. An additional year spent at the top of the life satisfaction scale (at a level of 10) is worth more WELLBYs than an existing year spent in excellent health because people care about more than just their health and hence are willing to forego some health quality for other factors (such as their children's welfare). We dissect these two components: the value of a year of life versus the quality measured in two different ways (health versus wellbeing).

In the nationally representative Understanding Society panel data for the United Kingdom, the average life satisfaction of someone in self-declared 'excellent' health was 5.88 on a 1-to-17 scale in Wave 8 (2016–18). In Wave 7 (2015–17), it was 5.85. If we translate this to a 0-to-10 scale using the response formula of Parducci (1995), explained in van Praag and Frijters (1999) and in the appendix to chapter 3, we find the average life satisfaction of someone in self-declared 'excellent' health was 7.95 and 7.91, respectively, in these periods. That is almost an 8, and above the average life satisfaction of the whole population, which was around 7.8 in 2019.[3]

[2] In a 2016 What Works Centre for Wellbeing discussion paper, Richard Layard maps several outcomes to life satisfaction, including EQ5D, SF6D, GQH12, self-reported health, the other ONS personal wellbeing measures, and various measures similar to life satisfaction such as the Warwick-Edinburgh Mental Well-Being Scale. The paper draws heavily on Mukuria et al. (2014). In this chapter, we go into greater conceptual and empirical depth on the relationship between WELLBYs and QALYs but do not cover the other outcomes as they are out of our scope. We should mention, however, that most of the results in the paper are still reasonably in line with the literature, except for the QALY measure, which appears to weigh too high, probably due to the fact that the underlying sample is rather small.

[3] The underlying ONS data (on a scale from 0-to-10) are available at: https://www.ons.gov.uk/peoplepopulationandcommunity/wellbeing.

Since a level of 2 in life satisfaction is our current best-estimate for the equivalent life satisfaction value of death (see chapter 2), an additional year in excellent health can be translated into six WELLBYs.[4] So one QALY via the 'LY' bit is worth six WELLBYs.

But how much is one QALY worth if only the 'QA' component moves up by one, holding the 'LY' bit constant? Because wellbeing covers more dimensions of life than health, including, for example, social relationships, employment, or social status, one would expect it to cost less than six WELLBYs if someone goes from excellent health to 'zero' health, holding all else constant.

How much lower is life satisfaction then if health deteriorates such that there is a one-point reduction in QALYs? This is ultimately an empirical question. Huang et al. (2018) looked at that question for a large sample (over ten thousand individuals) followed over time in Australia, using changes in health to identify its effect. This treats health changes, and particularly negative health shocks, as surprises to individuals, allowing for a causal interpretation of the effect of health shocks on life satisfaction. The basic answer the authors come up with is that 1 QALY (via changes in the 'QA' bit) buys about 2.5 WELLBYs. So a change in QALYs of 1 through an increase in length of life translates into a change in WELLBYs of 6, whereas a change in QALYs of 1 through improved health is worth 2.5 WELLBYs. One way to phrase this is to say that health, as measured by QALYs, makes up about 42 per cent (=2.5/6) of what constitutes a satisfied life, not too dissimilar frpm the share of health in the explained variance in adult life satisfaction shown in Figure 2.5 in chapter 2.

With this in mind, we can estimate the minimum social production costs of a WELLBY if we had a figure for how much it would cost the state to increase length of life at a given level of health or improve health. This figure may well differ between countries, depending on the public health system.

In the United Kingdom, this key figure comes from the Department of Health and Social Care, which assumes in its calculations that the NHS produces a QALY for £15,000 (Claxton et al., 2015; Lomas et al., 2019; see also Department of Health and Department of Education, 2017). We can interpret this to translate into 2.5 WELLBYs if we make the reasonable assumption that it buys health quality, and we can interpret this to translate into six WELLBYs if we assume it buys longevity. The Department of Health and Social Care uses the £15,000 for both of them, so to be conservative, we take the higher number. The six WELLBYs that an additional year of healthy life is worth means that the current NHS is assumed to buy a WELLBY at a rate of £2,500, which thereby represents the marginal social production costs of wellbeing.

[4] This uses the current best-estimate that the zero point of life satisfaction at which an individual is indifferent between life and death is two on a 0-to-10 scale (Peasgood et al., 2018).

We should mention here that the key studies on the monetary value of a QALY do not really justify that the NHS can buy an additional year of life for £15,000: Claxton et al. (2015) looked at improvements in health quality when they estimated that the NHS can buy one additional QALY at the price of around £12,936 (in 2008 prices) or around £15,000 in 2017 money, using the Consumer Price Index (CPI) as deflator. This is thus their calculated social production costs of one QALY via improvements in health, not via life expectancy.

In appendix 2 of their paper, Claxton et al. (2015) also estimate that an additional year of life can be bought by the NHS for about £33,333 in 2009 or about £42,500 in 2017 prices, adjusting for inflation. The authors obtain these estimates by focusing more on mortality-related types of health budgets. There is, therefore, a good argument to be made that the Department of Health and Social Care should differentiate the minimum social production costs for a QALY bought by health improvements from those for a QALY bought by longevity improvements. If we assume that the NHS produces 2.5 WELLBYs for £15,000 (through health improvements), we obtain a cost per WELLBY of £6,000.

Taken together, we estimate the minimum social production cost of wellbeing to be between £2,500 and £6,000. The conservative figure used throughout the text is £2,500.

Finally, let us note that we suspect the total wellbeing value of the NHS to be far higher than estimated by Claxton et al. (2015), essentially for reasons discussed in chapter 2: we know from the extension of health insurance in the United States that health programmes have large and permanent beneficial effects on wellbeing that are far higher than one would expect from the health effects alone. This is because insurance has other effects, such as less anxiety that one will be financially ruined by unexpected, catastrophic health costs, and the more general feeling that one is accepted by society when one shares the umbrella of the welfare state. There are also likely to be social multipliers on those close to the insured, as shown in the example of IAPT programme in chapter 3. Nevertheless, we leave the exploration of these issues for future research.

Now that we have narrowed down the marginal social production costs of wellbeing, we next turn to the individual willingness to pay for wellbeing.

The Willingness-to-Pay for Wellbeing

Existing cost-benefit analyses take a market approach to the monetary valuation of benefits, looking for a market price to determine the willingness to pay for something, including wellbeing. The UK Treasury Green Book recommended methodology, therefore, looks for what a rational individual would be willing to pay for one WELLBY. Particular approaches include stated-preference approaches (which directly ask individuals); revealed-preference approaches such as hedonic pricing (which indirectly infers the willingness-to-pay from price changes in complementary markets), or (preferably) deriving the monetary valuation of a WELLBY directly from money by comparing the wellbeing of individuals with different levels of income.

We suggest two quite different approaches to ascertain an individual's willingness to pay for a WELLBY: via the implied willingness to avoid risks of death in traffic and via the observed relation between income and life satisfaction when using particularly visible reductions in finances akin to large payments. Both turn out to yield almost the same result.

In terms of the willingness to avoid risks of death in traffic, the long-standing estimate by the Department for Transport[5] has been that individuals are prepared to pay £60,000 to reduce risks of death in traffic such that they, in expectation, would live another year in their current health (HM Treasury, 2018, page 73; Glover and Henderson, 2010; see also Department of Health and Department of Education, 2017). As this can be expected to be in reasonable health, average life satisfaction for people in good health applies to these individuals, meaning that for them too the life satisfaction level they could expect in that extra year would be about an 8, contrasted with a 2 for death. Therefore, the extra year is likely to be close to six WELLBYs. Hence, the implied willingness-to-pay for a WELLBY via the willingness to avoid risks of death in traffic is about £10,000.

A quite different approach is to look at how much self-reported reductions in finances, which are like visible payments, affect life satisfaction. Huang et al. (2018) applied this approach: they use self-reported reductions in finances as identifying variation in how much reductions in income (which then could be linked to self-reported reductions in finances) would decrease wellbeing. Somewhat remarkably, they too found that the implied willingness-to-pay for a WELLBY was about £9,000 (Huang et al. 2018). This is our preferred figure, because it is clearer what the value of money was for individuals.

What this means is that if one wanted to stick to existing CBA and simply wanted to put a monetary value on a found improvement in wellbeing, using whatever methodology, one could simply use £9,000 as a conversion factor.

Is this type of willingness-to-pay truly appropriate though? Does it make sense from the point of view of maximizing the social welfare or wellbeing of the UK population? That begs the question of how money and wellbeing relate to each other in general, which is what we discuss next. It will bring out the underlying issues of rationality and externalities.

[5] For example, see https://assets.publishing.service.gov.uk/government/uploads/system/uploads/attachment_data/file/664442/MHGP_IA.pdf for how £60,000 is used to value health improvements in cross-government comparisons.

Money and Wellbeing

How much wellbeing is an additional £ worth to individuals and society? There are different answers to this question depending on the circumstances surrounding that additional £. It matters if the additional £ is given to or taken away from an individual. It matters whether we want to know the wellbeing benefit of the additional £ to the individual who receives it or to society as a whole. It matters how visible the additional £ is to the individual, whether given or taken away. It matters how visible the spending of the additional £ is to everyone else. And it matters whether the additional £ is in government or private spending. What one takes to be the 'right' amount of wellbeing per £ thus requires one to decide on whether to take the individual or social perspective, to choose between visible and unnoticed changes in £, to decide on the visibility to others of what the £ is spent on, and by whom the £ is spent.

The highest wellbeing value of a £ is probably in government spending on social relationship investments, where we now think we can buy one WELLBY for around £500 or less. The social programmes of the UK National Lottery had that kind of effect (see chapter 3 for details). The UK City of Culture initiative in Kingston upon Hull had that kind of effect (see chapter 5 for details). The Incredible Years parenting programme for parents with children who have conduct disorders had that kind of effect (see chapter 2 for details). And the Increasing Access to Psychological Therapies (IAPT) programme had that kind of effect (see chapter 3 for details). The United Kingdom as a whole could spend billions of £ per year with that kind of return.

If we take these 'minimum social production costs of wellbeing' as the relevant wellbeing value of a £, then one WELLBY is worth £500. This would be the appropriate figure in cases where we spend each additional £ possible on those areas with the greatest wellbeing gains, refusing to spend discretionary funds on anything else.

The lowest wellbeing value of a £ probably comes from increasing highly visible private consumption, such as houses or luxury cars, only counting the change in societal wellbeing as actual wellbeing gain. This can be estimated as the effect of individual income and national income on individual wellbeing, taking relative income and government activity as constant.

The literature is not quite united on that value. At best, at the national level that kind of 'conspicuous consumption' has an effect of income on wellbeing in log-terms of about 0.16 per doubling of incomes (Clark et al., 2018). It is the effect of individual income on life satisfaction found in panel data studies in the United Kingdom (see Blanchflower and Oswald (2004), for example). It is also the number that emerges in cross-country analyses where the level of government spending is given, implying that we are indeed looking at the effect of private consumption. In a recent study, Kapteyn et al. (2019) found that the effect of log-income on life satisfaction, holding relative income constant, is about 0.15 (Table 3 Columns 2 and 5).

In the United Kingdom, where average annual income per individual (that is, average GDP per capita) is about £35,000, an estimated 0.16 log-effect of income on wellbeing means that £218,750 (=35,000/0.16) spread out over average-income individuals would buy one WELLBY.

If we take the total UK wellbeing effect of individual conspicuous consumption as the relevant effect of money on wellbeing, then the value of one WELLBY is £219,000. This estimate is 438 times larger than what we would count as the value of wellbeing if we looked at the minimum social production costs of wellbeing. That is a rather large range.

We obtain values in between when we vary the key elements of the circumstances surrounding the additional £: is it spent by individuals or government? Is it spent on average programmes or the best programmes in terms of returns to wellbeing? Is individual spending visible to individuals themselves, to others, or not? And are we talking about a £ increase or a £ decrease?

The following rules of thumb apply:

1. To an individual, the additional £ is worth around half the amount of wellbeing that taking away a £ costs. These are the classic endowment and loss-aversion effects by Kahneman and Tversky (1979). We find this also in self-reports when comparing how people react asymmetrically to financial increases and decreases (Frijters et al., 2011). This means that the willingness-to-pay for one WELLBY is basically half the value of the willingness-to-accept for a decrease by one unit.
2. A largely unnoticed income change by an individual is, in the short run, worth a fraction of a highly visible one in terms of wellbeing. Huang et al. (2018), for instance, found for Australian panel data that the effects of a self-reported decrease in finances is much higher in the short run (by a factor of 100) than other changes in finances. The different effects of salient financial shocks versus unnoticed ones also shows up in the effects of stock market changes: Frijters et al. (2015) found that the effects of stock market changes in the period 2001 to 2006 that were not strongly mentioned in the media (i.e. no spectacular crash) were close to zero, compared to much larger effects in the period 2007 to 2012 when stock markets were constantly in the news, holding relative losses constant.[6] Visibility hence matters greatly.

[6] The implied effect of a 100-points movement in the AEX was 0.02 in the visible period. A 100-points is about 2.5 per cent of the value of stocks, making the implied effect of a 1 per cent increase on life satisfaction equal to 0.008 (which is very high considering that most individuals own very few stocks). Yet, the effect also holds for non-owners, implying that the effect is probably more about national mood and future economic expectations.

3. The long-run value of money which an individual is aware of but has gotten used to, like the long-run effect of income increases, is probably best approximated by the identified wellbeing effect of large lottery wins several years after the event. The best study in this context is by Lindqvist et al. (2020) for Sweden, discussed in chapter 2, which found that one additional WELLBY was worth about £80,000 (which corresponds to a log-effect of 0.4). If one considers the individual wellbeing effect of long-run increases in money, such as, for instance, from improved education or skills, this is probably the most appropriate number to use.
4. As a rule of thumb, it seems that highly contested public costs are like visible personal costs to individuals: the implicit valuation of health care by individuals, for instance, coincides almost perfectly with what the government is openly willing to pay for additional health via new medicines (Huang et al., 2018). That suggests that the health budget is basically set in conditions whereby the electorate calculates their willingness-to-pay as if they buy it visibly as individuals. This coincides with a value of one WELLBY of £9,000, which is our preferred figure. It also coincides with a willingness-to-pay in order to avoid risks of accidental deaths in regular life (such as via safer transport) of around £60,000 per healthy life year (that is, a year spent in excellent health, cf. HM Treasury, 2018, page 73; Glover and Henderson, 2010; see also Department of Health and Department of Education, 2017). For highly visible individual willingness-to-pay situations, this is probably the most appropriate number to use.
5. As a rule of thumb, status externalities reduce the effect of more private consumption at the societal level. To account for this, we suggested using an Easterlin Discount. As argued in chapter 3 and later on in this chapter, it is disputed whether that should be a 100 per cent discount, but it is certainly at least 50 per cent and the current body of evidence would put it at 75 per cent. It is the element of the income effect that disappears when keeping relative income constant (Kapteyn et al., 2019).

Within the logic of current CBA, the most appropriate value of wellbeing changes is arguably the willingness-to-pay of individuals for very visible increases in wellbeing when the price to pay is also highly visible. Note that this ignores the evidence on private consumption externalities and hence does not mean that the £9,000 truly buys society one WELLBY.

We may note that if one adopts this number as the appropriate one for CBA, one effectively weighs wellbeing as if its drivers were highly visible. For consistency, one would then have to value every other cost and benefit as if it was highly visible too. That would constitute a considerable change with current practice wherein it is not deemed important whether costs and consumption are highly visible or not.

On the other hand, within the logic of wellbeing CEA, one would want to use the marginal social production costs of producing one WELLBY, which, taking the example of the NHS in the United Kingdom, is taken to be £2,500 per WELLBY. Moreover, within the logic of wellbeing CEA, one would convert private consumption increases into wellbeing using the best estimates of the actual effects of income levels on life satisfaction, which in chapter 2 was argued to be a 0.4 effect of a one-unit log-change. This is far less than the effect of highly visible changes in income and far more than the usual cross-sectional effect of reported changes in income on life satisfaction. Rather, it reflects the effect of income that individuals have gotten used to and that truly changes their private consumption levels in a permanent way.

Reflections: Why Do These Numbers Differ So Much?

The huge differences in the estimated monetary values of wellbeing reflect four main differences between current cost-benefit and wellbeing CEA:

1. Wellbeing CEA does not assume that individuals are rational in the sense that individuals are fully aware of everything at all times. That makes visibility part of the wellbeing cost-effectivenss analysis policy evaluation question. Current CBA, however, does assume rationality and full awareness as the default, an assumption under which visibility is irrelevant because individuals are assumed to be fully aware of everything at all times. That difference is why, for example, accrediting particular experience goods is important for wellbeing policy-making; why certain disamenities are not properly reflected in market prices (for example, air pollution not fully internalized in real estate prices); and why barely noticed changes in income buy far less wellbeing than very visible ones. Within the wellbeing lens, individuals are more manipulable in terms of what they know and what they view as high status than under current CBA, where individual preferences are set in stone and rational people know everything at all times.
2. Wellbeing CEA assumes that social comparisons are important and that hence additional private consumption beyond the welfare state level is largely offset by an increase in negative social comparisons with others. Current CBA, however, assumes that such negative private consumption externalities are absent.
3. Wellbeing CEA takes the perspective of how government can maximize wellbeing given its budget, leading to the marginal social production costs of wellbeing as the appropriate monetary value of wellbeing. Current CBA,

hoewever, assumes that the willingness-to-pay is the appropriate measure of value, leading to an individual willingness-to-pay for a wellbeing improvement as the appropriate starting point for the monetary value of wellbeing. Depending on how visible the costs and how aware individuals are of what they might be buying, that then leads to a value of wellbeing in current CBA that is far higher than the social production costs of wellbeing.

4. Wellbeing CEA, in principle, uses empirical evidence from the literature for supposed effects, which means that the symmetry between different types of expenses made by different actors is broken: different expenses by different actors (departments, individuals, government as a whole) have different wellbeing effects, each needing to be empirically established. In contrast, current CBA does exactly the opposite: changes in government expenses and consumption of all actors are measured in £ and just added up, while the same wellbeing effects of different sources (such as the environment or noise) are valued differently depending on how much willingness-to-pay might differ for them.

One of the key differences between current CBA and wellbeing CEA are thus negative private consumption externalities, which have been found to be large and not negligible. This finding could, in principle, be incorporated into current CBA by measuring consumption externalities wherever relevant. It would lead to large changes in nearly all existing economic CBA, effectively because most of the individual benefit of higher private consumption is offset by jealousy effects on others, the key insight of the Easterlin hypothesis. For example, the wellbeing value of housing is unlikely to increase much merely because all housing prices increase, although this is precisely what is commonly assumed in current CBA of housing studies, in which a higher price of a house is assumed to reflect a higher consumption value rather than the effect of a zero-sum status race.

On the Difference in Rationality Assumptions between Traditional Cost-benefit and Wellbeing Cost-effectiveness Analysis

Traditional CBA comes out of a particular stream of economics and reflects the standard view of the world in economics of around 1985. A key part of that world view is the idea that consumers are, roughly speaking, rational: consumers are assumed to manage, even if only in an approximate way, to maximize their utility based on their understanding of the world.

That rational view of the world is why CBA takes the market price of a good or service as a valid indication of its consumption value: individuals are assumed to know what purchases do for them and hence only buy something that they know they value, at least as much as they value the purchasing costs.

Taken literally, the assumption that people knew everything with perfection and that hence their choice behaviour revealed how much things were valued was always highly problematic. It required a super-human 'procedural rationality' on the side of people to understand the world, including such things as 'the expected distribution of the interbank interest rate in twenty years' time'. Individuals are not super-computers, nor do they have a reasonable understanding of everything that affects their life, such as the economy and the political system. Yet, rationality was adopted as the default assumption because, as Christopher Sims famously said, it is clear what rationality means while there is a 'wilderness of "disequilibrium economics"' (Sims, 1980).

Complete rationality is highly problematic as an assumption for almost any decision, but it is equally unreasonable to assume that individuals are completely unaware of their own limitations and do not adopt heuristics to get it roughly right. They might, for instance, not be able to know beforehand what it is like to be married and to have children, but they can be expected to have a good look at others with marriages and children to deduce from their observations how getting married and having children might work out for them.

It is important to be fair to the basic assumption of rationality because it leads one to take people seriously. We should not, for instance, conclude from the fact that 40 per cent of marriages fail that people should not have gotten married in the first place. There are a lot of unanticipated complexities and shocks that make people change their minds over time, which make many choices seem irrational that were probably the right choice to make at the time with the information available then.

On the other hand, some choices are known to be irrational from a reasonable point of view (such as substance addictions), and there is a recognized role for (state) institutions to protect the public from things they cannot be expected to work out for themselves in all cases. This is, for instance, why we have food standard agencies that enforce hygiene at all food outlets: it is not reasonable to expect consumers to check the bacteria count at every restaurant they frequent and it is simply more efficient to have a system that can be relied upon. Our institutions, therefore, already assume there are some areas where people are somewhat rational (for example, when it comes to marriage) and some areas where they need more information or whole systems with expert knowledge (for example, when it comes to health).

As a rule of thumb, we expect decisions that people deliberate over for a long time and which they have good information about, to be 'more rational' and more in line with wellbeing maximization. This means that, when individuals have good information and the choice involves a lot of situation-specific information that is highly idiosyncratic, we do not expect major increases to personal wellbeing to go unrecognized by people. Individuals remain somewhat responsible for their own wellbeing.

However, it is ultimately an empirical question whether people are roughly rational about some of life's major choices, and we already know a lot about choices and wellbeing effects. The section on experience goods in chapter 2 and the many examples of them are explicitly about the limits to individual rationality: individuals do not always correctly anticipate how important some things are to them and it is often the job of the state to provide credible information. This was the case with passive smoking and is now the case with many areas of mental health, socio-emotional skills, or forms of selflessness.

Hence, choice data are not necessarily all that informative, as smoking choices in the 1960s attest to. Likewise, the enormous importance of visibility for how much people value something, which can easily move the importance of money up by a factor of ten, tells us that we cannot take classic economic rationality as an appropriate starting base in all market transactions. Individuals might be doing a reasonable job of making choices given what is known to them, but just what is known to them is largely dictated by others who bring things to their attention. Hence, being alerted to something matters an awful lot for choices, which is well understood in politics and marketing, yet does not fit the classic economic notion of rationality.

Just as we now have over a hundred identified 'violations of rationality' in consumer behaviour, so too is the wellbeing literature learning to identify failures of reasonable rationality in some of life's big decisions. In chapter 2, we offered a checklist on whether the state should encourage a candidate solution to a supposed experience good: is there evidence something really works; is it something people have opposite and wrong expectations about; and is the solution cost-effective?

What do individuals not understand well? One key lack of understanding is of things they have never experienced and of which they cannot see how others have experienced them, because they cannot look into the minds of others. They therefore find it hard to understand the concept of mental health until they experience it changing; the concept of other types of social relationships; other types of environments and cultures; or other reference points. Individuals also make particular mistakes and get anxious when their consumption plans are threatened by things they cannot control, which is largely why providing a basic comfort level has such high wellbeing benefits.

Another key lack of understanding comes from the sheer complexity of the world. Few individuals, if any, can be expected to know the full workings of the economy, or the impact of the environment on their mental health, or all the effects particular foods might have on them. This complexity gives rise to the need for individuals and society as a whole to discover how things work and to share that information. With very complex issues which take a lot of expertise to figure out, this role is taken up largely by people paid to do so by the rest of society, for instance via academic researchers and dedicated government agencies. This is a dynamic process, though, and at any moment in time it will be the case that some part of the whole system has already figured out something (like the effect of air pollution on mental health) that most of the rest is not aware of, meaning, for instance, that market prices (such as house prices in polluted areas) do not yet reflect a shared full understanding.

The next question is then how existing cost-benefit analyses could incorporate some wellbeing insights without adopting its main arguments and findings wholesale. There are three suggested add-ons: Easterlin Discounts to private consumption and wealth; using wellbeing estimates as an additional source of information about important effects; and using a willingness-to-pay measure for wellbeing derived from the literature. We extensively covered the issue of willingness-to-pay and now discuss the first two of these in more depth.

Easterlin Discounts

One possible way to incorporate one of the main insights of the wellbeing literature without switching from current practice to wellbeing CEA is to apply an Easterlin Discount to all changes in private consumption and wealth in any CBA, just as an Easterlin Discount should be applied to all changes in wellbeing due to private consumption and wealth in wellbeing CEA (see chapter 3). This Easterlin Discount is the percentage of the private consumption effect offset by negative private consumption externalities. Richard Easterlin himself maintains that the proper discount is 100 per cent, and even those who challenge this find that the implied strength of the consumption externality is large (see Proto and Rustichini (2013), for example). Part of the controversy is about separating the effects of income at the national level from things that generate income (such as good governance and a stable economic environment), as well as from things that income can buy but that are dependent on policy (such as public goods paid by taxation). Yet, there is widespread agreement that private negative consumption externalities at the individual level are large on visible goods such as houses, cars, expensive holidays, or other goods and services that economic surplus often buys (see chapter 2 and Clark et al. (2008), for example).

An Easterlin Discount would naturally apply to changes in private consumption and wealth, but not on government spending which is largely on public goods and services (for example, safety nets). The logic is that private surplus leads to more visible consumption which is subject to negative private consumption externalities, but public goods and services apply to everyone equally. The wellbeing value of public goods and service is then only a matter of statistical evidence, where for many public goods and services strong effects have been found (see chapter 2). Yet, the basic principle would be to apply the Easterlin Discount to all goods and services that are an important part of the relative status between individuals within a country. Ultimately, the size of the discount should be estimated empirically, and one can think to have, at some point, different discounts applied to different types of private consumption (similar to different value added taxes for different consumption goods), depending on how high the estimated effect of relative comparisons is. To implement that kind of sophisticated discounts would require additional research and it hence makes sense to have a default Easterlin Discount for all private consumption that would apply unless there is robust empirical evidence to apply something more appropriate.

Direct studies of how much people's reference position changes with other people's incomes (which is the direct channel of dissipation) suggest that the Easterlin Discount is at least 60 per cent (Clark et al., 2008; van Praag and Frijters, 1999). The absence of wellbeing growth in the United States during the last fifty years or so despite large increases in average private consumption suggests it is closer to 100 per cent.

What this means in practice is that non-visible forms of additional private consumption (where the consumption, for instance, is given in private and effort is made to keep it hidden) are worth more than visible forms. Yet, we suggest that the difference in how much additional national discretionary average consumption buys more national wellbeing versus how much additional individual discretionary average consumption buys more individual wellbeing is the most appropriate source of an empirical estimate for an average Easterlin Discount. At present, this would be about 75 per cent (see chapter 2).

One could interpret an Easterlin Discount of 100 per cent as effectively switching the burden of proof of social value between wellbeing and GDP: with a 100 per cent Easterlin Discount, private economic surplus is irrelevant unless one can effectively demonstrate non-private-consumption benefits of it (such as effects on unemployment or social cohesion), whereas with a 0 per cent Easterlin Discount GDP is taken as the default measure of social value and non-market effects have to prove themselves. The key difference that the 'habit' of ignoring status concerns in current CBA makes is that it leads to much greater weight on private consumption increases, for example from reduced taxation. It thereby reduces the appreciation of the wellbeing effects of, for example, expenses on social safety nets that are not subject to status concerns. It also reduces the importance of some other non-private consumption considerations like inclusive growth or environmental sustainability. Thus, the Easterlin Discount is a weathervane for how seriously these non-GDP considerations are taken in actual calculations.

Importantly, the habit of ignoring status considerations in current CBA has little implications for the importance of economic growth: in wellbeing CEA, more economic growth that does not come at the expense of something else is always welcome, if only because of higher tax receipts and greater resilience of individuals and regions to shocks. Thus, even though status considerations reduce the wellbeing value of economic growth because it reduces the importance of private consumption, it does not lead one to be anti-growth. Indeed, any policy that has little direct wellbeing effects but raises taxation via raising the economic pie, such as (arguably) education expansions, are policies supported under any of the approaches discussed here.

Looking over the Shoulder at Wellbeing Knowledge

Another way of including wellbeing insights into current CBA is to look at the wellbeing literature for inspiration as to where there may be wellbeing effects that could be valued in a monetary manner.

One example of such wellbeing effects is the finding that fear of crime is a multiple of actual levels of crime and has large effects on mental wellbeing (see chapter 2). One could take an estimate for that effect and use it to value fear of crime in an otherwise standard CBA of some relevant intervention (say, an anti-recidivism policy).

The example of air pollution in chapter 3 also illustrates the benefit of 'looking over the shoulder' at wellbeing knowledge: it is from studies such as Luechinger (2009), but also some of the UK work on the same topic by Dolan and Laffan (2016) and Powdthavee and Oswald (2020), that it was discovered that there are significant wellbeing gains of reduced air pollution. One might think that this was already known from the extensive work in the medical literature on the physical health effects of air pollution and that the wellbeing literature merely discovered another way of measuring the same link. However, this is not the case: a large part of the wellbeing effect is due to mental health effects, thus making the total effect far larger, going beyond the more well-known physical health effects (see Zhang et al. (2017), for example).[7] Essentially, air pollution disrupts thought processes and makes individuals more miserable and irritable, with wellbeing losses additional to physical health problems. Importantly, Luechinger (2009) and others have shown that only little—no more than 5 per cent—of the air pollution effect is incorporated at present in real estate prices, indicating that individuals do not know these effects (or markets do not function properly to internalise them via the price mechanism). This means that apart from countering air pollution, accrediting and disseminating the knowledge of just how negative the consequences of air pollution can be is a policy in and of itself.

[7] These authors look at the effect of air pollution on mental health and wellbeing using the China National Longitudinal Survey matched with contemporaneous air quality and weather conditions at the time and place of each interview. They find that one standard deviation improvement in a single-day air quality is associated with 0.03 to 0.04 standard deviations improvement in mental health.

Another example is how to think of time not spent at work, particularly commuting. In current CBA by the Department for Transport in the United Kingdom, for example, commuting time is valued as lost production to the tune of the prevailing wage rate. Some allowances are made for mode of transport, partly because different people commute in different modes and their wage rates differ (Dickerson et al., 2014; Stutzer and Frey, 2008). However, it is still assumed that an hour spent commuting by bike to work is a net negative to society, even though at Sports England, an hour additionally spent on the bike counts as a net positive.

From a wellbeing perspective, the effect of time not spent at work, even if it is commuting, is not lost production, but whatever the effect of how that time is spent on wellbeing happens to be. It needs to be estimated. Current estimations typically find that the difference between commuting and leisure is surprisingly small, suggesting that for many commuters, time is not quite 'lost' but spent on activities that would otherwise have taken place anyway, such as reading a newspaper, listening to music, spending time on social media, riding a bike, walking, or thinking about the day (see the references in Table 2.2 of chapter 2). We discuss this in greater detail in chapter 5, where we present a particular study on the life satisfaction effects of commuting commissioned by the Department for Transport in the United Kingdom.

The value of different activities to individuals is often equated in current CBA to be the market price for these activities, often approximated by the time value and hence wages. Yet, from a wellbeing perspective, other considerations come into view, such as whether those activities harm social relationships between people, whether the time spent in those activities is a relatively happy time, and whether there are any mental health costs or benefits from those activities. Hence, in addition to taking wages as an appropriate approximation of the value of time, a wellbeing perspective would additionally look at non-monetary aspects and whether individuals are really aware of these effects and the alternatives they could have. Individuals would certainly not be assumed to be rationally optimizing and doing the best possible thing they could do.

On the issue of just using market prices, there are many forms of leisure that people do not pay for, which arguably includes the most important social activities that people undertake, such as caring for partners and children. GDP explicitly does not value the time people spend on caring for children even though it is difficult to envisage any economy in which that does not occur for any length of time. In contrast, within wellbeing CEA, family time is, arguably, one of the more 'wellbeing productive' moments of the day, with the loss in market consumption from not working even longer hours' worth much less.

There are other key differences to mention in terms of how the default assumptions lead one to look in different places, but the basic point is always the same: wellbeing CEA takes its cues from the perspective of what increases wellbeing, which leads one to put a lot of weight on things like mental health and social relationships.

It is possible to incorporate the same insights as to what is important for wellbeing into current CBA, but it does not come naturally because its current focus is to look at the volume of things that are bought and sold. The 'evidence bar' that changes in marketed goods and services have to meet to be included in current CBA is low, while the evidence bar for including non-market aspects of life (our inner feelings, social relationships, or how jealous we are) is high. The exact opposite holds for wellbeing CEA, which naturally acquaints one with the relative importance of different non-market aspects as well as with marketed goods and services involving strong social externalities such as status considerations that limit their importance from a national wellbeing point of view.[8]

A careful look at the inner life of individuals thus yields insights that are not always 'obvious and already known'. The wellbeing literature could therefore simply join many other literatures as background information to existing CBA, but doing so seriously would change how virtually every CBA is undertaken.

Business Cases and the Value of Wellbeing

CBA is about total value, yet government departments can also be asked how much societal value a policy creates for the invested public funds, a so-called *business-case analysis*. That logic is much closer to wellbeing CEA as the opportunity costs of public funds is then a key consideration. Yet business cases usually have a very specific outcome in mind, such as, say, recidivism of prisoners, and primarily calculate the public costs per unit of that particular outcome. The question is then how other effects are counted, where we think of other effects as a change in wellbeing (denoted by ΔW).

If one is looking at ΔW in the context of a business-case analysis, the change in wellbeing is a particular effect of a policy, potentially alongside several other outcomes that are not monetized. This fits cases in which one is interested in a different outcome using public funds, but where additional effects are in terms of ΔW. One could, for instance, think of a health policy or an education policy where the primary objective is something very different (like QALYs or test scores). This would go against the wellbeing perspective we describe in this book but fits many current practices in governments as it fits the specialization of government departments that are 'charged' with some specific deliverables for which

[8] One can rightfully ask why public goods and services are then thought to have such large effects. Essentially, things like jealousy are not very relevant to health, basic education, basic housing, clean air, defence, basic social safety nets, and other key public goods and services.

they have a budget. Wellbeing effects over and beyond the primary objective are then a kind of 'unintended bonus' for which one needs to find an appropriate monetary value.

Within the logic of that 'other primary outcome' approach, one should see ΔW in terms of an output of the public sector as a whole. This is the consequence of the whole-of-government approach which assumes that any particular output achieved anywhere is of equal overall value. The question is then what monetary value to put on that ΔW.

One way to think about this is then again the opportunity-cost approach, applied to the public sector as a whole. The question is thus not what the monetary equivalent is that would make an individual as well off in terms of wellbeing gain, but how much resources would minimally have to be spent elsewhere in the public system to achieve the same wellbeing gain. One in that case wants to use $(1/\lambda)$, i.e. the amount of money needed in the marginal project to get one unit of wellbeing.

Cost-effectiveness Analysis versus Social-Rate-of-Return Analysis

In the United Kingdom, social-rate-of-return analysis has increased in popularity in policy circles as an acceptable way of making the case for a policy. Social-rates-of-return analysis relates to the concept of net additional public costs of a policy, which can be written as:

$$\text{Net Additional Public Costs} = \text{Direct Costs} - \text{Net Additional Public Savings} \quad (4)$$

This formula disaggregates the net additional public costs of a policy into its direct costs and its resulting net additional public savings elsewhere in the public sector. This distinction reflects the reality that most policies require some initial costs that have to be approved, either by councils, ministers, or politicians.

Social-rate-of-return analysis then focuses on the difference between direct costs and the net additional public savings, a common feature it shares with business-case analysis, which typically represents policies in terms of net additional present value (which is essentially net additional public savings less direct costs) or cost-return ratios (a ratio between monetary returns and direct costs).

Social-rate-of-return analysis looks at the annualized return on the direct costs implied by the net additional public savings (that is, rate of return). A classic example that has been widely studied is the rate of return on investments in education, where the direct costs are tuition fees and the costs of schools and universities, and the net additional public savings are primarily the additional tax returns in later life.

As a rule of thumb, rates of return on post-compulsory education are around 6 per cent per year, which may serve as a benchmark return against which to compare other public investments.[9] In case of education, we do not believe that additional average life satisfaction gains are very large (see Blanchflower and Oswald (2004), for example), but we do believe that almost everything one cares about improves with education, such as life expectancy, civic responsibility, and investments in children, i.e. indirect as opposed to direct effects of education on wellbeing. Hence, the rate of return to post-compulsory education is at least 6 per cent per year.

The link between social-rate-of-return analysis and wellbeing CEA is then that, implicitly, standard social-rate-of-return analysis does not monetize changes in wellbeing or effects that look like it (such as improvements in mental health) but only counts monetary flows in and out of the public purse. In fact, social-rate-of-return analysis is all about public costs and not about monetizing many of the benefits (they sometimes valuate physical health benefits via QALYs, yet ignore many of the mental health effects), implicitly presuming that benefits are positive anyway.

There is no difference in basic principles between social-rate-of-return analysis and wellbeing CEA: both are a measure of social value for public money. The difference is more in the habits and defaults used to generate the actual numbers. In wellbeing CEA, there is immediate attention to quantifying all the benefits to individuals' lives in terms of wellbeing (including, per default, inner lives). Often, this is not done in social-rate-of-return analysis (though it would be possible, in principle), where the main focus is on whether the intervention pays itself back or not in terms of money flowing in and out of the public purse.

One could, however, conduct more sophisticated social-rate-of-return analyses in which the benefits of a policy are not merely the net additional public savings, but also the monetary equivalent value of other changes. Social-rate-of-return analyses would then be just another flavour of cost-benefit analysis and differences to wellbeing CBA would fade or become negligible in case that all benefits are (monetized) wellbeing impacts.

[9] See, for example, Blundell et al. (2005), Dearden et al. (2002), and McIntosh (2006) for the United Kingdom; Oreopoulos and Petronijevic (2013) for the United States; and Psacharopoulos and Patrinos (2004) for a review of estimates from a wide range of countries.

Multi-criterion Analysis

This book is largely concerned with wellbeing calculations based on a one-dimensional notion of wellbeing. This reflects the economic and utilitarian concern with trade-offs and decisions, which invariably mean that one must compare different possibilities on some one-dimensional outcome so that one can make the choice that involves the higher overall outcome. Explicitly or implicitly, choices involve a judgement on how the huge complexity of the world is reducible to a single dimension in which judgements between very different possible choices can be made.

Nevertheless, there are many policy institutions and decision situations that avoid an open choice for a one-dimensional metric of outcomes. Instead, institutions might openly adopt a large multitude of outcomes that it considers part of wellbeing (or some other phrase that captures overall value). The UN Sustainable Development Goals, the OECD Framework for Measuring Well-being and Progress, and the Welsh Well-being of Future Generations legislative framework are just some of the many examples of this.

The UN Sustainable Development Goals (SDGs) now include an ever-expanding set of issues deemed important, currently summarized in seventeen overall goals which further subdivide into 169 actual empirical indicators. The number of dimensions and actual indicators keeps increasing, meaning that this current description is unlikely to remain accurate for long. Importantly, of course, the UN SDGs are not a method of government or of resource allocation. The UN is thus under no pressure to come up with a methodology that is workable for real choices.

Similarly, the OECD Framework for Measuring Well-being and Progress currently includes thirteen items, several of which are themselves an index of many more items, leading to a dashboard that does not bring with it a methodology for making real choices when public resources are scarce.

The Well-being of Future Generations (Wales) Act sets out four dimensions of wellbeing which are derived from the Government of Wales Act (2006) and the notion of sustainable development in Wales. These dimensions are termed economic wellbeing, social wellbeing, environmental wellbeing, and cultural wellbeing. These are the same terms that the UN uses in their definition of sustainable development, except for cultural wellbeing.

To provide further detail on what is meant by these four dimensions of wellbeing, the Well-being of Future Generations (Wales) Act puts in place seven wellbeing goals:

1. A prosperous Wales
2. A resilient Wales

3. A more equal Wales
4. A healthier Wales
5. A Wales of cohesive communities
6. A Wales of vibrant culture and Welsh language
7. A globally responsible Wales

As with the UN SDGs, there are national indicators to help measure progress towards these goals. Moreover, the sustainable development principle embodied in this approach includes five ways of working that public bodies are required to take into account:

- Looking at the long term so that the ability of future generations to meet their own needs is not compromised
- Taking an integrated approach so that public bodies look at all the wellbeing goals in deciding on their wellbeing objectives
- Involving a diversity of the population in the decisions that affect them
- Working with others in a collaborative way to find shared sustainable solutions
- Understanding the root causes of issues to prevent them from occurring

Each of these five ways of working, in turn, is associated with a set of guidelines, behaviours, and activities across public bodies in Wales. The seven statutory wellbeing goals relate to forty-six National Well-being Indicators for Wales and the Annual Well-being of Wales Report. In 2017, Wales developed an online tool map for the Wales wellbeing goals and national indicators to the seventeen SDGs.

As a result of this initiative, all schools in Wales, for example, now measure the life satisfaction of their students during teenage years, alongside various indicators of problems prevalent amongst teenagers, like bullying or social media abuse. The Well-being of Future Generations (Wales) Act also introduces a new collective entity called Public Services Boards (PSBs), regrouping all public services operating in a local area. The aim of PSBs is to encourage collaboration and integration in the delivery of public services. They have a duty to improve the economic, social, environmental, and cultural wellbeing of their area by contributing to the achievement of the wellbeing goals. To do that, they have to collectively assess the wellbeing of their area in order to select wellbeing objectives and prepare a local wellbeing plan.

The whole exercise is thus very much in the spirit of evidence-based policy-making, which starts with getting on top of where one is at the moment and where one wants to be in the future, guided by evidence as to how to best get there. One might see this as the whole government machinery becoming more self-aware and rational. The main enforcement mechanism is via mandatory plans that PSBs must have towards improving the wellbeing goals in their local areas, which can then be judged against local outcomes.

The obvious issue with a high-dimensional approach to wellbeing is that it does not easily lend itself to making consistent choices as to how to spend scarce resources: if something makes Wales a bit more prosperous but also a bit less healthy and less globally responsible (say, because of more motorways), then on what basis should a decision be made? How much health is a bit more prosperity worth? Also, if the plans begin to bite and the management of the PSBs is held accountable for progress, the temptation will emerge to game the indicators, which gets easier the more there are of them.

Somehow, for making choices between projects that have conflicting effects in these dimensions (not to mention the effect on the public purse, which is not in the seven dimensions), there has to be some procedure, formally or informally, to boil down the seven goals into one. Ideally, such a procedure is the same across PSBs, to make consistent choices across Wales. This implicit joint goal and joint procedure could arise top-down, or more bottom-up, or not at all, depending on local administrative culture.

Since the issue of trade-offs is always important, let us first sketch what a simple 'multi-criterion analysis' approach would look like when making decisions in a highly multi-dimensional space. Then, we sketch the current guidelines of the Future Generations Commissioner Wales on this topic.

Multi-criterion Analyses—A Primer

Multi-criterion analysis is a common tool for multi-dimensional decision situations, which arise in many organizations and institutions that distrust single measures of outcomes. The generic approach is to trust some group of final decision-makers with the ability to make consistent optimal choices (which obviously has its own problems) and to present them with a palette of choices, in which all the dimensions are described.

Taking life satisfaction as the measure for wellbeing, trust is ultimately put in the individuals' ability to judge their own lives, though there too one wants to rely on judgements made in the literature and by decision-makers within the policy process as to how much one can 'really' trust the results from data and analyses on life satisfaction. In the case of the Well-being of Future Generations (Wales) Act, trust is placed more explicitly inside the decision machinery of the civil service and public bodies, which includes the Future Generations Commissioner.

Mathematically speaking, multi-criterion analysis is the depiction of the option space in the multiple dimensions envisioned. Consider how this works in the Welsh case.

Suppose there is a given budget B and a large set of possible interventions INT^k where $k = 1, ..., K$. Each of the interventions is associated with net additional public costs of C^k and a final change in the total outcome j where $j = 1, \ldots, 7$ (representing the seven outcome dimensions) denoted as Y^{jk}. For each intervention, the option is to fund it or not, denoted as the binary indicators $I^{sk} = 1$ that $I^k \in \{0, 1\}$. A feasible choice set $s \in S$ is then any set of binary indicators that respects the budget condition:

$$\sum\nolimits_k I^{ks} * C^k \leq B \tag{5}$$

where the total outcome in each of the seven dimensions is then:

$$Y^{js} = \sum\nolimits_k I^{sk} * Y^{jk} \tag{6}$$

A single possible outcome s in the seven domains can be depicted as consisting of the point $(Y^{1s}, ..., Y^{7s})$ in the seven-dimensional space. The entire possibility space $M(Y^1, ..., Y^7)$ is then merely the entire set of feasible points.

In the two-dimensional space with marketed goods and services that have fixed prices, the possibility set of two goods and services under a finite budget is simply the budget line denoting all combinations of goods and services one can buy. The issue is the same in seven dimensions, but then with points instead of lines. In essence, this is the Lancaster (1968) model of consumption choice where each consumption good or service consists of a bundle of characteristics (in this case, seven characteristics).

The number of possible choices in this seven-dimensional space will quickly become extremely large when there are many possible interventions to consider. The main question in multi-criterion decision analysis is then (i) to weed out all the possibilities that are strictly dominated by another possibility; (ii) to get agreement on simple rules of thumb to weed out more possibilities; and (iii) to arrive at a smaller set of choices to consider that might be acceptable to the decision-maker.

The first of these issues is simple: one discards all possible allocations s for which there is another feasible allocation σ with higher outcomes in all seven dimensions, i.e. for which $Y^{js} < Y^{j\sigma}$ for all $j = 1, ..., 7$.

The second of these issues is more cumbersome, because it requires one to ask the (group of) decision-makers what the minimal trade-offs are that they would find acceptable between each of the seven dimensions in terms of a numeraire dimension, preferably a particularly important outcome. For illustration, suppose the numeraire outcome is 'A healthier Wales' ($j = 4$). Decision-makers would then be asked of each of the other six dimensions how much they would minimally and maximally be willing to trade one unit in that dimension for x_j^{min} and x_j^{max}

in the health dimension. Implicitly, in a single dimension measure of wellbeing $x_j^{\min} = x_j^{\max}$, so that the difference between $x_j^{\min}$ and $x_j^{\max}$ captures the degree to which decision-makers are unsure how much an outcome in one dimension is worth an outcome in another dimension.

Once decision-makers have nominated a set of $\{x_1^{\min}, ..., x_7^{\min}, ..., x_1^{\max}, ..., x_7^{\max}\}$, this can then be used to weed out more choices that are deemed inferior. Concretely, one can then discard all feasible choices s for which it is the case that there is at least one feasible choice σ which has as the property:

$$Y^{4\sigma} - Y^{4s} > \sum_{j \neq 4} (Y^{js} - Y^{j\sigma})\, x_j^{\min} * Y^{js} < Y^{j\sigma} + \sum_{j \neq 4} (Y^{js} - Y^{j\sigma})\, x_j^{\max} * Y^{js} > Y^{j\sigma} \tag{7}$$

which is a bit of a cumbersome formula, but denotes a very simple heuristic for ascertaining that choice σ is better than choice s: in the domains where choice s is superior to choice σ, i.e. $Y^{js} > Y^{j\sigma}$, one uses the high price $x_j^{\max}$ to value that advantage, whereas when the opposite holds, one uses the low price $x_j^{\min}$. This will generically weed out all choices which do well in just one dimension in a very marginal sense, where they are not strictly dominated by a choice that is better in all dimensions but something close to that does apply.

The possible choices that survive this culling can then either be explicitly enumerated if there are a few of them, or with key trade-offs made visible graphically or numerically. This also works the other way around: one can illustrate the difference between two distinct choices as implicit weights on the seven different dimensions.

Note that this all presumes that in each of the seven dimensions one has accepted an actual measurement to represent the final outcome in that dimension.[10] If one is not prepared to do that and wants to use several indicators for each domain independently, one effectively has more than seven dimensions, ending up with as many dimensions as one wishes to have indicators that one refuses to add up in a unique way. A way forward in such higher-dimensionsal multi-criterion analysis is then to apply the aforementioned methodology separately to each dimension, gradually reducing the decision problem.

[10] We understand that there are statutory definitions and guidance from the Future Generations Commissioner as to what they should entail and focus on, but we are not sure whether this means there are set-in-stone rules on how to get at a cardinal number for each of the seven dimensions.

How Does Multi-criterion Analysis Work in Practice?

If we now turn to the question of how this actually works in practice, looking at the example of Wales, we must admit that we do not quite know, but we can report parts of the guidelines given to the Future Generations Commissioner for Wales on how to implement it.

First, the Future Generations Commissioner advises against trade-offs and encourages public bodies to 'work harder and look for decisions which would have positive outcomes across all goals or dimensions, accepting that the benefits might be very different and small in some cases while others would be significant.' This essentially would encourage projects that have improvements on all dimensions, rejecting those with small losses in one diemnsion and huge gains in others.[11]

The Future Generations Commissioner's Office commented on these matters (via personal correspondence to the authors) that:

> It is worth noting that the Future Generations Commissioner for Wales has expressed her view that the Act moves us away from the traditional trade-offs approach to one of balancing in a more literal sense. This would require an approach which actively seeks to give equal consideration to different sets of needs in order to maximize contribution across all of these needs (albeit not always equal contribution). She has created different frameworks, which seek to help public bodies in Wales take the Act and its elements into account and ensure that equal consideration is given to each element of well-being.

The Future Generations Commissioner thus advises that equal consideration should be given to all goals and the selected options that damage any of the goals should be rejected and only decisions with positive impacts should be selected—appreciating this is a difficult exercise and one that requires a complete shift of mind and practice within the civil service. The decision rule on options is reportedly (i) to weed out the decision with negative impact on any goal; (ii) to weed out those with positive impact against only one or two goals; and (iii) to select the most balanced or widest benefits in the pool left.

Note that this reported decision rule puts a large weight on positive changes from an existing status quo, independent on the base level of that status quo. Hence, no obvious priority seems to be given to areas that have a very low starting level and that might be thought to yield higher marginal 'utility' relative to gains in areas that are already at high levels.

[11] This has strong incentive effects on the presentation of options. It would, for instance, appear to encourage the bundling of several projects into one such that there is a more visible expected increase in the different dimensions.

Benefits of Multiple Dimensions and Advocated Ways of Implementing Them

There can be good reasons to have a multi-dimensional approach to outcomes, essentially related to uncertainty and to the practicalities of policy-making discussed in chapter 1:

1. If what one ultimately cares about is a very non-linear function of a set of underlying dimensions, then any linear approximation inherent in weights is inappropriate. One would then ideally want to explicitly state that non-linear function, but it might well be the case that one only gradually learns over time what that function truly looks like. Multi-criterion analysis might thus be a practical procedure to gradually discover what one truly values, i.e. to discover what wellbeing actually means.
2. Different parts of the economy and the state machinery might be fruitfully focused on only a subset of outcomes without much concern for others. It might, for instance, be more practical and efficient to have the tax authorities worry about how to close down tax loopholes without being overly bothered to work out how each closed loophole might affect the resilience of the population. In this way, possible interventions proposed by different parts of the state machinery might simply not include all the relevant dimensions, or have an easy-to-compute link with the long-term wellbeing of the entire population. Openly accepting such limitations via a selective outcome focus (and thus a reporting focus) can then force one into multi-dimensionality, at least in the sense of initial reporting of policy outcomes by some group.
3. The politics of decision-making might preclude the ability of any group to openly adopt any explicit measure, and might involve various checks and balances where particular interests can veto plans that are too negative for them. Such mechanisms are central to many democracies which have a balance of power and explicit institutions with different mandates to care about different things. Testing whether something adheres to the rule of law and the constitution is, for instance, a different exercise to judging the wellbeing effect of something, done by different institutions and involving different weights. Multi-criterion analysis in that sense is merely a reflection of the fractured nature of practical policy-making, simply made more explicit by naming the key dimensions. However, if that is the main motivation, then one only wants to include those dimensions involved in checks and balances.
4. The main actual gain in wellbeing might well come from following simple heuristics, such as included in the five ways of doing things in Wales. If that

is the case, then it might be simpler to push for the direction in which the gains are likely to be made rather than force each part of the machinery to be involved in a 'level playing field' competition for resources.

What this boils down to is quite simple: the difference between the seven dimensions of wellbeing in Wales and the one-dimensional approach favoured in the classic economic approach advocated by most governments comes down to whether the likely gains in one-dimensional wellbeing are in the seven dimensions of the approach in Wales or not. If they are in the same direction, then there will be little difference in practical policy-making.

If we think about the technical advice given in the previous chapters, there is no large difference between multi-criterion analysis and wellbeing CEA. The technical difficulties all carry over: there is still the issue of bargaining over prices, the issue of a gradual discovery process versus one-offs, the issue of uncertainty, and so on. It just becomes even more complicated.

Wellbeing Frameworks around the World

The appeal of a single measure of wellbeing that policies orient around is partially due to the associated benefits of simplicity and accountability: it makes for a simple story of what policy-making is all about, whether local or national, and it allows others to challenge policies based on the science of wellbeing and statistics on actual outcomes. It thus fits a vision of policy-making that is 'enlightened and rational' in the sense of being oriented towards a clear goal that can be debated and improved upon over time.

If one accepts that vision of policy-making as something to move towards, the main question is whether there is a candidate measure of wellbeing that has the minimum characteristics one needs to use it in policy-making: it should be easy to collect and analyse, provide definitive answers on what needs to be done in order to improve it (and what not to do), and it is acceptable to politicians and the general public. This is the vision advocated in this book, and we make the argument that life satisfaction is the measure of wellbeing that most appropriately ticks all these boxes at present.

Yet, many think differently. So in this section, we discuss alternative visions of policy-making, which leads to an appreciation of other wellbeing measures and other roles of these measures.

One alternative scenario is a policy world in which there is little capacity to understand the many linkages between policies and where there is little capacity for continuous experimentation and learning. This is the reality in many developing countries, for example, and inside many institutions within developed countries where there is limited capacity to gradually optimize on the basis of a whole apparatus of measurement and reflection.

The experience of Bhutan is quite instructive in this regard. Its monarchy has been invested in the notion of 'Gross National Happiness (GNH)' from the 1970s onwards, but there were few university-trained civil servants in Bhutan, which has a population of just under a million and which is highly dispersed and quite diverse. Not until 2007 was there an actual attempt at measuring happiness, and even currently there is little in terms of organized learning about happiness within its small civil service. Bhutan simply lacks the general expertise and resources to implement the sophisticated policy systems which operate in richer and far larger countries.

What this primarily meant was that happiness-promoting policies were arrived at in a discretionary and top-down way, with the political elite of Bhutan simply enacting what it believed to be good for happiness, such as restricting tourism so as not to introduce cultural change and pressure on environmental resources due to tourism.

Many other countries in the world have a similar combination of a political desire to, in principle, improve the wellbeing of the population, but quite limited capacity to independently fine-tune local institutions based on sophisticated measurement and experimentation.

In this section, we introduce three of the most prevalent alternative approaches to wellbeing policy-making: (1) aspirational wellbeing decision systems (such as that of Bhutan), (2) wellbeing dashboard systems, and (3) policy-domain-specific wellbeing systems. The perspective that this gives allows us to reflect on the approach in this book, i.e. the pros and cons of a system that openly accepts a particular measure of wellbeing as decisive for policy trade-offs. We call such a decisive measure an *apex measure* and a system that openly accepts such a measure an *apex-measure-based system.*

Aspirational Wellbeing Decision Systems: The Case of Bhutan

An aspirational wellbeing decision system is one in which the policy elite has openly and seriously accepted that the goal of government is the wellbeing of the population, but where there is no actual measurement of wellbeing or real attempt at integrating scientific insights on wellbeing into policy-making.

To some degree, many countries in the world have been aspirational on wellbeing for many decades without incorporating scientific insights on wellbeing. The United States is a perfect example of this, with a constitution that for over two hundred and fifty years has advocated an inalienable right to the pursuit of happiness. Yet, the United States has no institutional mechanism to adopt insights on happiness into actual policy-making. There is no happiness accounting unit in Congress, or even a happiness advisory group informing the president about how the country fares in terms of the happiness of the population. Its constitutional advocacy of happiness has remained aspirational for over two hundred and fifty years, at least when it comes to federal government.

Probably the best-known long-standing commitment to wellbeing by a government comes from Bhutan, where the fourth King of Bhutan, King Jigme Singye Wangchuck, declared in 1972: 'Gross National Happiness is more important than Gross Domestic Product.'[12] This declaration was not mere idle talk either, as the religion of the country, Vajrayana Buddhism, has an explicit role for religious leaders in catering for the happiness of the population, for example through happiness-oriented meditation practices.

Making the population happier through meditation by dedicated priests 'beaming out' happiness to others is an actual policy, though it obviously does not fit within modern scientific ideas of how people affect each other. Yet, within the belief system of the majority religion of Bhutan, it is a serious proposition that particular types of meditation are the way to make others happy. It thus fits our definition of an aspirational wellbeing decision system: serious but without the application of science. As said before, there was no actual attempt in Bhutan to measure the wellbeing of the population until its first survey in 2007. Currently, it has a dashboard-measure of wellbeing (the GNH index) that is purportedly used as a checklist in policy-making.

It is important not to over-romanticize Bhutan: it has a population of less than a million, its life expectancy is about sixty-eight years, its GDP per capita is not even 10 per cent of that of the United Kingdom, and it has experienced internal unrest in recent decades, especially when it comes to the expulsion and marginalization of the Lhotshampa community, many of whom had arrived in the nineteenth century (Aris, 1979; Meier and Chakrabarti, 2016). Still, Bhutan exemplifies a natural trajectory in wellbeing policy-making: from aspirational, to some kind of explicit measurement and gradual adoption into policy processes, perhaps eventually to an apex-measure-based system.

Like Bhutan, many other countries have formally adopted some notion of wellbeing as its goal and even mandated it in laws. This includes France, where its Senate in 2015 passed the 'Sas Act' mandating the government to inform the country every year of its progress in ten areas, including subjective wellbeing (see Table 3.1 in Durand (2018), for example). Part of the ambition was to have new initiatives evaluated in terms of their likely effect on wellbeing. Similar aspirations and initiatives have been taken in Australia, Ecuador, India (Andhra Pradesh), Italy, New Zealand, and many other countries and regions during the past decades.

[12] See, for example: https://ophi.org.uk/policy/national-policy/gross-national-happiness-index/.

Ecuador is a good example of how limited and transient some of these aspirational initiatives have been. In 2013, Ecuador instituted a 'State Secretary for the Presidential Initiative for the Construction of a Society of Good Life'. This position holder had no budget, no measurement apparatus, and no political power to do much else than appear frequently on conferences and talk about the direction towards which the country should go in terms of wellbeing policies. When an opposing political party came into power four years later, the position was axed.

Wellbeing Dashboard Systems

There are literally hundreds of wellbeing dashboards and associated indices in the world, including both government-sponsored dashboards and privately sponsored ones. Government-sponsored dashboards include, for example, the International Well-being Index, the Global Youth Well-being Index, the OECD Better Life Index, or the Bhutan Gross National Happiness Index. Privately sponsored dashboards include the Sainsbury's Living Well Index or the Lloyds Bank Happiness Index. There is even a Salvation Army one. A report by the New Zealand Treasury nicely summarizes many of the best-known ones (King et al., 2018).

To discuss their general properties and uses, let us discuss two in greater depth: the Bhutan Gross National Happiness Index and the OECD Better Life Index, which was adopted in a slightly altered format by New Zealand in its 2020 wellbeing budget.

The Bhutan Gross National Happiness Index is best summarized by its official diagram (Figure 4.1).

One can see that it involves nine policy domains, each including two to four actual indicators. We do not comment here about the actual indicators that supposedly measure elements such as 'knowledge' or 'family', as the inherent issues with these kinds of 'representative variables' will be discussed later in the context of the OECD Better Life Index. For now, let us assume that there are reasonable indicators to capture most of what is meant by these nine policy domains.

A general issue with such wellbeing dashboard systems is that there exists no natural way of adding up the different dimensions into a single number that can be used for trade-offs between different elements in one policy domain. Essentially for simplicity, the four indicators within each policy domain are added up, and the nine domains are assigned equal weights. Whether these domains are actually distinct and whether either the population or the government thinks of each of them as equally important is often not a consideration in the construction of these indices.

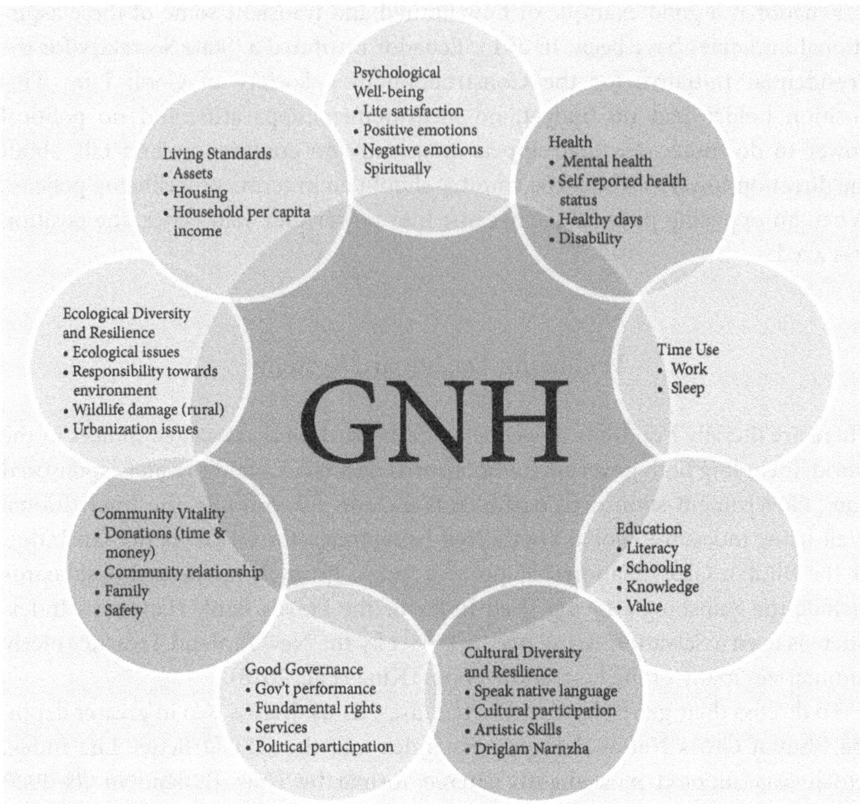

Figure 4.1 The nine domains of Gross National Happiness
Source: Centre for Bhutan Studies.

A related issue is that one suddenly has thirty-four indicators that may be affected by any candidate policy, meaning that one would want to know the causal effects of any policy on each of them over time. That is a rather daunting analytical task for any administrative system, and certainly so in the context of Bhutan which has a central bureaucracy roughly the size of that of a medium-sized UK city. There is simply no way it has the analytical capacity to truly contemplate how much policies would affect each of these thirty-four indicators, eventually leading to an appreciation of whether the overall index goes up or down.

Finally, it should be clear that many of the indicators in this index are not, reasonably speaking, final outputs. Rather, they are inputs or process outputs. For example, time spent on work and urbanization are neither by themselves positives or negatives: they are descriptions of what is going on, but not issues of innate value. Government performance and whether one speaks the language of the majority are similarly not obviously 'positive outputs' in themselves. They are, at best, inputs.

How is this index then actually used in policy decision processes in Bhutan? The advertised procedure followed by the government of Bhutan is that ministries advocating a new policy should submit a concept note for the policy to the Gross National Happiness Commission, which then gathers experts to apply a Gross National Happiness screening tool.[13] Essentially, this screening tool boils down to experts providing a qualitative judgement about whether the proposed policy is expected to have an uncertain, negative, neutral, or positive effect on the various policy domains. This is then, supposedly, taken into account by the government of Bhutan when making decisions. The situation seems similar in the United Arab Emirates, which also has a policy screening process based on a wellbeing dashboard system (Emirates, 2017). We do not know how this procedure is actually implemented.

The point is then that wellbeing dashboard systems are not very practical policy tools. They naturally fit discretionary systems where the dashboard is more a set of quick indicators that tells a powerful decision-maker how several different areas are going, but where actual decisions are largely made and motivated outside of the wellbeing frameworks.

This is not necessarily a critique as countries such as Bhutan have only a relatively small civil service with relatively few resources. However, it does mean that if one were to truly implement a wellbeing dashboard system in practice, one minimally needs a very large and highly trained civil service, which is something only highly developed countries will be able to afford.

The OECD Better Life Index is probably the best-known wellbeing dashboard. Figure 4.2 summarizes it and its supposed usage.

This wellbeing dashboard system has eleven policy domains, categorized under 'material conditions' and 'quality of life'. Each domain, in turn, consists of an evolving set of indicators. Once again, for simplicity, the wellbeing dashboard just adds up these eleven policy domains with equal weights to arrive at the OECD Better Life Index. Conceptually, the OECD sees the outputs in these eleven domains as coming from a production function that relies on four 'resources for future well-being', categorized under four different types of capital.

Let us first consider some of the indicators actually used in the eleven policy domains and whether they truly refer to wellbeing in the sense adopted by this book.

Civic engagement includes the percentage of the population that votes in elections. Not only is it by itself misleading to include voting in a 'quality of life' index, as voting can be a sign of dissatisfaction, but it also influences the conclusions as to which countries have high wellbeing. For example, voting is compulsory in Australia, which then receives a high civic engagement score. If a

[13] For more information, see: https://www.gnhc.gov.bt/en/?page_id=269.

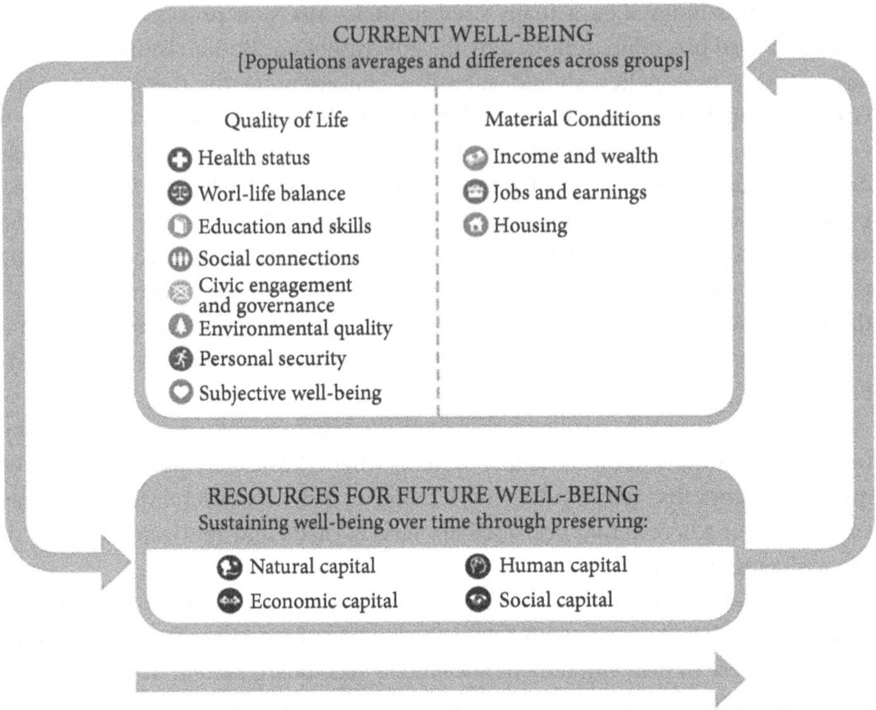

Figure 4.2 The How's Life framework for measuring wellbeing and progress
Source: OECD.

dictatorship thus wants to score high on civic engagement, by the logic of the OECD Better Life Index, achieving that would be as simple as making voting compulsory. So not only is this *not* a variable that unambiguously captures something positive about a society, but its inclusion creates perverse incentives if one were to take it seriously.

Next, child wellbeing includes the amount of public funding spent on particular forms of family support, derived from official statistics. This makes the variable partially dependent on how government measures its expenditures rather than their final destination. Moreover, such expenses depend on whether a society has many or few families with children and hence its age distribution. These expenditures can be a sign of problems rather than positive circumstances, for example providing evidence that families need public support they could not get elsewhere. Most importantly though, expenditures are inputs, not outputs. Our imaginary dictator who would want to game this item could for instance institute a new large public spending fund for family support, while at the same time instituting a new tax on families that takes away what was just given, so that wellbeing as measured via the OECD dashboard goes up but there is no net change in public funding for families. Once again hence, one would not want to take this dashboard seriously as a guide to increasing wellbeing because that would create perverse incentives.

There are similar problems with most indicators in this index. For example, education includes the test scores of students as reported by PISA studies, as well as the percentage enrolled in secondary school. The main problem is that these are inputs, not outputs. Housing includes the percentage of income spent on rents, which is strange because high housing costs for one are high rental incomes for another, so it is not clearly positive or negative if housing is expensive. Housing also includes the number of rooms per person. From a sustainability perspective, one might see a lot of rooms per person as a negative. In any case, it is once again an input, not an output. The same holds for many other indicators, ranging from time spent on hygiene (which could be seen as an indication of environmental degradation) to the time spent on work (which could be seen as good or bad depending on how pleasant work is).

One point to note is thus that many of the indicators used in the OECD wellbeing dashboard are not unambiguously good or bad. Another is that many indicators are not wellbeing outcomes at all, but, at best, inputs into a wider system that might or might not produce wellbeing.

What holds for this OECD dashboard holds for every wellbeing dashboard and indices derived from them:

1. Indices based on wellbeing dashboard systems use policy domain labels that make them 'cover' important domains of life, which are then 'populated' with indicators that have something to do with that domain. This makes the index appear to have captured the important elements of all these domains of life. As Nicholas Gruen noted, indices based on wellbeing dashboard systems are, therefore, first and foremost a kind of performance symbol whereby the organization adopting it uses it to seem to care about something (Gruen, 2017).
2. The actual indicators included in the Index are often ambiguous in terms of whether they capture something good or bad, often differ in their value for purely administrative reasons, and are often a mix of inputs, outputs, and circumstances. If one were to take such indices seriously as the object to optimize, the actual indicators involved may lead to perverse incentives.

It is therefore not surprising that indices based on wellbeing dashboard systems are seldom used to actually decide on competing policy priorities.

Notwithstanding these issues, New Zealand tried for about ten years to make the OECD Better Life Index operational (New Zealand Treasury, 2018),[14] unsuccessfully because of the second part of the diagram above: the four capitals

[14] For example, see the Treasury website for a history of the development of a living standards framework since 2011, which is available at: https://treasury.govt.nz/information-and-services/nz-economy/higher-living-standards/history-lsf.

categorized under the 'resources for future wellbeing'. The key issue is that there are no accepted summary measures for either natural capital or social capital, which makes it largely impossible to work out a system in which investments into these four forms of capital would lead to trade-offs in terms of wellbeing when it comes to competing policy priorities.

The reason why it has proven impossible so far to create a measure of natural capital is that environmental policy is far too complex to be collapsed into a simple, one-dimensional measure of capital. To see this, take the case of New Zealand, and consider the vast array of activities and measures involved in environmental policy: there are national parks, zoos, aquaria, and sea nurseries that one might see as forms of produced and maintained natural capital, but only if one explicitly measures and values things like biodiversity. If these were the only environmental activities, one might think that it should be possible to come up with a natural capital measure. Yet, New Zealand also tries to discourage the use of plastic bags and littering in parks. That is regulation tied ultimately to transient cultural ideas about nature ('clean parks' and 'plastic-free oceans'), not some amount of it. More blatantly still, New Zealand has regulations for insecticides and mandates that landowners control weeds, having an official list on what is considered a weed. This weed-control aspect is difficult to translate into natural capital as it implies a negative social value for certain species of plant, therefore involving some notion of 'bad nature' which, of course, is difficult to define and measure.

New Zealand also cares about the treatment of chicken in poultry farms, implying some care for how animals appear to feel in human captivity, yet not applying that same principle to animals in the wild: New Zealand is not in the habit of protecting birds against falling prey to other birds. Hence, care for animals is highly dependent on their relationship to humans, and not necessarily about the inner feelings of animals, which is exceedingly difficult to capture in an objective and simple one-dimensional measure of 'natural capital'. New Zealand similarly cares about carbon emissions, but not on the basis that it has worked out how much natural capital is being destroyed by its continued emissions.

In sum, environmental policies in New Zealand are like those in most developed countries: a very complicated mix of production, destruction, regulation, social and cultural notions of beauty and treatment of animals by humans, and rules of thumb on global environmental effects that one believes are good or bad for the planet. Some policies operate at the national level (carbon emissions) and some are highly local (clean parks). In many cases, policies are more oriented towards creating and maintaining useful social norms (for example, that park-littering is unacceptable) than actual measurement and control. Like other countries, New Zealand has not managed to condense those policies and practices into a measure of natural capital, recognizing that the policy reality is just too complex to lend itself to such a reductionist exercise.

The same considerations apply to social capital. While there exist specific indicators, such as trust in the community and how connected individuals in the population feel, the policy reality is again too complex to be reduced into a one-dimensional measure of 'social capital'. How should one, for instance, combine trust in the community, volunteering, tax morale, and the habit of tipping waiters into a single notion of social capital? No one as yet has a ready-to-use system for how this can be achieved.

One should thus look at wellbeing dashboard systems with a critical eye: they often contain many indicators that are ambiguous; indicators are often inputs and process indicators, not outputs; and they often involve concepts and indicators that do not really exist nor capture a policy-making reality that exists. They are more like a loose collection of policy domains and indicators that are at best vaguely related to wellbeing and that policy-makers are interested in, put together in one place in some suggestive way.

What did New Zealand then actually do in its 'wellbeing budget' in 2019/20? After all, the New Zealand government advertises that budget with its own index adapted from the OECD Better Life Index. How did it work?

Although one cannot be entirely sure, it appears from its documentation (New Zealand Treasury, 2019) that the actual policy framework was a combination of new policies and processes:

1. The New Zealand Treasury institutionally owned the wellbeing framework and advised other ministries what to implement in regard to wellbeing.
2. Spending ministries were instructed to choose the indicators in the index they thought their policies addressed, encouraging them to say how much their proposed and current policies contribute to those indicators.
3. Individual ministries were not required to work out how their policies affected the other indicators in the index, though in individual cases the Treasury negotiated with those ministries as to whether and how they should handle and report likely 'spillovers' of their policies to other policy domains.
4. There was approximately a 2 per cent discretionary budget which was spent on things that were advertised as core wellbeing: suicide prevention, mental health, and child wellbeing.
5. To a large extent, the announced new policies were reassessed and relabelled existing policies, including many long-standing ones, such as on economic growth.

It thus seems to be the case that the wellbeing budget in New Zealand combined a relabelling of existing policies with some discretionary spending in the direction of social relationships and mental health, as well as an evolving administrative system to induce spending ministries and organizations to start thinking about particular spillovers.

One should not think of this description as a critique at all, but rather as a reflection of the huge challenges involved in truly getting a machinery as complex as a civil service to move from its previous preoccupations to a wellbeing orientation. It simply takes time and the road inevitably involves aspirations, window dressing, ad hoc processes, and only a gradual adoption of new insights. One should not expect anything different but acknowledge that a reorientation of a civil service is an evolutionary process, not a revolutionary one. This, by the way, has its advantages because it makes policies dependable and credible: precisely because they cannot be changed wholesale from one decade to the next, the general population and the private sector have trust in many government programmes, like labour laws and social protection.

What to make of these indices and dashboards then? Given the discussions above surrounding wellbeing dashboard systems, it becomes difficult to ascertain whether this or that index of wellbeing, which invariably combines dozens of indicators, 'truly measures wellbeing'. Such indices are not used, or even usable, for practical policy-making, so their role is not really to measure 'the quality of life of the population'. Rather, the goal of wellbeing dashboard systems is to make particular groups of indicators quickly available and visible in one place.

In that light, very different questions arise regarding indices: do they combine the policy domains where there is a lot of improvement to make in the countries using them? Are the indicators involved leading the decision-making systems to perverse incentives, and if so, should they be taken seriously? Do the frameworks around these indices lead users to look in the most promising areas for wellbeing improvements? And in those cases in which they are just window-dressing and designed to make the funders feel useful, are they cheap forms of window dressing that have little negative effects?

These 'does this lead people to think of the right things' considerations are different from the question of whether indices 'truly measure wellbeing'. The answer to the latter question is that an index that combines inputs and outputs, personal facilitators and administrative measures, cannot possibly be the goal of any system. An inherent problem is then that dashboards and indices might well provide the right information at the right time, but one can only judge that from outside those indices. That judgement can come from the political process, the democratic process, or some apex-measure of wellbeing.

Consider how one would construct a dashboard if one started with some accepted measure of wellbeing, an 'apex' measure that one trusts. One would then have a measure acceptable to both politicians and voters, combined with some broad understanding of where the most likely possible improvements in wellbeing lie. The existence of likely areas of improvement then suggest a wellbeing dashboard system that has indicators measuring the states of those potential areas of improvement and their policy levers. The weighting into an index would then go on the basis of the marginal contribution to overall wellbeing of each of the actual outcomes of that wellbeing dashboard (as in input-output models that use satisfactions with domains of life, which works as a wellbeing dashboard for individuals, but unfortunately not countries; see van Praag et al. (2003), for example).

As far as we know, no such wellbeing dashboard system exists and no index has been constructed in this way. The problem is, of course, that the many groups and interests involved in the construction of any index have different apex-measures and purposes in mind, leading to indices that have conflicting and contradictory elements in them, which usually leads to the arbitrary practice of equally weighting their constituent elements.

Other Alternative Measures

The number of suggested alternatives to what is implicitly valued by government bureaucracies by now number in the thousands. They include 'GDP plus' type measures such as 'Green Accounting', 'Adjusted Net Savings', and 'Ecological Footprint'. Many of these measures were surveyed by Fleurbaey and Blanchet (2013). They discussed the methodology involved in these measures and what their pitfalls are. In sum, they cannot replace GDP as the apex measure because GDP is not the basis of cost-benefit accounting in government bureaucracies anywhere. This is partly because GDP shares some of the same limitations, which are:

1. These measures are not 'fine grained' enough to allow for sensible cost-benefit analyses (CBAs) of projects of only a few million or even smaller. They simply lack the methodology to easily link the thousands of projects across the whole public sector machinery to estimates of value.
2. There is no large literature on how any of these measures are causally affected by many things that governments, departments, councils, and organizations are interested in: how health, education, and employment affect them for instance. So they do not fill all that many gaps in the existing methodology whilst creating many new gaps.
3. There is no accepted or long-standing methodology for how to measure them across time, countries, and people. We for instance do not yet know how easy it is to game the measures of natural capital or 'social wealth'. We do not know how to apply these measures in different cultures that lack the same administrative rules on bank accounts, monetary versus social wealth, and regulations around allowed uses of wealth.

All this essentially means it would take decades for the methods to mature enough to the level that it can be used by a bureaucracy, whether private or public. They are, at best, at the aspirational stage of inclusion in decision-making processes. That situation has hardly changed since 2010 for the basic reason that GDP is not the explicit basis of policy choices inside bureaucracies, so alternatives that venture to go 'beyond GDP' don't start from the actual basis of trade-off calculations.

Policy-domain-specific Wellbeing Systems

Throughout the world, many countries have policies in particular policy domains that one could reasonably label 'wellbeing oriented'. One could, for example, label much of mental health policy in that light. One could also label various school philosophies as such, including the many initiatives that openly set themselves the task of guiding children to become happy, well-adjusted citizens who care for society. One could label many public safety and health systems as such, particularly if they also include mental health within their remit.

The United Kingdom, for example, has created many local wellbeing systems through the Care Act 2014 which mandated local councils to care for the wellbeing of the local population (HM Government, 2014), leading to a large proliferation of different initiatives and systems that rose to this challenge. Local initiatives in the United Kingdom alone now range from local citizen participation initiatives to whole regional programmes of wellbeing, such as the Thrive2020 initiative in Guernsey or the Happy Cities initiatives.

We describe one particular programme in greater depth to illustrate the complexities of such programmes, the time it takes to set them up, and the subtleties they involve when local government services try to meet local 'wellbeing needs'.

Our example is the 'safety at school' initiative in the Netherlands launched in 2016. In 2016, the Dutch parliament passed a law mandating schools to provide a safe environment for children in secondary schools, with wellbeing as a desired object of more safety. A prime concern was bullying at school, but any other source of low wellbeing was also explicitly included as important in the legislation.

In the years around this passage of the new 'wet veiligheid op school' (safety at school) law, the ministry of education gradually worked out what schools actually had to do, with quite a few changes along the way from what the original plans were in 2014/15. The key components of the system currently in operation are:

1. Schools are required to have an annual measurement of safety and wellbeing. However, they can each individually choose from a large list of accredited survey organizations they can use, negotiating what to measure and how (for example, on-site or online).

2. In their annual reports to the school inspectorate, schools have to briefly state how things are going regarding the safety of children at school, but if there are no notable problems, schools do not need to mention any set of policies or in-depth measurement.
3. If there are notable problems, particularly if these are ongoing, schools are supposed to draw up plans on how to handle them, often involving other schools in the area, but also social workers, psychologists, councils, and many other organizations in the field of child education (having more than ten organizations involved simultaneously is not uncommon).
4. If there are major problems, the approach and process would be part of the more in-depth reports and visits of the school inspectorate that normally happen once every four years. Again, the process is more oriented towards signalling unusual problems and discussing what resources and cooperation is needed to address them, rather than reporting compliance with advice from up high.

In a period of about four years, a system was developed in the Netherlands that takes great interest in the wellbeing of children in secondary (and many other) schools. It is characterized by a high degree of responsibility of individual schools which are free to define wellbeing in consultation with private suppliers of measurement. Schools are expected to seek cooperation with public organizations if there are notable problems. This would often involve charities and local publicly funded bodies. There is a general principle of 'when there are no problems, don't put much effort into reporting'.

Over time, this led to the development of all kinds of local resources, such as individual groups of teachers writing up recommendations for all other teachers in that area as to how to deal with autism, or how to recognize substance abuse. Local and national charities as well as other public bodies gradually learnt how to slot into this new system, for example by taking on the role of intermediaries to local religious organizations, or volunteer services for additional monitoring of vulnerable children after school hours.

These systems by and large work well in the Netherlands, with the PISA results showing Dutch students having amongst the highest levels of recorded prosociality and wellbeing in the world (OECD, 2019). The somewhat egalitarian ethos and habit of cross-organizational cooperation that make this work are not transportable to very different administrative systems, though: top-down systems do not work in the same way. Still, there are several general lessons to take from this example:

1. It takes time to build an actual wellbeing policy system in a particular policy domain, involving years of work. There is a high degree of local specificity

and adjustment of existing prior arrangements, potentially involving many organizations not originally involved in the legislative effort.
2. The eventual policy system is never 'done' but continuously evolving and subtly different in different localities, reflecting local habits, local problems, local sensitivities, and local strengths.
3. One does not necessarily need a recognized main 'measure of wellbeing' to have a wellbeing policy system in place. In the case of the Netherlands, where there is a fairly broad consensus on what is valued and what is wanted for children, it suffices to have a national accreditation system for providers of wellbeing measurement, with only small actual variations in local interpretations of what wellbeing means.
4. If there is general goodwill towards a wellbeing policy objective, high levels of professionalism throughout the adopting system, and a general culture of seeking cooperative solutions, the role of the central government can remain small. In this specific case, that role was a small amount of funding and organizing a few key administrative issues (the role of the school inspectorate, the accreditation of survey providers, and picking up on national trends that threaten safety, such as, for instance, drug problems).

You see similar dynamics with more top-down approaches to wellbeing as well: policies get more complex and integrated with other systems over time, measurement evolves, reporting bends to where the problems and the interests are, and it takes a lot of labour to work through and set up a whole system.

It is perhaps easiest to see the work and the judgements involved in the Dutch safety-at-school system if one considers the alternative choices that would arise more naturally in a top-down approach. Instead of having private providers of wellbeing measurement, one could have had a mandated national public provider offering a single standard package. Instead of local schools working out with the school inspectors what to report on and what to expand, one could have had mandatory reporting requirements that were the same across thousands of schools. Instead of having local schools and teachers being the ringleaders in terms of involving other local organizations, one could have a nominated institution that did the coordination, involving budgets and convening powers. Instead of having local schools decide what is important in terms of safety and wellbeing, one could have an official definition, with targets and progress indicators.

This alternative top-down approach has some advantages over the decentralized Dutch system, such as that it avoids the reinvention of the wheel in several places and that it has the potential of mandating a clear best-practice everywhere. It also has disadvantages, which are less local motivation and buy-in, as well as less responsiveness to local circumstances. The top-down approach works better if the situation is similar everywhere and there is a high degree of expertise and trust at the top. The devolved approach works better with more knowledge, expertise, and goodwill locally.

What this brings into view is the importance of an understanding of the culture and organization of the administrative system adopting wellbeing. Some general rules of thumb are possible as to what to look out for in different situations, but this is ultimately an issue of public administration that is probably best looked at and judged by experts within the public system or other existing organizations.

The main take-away is that different administrative systems naturally have different optimal approaches as to how to work towards the wellbeing of the population. Our suggested rules of thumb are:

1. If the main expertise and political power is concentrated at the top (as in case of Bhutan and the United Arab Emirates), it is probably best to have executive decision-making on specific wellbeing-related policies, with little use for a large measurement or experimental apparatus due to the aspirational nature of wellbeing policies.
2. In a highly diverse policy environment that has a top-down culture (like the United Kingdom or New Zealand), openly adopting broad principles helps with 'giving permission' to many individual institutions, though actual policies and practices will have to slowly evolve as the system works through the interdependencies in each terrain.
3. In a professional and cooperative system that has a strong shared sense of what wellbeing is (such as in the Nordic countries of Europe), the main role of the centre is to encourage and facilitate a lot of local experimentation in local service provision, combined with local measurement, with the ensuing generalizable information gradually being picked up organically by the whole system.

Conclusion and the Way Ahead

In this chapter, we compared wellbeing CEA to CBA as currently practiced in the United Kingdom and other countries. We showed there are four key differences between both approaches and broadly outlined how current CBA could account for these differences:

1. Wellbeing CEA is keenly aware of negative private consumption externalities, whereas current CBA does not take them into account. This means that wellbeing CEA, by default, discounts some of the wellbeing effects of changes in private consumption and wealth, including, in particular, highly visible changes. Current CBA could be extended to account for this insight

of the wellbeing literature by applying an Easterlin Discount on changes of private consumption and wealth.

2. Wellbeing CEA only assumes that people are 'rational' if the choice set is highly visible and individuals have had long exposure or otherwise have 'good' information about it, whereas current CBA, by default, assumes that individuals are fully rational and fully aware of everything at all times. This matters, in particular, when it comes to experience goods and asymmetric information, where there is a clear role for government to accredit and disseminate evidence on what works and what not. Limited rationality also matters for the monetary valuation of wellbeing because the wellbeing value of both income and many other inputs depends greatly on visibility and awareness, which creates a public role for deliberate (in)visibility. For instance, taxes that are hardly noticed have far less negative wellbeing effects than those that are highly visible and openly debated.
3. Wellbeing CEA takes the perspective of how government can maximize wellbeing given its budget, leading to minimum social production costs of wellbeing as the appropriate monetary value of wellbeing. This is closer to business cases and value per £ of public expenses. Current CBA assumes that the willingness-to-pay is the appropriate measure of value, implying that the individual willingness-to-pay for a wellbeing improvement is the appropriate starting point for the value of wellbeing. Depending on how visible the costs and how aware individuals are of what they might be buying, this leads to an actual value of wellbeing under current CBA. The implied monetary value of wellbeing is usually much higher than the minimum social production costs of wellbeing.
4. Wellbeing CEA uses, in principle, empirical evidence for all supposed wellbeing effects, which means that the symmetry between many different types of expenses made by different actors is broken: in a wellbeing CEA, it is not assumed that expenses made by different departments and institutions buy the same amount of wellbeing. In contrast, standard CBA does add up additional discretionary monetary surplus of different actors (consumers, producers, and the public sector) as if they each buy the same amount of utility (the differential effect is not, usually speaking, estimated). So in wellbeing CEA one adds wellbeing changes linearly, but not changes in non-government expenses and consumption, as each is valued according to how much total wellbeing it actually leads to. In contrast, current CBA does exactly the opposite: changes in non-government expenses and consumption of all actors are measured in £ that are simply added up, perhaps with distributional weights but not based on empirical evidence for actual wellbeing effects.

Moving from current CBA to wellbeing CEA can hence occur by doing away with any of the four key differences in any order, either in one go or via a transition. Practically speaking, one goes a long way towards wellbeing CEA if current CBA adopts an Easterlin Discount, uses the literature on wellbeing for inspiration about where to look for large, hitherto ignored pathways, or focuses on the business case (effect per £ of net additional public costs).

Looking ahead, merging knowledge on wellbeing with existing knowledge embedded in hundreds of cost-benefit analyses practices that are maintained by governments around the world would take years and a lot of analytical skill to do. It is part of a longer trajectory to professionalize evidenced-based policy-making, to standardize experiments and ex post policy analysis, and to increase the shared knowledge and training in wellbeing insights.

Literature

Akay, A., Bargain, O., Dolls, M., Neumann, D., Peichl, A., and Siegloch, S. (2012). Happy Taxpayers? Income Taxation and Well-Being. *IZA Discussion Paper* 6999.

Aris, M. (1979). *Bhutan: The Early History of a Himalayan Kingdom.* Warminster: Aris & Phillips.

Béllet, C., and Frijters, P. (2019). Big Data and Well-being. *World Happiness Report 2019.* New York: Sustainable Development Solutions Network.

Benjamin, D. J., Heffetz, O., Kimball, M. S., and Szembrot, N. (2014). Beyond Happiness and Satisfaction: Toward Well-being Indices Based on Stated Preference. *American Economic Review* 104(9): 2698–735.

Blanchflower, D. G., and Oswald, A. J. (2004). Well-being over Time in Britain and the USA. *Journal of Public Economics* 88(7–8): 1359–86.

Blundell, R., Dearden, L., and Sianesi, B. (2005). Evaluating the Impact of Education on Earnings: Models, Methods and Results from the NCDS. *Journal of the Royal Statistical Society Series A* 168(3): 473–512.

Boardman, A. E., Greenberg, D. H., Vining, A. R., and Weimer, D. L. (2017). *Cost-Benefit Analysis: Concepts and Practice.* Cambridge: Cambridge University Press.

Campbell, H. F. and Brown, R. P. C. (2016). *Cost-Benefit Analysis: Financial and Economic Appraisal using Spreadsheets.* Routledge.

Clark, A. E., Diener, E., Georgellis, Y., and Lucas, R. E. (2008). Lags and Leads in Life Satisfaction: A Test of the Baseline Hypothesis. *Economic Journal* 118(529): F222–F243.

Clark, A. E., Flèche, S., Layard, R., Powdthavee, N., and Ward, G. (2018). *The Origins of Happiness: The Science of Well-Being over the Life Course.* Princeton: Princeton University Press.

Clark, A. E., Frijters, P., and Shields, M. A. (2008). A Survey of the Income Happiness Gradient. *Journal of Economic Literature* 46(1): 95–144.

Claxton, K., Martin, S., Soares, M., Rice, N., Spackman, E., Hinde, S., … and Sculpher, M. (2015). Methods for the Estimation of the National Institute for Health and Care Excellence Cost-effectiveness Threshold. *Health Technology Assessment* 19(14): 1–503.

Dearden, L., McIntosh, S., Mychk, M., and Vignoles, A. (2002). The Returns to Academic and Vocational Qualifications in the UK. *Bulletin of Economic Research* 54(3): 249–74.

Deaton, A. (2008). Income, Health, and Well-Being around the World: Evidence from the Gallup World Poll. *Journal of Economic Perspectives* 22(2): 53–72.

Department of Health and Department of Education, (2017). Transforming Children and Young People's Mental Health Provision: A Green Paper Impact Assessment (IA). Available at: https://assets.publishing.service.gov.uk/government/uploads/system/uploads/attachment_data/file/664442/MHGP_IA.pdf.

Dickerson, A., Hole, R. A., and Munford, L. A. (2014). The Relationship between Wellbeing and Commuting Revisited: Does the Choice of Methodology Matter? *Regional Science and Urban Economics* 49: 321–9.

Dolan, P. (2008). Developing Methods that Really Do Value the Q in the QALY. *Health Econonomics Policy and Law* 3: 69–77.

Dolan, P., and Laffan, K. (2016). Bad Air Days: The Effects of Air Quality on Different Measures of Subjective Well-being. *Journal of Benefit-Cost Analysis* 7(1): 147–95.

Dupuit, Jules (1848). De la mesure de l'utilité des travaux publics. Annales des Ponts et Chaussées, Mémoires et documents relatifs à l 'art des constructions et au service de l'ingénieur. Series 2, 2, 2e semestre, 332–375, Pl. 75. (On thc Measurement of the Utility of Public Works. In Kenneth J. Arrow and Tibor Scitovsky (eds), *Readings in Welfare Economics*. 1969. London: Allen and Unwin, pp. 255–83.

Durand, M. (2018). Countries' Experiences with Well-being and Happiness Metrics. *Global Happiness Policy Report*. Global Happiness Council.

Easterlin, R. A. (2015). Happiness and Economic Growth—The Evidence. In W. Glatzer, L. Camfield, V. Moller, and M. Rojas (eds), *Global Handbook of Quality of Life: Exploration of Well-Being of Nations and Continents*. Dordrecht: Springer, pp. 283–99.

Emirates, U. A. (2017). Happiness Policy Manual. Available at: https://www.mocaf.gov.ae/docs/default-source/default-document-library/happiness-manual.pdf.

Fleurbaey, M., and Blanchet, D. (2013). *Beyond GDP: Measuring Welfare and Assessing Sustainability*. Oxford: Oxford University Press.

Frijters, P., Clark, A. E., Krekel, C., and Layard, R. (2020). A Happy Choice: Wellbeing as the Goal of Government. *Behavioural Public Policy* 4(2): 126–65.

Frijters, P., Johnston, D., and Shields, M. A. (2011). Happiness Dynamics with Quarterly Life Event Data. *Scandinavian Journal of Economics* 113(1): 190–211.

Frijters, P, Johnston, D., Shields, M., and Kompal, S. (2015). A Lifecycle Perspective of Stock Market Performance and Wellbeing. *Journal of Economic Behavior & Organization* 112: 237–250.

Glover, D., and Henderson, J. (2010). Quantifying Health Impacts of Government Policies. London: Department of Health. Available at: https://assets.publishing.service.gov.uk/government/uploads/system/uploads/attachment_data/file/216003/dh_120108.pdf.

Gruen, N. (2017). What Have Wellbeing Frameworks Ever Done for Us? *The Mandarin*. Available at: https://www.themandarin.com.au/84848-nicholas-gruen-what-have-wellbeing-frameworks-ever-done-for-us/#fn5.

HM Government (2014). Care Act 2014. Available at: https://www.legislation.gov.uk/ukpga/2014/23/contents/enacted.

HM Treasury (2018). *The Green Book: Central Government Guidance on Appraisal and Evaluation*. London: HM Treasury.

Huang, L., Frijters, P., Dalziel, K., and Clarke, P. (2018). Life Satisfaction, QALYs, and the Monetary Value of Health. *Social Science & Medicine* 211: 131–6.

Kahneman, D., and Tversky, A. (1979). Prospect Theory: An Analysis of Decision under Risk. *Econometrica* 47(2): 263–91.

Kahneman, D., Wakker, P. P., and Sarin, R. (1997). Back to Bentham? Explorations of Experienced Utility. *Quarterly Journal of Economics* 112(2): 375–406.

Kahneman, D., Krueger, A., Schkade, D., Schwarz, N., and Stone, A. (2004). A Survey Method for Characterizing Daily Life Experience: The Day Reconstruction Method. *Science* 306: 1776–80.

Kapteyn, A., Montgomery, M., Smith, J. P., and van Soest, A. (2019). Life Satisfaction within and across Countries: The Role of Societal Capital and Relative Income. Keynote address at the SABE conference in Dublin, 2 September.

King, A., Huseynli, G., and MacGibbon, N. (2018). Wellbeing Frameworks for the Treasury. *New Zealand Treasury Discussion Paper* 18/01.

Lachowska, M. (2017). The Effect of Income on Subjective Well-Being: Evidence from the 2008 Economic Stimulus Tax Rebates. *Journal of Human Resources* 52(2): 374–417.

Lancaster, K. J. (1968). *Mathematical Economics*. London: Macmillan.

Layard, R. (2016). Measuring Wellbeing and Cost-effectiveness Analysis Using Subjective Wellbeing. What Works Centre for Wellbeing report. Available at: https://whatworkswellbeing.files.wordpress.com/2016/08/common-currencymeasuring-wellbeing-series-1-dec-2016.pdf.

Lindqvist, E., Östling, R. and Cesarini, D. (2020). Long-Run Effects of Lottery Wealth on Psychological Well-Being. Review of Economic Studies: 87(6), 2703–26.

Lomas, J., Martin, S., and Claxton, K. (2019). Estimating the Marginal Productivity of the English National Health Service from 2003 to 2012. *Value in Health* 22(9): 995–1002.

Lucas, R. E., Wallsworth, C., Anusic, I., and Donnellan, M. B. (2020). A Direct Comparison of the Day Reconstruction Method (DRM) and the Experience Sampling Method (ESM). *Journal of Personality and Social Psychology.*

Luechinger, S. (2009). Valuing Air Quality Using the Life Satisfaction Approach. *Economic Journal* 119(536): 482–515.

Meier, B. M., and Chakrabarti, A. (2016). The Paradox of Happiness: Health and Human Rights in the Kingdom of Bhutan. *Health and Human Rights* 18(1): 193–208.

McIntosh, S. (2006). Further Analysis of the Returns to Academic and Vocational Qualifications. *Oxford Bulletin of Economics and Statistics* 68(2): 225–51.

Mukuria, C., Rowen, D., Peasgood, T., and Brazier, J. (2015). An Empirical Comparison of Well-being Measures Used in the UK. Policy Research Unit in economic evaluation of health and care interventions. *EEPRU Research Report* 027.

New Zealand Treasury (2018). The Treasury Approach to the Living Standards Framework. Wellington.

New Zealand Treasury (2019). The Wellbeing Budget. Wellington.

OECD (2011). *How's Life?: Measuring Well-being.* Paris: OECD Publishing.

OECD (2019). *PISA 2018 Results (Volume III): What School Life Means for Students' Lives.* Paris: PISA, OECD Publishing.

Oreopoulos, P., and Petronijevic, U. (2013). Making College Worth It: A Review of the Returns to Higher Education. *The Future of Children* 23(1): 41–65.

Parducci, A. (1995). *Happiness, Pleasure, and Judgment: The Contextual Theory and its Applications.* Mahwah, NJ: Lawrence Erlbaum Associates.

Peasgood, T., Mukuria, C., Karimi, M., and Brazier, J. (2018). Eliciting preference weights for life satisfaction: A feasibility study. Mimeo.

Powdthavee, N., and Oswald, A. J. (2020). Is There a Link between Air Pollution and Impaired Memory? Evidence on 34,000 English Citizens. *Ecological Economics* 169: 106485.

Proto, E., and Rustichini, A. (2013). A Reassessment of the Relationship between GDP and Life Satisfaction. *PLOS ONE* 8(11): e79358.

Psacharopoulos, G., and Patrinos, H. A. (2004). Returns to Investment in Education: A Further Update. *Education Economics* 12(2): 111–34.

Rojas, M. (2020). Happiness, Public Policy and the Notion of Development. *Behavioural Public Policy* 4(2): 1–11.

Sims, C. (1980). Macroeconomics and Reality. *Econometrica* 48(1): 1–48.

Social Value UK (2009). A Guide to Social Return on Investment. Available at: http://www.socialvalueuk.org/resources/sroi-guide/.

Stevenson, B., and Wolfers, J. (2008). Economic Growth and Subjective Well-Being: Reassessing the Easterlin Paradox. *Brookings Papers on Economic Activity* 39(1): 1–102.

Stutzer, A., and Frey, B. S. (2008). Stress That Doesn't Pay: The Commuting Paradox. *Scandinavian Journal of Economics* 110: 339–66.

Ura, K., Alkire, S., Zangmo, T., and Wangdi, K. (2012). *A Short Guide to Gross National Happiness Index*. Thimphu, Bhutan: The Centre for Bhutan Studies.

van Praag, B. M. S., and Frijters, P. (1999). The Measurement of Welfare and Well-being: The Leyden Approach. In D. Kahneman, E. Diener, and N. Schwarz (eds), *Well-being: The Foundations of Hedonic Psychology*. New York: Russell Sage, pp. 413–32.

van Praag, B. M. S., and Frijters, P. (1999). Economics, Welfare Policy and the History of Economic Thought: Essays in Honour of Arnold Heertje. In M. M. G. Fase, W. Kanning, and D. A. Walker (eds), *Different Data Sources for Studying Behaviour*. Cheltenham: Edward Elgar, pp. 290–309.

van Praag, B. M. S., Frijters, P., and Ferrer-i-Carbonell, A. (2003). The Anatomy of Subjective Well-being. *Journal of Economic Behavior & Organization* 51(1): 29–49.

Zhang, X., Zhang, X., and Chen, X. (2017). Happiness in the Air: How Does a Dirty Sky Affect Mental Health and Subjective Well-being? *Journal of Environmental Economics and Management* 85: 81–94.

Appendix: The Monetary Value of Wellbeing in Mathematical Notation

The standard method used so far to derive the individual willingness-to-pay for a public good or service via its wellbeing impacts relies on regressions that yield an estimated relationship between wellbeing and the public good or service in question. This can be referred to as experienced-preference valuation (since life satisfaction can be referred to as 'experienced utility', cf. Kahenman et al., 1997), to make it distinct from stated-preference (including contingent valuation or discrete choice experiments) and revealed-preference valuation (in particular hedonic pricing). For illustration, suppose, that one is interested in the relationship between life satisfaction, income, and air quality at the individual level. One estimates this relationship as follows:

$$LS_{it} = \alpha \ln(y_{it}) + \beta AirQ_{it} \tag{A1}$$

where LS_{it} is life satisfaction of individual i at time t,$\ln(y_{it})$ is the log of net annual individual income, and $AirQ_{it}$ is some measure of air quality as experienced by individual i at time t. An existing practice is to infer the individual willingness-to-pay of individuals for air quality improvements by working out how much one could decrease net annual individual income when there is air quality improvement such that life satisfaction is unchanged. Mathematically, the individual willingness-to-pay WTP_{it} for an air quality improvement Δ can thus be found by solving:

$$\alpha \ln(y_{it}) + \beta AirQ_{it} = \alpha \ln(y_{it} - WTP_{it}) + \beta(AirQ_{it} + \Delta) \tag{A2}$$

which, after some basic algrebraic manipulations, yields:

$$WTP_{it} = y_{it}\left(1 - \exp\left(\frac{-\beta\Delta}{\alpha}\right)\right) \tag{A3}$$

Similarly, one could calculate the individual willingness to accept a decrease in air quality by Δ from finding the income change that keeps life satisfaction constant. Mathematically, the individual willingness to accept WTA_{it} for an air quality reduction (denoted by Δ) can thus be found by equating:

$$\alpha \ln(y_{it}) + \beta AirQ_{it} = \alpha \ln(y_{it} + WTA_{it}) + \beta(AirQ_{it} - \Delta) \tag{A4}$$

which is solved by:

$$WTA_{it} = y_{it}\left(\exp\left(\frac{\beta\Delta}{\alpha}\right) - a\right) \tag{A5}$$

This value can be calculated for any individual with a particular income once it is known what α and β are.[15] The common approach to solve this problem was to find a dataset in which one could estimate equation A1, yielding estimates for both α and β within that dataset, denoted as $\hat{\alpha}$ and $\hat{\beta}$. If one took the income coefficient from this estimation, it would probably be heavily biased as variation in income is not random. We know, for instance, that people make mistakes in recording their own income and many changes in income are related to other life events that have their own effects (like promotions or inheritances).[16]

A cleaner approach to this problem is to distrust estimates unless the underlying source of variation that identifies them is very similar to the intervention one has in mind. This means that, in practice, one would prefer an estimate of income that comes from the best-available studies looking at how wellbeing is affected by random variation in income that resemble the unexpected income change associated with a policy change, such as perhaps due to a tax change or a large lottery win. Similarly, one would generically prefer an estimate of the variable of main interest that is identified from the best-available studies. In case of air quality, it could come from studies looking at, for example, air quality improvements due to mandatory changes to power stations (see Luechinger (2009), for example) or interventions related to traffic pollution.

[15] Most likely, the importance of income changes differs for increases and decreases of income, particularly when individuals are alerted to decreases. Technically, this simply means that a different α is likely to apply for the willingness to pay than for the willingness to accept.

[16] One might think that this problem does not show up if one uses administrative data, such as tax declarations. However, this is not true: many other problems show up in administrative data such as, for example, deliberate underreporting of income, creative use of tax offsets, or strategic spreading of income over spouses and family. Tax data do, of course, not include all sources of income either as they miss out in-kind transfers (such as free school meals or subsidized housing). Hence, measurement problems apply to administrative data just as well.

The approach sketched above, experience-preference valuation, is now a standard tool for valuing non-market goods in CBA. As one can see, it ignores the possibility that income changes of one person affect the wellbeing of someone else and thus ignores consumption externalities, meaning it identifies individual trade-offs, not societal trade-offs.[17] Note that we have used annual net individual income as the relevant income measure to calculate the based willingness-to-pay and the willingness to accept. This is because we can then ignore the issue of taxation. The situation sketched is therefore as if an individual is buying (or selling) a certain good (air quality) on a market with his or her disposable income.

Even this cleaner approach, however, makes several assumptions that have been found to be wrong:

1. The method assumes no 'kink' at the origin: small losses are treated symmetrically to small gains. A huge literature on loss aversion and endowment effects has shown that gains and losses are not treated symmetrically at all. However, an aysmmetry around the origin is difficult to implement in standard regression analyses where one typically does not have a good measure of the 'endowment' or 'reference position'.
2. The method assumes that individuals are rational in the sense of being fully aware of their income and any small changes to it at all times, with attention drawn to income changes deemed irrelevant. We now know that individuals are not fully aware of their income and other resources they can draw on, and that drawing attention to almost anything increases its importance for how people feel about it, an effect often termed as *focusing illusion*. In analyses of wellbeing, this turns out to be crucial, with noticed income changes being easily ten times as important to life satisfaction as unnoticed ones.
3. The method assumes that the circumstances leading to income changes are not so important, while in reality noticed changes in income, both positive and negative, come from sources that can have strong other effects. For example, income changes due to bequests typically relate to the death of a close relative, something that has a direct effect on wellbeing. Income changes due to promotions or demotions come with many side effects, such as pride of being promoted or shame of being demoted. Similar violations of the *ceteris paribus* condition apply to nearly all sources of income changes, rendering it difficult to convincingly show causality.

As a result of these difficulties, the literature does not have a recognized 'best' estimate of a change in income on wellbeing due to a 'normal' policy change (i.e. a change in taxes, welfare, or prices of government goods or services), and has relied on other sources of income changes (for example, inheritances or lottery wins), which means that it is quite possible that the current best estimate of how much income matters for individual well-being is too low.

There are conflicting results in the (scarce) literature looking at the effects of changes in taxation on wellbeing. Akay et al. (2012) look at variation across time and space in Germany in terms of changes in payroll and income taxes, finding no significant effect at the individual level. Looking at a specific tax change (the 2008 US tax rebate), Lachowska (2017) finds relatively high effects (of about 0.01 WELLBYs per 1 per cent income rise), but the question there is whether that holds for the longer run or is due to media attention and elation. Another factor is that individuals care far more about something that is visibly

[17] A simple change would remedy this, though: to go from information at the individual level to the group level at which externalities occur. This would require a group-level analysis. The same issue of random variation still applies, but one would automatically be including externalities between individuals.

taken away from them as opposed to something that is taken away from everybody or that they did not really know they had in the first place.

Pension wealth is a good example of a source of income that many people have only limited awareness of, making them less upset if it is reduced by one £ (for example, via pension fund fees) than if they were forced to give up a £ in the street. This is because individuals do not merely care about the consumption that a £ buys, but also about whether they feel their dignity and social position is being disrespected or undermined, which is about visibility.

Individuals can care an awful lot about very small decreases in their disposable income if it is visibly taken away from them (an effect that has been shown by many laboratory experiments in the field of behavioural economics), while being unperturbed by the same change if it is much less visible to themselves or others. This means that the relevant 'wellbeing effect of income' is highly dependent on the source and visibility of the income change—an area that is not yet well researched.

The conservative approach is then to use estimates of the effect of income on wellbeing that are highly visible to people, such as changes in income they themselves report to be shocks. The importance of financial shocks is easily ten times higher than general income changes (Huang et al., 2018). By using these larger coefficients, the estimated willingness-to-pay becomes much lower and much closer to what one would find in stated-preference and revealed-preference valuation techniques. Yet, if changes in disposable income are not very visible, then the more appropriate number is the long-run relation between incomes and wellbeing. Notable here is also that the media and the political process can deliberately make changes in income more visible, such as during election campaigns where voters are reminded of the costs of policies proposed by others, which increases the relevant wellbeing effect above normal levels.

5

Applying Wellbeing Insights to Existing Policy Evaluations and Appraisals

Preview

In this chapter, we show how insights from wellbeing could complement existing policy evaluations and appraisals, using real-world case studies from government departments and agencies. Although our focus is primarily on the United Kingdom, these examples are easily generalizable to other countries. For each case study, we first summarize the current evaluation or appraisal approach, including its internal logic. We also make general remarks to give some academic and policy context. We then show how insights from wellbeing could be brought to bear on these cases. In most cases, we sketch what a wellbeing augmented cost-benefit analysis (CBA) or a fully fledged wellbeing CEA might look like.

The last case study applies a wellbeing CBA at the global level for illustrative purposes to assess two very different policy responses during the Covid-19 crisis, one being a laissez-faire, business-as-usual response to the pandemic and one being a containment and eradication response involving the kind of lockdowns and preventive measures we have seen in most countries worldwide.

To quickly summarize the seven case studies:

- Case Study 1 is a traditional CBA of a large labour market programme undertaken in Wales in which about 16,000 young people aged 16 to 18 undertook skills training during the period 2015 to 2018, with the aim to increase their chances of finding a job. Sometimes, these 16 to 18 year olds were just trained in how to apply for a job. Other times, they obtained vocational training or work experience with employers. Yet other times, they completed hybrid programmes. Our contribution is to value the additional wellbeing benefits of such job training programmes that are not in the current standard evaluation: the avoidance of spillovers of unemployment on social relationships, the health cost savings from fewer mental health problems due to unemployment, the wellbeing impacts of higher job quality, and the benefits to the tax-and-public-spending system. All these benefits relate primarily to the success of the programme in making young people more

A Handbook for Wellbeing Policy-Making: History, Theory, Measurement, Implementation, and Examples. Paul Frijters and Christian Krekel, Oxford University Press (2021). © Paul Frijters and Christian Krekel.
DOI: 10.1093/oso/9780192896803.003.0005

employable than otherwise, so a wellbeing lens fits closely to the existing object of the programme but changes the calculation considerably.

- Case Study 2 is a CBA of the Human Henge project in which a group of people who suffer from mental ill health were taught about Stonehenge and other local historical sites. They were given on-site seminars and participated in group activities such as singing, making art, and walking. These were meant to engage these individuals in a participatory way with heritage as a link to a common past and ancestry, thereby improving their mental health. We conduct a wellbeing CEA, summing up the wellbeing benefits and relating them with the costs of the programme. We also make comparisons with other programmes that have similar elements.
- Case Study 3 is the evaluation of the City of Culture initiative in the United Kingdom, in which Kingston upon Hull became City of Culture and had a whole year of festivals and various artistic activities in schools and museums, which generated a lot of positive media coverage locally. We conduct a wellbeing CEA and comment on where we expect the key wellbeing benefits, which were not already in the evaluation, arose.
- Case Study 4 is a research study commissioned by the Department of Transport in the United Kingdom on commuting, conducted by the University of the West of England. The study covers 40,000 respondents in the UK Household Longitudinal Survey (Understanding Society) and looks at how changes in commuting affect individual and family life. In their most restrictive specifications, the authors do not find an effect of commuting on life satisfaction. We discuss the complicated macro-socio-economic issues that arise when attempting to fully value commuting and infrastructure investments into less commuting. We also illustrate how one would value commuting from a wellbeing perspective if one was to take lost taxes and possible spillovers between family members into account.
- Case Study 5 is about the London-Heathrow runway extension appraisal carried out by the Airports Commission. We show how one could augment this traditional CBA with more insights from the wellbeing literature. We also use this case study to illustrate how one could transition between the existing CBAs and a complete wellbeing evaluation. The case study touches on many of the differences between existing CBAs and how one would look at projects from a wellbeing lens, with a particular focus on consumption externalities.
- Case Study 6 is a survey into the usefulness of an additional public employment service in the United Kingdom (called Fit for Work) which targeted individuals who were absent from their primary job for extended periods due to health or caring issues. The aim of the service was to bring people back to work as early and smoothly as possible. We make suggestions on how to measure wellbeing and how to restructure such surveys as well as other methods for evaluating the effectiveness of public services.

- Case Study 7 deals with the Covid-19 pandemic. We conduct a simple, illustrative wellbeing CBA at a global level for two policy responses, one being a laissez-faire, business-as-usual scenario and one being a containment and eradication scenario. We study, from a wellbeing perspective, which of these two policy options leads to lower losses in wellbeing at the global level and also ask how deadly a virus must be to justify radical containment and eradication policies.

We should remind ourselves of some of the key differences between traditional CBA and wellbeing cost-benefit or wellbeing CEA, as outlined extensively in chapters 3 and 4:

- The most appropriate monetary value of wellbeing in wellbeing CEA is the opportunity cost of public money and thus the marginal cost of producing more wellbeing. In the United Kingdom, spending by the National Health Service (NHS) is a suggested initial anchor for this, implying a monetary value of a WELLBY of about £2,500. In contrast, in standard CBA, the typical monetary value used is the willingness of individuals to pay for an increase in their own wellbeing when such a payment is highly visible. An appropriate number can be derived from an individual's willingness to pay for health improvements or reduced risks of death, which amounts to about £9,000 per WELLBY. Thus, within standard CBA one would value items that demonstrably increase wellbeing higher than in wellbeing CEA, by a ratio of about four to one, which is similar to the difference between the marginal social production costs of QALYs (about £15,000, cf. Claxton et al., 2015; Lomas et al., 2019; see also Department of Health and Department of Education, 2017) and the actual value used by many government departments and agencies in the United Kingdom (about £60,000, cf. HMT Green Book, 2018, page 73; Glover and Henderson, 2010; see also Department of Health and Department of Education, 2017). There is, therefore, a four-to-one difference between the value of money when spent optimally by the state bureaucracy versus the value of money when spent by individuals.
- By using wellbeing as the primary outcome through which non-monetary life circumstances such as health or social relationships are valued, the monetary value of physical health decreases compared to the current practice of monetarily valuing a QALY at about £60,000. Instead, the monetary value of improved health in terms of one QALY more of health is worth about 2.5 times the monetary value of a WELLBY,[1] i.e. about £2,500 × 2.5 = £6,250 for wellbeing CEAs and about £9,000 × 2.5 = £22,500 for traditional CBAs. The

[1] The average life satisfaction of a person in perfect health (i.e. a QALY of one) is about 2.5 points higher than the average life satisfaction of a person with a QALY of zero (Huang et al., 2018).

value of an additional year of life in good health is worth six WELLBYs, i.e. about £2,500 × 6 = £15,000 for wellbeing CEAs and £9,000 × 6 = £54,000 for traditional CBAs.

- In wellbeing CEA, public spending is typically taken to have higher wellbeing effects than private spending because many forms of private spending are subject to private consumption externalities. By contrast, many forms of government spending, for example by the welfare state, have not been found to have such externalities as they are available to everyone and their main role is to alleviate anxieties about health, wealth, and safety. Thus, wellbeing CEA breaks the symmetry between private and public expenditure in terms of social value. On the other hand, it enforces symmetry on the value of wellbeing changes arising from various sources, independent of any differences in the willingness to pay of individuals.

We now turn to our case studies. In each, case study, we attempt to answer three questions:

1. Taking the basic methodology and way of thinking as given, what could more insights from the wellbeing literature add?
2. If we were to go towards a wellbeing CBA or CEA, what would the policy evaluation or appraisal look like then? What would change?
3. If applicable: what is our best-guess in terms of cost-per-WELLBY in each case study?

Case Study 1: A Youth Traineeship Programme

We first look at the evaluation of a youth traineeship programme—the Welsh Government's Traineeships programme between 2015 and 2019—conducted by the Learning and Work Institute and Wavehill Research. Our evaluation is based on the 154-page report of that programme, which we use to give a brief overview. We refer the interested reader to this report for additional details and references.[2]

The youth traineeship programme had various predecessors that were merged into this programme, including the Work-Based Learning programme that operated in 2011 and 2015 which was set up after the Global Financial Crisis, when there were many young people with NEET (not in education, employment, or training) status. About 15 per cent of the 16 to 24 year olds in Wales had this status during this period, slightly more than in earlier periods, and about one to

[2] The full evaluation report can be found at: https://gov.wales/sites/default/files/statistics-and-research/2019-06/evaluation-of-the-traineeships-programme-2015-2019.pdf.

1.5 percentage points above the UK national average.[3,4,5] The programme consisted of a variety of sub-programmes, ranging from job-finding services to vocational-type qualifications, work-placements, and various combinations of learning and working.

The target population of the programme were young people aged 16 to 18 who were referred to the programme by Careers Wales, a government job-intermediary organization that operates at careers offices and partner premises throughout Wales, in schools, and online. To get admitted, one required a written referral on or before the traineeship start date. All referrals entering a traineeship—these were called Engagement Traineeships—had to undertake an initial diagnostic assessment of skills.

The youth traineeship programme had an intake of 15,917 trainees from January 2014 to December 2018. Twelve months after entry, about 50 per cent of the intake obtained a qualification, 31 per cent were in employment, 14 per cent were in further education, and 22 per cent remained unemployed.

The conclusion of the evaluation report, mainly based on *ex post* interviews with employers, trainees, and officials running the programme, was that the programme managed to give young people who had NEET status additional basic education (such as numeracy and literacy) and soft skills, such as confidence, self-management, and motivation. Yet, the programme did not measure those skills, which means an alternative way to evaluate the programme in future editions would be to measure these skills before and after, both for the participants and for a wider control group.[6] We know from the large literature on the life-long effects of education on income that many skills have long-term effects, meaning that short-term improvements in skills likely reflect long-term outcomes as well, thus offering a simple avenue for future evaluations.

The traditional CBA of the evaluation report is based on an assessment of the counterfactual question—what would have happened to the same people if they

[3] For more information, see https://gov.wales/young-people-not-education-employment-or-training-neet.

[4] The harmonized definition used to define the UK Annual Population Survey NEET estimates allows for some comparison across UK countries and English regions. However, there are differences, for example: the use of the Labour Force Survey or the Annual Population Survey, the use of different age groups, the use of academic age versus actual age, or differences in adjustment methodology used in apportioning missing values, or differences in education systems across the United Kingdom. As such, comparisons of figures of youth with NEET status across the United Kingdom should be taken with caution.

[5] Up to two percentage points higher each year for 16 to 18 year olds and one to four percentage points higher for 19 to 24 year olds.

[6] An advantage of direct measurement of skills is that one would not have to measure other outcomes into the far future as one could rely on the large literature that relates skills to later-life outcomes. A disadvantage is that it involves lengthier interviews and diagnostic assessments with both a representative sample of those in the programme as well as a sufficiently large control group, both of which need to be tracked over the period of the programme. To get some confirmation of additional skills, the programme asked the trainees afterwards whether their skills had improved (see Figure 11 on page 87 of the evaluation report).

had not participated in this programme. This is a standard quasi-experimental approach. We should note that it is inherently tricky to find a counterfactual to a programme that is meant to cover a whole population with particular difficulties (the population of 16 to 18 year olds who have NEET status). Any group that may lend itself as a potential comparison will, by definition, be different from the treatment group in at least some aspects. So taking the best control group one can find outside of the target population can only be a second-best compared to a control group one would have obtained when using a clear-cut randomized controlled trial. This, however, is often not politically feasible.

In fact, to truly get a clean estimate of what such wide coverage programmes can add, one would need either a whole region which, for some random reason, did not participate in the programme or else have some random variation in participation across individuals. Well-known options include the happenstance where a programme was introduced very suddenly, allowing researchers to compare just-before with just-after outcomes. Also possible, yet more difficult, is to find an otherwise identical region where such a programme did not operate. Often the best way would be some kind of randomization whereby some individuals got entry into the programme and some did not for somewhat accidental reasons (such as a postcode lottery, staggered introduction, or because of some administrative reason like limited capacity so that not everyone could be served at the time.)

The route the evaluation of this youth traineeship programme took was to leverage the Longitudinal Education Outcomes (LEO) dataset, existing administrative data that included the 16 to 18 year old population in Wales. From LEO, the study took individuals who had similar characteristics (age, gender, education, and residence), and matched them to the participants in the traineeship programme. The key criterion for matching was that the counterfactual control group had to have only Level 1 or entry-level education, similar to that of the trainee group.[7]

The evaluation report found that trainees had about thirty-four days more employment than the control group during the first twelve months and sixty-two days more in the second twelve months after entry. That result drove the higher earnings and the vast bulk of the reported benefits to this programme, such that even in their most pessimistic scenario the calculated economic benefits are at least twice as high as the calculated costs within three years of entry. These outcomes are strong. To have about three months of additional employment

[7] A suggestion for future evaluations is to leverage the Careers Wales database that assesses the eligibility of people applying, exploiting that some applicants who fall just below the cut-off for particular programmes would make a good counterfactual control group for those who just make the cut-off. Another suggestion is to look at a broader range of outcomes, including socio-emotional skills.

every year implies a huge benefit of this programme, both to individuals and the exchequer.

Card et al. (2018) provide a perspective on the benefits of active labour market programmes including job search, vocational education, or traineeships. The authors evaluated over two hundred programmes in mostly developed countries, concluding that:

> We conclude that: (1) average impacts are close to zero in the short run, but become more positive 2–3 years after completion of the program; (2) the time profile of impacts varies by type of program, with larger average gains for programs that emphasize human capital accumulation; (3) there is systematic heterogeneity across participant groups, with larger impacts for females and participants who enter from long-term unemployment; (4) active labor market programs are more likely to show positive impacts in a recession.

Much of this fits with the evaluation of the youth traineeship programme in this case study, which focuses on skills acquisition and also shows strengthened effects over time. The programme follows advice by Card et al. (2018), for example, by focusing on getting individuals into jobs as soon as possible and by focusing on getting them into non-public jobs. Indeed, Card et al. (2018) find that programmes focusing on both education and employment are more successful at 'activating' young people who have NEET status. However, they also report that it is normal for any programme to have effects of only about 1 per cent to 3 per cent on employment in the first year, climbing to up to 10 per cent in subsequent years, with the average training programme having effects of about 7 per cent in the long run.

In comparison, the youth traineeship programme in Wales had an effect of about 13 per cent in the first twelve months (based on the rule of thumb that a normal full-time UK working year has about 240 days), climbing to about 25 per cent in the second year. That makes this youth traineeship programme look like one of the most successful programmes in the world in terms of employment, which puts extra pressure on the question whether the matched control group is a good comparison group.

Although Card et al. (2018) do find that there is little difference in results for experimental and non-experimental studies, they included only studies published in high-ranked journals, implying that there is a high bar to be met by included non-experimental studies, leaving aside issues of publication bias.[8]

[8] A technical point to note is that the authors run out of degrees of freedom when looking at the importance of experimental design, which forces them to pool the short and longer-term effects of programmes, thus pooling the stronger short-term effects of experimental studies with their weaker longer-term effects, yielding the basic finding that non-experimental studies do have larger effects,

The authors also warn of high variation in difficulties faced by young people who have NEET status, implying that the choice of the counterfactual really matters. Yet, even if one substituted the reported results of this youth traineeship programme with medium-sized estimates of equivalent programmes reported by Card et al. (2018), the programme would look cost-effective.

Traditional CBA versus Wellbeing-augmented CBA

The evaluation uses matched Longitudinal Education Outcomes (LEO) data to calculate costs and benefits of the programme to participants, both of which cannot be known with certainty: costs for the control group, for example, were taken from Wales Audit Office (WAO) calculations for entry-level training costs for Further Education. Additionally, not all elements of the programme are easy to cost precisely, such as the contribution to costs of Careers Wales or the precise economic costs of the trainee programmes which will have involved invested time by private employers. Also, the sheer complexity of the programme, with its mix of interventions and various participants leaving the programme prematurely (often for education or a job), makes it a difficult programme to ascertain costs and benefits for. As a result, we follow the evaluation report closely by talking in general terms.

The main thing to say from a wellbeing perspective is that the big-ticket wellbeing item in this regard is employment versus unemployment, with a year in unemployment costing about one WELLBY relative to being in full employment (see chapters 2 and 3). Relatedly, mental health problems associated with unemployment and with fear of future unemployment have an unknown but probably quite large additional negative effect on those close to participants (see Clark et al. (2018), for example), including family, friends, and whole neighbourhoods, particularly if a lack of regular employment perspectives lead to crime. A wellbeing-augmented CBA of the same programme would, therefore, largely focus on whether or not the programme manages to make the participants employable or employed. Other aspects would be knock-on considerations, such as the negative effects of being out of work on social relationships. So just like the evaluation report, a wellbeing-augmented CBA or a fully fledged wellbeing CEA would put most emphasis on knowing whether the programme helped individuals out of unemployment and into employment, or at least into a gainful activity of some sort, which could include education, volunteering, or home-making. Unemployment is the main thing to avoid here from a wellbeing perspective.

but with such high standard deviations that this is no longer statistically significant (though economically very significant).

Unfortunately, the report does not *actually* say how less likely participants in the programme were to be unemployed. However, it does compare the length of time matched individuals in the treatment and counterfactual control group are in receipt of welfare benefits as a proxy for unemployment.

Some remarks on the findings in the evaluation report:

1. In a nutshell, the programme is a form of additional education for a treatment group that would otherwise not receive it, leading to higher employability.
2. The programme finds an effect of about 0.1 jobs (i.e. a percentage point increase of about 10 per cent of finding a new job) in the first year, increasing to about 0.2 jobs in the second year and ensuing years. The individual-level value of these employment effects is, therefore, in the order of £1,800 per year (in terms of willingness to pay in the second year). If one assumes an effect such as this over many years, the discounted benefit becomes large compared to the up-front public cost.
3. The evaluation also concerns the uptake of the Welsh language. We do not comment on this language aspect of the programme as it is separate from the issue of generic interest across the world: whether this type of programme increases the likelihood of job finding and earnings.

We first look at a basic CBA of the programme, and then see what a wellbeing-augmented CBA, which takes into account specific insights from the wellbeing literature, could look like. Finally, we conduct a wellbeing CEA, where we make some strong assumptions, largely for illustrative purposes. Our aim is to compare these approaches so as to illustrate what drives the differences between them.

For each of the three approaches, we assume three distinct time periods (year 1, year 2, and year 3) which differ regarding costs and benefits. Benefits in terms of increased total individual income per participant are taken from the impact evaluation report. Programme costs per participant (£1,145) are calculated as net present value of costs (£18,218,364) divided by number of participants (15,917). Both figures are taken from the evaluation report (table 3 on page 81 and table 8 on page 98, respectively).

Traditional CBA

Table 5.1 shows the traditional CBA: the programme increases total individual income per participant in the first period, and even more so, in periods two and three.

The increase in individual income can be further subdivided into higher personal consumption (which is, assuming a tax rate of a maximum of 20 per cent for

Table 5.1 Traditional CBA

Traditional Cost-Benefit Analysis				
Period	**1**	**2**	**3**	**Combined total**
Increased total individual income per person	642	1,811	1,811	4,264
Higher personal consumption	514	1,449	1,449	3,411
Higher taxes	128	362	362	**853**
Crime cost savings	40	80	80	**200**
Healthcare cost savings	9	17	17	**43**
Programme costs per participant				**1,145**
Benefits minus costs				**3,362**

Note: For simplicity, the discount rate used here is 0 per cent.
Source: Own calculations.

lower incomes, about 80 per cent) and higher taxation (about 20 per cent). We note that this is likely to be an overestimate of the proportion of earned income actually going into higher personal consumption and an underestimate of the proportion of earned income flowing back to the state because it misses reductions in welfare payments. These can include unemployment benefits, housing benefits, reduced council tax, and other subsidies that are means-tested and thus decrease as earnings increase.

Note that one would ideally want to have estimates on the effective marginal tax rates (EMTRs) of participants in this programme to ascertain how much of an additional £ of earnings reduce various welfare benefits. For example, it is known from the poverty-trap literature that EMTRs can be high when several welfare payments reduce at the same time as earnings increase. EMTRs are particularly large in the United Kingdom for low-income families with two adults, where they go up to almost 73 per cent.[9] As EMTRs depend strongly on family structure, we cannot easily guess what the average would be for this group of trainees without more detailed calculations, although we suspect average EMTRs to be at least 50 per cent. Nevertheless, as a highly conservative estimate, we go with a 20 per cent income tax rate. This does not actually matter for traditional CBA, but it does matter for cost-effectiveness and the exchequer.

We also assume other benefits to the public purse: a higher rate of job finding of 10 per cent in the first and 20 per cent in the second and third periods, on average, yields cost savings in the areas of healthcare and crime. Public Health England's

[9] For example, see the discussion in Williams (2019), which is heavily based on updated 2015 EMTR calculations by the OECD (Beighton et al., 2018).

Return on Investment Tool[10] (PHE, 2018) suggests that bringing a person back to work yields healthcare cost savings of about £85 and crime cost savings of about £400.

Adding up the benefits (higher personal consumption and higher taxation) and cost savings in the areas of healthcare and crime while subtracting programme costs per participant yields a total benefit of the programme of £3,362 under traditional CBA.

Wellbeing-augmented CBA

Table 5.2 shows a wellbeing-augmented CBA. This type of analysis builds on the traditional CBA but takes it one step further, leveraging the insights from the wellbeing literature to enrich both the benefits and the costs sides.

In our case, we start by recognizing that, in the wellbeing literature, unemployment has a detrimental impact on life satisfaction that goes over and beyond the negative effect of income loss alone. Keeping income constant in a regression analysis framework, unemployment has been shown to reduce life satisfaction in the United Kingdom by about 0.46 points on a 0-to-10 scale (see chapter 2). Noting that the training programme increases the likelihood of finding a job by

Table 5.2 Wellbeing-augmented CBA

Wellbeing-Augmented Cost-Benefit Analysis				
Period	**1**	**2**	**3**	**Combined total**
Increased total individual income per person	642	1,811	1,811	4,264
Higher personal consumption	514	1,449	1,449	**3,411**
Higher taxes	128	362	362	**853**
LS effect of unemployment	−0.4600	−0.4600	−0.4600	
LS effect of reduced unemployment	0.0460	0.0920	0.0920	
WTP for reduced unemployed	414	828	828	2,070
Accounting for social multiplier				***4,140***
Crime cost savings	40	80	80	**200**
Healthcare cost savings	9	17	17	**43**
Programme costs per participant				**1,145**
Benefits minus costs				**7,502**

Note: For simplicity, the discount rate used here is 0 per cent.

Source: Own calculations.

[10] For further information see: https://cvd-prevention.shef.ac.uk/.

about 10 per cent in the first and by about 20 per cent in the second and third years, on average. Assuming the additional employment replaces unemployment, we can thus add 0.046 life-satisfaction points in the first and 0.092 in the second and third year to the benefits of the programme. We then convert these life-satisfaction gains from less unemployment by using our estimate for the individual willingness-to-pay for a WELLBY of £9,000, which yields an additional, monetized benefit of reduced unemployment due to programme participation of about £2,070.

A further insight from the wellbeing literature is that there exist spillovers from individuals whose wellbeing changes to their family and friends, especially for negative life shocks. Clark et al. (2018) suggest a multiplier of about two, which then doubles monetized benefits of reduced unemployment to about £4,140.

Keeping everything else as in the traditional CBA, incorporating these simple insights from the wellbeing literature increases the total benefit to £7,502. In other words, it more than doubles the original total benefit which considers only higher personal consumption as the individual benefit of programme participation.

Wellbeing CEA

Table 5.3 shows a fully fledged wellbeing CEA. Different from the previous analyses, it takes an alternative angle: it divides the sum of wellbeing benefits of the programme by its net public costs.

To arrive at the numerator, i.e. the sum of wellbeing benefits, we start by noting that log annual net household income is typically found to increase life satisfaction in the United Kingdom, measured on a 0-to-10 scale, by about 0.4 points. In other words, a 1 per cent change in average annual net household income raises life satisfaction by 0.004 points—a rather small effect. We assume that the average annual net household income of low-income households in Wales is about £15,000. We use these figures to calculate the life-satisfaction effects of higher personal consumption due to programme participation in each period, which we then sum up after applying an Easterlin Discount of 75 per cent to account for negative private consumption externalities between individuals.

The life-satisfaction effects of reduced unemployment in each period remain as before in the wellbeing-augmented CBA. However, unlike in the wellbeing-augmented CBA, we do not monetize any life-satisfaction effects, either for higher personal consumption or for reduced unemployment. This is a key difference: wellbeing CEA does not rely on translating wellbeing benefits into a monetary unit of account. This makes far fewer assumptions than are typically required during such translations.

Table 5.3 Wellbeing CEA

Wellbeing Cost-Effectiveness Analysis				
Period	**1**	**2**	**3**	**Combined total**
Increased total individual income per person	642	1,811	1,811	4,264
Higher personal consumption	514	1,449	1,449	3,411
LS effect of log annual household income	*0.4000*	*0.4000*	*0.4000*	
LS effect of higher consumption	*0.0137*	*0.0386*	*0.0386*	
Easterlin discounted LS effect of higher consumption	*0.0034*	*0.0097*	*0.0097*	*0.0227*
LS effect of unemployment	*−0.4600*	*−0.4600*	*−0.4600*	
LS effect of reduced unemployment	*0.0460*	*0.0920*	*0.0920*	*0.2300*
Accounting for social multiplier				*0.4600*
Crime cost savings	40	80	80	200
Healthcare cost savings	9	17	17	43
Higher taxes	128	362	362	853
Programme costs per participant				1,145
Net public costs				49
WELLBY per pound of net public costs				0.009795

Note: For simplicity, the discount rate used here is 0 per cent.
Source: Own calculations.

As before, we note that programme participation brings with it cost savings in the areas of healthcare and crime as well as higher taxation, which, when subtracted from the programme costs per participant, yield a net public costs of £49, close to zero. We note that if we use EMTRs instead of income tax rates as the estimate for how much the exchequer receives from the additional earned income, then the total public costs per person would almost certainly be negative (because the EMTRs are probably about 50 per cent, versus an additional marginal tax rate of about 30 per cent).

The resulting wellbeing cost-effectiveness ratio is the sum of wellbeing benefits (Easterlin Discounted life-satisfaction effects of higher private consumption plus life-satisfaction effects of reduced unemployment misery on individuals and their social surroundings) divided by net public costs. It is 0.0096, and thus easily passes the suggested cost-effectiveness threshold of 0.0004 (1/2,500) derived from the NHS and its monetary valuation of a QALY. At a cost per WELLBY of a little over £100, the youth traineeship programme thus turns out to be highly cost-effective.

Summary

Traditional CBA, wellbeing-augmented CBA, and wellbeing CEA all suggest that the youth traineeship programme in Wales was worth the costs. Benefits are already visible in the traditional CBA which considers only higher personal consumption and taxes as benefits. Augmenting this traditional analysis with insights from the wellbeing literature, in particular on the detrimental effect of unemployment on individuals and their families and friends above and beyond income losses, suggests that adding the non-monetary benefits of reduced unemployment due to programme participation more than doubles the benefits of the programme. This is highly dependent on just how much unemployment the programme prevented though, which is still somewhat uncertain because of the lack of a randomized controlled trial.

It is important to note that moving to a fully fledged wellbeing CEA leads us to the same conclusion: the programme was worth the costs. However, the mechanisms for why it was worth the costs are different. Under wellbeing CEA, it is much less about higher personal consumption. Even the small beneficial wellbeing benefit of more personal income is largely lost due to negative status effects in others (recall that the Easterlin Discount is 75 per cent). Rather, it is about the reduced hardship of unemployment for the affected individual and their social surroundings.

This is then also the clear message for future evaluations of this type of programme: the wellbeing effects are dominated by employment versus unemployment and by what happens to those close to the one affected, such as family and friends.

Case Study 2: Human Henge

We next discuss the Human Henge project, a UK pilot into the efficacy of using historic landscapes for improving mental health outcomes. It is based on the notion that connection with historic landscapes could play a vital role in recovery from mental illness, which is an active research area. The project was based primarily at Stonehenge, hence the name. It was aimed at engaging people from Wiltshire living on low incomes and with long-term mental health conditions to 'explore the ancient landscapes of Stonehenge in creative ways that are unfamiliar yet safe, rejuvenating, and revitalising'.

The original impact evaluation of this project simultaneously evaluated Human Henge Stonehenge and a twin project—Human Henge Avebury—to increase sample size. Both projects had the same background and motivation as well as similar participants and treatments. The impact evaluation period was from September 2016 to December 2018.

The Intervention

The Human Henge project involved ten weekly, three-hour long, on-site sessions on Friday mornings. They included workshops led by co-facilitators, in particular a mental health professional and an archaeologist, on various topics related to the historic landscape. Each workshop incorporated an on-site walk that included singing, dancing, lectures, art activities, and other activities oriented towards actively engaging participants in the Neolithic site. There were elements of meditation and sensory experiences, somewhat reminiscent of mindfulness practices. The programme also involved a night-time walk and an early-morning ceremony designed by participants themselves. This was well received: due to popular demand by participants, three additional get-togethers were organized (the last event took place in March 2019), including walks and picnics. Sessions were delivered to participants free of cost and were clearly structured.

Mechanisms through which this treatment may bring about positive mental health outcomes are threefold: first, there is a growing evidence base on mindfulness interventions, in part impact-evaluated using randomized controlled trials (Bohlmeijer et al., 2010; Gu et al., 2015). It shows that, for example, mindfulness-based cognitive therapy, when complementing treatment-as-usual, can reduce both short-term and longer-term depressive symptoms, reduce rates of relapse into depression (especially for patients with long-term depressive symptoms), and improve overall quality of life (Godfrin and van Heeringen, 2010).

Second, psychological self-determination theory articulates the fundamental human needs of autonomy, relatedness, and competence (Ryan and Deci, 2000). Treatment tried to cater to these needs: it attempted to build autonomy by helping participants discover themselves in relation to a historic landscape in their local environment; it attempted to build relatedness by fostering friendship, connection, and social trust within the gathering of similar people in their local community; and it attempted to build competence by helping participants experience for themselves how small behavioural changes to their daily routines could make large differences to their mental health.

There is evidence from randomized controlled trials that treatment rooted in psychological self-determination theory can have strong positive impacts on mental wellbeing and pro-sociality (see Krekel et al., 2020, for example). The original impact evaluation provides evidence for the connectedness pathway: for example, participants from the second group created a closed Facebook group that continued to be in use after the intervention ended.

Finally, there is the historic landscape itself which may bring about positive mental health outcomes, over and beyond the other two mechanisms, in two ways: first, a central element of the programme is that participants spend time and are physically active in nature. There is, for example, evidence that exposure to greenery has positive impacts on wellbeing, by raising physical and mental health and by improving overall life satisfaction (White et al., 2013; Alcock et al., 2014; Bertram and Rehdanz, 2015; Krekel et al., 2016). These impacts, however, are typically rather small and become quantitatively relevant only when aggregated across many individuals. Beyond such nature-related effects, the specific site itself, combined with the narratives about its previous purposes, may have positive placebo-type impacts on wellbeing.

In sum, the treatment targeted disadvantaged individuals with long-term mental health conditions. It had an educational and a therapeutic component. Both were high quality: participants were granted exclusive access to the Stonehenge circle as well as interaction with professionals and volunteers.

In what follows, we focus on the therapeutic component of the programme, which was the focus of the (quantitative) original impact evaluation.

Costs

Table 5.4 lists the costs of the programme, separately for Human Henge Stonehenge (column 1) and Human Henge Avebury (column 2). The third column lists the average costs per category.

Note that these costs do not include allocated fixed costs for overheads overheads, and neither allocated fixed costs for the maintenance of the historic site itself.

Original Impact Evaluation

The original impact evaluation is described in Heaslip and Darvill (2017) and Drysdale (2018). We base our wellbeing CEA on these documents. Wherever suitable, additional sources are used to complement the analysis.

Participants

For the original Human Henge Stonehenge impact evaluation, thirty-two participants were recruited, of which twenty-three attended the programme as

Table 5.4 Cash and non-cash costs of Human Henge project

	Human Henge Stonehenge, £	Human Henge Avebury, £	Average, £
Cash	18,473	6,275	12,374
Non-cash	35,304	17,608	26,456
Total	53,777	23,883	38,830

Source: Obtained from personal communication with Historic England.

committed participants (defined as those attending at least half of the sessions, and in reality, more than eight). They were divided into two groups, whereby the first group received treatment in autumn 2016 and the second in spring 2017. Each group itself had about as many males as females. The age range of participants was from 26 to 77, with a mean age of 48.

Three of the initial twenty-three participants dropped out before the end of the programme due to deteriorating mental health and one dropped out due to a new job, with presumably no deteriorating mental health. Given the seriousness of mental health issues of some of the participants, a mental-health-related drop-out rate of 3/23 = 0.13 (13 per cent) is not unusual (and maybe even small). Twelve of the remaining nineteen participants were available for a follow-up interview one year after the programme had ended.

It should be noted that participation in the programme was voluntary: potential participants were all clients of a charity for people living with mental health challenges. They were screened by the charity against eligibility criteria for community support and complex needs services for people aged 18 and above in Wiltshire. These complex needs could include, for example, temporary admission to a mental health hospital or severe mental illness. Human Henge itself was not advertised as a mental health service.

Data and Methods

Data collection, which was survey based, occurred at baseline (week 1 of the programme), midline (week 5), and endline (week 10). The follow-up survey was distributed in week 62, one year after the programme had ended.

Besides demographics and questions about the programme itself, the primary outcome to measure mental health improvements was the seven-item five-point Short Warwick-Edinburgh Mental Well-being Scale (WEMWBS), which is similar to other wellbeing scales.[11]

It should be noted that the impact evaluation design was a simple before-and-after comparison of participants, not a randomized controlled trial. Of course, large trials are expensive, but they do exist for mental health, and those could be taken as comparators in terms of value for money.

Findings

The original impact evaluation, which compares outcomes recorded before the intervention with those recorded after, finds that treatment has a positive impact on mental health and wellbeing in the short run. Although there is some indication regarding long-run impacts, as Drysdale (2018) describes, it is difficult to evaluate these given the small sample size, suggesting the need for a study with a

[11] For more information, see the figure on page 23 of Stewart-Brown and Janmohamed (2008) and Tennant et al. (2007).

larger sample size. Thus, to say something sensible about long-run impacts, we have to rely on rules of thumb on wellbeing that originate from larger intervention studies. We know, for example, that cognitive-behavioural-therapy-type mental skills are quite persistent (see chapter 3) whilst community-building needs to be sustained to have a long-run impact (see chapter 2 and the case study on the UK City of Culture later in this chapter). We know festivity-type effects are short lived, often only lasting weeks or months (see chapter 3 and again the case study on the UK City of Culture).

A limitation of the original impact evaluation by Drysdale (2018) is that the document makes little reference to effect sizes. Heaslip and Darvill (2017) show figures but collapse the items of the WEMWBS from five to three points, showing only percentages per category. The original scale has seven items with five points each, which would yield a summary score between 7 and 35 for each participant in the programme, whereby higher scores indicate higher positive mental wellbeing. Changes in the summary score between before and after the programme would yield the individual mental wellbeing impact of the programme, or when averaged across all participants, the average impact of the programme. We are, however, able to restore this summary score to some extent.

Tables 3 to 9 in Heaslip and Darvill (2017) show the share of responses in percentages for each of the (collapsed) categories of the WEMWBS. We calculate the percentage point difference between baseline and endline, take the absolute value, and then calculate the average percentage point difference. As almost all categories 'move in the right direction', the resulting absolute average percentage point difference between baseline and endline of 12.6 suggests an improvement in mental wellbeing between before and after the programme.[12]

To translate this absolute average percentage point difference into an actual level difference, we assume that, for each item, categories take the values 1 for category one (the lowest), 2 for category two (the middle), and 3 for category three (the highest). Note that percentage shares do not sum up to 100 due to missing values, and that the sum at baseline is, on average, 96 and at endline, 83—a thirteen percentage point difference. We adjust the percentage shares at endline by adding $13/3 = 4.3$ percentage points to each category. This gives us average levels at baseline and endline of, respectively, 12.5 and 14.1. The level difference is, therefore, 1.6. In other words, treatment shifted participants from, on average, 12.5 at baseline to, on average, 14.1 at endline on a 7-to-21 scale. Adjusting this scale to the original WEMWBS (which goes from 7 to 35) gives us a level difference of $1.6 \times (35/21) = 2.7$.

[12] The midline data were still being collected at the moment of writing and so could not be used for this evaluation.

We choose a conversion rate dLS/dWEMWBS between life satisfaction (LS), measured on a 0-to-10 scale, and the WEMWBS of 0.25 (see the conversion tables in chapter 3 or Layard, 2016). This implies that, for a 1-unit change in WEMWBS, LS increases by 0.25. Accordingly, the corresponding value for life satisfaction is $0.25 \times 2.7 = 0.68$.

In other words, Human Henge improved the life satisfaction of participants by 0.68 points on a 0-to-10 scale, a large but not unrealistic effect. By comparison, the 'Exploring What Matters' course by Action for Happiness, which is a local community intervention that is group-based and also rooted in psychological self-determination theory, improved the life satisfaction of participants by an entire point (Krekel et al., 2020).

Preliminary Discussion

There is some reason to believe that the estimated effect of Human Henge is an upper bound of its true effect. There has been selective attrition, with some participants dropping out of the programme due to a deterioration of mental health, leaving the relatively healthier in the sample. This yields upward bias. Answers may also have been subject to social desirability bias, with participants being inclined to answer in a more positive manner because it might be seen as impolite to do otherwise. This is difficult to verify *ex post*. It would also lead to upward bias.

The authors of the original impact evaluation add the caveat that the sample size is small. Estimates should therefore be interpreted with caution. Moreover, the impact-evaluation design is based on a simple before-and-after comparison without a proper control group (although during a relatively short period of time) rather than a randomized controlled trial. This implies that causality is less certain. Besides such issues of internal validity, there is also the question of external validity, and in particular, whether the estimated effects would translate from Stonehenge and Avebury to other historic landscapes, if one were to replicate the programme elsewhere.

Although the focus of this initial trial was not on achieving cost-effectiveness but to draw attention to the opportunities to use historic landscapes for improving mental health and wellbeing, the question naturally arises how cost-effective the trial was. To answer this question, we now conduct a wellbeing CEA.

Wellbeing CEA

We start by noting that treatment improves life satisfaction by 0.68 points on a scale from 0-to-10, and that treatment was given to twenty-three participants taken to be committed. This is a conservative approach: some of the early dropouts surely must have had at least some life-satisfaction benefits, although there were also some who dropped out because their health worsened. Further, we assume that treatment lasts one year: evidence for long-run impacts is weak and inconclusive. This is a conservative approach which seems justified as the estimated effect is likely to be biased upwards due to, amongst others, selective attrition and social desirability bias.

Summing up the life-satisfaction benefits over 20 participants yields a total life-satisfaction benefit of $0.68 \times 20 = 13.6$. The total costs of the mental health part of the Human Henge project was £38,830. This gives us a wellbeing cost-effectiveness ratio of 13.6/38,830 = 0.00029. It falls a bit short of the benchmark ratio of 1/2,500 = 0.0004.[13] Put equivalently, the resulting cost-per-WELLBY is £38,830/13.6 = £2,855.

This is clearly higher than the cost-per-WELLBY of the NHS IAPT scheme, which is probably cost-saving, but even at an extremely conservative estimate has a cost-per-WELLBY of £650/0.4 = £1,625, cf. chapter 3. Thus, in terms of other social investments in wellbeing via mental health improvements, the Human Henge project looks somewhat expensive.

One could argue this is a borderline case though. As discussed above, the obtained wellbeing cost-effectiveness ratio is a conservative lower bound: if we were to assume that all initial participants experienced a life-satisfaction improvement of 0.68 (lasting for one year), the resulting threshold would be just above 0.0004. In this case, Human Henge would be wellbeing cost-effective. Likewise, if all final participants had permanent improvements of about 0.5, the programme would be very cost-effective within just three years. One could similarly argue there would be economies of scale to wider implementation. If the participants were partnered, we could assume that there are intra-household wellbeing spillovers. In fact, Mervin and Frijters (2014) estimate that such spillovers are of the order of 15 per cent. If there were also children, the resulting threshold would be close to 0.0004.

Related, the original impact evaluation does not study the effects of the treatment on volunteers leading the workshops. There is, however, an established literature documenting that volunteering (Meier and Stutzer, 2008), or pro-social action more generally (Dunn et al., 2008), can bring about positive wellbeing benefits. To the extent that volunteers, practitioners, or even partners in participating organizations may have profited from delivering the treatment, their wellbeing benefits should be counted. Since they do not suffer from the same mental health issues as the participants in the trial, to account for their wellbeing benefits, a broader measure of wellbeing should be used, ideally life satisfaction.

[13] The wellbeing cost-effectiveness threshold is taken from the Department of Health estimate that the NHS buys an additional year in good health for £15,000 (Claxton et al., 2015; Lomas et al., 2019; see also Department of Health and Department of Education, 2017). As discussed in chapter 4, that translations to a cost-per-WELLBY of £2,500. The WELLBY per £ ratio is then 1/2,500 = 0.0004.

Nevertheless, one could also argue the other way and consider the importance of allowing for an optimism bias in any positive claims. The HMT Green Book mandates an accounting-for-optimism bias, which would, in turn, reduce the cost-effectiveness of the intervention.

The most important consideration in this context is whether there are in fact long-run impacts. As discussed above, evidence is weak and inconclusive. If treatment equipped participants with certain socio-emotional skills such as resilience or coping skills similar to those cognitive behavioural therapy cultivates, there may well be long-run impacts. We know from the evidence on cognitive behavioural therapy, for example, that relapse rates into depression are low, and that impacts can be detected several years post-treatment (Fava et al., 2004; Wiles et al., 2013, 2016). In fact, the aim of Human Henge included that 'committed participants demonstrate new communication skills' (Drysdale, 2018, page 4), 'self-confidence and self-esteem' (page 14), 'trust', and 'creative skills' (page 18). To the extent that this aim was achieved, there may well be long-run impacts, yielding a more favourable wellbeing cost-effectiveness ratio above the benchmark. Yet, this would have to be shown because the identified short-run increase is not spectacular relative to cognitive behavioural therapy or simple community events like those of the wellbeing programmes financed by the UK National Lottery Community Fund (see chapter 3).

This question remains an interesting avenue for future research, and potentially, for refining the treatment towards a stronger focus on cultivating certain socio-emotional skills. Other interesting questions that a more rigorous impact-evaluation design should attempt to answer are: can the treatment be replicated for historic sites other than Stonehenge and Avebury? Do different historic sites yield different wellbeing benefits? And what are the specific mechanisms through which these benefits manifest themselves? In any case, the positive mental health effects of historical landscapes and their potential use for therapeutic purposes remains an active and interesting research area.

Case Study 3: The UK City of Culture

In 2013, Kingston upon Hull successfully won the bid to be the UK City of Culture, an initiative that nominates a different city once every four years. In 2017, this meant a whole-year-long programme of cultural activities, including exhibitions, art projects, music, cinema, theatre, and literary festivals. Central government public funding was £32.8m, on top of which there was large-scale involvement of private donors and volunteers.

The evaluation report of the programme by the University of Hull was largely based on purpose-built surveys amongst stakeholder groups in Hull, including the general population (surveyed in 2015, 2016, and 2017), the private sector, special groups (for example, schoolchildren), and project staff. What the evaluation report does is to report on both levels of important outcomes in the project period and, where possible, changes in those levels during that period. The report looks at many outcomes but focuses predominantly on economic activities (tourism and jobs), measures of community cohesion (pride in Hull and feelings of connectedness to the local community), wellbeing (life satisfaction), and visibility (media coverage, volunteering levels, and awareness of cultural activities in Hull). The report declared the scheme a great success.

Given that there were eighty funding institutions, several hundreds of involved public and private institutions, and activities that ranged from one-off events to longer-term investments into art-relevant skills amongst schoolchildren, Hull 2017 is a massive and incredibly complex project to evaluate. To do all aspects of it full justice is not possible here, so we will focus on the key parts relevant for a wellbeing CEA.

To see the contrast between a business-as-usual and a wellbeing approach, we first sketch how traditional CBA advocated by the HMT Green Book would look like, which, when it comes to supposed social benefits follows the adage: when in doubt, leave it out.

From Traditional Cost-benefit to Wellbeing CEA

If we take a conservative standard economic view of the UK City of Culture programme, one thinks of costs in terms of opportunity costs and thus as any resources the United Kingdom could have spent otherwise. The seed funding came from organizations underlying the UK City of Culture initiative (such as the National Lottery) and amounted to about £23m. This was then increased by further charitable funding and corporate sponsorship to a total amount of about £32.8m. One should add to this the time-investments made by volunteers valued at the appropriate market price which is the gross wage they could have otherwise earned, which the report values at about £5.4m. Thus, the up-front costs from the point of view of UK spending were about £38.2m.

What these investments bought were the jobs and time needed to plan, organize, and deliver Hull 2017. Importantly, costs from the perspective of the United Kingdom will not always be costs from the perspective of the region: whatever comes from outside as additional resources is not a cost to local budgets. It is difficult to verify which charitable funding is Hull-specific and which is not, particularly given the involvement of so many institutions, but at the very least the volunteer work is nearly all from Hull and so counts as an investment by Hull itself. As a reasonable guess, nearly all private sponsorship and charity comes from the region itself too, so the total investments from within Hull are in the order of about £15m.

If we then think of the local benefits, the main one is value added in the tourism industry (mainly hotel occupancy) from within the United Kingdom. There is no direct evidence that individuals came to Hull for Hull 2017, so we must look at general trends to see what likely happened. We see no increase in international tourism to Hull in 2017 compared to 2016 (nor a large decrease in 2018), but there is a strong overall domestic tourism increase of 10 per cent in Hull in 2017, which remained stable in 2018, which we must compare to the rest of England.

A recent parliamentary report showed that domestic overnight tourism expenditure was up by about 3 per cent in England in 2017 relative to 2016, which seems the best comparator for the trend in Hull, implying that one should count Hull 2017 as having increased domestic tourism by about 7 per cent.[14] This is 7/10th of the increase in tourism in 2017. If we accept the judgement in the evaluation report that the value added is 56 per cent of the increased spending, then the additional value added due to Hull 2017 is about £11m (this is 56 per cent of 7/10 of the £28m increased tourism in Hull spending in 2017).

The jobs directly paid for by Hull 2017 would not normally count as net additional jobs unless a case can be made that the individuals involved would otherwise not be gainfully employed. This is because of the underlying economic assumption of an efficient labour market, which essentially holds that unemployment is due to labour market frictions (workers and jobs cannot immediately find each other) and that net increases in employment would have to come from overcoming those frictions, which is not the case in this one-off programme.

In times of high unemployment one can more easily make the argument that the jobs created would keep people employed who would otherwise be unemployed, and our understanding is that in such circumstances truly new permanent jobs are counted by the UK Department of Housing, Communities and Local Government as additional employment lasting five years. However, since this was a period of relatively high levels of employment, it would not be normal to count the jobs immediately paid for as an additional benefit since the assumption is that the same individuals would otherwise be working in a different sector and paid a gross wage. Moreover, the type of job was transient since the event were transient. In such circumstances, the benefit of employing people is then not that they are employed but what they produce. The gross wage they would otherwise make is, from a traditional economic point of view, the investment made by the United Kingdom into the activities they undertake as volunteers.

The main benefits, both local and national, of the programme were the many activities and festivities. The report claims 2,800 events and 5.34m audience visits. These include large events such as exhibitions and festivals as well as small events

[14] See Kantar TNS (2018) and Foley and Rhodes (2019).

such as workshops in schools. These activities were a main aim of Hull 2017 and a natural question is just how much economic value they created. From a standard economic point of view, these would mainly be forms of entertainment for which one would want to count the value that alternative 'just as good' entertainment would have cost those who enjoyed it. One would preferably want some notion of a market price for these activities.

Since the vast majority of the initiatives were provided to visitors well below cost-price, one lacks a market signal. An option would have been to run 'willingness-to-pay' surveys amongst attendees, or alternatively, to try and see how much they enjoyed the initiatives relative to others with known prices, such as going to the movies. Yet, this was not done, so one is then left with having to calculate the costs per attendee.

There is the question of whether one should count the joy created among volunteers and in the city as a whole. From a traditional point of view, one could not easily count the enjoyment of the volunteers or the city as a whole in a CBA, though we should recognize that many joy-creating activities are publicly funded in the United Kingdom without a CBA that 'shows' their value. Public events such as fireworks and Christmas celebrations have been subsidized by community funds for many decades, but have always struggled to justify themselves in terms of market-priced enjoyment. So the joy created does matter, but it has hitherto been hard to make it visible in money terms. Still, the joy created is one of the main outcomes paid for.

Nevertheless, if we restrain ourselves to what is traditional economic activity, the costs to Hull would be in the vicinity of £15m (made up by the volunteering, the private subsidies, and the local charities), with the additional economic activity due to tourism in the vicinity of £11m, yielding a cost-benefit ratio below unity. As a comparison, for the NHS, the Department of Health in the United Kingdom assumes that it can generate a unit of health (a QALY) for £15,000 (Claxton et al., 2015; Lomas et al., 2019; see also Department of Health and Department of Education, 2017), while it counts as benefits to that unit of health some £60,000 (HMT Green Book, 2018, page 73; Glover and Henderson, 2010; see also Department of Health and Department of Education, 2017), yielding a cost-benefit ratio of four.

From the point of view of the United Kingdom as a whole, matters look very different. That is because for the United Kingdom as a whole, the additional tourism from within the United Kingdom probably replaces tourism elsewhere, and subsidies from outside Hull but within the United Kingdom are just as much costs as those from within Hull. Hence, in terms of directly observed economic costs one would then count £38.2m. On the economic benefit side one would have nothing clearly observable. The negative net present value is then basically the costs that were incurred for the unknown value of the many initiatives. That negative value is about £38.2m. Given that there were about 5.3 million audience visits, one should view this negative value as an implicit cost per audience visit of about £7, about the price of seeing a film in the cinema.

This traditional CBA is summarized in Table 5.5.

Table 5.5 Traditional CBA of Hull 2017: economic benefits only

	Additional surplus in Hull	Additional surplus in the United Kingdom
Monetized costs and benefits		
Benefits		
Rise UK tourism	£11m	£11m
Rise foreign tourism	0	0
Loss tourism/spending elsewhere United Kingdom		–£11m
Costs		
Public investment	£10.0m	£32.8m
Volunteering	£5.4m	£5.4m
Net present value 2017	–£4.4m	£-38.2m
Non-monetized direct benefits		
2,400 engaged volunteers	+	+
5.3 million art experiences	+	+
Additional pride/cohesion in Hull	+	?
100 schools involved	+	?
56,000 kids and volunteers art-exposed	+	+
More involvement in art	?	

Source: Own calculations.

This table reflects the following considerations not yet described above:

- Local tourism, reasonably speaking, crowds out tourism in other places in the country (unless proven otherwise), so only additional non-domestic tourism is a UK benefit. However, there was no upward trend in foreign tourism in Hull in 2017.
- The report mentions a range of additional factors but these would normally only show up in a traditional CBA according to the UK HMT Green Book if there is strong evidence for them. The default is that one mentions them together with an indication of whether they add positively or negatively beyond the quantifiable net present value.
- The volunteers who reportedly enjoyed their involvement are a probable positive, but the default economic supposition is that their time on this is substituted away from other activities just as enjoyable or important for GDP.
- Pride and cohesion are noted to go up, a probable positive, but not given a monetary value in the report. From a UK perspective, there is the question whether the increased pride in Hull is at the expense of pride elsewhere.

- Art exposure of children, volunteers, and participants is another probable positive, but unless explicitly market-valued (that is, there is a price and someone pays for it or the imputed value of buying something in a complementary market), the default is that these have no quantifiable worth.
- Long-term benefits of having more art of the variety on offer are unknown and neither clearly positive nor negative. One can argue that people's capacity for enjoyment and fulfilment is permanently increased, and one can argue that popular culture provided by the market is already very rich and that there is no obvious market failure involved, nor evidence that additional cultural activities increase wellbeing relative to 'culture-poor' populations.

The table thus reflects standard economic thinking on costs and benefits of public expenditure in a difficult-to-quantify area like culture and art. The key thing that leads to a strongly negative net present value is that the default assumptions in the HMT Green Book are somewhat set up against this kind of initiative: local economic benefits via local spending or some other local demand expansion are assumed to be offset by a decrease elsewhere in the United Kingdom unless there is a shown productivity increase or improvement in labour market matching; volunteering, pride, or community cohesion are not assumed to have value until it is shown that the initiative changed things for the better relative to the opportunity costs (i.e. the situation that otherwise would have arisen). Because the report neither discusses nor shows what the volunteers were likely to have contributed otherwise, the default assumption is no added economic value.

The two columns in the table adopt different perspectives: the first column calculates costs and benefits from the point of view of Hull, the other from the point of view of the United Kingdom as a whole. Note that HM Treasury guidance on this in the Green Book has changed over the years, with previous practice enforcing a UK perspective on a CBA, but with more recent changes allowing authorities to make the case on the basis of a regional calculation and thus allowing decision-makers to decide whether particular regions at particular times should have precedence over other regions in the United Kingdom in terms of public funds.

Importantly, what this exercise also shows is that traditional CBA according to the HMT Green Book is not truly what drives policy in this area. In the area of culture and art, different outcomes are taken to be the goal, namely exposure to art, the quality of cultural life, and cultural activities that are seen to be spaced out across the country. Taking such 'area' goals as given, which is not obviously related to either economic surplus nor the concepts of social value referred to in the HMT Green Book, one can then measure how cost-effective the intervention was in reaching those 'area' goals.

One should not see this as criticism, but rather a reflection of the difficulties of complex policy problems mentioned in the previous chapters: there is a general recognition that art is an important human activity that governments have a role in subsidizing, but the economic methodology developed for traditional CBA is not yet set up to measure and value that role, As a result, policy-making reverts to different heuristics to rationalize it anyway.

The obvious problem with the current set-up is that one essentially relies on implicit frameworks and gut feelings to rationalize budget allocations over different 'area' goals. One leaves the world of a single outcome metric against which all is judged and essentially takes 'area' goals in isolation while leaving the link to the wider impacts and the overall objective to judgement. This is not desirable either.

Wellbeing-augmented CBA

The most important items about Hull 2017 from a wellbeing perspective are the various pieces of evidence about exposure to art, volunteering, pride, and cohesion in Hull during 2017. In order to avoid double-counting, one cannot count these various non-monetary benefits at the same time but must see something as the final benefit towards which all of these elements contribute.

The logical final outcome to consider is overall wellbeing. The project evaluation ran surveys from 2015 to 2018 that included the ONS question on life satisfaction, asking respondents: 'Overall, how satisfied are you with your life nowadays?' Answer possibilities range from 0 ('not at all') to 10 ('completely').

In terms of survey design and asking about life satisfaction, one has to be careful not to prime respondents and get artificially higher answers in some years by asking more positively skewed questions before the life-satisfaction question. We know that more positive prior questions have been found to elicit higher responses on the subsequent question on life satisfaction, so one needs to look at how the survey changed over the years. The survey in 2015 asks about community pride just before asking about life satisfaction, and in particular, asks respondents whether they feel pride in the community and feel they can challenge other community members. Fortunately, the 2016, 2017, and 2018 surveys had the same question on community pride preceding the question on life satisfaction, so the answers should be comparable. We show here the findings over time for community pride (the preceding question, Figure 5.1) and life satisfaction (the subsequent question, Figure 5.2).

We can see some evidence of an increase in both community pride and life satisfaction in Hull in 2017. If we were to look at averages, which exhibit the same pattern as the percentages show above, then life satisfaction was up by at least 0.1 points on a 0-to-10 scale in Hull in 2017. Compared to 2018, it was up by at least 0.2.

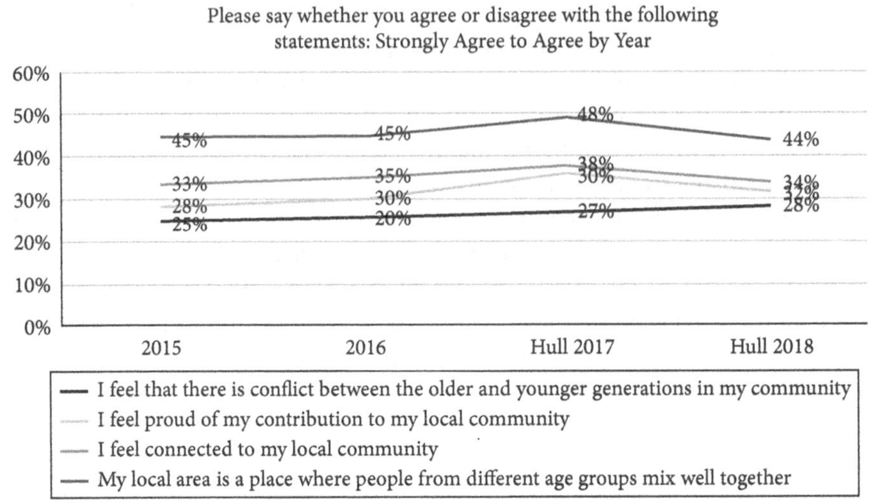

Figure 5.1 Community pride before and after Hull 2017
Source: University of Hull Impact Evaluation.

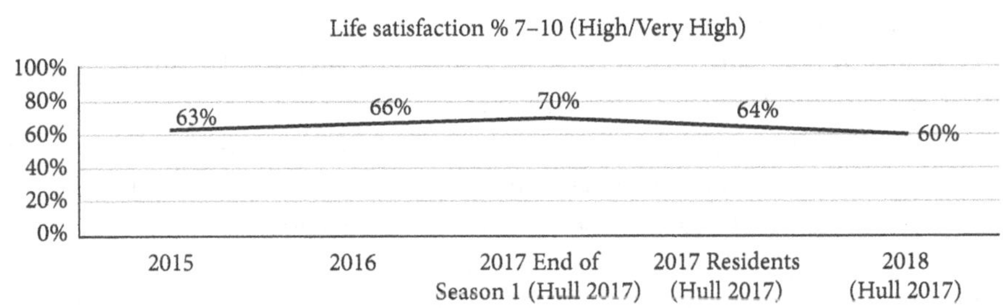

Figure 5.2 Life satisfaction before and after Hull 2017
Source: University of Hull Impact Evaluation.

Given that the population of Hull is over 280,000, this increase in life satisfaction is large when aggregated over all affected individuals. However, one has to wonder whether these are significant differences, statistical artefacts due to relatively small numbers of respondents in surveys, or even just general UK trends. As the surveys using in the evaluation included about 2,700 respondents in Hull in 2017 and the standard deviation of the average life satisfaction is about 0.04, these differences are statistically significant at the 1 per cent level.[15] To check whether they just reflect general UK trends, we need to look at available national information that includes Hull.

[15] This is the standard deviation of life satisfaction at the individual level (which is about 2) divided by the square root of the number of respondents (which is then about 52).

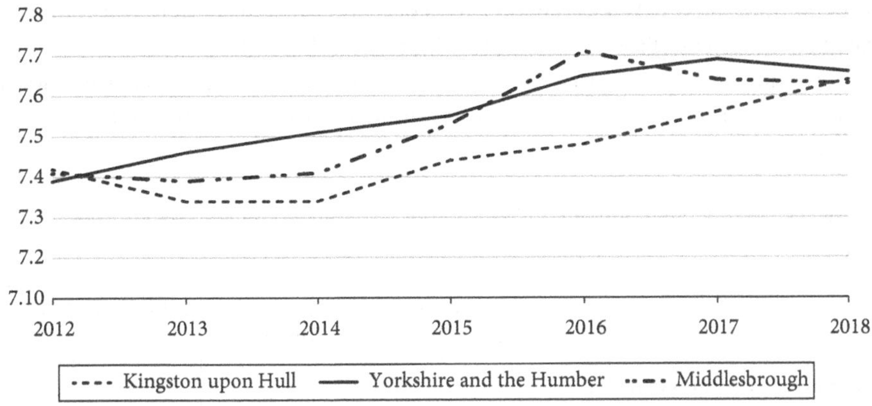

Figure 5.3 Life satisfaction in Hull and the nearby region over time
Source: ONS.

The regional data from the ONS over the 2016 to 2018 period gives some support to the belief that there is no large wellbeing benefit to populations far from Hull: as one can see in Figure 5.3, one does not see life satisfaction in cities close to Hull increase in the same way as that in Hull does. Note that fluctuations in city-level life satisfaction are quite high and that it is, therefore, difficult to be certain that the increase in Hull is due to the Hull 2017 events. Still, it is true that life satisfaction in Hull in 2017 is quite a bit up during the 2016 to 2018 period compared to the rest of the East Yorkshire and the Humber region. We should note that these numbers are based on somewhat lower sample sizes: the surveys run by the ONS include no more than a few hundred interviews in the Hull region per year and thus mainly confirm that 2017 indeed was a year with a higher life satisfaction in Hull than in the preceding years.

Given that the population of Hull is about 280,000, an increase of 0.1 points in life satisfaction on a 0-to-10 scale for one year amounts to about 28,000 WELLBYs. One can make deductions for children too young to fully experience all aspects of the event (for example, the 0-to-10 age range) and additions for populations outside of Hull that also feel part of Hull (for example, because they live or work there), but neither of those will make a major difference to the basic claim that the programme delivered 28,000 WELLBYs to the UK population that would otherwise not have occurred. For a CBA, these should be valued at the willingness-to-pay for a WELLBY, estimated in chapter 4 to be £9,000 per WELLBY.

The decrease in life satisfaction in Hull following the years after 2017 suggests that the events should mainly be read as a set of enjoyable activities and festivities, as we typically find that effects of activities and festivities do not last. Similar results were found for most of the activities of the UK National Lottery wellbeing programmes after 2011 (see chapter 3). There too, the effects were not found to last beyond a year (Breeze et al., 2010; CLES and NEF, 2013).

If we now use the information in the evaluation report on the increase in local wellbeing and integrate this into the traditional CBA, one would obtain a very different table.

Table 5.6 Wellbeing-augmented CBA of Hull 2017: economic and social value benefits

	Additional surplus in Hull	Additional surplus in the United Kingdom
Monetized costs and benefits		
Benefits		
28,000 WELLBYs × £9,000	£252m	£252m
Additional tourism value added	£11m	0
Costs		
Public investment	£10m	£32.8m
Volunteering	£5.4m	£5.4m
Net present value 2017	+£247.6m	+£213.8m
Non-monetized costs and benefits		
Long-run effect of art-exposure	?	?
Public health costs 2017	?	?
Crime costs 2017	?	?
Improved governance	+	+
Greater within UK equality	+	+

Source: Own calculations.

Table 5.6 reflects the following key considerations:

- The report shows how life satisfaction in a representative sample of 2,700 respondents in Hull (that is, about 1 per cent of the total population of about 280,000) increased by about 0.1 points on a scale from 0-to-10 in 2017 relative to both before and after. This tallies in a rough sense with the observed increase in life satisfaction in Hull seen in the ONS regional life-satisfaction tables compared to trends in the region. Scaled up to the population, this means there was a WELLBY benefit of 28,000.
- Because the vast majority of the visitors, attendants, or volunteers were local (over 80 per cent in each category), it is not plausible that the positive life-satisfaction effect on residents in Hull is offset by a negative outside of Hull (for example, due to jealousy): the media on the event was largely local, reflected in the fact that only 1 per cent of the visitors were foreign (though they made up 11 per cent of the hotel bookings). Thus, the social UK value is reasonably the same as the local social value.

- We have used £9,000 as the monetary value of a WELLBY as this is how much individuals are willing to pay for an increase in wellbeing, which is the standard approach in which wellbeing-augmented CBA values non-market outcomes (see chapter 4). Remember that the individual willingness-to-pay-for a WELLBY is much higher than the minimum social production costs of wellbeing.
- Because the WELLBY benefits are based on the average life-satisfaction effects for the whole population, they include many benefits, including to the economy, social relationships, or arts and festivities. Thus, to remain conservative and avoid double-counting, all other benefits have been taken out of the economic benefit side. They also no longer appear on the 'non-monetized' list because they have now implicitly been monetized. By monetarily valuing the WELLBY benefits, all reasonable pathways that involve inner-life issues have been included to some extent. To include even more benefits would require a model with direct and indirect effects.
- In terms of public investment, the conclusion remains the same: the project now has a large, positive net present value.

Note that the scope of this wellbeing-augmented CBA implicitly addresses the question of negative private consumption externalities: the WELLBY benefits have already been calculated at the level where status effects would appear—the region of Hull where the exposure and involvement were concentrated—so that there is no need to apply an Easterlin Discount.

In terms of comparison, we should mention that the 2012 London Olympics were also found to have a positive yet temporary life-satisfaction benefit to those living in London, but the costs per WELLBY were far higher.[16] Similar results were found for most of the activities of the UK National Lottery wellbeing initiatives, which included a range of community activities.[17] There too, the effect did not last beyond a year (see chapter 3).

Thus, from a wellbeing perspective, the UK City of Culture initiative should be seen as a festivity that has positive, short-run effects on local wellbeing. Its long-run legacy effects are probably positive but much less certain. They are difficult to research. Yet, from a wellbeing perspective, there is nothing wrong with temporary wellbeing benefits. The question boils down to whether those benefits are bought cheaply or expensively.

Wellbeing CEA

We now turn to our final table in this section (Table 5.7). Here, we adopt the perspective that wellbeing is our ultimate outcome of interest. That said, we do not value wellbeing monetarily but use it as our primary policy metric:

[16] See Dolan et al. (2019).
[17] See Breeze et al. (2010) and CLES and NEF (2013).

Table 5.7 Wellbeing cost-effectiveness analysis of Hull 2017: wellbeing benefits

	Additional surplus in Hull	Additional surplus in the United Kingdom
Cost-effectiveness calculation		
Additional WELLBYs	28,000	28,000
Costs		
Public investment	£10m	£32.8m
Cost per WELLBY	**£357**	**£1,171**
Non-monetized costs and benefits		
Long-run effect of art-exposure	?	?
Public health costs 2017	+	+
Crime costs 2017	+	+
Improved governance	+	+
Greater within UK equality	+	+
Value of a cultural elite	?	?

Source: Own calculations.

Table 5.7 reflects the following key considerations:

- Most importantly, the table has done away with a conservative estimate of the opportunity cost of wellbeing and presents the benefits in units of well-being only (rather than £).
- The table has now suppressed the value of tourism and the cost of volunteering because they are relatively small compared to the WELLBY benefits.
- On top of the previous, non-monetized potential benefits, an extended wellbeing perspective would also lead one to think of how cultural elites that are empowered and stimulated through initiatives like the UK City of Culture benefit the nation as a whole. This is a hugely complex issue that raises question of, on the one hand, whether a cultural elite helps to raise and retain highly talented individuals. On the other hand, one might see all sorts of negatives in elitism. It is not obvious what the balance of the effects are. It is mentioned here as a consideration that is likely to come up in real decision-making, but without a clear answer as of yet.

The key figure is a cost-effectiveness ratio of £1,171 per WELLBY for the UK City of Culture initiative. It is important to put this figure into perspective, both nationally and internationally.

From a national perspective, the implied cost per WELLBY is lower than how much one would pay for a unit of wellbeing in marginal NHS spending. The figure is about seven times lower than the implied cost per WELLBY from the 2012

London Olympics (which is about £8,000 per WELLBY), but somewhat higher than implied cost per WELLBY from the UK National Lottery wellbeing programmes (see chapter 3), which bought a WELLBY for about £400. It is higher than the advocated estimate of the marginal social production costs of a WELLBY through the NHS, which is £2,500. On balance, the UK City of Culture initiative seems to be high value for money from a national perspective.

From an international perspective, the best comparison is the wellbeing benefits of the European City of Culture. Steiner et al. (2015) looked at the before-during-after effects of being the European City of Culture and found no positive economic effects of the programme. The authors even found short-run negative effects on wellbeing, but no evidence for long-run (or legacy) effects beyond the year of the festivities. Relative to that, Hull 2017 can be seen as a successful event, being able to avoid the negatives of the European City of Culture initiative.

We can only speculate why there is this difference, but the arguments in Steiner et al. (2015) combined with the findings in the Hull 2017 evaluation report suggest a combination of factors. First, European Cities of Culture often need to use their own funding to run the event and cities are comparably larger with larger economies, making it difficult to detect a positive effect. To some extent, cities 'buy' the title. This also seems likely to drive the negative wellbeing effect: the local populations see it as a prestige project that is at their expense. There is thus a likelihood that the effects of the European City of Culture are largely status effects, benefiting only a small group of local elites at the expense of their populations, having negative wellbeing effects in total.

That explanation would also hold important lessons for the UK City of Culture initiative and initiatives like it: what makes it work is that it is small-scale enough to avoid the charge of leading to lots of local nuisance, and yet the event is seen to be done by and for the local population.

Moreover, there is an important question of whether the wellbeing effects are likely to be status-related or not. After all, if the programme's effect is solely from more national prestige directed toward residents of Hull, taking away from the general prestige of all other cities and regions, then the gain for the population of Hull would be compensated with a decrease everywhere else, a decrease that would have been far too small to see in national data which reflects thousands of shocks to the whole country. This goes partly to the question of what the content was of the Hull 2017 activities (status-oriented or otherwise) and how it was perceived.

The evaluation report gives important clues about how it was perceived in the media, which primarily celebrated the various activities, probably displacing 'regular news' which is a mixture of negatives and positives. The content of the activities was largely participatory, involving school children doing activities, and volunteers explaining Hull and the festivities to visitors. So by and large, it is likely that the status element was rather small. Most events were cheap and free, public goods that were in principle available to all in the United Kingdom. It was largely like a party in which one temporarily is less oriented towards bad news. However, it cannot be denied that there was some status element to the whole idea and events: by showing that Hull is no longer deprived, places that are still deprived go down in the deprivation pecking order.

The international wellbeing literature has some indicative evidence that it is possible to have a high degree of pride in something local without this meaning that the pride of others in their places goes down. The demise of the Eastern European communist block saw great reductions in how well their populations thought about their region, but this did not lead to great euphoria in the non-communist countries close by, for the basic reason that they did not compare themselves with former communist countries in the first place. So too is it likely with cities: everyone can have great pride in their own city for local reasons.

However, there is no consensus about this question. Indeed, the question of whether city populations see themselves in a status race with other cities, decided by who has the more impressive art events, has not been posed in any serious way in the wellbeing literature. As a preliminary judgement, the implicit belief of the evaluation report that the wellbeing benefits to Hull from its festivities did not lead to significant jealousy elsewhere seems reasonable. In this regard, it is important to note that the media activities about this event were highly locally concentrated. Residents in other cities would not have known about Hull 2017 to the same degree as Hull residents.

Additional Considerations

In terms of longer-run impacts after 2017, the evaluation report looks at knock-on economic activity, knock-on grants for further cultural activities, and the possible skills in participants.

Greater economic activity in Hull and more grants coming to Hull are, of course, desirable for locals but are not clearly of benefit to the United Kingdom as a whole: we must stick to the basic economic insight that, in the longer-run, economic activity is simply tied to wherever populations are, and that grants to one place come at the expense of grants to another. Hence, more businesses, activity, and grants coming to Hull might be seen as benefits to Hull but are not clearly increasing either the economy or the wellbeing of the United Kingdom as a whole.

The same insight also applies to non-domestic tourism, which was probably small in the case of Hull 2017. In the long run, jobs in the tourism industry should be seen as something that people do instead of doing something else. In order to count them as a net benefit to the United Kingdom, one would have to argue that jobs in the tourism industry are especially happy and tax-raising jobs compared to the other jobs they replace in the long run. That might be the case, but it is not clear. There is, therefore, no obvious reason to subsidize tourism over other sectors because any subsidy always implicitly taxes the other sectors that pay for the subsidy.[18]

Taken together, we do not need to look at knock-on economic activity or grants for further cultural activities for a UK wellbeing evaluation of Hull 2017, although it is entirely understandable that this is a major reason for locals to be involved in the initiative. There is nothing innately wrong with that from a wellbeing perspective, but it is not much different from being agnostic at the national level about the decisions of competing businesses: part of normal economic activity.

In terms of the evaluation report's data on skills and changes to the communities and attitudes of volunteers, the key point to make is that those are local benefits that one would expect to show up in the local wellbeing statistics, i.e. the life satisfaction of the city. If it is true that the wellbeing benefit subsided after 2017, then it is probably also the case that the community cohesion and social capital benefits were temporary too, or at least too small in terms of long-run effects to continue to show up as a significant wellbeing benefit. If one then looks at the wellbeing literature, one essentially would think the same: communities need regular activities to exist and strengthen, and without continued additional activities their strength returns to 'normal'. Here again, it is probably a good thing for wellbeing in Hull that it has attracted more funding for continued cultural activities in the future. This is possibly why the ONS data do not show the decrease in life satisfaction in 2018 that the city-wide surveys at the end of 2017 show. However, that wellbeing benefit should be properly counted to further investments of granting agencies, not Hull 2017.

Socio-emotional and mental skills are known to have long-run benefits that can last (Fava et al., 2004; Lordan and McGuire, 2019; Wiles et al., 2013, 2016), but the skills that were cultivated in Hull 2017 are not likely to be of that kind: Hull 2017 was about being a community in the way that volunteers and organizers knew how to organize. They were thus applying socio-emotional and mental skills already learned previously. For sure, there was implicit training and amplification that comes from applying skills, but the same could be said for the activities that volunteers and organizers would otherwise have been doing, such as activities in their communities or businesses.

In sum, on the benefits side, a large number of people visited, paid for, and participated in Hull 2017. The additional benefit of activities and festivities to the population and volunteers about Hull is likely to have been 0.1 points on a 0-to-10 life-satisfaction scale or higher during 2017.

When it comes to the costs side, from the perspective of national wellbeing cost-effectiveness, the question boils down to how much public resources have

[18] As discussed previously, if jobs are truly new and would otherwise not exist, such as in a deep depression, different rules of thumb apply, but this was a period close to full employment.

gone into Hull 2017 that would otherwise not have been spent. In case of Hull 2017, this is a difficult question as there were eighty funders, both public and private (though the vast majority were public), and there are many plausible public cost benefits not captured by the data in the evaluation report. We must, therefore, look carefully at which subsidies by those eighty funders really count as net public costs to the UK public sector, as well as which possible benefits might have occurred elsewhere in the public sector.

In terms of the direct costs of £32.8m, 69 per cent came from direct public subsidies and UK National Lottery funding, which clearly count as public costs. Another 12.5 per cent came from trusts and foundations that have their own decision-making procedures, but these were, crucially, national and not international funders, so subsidies to Hull 2017 probably came at the expense of other causes in the United Kingdom. The 18.5 per cent that came from corporate sponsors also seems to have come from internal budgets earmarked for philanthropic and community purposes. While debatable, it is probably right to count these expenses as net public expenses in the sense that all of these funders 'should' have a UK wellbeing perspective and would have spent these funds on something else if it offered a higher return. The direct costs were, therefore, likely to be about £32.8m.

Somewhat related is the question of how to value the time of volunteers, which is currently valued at about £5.4m in the evaluation report. In a traditional CBA, volunteering time is simply an investment into the outputs of Hull 2017, worth whatever the outputs were worth, displacing other activities that would have generated tax returns for the United Kingdom as a whole (for example, income or corporate tax).

From a wellbeing cost-effectiveness perspective, one has to distinguish between the investment of these people as individuals and the implicit investment by society if the same volunteers would have otherwise been engaged in taxed activities and thus contributed more to public goods (via taxation). As a rule of thumb, the UK public sector as a whole taxes economic activity at a rate of 40 per cent, which is roughly the government expenditure to GDP ratio. Thus, one could interpret the £5.4m of volunteering time as a private gift of £3.24m (0.6 × £5.4m) of volunteers to Hull 2017 that they would have otherwise spent on themselves (their after-tax consumption) and £2.16m (0.4 × £5.4m) as the additional tax gift by the UK public sector to Hull 2017. One could argue that these volunteers have probably had wellbeing benefits by giving to their community, but those benefits are already included in the wellbeing figures and one should, therefore, not count them again on the benefit side. Because of its involvement, the UK public sector forewent £2.16m in taxes that one could count on the net public cost side of this programme. We did not include this item in Table 5.7, but it would not change the conclusions materially.

In this regard, one might also note that all the additional private economic activity related to Hull 2017 (for example, hotels or restaurants) would have increased the tax receipts of Hull, but there is no good reason to think it would have increased the tax receipts of the United Kingdom as a whole unless one can argue that productivity went up as a result of Hull 2017, which seems rather far-fetched. Thus, while Hull as a city is rightfully interested in local economic activity and taxes stimulated by the tourism increase due to Hull 2017, this does not count as a clear UK benefit.

On the other hand, we need to add or deduct from these costs the benefits of Hull 2017 in terms of increased or decreased public expenses in other major spending programmes. This goes to the question of whether there were health benefits leading to NHS costs. It also goes to the question of whether greater community cohesion will likely have led to less crime.

The evaluation report does not include many of these non-monetary benefits or costs, and additional data on health and crime in Hull in this period (available on request) do not show patterns in non-monetary outcomes that are clearly related to public costs or benefits. What this means is that there were probably too many other changes in this region and period to confound the impact of Hull 2017 itself. Given that the region is a multi-billion £ economy, it is not entirely unexpected that a project of 'only' £32.8m would not register hugely in terms of non-monetary benefits or costs. It is somewhat remarkable that the change in life satisfaction is pronounced enough to be seen at the aggregate level at all, suggesting the value of such events for (temporary) wellbeing gains.

In Conclusion

Taking the perspective of a traditional CBA, Hull 2017 does not look like the most desirable project, but under reasonable assumptions of additional WELLBYs created, Hull 2017 looks like a high positive net present value project. In fact, if we adopt a wellbeing cost-effectiveness lens, we find that Hull 2017 bought the United Kingdom 28,000 WELLBYs at a unit cost of £1,171, which is better value for money than the 2012 London Olympics. It is also better value for money than the advocated best estimate of the marginal social production cost of a WELLBY (about £2,500).

There are major unknowns in an area as complicated as spending on arts and culture, which would require major research efforts. Among the likely additional positive aspects of Hull 2017 is the likely pro-social behaviour and community cohesion, the community life in Hull more generally, and the possible longer-term benefits of exposure to art and culture amongst many layers of the population.

We showed both how insights from the wellbeing literature can augment traditional CBA in this area and how it might replace it entirely in terms of both wellbeing CEA and a change in what one looks for in such initiatives.

Case Study 4: The Wellbeing Costs of Commuting

This case study is based on a study on commuting, originally conducted by the University of the West of England (Chatterjee et al., 2017). We first give some background on how this study (which we refer to as the 'Bristol study' from here on) fits into traditional CBA, and then we discuss the findings of that study in more detail.

The Value of Better Transport

When building or improving transport infrastructure, the costs of doing so to society are often quite clear and measurable, pertaining mostly to the material resources needed to build the infrastructure, measured in terms of capital, equipment, and labour.

However, the benefits of new or improved infrastructure are diverse and more difficult to estimate: short-term benefits include the lower marginal costs of transport which can often be well measured, for example, pertaining to less wear and tear of vehicles or lower costs of tickets. Another important short-term benefit of better transport is the reduction in travel time, which is more difficult to measure because it is often not that easy to classify time spent in transport: is it consumption, leisure, or production time?

Long-term benefits of better transport include the different patterns of economic and social activity that come with new or improved infrastructure. These benefits are well discussed in the academic literature and potentially huge, yet difficult to pin down statistically. They include the increased specialization from having more people in a single market with less barriers, and the decrease in conflict when trade ties improve relations between regions. Both pertain to the potential advantages of price equalization across regions and cross-fertilization in terms of people and technology. These longer-term benefits are very difficult to pin down and rather general in nature, rendering it difficult to use them to argue for small additional bits of infrastructure that improve, say, ten roads in a village in some place.

Practically speaking, transport departments in many countries, therefore, rely heavily on the value of estimated reductions in travel times of various transport users to argue for the value of new or improved infrastructure. This reflects the fact that departments often use models of traffic flows in which the value of time can be inserted in order to calculate the total benefits of new transport facilities. Thereby, departments make many distinctions between modes and types of travel, including such concepts as personal travel, work trips, regular commuting travel, transit movements, heavy-truck movements, peak-hour travel, or congestion-adjusted travel.

When thinking about commuting, which is one of the largest categories of transportation usage and hence a major element in estimates of benefits to more infrastructure, many considerations are relevant when estimating the value of reducing commuting time. This includes the question of just how much of the commuting time is actually spent working, what activities are being crowded out, and what the actual costs of commuting are (for example, in terms of tickets or fuel). Judgements on these elements are crucial to arrive at what one might term 'the time value of commuting', which tells one how much value there would be to individuals or society in reducing travel time and allowing individuals to choose another way to spend that time.

Different countries have different rules of thumb on how to value this time spent on commuting, where commuting is understood as movements between a domicile and a place of work. The United States, for instance, has adopted a 50 per cent wage rule on commuting, which means they count half the time spent on commuting as lost production valued at the wage of the commuter.[19]

The United Kingdom, like many other European countries, mainly relies on the willingness of commuters to pay in order to reduce their travel times to estimate the implied time value of commuting (estimated either via a revealed or a stated willingness-to-pay approach).[20] France has a similar approach, with some of their researchers (Meunier and Quintet, 2015) admitting that their approach is pragmatic when they say 'the models [in this line of work] often do not follow the principles of micro-economic theory (in technical terms, the demand functions cannot be integrated).' An alternative to blanket assumptions like in the United States or willingness-to-pay studies in the United Kingdom or France is to base the estimate of the value of time during commuting on well-being. Interestingly, we know that the actual activity of commuting is rather low rated in terms of how people actually experience that activity, but in chapter 2 we already learned that low levels of immediately experienced happiness do not necessarily show up in life satisfaction, for example, if the activity is seen as high in social status and meaning.

[19] See Kruesi (1997) and White (2016).

[20] The basic theoretical framework is the standard partial-equilibrium time-budget approach explained in Small (2012).

All this leads us to the Bristol study which attempts to measure the value of less commuting time using wellbeing data. The study was aimed to find:

1. The effects of one hour spent commuting on life satisfaction and other measures of wellbeing, by transport type and type of user.
2. A scaling factor between those wellbeing effects and money to obtain a monetary value that can be plugged into traditional CBA, in order to help appraise the value of new or better transport infrastructure.

The Bristol Study

The study analyses 40,000 individuals in the Understanding Society panel data, looking at how changes in commuting affects individual and family life. The authors look at a large range of outcomes, including job satisfaction, leisure satisfaction, life satisfaction, and mental health, distinguishing the effects of different modes of commuting.

The key finding on life satisfaction that Chatterjee et al. (2017) find is:

> When comparing individuals, we found that longer duration commutes are associated with lower life satisfaction after accounting for other differences between individuals (by 0.015 points on the 7-point scale for every extra ten minutes each way). This applies to both men and women but it represents a relatively small effect (working part-time is associated with a higher life-satisfaction score of 0.12 points). For the same individuals we did not find lower life satisfaction on occasions when they have longer duration commutes.

This finding tallies perfectly with the stylized understanding of the literature in chapter 2: we know from studies like Stutzer and Frey (2008) that those who commute have worse jobs and lower life satisfaction, hence the negative association found when comparing individuals who commute more with individuals who commute less. Stutzer and Frey (2008) used German data but the same result holds for the United Kingdom, although the effect sizes are not huge: commutes rarely take more than 100 minutes and even going from zero to 100 minutes reduces life satisfaction by 'only' 0.15 points on a 1-to-7 scale in a cross-section, no more than a quarter of the effect of being unemployed. Thus, compared to having no job, a long commute of an hour each way reduces life satisfaction no more than a sixth of the effect of being unemployed. Still, that is taking the between-individual effect at face value.

It should be noted that the link between commuting and life satisfaction is exceptionally difficult to pin down precisely as most of the literature lacks random variation in commuting times, implying that most studies suffer from the problem that people and jobs with longer commutes are usually different from people and jobs with shorter commutes. Someone prepared to commute for longer usually does so to either go to a better job than he or she would otherwise have, which biases the estimated effect of commuting downwards, even when comparing the same individual over time. Similarly, there are likely to be some people who dislike commuting more than others and who will work from home or take a job closer to home, which also biases the found effect of commuting downwards when comparing these different types of individuals. So it is likely that the between-estimates are more negative than the true causal relation.

Researchers have mused about the kind of data and methods they need to identify the causal effect of commuting on wellbeing, such as, for example, accidental increases in commuting times due to major road or rail repairs that unexpectedly increase commuting times for a longer period of time (say, for a year). However, as far as we know, no large study in that vein exists for the United Kingdom.

Going back to the Bristol study, to put a monetary value on commuting, Chatterjee et al. (2017) use a coefficient of income that comes out of their own regressions to calculate income equivalents. As we argued in chapters 2, 3, and 4, changes in self-reported income on a year-to-year basis in panel data have huge measurement errors, often coming from changes in income that have little to do with purchasing power. The variation in measured income often comes from whether a household gained or lost another adult, and they involve increases and decreases in income that individuals may not be aware of. As a result, one typically obtains income coefficients in the order of an increase in life satisfaction by 0.15 points on a 0-to-10 scale for a doubling in income, while the more careful studies find a coefficient of about 0.4 (see Lindqvist et al. (2020), for example). Even these higher estimates probably do not relate to the effect of very visible changes in income which affect individuals much more than many sources of income changes that people may not be aware of. The income coefficient used in the Bristol study is, therefore, probably much lower than the more apt effect one should apply, which is the effect of very visible changes in income since that is the effect most applicable to visible changes in prices and costs paid by an individual. In contrast, Fujiwara and Campbell (2011), who account for the direct and indirect effects of income (using a three-step adjustment methodology), typically find coefficients of income which are about ten times larger than in the Bristol study.

We advocated in chapter 4 to use a standard single measure for the willingness-to-pay for a WELLBY of £9,000, which is derived from the effect of visible changes in financial positions on wellbeing, but which is also close to the implied value of a WELLBY if we accept that people are willing to spend about £60,000 per healthy life-year (QALY) when they make expenses to avoid risks of death (HMT Green Book, 2018, page 73; Glover and Henderson, 2010; see also Department of Health and Department of Education, 2017). When thinking of cost-effectiveness (as opposed to cost-benefit), we advocated a different number, namely the minimum marginal social production cost of a WELLBY, which is £2,500. Thus, depending on whether one augments traditional CBA or applies a fully fledged wellbeing CEA, one uses either £9,000 or £2,500 per WELLBY. Yet, within the logic of the cost-benefit analyses run by transport departments, a willingness-to-pay measure is the appropriate value.

When using their own (rather low) estimate of the effect of income on wellbeing, the authors obtain income equivalent effects of commuting that are rather large: if income has rather small effects, it takes more additional income to obtain a large wellbeing effect. The study's key figure for the income equivalent effect is then:

> An additional ten minutes (each way) of commuting time is associated with the equivalent effect on life satisfaction as a reduction of £490 per month in gross personal income (or £5,880 per annum).

Note that this income equivalent is based on a cross-sectional estimate of commuting on wellbeing, rather than the normally preferred longitudinal estimate, and that the low estimate of the effect of income leads to a rather large number.

We may note that a ten-minute (each way) change is about seven hours less commute per month, based on twenty-one working days per month. This implies that the per-hour disutility of commuting according the key figure of the study is about £50 per hour. The UK Department of Transport advocated value is close to £15 per hour (derived from hourly earnings, varying with mode of transport, i.e. more for cars than for walking), which is substantially lower.[21]

The most appropriate estimate in the Bristol study, however, comes from longitudinal data (see the appendix of the study). This estimate is essentially zero. Hence, we would currently put a value of zero on the additional commute because that is what the longitudinal effect of commuting on wellbeing is found to be. Note that this does not preclude including a negative effect of longer commutes on tax receipts in a traditional CBA, because tax receipts are an externality for the individuals involved and thus not likely part of their own wellbeing. Additional monetary costs of travelling (for example, a ticket) are then, of course, also a straight cost.

Interestingly, the authors find that changes in mode of commuting have little long-run effect on physical or mental health outcomes, essentially because people seem to get used to their travel mode.

[21] Department for Transport (2019). TAG (Transport and Analysis Guidance) Data Book. Available at: https://www.gov.uk/government/publications/tag-data-book.

The bottom line from a critical reading of the study is, therefore, that commuting is likely to have no or little impact on our preferred measure of wellbeing because in the specification that is the more convincing one (the longitudinal estimate in the appendix of the Bristol study report), the found effect is zero. It is true that the authors find some non-zero wellbeing effects for particular groups of people, but those are artificial effects in the sense that the overall effect can only be zero if the positive effects on some groups are counterbalanced by negative effects on others.

An obvious question is then what the health effects are worth on their own. There, the study (on page 21), similar to the literature they quote, finds small and insignificant effects of longer commuting on physical health, which is really what one expects: there is nothing particularly healthy or unhealthy about commuting time. Hence, there are no obvious physical health costs or benefits if commuting changes. This does vary, of course, by mode of transport, where the study suggests cycling is healthy and taking the bus is not. The results on cycling make sense from an exercise point of view, although the results on taking the bus depend on methodology as longer bus commutes have not been found to have effects for the same individual. The cross-sectional estimate is probably subject to self-selection (that is, less healthy people take the bus). Still, their overall finding is that there are no significant health benefits or costs of longer commutes.

Hence, at closer inspection of the results of the Bristol study, there seems to be a zero effect of commuting on wellbeing and thus no individual gain or loss to consider.

If we think of what more could have been done with the basic theories on wellbeing in mind, we can make two substantive comments:

1. There is the question of whether there is some loss to social relationships, such as with one's partner or children. An individual who commutes longer might get used to it, essentially when spending more leisure time or even just working during commutes, but there might be some loss to social relationships that is not accounted for in analyses focusing on the commuter rather than the whole family. There is an older literature that strongly suggests such losses (see Green et al. (1999), for example) and quite a few recent studies (see Sandow (2019), for example that suggest more family stress when someone commutes longer, particularly due to less time spent with children and spouses.[22] However, as with the effect of commuting on one's own life satisfaction, we could find no studies with strong causal

[22] Green et al. (1999) look at British households with a long-distant commuter and claim that: The evidence points to increasing complexity in home and working lives, with important implications for housing, transport, and human resource management policies, as well as for family life. Long-distance weekly commuting may yield substantial financial and career benefits for the commuter, but the majority of costs are borne by his/her partner. For some individuals and households, such a life-style

designs. Still, the argument is plausible that there may be a loss to others that is not picked up in a commuter's own life satisfaction. Men, in particular, have been found to be somewhat unaffected by the mental health problems of their spouses (Mervin and Frijters, 2014), allowing for the possibility that longer-commuting men might be less affected by the loss their commute causes to others in their immediate surroundings (Sandow, 2019).

2. We can sketch how to use wellbeing derived Value of Travel Time Savings (VTTS), a term that originates from the UK Department of Transport, in traditional CBA. Traditional CBA would roughly say: an hour of commuting costs the ticket plus the willingness-to-pay income equivalent of the total wellbeing effect of the time spent in commuting itself. A wellbeing CEA, on the contrary, would compare the total wellbeing effect of the longer commute, including the wellbeing effects of the actual transport costs (Easterlin discounted) versus the net public costs which could include forgone taxation if production is lower with longer commuting. To calculate the wellbeing effects of changes in income one would use long-term actual income effects (hence neither willingness-to-pay or minimum social production costs), Easterlin discounted. The wellbeing effects would also include effects on the family. For an example of how one can populate and structure these calculations, we refer the reader to the case study on the youth traineeship programme in Wales earlier in this chapter.

Reflections: Can the Effect of Commuting Be Zero? Why Have More Infrastructure At All Then?

We should reflect on whether it can really be true that commuting has no negative marginal effect on the wellbeing of an individual or on his or her loved ones. We should additionally reflect on how the case for infrastructure would change if one does not base it on commuting time changes.

At the outset, it should be admitted that, from a wellbeing literature perspective, one would not expect a 'zero effect' of commuting on wellbeing, although the expected effect would be somewhat small because a wellbeing effect worth £10 per hour is very small.

We would expect a negative effect because we know people dislike the experience of commuting (see the studies referenced in chapter 2); we know there is a natural limit to how much time people can and are often willing to spend commuting; because there is clear evidence of a positive willingness-to-pay in order to avoid long commutes; because commuting decisions are made in

is one to be 'enjoyed', and is seen as sustainable over the medium term, whereas for others it is a case of 'enduring suffering' until the family home and the workplace may be brought into closer alignment.

situations where people are reasonably familiar with various experiences of commuting and thus should be 'wellbeing rational'; and because the cross-sectional evidence on wellbeing shows a suggested trade-off.[23]

In such circumstances, where one has very good reasons to suspect the true effect must be negative, but the data available shows a nil finding, the initial suspicion is that the data are simply not random and clean enough to show the actual (probably small) relation between wellbeing and commuting. There is indeed no study so far that exploits a strong, convincing random variation in commuting time. If we think of what the best data on this would be, they would have to come from something like disruptions to commuting times that last a long time (for example, coming from major upgrades or repairs that take several months) and that apply to a large number of individuals followed over time. That kind of study still needs to be done.[24]

Another suspicion is that the effect is simply too small to be picked up, even with thousands of observations. This reflects the fact that the standard deviation of average life satisfaction of a sample of 10,000 individuals is still about 0.015, which is in the same ball-park as what one expects the effect of an hour more commuting per week to be. This shows one of the disadvantages of life satisfaction as a measure: only quite large effects show up as statistically robust in most studies.

Nevertheless, unexpected data should not be dismissed without at least musing why, at the individual level, there could truly be a relatively low longer-run marginal effect of commuting on wellbeing:

i) Perhaps individuals face a menu of housing, job, and commuting choice bundles that are close to each other in terms of total wellbeing value so that a longer commute may simply lead an individual to pick a different job or place to live such that wellbeing remains close to the original level. In traditional economic parlance one could say they were already close to indifferent to other choices in the longer run. There may thus be benefits to being forced to change working or housing practices when commuting times get 'too long' such that the eventual effect on wellbeing may be close to zero.

[23] Importantly, individuals could enjoy commuting themselves but still be willing to pay to reduce their commuting times, for example if there is a loss to the rest of the family.

[24] Jacob et al. (2019) attempt to hone in on more random changes in commuting by using changes in self-reported commuting over time in the Understanding Society panel data for those individuals who remain in the same job and the same home address. They find small negative effects of commuting on the wellbeing of women, but not of men. The problem in this paper remains that the source of these changes in commuting times is unknown and the observed changes in commuting times might well reflect measurement error (which biases results towards zero). Indeed, the finding that men are not negatively affected by higher commuting times suggests they might not personally suffer (but that their family does) or that the change in commuting times reflects some other change in job circumstances (or modes of commuting).

ii) Perhaps individuals work while commuting, effectively substituting the workplace for the mode of transport used. Similarly, perhaps individuals substitute other forms of leisure time for commuting time such that they read or do sports when commuting on foot or by bike. Then, the cost of commuting is just equal to the transport costs as the commuting activity is effectively the same activity that would be done under a different heading even without any commuting. There is, of course, a limit to how much other forms of leisure or at-work time can be substituted with commuting time, but perhaps for the vast majority of commuters that limit is not reached.

These are merely speculations because, since we lack truly good causal studies on the effect of commuting on wellbeing, we also lack good causal studies on how people adjust to large changes in commuting time. Nevertheless, they tally with the general observation on wellbeing that levels of wellbeing are high for individuals living in suburbs and for people with higher socio-economic status who do a lot of international business travel, holding everything else (especially compensatory factors such as higher incomes) constant.[25] There may also be individuals for whom there exists an optimal, non-zero amount of time spent commuting, for example because they walk or cycle to work and thus combine physical exercise with commuting. In other words, not all travel-to-work time is necessarily detrimental to wellbeing.

A Wider Case for Transport

When it then comes to the economic case for transport, a recent paper on the longer-term development of London in the nineteenth century (and beyond) makes important general observations on transport, city density, and the economy. Heblich et al. (2020) argue that reductions in transportation costs in the long run do not strongly affect commuting times but rather the size of the city: the quicker one can get everywhere in a city, the larger it becomes. People simply travel further. The nature of activities in a city also changes with size: the centre stops being the place where people live and starts to be the place where people work in large numbers, with the opposite pattern starting to emerge at the urban fringes.

Within this logic of the 'transportation changes the equilibrium size and structure' theory of transport and urban development, the key benefit of new and better transport infrastructure is not in reduced commuting time but rather in economic agglomeration benefits arising from a bigger city and more

[25] For instance, business travel is a form of high-status commuting definitely not associated with low wellbeing (Derudder and Witlox, 2016).

interconnected regions, i.e. increased specialization and returns to scale. In turn, increased specialization has immensely complex effects on society as a whole through many different channels. For example, it gives rise to longer, more specialized education and different social structures as it leads to more choice and the demise of large groups that identify themselves by doing the same professional activities (such as farming or coal mining). Specialization also has many economic benefits, such as more goods and services being transported as whole regions specialize and become interconnected. International value chains start to emerge, combining the specializations of lots of smaller populations and places around the globe. This creates interdependences between regions with all sorts of effects, including arguably very positive effects like strong incentives for cooperation, reducing levels of conflict (Pinker, 2012).

The case for new and better transport infrastructure thus changes from being based on individual commuting times to being based on general equilibrium effects of bigger cities, interconnected regions, and the higher degree of specialization and larger economies resulting from these developments. From a wellbeing perspective, a larger economy pays more taxes and thus more public goods and services, as long as it does not, of course, come at the expense of other public goods such as environmental capital. It is likely that the overall wellbeing benefits of higher private consumption due to higher specialization are quite small as the effects of higher income on wellbeing are quite small and subject to negative private consumption externalities. Rather, it is the larger number of public goods and services paid by higher taxes from the additional economic activity that provides the main wellbeing benefits (see chapters 2 and 4). The pacification effect of trade also looms large in a full wellbeing calculation.

So, in conclusion, the Bristol study, like others before it, fails to find a significant effect of longer commuting times on life satisfaction or health, meaning that individual costs of commuting time are not that large, though future studies might reverse that conclusion. The wellbeing case of more infrastructure then revolves around the overall effects of the greater specialization and interconnectedness.

Case Study 5: The London-Heathrow Runway Expansion

Pre-amble: From Traditional CBA to Wellbeing CEA

In reality, different government departments and agencies are at different stages of implementation of a more evidence-based system of policy-making. Some are getting used to the idea of gathering data and conducting experiments. Others are used to gathering data only, although not necessarily data on wellbeing but on other, loosely associated indicators. Yet others are used to data and evidence but are only doing economic surplus calculations when it comes to policy evaluation and appraisal.

In chapter 4, we suggested various ways in which traditional CBA could be augmented with insights from wellbeing or, at a later stage, even be replaced with fully fledged wellbeing CEA. Here, we want to illustrate that transition by looking at the example of a proposed London-Heathrow airport runway expansion. In particular, we ask the following questions:

1. Keeping the basic methodology and thinking as is, how could insights from wellbeing augment the traditional CBA?
2. If we were to take a wellbeing-augmented CBA instead and apply a 50 per cent Easterlin Discount, what would the new appraisal look like?
3. If we were to switch to a fully fledged wellbeing CEA, what would the new appraisal look like then?

The Economic Case for the London-Heathrow Runway Expansion

A 2015 report by the Airports Commission (Airports Commission, 2015b), a government appointed body, presented the basic case for the expansion of London-Heathrow airport by adding a third runway and associated infrastructure facilities (such as more public transport) in order to reduce congestion and travel time.

The report itself refers to several separate studies on the economic impact, the financing arrangements, and the quality of life impacts of a third runway.[26] It is based largely on economic modelling of changes in consumer demand for air flight, but augments this with add-on models of within-UK transportation, the competition between the different UK airports, and various scenarios for how a proposed carbon price might be implemented over time.

The basic economic case is illustrated below in the following three figures, where prices (P) are on the vertical and the volume of passengers (Q) is on the horizontal axis.

This first diagram (Figure 5.4) introduces the main elements of the economic case, which are demand curves for air flights, a marginal cost curve (MC) for airlines, and a capacity constraint on the number of landing spots at London-Heathrow airport (or the United Kingdom as a whole). The picture shows that the

[26] See Airports Commission (2015b), particularly page 87 (hat-tip to one of our sponsors).

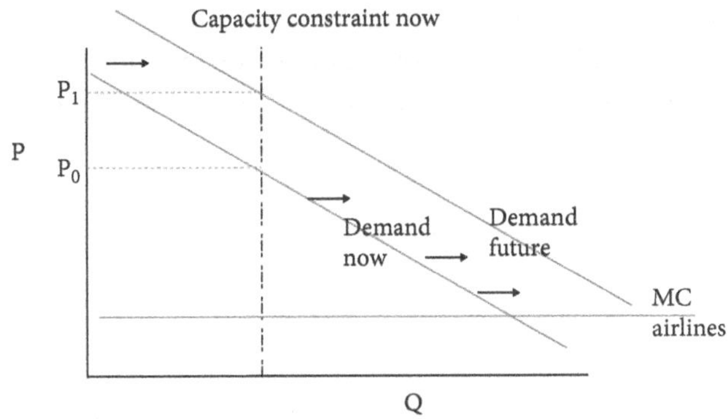

Figure 5.4 Basic economic case for airport expansion benefits: status quo assumptions
Source: Own illustration.

demand is assumed to increase over time, which, in the case that prices are set by the marginal consumer, would lead to an increase in prices to consumers from P_0 to P_1 if there is no increase in capacity. The actual modelling is, of course, far more complicated, with regulators preventing the price from being too high, with different types of services (such as international-to-international transfers, domestic flights, and international flights), and far more dynamics than just two time periods. However, the basic rationale of the economic case is this somewhat standard economic demand-supply framework in which the capacity interacts with demand to produce a price. So one imagines they have to make a decision at time 0, facing a possible future time period 1 in which prices would rise as demand increases but capacity remains fixed.

The basic idea of the capacity increase is then to increase total volume and reduce prices for consumers, which is illustrated in Figure 5.5.

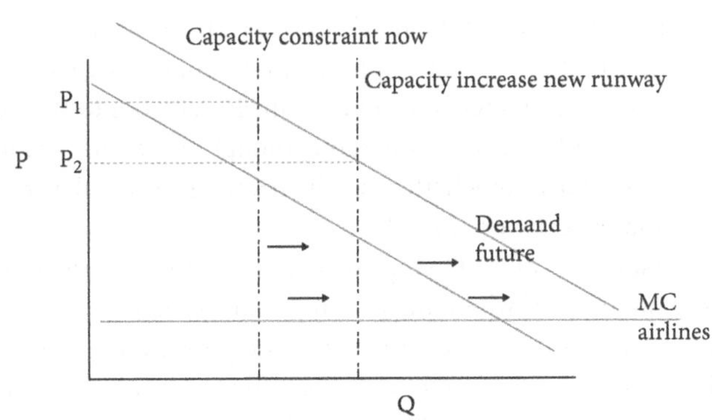

Figure 5.5 Basic economic case for airport expansion benefits: capacity increase
Source: Own illustration.

Here, P_2 is the new, lower price of future air flights relative to the anticipated status quo price P_1. Within the logic of standard economic analysis, this then leads to changes in both consumer and producer surplus, which are illustrated in Figure 5.6.

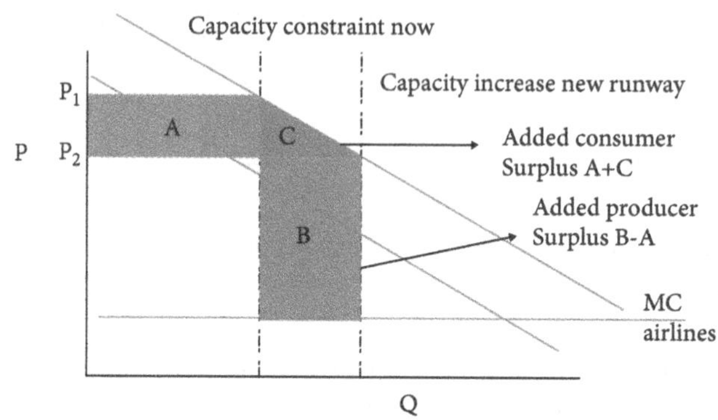

Figure 5.6 Basic economic case for airport expansion benefits: capacity increase effect on surplus

Source: Own illustration.

Consumers gain A+C from the increased capacity while producers gain B–A: the decrease in the price comes at the expense of profits, but producers are more than compensated by a higher profit volume coming from additional consumers.

One might think that this result is quite sensitive to assumptions on how competition in the airline industry works, for example because airports have market power relative to the airlines and can hence charge airlines. However, this is largely a matter of labelling. If one thinks of the price in the above diagrams as the total price charged to consumers, then the difference between the consumer price and the marginal cost of airlines is the value that airports can bargain over with airlines. If airports have all the market power, this is what they could charge airlines. The change in the eventual surplus from the runway expansion would still be the same, but now the change in producer surplus all goes to the airport rather the airlines. The basic idea remains the same, though these nuances matter to the United Kingdom insofar as to whether profits from airlines and airport operators are distributed domestically or abroad.

From the perspective of wellbeing, which is oriented towards the national population, the question of where the producer surplus goes to is highly relevant, as it is for any other policy which is related to the public purse, such as health or education. However, in which circumstances one should make a distinction between domestic or foreign beneficiaries is largely a discussion for a different forum because it is not truly wellbeing-specific but arises for any measure of social welfare. One can see 'equal treatment for foreign and domestic entities' in particular realms as something that arises from international negotiations and thus from larger strategic considerations.

The London-Heathrow Runway Expansion Appraisal

We take the appraisal results in the final report by the Airports Commission (2015a) at their face value. The report states:

> Against the objective of maximizing *economic benefits* and supporting the competitiveness of the UK economy the Heathrow Airport Northwest Runway option performs most strongly, generating £69.1 billion of benefits, compared to £58.7 billion from the Extended Northern Runway scheme and £60.1 billion from the Gatwick Second Runway. (page 149)

This final recommendation thus delineates economic benefits from other benefits, though this is not well defined, and puts weight on the particular figures in Table 5.8 that summarizes various costs and benefits.

Table 5.8 Appraisal results for London-Heathrow Airport Northwest Runway scheme, present value (£billion, 2014 prices)

Appraisal results	Assessment of needs	
	Carbon traded (CT)	Carbon capped (CC)
Monetized*		
Consumer surplus	54.8	33.6*
Producer surplus	−38.4	−25.8*
Government revenue	1.8	1.9*
Delays	1.0	3.0
Wider economic impacts	11.5	7.7*
Noise	−1.0	−1.5
Air quality	−0.8	−0.8
Carbon emissions	−0.9	−0.7
Biodiversity	0	0
Total benefits	69.1	46.2
Total dis-benefits	−41.1	−28.8
Net social benefit	**28.0**	**17.4**
Scheme capex and surface access cost	−16.1	−16.0
NPV (net social benefits and PVC)	**11.8**	**1.4**
Non-monetized*		
Surface access	↑	
Quality of life	→	
Community	↓	
Place	↓	

Continued

Table 5.8 *Continued*

Appraisal results	Assessment of needs
Local economy	↑↑
Water and flood risk	↓

Notes: *indicates the demand reduction sensitivity results. Arrows are used to represent the Commission's view of the likely direction of the non-monetized impacts: ↓↓ is strongly negative, ↓ is slightly negative, → is neutral, ↑ is slightly positive, and ↑↑ is very positive.

Source: Airports Commission (2015b).

The two columns compare two different pricing mechanisms that are supposed to keep the runway expansion carbon-neutral, which means they involve different levels of carbon pricing: carbon-traded (CT) pricing of the additional carbon generated by the additional air flights would involve buying off-sets and would be relatively cheap. On the other hand, carbon-cap (CC) would be more expensive, although the implementation of this mechanism is somewhat unclear as a cap might mean that Heathrow is only allowed to have so much emissions from airplanes, presumably implying a shift to less carbon-intensive airplanes.

The table implicitly uses discounted values over a long time horizon. The net present value (NPV) is basically total benefits minus costs. One can see that the bulk of the value change is taken up by producer and consumer surplus (the areas in Figure 5.6), with the rest calculated to be a different kind of consumer or producer surplus accruing to different agents, such as those living near. Government revenue is valued similar to personal consumption, not at the value to consumers that government spending would entail, that is the degree to which government spending has higher overall wellbeing effects than personal consumption. Noise is essentially treated as a negative consumption good that is valued via the effect of noise on health, which is then valued using estimates from the NHS.

The table is thus rooted in the logic of classic economics, where goods are valued by market prices and government consumption is added linearly to private consumption. When there are goods that are not marketed (and hence not in GDP), such as noise, the approach is to try and find substitutes close to them and use their market value. Interestingly though, consumer surplus is itself a valuation of an intangible because it relates to how much more consumers would be willing to pay for something they obtain at a particular price. It is not directly observed but inferred from estimated elasticities of demand curves. Consumer surplus is thus some form of pleasure ('utility') derived from consumption over and beyond the displeasure of the price paid.

There are several things to note about the elements in this table even before discussing how insights from wellbeing might change the figures. The first point to note is, of course, that the table shows various domains in which the runway expansion is acknowledged to worsen wellbeing, for example, community and places like heritage sites. Yet, their value is implicitly set to zero and does not enter the final recommendation of the Airports Commission in a similar fashion as 'economic benefits' do. So 'noise' and pleasure from cheaper air travel consumption is taken as an economic benefit, but displeasure from the erosion of communities or places like heritage sites is not. The table and the final recommendation is, therefore, a perfect illustration of the old adage that if something is not measured it does not count: community, place, heritage, or quality of life are deemed economically worthless because there is no acknowledged measure to assign them a monetary value.

A second point to note is that the figures are not very sensible even within the stated methodology. As one can see from the very high, positive increase in consumer surplus, the runway expansion is assumed to lead to lower prices and more passengers. It is also supposed to lead to much lower producer surplus, i.e. profits. Given that the airlines operate in a highly competitive industry with very low profit margins (Doganis, 2013), the supposed decrease in producer surplus from airline profit decreases seems uncertain. Indeed, the expansion is supposedly organized and largely financed by the airport operator—a private business—that is assumed to recoup its investment through higher 'aero charges' allowed by a regulator, which would be an increase in producer and decrease in consumer surplus. So the stated presumed drop in producer surplus is not truly what is expected at all, and deep in the report on page 89 the point is conceded that the regulator is expected to allow an increase in 'aero charges', meaning the headline advertised increase in consumer surplus is not truly what is expected. This results in an artificially high 'economic benefit' in the concluding remarks.

Another point to note is that the table counts all consumer and producer surplus equally, although the report does mention that about 30 per cent of the passengers are foreign, implying that the supposed increase in consumer surplus will benefit different countries. If one were to subtract 30 per cent off the claimed consumer benefit, it would make the net present value negative to the United Kingdom. This is, therefore, a clear case where it matters just whose benefits count for the country. However, given that the point before made clear that the claimed consumer surplus increase is unlikely, it is largely irrelevant whether it is foreign or domestic.

A regulatory question is why the expansion proposal is not compared with increased taxation on tourists to keep prices constant, for example by levying a tax on landing in the United Kingdom that keeps pace with demand increases, converting much of the surplus into domestic tax.[27] Such proposals may be outside the remit of the Airports Commission, but surely relevant to the United

[27] There are already taxes on landing. Many countries in the EU have city-based or airport-based tourist taxes of some form or another. For an overview, see https://ec.europa.eu/growth/

Kingdom as a whole. So there is much to argue about if one really delves into the report.

However, this is not the place to analyse this report in depth and critique every aspect of it, also because the report explicitly admits that it is not HMT Green Book compliant (because, for example, it does not calculate net public costs). It should suffice to say that each aspect of this table can be reasonably questioned even under conventional viewpoints, as would be true with almost any other appraisal. We mainly pointed out some major issues to make clear that these cost-benefit calculations are not done in a political or business vacuum.

Let us now consider how this table would change if we were to adopt more wellbeing knowledge in two particular classic wellbeing areas: noise and air pollution.

Noise

On noise, the report takes a QALY approach, stating that:

> This approach values the noise impacts by estimating the number of years of life lost or spent with a disability, to get the number of QALYs lost, and uses established values for each QALY lost to arrive at the total monetised noise impact. The quantified and monetised impacts of noise cannot fully reflect people's individual experience of noise.

Augmenting the traditional CBA with wellbeing insights on noise would mean to focus primarily on the estimated impact of airport noise on wellbeing and then to value that impact using the willingness-to-pay for a WELLBY of £9,000. Estimates of the impact of airport noise on wellbeing can be found in Lawton and Fujiwara (2016), for example. The general relationship between noise and wellbeing as well as mental health has been subject of many studies in the wider academic literature (see van Praag and Baarsma (2005), for a prominent example of airport noise) and reviewed in Beutel et al. (2016). To be fair, there is not yet a definitive study with a very strong causal randomized design that can be relied on to yield a short-run and long-run estimate of the causal effects of different types of noise on wellbeing, but there is an established body of literature showing that, in particular, unexpected noise (as from airplanes) negatively affects wellbeing and mental health, so the general direction of impacts is established.

Over and above the wellbeing impact would be the cost to the public of the health effect of noise. One would not additionally value the health effect itself, because it would already be included the WELLBY cost, but one would add the likely cost to the public health system because that is a further externality to

sectors/tourism/business-portal/financing-your-business/tourism-related-taxes-across-eu_en and PwC (2017).

the public purse. These additional costs will come from both the mental and the physical health effects: noise has negative effects on mental health and reduced mental health is known to increase physical health costs at any given level (see the example on the IAPT programme in chapter 3).

On balance, because noise has mental health effects that are not fully reflected in the QALY methodology of the report, but that would be reflected in a WELLBY methodology which more strongly relates to mental health, the total cost of noise would be expected to be higher when valued using WELLBYs. It is interesting to note what the report says in this regard:

> Locally, the impacts of airport development include impacts of aircraft noise . . . The literature review suggests that there is significant evidence linking these impacts to people's subjective wellbeing. Testing this using the Annual Population Survey (APS) and Mappiness data gives some interesting results . . . living in a daytime noise contour (over 55dB) is negatively associated with all subjective wellbeing measures while living in a night time aircraft contour was not associated with any effect on subjective wellbeing.

We agree with their statement of the literature, since Lawton and Fujiwara (2016), and indeed many studies find evidence of lower life satisfaction and mental health due to noise. Yet, we should also point out their use of the experience sampling methods like Mappiness to inform their question. As we explained in chapter 2, these methods fail to pick up how people think about their own life. Experience sampling, which in the case of Mappiness consists of asking people via their mobiles how they feel right now, does not pick up many mental health issues, nor does it correlate that highly with life satisfaction. This is why Daniel Kahneman and others have now abandoned these measures as proxies for well-being. So exactly what mental health damage individuals are aware of with noise is likely missing from Mappiness-type data. Using a less well-established wellbeing measure which yields a (conveniently) low estimate of the effects of noise thus illustrates how one can be selective with the term wellbeing if there is not a clear adopted standard.

We thus think it is better to go with the estimates of the strongest research study one can find rather than rely on own estimations of small ad hoc studies to dismiss an effect. After all, the report does not empirically investigate the health effects of noise but takes recommended estimates.

Air Pollution

When it comes to air pollution, the report looks at health and buildings:

> For the air quality impacts for the carbon-traded scenario, Department for Environment, Food and Rural Affairs (DEFRA) values of damage cost per

tonne of emissions of NOx and PM10 have been used to monetise the air quality impacts on health and morbidity as well as damage to buildings.

Here too, we would recommend relying more on estimates of the wellbeing effects of air pollution, such as from the study by Luechinger (2009) mentioned in chapters 2 and 3. These wellbeing effects can then be converted into a monetary value using the willingness-to-pay measure. Since Luechinger (2009) and others have found that air pollution has negative effects on wellbeing and mental health that individuals seem to be poorly aware of and that are only limitedly reflected in real estate prices, we expect the effects of air pollution to turn out to be much higher under a wellbeing lens. These wellbeing effects include the mental health costs over and above the physical health costs, and are far higher than when looking at measures derived from property prices.

Now, in an analogous manner, Table 5.9 highlights where insights from wellbeing would likely make changes to the standard CBA shown previously:

In short, the key changes would be:

Table 5.9 Appraisal results for London-Heathrow Airport Northwest Runway scheme, present value (£billion, 2014 prices). Improved intangible valuation

Appraisal results	**Assessment of needs**	
Carbon-traded (CT)/capped (CC)	CT	CC
Monetized*		
Consumer surplus	54.8	33.6*
Producer surplus	−38.4	−25.8*
Government revenue	1.8	1.9*
Delays	1.0	3.0
Wider economic impacts	11.5	7.7*
Noise	−1	−1.5
Air quality	−0.8	−0.8
Carbon emissions	−0.9	−0.7
Biodiversity	0	0
Total benefits	69.1	46.2
Total dis-benefits	−41.1	−28.8
Net social benefit	**28.0**	**17.4**
Scheme capex and surface access cost	−16.1	−16.0
NPV (net social benefits and PVC)	**11.8**	**1.4**
Non-monetized*		
Surface access	↑	
Quality of life	→	
Community	↓	
Place	↓	
Local economy	↑↑	
Water and flood risk	↓	

Note: *indicates the demand reduction sensitivity results. Arrows are used to represent the Commission's view of the likely direction of the non-monetized impacts: ↓↓ is strongly negative, ↓ is slightly negative, → is neutral, ↑ is slightly positive, and ↑↑ is very positive.

Source: Airports Commission (2015a, 2015b).

1. Insights from wellbeing knowledge could be used to value loss of community cohesion and heritage sites as well as changes in flood risks.
   a. The valuation of community cohesion and heritage sites (or place) has three elements: first, the impact of the runway expansion on place and key aspects of communities (cohesion primarily); second, the impact of these intermediary outcomes on wellbeing (ideally taken from the literature); third, the monetary valuation using the accepted monetary value of a WELLBY, which, following the logic of this table, would be the willingness of individuals to pay for one WELLBYs (valued at £9,000).
   b. The valuation of changes in flood risks would include standard elements (such as damage to property) but also a wellbeing-based valuation of loss-of-life (based on the fact that every year of lost life is counted as a loss of about six WELLBYs). The relevant value of a WELLBY would, following the logic of this table, be the willingness of individuals to pay for one WELLBY (again valued at £9,000).
2. The valuation of delays and air quality is likely to change significantly when using insights from wellbeing knowledge because we know that noise has effects on wellbeing and mental health that are only insufficiently captured in real estate prices or physical health. We also know that delays are presumably less detrimental to wellbeing than you would probably think from valuing them at the hourly wage of individuals. Hence, the anticipated negative effect of more noise is likely to increase and the anticipated positive effect of less delays is likely to decrease when using insights from wellbeing.
3. Of course, the same in principle would go for the non-monetized aspects which are currently highlighted in green: there too, one would value intangibles using wellbeing.

Let us discuss the 'belonging' aspect of the runway expansion, that is the disruption to community life if several homes are displaced and communities affected. The report states:

> As noted above, *783 homes* are expected to be lost to enable the delivery of the additional runway and further could be required due to associated surface access infrastructure. In addition, a small number of community facilities would also be lost, including a *primary school, community centres and a recreation ground.* Financial support and the likely availability of alternatives nearby would mitigate the lost facilities, and compensation would need to be provided for housing loss.

Now, what buying houses does is to compensate individuals for the loss of current consumption value of their home. As the report acknowledged, it does not compensate for the discomfort of having to build a new life elsewhere, which would be an unanticipated inconvenience for many: people who voluntarily move from home to home have some life elsewhere in mind, but people forced to move are less likely to have a clear alternative. Perhaps most importantly, the displacement of 783 homes can have very negative consequences for community cohesion. Many of the social relationships and expectations built up between people living in these homes may be lost. Since social relationships and interpersonal expectations are not privately owned, they cannot be bought.

Yet, disruptions to community cohesion happen often due to economic activity or natural processes such as demographic changes. One way to see this disruption to community life is, therefore, to view the social relationships between people, captured in indicators like trust or community cohesion, akin to employer-employee relations. When considering the unemployment effects of economic change one thinks of the natural rate at which the newly unemployed find different jobs elsewhere. The total disruption is then the discounted loss of employment as people adjust until a new equilibrium is reached. So too can one view disruption in social relationships: it depends on the natural rate at which people involved find new friends and new communities elsewhere. The total discounted loss in social relationships and community cohesion would then need to be translated into a WELLBY effect based on the effects of social relationships and community cohesion on life satisfaction.

Those calculations cannot be done as yet because the literature on building social relations does not yet have a clear estimate of the natural rate of relationship formation. Yet, there are some indicators for these rates, such as the estimated speed with which migrants in a new region or country adapt to the wellbeing and economic life of their adopted region (see the World Happiness Report (2018), for example). Estimates of the speed of adaptation for different combinations of migrants and recipient communities could be converted to some notion of the total number of days of normal social relations lost when individuals are forced to move, which in turn could be used as an estimate in forced disruptions like those involved in major infrastructure projects.

An Easterlin Discount

A more substantive shift away from traditional CBA would occur if we allow for negative private consumption externalities, also referred to as *status effects*, which we introduced in chapter 2 and further developed in chapters 3 and 4.

The basic idea is that negative private consumption externalities should be taken into consideration. As a default, no status effects are assumed for public goods (which belong to everyone) or welfare-state expenses (which are accessible by everyone). A blanket status effect is assumed for all private economic surplus, including after-tax income and profits.

Importantly, this introduces distinctions not made in the original runway expansion report, particularly between government revenue and the economic surplus of consumers and producers. Unlike the youth traineeship programme in

Wales discussed earlier, the original runway expansion does not calculate 'Exchequer effects' of the runway expansion and thus does not differentiate between higher private consumption and higher tax revenue. Yet, for a proper application of the Easterlin Discount that distinction is crucial. It is also crucial for a government business case and for social rates-of-return analyses because they too put heavy emphasis on how much money flows in and out of the public purse because of an intervention.

The original runway expansion does not calculate for any scenario whether the public purse gains or loses, although some forms of public-purse effect do show up, such as government revenue via taxes on flights or a 'tax wedge' applying to certain additional economic activities involved in expansion. However, private surplus is not differentiated into private after-tax surplus and additional taxes, nor is 'additional economic activity' differentiated in more private value added and changes in the total tax take.[28] Similarly, the 'surface access costs' that are estimated to be £5 billion are said in the report to be split between the private sector and the government, although that split is not explicitly depicted.

As a result, we cannot properly apply an Easterlin Discount to items where it is appropriate and where it is not. We can only sketch how it might look like by applying an Easterlin Discount to all items of private surplus if we make a guess about the likely changes in tax revenue involved.

Taking a conservative estimate for the Easterlin Discount (50 per cent) would imply see imply several changes, as depicted in Table 5.10.

Table 5.10 Appraisal results for London-Heathrow Airport Northwest Runway scheme, present value (£ billion, 2014 prices): 50 per cent Easterlin Discount and re-arranged

Appraisal results	Carbon-traded (CT)	
With or without Easterlin Discount (ED)	Without ED	With ED
Monetized		
Consumer surplus	54.8	27.4
Producer surplus	−38.4	−19.2
Scheme capex and private paid surface access cost	−13.6	−6.8
Primary surplus change	2.8	1.4
Delays	1.0	1.0
Wider economic impacts post-tax	6.9	3.45
Noise	−1.0	−1.0

Continued

[28] Another aspect that is unclear in the original evaluation report is that the additional capital expenditure (referred to as the *Scheme Capex*) shows up as a cost, but it is not clear from the basic appraisal table where the supposed returns to that investment are. The report states on page 89 that 'the airport scheme would be financed privately and offset via rising aero charges levied on the passengers and users of the airport (not accounted for in this calculation)'. This is unclear: even after granting that an aero charge is a transfer from consumer to producer surplus and hence does not change the total surplus, it means the headline consumer surplus benefit is actually anticipated to be less than reported. To allow for a decent return on the capex (which is assumed) would need far less consumer and more producer surplus.

Table 5.10 *Continued*

Appraisal results	Carbon-traded (CT)	
With or without Easterlin Discount (ED)	Without ED	With ED
Air quality	−0.8	−0.8
Carbon emissions	−0.9	−0.9
Biodiversity	0	0
Government paid surface access costs	−2.5	−2.5
Taxes (40%) from wider economic impact	4.6	4.6
Government revenue	1.8	1.8
NPV (net social benefits and PVC)	**11.9**	**7.05**
Non-monetized		
Surface access	↑	
Quality of life	→	
Community	↓	
Place	↓	
Local economy	↑↑	
Water and flood risk	↓	

Note: Arrows are used to represent the Commission's view of the likely direction of the non-monetized impacts: ↓↓ is strongly negative, ↓ is slightly negative, → is neutral, ↑ is slightly positive, and ↑↑ is very positive.

Source: Own illustration, based on Airports Commission (2015b).

Let us go over these changes:

1. We have rearranged what seem to be the primary impacts of the runway expansion on passengers, airlines, and the airport operator, which we call the primary surplus. This makes it visible what the assumed commercial point of the exercise is, which is that the anticipated total increase in surplus (even with aero charges) is more than the capex costs of the scheme as paid for by the airport operator. The fact that the report can claim the airport operator is confident of being able to raise the funding means confidence in high enough future demand so that the new capacity constraint can be hit even with all passengers paying higher aero charges.
2. We have rearranged all the non-government benefits that do not immediately accrue to passengers, airlines, or the airport operator so as to highlight the strong importance of the assumed additional economic benefits and the low relative importance of noise and other intangibles.
3. We have put all the supposed government public purse effects into one group, where we made the assumption that the government would pick up half the 'surface access cost' and obtains 40 per cent of the additional economic activity via taxes (where 40 per cent is the government to GDP ratio). This shows what the public purse 'gets out of it', where we still neglect the actual public costs involved in air and noise pollution, loss of community cohesion and heritage sites, and so on. So we are still following the assumption that these costs are not borne by the public purse or are zero.

4. We have applied the Easterlin Discount (in column 2) to all private-surplus-related elements, which includes wider economic activity. This treats all forms of market-related consumer surplus as subject to a private negative consumption externality of 50 per cent unless proven otherwise. We would actually prefer to directly apply it to the presumed increase in surplus rather than the consumer and producer surplus separately since the report itself already suggests that the actual division is different from the one shown because of the aero charges that were not deducted from consumer surplus but that have to pay for the capex.
5. Importantly, we have also applied an Easterlin Discount to the capex even though this investment is in large parts a transfer in assets from the previous owners of the land, who are bought out, to the new owners. This follows the logic of wanting to apply both the Easterlin Discount and the calculation of net present value to the change in total consumption. That change is the supposed aero charges minus the capex, though this does assume that the former owners of the land bought have no private consumption value from owning that land or its buildings (no one is jealous of their runway).
6. The Easterlin Discount does not apply to government revenue because that is at the margin not spent on private consumption but on public goods and services for everyone (with strong benefits to wellbeing to everyone, as discussed in chapters 2 and 3).
7. The Easterlin Discount does not apply to largely invisible private non-monetized items, such as noise, or non-personal negative external effects such as carbon emissions. This is partly because individuals are not well aware of what causes reductions in their mental health (see Luechinger (2009), for example). It is also partly because lack of noise is seen as a basic good (a 'universal right') which is not a status good but more of a general entitlement applying to everyone.

Wellbeing CEA

Now that we have augmented the traditional CBA in the original evaluation report with insights from the wellbeing literature, we ask: what would happen in terms of policy appraisal if we were to move to a fully fledged wellbeing CEA?

Many of the monetary estimates coming out of the traditional CBA would be translated into wellbeing estimates. To do so, we use, as a conversion factor, an income coefficient of 0.4 for a doubling of income, which originates from a study exploiting Swedish lottery wins as a source of exogenous variation in income (Lindqvist et al., 2020). An Easterlin Discount would then be applied, implying that the consumer and producer surplus changes would be worth relatively little in wellbeing terms.

We give an illustrative calculation if we take these numbers at face value, which we do not think is realistic, but just to illustrate. If we make the assumption that the median income of those who obtain the additional surplus is £30,000 (which is a little lower than average GDP, hence a conservative estimate), then the additional £4.9 billion in private economic surplus (primary surplus plus the wider economic activities) would be worth about 40,000 WELLBYs (=0.4×4,900,000,000/30,000). The effects of air and noise pollution as well as other of non-monetized costs and benefits would also be translated into WELLBYs. All of this would then be summed up and related to the total discounted change in the public purse, which is assumed to be positive (£3.9 billion, mainly due to the taxes on the wider economic activities). Thus, unless the estimated total WELLBY effects become negative or the public costs turn negative, there is actually a negative cost per WELLBY from the runway expansion, even when applying an Easterlin Discount.

A fully fledged wellbeing CEA of the policy options around Heathrow would also entail a consideration of other factors that are wellbeing relevant. To name just a few of these factors, of which some but not all are briefly considered in the original evaluation report: who should make profits from increased tourism, central government (via airport taxes) or private airport operators (which can be foreign)? Do we want decreases in private economic surplus, for example, because of its footprint on the world's resources and the potential neglect of other activities?

So in a fully fledged wellbeing CEA, economic activity is a mere input, mainly important to sustain full employment and tax revenue. Sustainability, pleasure, and the question of how (and importantly, with whom) we want to spend our time become primary concerns.

Summing up

We have used the controversial example of the London-Heathrow airport runway expansion to illustrate the differences between traditional CBA, wellbeing-augmented CBA, and a fully-fledged wellbeing CEA. This ranged from using slightly different approaches to valuing air and noise pollution to a full-on consideration of negative private consumption externalities and the public purse costs per WELLBY.

While we commented on many aspects of the original evaluation report by the Airports Commission, we are not in the position to make any judgement on its methodology, merely pointing out that even the presentation of appraisals would differ, such as by splitting private surplus from changes in the public purse, which is irrelevant for net present value yet crucial for cost-effectiveness calculations.

Case Study 6: The Health and Wellbeing at Work Survey

This case study is about the design and findings of the Health and Wellbeing at Work Survey in 2014, conducted by the Department for Work and Pensions in the UK. The survey was developed with reference to an earlier survey conducted in 2011. Different from this earlier survey, the Health and Wellbeing at Work Survey in 2014 had a particular focus on sickness absence and support provided by employers to help employees with health conditions remain in work or return to work after an extended period of sickness absence. It also studied attitudes towards Fit for Work, which was then a new, independent health and work advice and referral service—largely modelled after the existing Health and Work Service in the United Kingdom—to be launched at the end of 2014 (after the survey had been conducted). So the survey was partly scanning the demand and support for the planned Fit for Work service.

Relevantly, part of the Fit for Work service stopped in 2018 because it was hardly used, but that was, of course, not known at the time of the survey. We base our observations on the research report on the Health and Wellbeing at Work Survey in 2014 (Department for Work and Pensions, 2015). However, lessons learnt from this survey about wellbeing at work, and about wellbeing services for work more generally, are transferable to similar surveys and services throughout the world.

The Fit for Work service targeted employees who reached or were expected to reach four weeks of sickness absence. After this time, there is an increased risk of longer-term absence which accounts for 40 per cent or more of work time lost (Black and Frost, 2011). Eligible employees were referred to the service by their general practitioners and use of the service was consent based. During the intake session, an assessment was conducted by an occupational health professional who looked at issues preventing the employee from returning to work, who gave recommendations on how to return more quickly, and who provided information on how to get appropriate help and advice.

An important element of the service was the creation of an individual return-to-work plan, which identified barriers to returning to work and derived strategies on how to overcome these barriers. Finally, Fit for Work gave employers, employees, and general practitioners access to general health and work advice via phone and online (www.fitforwork.org). This last element (the advice lines) still existed at the end of 2019, and we understand that new initiatives are likely to fill the void left by lack of direct help in planning the future work relationship.

Let us briefly consider the question how one might in principle want to evaluate the Fit for Work service using surveys, because the Health and Wellbeing at Work Survey in 2014 was partially set up to evaluate the demand by employees and employers for such a service.

In terms of finding out what employees with health problems might think of an intended new service, just asking them via a survey seems a sensible thing to do. To find out whether the service had the intended outcomes would need more than surveys, though, as it would require an understanding of what change the service would make. Partly, this is about simply checking whether the service was used at all. Supposing it was, one would then have to follow individuals over time (before-and-after) and to have a comparable group that did not have access to the service during the same period (a control group). In fact, to evaluate the impacts of a programme in wide use, the first-best would be to consciously randomize who has access to the service and compare the group with access (i.e. the treatment group) to another group without (i.e. the control group). That would require one to follow both groups over time though, which could be quite costly.

A cheaper way to evaluate the impact of a programme such as Fit for Work would be to see if it was introduced gradually and in a staggered way across the country so that one can compare the changes in outcomes for regions that were early adopters with those for regions that were later adopters. Another possibility would be to identify workers who fell just below the eligibility criteria of four weeks of sickness absence, and compare those with the ones who were just eligible. If there was differential awareness and usage across workplaces, that could also be exploited.

Second-best options to evaluate the impacts of a programme such as Fit for Work would be to ask employers and employees what their experiences were and whether they would recommend the service, or to simply look at before-and-after outcomes for sick employees in organizations around the time of introduction. A quick survey or simple before-and-after analyses of current data has the advantage of being fairly cheap relative to collecting longitudinal data in a proper randomized controlled trial.

Wellbeing and Health at Work

To give some background, wellbeing at work is increasingly recognized as a priority area for policy. Annual costs of ill health due to workdays lost (i.e. absenteeism) and worklessness (i.e. presenteeism) are estimated to be above £100 billion (Black, 2008). Of these, sickness absence is estimated to be about £15 billion, largely due to lost output (Black and Frost, 2011). Leakages in productivity due to inactivity, therefore, make up the bulk of the costs to the economy. Together, the combined costs of sick pay and other costs involved in managing sickness absence are estimated to be about £9 billion to employers.

Against this background, Fit for Work's aim was to reduce wellbeing-related ill health that leads to costly absenteeism and presenteeism. The general findings of the related Health and Wellbeing at Work Survey in 2014 were (Department for Work and Pensions, 2015, page 3):

- Almost a third of employees had a health condition in the twelve months preceding the survey, defined in the survey as a long-term health condition or disability, or an illness or injury that affected the work they could do.
- Just over one-third of employees with a health condition had not discussed it with their employer, even in cases where it had affected their work. Those with a mental health condition were less comfortable discussing their condition than those with a physical health condition.
- About two-fifths of employees had experienced at least one period of sickness absence. Seven per cent had experienced sickness absence lasting more than two weeks and five per cent more than four weeks.
- Employees who reported a period of sickness absence lasting more than two weeks were more likely to be female, have both a mental and a physical health condition, be employed on a permanent basis and work in a large organization.
- Having a supportive employer and discussing any health condition at an early stage reduced the likelihood of sickness absence of more than two weeks.
- Most employees who had experienced a period of sickness absence lasting more than two weeks or who had a health condition had made adjustments. The most common adjustment was the possibility of taking time off at short notice, followed by flexible hours. Provision of these types of adjustments was more likely for employees who only had a physical health condition.
- Enrolment in workplace pensions, access to flexible working, provision of injury prevention training and occupational health had increased since 2011. An increase did not occur in the provision of policies associated with mental health—stress management training and independent counselling or advice.
- More than four-fifths of employees, including those who had experienced a sickness absence lasting four weeks or more, perceived Fit for Work to be a useful service.

In what follows, we first look at the overall importance of wellbeing at work, by providing empirical evidence on which workplace characteristics matter for wellbeing and, importantly, on how wellbeing matters for employee productivity and firm performance. We then comment on the implementation and findings of the Health and Wellbeing at Work Survey in 2014, with a particular focus on its components capturing wellbeing and attitudes towards Fit for Work.

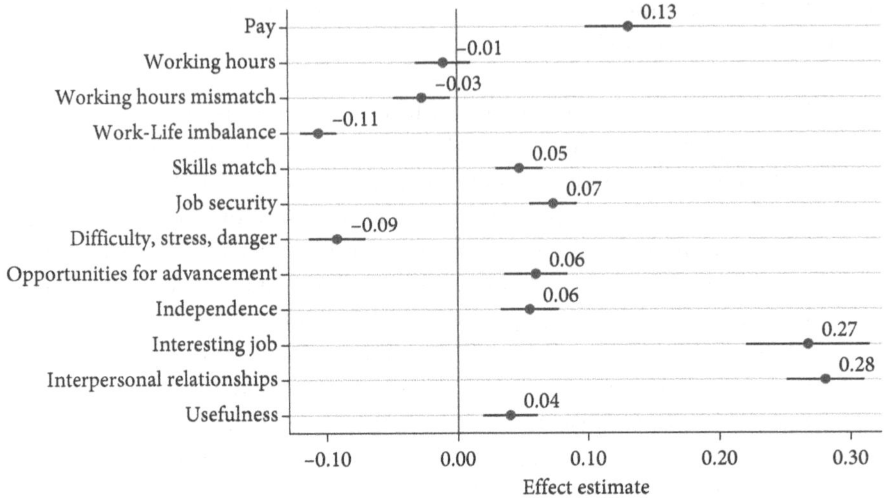

Figure 5.7 Effect of workplace quality on job satisfaction (International Social Survey Programme, Module on Work Orientations, 2015; confidence intervals 95 per cent)

Notes: The figure plots effect estimates obtained from regressing job satisfaction on different domains of workplace quality. All variables (both left-hand side and right-hand side) are standardized with mean zero and standard deviation one; regressors are thus beta coefficients. Squaring a regressor yields the respective share in the variation of job satisfaction that this regressor explains. *Pay, Working Hours Mismatch, Work-Life Imbalance, Skills Match, Difficulty, Stress, Danger, Independence, Interpersonal Relationships*, and *Usefulness* are principle components obtained from separate principle component analyses that condense various variables in the respective domain of workplace quality into a single indicator; see Krekel et al. (2019a) Section 4 for a description of the procedure. The sample is restricted to all individuals who state that they are working and who report working hours greater than zero.

Source: Krekel et al. (2019a).

The Importance of Wellbeing at Work

Before we comment on the survey and the Fit for Work service, let us first take one step back and look at the importance of wellbeing at work, which goes far beyond absenteeism and presenteesim due to mental ill health. It is subdivided into two parts: the first draws on Krekel et al. (2019a) and provides evidence on which specific workplace characteristics matter most for wellbeing at work. The second draws on Krekel et al. (2019b) and provides evidence on how wellbeing at work matters for employee productivity and firm performance.

In both sub-sections, our measure of wellbeing is job satisfaction, which one can see as the part of life satisfaction generated by work-related conditions. Key additional outcomes are worker productivity and firm profits.

Which Workplace Characteristics Matter for Wellbeing at Work

Figure 5.7 shows the key findings on the relationship between workplace characteristics and wellbeing at work from Krekel et al. (2019a). This table uses the latest module on work orientations of the International Social Survey Programme (ISSP)—a comprehensive, internationally comparable survey that reports, for thirty-seven countries across all regions in the world, on a wide array of working conditions alongside wellbeing.

Probably the most interesting finding is that, although pay matters a great deal, it is not the most important determinant of job satisfaction. In fact, the most important determinants are interpersonal relationships at work, especially with management, and having a genuinely interesting job. Both are almost twice as important as pay, and are themselves not statistically significantly distinguishable from each other.

Another interesting finding is that working hours per se have no statistically significant correlation with job satisfaction. What seems to matter, however, is working hours mismatch—the difference between actual and desired working hours, a measure of work-life balance. The negative impact of work-life imbalance is almost as detrimental for job satisfaction as having a difficult, stressful, or even dangerous job.

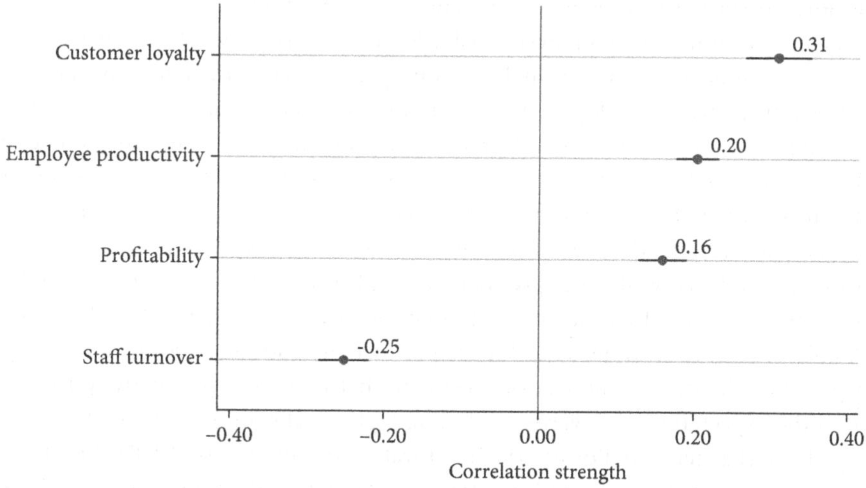

Figure 5.8 Correlation between employee satisfaction with company and firm performance (Gallup Client Database, years 1994 to 2015; confidence intervals 95 per cent)

Notes: The figure plots adjusted average correlation coefficients between employee satisfaction and different performance outcomes originating from a meta-analysis of 339 independent research studies that include observations on the wellbeing of 1,882,131 employees and performance of 82,248 business units. See Krekel et al. (2019b) Section 3 for a description of the procedure.

Source: Krekel et al. (2019b).

All other workplace characteristics—skills match, job security, opportunities for advancement, independent, and usefulness—take a midfield position when it comes to their importance for wellbeing at work.

How Wellbeing at Work Matters for Employee Productivity and Firm Performance

Figure 5.8 presents the key findings from Krekel et al. (2019b). It is based on a meta-analysis that leverages the Gallup client database. Over the years, Gallup has accumulated 339 independent research studies—conducted as proprietary research for clients—that include data on employee wellbeing as well as firm performance. In total, these studies include (partly repeated) observations on the wellbeing of 1,882,131 employees and performance of 82,248 business units, originating from 230 independent organizations across forty-nine industries in seventy-three countries.

Figure 5.8 shows aggregate correlations of employee satisfaction with employee productivity and three key firm performance indicators (customer loyalty, profitability, and staff turnover). To arrive at these aggregate correlations, the authors first calculated separate correlations for each of the 82,248 business units in the Gallup client database. They then employed meta-analytic methods that enabled them to aggregate the correlations and produce generalizable insights. These methods control for differences resulting from sample size, measurement error, or other artefacts to eliminate biases (Hunter and Schmidt, 2015).

Figure 5.8 shows that employee satisfaction is strongly positively correlated with employee productivity and strongly negatively correlated with staff turnover. The correlation between employee satisfaction and customer loyalty is even stronger. Though these correlations are not proof of causality, they are at least suggestive of the idea that higher employee productivity and customer loyalty, as well as lower staff turnover, trickle down to higher profitability at the business-unit level.

There are various theoretical reasons why one might expect a positive relation between employee wellbeing, productivity, and firm performance. Human relations theory states that higher employee wellbeing is associated with higher morale, which, in turn, leads to higher productivity (Strauss, 1968). Conversely, expectancy theories of motivation postulate that employee productivity follows from the expectation of rewards (including higher wellbeing) generated by eliciting effort (Lawler and Porter, 1967; Schwab and Cummings, 1970). Emotions theory argues that employees' emotional states affect their productivity (Staw et al., 1994), and in particular, that positive emotions lead to heightened motivation, and hence better job outcomes and organizational citizenship (Isen and Baron, 1991). A further channel is through positive, stimulating arousal, which can result in more creativity (Isen et al., 1987) or positive changes in attitudes and behaviour (Baumeister et al., 2007).

These studies are thus supportive of the idea that good social relations are important in making work pleasant and healthy, and that high wellbeing at work translates back into higher productivity and profits. With this in mind we can turn to the Health and Wellbeing at Work Survey.

The Health and Wellbeing at Work Survey in 2014

The Health and Wellbeing at Work Survey was conducted in 2014 to support the Health and Work Policy Programme by the Department for Work and Pensions in the United Kingdom. It was commissioned in response to recommendations by the Independent Review of Sickness Absence released in 2011, and includes the Health, Work and Wellbeing indicator set developed in 2010.

The target group of the Health and Wellbeing at Work Survey were paid employees aged 16 and above in Great Britain. There are 2,013 respondents in the main sample plus two boosters of 219 and 139 respondents, respectively, targeting individuals who were off work for more than two weeks, given a low prevalence of employees who had been off work for more than two weeks in the past twelve months. Taken together, there are 2,371 survey respondents in total. Interviews lasted, on average, twenty minutes.

The main sample, which comprises 2,013 respondents, was collected using computer-assisted telephone interviews and random digit-dialling of both landline and mobile phone numbers so as to reach all parts of the phone-using population. Respondents were called at different times of the day and at different times of the week to ensure a nationally representative sample. Field work, which was conducted by NatCen Social Research and the Work Foundation, was from January to April 2014. The response rate for the main sample was about 25 per cent, which is very reasonable for a survey of this type.

The first booster sample, comprising 219 respondents, was collected by following up respondents from the Health Survey for England, Scottish Health Survey, and Welsh Health Survey. Respondents with certain characteristics that made them more likely to have been off work for more than two weeks (i.e. reported health problems and being in work or close to the labour market) were contacted. The second booster sample, comprising 139 respondents, was collected using the contact details of respondents from a consumer access panel (Panelbase).

All three sub-samples were combined and weighted to make the combined, final sample nationally representative of the population of employees aged 16 and above in Great Britain.

Wellbeing

The Health and Wellbeing at Work Survey included the measures on wellbeing from the ONS 'Measuring National Well-being' Programme (Office for National Statistics, 2019), the so-called *ONS-4*, recommended by Dolan and Metcalfe (2012).

They key findings of the Health and Wellbeing at Work Survey in 2014 with respect to wellbeing were (Department for Work and Pensions, 2015, pages 16 and 17):

- Eighty-three per cent of employees reported high to medium life satisfaction.
- Employees with a mental health condition reported lower life satisfaction, as did those with both a mental and physical health condition.
- Higher life satisfaction was associated with employees having more control over their work, better workplace relationships, a greater sense of accomplishment at work, and lower stress at work and at home.

As to health and wellbeing, the survey finds that (Department for Work and Pensions, 2015, page 36):

- Employees with a mental health condition were considerably more likely than those with just a physical condition or without any condition to be in the 'very low' category [of life satisfaction]. Twenty-one per cent of those with only a mental health condition were in the 'very low' category, compared to 3e per cent of those with only a physical condition and 2 per cent of those without a health condition.

These results resonate well with the literature on life satisfaction. Across countries, studies typically find that mean life satisfaction, measured on a scale from 0 to 10, is about 7, with a standard deviation of 2 (Clark et al., 2018). This finding, therefore, fits well with the finding of the survey and the way life satisfaction is collapsed there: categories ten and nine denote 'high', seven and eight 'medium', five and six 'low', and categories four to zero 'very low' life satisfaction.

It is also well-documented that individuals with lower mental health report lower life satisfaction. In fact, Flèche and Layard (2017) find that mental illness is not only highly correlated with poverty and unemployment, but also contributes more to explaining very low life satisfaction (0 to 4) than is explained by either poverty or unemployment alone.

On the relative importance of employee and workplace characteristics for life satisfaction, the survey finds (ranked in order of importance):

- Home life being 'not at all' stressful, compared with it being slightly stressful or very stressful.

- Accomplishing your best at work 'most days' compared with 'not very often'.
- Having a high level of control over work compared with a very low-level of control.
- Feeling comfortable with discussing mental health conditions at work if required.
- Not having a health condition in the previous twelve months.
- Having children under four years old, compared with not having children in the household.
- Work being 'not at all' stressful, compared with it being slightly stressful or very stressful.
- Being female.
- Strongly agreeing that relationships with colleagues are good.
- Being in the youngest age group, compared to middle age groups.

Some of these employee and workplace characteristics, although coarse, mimic the variables of workplace quality studied by Krekel et al. (2019a). Just as that study, the Health and Wellbeing and Work Survey also finds that stress and lack of work-life balance are the most detrimental to wellbeing at work, whereas having good interpersonal relationships and an interesting job are amongst the most positive influential factors.

In sum, the Health and Wellbeing at Work Survey results are very much in line with the findings in the literature. It should be noted that the survey reports an increase in health and wellbeing policies and initiatives in firms as well as a trend in workplace culture pointing towards greater awareness of the significance of wellbeing at work. This is an important development.

The Fit for Work Service

The Health and Wellbeing at Work Survey in 2014 includes a battery of items asking respondents about their attitudes towards a newly planned, independent health and work advice and referral service at the time. The key findings are (Department for Work and Pensions, 2015, pages 20 and 21):

- The vast majority of employees felt that Fit for Work sounded useful (84 per cent) and two-thirds (67 per cent) thought that they would use it if they were off sick for more than four weeks.
- Fit for Work was viewed slightly more positively amongst those with a mental health condition than those with a physical health condition or both conditions.
- Overall, employees viewed Fit for Work more positively when they worked in large organizations, the public sector, sales and customer service occupations, and organizations that had a good range of health and wellbeing policies and initiatives in place.

- Employees who had experienced sickness absence of more than four weeks also viewed Fit for Work positively: 73 per cent said they would use the service.
- There was some indication that those in older age groups felt less positively about Fit for Work than younger age groups.
- Of those who reported being unlikely to use Fit for Work, most did so because they felt that their employer would help them without it (70 per cent) or because they already had access to occupational health services at work (37 per cent). Almost a quarter, however, reported that they were unlikely to use it because they would feel uncomfortable involving their employer with the service (23 per cent).
- Eighty-four per cent of employees felt that they would be comfortable sharing a Return to Work Plan with their employer. There was some variation between groups however, with a suggestion that those with mental health conditions would be less willing to share a Return to Work Plan than those with a physical health condition only or no condition at all.
- Eighty-five per cent were confident that their employer would act on the Return to Work Plan, with 6 per cent thinking it was not at all likely.
- Five per cent of respondents would have been eligible to use the service (i.e. they had more than four weeks of sickness absence) in the previous twelve months.

Given how the actual Fit for Work service was cancelled because it was hardly prescribed by general practitioners, the above findings mainly indicate the potential demand for a return-to-work service. The actual respondents, however, had little idea as to how the scheme could be accessed or would be activated, so they were not the people to ask about that. So questions like whether they would use the service were not indicative of how much take-up there would actually be as the decision to activate the service was not just theirs to make. There was also likely a strong degree of social desirability bias involved with respondents in principle agreeing with the idea of a service that would be 'on their side' when it came to their continued workplace involvement.

In terms of the stream of ideas from which the Fit for Work service came, one can think of it as a component, amongst others, of an active labour market programme. There is evidence in the literature that active labour market programmes, in general, have positive impacts on wellbeing, in particular on evaluative measures such as life satisfaction (Sage, 2015). Besides raising perceived job security (which clearly matters for wellbeing at work, cf. Krekel et al., 2019a), they raise resilience to the health risks of being out of the job and increase the likelihood of job reintegration (Coutts et al., 2014). There is evidence that active labour market programmes which are work-oriented are more effective in promoting life satisfaction than, for example, employment assistance (Sage, 2015).

Another potential benefit of the Fit for Work programme was that it aimed at procedural fairness (Frey et al., 2004; Frey and Stutzer, 2005) which fits the findings that economic agents care about the way processes are organized around them and the way in which they are treated. When they feel treated as equals, they have a stronger sense of belonging to their workplace. The integrative part of the Fit for Work programme thus had the potential for giving process-related wellbeing to the workers.

The return-to-work plan was itself a promising tool, backed up by an established literature in psychology showing that goal-setting and planning tools, even if they take the form of simple if-then plans in case of what to do when facing distractions from goals or obstacles, are promising ways to move from intention to actual behaviour (Gollwitzer and Oettingen, 2011). To be most effective, such plans should be structured.

What is less clear is whether a return-to-work plan should be set up by an outside consultant or by the employee in direct consultation with employers and co-workers. The apparent scepticism of general practitioners and employers about Fit for Work, as manifested by low demand for the service, might well have related to the external nature of the advice. The low take-up might also be due to the fact that 2015 to 2018 was a period of relatively high employment which reduced the pressure on employees to hang on to existing jobs and made it easier to find new ones.

Discussion

The Fit for Work Service

The Fit for Work service was a *preventative* measure to avoid costly absenteeism and presenteeism due to ill health. We should again note that many aspects of Fit for Work were scrapped in 2018, though its cheapest elements (the website and free online phone service to general practitioners, employees, and employers) have remained intact and are still funded. What was scrapped was the hands-on return-to-work planning activities.

In its response to the 'Work, health and disability green paper' consultation, the government noted that 'Fit for Work, the DWP-commissioned service for offering free OH [Occupational Health] assessments, has had very low take-up', indicating that the 'current model of OH provision does not meet the needs of employers or individuals'.

As an explanation for the decision to scrap the main elements of the scheme in 2018, it was reported that: 'Since its launch in 2015, the Fit for Work service has consistently struggled with a low public profile and scepticism among both GPs and employers about its use and usefulness. A survey by *GP* magazine last summer found that 65 per cent of GPs had not referred a single patient to the service and that a lack of publicity was the cause. And a study by Willis Towers Watson last March found only 21 of HR professionals said they had used it.'[29]

Coverage of Items

Overall, the survey has been well implemented. It integrated the ONS-4 item battery—life satisfaction, happiness, anxiety, and worthwhileness. It may also have been useful to ask additional questions related to domain satisfactions, which would provide domain-specific evaluative measures of wellbeing. The survey could measure satisfaction with certain elements of the job (such as with management or colleagues), or satisfaction with other domains of life that are indirectly related to work (such as with leisure time or family life). Job satisfaction, in particular, is an established measure that is highly predictive of job quits (Lévy-Garboua et al., 2007) and that appears in many other employee surveys because it is so informative as to the circumstances in workplaces.

Another key measure to include 'next time' is employee engagement: being engaged with a job requires employees to be positively absorbed by what they do, and to be committed to advancing their firm's interests. Employees who are engaged identify themselves with the firm and represent their firm even outside formal working hours. The Gallup Organisation, for example, is sampling employee engagement regularly in its client surveys via the Gallup Q^{12} instrument (this instrument is proprietary, though). Developing a comparable, valid instrument to measure employee engagement, and incorporating it in future versions, may be a promising way ahead to capture some of the main circumstances that make good jobs and bad jobs.

Positioning of Items

It should be noted that the positioning of the ONS-4 item battery within the survey is problematic: it appears just after workplace characteristics, and in particular, emotional items, for example, how often respondents feel they accomplish their best at work, whether they feel they get rewarded appropriately, and whether they enjoy good relations with colleagues. There is evidence that items such as life satisfaction are strongly influenced by the preceding items (Schwartz et al., 1987). Answer behaviour may thus be shaped by what is currently salient in memory (primed by preceding items) and towards what attention is directed. That artificially makes emotional circumstances at work more important for the measure of life satisfaction than they would normally be.

In future versions, ideally, the ONS-4 item battery should be placed towards the beginning of the survey, after some introductory questions to ease respondents.

[29] https://www.personneltoday.com/hr/fit-work-service-scrapped-workplace-health-policy-overhaul/.

The assumption behind this approach is that any priming just before the survey starts is, on average, white noise.

Wording of Items

There may be a potential gap between the stated willingness to use Fit for Work and actual usage. The service is a public good: when asking respondents directly about whether they would use it or not, they may not—consciously or subconsciously—reveal their true willingness. For example, they may express their intrinsic attitudes towards the service, or answer in a strategic or socially desirable way. This potential gap between stated and actual usage is, to a certain extent, already visible when comparing the rating of the service with the stated willingness to use it (84 per cent rate service as very or quite useful, yet only 67 per cent think they would use it if eligible).

It should further be noted that the language describing the service is rather positive, using words such as 'new', 'independent', 'help', or 'with you', all of which bear positive connotations. This amounts, to a certain extent, to framing, and may further increase the wedge between stated and actual willingness to use the service. Given the low eventual uptake, this seems indeed likely.

Survey Mode

Finally, the survey was conducted via phone. While this does not constitute a problem per se, it should be noted that, when sampled, life satisfaction has been shown to be prone to contextual effects (for example, whether other individuals are present during the interview, cf. Kavetsos et al., 2014) and survey mode (for example, whether the interview is conducted in person or on the phone, cf. Dolan and Kavetsos, 2016).

In particular, it has been shown that respondents report consistently higher life satisfaction in phone interviews compared to face-to-face settings, and that life circumstances tend to matter less when reported over the phone. This should be kept in mind when interpreting findings from this survey.

Case Study 7: A Wellbeing CBA of Covid-19 Containment and Eradication Policies

The Covid-19 pandemic presented enormously complex and dynamic problems to governments, businesses, and individuals around the world. What should be done about the threat, and whether to do anything at all, were extremely difficult questions, answered differently by different governments on the advice of different scientists from different disciplines.

One of the key issues decision-makers were facing was that there were so many diverse effects of government policies. Border controls, national or regional lockdowns, physical distancing, track-and-trace systems, and many other policy options have effects on many different domains of life: there are effects on physical health, mental health and loneliness, risks of dying of various other diseases, personal rights and freedoms, employment, social relationships, trust and volunteering, crime, air quality and carbon emissions, and many others. And, of course, these effects differ for different persons and households.

Generically, these policy options present trade-offs across very different domains of life: lockdowns and distancing are expected to reduce the number of premature deaths from Covid-19, but at a predictable cost in terms of reduced economic activity, business closures, unemployment, and loneliness, as well as many other negative consequences of major recessions that go beyond the sheer loss of income. These costs and benefits also have a temporal dimension: benefits in terms of prevented deaths from Covid-19 accrue within weeks and months, whereas costs in terms of economic activity and unemployment are probably felt for years to come, though costs of loneliness accrue right away.

A major complication for many governments was that they lacked a reasonable way to weigh the expected net benefits of different policy options in various life domains against each other. This is the key strength of wellbeing CBA and CEA championed in this book: the expected effects of different policies in various life domains can be quite easily translated into a single metric that can be compared across different policy options so that policy-makers can make a rational decision based on how important different domains are to the wellbeing of those affected.

Both authors were heavily involved in several projects on these issues (Frijters 2020a, 2020b; Layard et al., 2020),[30] openly advocating the policies that came out better in their favoured wellbeing calculus. We essentially argued early on that the negative effects of unemployment and social misery caused by various policies aimed at reducing the spread of the virus heavily outweighed the positive effects of the reduced number of premature deaths from Covid-19.

Here, we illustrate this line of thinking by giving a stylized wellbeing CBA of what the world governments as a whole, and not just the United Kingdom or even a region, decided to engage in when reacting with containment and eradication policies to the emergence of Covid-19. Crucial are the two scenarios compared, the 'business as usual' and the 'containment and eradication' scenario. We take a five-year horizon and sketch the two scenarios. Needless to say, the crisis is highly dynamic and figures were changing daily at the time of working on this chapter (August and December 2020), making the subsequent analysis highly

[30] Frijters (2020a): https://clubtroppo.com.au/2020/03/21/the-corona-dilemma/; Frijters (2020b): https://clubtroppo.com.au/2020/04/08/how-many-wellbys-is-the-corona-panic-costing/; Layard et al. (2020): http://cep.lse.ac.uk/pubs/download/occasional/op049.pdf.

uncertain. Nevertheless, decisions in real time are also inherently based on uncertain, evolving information. Our calculations show how a wellbeing perspective can, in real time, support very difficult, high-stakes policy decisions, even those involving trade-offs between life and death in crisis situations such as Covid-19.

The Business-as-usual Scenario

The business-as-usual scenario would have meant that the world governments treated Covid-19 just as they have treated seasonal flu, Asian Flu, Swine Flu, and most other infectious diseases of the recent decades: no drastic attempt at containment or wholesale eradication but mainly treating those who fell ill and handing out advice on risks and voluntary precautionary measures. Importantly, this was the advice the World Health Organization (WHO) gave in a report in October 2019, so just before the emergence of the Covid-19. That report came to the conclusion that the costs of containment and eradication of a virus such as Covid-19 were higher than the benefits once it had become a pandemic and so widely spread that it could not realistically be contained forever (WHO, 2019).

Given the characteristics of Covid-19, this would have meant negligible disruptions to the economy since the overwhelming majority of serious cases were amongst those above 60 years of age (Verity et al., 2020) or with certain medical preconditions (high blood pressure, diabetes, heart disease, and lung disease, cf. Chen et al., 2020; Fang et al., 2020), a group that is not a major part of the workforce. As a result, the world economy would have kept growing at its anticipated long-run growth rate of 2 per cent per year. As government revenue is roughly 30 per cent of world GDP, this allows us to calculate the expected rise in resources available to the public purse during the five-year time horizon. There would be little change in unemployment, mental health, loneliness, or social cohesion.

Of course, there is the key question of how many people would have died under this business-as-usual scenario, how many years those individuals would have had left to live, and whether there would have been knock-on deaths because of the overwhelming of the emergency departments in hospitals in many countries. To be generous towards the benefits of containment and eradication, we assume that the emergency departments in hospitals would have sent away any Covid-19 patients for whom there was no more room.

As there would have been no attempt at containment or eradication in the business-as-usual scenario, we assume that the vast majority of the world population would have been exposed to Covid-19. Importantly, we should note that exposure does not mean everyone would be heavily infected, as many individuals would get mild infections that could be more easily overcome than heavy infections or would be asymptomatic altogether. The current best estimate of the fatality rate with mass exposure is about 0.2 per cent on 22 May 2020, according to the Centers for Disease Control (CDC) in the United States,[31] which is roughly the fatality rate observed in New York City and some other cities where the vast majority of the population was likely exposed to some degree. Yet, as of December 2020, there was no country above a million inhabitants with a fatality rate above 0.16 per cent. Still, to be generous and account for the fact that in many countries access to accident and emergency care is limited, let us assume double the infection fatality rate, thus saying that 0.4 per cent of the world population would have died under no containment or eradication policy. Given that there are 7.7 billion individuals, this yields about 30 million deaths.

We now need to consider how many WELLBYs these deaths would have represented, for which we need to know how many more years these victims would have had left to live and how high their wellbeing would have been. Again, to be generous, we assume they would have had another five years to live, on average, enjoying a life satisfaction of 6, on average, measured on a 0-to-10 scale during this period. This estimate of remaining life years is similar to the one used by Layard et al. (2020), who formally derive a value of six years from the ONS Life Tables, or by Dolan and Jenkins (2020). We thus obtain $(6-2)\times5\times30{,}000{,}000 =$ 600 million WELLBYs lost due to 30 million deaths worldwide. Recall that the number 2 represents the zero point of life-satisfaction, i.e. the level which individuals themselves rate as not worth living if that is what life would be like for the rest of their lives (see chapter 3).

Now that we have obtained a total WELLBY value for the business-as-usual scenario, we need to sketch the 'containment and eradication' scenario, which is largely the choice the world as a whole made.

The 'Containment and Eradication' Scenario: Effects of Containment and Eradication Attempts

In sketching the effects of containment and eradication attempts, we face the problem that we do not yet have five years of knowledge about the various policies still to be chosen by many countries. Hence, we need to construct a reasonable scenario that does justice to the possible benefits of the choices made so far.

Let us be optimistic about containment and eradication and assume that the world is going to successfully eradicate the virus at a cost no higher than three million deaths, either via vaccines or eradication by containment. Relative to the

[31] These figures were used for the prediction model. But they are updated regularly at the moment and depend on the respective country and time horizon. For an overview, see: https://www.cebm.net/covid-19/global-covid-19-case-fatality-rates/.

30 million deaths under for 'business-as-usual' scenario, this is a gain of 27 million lives. Yet, the three million deaths would be a loss of $(6-2) \times 5 \times 3{,}000{,}000 = 60$ million WELLBYs, a small figure and a difference of 540 million WELLBYs relative to the business-as-usual scenario (a loss of 600 million WELLBYs).

Let us also be optimistic about what is required to get at that relatively low loss of life due to Covid-19 and assume that it takes the world three months of UK Tier-4-style lockdowns and physical distancing, and that it can otherwise return to normal life thereafter, including economic and social recovery. In some countries, lockdowns lasted far longer while in other countries they were much shorter and much lighter, so the notion of three months is then a middle-of-the-road average. This means that the 'costs' of containment and eradication are the costs due to the negative effects of being in lockdown, physical distancing, social isolation and loneliness, and so on, as well as the expected costs of the disruption to the world economy and the social system over a time period of five years, i.e. the 'pain' during economic and social recovery. Moreover, let us be optimistic and assume that costs other than loss of income and unemployment would disappear immediately after three months. This is overly optimistic for many countries in Europe, but perhaps pessimistic for countries in East Asia and Africa where the disruption has been much less.

Finally, let us be optimistic about any knock-on health effects of shutting down public health systems to many other, Covid-19-unrelated patients and health needs during this period and simply assume that these costs, which we know in reality are rather large, do not occur. That is, to keep the argument as simple as possible, we do not count the loss of WELLBYs due to disrupted cancer screening and operations, delayed inoculation programmes around the world, increased suicides amongst the depressed, the loss in the will to live amongst the elderly locked away from their family and friends, abuse in households, disruption to education of children, delayed labour market entries of youth, and so on. Although all of these effects are well documented and we ourselves argued for their importance, let us not count them to make the case for containment and eradication as generous as possible.

The costs of the three months of UK Tier-4-style lockdowns and physical distancing, however, have three major items we do count. The first is the general reduction in the wellbeing of the whole population which is no longer able to work (in a normal manner), socialize, meet new people and partners, and generally enjoy life. The second is the reduction in wellbeing due to the rise in unemployment during the five-year time horizon. The third is the total loss in government revenue due to the loss in world GDP.

Turning to the first element, which is the general reduction in the wellbeing of the whole population, we estimate this to be, on average, about 0.5 points on a 0-to-10 life-satisfaction scale, for everyone in the general population based on the effects of loneliness on wellbeing (Clark et al., 2018).[32] This is a realistic estimate: several UK studies have now put the likely figure between 0.4 and 1.0 points for the general population, whereby reductions were most pronounced for individuals who were prevented from going to work (the effect on those in regular employment or in 'essential jobs' was almost zero, showing that the drop was largely due to work-related quality of life). An assumed effect of 0.5 points is hence a good estimate of the general reduction in the wellbeing of the whole population under UK Tier-4-style lockdowns and physical distancing. As we assume that these effects would only last for three months, we need to divide this figure by four to obtain a quarterly figure of 0.125 points (recall that the WELLBY is an annual measure). This applies to the general population worldwide, yielding a total WELLBY loss of about $0.125 \times 7{,}700{,}000{,}000 = 963$ million.

Turning to unemployment next, we assume that world effective unemployment rose by 10 per cent of the labour force due to containment and eradication policies. We make a generous V-shape assumption on how quickly those who became unemployed will be re-employed, assuming that they will be re-employed at a steady rate within three years. With a worldwide labour force of about 3.4 billion, this implies a peak 340 million additional unemployed, taking three years to regain employment, yielding $1.5 \times 340 = 510$ million unemployment years (the factor 1.5 comes from the V-shaped unemployment-re-employment curve and the assumption that re-employment occurs within three years, which presupposes an average time to re-employment of 1.5 years). We know that unemployment results in a loss of about 0.7 WELLBYs per unemployment year (Clark et al., 2018), yielding a total WELLBY loss of $510 \times 0.7 = 357$ million.

Finally, we turn to the loss of world GDP. We are again generous and make the assumption that the world will actually catch up in GDP growth terms with the business-as-usual scenario after three years, with economic recovery starting after the three-months of lockdowns and physical distancing measures. Given how world GDP dropped by about 4 per cent relative to its pre-crisis expected growth rate of three per cent, a three-year catch-up implies a lower average level of world GDP of about 5 per cent for three years, which is (roughly because of the eventual GDP growth) a 15 per cent loss of world GDP for one year. World GDP was about $88 trillion in 2019. Since we only want to count the loss in government revenue (and government revenue is about 30 per cent of world GDP), we obtain a loss of government revenue of about $88 \times 0.15 \times 0.3 = \$3.96$ trillion.

We then need to consider how many WELLBYs are lost when government services reduce. In this book, we have so far used the number of £2,500 as the marginal social production costs of a WELLBY, but that was based on somewhat

[32] Importantly, Clark et al. (2018) find that an increase in loneliness by one point is associated with a decrease of 0.49 points in life satisfaction measured on a 0-to-10 scale. The cost of loneliness was thus known well before the Covid-19 crisis.

generous assumptions on how productive the UK NHS was. In line with our desire to use optimistic but defensible assumptions on the benefits of containment and eradication policies, let us take the willingness-to-pay number of £12,500 per WELLBY as a more generous indication of the value of government spending. Then, we obtain a total WELLBY loss of about (3,960,000,000,000)/(12,500) = 317 million.

Taking stock, we obtain the following ballpark figures for the business-as-usual scenarios versus the 'containment and eradication' scenario:

Business-as-usual scenario		
Costs		
Costs		
Loss of life	−600	Million WELLBYs
'Containment and eradication' scenario		
Costs		
Loss of life	−60	Million WELLBYs
General reduction in population wellbeing	−963	Million WELLBYs
Unemployment	−357	Million WELLBYs
Loss of government revenue	−317	Million WELLBYs
Total costs	−1,697	Million WELLBYs

Cost-benefit ratio of containment and eradication scenario versus business-as-usual: about 2.83.

This simple, back-of-the-envelope wellbeing CBA thus finds that the 'containment and eradication' scenario is almost 3 times more costly in terms of wellbeing than the laissez-faire, business-as-usual scenario. And that ratio uses assumptions and numbers which are blatantly pessimistic about 'business-as-usual' and blatantly optimistic about 'containment and eradication'. Under more reasonable assumptions the costs are easily fifty times larger under the containment strategy than the business-as-usual strategy.

Even if we did not count the general reduction in population wellbeing and focus more on the more classic economic case of unemployment and the loss of government revenue, the 'containment and eradication' scenario is still more costly in terms of wellbeing. These calculations thus point out the huge costs to world wellbeing of disruptions to the economic and social system, disruptions that very quickly dwarf even the effects of millions of lives lost, basically because with over seven billion people small changes in average wellbeing count higher when being summed up.

We should mention that we have tried to value several other aspects of the policy reactions and the trade-off between business-as-usual and containment and eradication only looks worse if one expands the set on the latter side. Indeed, the disruption to public healthcare systems alone may potentially lead to more loss of life than were saved in terms of reduced infections (Barach et al., 2020; Metzler et al., 2020; Robertson et al., 2020). Many of these lives lost are individuals who are, on average, younger than those who die of Covid-19 and hence yield more years of life lost.

When Would Containment and Eradication Be Sensible?

We can also apply our wellbeing perspective to give a ballpark figure for how bad a pandemic must be before it makes sense to take the radical steps governments took around the world. We do this here for illustrative purposes.

We ask: 'What death toll would have been worth the effects of three months of complete UK Tier-4-style lockdowns and physical distancing?' To answer this question, we use some of the same figures as above, which were generous towards the idea of a speedy recovery from a total lockdown: the total WELLBY loss from the general reduction in population wellbeing is 963 million and the total WELLBY loss from unemployment is 357 million. For illustrative purposes, let us then take the marginal costs for producing a WELLBY via government expenditure in the world to be about $1,100. This reflects the fact that average world income is about a third of that of the United Kingdom and that we should use about one third of the UK threshold number (£2,500) for other countries, and then adjust for the $ to £ exchange rate. With that threshold, the 3.96 trillion loss in government revenue implies a 3.6 billion loss in WELLBYs through less government services over the whole lifetime of the whole world population. In other words, the cost of containment and eradication is about 4.92 billion WELLBYs.

An average world citizen experiences about four WELLBYs per year, which is the difference between the average life satisfaction in the world (a bit under 6) and the minimum level at which individuals are indifferent between additional life versus death (estimated to be around 2). With a world population of 7.7 billion individuals, the WELLBY costs is equivalent, roughly, to 1.92 months of life for everyone on the planet, or equivalently 41 million individuals who had an average of thirty more years left to live. This would imply a fatality rate of about 0.5 per cent if it was a disease that is equally lethal for everyone on the planet (so more like the Spanish Flu). For a disease like Covid-19 where victims had (generously) only five good years left on average, the equivalent fatality rate should be about 3.2 per cent to break even and make a radical containment and eradication policy worthwhile, presuming that would actually eliminate the disease.

The WELLBY framework, and the policy evaluation and appraisal techniques championed in this book, are thus suitable to generate quick and reasonable figures for such general trade-offs.

Conclusion and the Way Ahead

In this chapter, we went over seven examples, mostly from government departments and agencies, of how to inject more wellbeing into policy evaluations and appraisals as well as evaluation methodologies like survey instruments. We applied many of the recommendations we made in chapters 3 and 4, showing what difference these would make to the status quo procedures.

We should reiterate that the recommendations made are not set in stone but should be expected, like all aspects of policy evaluation and appraisal practice over the decades, to be subject to challenge and negotiation such that they evolve. The examples should, therefore, be read in a generic sense of 'this is the kind of thing we at this moment think should be done' rather than 'this is what should be done'.

If we look at the many guidelines and examples of the many government departments and agencies that undertake policy evaluations and appraisals, it seems to us that getting used to thinking more in wellbeing terms will take time and is a matter of evolution. It will require more training of analysts and policy-makers in the basic lessons, data, and methodology of wellbeing. It will involve trial and error with methods and with the various ways in which knowledge can be generated and retained. It will need more research and preferably a gradual move towards a more experimental, self-learning bureaucracy.

There is hence much to be done.

Literature

Airports Commission (2015a). Final Report. Available at: https://mycouncil.surreycc.gov.uk/documents/s24198/Annex%20A%20airports-commission-final-report.pdf.

Airports Commission (2015b). Business Case and Sustainability Assessment—Heathrow Northwest Runway. Available at: https://assets.publishing.service.gov.uk/government/uploads/system/uploads/attachment_data/file/440315/business-case-and-sustainability-assessment.pdf.

Alcock, I., White, M. P., Wheeler, B. W., Fleming, L. E., and Depledge, M. H. (2014). Longitudinal Effects on Mental Health of Moving to Greener and Less Greener Urban Areas. *Environmental Science and Technology* 48(2): 1247–55.

Barach, P., Fisher, S. D., Adams, M. J., Burstein, G. R., Brophy, P. D., Kuo, D. Z., and Lipshultz, S. E. (2020). Disruption of Healthcare: Will the COVID Pandemic Worsen Non-COVID Outcomes and Disease Outbreaks? Progress in Pediatric Cardiology. DOI: 10.1016/j.ppedcard.2020.101254.

Baumeister, R. F., Vohs, K. D., DeWall, C. N., and Zhang, L. (2007). How Emotion Shapes Behavior: Feedback, Anticipation, and Reflection, Rather Than Direct Causation. *Personality and Social Psychology Review* 11(2): 167–203.

Beighton, L., Draper, D., and Pearson, A. (2018). The Taxation of Families International Comparisons 2017. CARE Research Paper. Available at: https://care.org.uk/sites/default/files/26817_CARE%20TAX%20REPORT%202017%20FINAL.pdf.

Bertram, C., and Rehdanz, K. (2015). The Role of Urban Green Space for Human Well-being. *Ecological Economics* 120: 139–52.

Beutel, M. E., Jünger, C., and Klein, E. M. (2016). Noise Annoyance Is Associated with Depression and Anxiety in the General Population—The Contribution of Aircraft Noise. *PLOS One* 11(5): e0155357.

Black, C. (2008). *Working for a Healthier Tomorrow: Health and Work in Britain.* London: The Stationery Office.

Black, C., and Frost, D. (2011). *Health at Work—An Independent Review of Sickness Absence.* London: The Stationery Office.

Blanchflower, D. G., and Oswald, A. J. (2004). Well-being over Time in Britain and the USA. *Journal of Public Economics* 88(7–8): 1359–86.

Bohlmeijer, E., Prenger, R., Taal, E., and Cuijpers, P. (2010). The Effects of Mindfulness-based Stress Reduction Therapy on Mental Health of Adults with a Chronic Medical Disease: A Meta-analysis. *Journal of Psychosomatic Research* 68(6): 539–44.

Breeze, J., Qureshi, N., and Abdallah, S. (2010). Big Lottery Fund National Well-being Evaluation. Available at: http://www.cles.org.uk/wp-content/uploads/2011/01/Gholderconf-03.10-CLES-w.pdf.

Card, D., Kluve, J., and Weber, A. (2018). What Works? A Meta analysis of Recent Active Labor Market Program Evaluations. *Journal of the European Economic Association* 16(3): 894–931.

Chatterjee, K., Clark, B., Martin, A., and Davis, A. (2017). The Commuting and Wellbeing Study: Understanding the Impact of Commuting on People's Lives. UWE Bristol, UK.

Chen, T., Wu, D., Chen, H., Yan, W., Yang, D., Chen, G., Ma, K., Xu, D., Yu, H., Wang, H., Wang, T., Guo, W., Chen, J., Ding, C., Zhang, X., Huang, J., Han, M., Li, S., Luo, X., Zhao, J., and Ning, Q. (2020). Clinical Characteristics of 113 Deceased Patients with Coronavirus Disease 2019: Retrospective Study. *BMJ* 368: m1091.

Clark, A. E., Flèche, S., Layard, R., Powdthavee, N., and Ward, G. (2018). *The Origins of Happiness: The Science of Well-being over the Life Course.* Princeton, NJ: Princeton University Press.

Clark, A. E., and Jung, S. (2017). Does Compulsory Education Really Increase Life Satisfaction? Inha University, Institute of Business and Economic Research, No. 2017–6.

Claxton, K., Martin, S., Soares, M., Rice, N., Spackman, E., Hinde, S., Devlin, N., Smith, P., and Sculpher, M. (2015). Methods for the Estimation of the NICE Cost Effectiveness Threshold. *Health Technology Assessment* 19(14): 1–503.

CLES Consulting, and new economics foundation (2013). Big Lottery Fund National Well-being Evaluation. Available at: https://www.nurturedevelopment.org/wp-content/uploads/2016/01/National-Well-being-Evaluation-Final-Report-August-2013.pdf.

Coutts, A. P., Stuckler, D., and Cann, D. J. (2014). The Health and Wellbeing Effects of Active Labor Market Programs. In C. L. Cooper (ed.), *Wellbeing: A Complete Reference Guide.* London: John Wiley & Sons.

Department for Transport (2019). TAG (Transport Analysis Guidance) Data Book. Available at: https://www.gov.uk/government/publications/tag-data-book.

Department for Work and Pensions (2015). Health and Wellbeing at Work: A Survey of Employees, 2014. Research Report no. 901.

Department for Work and Pensions and Department of Health (2017). Improving Lives: The Future of Work, Health and Disability. Available at: https://assets.publishing.service.gov.uk/government/uploads/system/uploads/attachment_data/file/663399/improving-lives-the-future-of-work-health-and-disability.PDF.

Department of Health and Department of Education (2017). Transforming Children and Young People's Mental Health Provision: A Green Paper Impact Assessment (IA). Available at: https://assets.publishing.service.gov.uk/government/uploads/system/uploads/attachment_data/file/664442/MHGP_IA.pdf.

Derudder, B., and Witlox, F. (2016). *International Business Travel in the Global Economy*. London: Routledge.

Dickerson, A., Hole, A., and Munford, L. (2014). The Relationship between Well-being and Commuting Revisited: Does the Choice of Methodology Matter? *Regional Science and Urban Economics* 49: 321–9.

Doganis, R. (2013). *Flying Off Course: The Economics of International Airlines*. London: Routledge.

Dolan, P., and Jenkins, P. (2020). Estimating the Monetary Value of the Deaths Prevented from the UK Covid-19 Lockdown—and the Value of 'Flattening the Curve'. Mimeo.

Dolan, P., and Kavetsos, G. (2016). Happy Talk: Mode of Administration Effects on Subjective Well-being. *Journal of Happiness Studies* 17(3): 1273–91.

Dolan, P., and Metcalfe, R. (2012). Measuring Wellbeing: Recommendations on Measures for Use by National Governments. *Journal of Social Policy* 41(2): 409–27.

Dolan, P., Kavetsos, G., Krekel, C., Mavridis, D., Metcalfe, R., Senik, C., Szymanski, S., and Ziebarth, N. R. (2019). Quantifying the Intangible Impact of the Olympics Using Subjective Well-being Data. *Journal of Public Economics* 177: 104,043.

Drysdale, L. (2018). Human Henge Evaluation Report for the Heritage Lottery Fund.

Dunn, E. W., Aknin, L. B., and Norton, M. I. (2008). Spending Money on Others Promotes Happiness. *Science* 319: 1687–8.

Egglestone, C., Aylward, N., Melville, D., Bivand, P., Allies, O., and Burgess, A. (2019). Evaluation of the Traineeships Programme: Final Report 2015–2019. Available at: https://gov.wales/sites/default/files/statistics-and-research/2019-06/evaluation-of-the-traineeships-programme-2015-2019.pdf.

Everett, D. L. (2005). Cultural Constraints on Grammar and Cognition in Pirahã. *Current Anthropology*: 46, 621–46.

Everett, D. L. (2008). *Don't Sleep, There Are Snakes: Life and Language in the Amazonian Jungle*. New York: Vintage Books.

Fang, L., Karakiulakis, G., and Roth, M. (2020). Are Patients with Hypertension and Diabetes Mellitus at Increased Risk for COVID-19 Infection? *Lancet Respiratory Medicine* 8(4): e21.

Fava, G. A., Ruini, C., Rafanelli, C., Finos, L., Conti, S., and Grandi, S. (2004). Six-year Outcome of Cognitive Behavior Therapy for Prevention of Recurrent Depression. *American Journal of Psychiatry* 161: 1872–6.

Flèche, S., and Layard, R. (2017). Do More of Those in Misery Suffer from Poverty, Unemployment or Mental Illness? *Kyklos* 70(1): 27–41.

Foley, N., and Rhodes, C. (2019). Tourism: Statistics and Policy. House of Commons Library Briefing Paper no. 06022. Available at: http://researchbriefings.files.parliament.uk/documents/SN06022/SN06022.pdf.

Frey, B. S., Benz, M., and Stutzer, A. (2004). Introducing Procedural Utility: Not Only What, But Also How Matters. *Journal of Institutional and Theoretical Economics* 160(3): 377–401.

Frey, B. S., and Stutzer, A. (2005). Beyond Outcomes: Measuring Procedural Utility. *Oxford Economic Papers* 57(1): 90–111.

Frijters, P., Béllet, C., and Krekel, C. (2019). Micro-Macro Simulations for Wellbeing. Mimeo.

Fujiwara, D., and Campbell, R. (2011). Valuation Techniques for Social Cost-Benefit Analysis. London: HM Treasury. Available at: https://www.gov.uk/government/publications/valuation-techniques-for-social-cost-benefit-analysis.

Godfrin, K. A., and van Heeringen, C. (2010). The Effects of Mindfulness-based Cognitive Therapy on Recurrence of Depressive Episodes, Mental Health and Quality of Life: A Randomized Controlled Study. *Behaviour Research and Therapy* 48(8): 738–46.

Gollwitzer, P. M., and Oettingen, G. (2011). Planning Promotes Striving. In K. D. Vohs and R. F. Baumeister (eds), *Handbook of Self-regulation: Research, Theory, and Applications*. New York: Guilford.

Gordon, P. (2004). Numerical Cognition without Words: Evidence from Amazonia. *Science* 306(5695): 496–9.

Glover, D., and Henderson, J. (2010). *Quantifying health impacts of government policies*. London: Department of Health. Available at: https://assets.publishing.service.gov.uk/government/uploads/system/uploads/attachment_data/file/216003/dh_120108.pdf

Green, A. E., Hogarth, T., and Shackleton, R. E. (1999). Longer Distance Commuting as a Substitute for Migration in Britain: A Review of Trends, Issues and Implications. *International Journal of Population Geography* 5(1): 49–67.

Gu, J., Strauss, C., Bond, R., and Cavanagh, K. (2015). How Do Mindfulness-based Cognitive Therapy and Mindfulness-based Stress Reduction Improve Mental Health and Wellbeing? A Systematic Review and Meta-analysis of Mediation Studies. *Clinical Psychology Review* 37: 1–12.

Heaslip, V., and Darvill, T. (2017). Human Henge Wellbeing Research: First Report.

Heblich S., Redding, S. J., and Sturm, D. M. (2020). The Making of the Modern Metropolis: Evidence from London. *Quarterly Journal of Economics* 135(4): 2059–133.

Huang, L., Frijters, P., Dalziel, K., and Clarke, P. (2018). Life Satisfaction, QALYs, and the Monetary Value of Health. *Social Science & Medicine* 211: 131–6.

Hull City Council (n.d.). Public Health Outcomes Framework. Available at: http://www.hullcc.gov.uk/pls/hullpublichealth/phof.html.

Hunter, J. E., and Schmidt, F. L. (2015). *Methods of Meta-analysis: Correcting Error and Bias in Research Findings*. Newbury Park, CA: Sage.

Isen, A. M., and Baron, R. A. (1991). Positive Affect as a Factor in Organizational Behavior. *Research in Organizational Behavior* 13: 1–53.

Isen, A. M., Daubman, K. A., and Nowicki, G. P. (1987). Positive Affect Facilitates Creative Problem Solving. *Journal of Personality and Social Psychology* 52(6): 1122–31.

Jacob, N., Munford, L., Rice, N., and Roberts, J. (2019). The Disutility of Commuting? The Effect of Gender and Local Labor Markets. *Regional Science and Urban Economics* 77: 264–75.

Kahneman, D., Wakker, P. P., and Sarin, R. (1997). Back to Bentham? Explorations of Experienced Utility. *Quarterly Journal of Economics* 112(2): 375–405.

Kantar TNS, (2018). The GB Tourist 2017 Annual Report. Available at: https://www.visitbritain.org/sites/default/files/vb-corporate/Documents-Library/documents/England-documents/40413193-260c_gb_tourist_2017_annual_report_v18.pdf.

Kavetsos, G., Dimitriadou, M., and Dolan, P. (2014). Measuring Happiness: Context Matters. *Applied Economics Letters* 21(5): 308–11.

Krekel, C., De Neve, J.-E., Fancourt, D., and Layard, R. (2020). A Local Community Course That Raises Mental Wellbeing and Pro-sociality. *CEP Discussion Paper* 1671.

Krekel, C., Kolbe, J., and Wüstemann, H. (2016). The Greener, the Happier? The Effect of Urban Land Use on Residential Well-being. *Ecological Economics* 121: 117–27.

Krekel, C., Ward, G., and De Neve, J.-E. (2019a). What Makes for a Good Job? Evidence Using Subjective Wellbeing Data. In M. Rojas, (ed). *The Economics of Happiness*. Cham: Springer, pp. 241–68.

Krekel, C., Ward, and De Neve, J.-E. (2019b). Employee Wellbeing, Productivity and Firm Performance. CEP Discussion Paper 1605.

Kruesi, F. E. (1997). Departmental Guidance for the Valuation of Travel Time in Economic Analysis. US Department of Transportation, Office of the Secretary of Transportation. Available at: https://cms7.dot.gov/file/68931/download?token=CiKLuT8o.

Lawler, E. E. III, and Porter, L. W. (1967). The Effect of Performance on Job Satisfaction. *Industrial Relations* 7: 20–8.

Lawton, R. N., and Fujiwara, D. (2016). Living with Aircraft Noise: Airport Proximity, Aviation Noise and Wellbeing in England. *Transportation Research Part D: Transport and Environment* 42: 104–18.

Layard, R., Clark, A. E., De Neve, J.-E., Krekel, C., Fancourt, D., Hey, N., and O'Donnell, G. (2020). When to Release the Lockdown: A Wellbeing Framework for Analysing Costs and Benefits. CEP Occasional Paper 49.

Lévy-Garboua, L., Montmarquette, C., and Simmonet, V. (2007). Job Satisfaction and Quits. *Labour Economics* 14: 251–68.

Lindqvist, E., Östling, R., and Cesarini, D. (2020). Long-Run Effects of Lottery Wealth on Psychological Well-Being. Review of Economic Studies: 87 (6), 2703–26.

Loewenstein, G., and Schkade, D. A. (1999). Wouldn't It Be Nice? Predicting Future Feelings. In D. Kahneman, E. Diener, and N. Schwarz (eds), *Well-Being: The Foundations of Hedonic Psychology*. New York: Russell Sage, pp. 85–105.

Loewenstein, G., and Adler, D. (1995). A Bias in the Prediction of Tastes. *Economic Journal* 105(431): 929–37.

Loewenstein, G., O'Donohue, T., and Rabin, M. (2003). Projection Bias in Predicting Future Utility. *Quarterly Journal of Economics* 118(4): 1209–48.

Lomas, J., Martin, S., and Claxton, K. (2019). Estimating the Marginal Productivity of the English National Health Service From 2003 to 2012. *Value in Health* 22(9): 995–1002.

Lordan, G., and McGuire, A. (2019). Widening the High School Curriculum to Include Soft Skill Training: Impacts on Health, Behaviour, Emotional Wellbeing and Occupational Aspirations. IZA Discussion Paper 12439.

Luechinger, S., (2009). Valuing Air Quality Using the Life Satisfaction Approach. *Economic Journal,* 119(536): 482–515.

Meier, S., and Stutzer, A. (2008). Is Volunteering Rewarding in Itself? *Economica* 75 (397): 39–59.

Mervin, M. C., and Frijters, P. (2014). Is Shared Misery Double Misery? *Social Science & Medicine* 107: 68–77.

Metzler, B., Siostrzonek, P., Binder, R. K., Bauer, A., and Reinstadler, S. J. (2020). Decline of Acute Coronary Syndrome Admissions in Austria since the Outbreak of COVID-19: The Pandemic Response Causes Cardiac Collateral Damage. *European Heart Journal* 41(19): 1852–3.

Meunier, D., and Quinet, E. (2015). Value of Time Estimations in Cost-Benefit Analysis: The French Experience. *Transportation Research Procedia* 8: 62–71.

National Audit Office (2020). Overview of the UK Government's Response to the Covid-19 Pandemic. Available at: https://www.nao.org.uk/wp-content/uploads/2020/05/Overview-of-the-UK-governments-response-to-the-COVID-19-pandemic.pdf.

Office for National Statistics (n.d.). Measures of National Well-being Dashboard. Online: http://www.ons.gov.uk/peoplepopulationandcommunity/wellbeing/articles/measuresofnationalwellbeingdashboard/2018-04-25.

Pinker, S. (2012). *The Better Angels of our Nature: A History of Violence and Humanity*. London: Penguin Books.

Plumplot (n.d.). Hull Violent Crime Statistics. Available at: https://www.plumplot.co.uk/Hull-violent-crime-statistics.html.

Police UK (n.d.). Crime in Kingston upon Hull Compared with Crime in Other Similar Areas. Available at: https://www.police.uk/humberside/69/performance/compare-your-area/.

PricewaterhouseCoopers LLP (PwC) (2017). The Impact of Taxes on the Competitiveness of European Tourism. Available at: https://ec.europa.eu/docsroom/documents/26445/attachments/1/translations/en/renditions/native.

Public Health England (PHE) (2018). Cardiovascular Disease Prevention Return on Investment Tool: Final Report. Available at: https://assets.publishing.service.gov.uk/government/uploads/system/uploads/attachment_data/file/784208/Cardiovascular_disease_prevention_ROI_tool.pdf.

Roberton, T., Carter, E. D., Chou, V. B., Stegmuller, A. R., Jackson, B. D., Tam, Y., . . . and Walker, N. (2020). Early Estimates of the Indirect Effects of the COVID-19 Pandemic on Maternal and Child Mortality in Low-income and Middle-income Countries: A Modelling Study. *Lancet Global Health* 8(7).

Ryan, R. M., and Deci, E. L. (2000). Self-determination Theory and the Facilitation of Intrinsic Motivation, Social Development, and Well-being. *American Psychologist* 55(1): 68–78.

Sachs, J. D., Layard, R., and Helliwell, J. F. (eds) (2018). *World Happiness Report 2018*. Available at: https://worldhappiness.report/ed/2018/.

Sage, D. (2015). Do Active Labour Market Policies Promote the Subjective Well-being of the Unemployed? Evidence from the UK National Well-Being Programme. *Journal of Happiness Studies* 16(5): 1281–98.

Sandow, E. (2019). Til Work Do Us Part: The Social Fallacy of Long-distance Commuting. In C. Lindkvist Scholten and T. Joelsson (eds), *Integrating Gender into Transport Planning: From One to Many Tracks*. Cham: Palgrave Macmillan, pp. 121–44.

Schwab, D. P., and Cummings, L. L. (1970). Theories of Performance and Satisfaction: A Review. *Industrial Relations* 9: 408–30.

Schwartz, N., Strack, F., Kommer, D., and Wagner, D. (1987). Soccer, Rooms, and the Quality of your Life: Mood Effects on Judgments of Satisfaction with Life in General and with Specific Domains. *European Journal of Social Psychology* 17(1): 69–79.

Small, K. A. (2012). Valuation of Travel Time. *Economics of Transportation* 1(1–2): 2–14.

Staw, B. M., Sutton, R. I., and Pelled, L. H. (1994). Employee Positive Emotion and Favorable Outcomes in the Workplace. *Organisational Science* 5: 51–71.

Steiner, L., Frey, B., and Hotz, S. (2015). European Capitals of Culture and Life Satisfaction. *Urban Studies* 52(2): 374–94.

Stewart-Brown, S., and Janmohamed, K. (2008). Warwick-Edinburgh Mental Well-being Scale. User Guide, Version 1. Available at: http://www.ocagingservicescollaborative.org/wp-content/uploads/2014/07/WEMWBS-User-Guide-Version-1-June-2008.pdf.

Strauss, G. (1968). Human Relations—1968 Style. *Industrial Relations* 7: 262–76.

Stutzer, A., and Frey, B. S. (2008). Stress That Doesn't Pay: The Commuting Paradox. *Scandinavian Journal of Economics* 110(2): 339–66.

Tennant, R., Hiller, L., Fishwick, R., Platt, S., Joseph, S., Weich, S., . . . and Stewart-Brown, S. (2007). The Warwick-Edinburgh Mental Well-being Scale (WEMWBS): Development and UK Validation. *Health and Quality of Life Outcomes* 5(1): 63.

Treasury, HM (2018). *The Green Book: Central Government Guidance on Appraisal and Evaluation*. London: HM Treasury.

University of Hull (2018). Cultural Transformations: The Impact of Hull UK City of Culture 2017: Preliminary Outcomes Evaluation. Available at: https://static.a-n.co.uk/wp-content/uploads/2018/07/Cultural-Transformations-The-Impacts-of-Hull-City-of-Culture-2017.pdf.

Van Praag, B. M., and Baarsma, B. E. (2005). Using Happiness Surveys to Value Intangibles: The Case of Airport Noise. *Economic Journal* 115(500): 224–46.

Verity, R., Okell, L. C., Dorigatti, I., Winskill, P., Whittaker, C., . . . and Imai, N. (2020). Estimates of the Severity of Coronavirus Disease 2019: A Model-based Analysis. *Lancet Infectious Diseases* 20(6): 669–77.

White, M. P., Alcock, I., Wheeler, B. W., and Depledge, M. H. (2013). Would You Be Happier Living in a Greener Urban Area? A Fixed-effects Analysis of Panel Data. *Psychological Science* 24(6): 920–8.

White, V. (2016). Departmental Guidance for Conducting Economic Evaluations Revision 2 (2016 Update). US Department of Transportation, Office of the Secretary of Transportation. Available at: https://www.transportation.gov/sites/dot.gov/files/docs/2016%20Revised%20Value%20of%20Travel%20Time%20Guidance.pdf.

WHO (2019). Non-pharmaceutical Public Health Measures for Mitigating the Risk and Impact of Epidemic and Pandemic Influenza. Geneva: WHO.

Wiles, N. J., Thomas, L., Abel, A., Ridgway, N., Turner, N., Campbell, J., Garland, A., Hollinghurst, S., Jerrom, B., Kessler, D., Kuyken, W., Morrison, J., Turner, K., Williams, C., Peters, T., and Lewis, G. (2013). Cognitive Behavioural Therapy as an Adjunct to Pharmacotherapy for Primary Care-based Patients with Treatment Resistant Depression: Results of the CoBalT Randomised Controlled Trial. *Lancet* 381: 375–84.

Wiles, N. J., Thomas, L., Turner, N., Garfield, K., Kounali, D., Campbell, J., Kessler, D., Kuyken, W., Lewis, G., Morrison, J., Williams, C., Peters, T. J., and Hollinghurst, S.

(2016). Long-term Effectiveness and Cost-effectiveness of Cognitive Behavioural Therapy as an Adjunct to pharmacotherapy for Treatment-resistant Depression in Primary Care: Follow-up of the CoBalT Randomised Controlled Trial. *Lancet Psychiatry* 3: 137–44.

Williams, J. (2019). Taxing Families in the UK. [Blog post]. 18 June. Available at: https://ifstudies.org/blog/taxing-families-in-the-uk.

Index

Note: Tables and figures are indicated by an italic '*t*' and '*f*', respectively, following the page number.